COOK'S ILLUSTRATED

~ 2018 ~

COOK'S ILLUSTRATED INDEX 2018

A

Acme Rotary Mincer ... Jan/Feb 18 ... 30
Aglio e Olio (Garlic and Oil Sauce) ... Mar/Apr 18 ... 17
Air fryers, testing of ... May/Jun 18 ... 32
Aji amarillo chile paste ... Jul/Aug 18 ... 28
Alliums, powdered, seasoning dressings with ... Nov/Dec 18 ... 14
Almond(s)
    and Arugula Pesto ... May/Jun 18 ... 7
    Belgian Spice Cookies (Speculoos) with ... Sep/Oct 18 ... 23
    cream ... Nov/Dec 18 ... 15
    flour vs. meal ... Nov/Dec 18 ... 23
    Orange Butter ... May/Jun 18 ... 13
    Torta Caprese (Italian Chocolate-Almond Cake) ... Nov/Dec 18 ... 22–23
Aluminum foil, neater blind baking with ... Jan/Feb 18 ... 3
Amaretto Whipped Cream ... Nov/Dec 18 ... 23
Amatriciana ... Mar/Apr 18 ... 17
American cheeses, field guide ... Mar/Apr 18 ... BC
Anchovies
    meaty flavor boosted by ... Nov/Dec 18 ... 17
    Puttanesca ... Mar/Apr 18 ... 16
Appetizers and first courses
    Chinese-Style Barbecued Spareribs ... Jan/Feb 18 ... 6–7
    Falafel ... Sep/Oct 18 ... 12–13
    Gougères ... Jan/Feb 18 ... 14–15
        with Aged Gouda and Smoked Paprika ... Jan/Feb 18 ... 15
        with Manchego and Black Pepper ... Jan/Feb 18 ... 15
    Japanese Grilled Steak and Scallion Rolls (Negimaki) ... Sep/Oct 18 ... 8–9
    Japanese shishito peppers, preparing at home ... Mar/Apr 18 ... 28
    Marinated Grilled Tomatoes with Fresh Mozzarella ... Jul/Aug 18 ... 15
    Peruvian Fish Ceviche with Radishes and Orange ... Jul/Aug 18 ... 18–19
Apple(s)
    coring and peeling ... Sep/Oct 18 ... 19
    juice shed by peaches vs. ... Jul/Aug 18 ... 23
    peels, flavor compounds and pigments in ... Sep/Oct 18 ... 18
Apple corers, technique for ... Sep/Oct 18 ... 19
Applesauce ... Sep/Oct 18 ... 18–19
    apple varieties for ... Sep/Oct 18 ... 19
    Dessert-Worthy, with Brown Sugar and Rum ... Sep/Oct 18 ... 19
    Savory, with Beets and Horseradish ... Sep/Oct 18 ... 19
Appliances
    cleaning
        compressed air duster for crevices ... Nov/Dec 18 ... 2
        steam-cleaning grooves in cooking surfaces ... Mar/Apr 18 ... 3
        under-appliance dusters, testing of ... May/Jun 18 ... 32
    testing of
        air fryers ... May/Jun 18 ... 32
        Behmor Connected 8-Cup Brew System ... May/Jun 18 ... 32
        blenders, high-end ... Jan/Feb 18 ... 24–25
        Cuisinart Automatic Cold Brew Coffeemaker ... Jul/Aug 18 ... 32
        Hestan Cue Smart Cooking System ... Sep/Oct 18 ... 32
        June Intelligent Oven ... Nov/Dec 18 ... 32
        pizza ovens, indoor ... Sep/Oct 18 ... 32
Apricots, Dried, Barley with Fennel, Orange and ... May/Jun 18 ... 18
Arbol chiles ... Nov/Dec 18 ... 13
Arugula
    and Almond Pesto ... May/Jun 18 ... 7
    field guide ... May/Jun 18 ... BC
    Italian Pasta Salad ... Sep/Oct 18 ... 21
    Warm Bread Salad, Roast Chicken with ... May/Jun 18 ... 8–9
Asian (cuisines)
    See also Chinese (cuisine)
    Gochujang Paste ... Jul/Aug 18 ... 5
    ingredients
        Chinese cooking wines ... Mar/Apr 18 ... 21
        lo mein noodles ... May/Jun 18 ... 29
        nuoc cham ... Jul/Aug 18 ... 10
        rice noodles ... Jul/Aug 18 ... 11
        Sichuan peppercorns ... Nov/Dec 18 ... 13
        white miso paste, tasting of ... Sep/Oct 18 ... 28
    Japanese Grilled Steak and Scallion Rolls (Negimaki) ... Sep/Oct 18 ... 8–9
    Nuoc Cham (recipe) ... Jul/Aug 18 ... 11
    shishito peppers, preparing at home ... Mar/Apr 18 ... 28
    tangzhong (bread-baking technique) ... Nov/Dec 18 ... 16
        falafel and ... Sep/Oct 18 ... 12, 13
    Thai-Style Chicken Salad with Mango ... May/Jun 18 ... 15
    Vietnamese Grilled Pork Patties with Rice Noodles and Salad (Bun Cha) ... Jul/Aug 18 ... 10–11
Asparagus
    Buttery Spring Vegetables ... May/Jun 18 ... 22
    Roasted ... Sep/Oct 18 ... 16
Avocado
    dicing, for guacamole for a crowd ... Jan/Feb 18 ... 31
    ricing, for supersmooth guacamole ... Mar/Apr 18 ... 2

B

Bacon, turkey
    best way to cook ... Mar/Apr 18 ... 30
    tasting of ... Mar/Apr 18 ... 28
Bag clips, keeping filled soft tacos closed with ... Mar/Apr 18 ... 2
Baguette, field guide ... Sep/Oct 18 ... BC
Baked goods, baking soda's enhancement of flavor
    ... Mar/Apr 18 ... 13
    ... Nov/Dec 18 ... 17
Bakeware and baking supplies
    See also Baking sheets
    baking pans
        aluminum, as nonstick cover for casserole ... May/Jun 18 ... 2
        quick-softening butter for greasing ... May/Jun 18 ... 3
    cookie press, Danish ... Nov/Dec 18 ... 30
    parchment paper
        crumpling for blind baking ... Jul/Aug 18 ... 2
        testing of ... Mar/Apr 18 ... 24–25
        waxed paper vs. ... Mar/Apr 18 ... 31
    pastry brushes ... Jul/Aug 18 ... 30
        natural-fiber, testing of ... Jul/Aug 18 ... 32
        silicone, testing of ... Nov/Dec 18 ... 32
    pastry wheels, fluted ... Sep/Oct 18 ... 22
    silicone baking mats, testing of ... Mar/Apr 18 ... 32
Baking sheets
    hot, handling ... Nov/Dec 18 ... 3
    old, dull, more effective for browning food ... Sep/Oct 18 ... 31
    rimmed, as nonstick cover for casserole ... May/Jun 18 ... 2
    transporting raw and then cooked meat on ... Jul/Aug 18 ... 2
Baking soda
    flavor contribution of, to baked goods
        ... Mar/Apr 18 ... 13
        ... Nov/Dec 18 ... 17
    Irish soda bread
        Brown (recipe) ... Mar/Apr 18 ... 12–13
        hearth-baked original ... Mar/Apr 18 ... 13
        white ... Mar/Apr 18 ... 12
    nontraditional uses for ... Nov/Dec 18 ... 17
Bang Bang Ji Si (Sichuan-Style Chicken Salad) ... May/Jun 18 ... 15
Barbecued Spareribs, Chinese-Style ... Jan/Feb 18 ... 6–7
Barbecue sauces
    Mustard, South Carolina ... Mar/Apr 18 ... 5
    Sweet and Tangy ... Mar/Apr 18 ... 5
    Vinegar, Lexington ... Mar/Apr 18 ... 5
Barley
    with Celery and Miso Dressing ... May/Jun 18 ... 18
    with Fennel, Dried Apricots, and Orange ... May/Jun 18 ... 18
    with Lemon and Herbs ... May/Jun 18 ... 18
    pasta cooking method for ... May/Jun 18 ... 18
Bars and bar cookies
    granola bars, chewy ... Jul/Aug 18 ... 12–13
        with Hazelnuts, Cherries, and Cacao Nibs ... Jul/Aug 18 ... 13
        Nut-Free ... Jul/Aug 18 ... 13
        with Walnuts and Cranberries ... Jul/Aug 18 ... 13
    Lemon Bars, Best ... Mar/Apr 18 ... 22–23
    portioning with bench scraper ... Nov/Dec 18 ... 31
Basil
    Italian Pasta Salad ... Sep/Oct 18 ... 21
    and Lemon Butter ... Sep/Oct 18 ... 17
    Pesto, Classic ... Mar/Apr 18 ... 16

BASIL/
BUTTER

COOK'S ILLUSTRATED INDEX 2018

Basil *(cont.)*
Thai vs. Italian ..... Mar/Apr 18 29
Basmati rice
aging process and ..... Sep/Oct 18 24
jasmine rice vs. ..... Sep/Oct 18 28
tasting of ..... Sep/Oct 18 24–25
Basque-Style Herb Sauce (Tximitxurri) ..... Nov/Dec 18 11
Bâtard, field guide ..... Sep/Oct 18 BC
Bay, dried vs. fresh ..... Sep/Oct 18 4
Bean(s)
See also Green beans
canned
dried beans vs. ..... Nov/Dec 18 18
rinsing, sodium reduced by ..... Mar/Apr 18 29
chickpea(s)
baking soda's impact on cooking ..... Nov/Dec 18 17
canned, tasting of ..... Jan/Feb 18 28
Falafel ..... Sep/Oct 18 12–13
and Lentil Soup, Moroccan (Harira) ..... Mar/Apr 18 14
pie-weight, cooking and eating after use ..... Mar/Apr 18 30
Red Wine Risotto with (Paniscia) ..... Jan/Feb 18 11
White, and Mushroom Gratin ..... Nov/Dec 18 18
Beef
Grilled Steak and Scallion Rolls, Japanese (Negimaki) ..... Sep/Oct 18 8–9
ground
and Cheese Enchiladas ..... Jan/Feb 18 4–5
Italian-Style Meat Sauce, Simple (for pasta) ..... Mar/Apr 18 17
Tacos, Crispy (Tacos Dorados) ..... Jul/Aug 18 8–9
roast
mini, for family dinner ..... Nov/Dec 18 7
and potatoes for company ..... Nov/Dec 18 6–7
Top Loin, with Potatoes ..... Nov/Dec 18 7
top loin or "strip roast" for ..... Nov/Dec 18 6
skirt steak
Grilled Mojo-Marinated ..... May/Jun 18 4–5
marinating (science) ..... May/Jun 18 5
shopping for ..... May/Jun 18 5
tough, thin steaks, how to slice ..... May/Jun 18 31
Beer and Lime Cocktail, Mexican (Michelada) ..... Jul/Aug 18 9
Beets, Savory Applesauce with Horseradish and ..... Sep/Oct 18 19
Behmor Connected 8-Cup Brew System, testing of ..... May/Jun 18 32
Beijing-Style Meat Sauce and Noodles (Zha Jiang Mian) ..... May/Jun 18 19
Belgian endive, field guide ..... May/Jun 18 BC
Belgian Spice Cookies (Speculoos) ..... Sep/Oct 18 22–23
with Almonds ..... Sep/Oct 18 23
Bench scrapers
turning coffee can lid into ..... Jan/Feb 18 3
uses for ..... Nov/Dec 18 31
slicing ice cream cake with ..... Sep/Oct 18 3
Beverages
See also Coffee
chilling for party ..... Nov/Dec 18 2
cocktails
bois lélé (swizzle stick) for ..... Jul/Aug 18 30
field guide ..... Nov/Dec 18 BC
Michelada (Mexican Beer and Lime Cocktail) ..... Jul/Aug 18 9
Biscoff ..... Sep/Oct 18 23
Bitter greens, field guide ..... May/Jun 18 BC
Black pepper, sensory effects of (science) ..... May/Jun 18 11
Blenders, high-end, testing of ..... Jan/Feb 18 24–25
Blind baking
cooking and eating pie-weight beans used for ..... Mar/Apr 18 30
crumpling aluminum foil for ..... Jan/Feb 18 3
crumpling parchment paper for ..... Jul/Aug 18 2
Bloody Mary, field guide ..... Nov/Dec 18 BC
Blueberry, Mango, and Kiwi Topping (for pavlovas) ..... Nov/Dec 18 21
Bois lélé (swizzle stick) ..... Jul/Aug 18 30
Boning knives, flexible, testing of ..... Sep/Oct 18 32
Bottles
glass water, testing of ..... Nov/Dec 18 32
narrow, cleaning with sponge attached to wooden spoon ..... May/Jun 18 3
socking up drips on ..... Sep/Oct 18 2
Bourbon, as emergency sub for vanilla extract ..... Nov/Dec 18 29
Bowls
shower cap as impromptu cover for ..... Nov/Dec 18 2
wooden salad, caring for ..... May/Jun 18 30
Boxed broth, pouring ..... Nov/Dec 18 2
Braises, low-liquid, searing meat for ..... Nov/Dec 18 16
Brazilian Shrimp and Fish Stew (Moqueca) ..... Mar/Apr 18 10–11
Brazil nut cream ..... Nov/Dec 18 15
Bread(s)
baking
Asian technique for (tangzhong) ..... Sep/Oct 18 12,13
..... Nov/Dec 18 16
improvised lame for ..... Jan/Feb 18 2
trusting eyes when judging doneness ..... Nov/Dec 18 30
crumbs, toasting in microwave ..... May/Jun 18 17
French, field guide ..... Sep/Oct 18 BC
Pita ..... Sep/Oct 18 14–15
Salad, Warm, Roast Chicken with ..... May/Jun 18 8–9
sliced, plugging holes in ..... Jul/Aug 18 3
soda, Irish
Brown (recipe) ..... Mar/Apr 18 12–13
hearth-baked original ..... Mar/Apr 18 13
white ..... Mar/Apr 18 12
Breakfast fare
Braised New Mexico–Style Pork in Red Chile Sauce (Carne Adovada) ..... Sep/Oct 18 6–7
Coffee Cake with Pecan-Cinnamon Streusel ..... Jan/Feb 18 18–19
Pancakes, Easy ..... May/Jun 18 12–13
Scrambled Eggs, Creamy French-Style ..... Jan/Feb 18 20
Brining
poultry and meat ..... Nov/Dec 18 16
turkey in cooler ..... Nov/Dec 18 31
Brioche à tête, field guide ..... Sep/Oct 18 BC
Broccoli, Roast ..... Sep/Oct 18 16
Broccolini, pan-steamed
with Ginger ..... Mar/Apr 18 15
with Shallot ..... Mar/Apr 18 15
Broth
See also Stock
boxed, pouring ..... Nov/Dec 18 2
Browning
baking soda and ..... Nov/Dec 18 17
in hot vs. "cold" (not preheated) skillet ..... Nov/Dec 18 16
on old, dull baking sheet ..... Sep/Oct 18 31
searing meat
low-liquid braises and ..... Nov/Dec 18 16
before vs. after roasting ..... Nov/Dec 18 16
sugars in honey vs. granulated sugar and ..... May/Jun 18 7
Brown Soda Bread, Irish ..... Mar/Apr 18 12–13
Brown sugar, molasses content of ..... Sep/Oct 18 23
Brushes, pastry ..... Jul/Aug 18 30
natural-fiber, testing of ..... Jul/Aug 18 32
silicone, testing of ..... Nov/Dec 18 32
Brussels Spouts, Roasted ..... Sep/Oct 18 17
Buckwheat flour, in Foolproof All-Butter Pie Dough ..... Sep/Oct 18 31
Bulgur, cooking in rice cooker ..... Sep/Oct 18 30
Bun Cha (Vietnamese Grilled Pork Patties with Rice Noodles and Salad) ..... Jul/Aug 18 10–11
Burrata, tasting of ..... Jul/Aug 18 28
Butter
Buttery Spring Vegetables ..... May/Jun 18 22
cow's diet and yellow shades of ..... Nov/Dec 18 24
creaming sugar and, impact on cake texture (science) ..... Nov/Dec 18 31
Cultured ..... Nov/Dec 18 29
flavored
Basil and Lemon ..... Sep/Oct 18 17
Ginger-Molasses ..... May/Jun 18 13
Orange-Almond ..... May/Jun 18 13
Foolproof All-Butter Pie Dough ..... Jan/Feb 18 21–23
for Double-Crust Pie ..... Jan/Feb 18 22
for Single-Crust Pie ..... Jan/Feb 18 23
whole-wheat, rye, or buckwheat flour in (science) ..... Sep/Oct 18 31
packaging of ..... Nov/Dec 18 24

Butter (cont.)
tips and techniques
cold, spreading	Nov/Dec 18	3
cubing with bench scraper	Nov/Dec 18	31
"orphans," storing	Sep/Oct 18	2
quick-softening, for greasing baking pan	May/Jun 18	3
unsalted, tasting of	Nov/Dec 18	24–25
Buttermilk, as by-product of Cultured Butter recipe	Nov/Dec 18	29
Butternut Squash, Roasted	Sep/Oct 18	17

C

Cabbage
chopping	Jan/Feb 18	31
Red Wine Risotto with Beans (Paniscia)	Jan/Feb 18	11

Cacao
beans, field guide	Jan/Feb 18	BC
nibs		
Chewy Granola Bars with Hazelnuts, Cherries and	Jul/Aug 18	13
field guide	Jan/Feb 18	BC
pod, field guide	Jan/Feb 18	BC

Caesar Salad, Chicken	May/Jun 18	15

Cakes
Coffee, with Pecan-Cinnamon Streusel	Jan/Feb 18	18–19
creaming's impact on texture of (science)	Nov/Dec 18	31
ice cream, slicing with bench scraper	Sep/Oct 18	3
Torta Caprese (Italian Chocolate-Almond Cake)	Nov/Dec 18	22–23

Cake tester, judging doneness of dense vegetables with	Sep/Oct 18	3
Candied Nuts, Quick	May/Jun 18	29
Caper-Currant Relish	Sep/Oct 18	11

Caramel
	Mar/Apr 18	18–19
accurately taking temperature of	Mar/Apr 18	19
judging by color alone vs.	Mar/Apr 18	30
-Braised Shallots with Black Pepper	Mar/Apr 18	19
Popcorn, Spicy	Mar/Apr 18	19
Sauce, All-Purpose	Mar/Apr 18	19

Caramelizing sugar in microwave	May/Jun 18	17
Carbon-steel skillets, caring for	Jan/Feb 18	30
Cardboard containers, spill-proof	May/Jun 18	2
Carne Adovada (Braised New Mexico–Style Pork in Red Chile Sauce)	Sep/Oct 18	6–7

Carrot(s)
bunched vs. bagged	Jan/Feb 18	13
chopped, salads	Jan/Feb 18	12–13
with Celery and Raisins	Jan/Feb 18	13
with Fennel, Orange, and Hazelnuts	Jan/Feb 18	13
with Mint, Pistachios, and Pomegranate Seeds	Jan/Feb 18	13
with Radishes and Sesame Seeds	Jan/Feb 18	13
shredded carrot salads vs.	Jan/Feb 18	13
Quick Pickled Turnips and, with Lemon and Coriander	Sep/Oct 18	29
Roasted	Sep/Oct 18	17
skin, texture and flavor of (science)	Jan/Feb 18	12
tops, cooking with	May/Jun 18	29

Cashew cream
in creamless creamy dressings	Nov/Dec 18	14–15
testing of other nut creams vs., as base for vegan cheeses and sauces	Nov/Dec 18	15

Casseroles
hot, homemade carrier for	Sep/Oct 18	2
nonstick cover for	May/Jun 18	2
White Bean and Mushroom Gratin	Nov/Dec 18	18

Cast-iron cookware
caring for	Jul/Aug 18	30
skillets, testing of handle covers for	Mar/Apr 18	32

Cauliflower, Roasted	Sep/Oct 18	17
Cayenne pepper, sensory effects of (science)	May/Jun 18	11
Celery, Chopped Carrot Salad with Raisins and	Jan/Feb 18	13

Ceviche, fish
how acid "cooks" fish in	Jul/Aug 18	18
how to buy freshest fish for	Jul/Aug 18	19
Peruvian, with Radishes and Orange	Jul/Aug 18	18–19
popcorn served with	Jul/Aug 18	19
shrimp	Jul/Aug 18	19

Champagne
cocktail, field guide	Nov/Dec 18	BC
flat, reviving with raisin	Nov/Dec 18	30

Champignon (bread), field guide	Sep/Oct 18	BC
Channellock pliers, retrieving hot pans from oven with	Nov/Dec 18	3

Charcoal grills
starting fire on	Jul/Aug 18	16
testing of	Jul/Aug 18	16
vents of	Jul/Aug 18	17

Cheddar, field guide	Mar/Apr 18	BC

Cheese(s)
See also Mozzarella
American, field guide	Mar/Apr 18	BC
burrata, tasting of	Jul/Aug 18	28
curds, field guide	Mar/Apr 18	BC
Gougères	Jan/Feb 18	14–15
with Aged Gouda and Smoked Paprika	Jan/Feb 18	15
with Manchego and Black Pepper	Jan/Feb 18	15
grating too far in advance	Mar/Apr 18	29
and Ground Beef Enchiladas	Jan/Feb 18	4–5
Pecorino Romano and Romano, tasting of	Mar/Apr 18	26–27
semisoft, grating	Jan/Feb 18	4

Chef's knives for kids, testing of	Jul/Aug 18	32

Cherry(ies)
Chewy Granola Bars with Hazelnuts, Cacao Nibs and	Jul/Aug 18	13
pitted, slicing in half efficiently	Nov/Dec 18	3
Sauce	May/Jun 18	21

Chia seeds, in Nut-Free Chewy Granola Bars	Jul/Aug 18	13

Chicken
Kung Pao	Nov/Dec 18	12–13
label claims	Jan/Feb 18	16
Piccata	Jan/Feb 18	10
Pulled, Indoor	Mar/Apr 18	4–5
roast	Jan/Feb 18	16–17
carving	Jan/Feb 18	17
Crisp	Jan/Feb 18	17
inserting thermometer into	Jan/Feb 18	17
resting	Jan/Feb 18	17
with Warm Bread Salad	May/Jun 18	8–9
Weeknight	Jan/Feb 18	16
salads	May/Jun 18	14–15
Caesar	May/Jun 18	15
perfect poached chicken for	May/Jun 18	15
Sichuan-Style (Bang Bang Ji Si)	May/Jun 18	15
Thai-Style, with Mango	May/Jun 18	15
Thighs, Grilled, Best	Jul/Aug 18	4–5
Three-Cup	Mar/Apr 18	20–21
tips and techniques		
brining	Nov/Dec 18	16
drying skin in a flash	Nov/Dec 18	3
overcooking dark meat for juiciness and tenderness	Nov/Dec 18	17
overnight baking soda rub for (science)	Jan/Feb 18	17
portioning paste on flesh and skin sides of	Jul/Aug 18	4
shredding with tongs	Mar/Apr 18	4
with tender meat and crisp skin (science)	Jul/Aug 18	5
Vesuvio	Sep/Oct 18	4–5
whole, tasting of	Jan/Feb 18	16

Chickpea(s)
baking soda's impact on cooking	Nov/Dec 18	17
canned, tasting of	Jan/Feb 18	28
Falafel	Sep/Oct 18	12–13
and Lentil Soup, Moroccan (Harira)	Mar/Apr 18	14

Chile(s)
aji amarillo, paste	Jul/Aug 18	28
arbol	Nov/Dec 18	13
blending into smooth puree	Sep/Oct 18	7
chipotles in adobo, freezing and prepping	May/Jun 18	2
dried, shopping, cleaning, and storing	Sep/Oct 18	29
New Mexican	Sep/Oct 18	7
Pepper Sauce	Mar/Apr 18	11
Red, Sauce, Braised New Mexico–Style Pork in (Carne Adovada)	Sep/Oct 18	6–7

Chili-Lime Salt	Sep/Oct 18	17

Chilling beverages for party	Nov/Dec 18	2
Chimney starters, tips for using	Jul/Aug 18	16
Chinese (cuisine)		
Barbecued Spareribs	Jan/Feb 18	6–7
Beijing-Style Meat Sauce and Noodles (Zha Jiang Mian)	May/Jun 18	19
chicken		
Kung Pao	Nov/Dec 18	12–13
Salad, Sichuan-Style (Bang Bang Ji Si)	May/Jun 18	15
Three-Cup	Mar/Apr 18	20–21
cooking wines	Mar/Apr 18	21
lo mein noodles, shopping for	May/Jun 18	29
Chipotles in adobo, freezing and prepping	May/Jun 18	2
Chips		
Plantain	Jul/Aug 18	29
tortilla, field guide	Jul/Aug 18	BC
Chocolate		
bar, field guide	Jan/Feb 18	BC
chips		
dark, tasting of	Jan/Feb 18	26–27
field guide	Jan/Feb 18	BC
shape of	Jan/Feb 18	26
Cream Pie	Jan/Feb 18	23
Dark, Fudge Sauce	Jul/Aug 18	21
Orange	Jul/Aug 18	21
field guide	Jan/Feb 18	BC
melting or tempering, in microwave	May/Jun 18	17
melting wafers, for easier dipping	Mar/Apr 18	28
Mexican drinking, field guide	Jan/Feb 18	BC
Semifreddo	May/Jun 18	20–21
Torta Caprese (Italian Chocolate-Almond Cake)	Nov/Dec 18	22–23
Cilantro	May/Jun 18	28
Cinnamon-Pecan Streusel	Jan/Feb 18	18–19
Citrus		
See also specific citrus fruits		
segments, technique for	Jul/Aug 18	29
zest, dehydrating in microwave	May/Jun 18	17
Clothespins		
pinning your place in recipe with	Jul/Aug 18	2
as thermometer holder for grill	Nov/Dec 18	2
Cloves, storing in glass vs. plastic	Jan/Feb 18	29
Cocktails		
bois lélé (swizzle stick) for	Jul/Aug 18	30
field guide	Nov/Dec 18	BC
Michelada (Mexican Beer and Lime Cocktail)	Jul/Aug 18	9
Cocoa butter, field guide	Jan/Feb 18	BC
Cocoa powder		
Dutching process for	May/Jun 18	23
field guide	Jan/Feb 18	BC
tasting of	May/Jun 18	23–25
past its expiration date	Jul/Aug 18	28
Coconut, toasting in microwave	May/Jun 18	17
Coconut milk, in Brazilian Shrimp and Fish Stew (Moqueca)	Mar/Apr 18	10–11
Cod, in Brazilian Shrimp and Fish Stew (Moqueca)	Mar/Apr 18	10–11
Coffee		
antique German roaster for	Mar/Apr 18	30
coffeemakers, testing of		
Behmor Connected 8-Cup Brew System	May/Jun 18	32
Cuisinart Automatic Cold Brew Coffeemaker	Jul/Aug 18	32
filters, separating easily	Mar/Apr 18	3
grinders, avoiding static in	Mar/Apr 18	2
preheating mug for	Mar/Apr 18	30
Coffee Cake with Pecan-Cinnamon Streusel	Jan/Feb 18	18–19
Coffee can lid, turning into bench scraper	Jan/Feb 18	3
Colby, field guide	Mar/Apr 18	BC
Colby Jack, field guide	Mar/Apr 18	BC
Compressed air duster, cleaning crevices in cookware with	Nov/Dec 18	2
Condiments		
See also Dressings		
butters		
Basil and Lemon	Sep/Oct 18	17
Cultured	Nov/Dec 18	29
Ginger-Molasses	May/Jun 18	13

Condiments, butters *(cont.)*		
Orange-Almond	May/Jun 18	13
Chili-Lime Salt	Sep/Oct 18	17
Harissa	Mar/Apr 18	29
Pomegranate Molasses, Tart	Jan/Feb 18	29
relishes		
Caper-Currant	Sep/Oct 18	11
Cucumber-Ginger	May/Jun 18	7
Scallion-Ginger	Mar/Apr 18	6
seasoning pastes		
Gochujang	Jul/Aug 18	5
Mustard-Tarragon	Jul/Aug 18	5
Shallots, Caramel-Braised, with Black Pepper	Mar/Apr 18	19
Turnips and Carrots, Quick Pickled, with Lemon and Coriander	Sep/Oct 18	29
Cookbooks, keeping open for cooking	Jan/Feb 18	2
Cookie(s)		
See also Bars and bar cookies		
Belgian Spice (Speculoos)	Sep/Oct 18	22–23
with Almonds	Sep/Oct 18	23
burnt, rescuing with rasp-style grater	Nov/Dec 18	3
dough, rolling, waxed paper for	Mar/Apr 18	31
meringue	Nov/Dec 18	20
Cookie press, Danish	Nov/Dec 18	30
Cookie spatulas, testing of	Jan/Feb 18	32
Cooler, brining turkey in	Nov/Dec 18	31
Coriander	May/Jun 18	28
Corkscrews, twist, testing of	Jan/Feb 18	32
Corn		
cutting from cob	Jul/Aug 18	20
field guide	Jul/Aug 18	BC
husks, field guide	Jul/Aug 18	BC
nuts, field guide	Jul/Aug 18	BC
Salad, Mexican (Esquites)	Jul/Aug 18	20
shucking		
microwave method for	May/Jun 18	17
removing clingy silk with rubber glove	Jul/Aug 18	3
Cornmeal, white, field guide	Jul/Aug 18	BC
Cornstarch		
cleaning frying oil with	Sep/Oct 18	31
slurry, microwaving, for fry batter	Jan/Feb 18	9
Couronne, field guide	Sep/Oct 18	BC
Couverture wafers, field guide	Jan/Feb 18	BC
Cranberry(ies)		
Chewy Granola Bars with Walnuts and	Jul/Aug 18	13
Orange, and Mint Topping (for pavlovas)	Nov/Dec 18	21
Creaming's impact on cake texture (science)	Nov/Dec 18	31
Cream of tartar	Mar/Apr 18	22
Cream Pie, Chocolate	Jan/Feb 18	23
Cremini Mushrooms, Roasted	Sep/Oct 18	17
Crowd, cooking for		
dicing avocados for guacamole	Jan/Feb 18	31
Roasted Whole Side of Salmon	May/Jun 18	6–7
Turkey and Gravy	Nov/Dec 18	4–5
Crusts, pat-in-the-pan	Mar/Apr 18	23
Cucumber		
Ginger Relish	May/Jun 18	7
primer	Jul/Aug 18	29
Cuisinart Automatic Cold Brew Coffeemaker, testing of	Jul/Aug 18	32
Cupcakes, hollowing out, for filling	Mar/Apr 18	3
Curly endive, field guide	May/Jun 18	BC
Currant-Caper Relish	Sep/Oct 18	11
Cutting boards		
preventing sliding of	Mar/Apr 18	2
small, testing of	Jan/Feb 18	32
steadying, then sanitizing	Sep/Oct 18	2
Cutting mats, flexible, testing of	Mar/Apr 18	32

D

Dandelion greens, field guide	May/Jun 18	BC
Danish cookie press	Nov/Dec 18	30
Dark Chocolate Fudge Sauce	Jul/Aug 18	21
Orange	Jul/Aug 18	21

Deep frying
- cleaning oil with cornstarch after ... Sep/Oct 18 ... 31
- tools for ... Sep/Oct 18 ... 13

Defatting
- "skimming" fat with suction ... Jan/Feb 18 ... 2
- stock for turkey gravy, flavor lost by ... Nov/Dec 18 ... 9

Delicata squash
- buying, storing, and prepping ... Nov/Dec 18 ... 29
- Roasted ... Nov/Dec 18 ... 11

Desserts and sweet snacks
- Applesauce with Brown Sugar and Rum ... Sep/Oct 18 ... 19
- Belgian Spice Cookies (Speculoos) ... Sep/Oct 18 ... 22–23
  - with Almonds ... Sep/Oct 18 ... 23
- bourbon as emergency sub for vanilla extract in ... Nov/Dec 18 ... 29
- Chocolate Cream Pie ... Jan/Feb 18 ... 23
- Chocolate Semifreddo ... May/Jun 18 ... 20–21
- Coffee Cake with Pecan-Cinnamon Streusel ... Jan/Feb 18 ... 18–19
- granola bars, chewy
  - with Hazelnuts, Cherries, and Cacao Nibs ... Jul/Aug 18 ... 13
  - Nut-Free ... Jul/Aug 18 ... 13
  - with Walnuts and Cranberries ... Jul/Aug 18 ... 13
- Lemon Bars, Best ... Mar/Apr 18 ... 22–23
- pavlovas ... Nov/Dec 18 ... 19–21
  - with Fruit and Whipped Cream ... Nov/Dec 18 ... 20
  - Individual, with Fruit and Whipped Cream ... Nov/Dec 18 ... 21
  - Mango, Kiwi, and Blueberry Topping for ... Nov/Dec 18 ... 21
  - Orange, Cranberry, and Mint Topping for ... Nov/Dec 18 ... 21
- Peach Tarte Tatin ... Jul/Aug 18 ... 22–23
- Torta Caprese (Italian Chocolate-Almond Cake) ... Nov/Dec 18 ... 22–23

Dessert sauces and toppings
- Cherry Sauce ... May/Jun 18 ... 21
- Dark Chocolate Fudge Sauce ... Jul/Aug 18 ... 21
  - Orange ... Jul/Aug 18 ... 21
- whipped cream
  - Amaretto ... Nov/Dec 18 ... 23
  - Orange ... Nov/Dec 18 ... 23

Deviled eggs, piping filling of ... Sep/Oct 18 ... 3
Deviled Pork Chops ... May/Jun 18 ... 10–11
"Deviling," origin of term ... May/Jun 18 ... 11

Dips
- creamless creamy dressings as ... Nov/Dec 18 ... 15
- guacamole
  - for a crowd (technique) ... Jan/Feb 18 ... 31
  - supersmooth, with ricer ... Mar/Apr 18 ... 2
- Salsa, Grilled Tomato ... Jul/Aug 18 ... 15

Dish-drying rack, storing pot lids in ... Mar/Apr 18 ... 3

DIY recipes
- Butter, Cultured ... Nov/Dec 18 ... 29
- Candied Nuts, Quick ... May/Jun 18 ... 29
- Harissa ... Mar/Apr 18 ... 29
- Pickled Turnips and Carrots with Lemon and Coriander, Quick ... Sep/Oct 18 ... 29
- Plantain Chips ... Jul/Aug 18 ... 29
- Pomegranate Molasses, Tart ... Jan/Feb 18 ... 29

Doorstops, rubber, stopping cutting boards from sliding in cabinet with ... Mar/Apr 18 ... 2

Dough
- See also Pie(s)—dough
- coating in flour before rolling out ... Sep/Oct 18 ... 15
- pretorn plastic wrap for ... Jan/Feb 18 ... 3
- rolling, waxed paper for ... Mar/Apr 18 ... 31
- shaping logs with bench scraper ... Nov/Dec 18 ... 31
- yeasted, that ferments in the refrigerator, colder water for ... Sep/Oct 18 ... 31

Dressings
- creamless creamy ... Nov/Dec 18 ... 14–15
  - Ginger-Miso ... Nov/Dec 18 ... 15
  - Green Goddess ... Nov/Dec 18 ... 15
  - Herb ... Nov/Dec 18 ... 15
  - Roasted Red Pepper and Tahini ... Nov/Dec 18 ... 15
  - Russian ... Nov/Dec 18 ... 15
- seasoning with powdered alliums ... Nov/Dec 18 ... 14
- small-batch, whizzing together ... Jan/Feb 18 ... 2

Dusters
- compressed air, cleaning crevices in cookware with ... Nov/Dec 18 ... 2
- under-appliance, testing of ... May/Jun 18 ... 32

Dutch ovens
- space-saving storage of, in refrigerator ... Sep/Oct 18 ... 2
- testing of ... Sep/Oct 18 ... 26–27

E

Échelle, field guide ... Sep/Oct 18 ... BC

Egg(s)
- candling ... Nov/Dec 18 ... 16
- deviled, piping filling of ... Sep/Oct 18 ... 3
- foam, whipping technique for ... Nov/Dec 18 ... 23
- nifty holder for ... Mar/Apr 18 ... 3
- salting, before incorporating into dough ... Jan/Feb 18 ... 15
- Scrambled, Creamy French-Style ... Jan/Feb 18 ... 20
- whites
  - See also Meringue(s)
  - measuring by weight or volume rather than egg count ... Nov/Dec 18 ... 21

Eggplant, drying in microwave for frying or sautéing ... May/Jun 18 ... 17
Emulsions (science) ... May/Jun 18 ... 31
Enchiladas, Ground Beef and Cheese ... Jan/Feb 18 ... 4–5

Endive
- Belgian, field guide ... May/Jun 18 ... BC
- curly, field guide ... May/Jun 18 ... BC

Equipment and product testing
- air fryers ... May/Jun 18 ... 32
- baking mats, silicone ... Mar/Apr 18 ... 32
- blenders, high-end ... Jan/Feb 18 ... 24–25
- brushes, pastry
  - natural-fiber ... Jul/Aug 18 ... 32
  - silicone ... Nov/Dec 18 ... 32
- coffeemakers
  - Behmor Connected 8-Cup Brew System ... May/Jun 18 ... 32
  - Cuisinart Automatic Cold Brew Coffeemaker ... Jul/Aug 18 ... 32
- corkscrews, twist ... Jan/Feb 18 ... 32
- cutting boards, small ... Jan/Feb 18 ... 32
- cutting mats, flexible ... Mar/Apr 18 ... 32
- dusters, under-appliance ... May/Jun 18 ... 32
- Dutch ovens ... Sep/Oct 18 ... 26–27
- fruit/vegetable peelers for kids ... Nov/Dec 18 ... 32
- funnels ... Sep/Oct 18 ... 32
- ginger graters ... Mar/Apr 18 ... 32
- glass storage containers ... May/Jun 18 ... 32
- glass water bottles ... Nov/Dec 18 ... 32
- grills
  - charcoal ... Jul/Aug 18 ... 16
  - gas ... Jul/Aug 18 ... 17
- handle covers for cast-iron skillets ... Mar/Apr 18 ... 32
- hand soap dispensers, automatic ... Jan/Feb 18 ... 32
- Hestan Cue Smart Cooking System ... Sep/Oct 18 ... 32
- June Intelligent Oven ... Nov/Dec 18 ... 32
- knives
  - boning, flexible ... Sep/Oct 18 ... 32
  - chef's, for kids ... Jul/Aug 18 ... 32
- oven mitts for kids ... Sep/Oct 18 ... 32
- parchment paper ... Mar/Apr 18 ... 24–25
- pizza ovens, indoor ... Sep/Oct 18 ... 32
- plastic food storage containers ... May/Jun 18 ... 26–27
- probe thermometers (update) ... Mar/Apr 18 ... 32
- salad spinners ... Nov/Dec 18 ... 32
- shears, kitchen ... May/Jun 18 ... 32
- sous vide circulators ... Mar/Apr 18 ... 7
- spatulas
  - compact or cookie ... Jan/Feb 18 ... 32
  - metal ... Nov/Dec 18 ... 26–27
- steamer baskets ... Jul/Aug 18 ... 32
- thermometers, digital ... Jul/Aug 18 ... 26–27
- tongs, 9-inch ... Jul/Aug 18 ... 32

Escarole, field guide ... May/Jun 18 ... BC
Esquites (Mexican Corn Salad) ... Jul/Aug 18 ... 20

F

Falafel ... Sep/Oct 18 ... 12–13
    how flour paste holds it together (science) ... Sep/Oct 18 ... 13
Farmer's cheese, field guide ... Mar/Apr 18 ... BC
Fennel
    Barley with Dried Apricots, Orange and ... May/Jun 18 ... 18
    Chopped Carrot Salad with Orange, Hazelnuts and ... Jan/Feb 18 ... 13
    Roasted ... Sep/Oct 18 ... 17
Field guides
    American cheeses ... Mar/Apr 18 ... BC
    bitter greens ... May/Jun 18 ... BC
    chocolate ... Jan/Feb 18 ... BC
    cocktails ... Nov/Dec 18 ... BC
    corn products ... Jul/Aug 18 ... BC
    French breads ... Sep/Oct 18 ... BC
Fire extinguisher recall for Kidde model FA110 (or FA110G) ... Mar/Apr 18 ... 32
First courses. *See* Appetizers and first courses
Fish
    See also Swordfish steaks
    anchovies
        meaty flavor boosted by ... Nov/Dec 18 ... 17
        Puttanesca ... Mar/Apr 18 ... 16
    ceviche
        how acid "cooks" fish in ... Jul/Aug 18 ... 18
        how to buy freshest fish for ... Jul/Aug 18 ... 19
        Peruvian, with Radishes and Orange ... Jul/Aug 18 ... 18–19
        popcorn served with ... Jul/Aug 18 ... 19
        shrimp ... Jul/Aug 18 ... 19
    cooking with residual heat ... Mar/Apr 18 ... 11
    salmon
        Roasted Whole Side of ... May/Jun 18 ... 6–7
        side of, buying and trimming ... May/Jun 18 ... 28
    and Shrimp Stew, Brazilian (Moqueca) ... Mar/Apr 18 ... 10–11
Fish spatulas
    conventional spatulas vs. ... Nov/Dec 18 ... 26
    testing of ... Nov/Dec 18 ... 26–27
Flour
    coating dough with, before rolling out ... Sep/Oct 18 ... 15
    paste, Asian (tangzhong) ... Nov/Dec 18 ... 16
        falafels and ... Sep/Oct 18 ... 12, 13
Fluted pastry wheels ... Sep/Oct 18 ... 22
Folding aerated ingredients, best technique for ... May/Jun 18 ... 30
Fond, turkey gravy and ... Nov/Dec 18 ... 9
Food storage containers
    glass, testing of ... May/Jun 18 ... 32
    plastic, testing of ... May/Jun 18 ... 26–27
Fougasse, field guide ... Sep/Oct 18 ... BC
French (cuisine)
    breads, field guide ... Sep/Oct 18 ... BC
    Creamy Scrambled Eggs ... Jan/Feb 18 ... 20
    Gougères ... Jan/Feb 18 ... 14–15
    Peach Tarte Tatin ... Jul/Aug 18 ... 22–23
Fries, Thick-Cut Oven ... Jan/Feb 18 ... 8–9
Frisée, field guide ... May/Jun 18 ... BC
Frosting, smoothing with bench scraper ... Nov/Dec 18 ... 31
Fruits
    See also specific fruits
    rinsing and draining on the go in zipper-lock bags ... May/Jun 18 ... 3
Fruit/vegetable peelers
    for kids, testing of ... Nov/Dec 18 ... 32
    slicing butter for quick softening with ... Nov/Dec 18 ... 3
Frying
    air fryers, testing of ... May/Jun 18 ... 32
    cleaning oil with cornstarch after ... Sep/Oct 18 ... 31
    tools for ... Sep/Oct 18 ... 13
Fudge Sauce, Dark Chocolate ... Jul/Aug 18 ... 21
    Orange ... Jul/Aug 18 ... 21
Funnels, testing of ... Sep/Oct 18 ... 32

G

Garlic
    Dried Mint Sauce, Spicy ... Sep/Oct 18 ... 11
    and Oil Sauce (Aglio e Olio) ... Mar/Apr 18 ... 17
    powder, seasoning dressings with ... Nov/Dec 18 ... 14
    products, convenience ... Sep/Oct 18 ... 29
    tips and techniques
        emulsifying sauces with ... Sep/Oct 18 ... 5
        grating safely ... May/Jun 18 ... 2
        lubricating with oil before adding to stir-fry ... Nov/Dec 18 ... 13
        raw, mellowing in microwave ... May/Jun 18 ... 17
        taming with lemon juice ... Sep/Oct 18 ... 5
Gas grills
    checking fuel level in propane tank ... Jul/Aug 18 ... 17
    testing of ... Jul/Aug 18 ... 17
    vents of ... Jul/Aug 18 ... 17
Gazpacho, Grilled Tomato ... Jul/Aug 18 ... 15
Genoa salami ... Jan/Feb 18 ... 28
German coffee roaster, antique ... Mar/Apr 18 ... 30
Ginger
    Cucumber Relish ... May/Jun 18 ... 7
    Miso Dressing, Creamless Creamy ... Nov/Dec 18 ... 15
    Molasses Butter ... May/Jun 18 ... 13
    Scallion Relish ... Mar/Apr 18 ... 6
    tips and techniques
        fresh, storing ... Jan/Feb 18 ... 29
        lubricating with oil before adding to stir-fry ... Nov/Dec 18 ... 13
        peeling ... Mar/Apr 18 ... 21
Ginger graters, testing of ... Mar/Apr 18 ... 32
Glass storage containers, testing of ... May/Jun 18 ... 32
Glass water bottles, testing of ... Nov/Dec 18 ... 32
Gloves, rubber
    removing clingy silk from fresh corn with ... Jul/Aug 18 ... 3
    used, cutting into rubber bands ... May/Jun 18 ... 3
Glutamate-rich ingredients ... Nov/Dec 18 ... 17
Gochujang Paste ... Jul/Aug 18 ... 5
Gouda, Aged, Gougères with Smoked Paprika and ... Jan/Feb 18 ... 15
Gougères ... Jan/Feb 18 ... 14–15
    with Aged Gouda and Smoked Paprika ... Jan/Feb 18 ... 15
    with Manchego and Black Pepper ... Jan/Feb 18 ... 15
Grains
    See also specific grains
    cooking
        baking soda's impact on ... Nov/Dec 18 ... 17
        in rice cooker ... Sep/Oct 18 ... 30
Granola bars, chewy ... Jul/Aug 18 ... 12–13
    with Hazelnuts, Cherries, and Cacao Nibs ... Jul/Aug 18 ... 13
    Nut-Free ... Jul/Aug 18 ... 13
    with Walnuts and Cranberries ... Jul/Aug 18 ... 13
Grapes, slicing in half efficiently ... Nov/Dec 18 ... 3
Graters
    ginger, testing of ... Mar/Apr 18 ... 32
    safe handling of garlic cloves and ... May/Jun 18 ... 2
Gratin, White Bean and Mushroom ... Nov/Dec 18 ... 18
Gravy
    keeping hot for serving in ceramic teapot ... Jan/Feb 18 ... 3
    turkey ... Nov/Dec 18 ... 8–9
        browning roux for ... Nov/Dec 18 ... 9
        gluten- (or alcohol-) free ... Nov/Dec 18 ... 9
        Our Favorite ... Nov/Dec 18 ... 9
        Turkey and, for a Crowd ... Nov/Dec 18 ... 4–5
Green beans
    cooking for long time or over high heat ... Sep/Oct 18 ... 20
    Roasted ... Sep/Oct 18 ... 17
    Skillet-Charred ... Sep/Oct 18 ... 20
        with Crispy Bread-Crumb Topping ... Sep/Oct 18 ... 20
Green Goddess Dressing, Creamless Creamy ... Nov/Dec 18 ... 15
Greens, bitter, field guide ... May/Jun 18 ... BC

Grilled (foods)
cheese sandwiches, plugging holes in bread for ..... Jul/Aug 18 3
chicken
    with tender meat and crisp skin (science) ..... Jul/Aug 18 5
    Thighs, Best ..... Jul/Aug 18 4–5
Pork Patties with Rice Noodles and Salad,
    Vietnamese (Bun Cha) ..... Jul/Aug 18 10–11
steak
    and Scallion Rolls, Japanese (Negimaki) ..... Sep/Oct 18 8–9
    Skirt, Mojo-Marinated ..... May/Jun 18 4–5
Tomato(es) ..... Jul/Aug 18 14–15
    Gazpacho ..... Jul/Aug 18 15
    Marinated, with Fresh Mozzarella ..... Jul/Aug 18 15
    Salsa ..... Jul/Aug 18 15

Grilling equipment
charcoal grills
    starting fire on ..... Jul/Aug 18 16
    testing of ..... Jul/Aug 18 16
    vents of ..... Jul/Aug 18 17
chimney starters, tips for using ..... Jul/Aug 18 16
cleaning ..... Jul/Aug 18 17
gas grills
    checking fuel level in propane tank ..... Jul/Aug 18 17
    testing of ..... Jul/Aug 18 17
    vents of ..... Jul/Aug 18 17
grill grates, oiling ..... Jul/Aug 18 17
lighter fluid ..... Jul/Aug 18 16
thermometer holder ..... Nov/Dec 18 2
wood chips, pantry ingredients tested as alternative to ..... Nov/Dec 18 17

Grill pans, cleaning crevices in ..... Nov/Dec 18 2
Grimwade's Quick-Cooker ..... Sep/Oct 18 30
Gruyère cheese, in Gougères ..... Jan/Feb 18 14–15
Guacamole
for a crowd ..... Jan/Feb 18 31
supersmooth, with ricer ..... Mar/Apr 18 2
Guanciale, Rigatoni with Pecorino Romano and
    (Pasta alla Gricia) ..... Nov/Dec 18 10

H
Hair dryer, drying chicken skin in a flash with ..... Nov/Dec 18 3
Hand soap dispensers, automatic, testing of ..... Jan/Feb 18 32
Harira (Moroccan Lentil and Chickpea Soup) ..... Mar/Apr 18 14
Harissa (DIY recipe) ..... Mar/Apr 18 29
Hazelnut(s)
Chewy Granola Bars with Cherries, Cacao Nibs and ..... Jul/Aug 18 13
Chopped Carrot Salad with Fennel, Orange and ..... Jan/Feb 18 13
cream ..... Nov/Dec 18 15
Herb(s)
Dressing, Creamless Creamy ..... Nov/Dec 18 15
dried vs. fresh ..... Sep/Oct 18 4
fresh, drying in microwave ..... May/Jun 18 17
Sauce, Basque-Style (Tximitxurri) ..... Nov/Dec 18 11
Hestan Cue Smart Cooking System, testing of ..... Sep/Oct 18 32
Hominy, field guide ..... Jul/Aug 18 ..... BC
Honey
for even browning ..... May/Jun 18 7
Spicy ..... Nov/Dec 18 11
Hoop cheese, field guide ..... Mar/Apr 18 ..... BC
Horseradish, Savory Applesauce with Beets and ..... Sep/Oct 18 19

I
Ice cream cake, slicing with bench scraper ..... Sep/Oct 18 3
Ice cube trays, freezing chipotle chiles in adobo sauce in ..... May/Jun 18 2
Ingredients
See also Tastings
keeping track of additions while cooking ..... Jan/Feb 18 3
Irish soda bread
Brown (recipe) ..... Mar/Apr 18 12–13
hearth-baked original ..... Mar/Apr 18 13

Irish soda bread (cont.)
white ..... Mar/Apr 18 12
Italian and Italian-American (cuisines)
Chicken Vesuvio ..... Sep/Oct 18 4–5
Chocolate Semifreddo ..... May/Jun 18 20–21
Pasta Salad ..... Sep/Oct 18 21
Pizza, One-Hour ..... Mar/Apr 18 8–9
Red Wine Risotto with Beans (Paniscia) ..... Jan/Feb 18 11
Torta Caprese (Chocolate-Almond Cake) ..... Nov/Dec 18 22–23

J
Jack cheeses
Colby, field guide ..... Mar/Apr 18 ..... BC
Monterey Jack
    grating ..... Jan/Feb 18 4
    Ground Beef and Cheese Enchiladas ..... Jan/Feb 18 4–5
Vella Dry, field guide ..... Mar/Apr 18 ..... BC
Japanese (cuisine)
Grilled Steak and Scallion Rolls (Negimaki) ..... Sep/Oct 18 8–9
shishito peppers, preparing at home ..... Mar/Apr 18 28
white miso paste, tasting of ..... Sep/Oct 18 28
Jasmine rice, basmati rice vs. ..... Sep/Oct 18 28
June Intelligent Oven, testing of ..... Nov/Dec 18 32

K
Kale, mechanically massaging ..... Sep/Oct 18 2
Kidde fire extinguisher recall ..... Mar/Apr 18 32
Kids, testing products for
chef's knives ..... Jul/Aug 18 32
fruit/vegetable peelers ..... Nov/Dec 18 32
oven mitts ..... Sep/Oct 18 32
Kiwi, Mango, and Blueberry Topping (for pavlovas) ..... Nov/Dec 18 21
Knives
boning, flexible, testing of ..... Sep/Oct 18 32
chef's, for kids, testing of ..... Jul/Aug 18 32
Korean Gochujang Paste ..... Jul/Aug 18 5
Kung Pao Chicken ..... Nov/Dec 18 12–13

L
Lame, improvised ..... Jan/Feb 18 2
Latin American (cuisines)
Brazilian Shrimp and Fish Stew (Moqueca) ..... Mar/Apr 18 10–11
Peruvian Fish Ceviche with Radishes and Orange ..... Jul/Aug 18 18–19
Legumes. *See* Bean(s)
Lemon(s)
Bars, Best ..... Mar/Apr 18 22–23
and Basil Butter ..... Sep/Oct 18 17
Chicken Piccata ..... Jan/Feb 18 10
for complexity, use every part (science) ..... Jan/Feb 18 10
flavor that lingers (science) ..... Mar/Apr 18 23
juice, garlic tamed with ..... Sep/Oct 18 5
Meyer vs. standard ..... Jan/Feb 18 28
Lemon grass, getting more out of ..... Jan/Feb 18 29
Lentil and Chickpea Soup, Moroccan (Harira) ..... Mar/Apr 18 14
Lexington Vinegar Barbecue Sauce ..... Mar/Apr 18 5
Lids, pot
for space-saving storage in refrigerator ..... Sep/Oct 18 2
storing in dish-drying rack ..... Mar/Apr 18 3
Lighter fluid ..... Jul/Aug 18 16
Lime
and Beer Cocktail, Mexican (Michelada) ..... Jul/Aug 18 9
Chili Salt ..... Sep/Oct 18 17
Linguine, dried, as lo mein alternative ..... May/Jun 18 29
Liquid smoke ..... Mar/Apr 18 5
Lobster, "sedating" ..... Nov/Dec 18 16
Lo mein noodles
Beijing-Style Meat Sauce and (Zha Jiang Mian) ..... May/Jun 18 19
shopping for ..... May/Jun 18 29

M

Macadamia nut cream .... Nov/Dec 18 ... 15
Maillard reaction, turkey gravy and .... Nov/Dec 18 ... 9
Main dishes
  beef
    Crispy Tacos (Tacos Dorados) .... Jul/Aug 18 ... 8–9
    Grilled Mojo-Marinated Skirt Steak .... May/Jun 18 ... 4–5
    Ground, and Cheese Enchiladas .... Jan/Feb 18 ... 4–5
    Japanese Grilled Steak and Scallion Rolls (Negimaki) .... Sep/Oct 18 ... 8–9
    Top Loin Roast with Potatoes .... Nov/Dec 18 ... 7
  chicken
    Caesar Salad .... May/Jun 18 ... 15
    Kung Pao .... Nov/Dec 18 ... 12–13
    Piccata .... Jan/Feb 18 ... 10
    Pulled, Indoor .... Mar/Apr 18 ... 4–5
    Roast, Crisp .... Jan/Feb 18 ... 17
    Roast, Weeknight .... Jan/Feb 18 ... 16
    Roast, with Warm Bread Salad .... May/Jun 18 ... 8–9
    Salad, Sichuan-Style (Bang Bang Ji Si) .... May/Jun 18 ... 15
    Salad with Mango, Thai-Style .... May/Jun 18 ... 15
    Thighs, Grilled, Best .... Jul/Aug 18 ... 4–5
    Three-Cup .... Mar/Apr 18 ... 20–21
    Vesuvio .... Sep/Oct 18 ... 4–5
  Falafel .... Sep/Oct 18 ... 12–13
  fish
    Peruvian Ceviche with Radishes and Orange .... Jul/Aug 18 ... 18–19
    Salmon, Roasted Whole Side of .... May/Jun 18 ... 6–7
    Swordfish Steaks, Pan-Seared .... Sep/Oct 18 ... 11
  Pasta alla Gricia (Rigatoni with Pancetta and
    Pecorino Romano) .... Nov/Dec 18 ... 10
  Pizza, One-Hour .... Mar/Apr 18 ... 8–9
  pork
    Beijing-Style Meat Sauce and Noodles (Zha Jiang Mian) .... May/Jun 18 ... 19
    Braised New Mexico–Style, in Red Chile Sauce
      (Carne Adovada) .... Sep/Oct 18 ... 6–7
    Chinese-Style Barbecued Spareribs .... Jan/Feb 18 ... 6–7
    Chops, Deviled .... May/Jun 18 ... 10–11
    Patties, Grilled, with Rice Noodles and Salad,
      Vietnamese (Bun Cha) .... Jul/Aug 18 ... 10–11
    Tenderloin Steaks, Perfect Pan-Seared .... Mar/Apr 18 ... 6
    Tenderloin Steaks, Sous Vide .... Mar/Apr 18 ... 7
  Red Wine Risotto with Beans (Paniscia) .... Jan/Feb 18 ... 11
  Turkey and Gravy for a Crowd .... Nov/Dec 18 ... 4–5
  White Bean and Mushroom Gratin .... Nov/Dec 18 ... 18
Mai Tai, field guide .... Nov/Dec 18 ... BC
Manchego, Gougères with Black Pepper and .... Jan/Feb 18 ... 15
Mango
  Kiwi, and Blueberry Topping (for pavlovas) .... Nov/Dec 18 ... 21
  Thai-Style Chicken Salad with .... May/Jun 18 ... 15
Manhattan (cocktail), field guide .... Nov/Dec 18 ... BC
Margarita, field guide .... Nov/Dec 18 ... BC
Marinades
  salt as most important ingredient in .... Nov/Dec 18 ... 17
  skirt steak and (science) .... May/Jun 18 ... 5
Martini, field guide .... Nov/Dec 18 ... BC
Measuring
  dry ingredients, leveling with bench scraper .... Nov/Dec 18 ... 31
  liquids halfway in dry measuring cups or spoons .... Nov/Dec 18 ... 3
Meat
  See also specific meats
  sauce
    and Noodles, Beijing-Style (Zha Jiang Mian) .... May/Jun 18 ... 19
    Simple Italian-Style (for pasta) .... Mar/Apr 18 ... 17
  tips and techniques
    baking soda as tenderizer for .... Nov/Dec 18 ... 17
    brining and salting .... Nov/Dec 18 ... 16
    dwindling heat during cooking .... Nov/Dec 18 ... 17
    searing before adding to low-liquid braises .... Nov/Dec 18 ... 16
    searing before vs. after roasting .... Nov/Dec 18 ... 16
    seasoning before stewing (science) .... Mar/Apr 18 ... 31

Meatless main dishes
  Falafel .... Sep/Oct 18 ... 12–13
  Pizza, One-Hour .... Mar/Apr 18 ... 8–9
  White Bean and Mushroom Gratin .... Nov/Dec 18 ... 18
Meat pounder, makeshift .... Jul/Aug 18 ... 3
Meaty flavor without meat .... Nov/Dec 18 ... 17
Meringue(s)
  cookies .... Nov/Dec 18 ... 20
  measuring egg whites for .... Nov/Dec 18 ... 21
  pavlovas .... Nov/Dec 18 ... 19–21
    with Fruit and Whipped Cream .... Nov/Dec 18 ... 20
    Individual, with Fruit and Whipped Cream .... Nov/Dec 18 ... 21
    Mango, Kiwi, and Blueberry Topping for .... Nov/Dec 18 ... 21
    Orange, Cranberry, and Mint Topping for .... Nov/Dec 18 ... 21
Mexican (cuisine)
  Corn Salad (Esquites) .... Jul/Aug 18 ... 20
  drinking chocolate, field guide .... Jan/Feb 18 ... BC
  Grilled Tomato Salsa .... Jul/Aug 18 ... 15
  Michelada (Mexican Beer and Lime Cocktail) .... Jul/Aug 18 ... 9
Meyer lemons, standard lemons vs. .... Jan/Feb 18 ... 28
Miche, field guide .... Sep/Oct 18 ... BC
Michelada (Mexican Beer and Lime Cocktail) .... Jul/Aug 18 ... 9
Microplane graters, for ginger, testing of .... Mar/Apr 18 ... 32
Microwave (ovens) .... May/Jun 18 ... 16–17
  anatomy and function of .... May/Jun 18 ... 16
  easy cleanup of .... May/Jun 18 ... 16
  paper towels for .... May/Jun 18 ... 17
  tips for heating food efficiently in .... May/Jun 18 ... 16
  unexpected ways to use .... May/Jun 18 ... 17
  waxed paper for .... Mar/Apr 18 ... 31
Middle Eastern (cuisines)
  Falafel .... Sep/Oct 18 ... 12–13
  Pickled Turnips and Carrots with Lemon and
    Coriander, Quick .... Sep/Oct 18 ... 29
  Pita Bread .... Sep/Oct 18 ... 14–15
  Tahini Sauce .... Sep/Oct 18 ... 13
Milk, hot, preventing from sticking to pans (science) .... Jul/Aug 18 ... 31
Milk frothers
  aerating one glass of wine with .... Nov/Dec 18 ... 2
  whizzing together small-batch dressings with .... Jan/Feb 18 ... 2
Millet, cooking in rice cooker .... Sep/Oct 18 ... 30
Mincer, Acme Rotary .... Jan/Feb 18 ... 30
Mint
  Chopped Carrot Salad with Pistachios, Pomegranate
    Seeds and .... Jan/Feb 18 ... 13
  Dried, Garlic Sauce, Spicy .... Sep/Oct 18 ... 11
  Julep, field guide .... Nov/Dec 18 ... BC
  Orange, and Cranberry Topping (for pavlovas) .... Nov/Dec 18 ... 21
Miso
  Dressing, Barley with Celery and .... May/Jun 18 ... 18
  Ginger Dressing, Creamless Creamy .... Nov/Dec 18 ... 15
  white, paste, tasting of .... Sep/Oct 18 ... 28
Mixer, stand, massaging kale with .... Sep/Oct 18 ... 2
Mojo-Marinated Skirt Steak, Grilled .... May/Jun 18 ... 4–5
Molasses
  in brown sugars .... Sep/Oct 18 ... 23
  Ginger Butter .... May/Jun 18 ... 13
Monterey Jack cheese
  grating .... Jan/Feb 18 ... 4
  Ground Beef and Cheese Enchiladas .... Jan/Feb 18 ... 4–5
Moqueca (Brazilian Shrimp and Fish Stew) .... Mar/Apr 18 ... 10–11
Moroccan (cuisine)
  Harissa (DIY recipe) .... Mar/Apr 18 ... 29
  Lentil and Chickpea Soup (Harira) .... Mar/Apr 18 ... 14
Mozzarella
  fresh
    Italian Pasta Salad .... Sep/Oct 18 ... 21
    Marinated Grilled Tomatoes with .... Jul/Aug 18 ... 15
    tasting of .... Jul/Aug 18 ... 24–25
  Pizza, One-Hour .... Mar/Apr 18 ... 8–9

COOK'S ILLUSTRATED INDEX 2018

Muenster, field guide .... Mar/Apr 18 BC
Mugs, preheating .... Mar/Apr 18 30
Mushroom(s)
    Cremini, Roasted .... Sep/Oct 18 17
    and White Bean Gratin .... Nov/Dec 18 18
Mustard
    Barbecue Sauce, South Carolina .... Mar/Apr 18 5
    sensory effects of (science) .... May/Jun 18 11
    Tarragon Paste .... Jul/Aug 18 5
Mustard greens, field guide .... May/Jun 18 BC

N

Narrow bottles, sponge for cleaning .... May/Jun 18 3
Negimaki (Japanese Grilled Steak and Scallion Rolls) .... Sep/Oct 18 8–9
Negroni, field guide .... Nov/Dec 18 BC
New Mexican (cuisine) .... Sep/Oct 18 6
    Braised Pork in Red Chile Sauce (Carne Adovada) .... Sep/Oct 18 6–7
New Mexican chiles .... Sep/Oct 18 7
Noodles
    See also Pasta
    Beijing-Style Meat Sauce and (Zha Jiang Mian) .... May/Jun 18 19
    Rice, and Salad, Vietnamese Grilled Pork Patties with
        (Bun Cha) .... Jul/Aug 18 10
North African (cuisines)
    Harissa (DIY recipe) .... Mar/Apr 18 29
    Moroccan Lentil and Chickpea Soup (Harira) .... Mar/Apr 18 14
Nucleotide-rich ingredients .... Nov/Dec 18 17
Nuoc cham (condiment) .... Jul/Aug 18 10
Nuoc Cham (recipe) .... Jul/Aug 18 11
Nut(s)
    See also specific nuts
    Candied, Quick .... May/Jun 18 29
    creams
        in creamless creamy dressings .... Nov/Dec 18 14–15
        testing various nuts as base for vegan
            cheeses and sauces .... Nov/Dec 18 15
    toasting in microwave .... May/Jun 18 17

O

Oil
    Aglio e Olio (Garlic and Oil Sauce) .... Mar/Apr 18 17
    for frying, cleaning with cornstarch and reusing ... Sep/Oct 18 31
    pouring from bottle
        in slow, steady stream .... Sep/Oct 18 3
        socking up drips .... Sep/Oct 18 2
Old-Fashioned (cocktail), field guide .... Nov/Dec 18 BC
Olives
    Italian Pasta Salad .... Sep/Oct 18 21
    steadying, for slicing .... Mar/Apr 18 3
Onion powder, seasoning dressings with .... Nov/Dec 18 14
Orange
    Almond Butter .... May/Jun 18 13
    Barley with Fennel, Dried Apricots and .... May/Jun 18 18
    Chopped Carrot Salad with Fennel, Hazelnuts and .... Jan/Feb 18 13
    Cranberry, and Mint Topping (for pavlovas) .... Nov/Dec 18 21
    Dark Chocolate Fudge Sauce .... Jul/Aug 18 21
    Peruvian Fish Ceviche with Radishes and .... Jul/Aug 18 18–19
    Whipped Cream .... Nov/Dec 18 23
Oregano
    dried vs. fresh .... Sep/Oct 18 4
    Mediterranean vs. Mexican .... Jul/Aug 18 29
Oven Fries, Thick-Cut .... Jan/Feb 18 8–9
Oven mitts for kids, testing of .... Sep/Oct 18 32
Ovens
    See also Microwave (ovens)
    June Intelligent Oven, testing of .... Nov/Dec 18 32
    preventing smoke in, with water bath .... Jan/Feb 18 7
    storing—and remembering—items in .... Jan/Feb 18 2

P

Pain au levain, field guide .... Sep/Oct 18 BC
Pain de mie, field guide .... Sep/Oct 18 BC
Pain d'epi, field guide .... Sep/Oct 18 BC
Pancakes
    butters for
        Ginger-Molasses .... May/Jun 18 13
        Orange-Almond .... May/Jun 18 13
    Easy .... May/Jun 18 12–13
    tips and techniques
        baking soda's enhancement of flavor .... Nov/Dec 18 17
        leftover, extending life of .... May/Jun 18 31
        lumpy vs. smooth batter .... May/Jun 18 13
        mix-in strategy .... May/Jun 18 28
        troubleshooting .... May/Jun 18 13
Pancetta, Rigatoni with Pecorino Romano and
    (Pasta alla Gricia) .... Nov/Dec 18 10
Panini presses
    cleaning crevices in .... Nov/Dec 18 2
    steam-cleaning .... Mar/Apr 18 3
Paniscia (Red Wine Risotto with Beans) .... Jan/Feb 18 11
Paper towels, for microwave .... May/Jun 18 17
Parchment paper
    crumpling for blind baking .... Jul/Aug 18 2
    testing of .... Mar/Apr 18 24–25
    waxed paper vs. .... Mar/Apr 18 31
Parmesan, grating too far in advance .... Mar/Apr 18 29
Pasta
    See also Noodles
    firmer when cool (retrogradation) .... Sep/Oct 18 21
    alla Gricia (Rigatoni with Pancetta and Pecorino Romano) .... Nov/Dec 18 10
    linguine, dried, as lo mein alternative .... May/Jun 18 29
    Roman quartet .... Nov/Dec 18 10
    Salad, Italian .... Sep/Oct 18 21
    sauces .... Mar/Apr 18 16–17
        Amatriciana .... Mar/Apr 18 17
        Basil Pesto, Classic .... Mar/Apr 18 16
        Garlic and Oil (Aglio e Olio) .... Mar/Apr 18 17
        Meat, Simple Italian-Style .... Mar/Apr 18 17
        Puttanesca .... Mar/Apr 18 16
        Tomato, Fresh .... Jul/Aug 18 6–7
        Tomato, Quick .... Mar/Apr 18 16
Pastry
    See also Pie(s)
    Gougères .... Jan/Feb 18 14–15
    Peach Tarte Tatin .... Jul/Aug 18 22–23
Pastry bag leaks, preventing .... Jan/Feb 18 30
Pastry brushes .... Jul/Aug 18 30
    natural-fiber, testing of .... Jul/Aug 18 32
    silicone, testing of .... Nov/Dec 18 32
Pastry wheels, fluted .... Sep/Oct 18 22
Pat-in-the-pan crust .... Mar/Apr 18 23
Pavlovas .... Nov/Dec 18 19–21
    with Fruit and Whipped Cream .... Nov/Dec 18 20
    Individual .... Nov/Dec 18 21
    Mango, Kiwi, and Blueberry Topping for .... Nov/Dec 18 21
    measuring egg whites for .... Nov/Dec 18 21
    Orange, Cranberry, and Mint Topping for .... Nov/Dec 18 21
Peach(es)
    juice shed by apples vs. .... Jul/Aug 18 23
    peeling and pitting .... Jul/Aug 18 31
    Tarte Tatin .... Jul/Aug 18 22–23
    yellow vs. white .... Jul/Aug 18 28
Peanut butter, crunchy, tasting of .... Nov/Dec 18 28
Pecan-Cinnamon Streusel .... Jan/Feb 18 18–19
Pecorino Romano
    grating too far in advance .... Mar/Apr 18 29
    tasting of .... Mar/Apr 18 26–27
    Rigatoni with Pancetta and (Pasta alla Gricia) ...... Nov/Dec 18 10
Peelers
    for kids, testing of .... Nov/Dec 18 32
    slicing butter for quick softening with .... Nov/Dec 18 3

Pepitas, in Nut-Free Chewy Granola Bars	Jul/Aug 18	13
Pepper(corns), black, sensory effects of (science)	May/Jun 18	11
Pepper(s)		
See also Chile(s)		
Roasted Red, and Tahini Dressing, Creamless Creamy	Nov/Dec 18	15
shishito, preparing at home	Mar/Apr 18	28
Pepperoncini, in Italian Pasta Salad	Sep/Oct 18	21
Pepper Sauce	Mar/Apr 18	11
Peruvian Fish Ceviche with Radishes and Orange	Jul/Aug 18	18–19
Pesto		
Arugula and Almond	May/Jun 18	7
Basil, Classic	Mar/Apr 18	16
Pickled Turnips and Carrots with Lemon and Coriander, Quick	Sep/Oct 18	29
Pie(s)		
Chocolate Cream	Jan/Feb 18	23
dough		
ensuring fray-free edges of	Jan/Feb 18	31
Foolproof, alcohol residue in	Nov/Dec 18	17
Foolproof All-Butter	Jan/Feb 18	21–23
mixing methods for (science)	Jan/Feb 18	21
rolling, waxed paper for	Mar/Apr 18	31
whole-wheat, rye, or buckwheat flour in (science)	Sep/Oct 18	31
leftover, storing	Jul/Aug 18	30
shells, blind baking		
cooking and eating pie-weight beans after	Mar/Apr 18	30
crumpling aluminum foil for	Jan/Feb 18	3
crumpling parchment paper for	Jul/Aug 18	2
Pinto beans, in Red Wine Risotto with Beans (Paniscia)	Jan/Feb 18	11
Pipe cleaners, as sturdier twist ties for plastic bags	Jan/Feb 18	2
Pisco Sour, field guide	Nov/Dec 18	BC
Pistachio(s)		
Chopped Carrot Salad with Mint, Pomegranate Seeds and	Jan/Feb 18	13
cream	Nov/Dec 18	15
Pita Bread	Sep/Oct 18	14–15
puffing of (science)	Sep/Oct 18	14
Pizza		
dough, proofing in takeout containers	May/Jun 18	3
One-Hour	Mar/Apr 18	8–9
Pizza ovens, indoor, testing of	Sep/Oct 18	32
Plantain Chips	Jul/Aug 18	29
Plastic bags		
sturdier twist ties for	Jan/Feb 18	2
zipper-lock		
facilitating opening of	May/Jun 18	3
piping deviled egg filling with	Sep/Oct 18	3
rinsing and draining fruits on the go in	May/Jun 18	3
Plastic food storage containers, testing of	May/Jun 18	26–27
Plastic salad greens boxes, reusing to store dry goods	Jul/Aug 18	3
Plastic wrap, tearing ahead for wrapping pastry or cookie dough	Jan/Feb 18	3
Polenta, field guide	Jul/Aug 18	BC
Pomegranate		
Molasses, Tart	Jan/Feb 18	29
Seeds, Chopped Carrot Salad with Mint, Pistachios and	Jan/Feb 18	13
Popcorn		
crimson, field guide	Jul/Aug 18	BC
served with ceviche	Jul/Aug 18	19
Spicy Caramel	Mar/Apr 18	19
yellow, field guide	Jul/Aug 18	BC
Pork		
Braised New Mexico–Style, in Red Chile Sauce (Carne Adovada)	Sep/Oct 18	6–7
butt		
breaking down	Sep/Oct 18	30
distinguishing features of pork shoulder vs.	Sep/Oct 18	28
Chops, Deviled	May/Jun 18	10–11
ground		
Beijing-Style Meat Sauce and Noodles (Zha Jiang Mian)	May/Jun 18	19
Vietnamese Grilled Pork Patties with Rice Noodles and Salad (Bun Cha)	Jul/Aug 18	10–11

Pork (cont.)		
Pancetta, Rigatoni with Pecorino Romano and (Pasta alla Gricia)	Nov/Dec 18	10
salt, in Amatriciana	Mar/Apr 18	17
shoulder, distinguishing features of pork butt vs.	Sep/Oct 18	28
spareribs		
Chinese-Style Barbecued	Jan/Feb 18	6–7
St. Louis–style vs. full rack	Jan/Feb 18	29
tenderloin roast, low oven vs. sous vide methods for	Mar/Apr 18	31
tenderloin steaks	Mar/Apr 18	6–7
Pan-Seared, Perfect	Mar/Apr 18	6
Scallion-Ginger Relish for	Mar/Apr 18	6
Sous Vide	Mar/Apr 18	7
Potato(es)		
Beef Top Loin Roast with	Nov/Dec 18	7
Chicken Vesuvio	Sep/Oct 18	4–5
Oven Fries, Thick-Cut	Jan/Feb 18	8–9
purple	May/Jun 18	29
Pot lids		
for space-saving storage in refrigerator	Sep/Oct 18	2
storing in dish-drying rack	Mar/Apr 18	3
Pouring neatly		
boxed broth	Nov/Dec 18	2
oil bottle in slow, steady stream	Sep/Oct 18	3
from one vessel to another	Jul/Aug 18	31
socking up drips on bottle	Sep/Oct 18	2
Pressure cooker, transporting soups and stews in	Mar/Apr 18	2
Probe thermometers		
deep frying and	Sep/Oct 18	13
testing of (update)	Mar/Apr 18	32
Propane tanks, checking fuel level in	Jul/Aug 18	17
Pulled Chicken, Indoor	Mar/Apr 18	4–5
Puttanesca	Mar/Apr 18	16

Q

Quinoa, cooking in rice cooker	Sep/Oct 18	30

R

Radicchio, field guide	May/Jun 18	BC
Radishes		
Buttery Spring Vegetables	May/Jun 18	22
Chopped Carrot Salad with Sesame Seeds and	Jan/Feb 18	13
Peruvian Fish Ceviche with Orange and	Jul/Aug 18	18–19
Raisins		
Chopped Carrot Salad with Celery and	Jan/Feb 18	13
reviving flat champagne with	Nov/Dec 18	30
Rasp-style graters		
rescuing burnt cookies with	Nov/Dec 18	3
when to retire	Mar/Apr 18	31
Recipes		
keeping cookbook open to, while cooking	Jan/Feb 18	2
marking ingredient additions in	Jan/Feb 18	3
pinning your place in	Jul/Aug 18	2
Red snapper, in Peruvian Fish Ceviche with Radishes and Orange	Jul/Aug 18	18–19
Red Wine Risotto with Beans (Paniscia)	Jan/Feb 18	11
Refrigerator, saving space when storing pots in	Sep/Oct 18	2
Relishes		
Caper-Currant	Sep/Oct 18	11
Cucumber-Ginger	May/Jun 18	7
Scallion-Ginger	Mar/Apr 18	6
Residual heat, cooking with	Mar/Apr 18	11
Rice		
basmati		
aging process and	Sep/Oct 18	24
jasmine rice vs.	Sep/Oct 18	28
tasting of	Sep/Oct 18	24–25
Chinese Restaurant–Style	Mar/Apr 18	21

Rice (cont.)
- risotto
  - ditching traditional rules for ..... Jan/Feb 18 30
  - Red Wine, with Beans (Paniscia) ..... Jan/Feb 18 11
- white, faster, easier ..... Nov/Dec 18 30

Rice cookers, other grains to cook in ..... Sep/Oct 18 30

Rice noodles
- and Salad, Vietnamese Grilled Pork Patties with (Bun Cha) ..... Jul/Aug 18 10
- two common types of ..... Jul/Aug 18 11

Ricers
- squeezing excess water from thawed chopped spinach with ..... Sep/Oct 18 3
- supersmooth guacamole with ..... Mar/Apr 18 2

Rigatoni with Pancetta and Pecorino Romano (Pasta alla Gricia) ..... Nov/Dec 18 10

Risotto
- ditching traditional rules for ..... Jan/Feb 18 30
- Red Wine, with Beans (Paniscia) ..... Jan/Feb 18 11

Roman (cuisine)
- Pasta alla Gricia (Rigatoni with Pancetta and Pecorino Romano) ..... Nov/Dec 18 10
- pasta quartet ..... Nov/Dec 18 10

Romano cheeses, tasting of ..... Mar/Apr 18 26–27
Rosemary, dried vs. fresh ..... Sep/Oct 18 4
Rose water ..... May/Jun 18 29

Roux
- browning ..... Nov/Dec 18 9
- emergency, in microwave ..... May/Jun 18 17

Rubber gloves
- removing clingy silk from fresh corn with ..... Jul/Aug 18 3
- used, cutting into rubber bands ..... May/Jun 18 3

Rum, Applesauce with Brown Sugar and ..... Sep/Oct 18 19
Russian Dressing, Creamless Creamy ..... Nov/Dec 18 15
Rye flour, in Foolproof All-Butter Pie Dough ..... Sep/Oct 18 31

S

Sachet, makeshift, for stock ..... Jan/Feb 18 3
Sage, dried vs. fresh ..... Sep/Oct 18 4
Salad bowls, wooden, caring for ..... May/Jun 18 30
Salad greens boxes, reusing to store dry goods ..... Jul/Aug 18 3

Salads
- Bread, Warm, Roast Chicken with ..... May/Jun 18 8–9
- carrot, chopped ..... Jan/Feb 18 12–13
  - with Celery and Raisins ..... Jan/Feb 18 13
  - with Fennel, Orange, and Hazelnuts ..... Jan/Feb 18 13
  - with Mint, Pistachios, and Pomegranate Seeds ..... Jan/Feb 18 13
  - with Radishes and Sesame Seeds ..... Jan/Feb 18 13
  - shredded carrot salads vs. ..... Jan/Feb 18 13
- chicken ..... May/Jun 18 14–15
  - Caesar ..... May/Jun 18 15
  - perfect poached chicken for ..... May/Jun 18 15
  - Sichuan-Style (Bang Bang Ji Si) ..... May/Jun 18 15
  - Thai-Style, with Mango ..... May/Jun 18 15
- Corn, Mexican (Esquites) ..... Jul/Aug 18 20
- Pasta, Italian ..... Sep/Oct 18 21

Salad spinners, testing of ..... Nov/Dec 18 32

Salami(s)
- common, distinguishing features of ..... Jan/Feb 18 28
- Italian Pasta Salad ..... Sep/Oct 18 21
- Red Wine Risotto with Beans (Paniscia) ..... Jan/Feb 18 11

Salmon, whole side of
- buying and trimming ..... May/Jun 18 28
- Roasted ..... May/Jun 18 6–7
  - cutting into perfect portions ..... May/Jun 18 6
  - honey for even browning of ..... May/Jun 18 7

Salsa, Grilled Tomato ..... Jul/Aug 18 15

Salt
- for airy puffs ..... Jan/Feb 18 15
- brining and salting techniques for poultry and meat ..... Nov/Dec 18 16
- Chili-Lime ..... Sep/Oct 18 17
- iodized vs. pure, tasting of ..... Sep/Oct 18 29
- as most important ingredient in marinade ..... Nov/Dec 18 17

Salt (cont.)
- seasoning meat vs. stew with (science) ..... Mar/Apr 18 31
- serving temperature and (science) ..... Jan/Feb 18 31

Sauces
See also Dressings; Gravy
- Arugula and Almond Pesto ..... May/Jun 18 7
- barbecue
  - Mustard, South Carolina ..... Mar/Apr 18 5
  - Sweet and Tangy ..... Mar/Apr 18 5
  - Vinegar, Lexington ..... Mar/Apr 18 5
- Caramel, All-Purpose ..... Mar/Apr 18 19
- Cherry ..... May/Jun 18 21
- creamy, garlic as emulsifier for ..... Sep/Oct 18 5
- Dark Chocolate Fudge ..... Jul/Aug 18 21
  - Orange ..... Jul/Aug 18 21
- Dried Mint–Garlic, Spicy ..... Sep/Oct 18 11
- Enchilada ..... Jan/Feb 18 5
- Herb, Basque-Style (Tximitxurri) ..... Nov/Dec 18 11
- Honey, Spicy ..... Nov/Dec 18 11
- Hot Pepper (Brazilian-style) ..... Mar/Apr 18 11
- Nuoc Cham ..... Jul/Aug 18 11
- pasta ..... Mar/Apr 18 16–17
  - Amatriciana ..... Mar/Apr 18 17
  - Basil Pesto, Classic ..... Mar/Apr 18 16
  - Garlic and Oil (Aglio e Olio) ..... Mar/Apr 18 17
  - Meat, Simple Italian-Style ..... Mar/Apr 18 17
  - Puttanesca ..... Mar/Apr 18 16
  - Tomato, Fresh ..... Jul/Aug 18 6–7
  - Tomato, Quick ..... Mar/Apr 18 16
- Tahini ..... Sep/Oct 18 13
- Tomato-Chile ..... Sep/Oct 18 13

Scallion(s)
- Ginger Relish ..... Mar/Apr 18 6
- Grilled Steak and, Rolls, Japanese (Negimaki) ..... Sep/Oct 18 8–9

Science
- cake texture, creaming and ..... Nov/Dec 18 31
- carrot skin, texture and flavor of ..... Jan/Feb 18 12
- chicken
  - baking soda in overnight rub for ..... Jan/Feb 18 17
  - with tender meat and crisp skin ..... Jul/Aug 18 5
- emulsions ..... May/Jun 18 31
- falafel held together by flour paste ..... Sep/Oct 18 13
- hot milk, keeping from sticking to pans ..... Jul/Aug 18 31
- juice shed by peaches vs. apples ..... Jul/Aug 18 23
- lemon
  - for complexity, use every part ..... Jan/Feb 18 10
  - flavor that lingers ..... Mar/Apr 18 23
- pie dough, mixing method for ..... Jan/Feb 18 21
- pita bread, puffing of ..... Sep/Oct 18 14
- salt and serving temperature ..... Jan/Feb 18 31
- skirt steak, marinating ..... May/Jun 18 5
- spicy ingredients, calibrating best burn from combination of ..... May/Jun 18 11
- stew, seasoning meat vs. ..... Mar/Apr 18 31
- swordfish steaks
  - benefits of frequent flipping ..... Sep/Oct 18 11
  - explanation for mushy texture ..... Sep/Oct 18 11

Scrambled Eggs, Creamy French-Style ..... Jan/Feb 18 20
Seafood. See Fish; Swordfish steaks

Searing meat
- low-liquid braises and ..... Nov/Dec 18 16
- before vs. after roasting ..... Nov/Dec 18 16

Semifreddo
- Chocolate ..... May/Jun 18 20–21
- folding technique for ..... May/Jun 18 30
- helping to resist melting ..... May/Jun 18 21

Serving temperature, salt and and (science) ..... Jan/Feb 18 31

Sesame seeds
- Chopped Carrot Salad with Raisins and ..... Jan/Feb 18 13
- Nut-Free Chewy Granola Bars ..... Jul/Aug 18 13

Shallots
- Caramel-Braised, with Black Pepper ..... Mar/Apr 18 19
- frying in microwave ..... May/Jun 18 17

Shaoxing wine .... Mar/Apr 18 21
Shears, kitchen
    testing of .... May/Jun 18 32
    uses for .... May/Jun 18 31
Shishito peppers, preparing at home .... Mar/Apr 18 28
Shower cap, as impromptu bowl cover .... Nov/Dec 18 2
Shrimp
    ceviche .... Jul/Aug 18 19
    cooking with residual heat .... Mar/Apr 18 11
    and Fish Stew, Brazilian (Moqueca) .... Mar/Apr 18 10–11
Sichuan peppercorns .... Nov/Dec 18 13
Sichuan-Style Chicken Salad (Bang Bang Ji Si) ... May/Jun 18 15
Side dishes
    Applesauce, Savory, with Beets and Horseradish ... Sep/Oct 18 19
    Asparagus, Roasted .... Sep/Oct 18 16
    barley
        with Celery and Miso Dressing .... May/Jun 18 18
        with Fennel, Dried Apricots, and Orange ... May/Jun 18 18
        with Lemon and Herbs .... May/Jun 18 18
    Broccoli, Roasted .... Sep/Oct 18 16
    broccolini, pan-steamed
        with Ginger .... Mar/Apr 18 15
        with Shallot .... Mar/Apr 18 15
    Brussels Sprouts, Roasted .... Sep/Oct 18 17
    Butternut Squash, Roasted .... Sep/Oct 18 17
    Carrots, Roasted .... Sep/Oct 18 17
    carrot salads, chopped
        with Celery and Raisins .... Jan/Feb 18 13
        with Fennel, Orange, and Hazelnuts ..... Jan/Feb 18 13
        with Mint, Pistachios, and Pomegranate Seeds ... Jan/Feb 18 13
        with Radishes and Sesame Seeds .... Jan/Feb 18 13
    Cauliflower, Roasted .... Sep/Oct 18 17
    Corn Salad, Mexican (Esquites) .... Jul/Aug 18 20
    Cremini Mushrooms, Roasted .... Sep/Oct 18 17
    Delicata Squash, Roasted .... Nov/Dec 18 11
    Fennel, Roasted .... Sep/Oct 18 17
    green beans
        Roasted .... Sep/Oct 18 17
        Skillet-Charred .... Sep/Oct 18 20
        Skillet-Charred, with Crispy Bread-Crumb Topping ... Sep/Oct 18 20
    Oven Fries, Thick-Cut .... Jan/Feb 18 8–9
    Pasta Salad, Italian .... Sep/Oct 18 21
    Rice, Chinese Restaurant–Style .... Mar/Apr 18 21
    Spring Vegetables, Buttery .... May/Jun 18 22
    Tomatoes, Grilled .... Jul/Aug 18 15
        with Fresh Mozzarella .... Jul/Aug 18 15
    Turnips and Carrots, Quick Pickled, with Lemon
        and Coriander .... Sep/Oct 18 29
Silicone baking mats, testing of .... Mar/Apr 18 32
Silicone brushes .... Jul/Aug 18 30
    testing of .... Nov/Dec 18 32
Skillets
    carbon-steel, caring for .... Jan/Feb 18 30
    cast-iron, testing of handle covers for ...... Mar/Apr 18 32
    hot vs. "cold" (not preheated), browning food in ... Nov/Dec 18 16
    as makeshift meat pounder .... Jul/Aug 18 3
Skirt steak
    Grilled Mojo-Marinated .... May/Jun 18 4–5
    marinating (science) .... May/Jun 18 5
    shopping for .... May/Jun 18 5
Smart cooking systems, testing of
    Hestan Cue Smart Cooking System .... Sep/Oct 18 32
    June Intelligent Oven .... Nov/Dec 18 32
Snacks
    Candied Nuts, Quick .... May/Jun 18 29
    granola bars, chewy
        with Hazelnuts, Cherries, and Cacao Nibs ... Jul/Aug 18 13
        Nut-Free .... Jul/Aug 18 13
        with Walnuts and Cranberries .... Jul/Aug 18 13
    Plantain Chips .... Jul/Aug 18 29
    Popcorn, Spicy Caramel .... Mar/Apr 18 19

Socking up bottle drips .... Sep/Oct 18 2
Soda bread, Irish
    Brown (recipe) .... Mar/Apr 18 12–13
    hearth-baked original .... Mar/Apr 18 13
    white .... Mar/Apr 18 12
Soppressata .... Jan/Feb 18 28
Soups
    Gazpacho, Grilled Tomato .... Jul/Aug 18 15
    Lentil and Chickpea, Moroccan (Harira) ... Mar/Apr 18 14
    transporting in pressure cooker .... Mar/Apr 18 2
Sous vide cooking
    low-oven method vs., for pork tenderloin roast ... Mar/Apr 18 31
    Pork Tenderloin Steaks .... Mar/Apr 18 7
    testing of circulators for .... Mar/Apr 18 7
South Carolina Mustard Barbecue Sauce .... Mar/Apr 18 5
Southeast Asian (cuisines)
    nuoc cham (condiment) .... Jul/Aug 18 10
    Nuoc Cham (recipe) .... Jul/Aug 18 11
    rice noodle varieties .... Jul/Aug 18 11
    Thai-Style Chicken Salad with Mango ...... May/Jun 18 15
    Vietnamese Grilled Pork Patties with Rice Noodles and
        Salad (Bun Cha) .... Jul/Aug 18 10–11
Spareribs
    Chinese-Style Barbecued .... Jan/Feb 18 6–7
    St. Louis–style vs. full rack .... Jan/Feb 18 29
Spatulas
    compact or cookie, testing of .... Jan/Feb 18 32
    fish vs. conventional .... Nov/Dec 18 26
    metal, testing of .... Nov/Dec 18 26–27
Speculoos (Belgian Spice Cookies) .... Sep/Oct 18 22–23
    with Almonds .... Sep/Oct 18 23
Spice(s)
    Cookies, Belgian (Speculoos) .... Sep/Oct 18 22–23
        with Almonds .... Sep/Oct 18 23
    pastes
        Gochujang .... Jul/Aug 18 5
        Mustard-Tarragon .... Jul/Aug 18 5
    tips and techniques
        advance prep of "spice kits" for favorite dishes ... Jul/Aug 18 3
        dried, judging freshness of .... Mar/Apr 18 14
        ground, storing in glass vs. plastic .... Jan/Feb 18 29
        surplus, reminder system for .... May/Jun 18 2
        whole, toasting in microwave .... May/Jun 18 17
Spicy Caramel Popcorn .... Mar/Apr 18 19
Spicy Dried Mint–Garlic Sauce .... Sep/Oct 18 11
**Spicy ingredients, calibrating best burn from
    combination of (science)** .... May/Jun 18 11
Spinach, thawed chopped, "ricing" water out of ... Sep/Oct 18 3
**Sponge attached to wooden spoon for cleaning
    narrow bottles** .... May/Jun 18 3
Spring Vegetables, Buttery .... May/Jun 18 22
Squash (winter)
    butternut, roasting .... Sep/Oct 18 16
    delicata
        buying, storing, and prepping .... Nov/Dec 18 29
        Roasted .... Nov/Dec 18 11
Stand mixer, massaging kale with .... Sep/Oct 18 2
Star anise, storing in glass vs. plastic .... Jan/Feb 18 29
Starters. *See* **Appetizers and first courses**
Steak
    Grilled, and Scallion Rolls, Japanese (Negimaki) ... Sep/Oct 18 8–9
    skirt
        Grilled Mojo-Marinated .... May/Jun 18 4–5
        marinating (science) .... May/Jun 18 5
        shopping for .... May/Jun 18 5
    tough, thin, how to slice .... May/Jun 18 31
Steamer baskets, testing of .... Jul/Aug 18 32
Stews
    seasoning meat before stewing and (science) ... Mar/Apr 18 31
    Shrimp and Fish, Brazilian (Moqueca) ...... Mar/Apr 18 10–11
    transporting in pressure cooker .... Mar/Apr 18 2

COOK'S ILLUSTRATED INDEX 2018

Stir-fries
    Kung Pao Chicken .... Nov/Dec 18   12–13
    lubricating garlic and ginger with oil for .... Nov/Dec 18   13

Stock
    makeshift sachet for .... Jan/Feb 18   3
    turkey
        defatting, flavor lost by .... Nov/Dec 18   9
        giblets and other parts to include in .... Nov/Dec 18   28
        making more flavorful .... Nov/Dec 18   8

Storage containers
    See also Food storage containers
    reusing salad greens boxes for dry goods .... Jul/Aug 18   3

Strawberry huller, hollowing out cupcakes for
    filling with .... Mar/Apr 18   3

Streusel, Pecan-Cinnamon, Coffee Cake with .... Jan/Feb 18   18–19

String cheese, field guide .... Mar/Apr 18   BC

Sugar
    brown, molasses content of .... Sep/Oct 18   23
    caramelizing, in microwave .... May/Jun 18   17
    creaming butter and, impact on cake texture (science) ..... Nov/Dec 18   31

Sugar nippers .... May/Jun 18   30
Sugar snap peas, in Buttery Spring Vegetables .... May/Jun 18   22
Sweet and Tangy Barbecue Sauce .... Mar/Apr 18   5
Swiss cheese, field guide .... Mar/Apr 18   BC
Swizzle stick (bois lélé) .... Jul/Aug 18   30

Swordfish steaks .... Sep/Oct 18   10–11
    accompaniments for
        Caper-Currant Relish .... Sep/Oct 18   11
        Spicy Dried Mint–Garlic Sauce .... Sep/Oct 18   11
    buying and prepping .... Sep/Oct 18   10
    Pan-Seared .... Sep/Oct 18   11
    science
        benefits of frequent flipping .... Sep/Oct 18   11
        explanation for mushy texture .... Sep/Oct 18   11

T

Tacos
    Crispy (Tacos Dorados) .... Jul/Aug 18   8–9
    filled soft, keeping closed .... Mar/Apr 18   2
    filling before frying .... Jul/Aug 18   8, 9

Tahini
    and Roasted Red Pepper Dressing, Creamless Creamy ..... Nov/Dec 18   15
    Sauce .... Sep/Oct 18   13

Takeout containers, proofing pizza dough in .... May/Jun 18   3
Tangzhong (Asian bread-baking technique) .... Nov/Dec 18   16
    falafel and .... Sep/Oct 18   12, 13
Tarragon-Mustard Paste .... Jul/Aug 18   5
Tarte Tatin, Peach .... Jul/Aug 18   22–23

Tastings
    basmati rice .... Sep/Oct 18   24–25
    butter, unsalted .... Nov/Dec 18   24–25
    cheeses
        burrata .... Jul/Aug 18   28
        mozzarella, fresh .... Jul/Aug 18   24–25
        Pecorino Romano and Romano .... Mar/Apr 18   26–27
    chicken, whole .... Jan/Feb 18   16
    chickpeas, canned .... Jan/Feb 18   28
    chocolate chips, dark .... Jan/Feb 18   26–27
    cocoa powder .... May/Jun 18   23–25
        past its expiration date .... Jul/Aug 18   28
    garlic products, convenience .... Sep/Oct 18   29
    lemons, Meyer vs. standard .... Jan/Feb 18   28
    oregano, Mediterranean vs. Mexican .... Jul/Aug 18   29
    peaches, yellow vs. white .... Jul/Aug 18   28
    peanut butter, crunchy .... Nov/Dec 18   28
    salt, iodized vs. pure .... Sep/Oct 18   29
    turkey bacon .... Mar/Apr 18   28
    turmeric, ground .... May/Jun 18   28
    white miso paste .... Sep/Oct 18   28

Teapot, ceramic, keeping gravy hot for serving in .... Jan/Feb 18   3
Tenderizer, baking soda as .... Nov/Dec 18   17

Testing. *See* Equipment and product testing

Tex-Mex (cuisine)
    Crispy Tacos (Tacos Dorados) .... Jul/Aug 18   8–9
    Ground Beef and Cheese Enchiladas .... Jan/Feb 18   4–5

Thai-Style Chicken Salad with Mango .... May/Jun 18   15

Thermometers
    digital
        caring for .... Jul/Aug 18   26
        testing of .... Jul/Aug 18   26–27
    grill, improvised holder for .... Nov/Dec 18   2
    probe
        deep frying and .... Sep/Oct 18   13
        testing of (update) .... Mar/Apr 18   32

Three-Cup Chicken .... Mar/Apr 18   20–21
Thyme, dried vs. fresh .... Sep/Oct 18   4

Tomato(es)
    balancing flavor in various parts of .... Jul/Aug 18   7
    cherry, slicing in half efficiently .... Nov/Dec 18   3
    Chile Sauce .... Sep/Oct 18   13
    Grilled .... Jul/Aug 18   14–15
        Gazpacho .... Jul/Aug 18   15
        Marinated, with Fresh Mozzarella .... Jul/Aug 18   15
        Salsa .... Jul/Aug 18   15
    halving, for grilling .... Jul/Aug 18   15
    paste, pushing out of can .... Jul/Aug 18   2
    sauces (for pasta)
        Amatriciana .... Mar/Apr 18   17
        Fresh .... Jul/Aug 18   6–7
        Meat, Simple Italian-Style .... Mar/Apr 18   17
        Puttanesca .... Mar/Apr 18   16
        Quick .... Mar/Apr 18   16

Tom Collins, field guide .... Nov/Dec 18   BC

Tongs
    9-inch, testing of .... Jul/Aug 18   32
    shredding chicken with .... Mar/Apr 18   4

Toothpicks, keeping filled soft tacos closed with .... Mar/Apr 18   2
Torta Caprese (Italian Chocolate-Almond Cake) .... Nov/Dec 18   22–23

Tortilla(s)
    chips, field guide .... Jul/Aug 18   BC
    Ground Beef and Cheese Enchiladas .... Jan/Feb 18   4–5
    tacos
        Crispy (Tacos Dorados) .... Jul/Aug 18   8–9
        filled soft, keeping closed .... Mar/Apr 18   2
        filling before frying .... Jul/Aug 18   8, 9
    white corn, field guide .... Jul/Aug 18   BC

Treviso, field guide .... May/Jun 18   BC
Turbinado sugar .... Sep/Oct 18   23

Turkey
    bacon
        best way to cook .... Mar/Apr 18   30
        tasting of .... Mar/Apr 18   28
    brining .... Nov/Dec 18   16
        in cooler .... Nov/Dec 18   31
    gravy
        browning roux for .... Nov/Dec 18   9
        gluten- (or alcohol-) free .... Nov/Dec 18   9
        Our Favorite .... Nov/Dec 18   9
    and Gravy for a Crowd .... Nov/Dec 18   4–5
    stock
        defatting, flavor lost by .... Nov/Dec 18   9
        giblets and other parts to include in .... Nov/Dec 18   28
        making more flavorful .... Nov/Dec 18   8
    temperature of, after standard 30-minute resting time ..... Nov/Dec 18   28

Turkey baster, "skimming" fat with .... Jan/Feb 18   2

Turmeric
    fresh .... Sep/Oct 18   29
    ground, tasting of .... May/Jun 18   28

Turnips
    Buttery Spring Vegetables .... May/Jun 18   22
    Quick Pickled Carrots and, with Lemon and Coriander ..... Sep/Oct 18   29

Twist ties for plastic bags, sturdier .... Jan/Feb 18   2
Tximitxurri (Basque-Style Herb Sauce) .... Nov/Dec 18   11

U

Under-appliance dusters, testing of .... May/Jun 18 — 2

V

Vanilla extract
    emergency sub for .... Nov/Dec 18 — 29
    substituting rose water for .... May/Jun 18 — 29

Vegan cooking
    See also Vegetarian cooking
    nut creams in .... Nov/Dec 18 — 14–15

Vegetable(s)
    See also specific vegetables
    baking soda's impact on cooking .... Nov/Dec 18 — 17
    dense, judging doneness with metal cake tester .... Sep/Oct 18 — 3
    Roasted, Everyday .... Sep/Oct 18 — 16–17
        Basil and Lemon Butter for .... Sep/Oct 18 — 17
        Chili-Lime Salt for .... Sep/Oct 18 — 17
    Spring, Buttery .... May/Jun 18 — 22

Vegetable oil spray
    for oven fries .... Jan/Feb 18 — 8
    to prevent hot milk from sticking to pan (science) .... Jul/Aug 18 — 31

Vegetable peelers
    for kids, testing of .... Nov/Dec 18 — 32
    slicing butter for quick softening with .... Nov/Dec 18 — 3

Vegetarian cooking
    meatiness without meat in .... Nov/Dec 18 — 17
    meatless main dishes
        Falafel .... Sep/Oct 18 — 12–13
        Pizza, One-Hour .... Mar/Apr 18 — 8–9
        White Bean and Mushroom Gratin .... Nov/Dec 18 — 18
    nut creams in .... Nov/Dec 18 — 14–15

Vella Dry Jack, field guide .... Mar/Apr 18 — BC

Vermouth, dry, shelf life of .... Mar/Apr 18 — 29

Vietnamese (cuisine)
    Grilled Pork Patties with Rice Noodles and Salad (Bun Cha) .... Jul/Aug 18 — 10–11
    nuoc cham (condiment) .... Jul/Aug 18 — 10
    Nuoc Cham (recipe) .... Jul/Aug 18 — 11
    rice noodle varieties .... Jul/Aug 18 — 11

Vinegar Barbecue Sauce, Lexington .... Mar/Apr 18 — 5

W

Walnut(s)
    Chewy Granola Bars with Cranberries and .... Jul/Aug 18 — 13
    cream .... Nov/Dec 18 — 15

Washing machine, chilling beverages for party in .... Nov/Dec 18 — 2

Water bath, preventing oven smoke with .... Jan/Feb 18 — 7

Water bottles, glass .... Nov/Dec 18 — 32

Watercress, field guide .... May/Jun 18 — BC

Watermelon, cutting into "sticks" .... Jul/Aug 18 — 2

Waxed paper
    parchment paper vs. .... Mar/Apr 18 — 31
    uses for .... Mar/Apr 18 — 31

Whipped cream
    Amaretto .... Nov/Dec 18 — 23
    folding technique for .... May/Jun 18 — 30
    Orange .... Nov/Dec 18 — 23
    Pavlova with Fruit and .... Nov/Dec 18 — 20
        Individual .... Nov/Dec 18 — 21

Whisks, cleaning .... Mar/Apr 18 — 2

White Bean and Mushroom Gratin .... Nov/Dec 18 — 18

White miso paste, tasting of .... Sep/Oct 18 — 28

Wholemeal flour, Irish, mimicking texture of .... Mar/Apr 18 — 13

Whole-wheat flour
    in Foolproof All-Butter Pie Dough .... Sep/Oct 18 — 31
    Irish wholemeal flour vs. .... Mar/Apr 18 — 13

Wine(s)
    aerating one glass of .... Nov/Dec 18 — 2
    bottles
        safely transporting more than one .... May/Jun 18 — 2
        socking up drips on .... Sep/Oct 18 — 2
    champagne
        cocktail, field guide .... Nov/Dec 18 — BC
        flat, reviving with raisin .... Nov/Dec 18 — 30
    cooking with
        cheap wines .... Nov/Dec 18 — 29
        Chinese cuisine and .... Mar/Apr 18 — 21
    Red, Risotto with Beans (Paniscia) .... Jan/Feb 18 — 11
    vermouth, dry, shelf life of .... Mar/Apr 18 — 29

Wire cooling rack, dicing avocados with .... Jan/Feb 18 — 31

Wood chips, pantry ingredients tested as alternatives to .... Nov/Dec 18 — 17

Wooden salad bowls, caring for .... May/Jun 18 — 30

Wooden spoons
    cleaning narrow bottles with sponge attached to .... May/Jun 18 — 3
    keeping cookbook open for cooking with .... Jan/Feb 18 — 2

Y

Yeast-fermented doughs
    shortcutting fermented flavor of .... Mar/Apr 18 — 9
    that ferment in the refrigerator, colder water for .... Sep/Oct 18 — 31

Z

Zha Jiang Mian (Beijing-Style Meat Sauce and Noodles) .... May/Jun 18 — 19

Zipper-lock bags
    facilitating opening of .... May/Jun 18 — 3
    piping deviled egg filling with .... Sep/Oct 18 — 3
    rinsing and draining fruits on the go in .... May/Jun 18 — 3

$35.00

Copyright © 2018 by The Editors of *Cook's Illustrated*
All rights reserved, including the right of reproduction
in whole or in part in any form.

Published by
America's Test Kitchen
21 Drydock Avenue, Suite 210E
Boston, MA 02210

Manufactured in the United States of America

ISBN: 978-1-945256-64-6
ISSN: 1933-639X

To get home delivery of *Cook's Illustrated* magazine, call 800-526-8442 inside the U.S., or 515-237-3663 if calling from outside the U.S., or subscribe online at www.CooksIllustrated.com/Subscribe.

In addition to *Cook's Illustrated* Annual Hardbound Editions available from each year of publication (1993–2018), America's Test Kitchen offers the following cookbooks:

The New Essentials Cookbook
Dinner Illustrated
Cook's Illustrated Revolutionary Recipes
Tasting Italy: A Culinary Journey
Cooking at Home with Bridget and Julia
The Complete Diabetes Cookbook
The Complete Slow Cooker
The Complete Make-Ahead Cookbook
The Complete Mediterranean Cookbook
The Complete Vegetarian Cookbook
The Complete Cooking for Two Cookbook
The Complete Cooking for Two Cookbook Gift Edition
Just Add Sauce
How to Roast Everything
Nutritious Delicious
What Good Cooks Know
Cook's Science
The Science of Good Cooking
The Perfect Cake
The Perfect Cookie
Bread Illustrated
Master of the Grill
Kitchen Smarts: Questions and Answers to Boost Your Cooking I.Q.
Kitchen Hacks: How Clever Cooks Get Things Done
100 Recipes: The Absolute Best Way to Make the True Essentials
The New Family Cookbook
The America's Test Kitchen Cooking School Cookbook
The Cook's Illustrated Meat Book
The Cook's Illustrated Baking Book
The Cook's Illustrated Cookbook
The America's Test Kitchen Family Baking Book
The Best of America's Test Kitchen (2007–2019 Editions)
The Complete America's Test Kitchen TV Show Cookbook (2001–2019)

Sous Vide for Everybody
Cook It in Your Dutch Oven
Multicooker Perfection
Food Processor Perfection
Pressure Cooker Perfection
Vegan for Everybody
Naturally Sweet
Foolproof Preserving
Paleo Perfected
The How Can It Be Gluten-Free Cookbook: Volume 2
The How Can It Be Gluten-Free Cookbook
The Best Mexican Recipes
Slow Cooker Revolution 2: The Easy Prep Edition
Slow Cooker Revolution
The Six-Ingredient Solution
The America's Test Kitchen Do-It-Yourself Cookbook
Cook's Illustrated Master Index 1993–2018

THE COOK'S ILLUSTRATED ALL-TIME BEST SERIES
All-Time Best Brunch
All-Time Best Dinners for Two
All-Time Best Sunday Suppers
All-Time Best Holiday Entertaining
All-Time Best Appetizers
All-Time Best Soups

COOK'S COUNTRY TITLES
One-Pan Wonders
Cook It in Cast Iron
Cook's Country Eats Local
The Complete Cook's Country TV Show Cookbook
Cook's Country Annual (2005–2018) Hardbound editions from each year of publication

Visit our online bookstore at www.CooksIllustrated.com to order any of our cookbooks listed above. You can also order subscriptions, gift subscriptions, and any of our cookbooks by calling 800-611-0759 inside the U.S., or at 515-237-3663 if calling from outside the U.S.

BC = Back Cover

NUMBER 150 JANUARY & FEBRUARY 2018

COOK'S
ILLUSTRATED

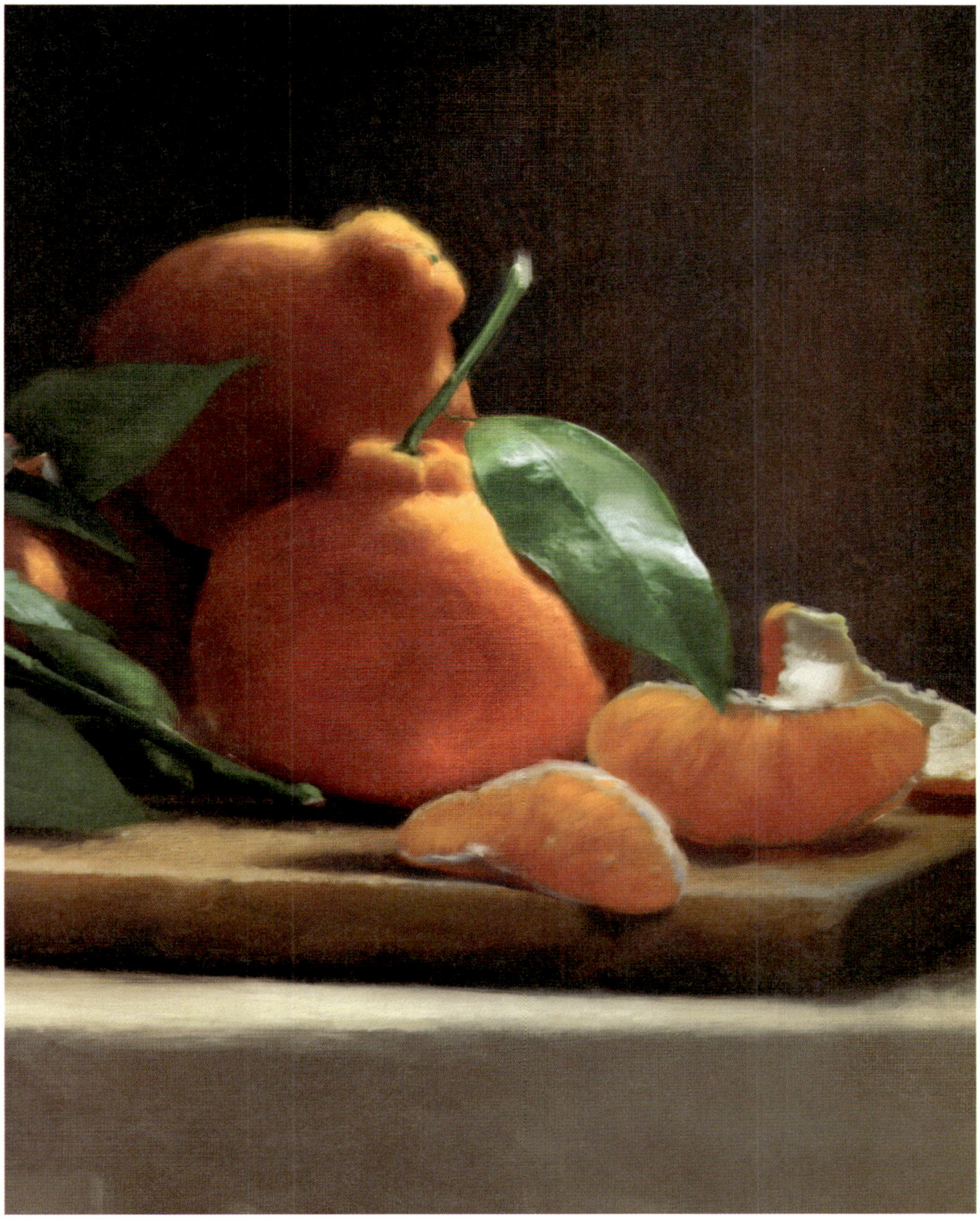

Supercrispy Oven Fries
The Secret's in the Starch

How to Roast Chicken
The Ultimate Guide

All-Butter Pie Dough
Utterly Foolproof

French-Style Scrambled Eggs
Lush and Creamy

Carrot Salad Revamp
Bold Flavor, No Grater

Choosing the Best Chocolate Chips

Testing High-End Blenders
Tender Coffee Cake
Chicken Piccata
Ground Beef Enchiladas

CooksIllustrated.com
$6.95 U.S.

Display until March 11, 2018

COOK'S ILLUSTRATED

JANUARY & FEBRUARY 2018

2 Quick Tips
Quick and easy ways to perform everyday tasks, from skimming fat from a soup or stew to making salad dressing. COMPILED BY ANNIE PETITO

4 Revamping Ground Beef Enchiladas
Say goodbye to the enchiladas you thought you knew. Techniques from both sides of the border produce a quicker—but still deeply flavorful—take on this Tex-Mex staple. BY STEVE DUNN

6 Chinese Barbecued Spareribs
Cantonese restaurants employ lengthy marinades and specialty ovens to produce these gorgeously lacquered ribs. We do it in 2 hours with common cookware. BY ANDREW JANJIGIAN

8 Really Good (Oven) Fries
Roasted potato planks aren't French fries. To mimic the real deal's delicately crispy crust and rich flavor in the oven, you first have to understand what makes a fry a fry. BY LAN LAM

10 Next-Level Chicken Piccata
For a sauce with deep citrus flavor, don't waste any part of the lemon. BY ANNIE PETITO

11 Red Wine Risotto with Beans
Northern Italians put an unexpected spin on risotto for a satisfying one-pot meal.
BY ANNIE PETITO

12 Great—Not Grated—Carrot Salads
Forget about your grater, your peeler, and any preconceptions of what carrot salad should be. We've got something better.
BY ANDREW JANJIGIAN

PAGE 5

14 Bringing Back Gougères
Airy, elegant French cheese puffs, known as *gougères*, deliver toasty flavor within delicately crisp shells. Bonus: Ours are a cinch to make.
BY LAN LAM

16 How to Roast a Great Chicken
Whether you need dinner on the table in a hurry or have time to pull out all the stops, we'll guide you to the best results.
BY ELIZABETH BOMZE

18 Rethinking Coffee Cake
Could we streamline the process for this breakfast treat and still produce a soft, tender crumb crowned with a crunchy, nutty streusel?
BY LAN LAM

20 Creamy French-Style Scrambled Eggs
For incredibly lush and creamy eggs, the key is to take things slow. BY ANDREA GEARY

21 Foolproof All-Butter Pie Dough
Our ultimate pie dough. It uses all butter, it's dead easy to roll, and it bakes up tender, crisp, and shatteringly flaky. BY ANDREA GEARY

24 Testing High-End Blenders
We investigate the new crop of pricey blenders to see what you get—and whether it's worth it—when the sky's the limit.
BY HANNAH CROWLEY

26 The Best Dark Chocolate Chips
With chocolate chips now coming in different shapes, sizes, and even cacao percentages, how do you choose? We tested 14 options to find a winner. BY LISA McMANUS

28 Ingredient Notes
BY ELIZABETH BOMZE, STEVE DUNN, ANDREW JANJIGIAN & ANNIE PETITO

30 Kitchen Notes
BY ANDREA GEARY, STEVE DUNN, LAN LAM & ANNIE PETITO

32 Equipment Corner
BY MIYE BROMBERG AND EMILY PHARES

BACK COVER ILLUSTRATED BY JOHN BURGOYNE

Chocolate

Inside the football-shaped **CACAO POD** harvested from the tropical evergreen tree (*Theobroma cacao*) sit **CACAO BEANS**, which are fermented, dried, roasted, and cracked to produce **CACAO NIBS**, a crunchy addition to baked goods or granola. When ground and pressed, the nibs are transformed into a paste of chocolate liquor. This paste is further processed to separate the fat, **COCOA BUTTER**, from the solids, which are dried and ground into **COCOA POWDER**. Chocolate liquor and cocoa solids are the building blocks of **BAR CHOCOLATE**, which is sold either unsweetened or sweetened. **CHOCOLATE CHIPS** can be shaped like disks or morsels. Manufactured specifically as coating chocolate, **COUVERTURE WAFERS** contain extra cocoa butter; when melted and set, they produce a particularly shiny, snappy layer. **MEXICAN DRINKING CHOCOLATE**, with rich traditions dating back to Mesoamerica, is often stone-ground and gritty.

America's Test Kitchen, a real test kitchen located in Boston, is the home of more than 60 test cooks and editors. Our mission is to test recipes until we understand exactly how and why they work and eventually arrive at the very best version. We also test kitchen equipment and taste supermarket ingredients in search of products that offer the best value and flavor. You can watch us work by tuning in to *America's Test Kitchen* (AmericasTestKitchen.com) and *Cook's Country from America's Test Kitchen* (CooksCountry.com) on public television and listen to our weekly segments on *The Splendid Table* on public radio. You can also follow us on Facebook, Twitter, Pinterest, and Instagram.

EDITORIAL STAFF

Chief Executive Officer David Nussbaum
Chief Creative Officer Jack Bishop
Editor in Chief Dan Souza
Executive Editor Amanda Agee
Deputy Editor Rebecca Hays
Executive Managing Editor Todd Meier
Executive Food Editor Keith Dresser
Senior Editors Andrea Geary, Andrew Janjigian, Lan Lam
Senior Editors, Features Elizabeth Bomze, Kristin Sargianis
Associate Editor Annie Petito
Lead Cook, Photo Team Daniel Cellucci
Test Cook Steve Dunn
Assistant Test Cooks Mady Nichas, Jessica Rudolph
Senior Copy Editor Krista Magnuson
Copy Editor Jillian Campbell
Senior Science Research Editor Paul Adams

Executive Editor, Tastings & Testings Lisa McManus
Deputy Editor, Tastings & Testings Hannah Crowley
Associate Editors, Tastings & Testings
 Miye Bromberg, Lauren Savoie, Kate Shannon
Assistant Editor, Tastings & Testings Emily Phares
Editorial Assistant, Tastings & Testings Carolyn Grillo

Director, Creative Operations Alice Carpenter
Test Kitchen Director Erin McMurrer
Assistant Test Kitchen Director Alexxa Benson
Test Kitchen Manager Meridith Lippard
Test Kitchen Facilities Manager Sophie Clingan-Darack
Senior Kitchen Assistant Receiver Kelly Ryan
Senior Kitchen Assistant Shopper Marissa Bunnewith
Lead Kitchen Assistant Ena Gudiel
Kitchen Assistants Gladis Campos, Blanca Castanza,

Creative Director John Torres
Design Director Greg Galvan
Photography Director Julie Cote
Designer Maggie Edgar
Senior Staff Photographer Daniel J. van Ackere
Staff Photographers Steve Klise, Kevin White
Photography Producer Mary Ball
Styling Catrine Kelty, Marie Piraino

Executive Editor, Web Christine Liu
Managing Editor, Web Mari Levine
Senior Editors, Web Roger Metcalf, Briana Palma
Assistant Editor, Web Molly Farrar

BUSINESS STAFF

Chief Financial Officer Jackie McCauley Ford
Director, Customer Support Amy Bootier
Senior Customer Loyalty & Support Specialist
 Rebecca Kowalski
Customer Loyalty & Support Specialist J.P. Dubuque
Production Director Guy Rochford
Imaging Manager Lauren Robbins
Production & Imaging Specialists Heather Dube,
 Dennis Noble, Jessica Voas

Chief Revenue Officer Sara Domville
Director, Special Accounts Erica Nye
Director, Business Partnerships Mehgan Conciatori
Partnership Marketing Manager Pamela Putprush
Director, Sponsorship Marketing & Client Services
 Christine Anagnostis
Client Services Manager Kate Zebrowski
Client Service & Marketing Representative Claire Gambee

Chief Digital Officer Fran Middleton
VP, Marketing Natalie Vinard
Marketing Director, Social Media & Content
 Strategy Claire Oliverson
Senior Social Media Coordinators Kelsey Hopper,
 Morgan Mannino

Senior VP, Human Resources & Organizational
 Development Colleen Zelina
Human Resources Director Adele Shapiro

Circulation Services ProCirc

Cover Art Robert Papp

PRINTED IN THE USA

LETTER FROM THE EDITOR

GET CLOSE

Dan Souza

Imagine you're standing on the edge of a giant tri-ply, heavy-bottomed, stainless-steel skillet, gazing into the vast, shiny basin before you. The foam soles of your shoes, like a good kitchen towel, are packed with tiny air pockets that insulate your feet from the searing-hot metal. Waves of radiant heat bathe your face. But you can't turn away. You are witnessing the death of an emulsion: A knob of butter lands with a slide, collapses into a puddle, and then reanimates as a noisy nest of bubbles. As the bubbles burst and subside you smell hazelnuts, toffee, maybe popcorn.

That close.

I dream about being that close to food and cooking. As a little kid at my grandmother's kitchen table in rural Maine, that meant removing my shirt before taking a fork to the wild blueberry pie. (Less material to get in the way.) Many years later at the Culinary Institute of America, it meant poring over Harold McGee's food science tome *On Food and Cooking* (2004) in search of a kind of x-ray vision for food. In professional kitchens in Boston and New York, it meant watching, making mistakes, and repeating. And almost a decade ago my need for an intimate connection to food meant coveting and landing my dream job: test cook, *Cook's Illustrated*.

With this issue I start a new chapter in my proximity to cooking. It is with intense excitement and a humble heart that I take the helm of a magazine that I've loved from the first time my mom handed me a dog-eared copy.

I don't know you personally, but I just have this hunch that if you're holding the 150th issue of *Cook's Illustrated* and you're reading my words, you also dream of being closer. You want more information and depth, not less. You're prone to asking "why?" and not just "how?" And you're not a foodie. You're a cook.

Perhaps you're here because you tried Andrea Geary's Peanut Butter Sandwich Cookies (March/April 2012) and realized that they made you just as happy as they did your 8-year-old (maybe happier?). Maybe you obsess over Quick Tips and Kitchen Notes (guilty!) because you take pleasure in refining your knowledge and skills in the kitchen. Or perhaps you've been part of the in-crowd since the early days and fell for *Cook's Illustrated* when you made Jack Bishop's Classic Bolognese Sauce (January/February 1999). Whatever the reason, it's good to have you.

OK. That's enough talk. We've got a lot of work to do for our next issue, and you've got some new recipes to try. Oh, and if while you're cooking through this issue something comes up (questions, comments, concerns), don't hesitate to reach out.

Dan Souza
Editor in Chief

Twitter and Instagram: @testcook
Email: Dan@americastestkitchen.com
Mail: Dan Souza, America's Test Kitchen,
21 Drydock Avenue, Suite 210E, Boston, MA 02210

FOR INQUIRIES, ORDERS, OR MORE INFORMATION

COOK'S ILLUSTRATED MAGAZINE

Cook's Illustrated magazine (ISSN 1068-2821), number 150, is published bimonthly by America's Test Kitchen Limited Partnership 21 Drydock Avenue, Suite 210E, Boston, MA 02210. Copyright 2017 America's Test Kitchen Limited Partnership. Periocicals postage paid at Boston, MA, and additional mailing offices, USPS #012487. Publications Mail Agreement No. 40020778. Return undeliverable Canadian addresses to P.O. Box 875, Station A, Windsor, ON N9A 6P2. POSTMASTER: Send address changes to *Cook's Illustrated*, P.O. Box 6018, Harlan, IA 51593-1518. For subscription and gift subscription orders, subscription inquiries, or change of address notices, visit AmericasTestKitchen.com/support, call 800-526-8442 in the U.S. or 515-237-3663 from outside the U.S., or write to us at *Cook's Illustrated*, P.O. Box 6018, Harlan, IA 51593-1518.

CooksIllustrated.com

At the all new CooksIllustrated.com, you can order books and subscriptions, sign up for our free e-newsletter, or renew your magazine subscription. Join the website and gain access to 25 years of *Cook's Illustrated* recipes, equipment tests, and ingredient tastings, as well as companion videos for every recipe in this issue.

COOKBOOKS

We sell more than 50 cookbooks by the editors of *Cook's Illustrated*, including *The Complete Mediterranean Cookbook* and *Vegan for Everybody*. To order, visit our bookstore at CooksIllustrated.com/bookstore.

EDITORIAL OFFICE 21 Drydock Avenue, Suite 210E, Boston, MA 02210; 617-232-1000; fax: 617-232-1572. For subscription inquiries, visit AmericasTestKitchen.com/support or call 800-526-8442.

QUICK TIPS

COMPILED BY ANNIE PETITO

Improvised Lame for Bread Baking
Ben Sobel of Cambridge, Mass., doesn't own a *lame*, a French tool with a fine blade used to slash the tops of rustic bread loaves before baking, so he devised a homemade alternative. He carefully holds a standard safety razor blade by the tabs on the short sides, bends the blade slightly, and then threads the narrow end of a chopstick through the holes on either side of the blade. The curved blade mimics the shape and function of a lame, and the chopstick is easy to grip.

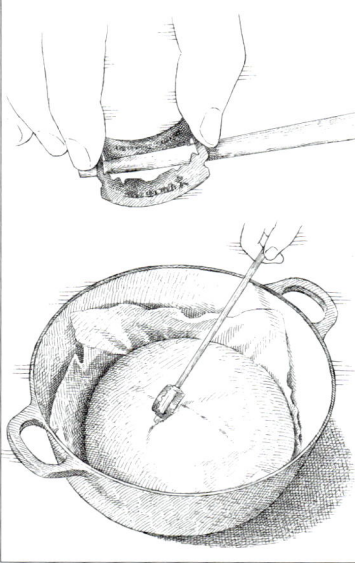

Keeping Cookbooks Open for Cooking
John Sauve of Toronto, Ontario, figured out a way to keep cookbooks open while he's cooking from them: He straps an elastic band to each side of the book on the page he wants open and braces the book with a wooden spoon on the cover side, spanning the spine like a cross. The book sits perfectly on the counter without bending the spine.

Whizzing Together Small-Batch Dressings
To quickly make a small batch of salad dressing, Michael Collins of Leesburg, Va., uses a handheld milk frother to blend the ingredients. The battery-operated tool helps emulsify the ingredients with little effort.

Sturdier Twist Ties for Plastic Bags
Taiya Barss of Halifax, Nova Scotia, often finds that the twist ties that come with plastic bags are too short or too weak to keep a bag tightly closed. She fashions sturdier ties from pipe cleaners, cutting each one in half and keeping a supply of them in a kitchen drawer.

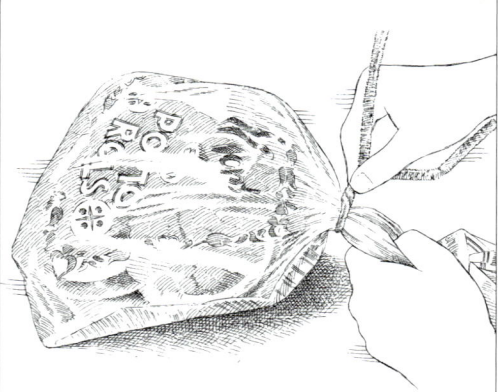

"Skimming" Fat with Suction
Holly Elmsley of Detroit, Mich., removes fat from the top of her pot of soup or stew with a turkey baster. The tool quickly suctions off the grease and can remove more at a time than a spoon can.

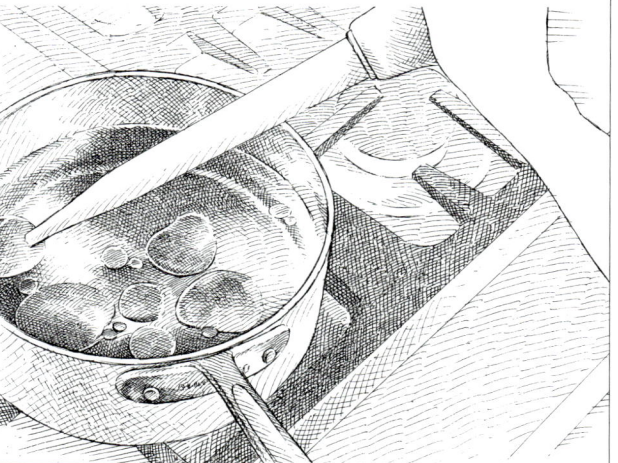

Storing—and Remembering—Items in the Oven
When Gayle Myers-Harbison of Lafayette, Colo., bakes and packages a lot of cookies during the holidays, she uses her oven as extra storage space to hold the full containers. To remind herself not to turn on the oven while the cookie packages are in there, she covers the control panel with blue painter's tape and writes "in use."

SEND US YOUR TIPS We will provide a complimentary one-year subscription for each tip we print. Send your tip, name, address, and telephone number to Quick Tips, *Cook's Illustrated*, 21 Drydock Avenue, Suite 210E, Boston, MA 02210, or to QuickTips@AmericasTestKitchen.com.

ILLUSTRATION: JOHN BURGOYNE

Pretorn Plastic Wrap
When Kristina Rasmussen of Madison, Wis., needs multiple sheets of plastic to wrap pastry or cookie dough for chilling, she tears all the sheets she will need before working with the dough and hangs the sheets from the edge of her counter. That way, she doesn't have to handle the box with her sticky fingers.

Marking Ingredient Additions
Sometimes Karen Toldt of Mequon, Wis., can't remember if she's already added an ingredient to a recipe. Her solution: Slip the printed recipe inside a clear page protector. As she adds each ingredient, she checks it off with an erasable marker. This method also works when making larger or multiple batches of a recipe; use hash marks to count each addition. When the recipe is complete, she wipes clean the page protector and uses it again for the next recipe.

A Pot for Hot Gravy
To keep gravy hot for serving, Kathleen Quinn of Wilmington, Del., stores it in a ceramic teapot instead of in a traditional gravy boat. The lidded pot keeps the gravy hotter than a gravy boat can, and the spout makes for tidy pouring.

Neater Blind Baking
Garry Carver of York, Pa., has found that pressing aluminum foil into a carefully formed and fluted pie shell (for filling with pie weights and prebaking) can distort its shape. He's found that it works better to shape the foil in an empty pie plate before placing it carefully on the shell.

Coffee Can Lid Turned Bench Scraper
Penny McDell of Maple Ridge, British Columbia, created her own bench scraper by cutting the plastic lid from a large coffee or shortening can in half. The sturdy but flexible lid makes it easy to scrape up pastry dough or scoop up everything from cut vegetables and herbs to flour.

Makeshift Stock Sachet
Michele Hershey of Kihei, Hawaii, uses the netting she's saved from onions, oranges, and other produce as a sachet when making stock. She places ingredients such as shrimp shells, garlic cloves, or herbs in the netting (using two layers of netting if the holes are large) and adds the bundle to the pot; once the flavors have been extracted, she can easily retrieve and discard the bundle.

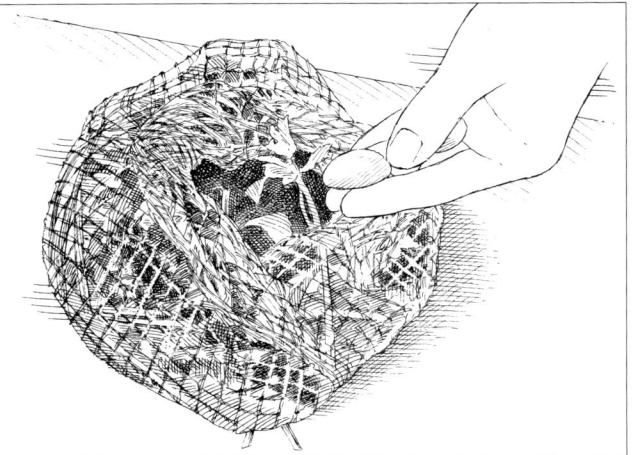

Revamping Ground Beef Enchiladas

Say goodbye to the enchiladas you thought you knew. Techniques from both sides of the border produce a quicker—but still deeply flavorful—take on this Tex-Mex staple.

≥ BY STEVE DUNN ≤

In Mexico, if a cook swaps out the cheese or chicken that is typically used as an enchilada filling for beef, there are no shortcuts. Fresh corn tortillas are lightly fried and rolled around a filling of tender, slow-braised shredded beef, and then smothered with a sauce made from dried chiles and topped with crumbled cheese. It's not hard to imagine the resulting enchiladas—they're deeply flavorful, complex, and entirely satisfying. There's only one downside, and it's a big one: The recipe can take quite a while to prepare, given its reliance on slow-cooked meat and a long-simmered sauce.

Then, of course, there are speedier Tex-Mex versions more familiar with Americans using ground beef, store-bought tortillas, loads of shredded cheese, and chili powder–infused tomato sauce. When I tried a few recipes to see how they compared with their Mexican cousins, there were no surprises: The fillings lacked the depth and velvety texture of braised beef, and some sauces were so full of tomato that they tasted Italian rather than Mexican. Many of the enchiladas were also greasy and weighed down with too much cheese. Surely, I could do better. I set out to use ground beef to develop my own quicker—but still deeply flavorful—enchiladas.

Not So Cheesy

I got started on the filling by sautéing finely chopped onion with plenty of minced garlic. Once the aromatics softened, I added a pound of 80 percent lean ground beef (to mimic the fat content of a beef steak or roast that might be used for the shredded version) seasoned with cumin and salt. I rolled the beef in store-bought corn tortillas that I'd briefly fried, topped them with a generic chile sauce, sprinkled on some cheese, and baked them for about 15 minutes.

It was a deflating first effort: The meat tasted bland, and its relative fattiness caused the greasiness problem I'd encountered in earlier versions. Switching to 90 percent lean beef helped the latter issue but made the filling taste too lean and dry. I needed to improve the texture of the beef without making it greasy.

Mixing the meat with a couple of spoonfuls of my sauce helped hydrate it and also deepened its

Before serving, we allow the enchiladas to sit for 10 minutes, which gives liquid a chance to be reabsorbed.

flavor, as did including ground coriander for citrusy tang. But the meat still seemed too lean. Some recipes call for sprinkling cheese over the filling prior to rolling it in the tortillas, so I gave that a try using a bit of shredded Monterey Jack, a great melter. But the cheese never fully coated the meat; it just sat in a gooey layer between the meat and the tortilla. To get the creamy-cheesy-beefy filling I had in mind, I doubled the amount of cheese (from 3 ounces to 6), but this time I stirred it directly into the hot beef after it finished cooking. The cheese melted beautifully, enrobing and enriching the beef. Lastly, I freshened up the filling's flavor by stirring in chopped cilantro.

Chasing Chile Flavor

With a moist and flavorful—and fast—beef filling ready to go, I shifted my attention to the sauce. Many Tex-Mex recipes call for a quick tomato-based concoction augmented with jarred chili powder, but an authentic Mexican enchilada sauce is a slow-cooked affair based on dried chiles. To guarantee complexity, I started with raisiny, mildly spicy dried anchos. I stemmed and seeded the chiles, tore them into pieces, and toasted them in a skillet to release their flavor before rehydrating them in beef broth (to bolster the ground beef's flavor) in the microwave.

Next, I sautéed a second batch of garlic and onions and, rather than add tomatoes, stirred in ¼ cup of tomato paste along with some earthy cumin. The tomato paste contributed concentrated sweetness without tasting overly tomatoey. I whizzed the onion mixture in a blender with the anchos and their hydrating liquid. And to mimic the flavor of a sauce made with multiple types of dried chiles, I also included some canned chipotle chiles in adobo sauce. Just 1 tablespoon added smoky spiciness—and it was as easy as opening a can. Finally, I simmered the sauce until it was thick enough to coat the tortillas.

But reducing the sauce turned out to be too lengthy a process and made me wonder if I could thicken it a different way. I tried using a roux (a cooked paste of flour and fat), as some recipes recommended. But tasters complained that it made the sauce seem artificially thick and robbed it of its vibrant flavor. Blitzing a tortilla into the sauce thickened it nicely (authentic recipes sometimes call for

FREEZE, THEN GRATE

Semisoft cheeses such as Monterey Jack can be a challenge to shred on box or paddle graters. They tend to smear on the face of the grater, break off in clumps, and clog up the holes. We found that freezing a block of cheese for 30 minutes before grating firmed it up so we could shred it more easily.

Keys To Success

We combined the deep flavor of Mexican enchiladas with the ease and speed of the Tex-Mex type.

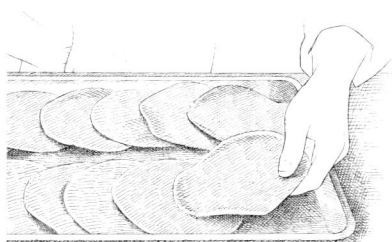

FLEXIBLE TORTILLAS
Usual Way: Flash-fry tortillas in oil.
Our Way: Brush tortillas lightly with oil and bake briefly.

DEEP CHILE FLAVOR
Usual Way: Slow-cook sauce made with multiple dried chiles.
Our Way: Make quick, flavorful sauce using dried anchos and canned chipotles.

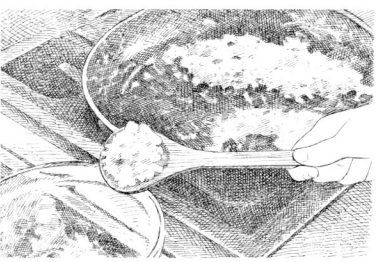

STREAMLINED AROMATICS
Usual Way: Season sauce and filling with separate batches of aromatics.
Our Way: Sauté 1 big batch of aromatics and add half to each component.

RICH BEEF FILLING
Usual Way: Braise beef, then shred it.
Our Way: Sauté ground beef, then mix in shredded cheese for extra richness.

---

using masa harina, or corn flour, for this purpose) but left me one wrapper short when building a dozen enchiladas. Ultimately, reducing the amount of broth from 3 cups to 2 worked best. My chile sauce had deep, faintly sweet, and spicy flavor—all in minutes.

As I prepared to assemble the enchiladas, I realized that the filling and sauce both included a mix of onion and garlic. I sautéed enough for both in a single batch and then split the mixture between the two components, simplifying the process and saving time.

Rolling Along

It was time to examine the tortillas. The traditional method of flash-frying tortillas in oil softens them enough to be filled and rolled. Could I eliminate the oil by just warming the tortillas in the microwave? I gave it a try and then filled the tortillas, slathered them with sauce, sprinkled them with a modest amount of Monterey Jack cheese, and popped them into a hot oven. Things seemed promising until serving time. The tortillas were so soggy that they fell apart into a raggedy mess when I tried to lift them onto plates. A fellow test cook posited that in addition to softening, the oil in the traditional method actually waterproofed the tortillas and kept them from absorbing too much sauce.

With that in mind, I tried giving the tortillas a light spritz of vegetable oil spray before briefly warming them in the oven. The spray helped but didn't fully mitigate sogginess. I had better luck using a pastry brush to fully cover both sides of the tortillas with a light coating of oil before briefly baking them.

I made a final batch, filling the oiled and baked tortillas with my cheesy cumin-and-coriander-spiced beef, ladling on the chile-laced sauce, and sprinkling extra cheese over the top. After baking for 15 minutes, the cheese was lightly browned and the tortillas were pliable without becoming waterlogged. My colleagues devoured the enchiladas, garnished with fresh cilantro, sour cream, scallions, and lime wedges.

GROUND BEEF AND CHEESE ENCHILADAS
SERVES 4 TO 5

Don't use ground beef that's fattier than 90 percent lean or the dish will be greasy.

Sauce
- 1½ ounces (3 to 4) dried ancho chiles, stemmed, seeded, and torn into 1-inch pieces
- 2 cups beef broth
- 1 tablespoon minced canned chipotle chile in adobo sauce
- 2 tablespoons vegetable oil
- 2 onions, chopped fine
- 6 garlic cloves, minced
- ¼ cup tomato paste
- 1 teaspoon ground cumin
- Salt

Enchiladas
- 3 tablespoons vegetable oil
- 1 pound 90 percent lean ground beef
- 1 teaspoon ground cumin
- 1 teaspoon ground coriander
- Salt
- 8 ounces Monterey Jack cheese, shredded (2 cups)
- 2 tablespoons minced fresh cilantro
- 12 6-inch corn tortillas
- 2 scallions, sliced thin on bias
- 2 tablespoons minced fresh cilantro
- Sour cream
- Lime wedges

1. FOR THE SAUCE: Adjust oven rack to middle position and heat oven to 400 degrees. Heat anchos in 12-inch nonstick skillet over medium-high heat, stirring frequently, until fragrant, 2 to 3 minutes. Transfer anchos to bowl, add broth, and microwave, covered, until steaming, about 2 minutes. Let stand until softened, about 5 minutes. Transfer anchos and broth to blender and add chipotle.

2. Heat oil in now-empty skillet over medium heat until shimmering. Add onions and cook, stirring occasionally, until translucent, about 5 minutes. Add garlic and cook until fragrant, about 1 minute. Transfer half of onion mixture to large bowl and set aside. Return skillet with remaining onion mixture to medium heat and add tomato paste and cumin. Cook, stirring frequently, until tomato paste starts to darken, 3 to 5 minutes. Transfer onion mixture in skillet to blender with ancho mixture and process until smooth, about 1 minute. Season sauce with salt to taste.

3. FOR THE ENCHILADAS: Heat 1 tablespoon oil in now-empty skillet over medium heat until shimmering. Add beef, cumin, coriander, and ½ teaspoon salt and cook for 2 minutes, breaking meat into ¼-inch pieces with wooden spoon. Add reserved onion mixture (do not wash bowl) and continue to cook until beef is no longer pink, 3 to 4 minutes longer. Return beef mixture to bowl; add 1½ cups Monterey Jack, cilantro, and ¼ cup sauce and stir to combine. Season with salt to taste.

4. Spread ½ cup sauce over bottom of 13 by 9-inch baking dish. Brush both sides of tortillas with remaining 2 tablespoons oil. Arrange tortillas, overlapping, on rimmed baking sheet and bake until warm and pliable, about 5 minutes. Spread ¼ cup filling down center of each tortilla. Roll each tortilla tightly around filling and place seam side down in dish, arranging enchiladas in 2 rows across width of dish.

5. Spread remaining sauce over top of enchiladas. Sprinkle with remaining ½ cup Monterey Jack. Bake until cheese is lightly browned and sauce is bubbling at edges, about 15 minutes. Let cool for 10 minutes. Sprinkle with scallions and cilantro. Serve, passing sour cream and lime wedges separately.

▶ **Watch Every Step**
A step-by-step video is available at CooksIllustrated.com/feb18

Chinese Barbecued Spareribs

Cantonese restaurants employ lengthy marinades and specialty ovens to produce these gorgeously lacquered ribs. We do it in 2 hours with common cookware.

≥ BY ANDREW JANJIGIAN ≤

Chinese barbecued spareribs are typically associated with Cantonese buffets and pupu platters, those medleys of vaguely authentic finger food that have been fixtures in Chinese American and Polynesian restaurants for decades. But unlike the questionable provenance of plattermates such as crab rangoons and chicken fingers, spareribs have real roots in Chinese cuisine. Their lurid red glow, lacquered sheen, and flavors redolent of hoisin and soy sauces, ginger, garlic, and five-spice powder indicate they are a form of *char siu*, the Cantonese-style barbecued pork you can find hanging in the windows of meat shops in any Chinatown. Their appeal is obvious—the meat is salty and sweet, with a deeply caramelized exterior and a satisfying resilient chew—and recipes for them have appeared in American newspapers, magazines, and cookbooks since the mid-20th century.

The distinct chew of Chinese barbecued spareribs sets them apart from the fall-off-the-bone tenderness of most American styles. They're also cooked very differently, since they're not actually barbecued. Like all forms of char siu, the ribs are marinated and then slow-roasted. In restaurants, this happens in large, boxy ovens where the meat hangs from hooks—a setup that allows fat to drip and hot air to circulate all around the meat so that it achieves its hallmark burnished finish. But this method also makes Chinese ribs tricky to replicate in a home oven, something I've always wanted to do in the winter months when I take a hiatus from the grill or when I don't feel like trekking to Chinatown for the real deal.

Take Cover

Spareribs are cut close to the belly of the pig. A whole rack can weigh more than 5 pounds since it includes the brisket bone and surrounding meat. To make smaller, evenly rectangular racks that are easier to fit on a grill or in the oven, butchers lop off the brisket portion and call this more svelte cut St. Louis–style spareribs (for more information, see "Understanding Spareribs" on page 29). They're meaty and flavorful and are our go-to cut for most rib recipes.

I started with two racks and mixed up a char siu marinade: soy and hoisin sauces, Chinese rice wine, garlic, ginger, five-spice powder, white pepper, and red food coloring (traditionally this color came from fermented rice or bean paste).

Whereas Southern-style ribs are known for their fall-off-the-bone texture, the Chinese style retains a satisfying chew.

▶ Look: Takeout at Home
A step-by-step video is available at CooksIllustrated.com/feb18

The recipes I found recommended marinating the ribs for many hours or even for days. In most cases, marinating meat for anything longer than an hour is overkill, since we've found that very few flavors penetrate much beyond the meat's surface, no matter how long it soaks. But here a longer marinade might actually be worthwhile, since the char siu marinade contains soy and hoisin sauces—powerhouse ingredients packed with salt and flavor-boosting glutamates, both of which we have found can penetrate deep into meat.

Since the layer of meat on ribs is thin, a 2-hour soak seemed like plenty of time. I went with that and tried three common cooking methods. The first re-creates the conditions of a Chinese barbecue oven by cooking a whole slab of ribs on a rack in a low oven, flipping it and basting it with a reduction of the marinade so that all sides of the rack get good exposure to the marinade and the heat. The results were chewy yet tender and had a lacquered coat, but this method required 3 to 4 hours of closely attended cooking in addition to marinating time—more of a commitment than I wanted.

The second, a speedier variation on that method, turns up the heat to about 350 degrees so that the ribs cook in 1 to 1½ hours. Unfortunately, the time savings came at the expense of the meat, which tended to dry out in the hotter oven. And the third, more common approach is to cut the rack into individual ribs and roast them in two stages: covered for 1 to 1½ hours so that they steam and tenderize and then brushed with a reduction of the marinade and roasted in a hot oven (or broiled) uncovered for about 15 minutes to dry out and color their exteriors.

Barbecued Ribs, Chinese Style

Chinese ribs are nothing like your average Southern barbecue. Not only are they not smoked, they're not even cooked on a grill. First, they're typically marinated in a mixture that includes the salty-sweet flavors of soy and hoisin sauces along with Chinese rice wine, loads of garlic and ginger, and red food coloring. The ribs are then roasted for several hours while dangling from hooks in large ovens, until they take on a rich mahogany color. The meat is intentionally pulled from the oven while it still retains some chew.

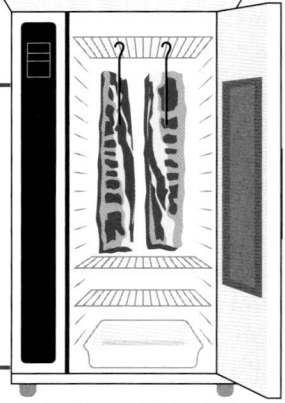

FLAVOR-PACKED INDOOR RIBS IN 2 HOURS

American barbecued ribs require you to spend the better part of a day tending a live fire. Our version of the Chinese approach uses the oven and takes 2 hours from start to finish.

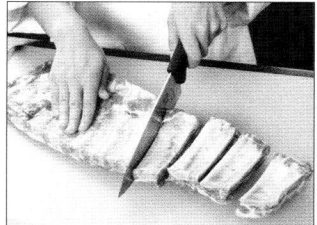

CUT RACK INTO RIBS
Individual ribs have more surface area than an uncut rack, which means each one is exposed to heat and to the marinade on all sides. (It's not necessary to remove the rack's membrane before slicing.)

BRAISE IN MARINADE
Moist heat quickly tenderizes the meat and accelerates the penetration of flavorful compounds (such as salt and glutamates), so the cooking time doesn't need to be long for the flavors to soak in.

ROAST IN HOT OVEN
Just 15 minutes in a hot oven dries the ribs' exteriors so that the glaze can set and caramelize.

The third method, moist heat followed by dry, was the most promising. Cutting the racks into single ribs speeds cooking and creates lots of surface area for painting on the flavor-packed glaze. And moist heat is a very efficient way to cook meat, since water conducts energy faster than air does. The drawback is that you don't want to baste ribs that you cover, since the steamy environment doesn't allow the first coat to dry and set, so you never get a substantial buildup of glaze. I'd have to get all my glazing done after I uncovered them, so I had to pack a lot of flavor into the glaze.

Braised and Glazed

My next move was to intensify the marinade so that when it reduced, a single coat of glaze would taste robust. I mixed up another batch with more soy and hoisin, more garlic and ginger (it was now more efficient to pulverize them in a food processor), and more spices. I also added honey, another typical char siu component that would lend the basting liquid more body.

But as I mixed up my new marinade, something occurred to me: If the ribs needed to soak in the marinade and moist heat was the most efficient way to cook them, why not do both at once by braising the ribs in the marinade before roasting them? Heat would also help the flavors penetrate the meat more quickly, so the cooking time wouldn't need to be long for the flavors to soak in. Then I could further reduce the braising liquid and use that to baste the ribs.

I made another batch of my marinade but this time thinned it with a little water and placed it in a Dutch oven. I added the ribs, brought the pot to a simmer, turned down the heat to low, covered the pot, and let the ribs cook on the stovetop until they were just tender, which took about 1 hour and 15 minutes. After straining and defatting the braising liquid, I returned it to the pot to simmer until it had reduced to a thick glaze; at this point, I also added some toasted sesame oil for further complexity. In the meantime, I heated the oven to 425 degrees and set a wire rack inside a rimmed baking sheet that I'd lined with aluminum foil and partially filled with water to catch the drips of fat and glaze that would otherwise cause the sheet to smoke (see "Prevent Oven Smoke with a Water Bath"). I tossed the ribs in the glaze and then placed them bone side up on the rack.

After 15 minutes, with a flip halfway through to brown the other side, they were done. The braising liquid's salty-sweet flavor had penetrated into the exterior of the meat, and the glaze had dried and left a lacquered sheen that gave way to the meat's satisfying chew. It was char siu to rival the best I'd had in Chinatown, but it was easy to make in my own kitchen.

Prevent Oven Smoke with a Water Bath

Partially filling the rimmed baking sheet with water creates a reservoir to catch drips of fat and glaze that would otherwise burn and smoke in the hot oven.

CHINESE-STYLE BARBECUED SPARERIBS
SERVES 6 TO 8 AS AN APPETIZER
OR 4 TO 6 AS A MAIN COURSE

It's not necessary to remove the membrane on the bone side of the ribs. These ribs are chewier than American-style ribs; if you prefer them more tender, cook them for an additional 15 minutes in step 1. Adding water to the baking sheet during roasting helps prevent smoking. Serve the ribs alone as an appetizer or with vegetables and rice as a main course. You can serve the first batch immediately or tent them with foil to keep them warm.

- 1 (6-inch) piece fresh ginger, peeled and sliced thin
- 8 garlic cloves, peeled
- 1 cup honey
- ¾ cup hoisin sauce
- ¾ cup soy sauce
- ½ cup Chinese rice wine or dry sherry
- 2 teaspoons five-spice powder
- 1 teaspoon red food coloring (optional)
- 1 teaspoon ground white pepper
- 2 (2½- to 3-pound) racks St. Louis–style spareribs, cut into individual ribs
- 2 tablespoons toasted sesame oil

1. Pulse ginger and garlic in food processor until finely chopped, 10 to 12 pulses, scraping down sides of bowl as needed. Transfer ginger-garlic mixture to Dutch oven. Add honey; hoisin; soy sauce; ½ cup water; rice wine; five-spice powder; food coloring, if using; and pepper and whisk until combined. Add ribs and stir to coat (ribs will not be fully submerged). Bring to simmer over high heat, then reduce heat to low, cover, and cook for 1¼ hours, stirring occasionally.

2. Adjust oven rack to middle position and heat oven to 425 degrees. Using tongs, transfer ribs to large bowl. Strain braising liquid through fine-mesh strainer set over large container, pressing on solids to extract as much liquid as possible; discard solids. Let cooking liquid settle for 10 minutes. Using wide, shallow spoon, skim fat from surface and discard.

3. Return braising liquid to pot and add sesame oil. Bring to boil over high heat and cook until syrupy and reduced to 2½ cups, 16 to 20 minutes.

4. Set wire rack in aluminum foil–lined rimmed baking sheet and pour ½ cup water into sheet. Transfer half of ribs to pot with braising liquid and toss to coat. Arrange ribs, bone sides up, on prepared rack, letting excess glaze drip off. Roast until edges of ribs start to caramelize, 5 to 7 minutes. Flip ribs and continue to roast until second side starts to caramelize, 5 to 7 minutes longer. Transfer ribs to serving platter; repeat process with remaining ribs. Serve.

TO MAKE AHEAD: At end of step 3, refrigerate ribs and glaze separately, covered, for up to 2 days. When ready to serve, bring glaze and half of ribs to simmer in Dutch oven over medium heat, then proceed with step 4. Repeat with remaining ribs.

Really Good (Oven) Fries

Roasted potato planks aren't French fries. To mimic the real deal's delicately crispy crust and rich flavor in the oven, you first have to understand what makes a fry a fry.

> BY LAN LAM <

Peel, cut, fry, let cool, fry again, drain. Repeat with remaining batches. Let oil cool and, finally, discard oil.

I think I speak for French fry lovers everywhere when I say that the tawny, crispy crusts and velvety interiors you get from a proper fry job are worth all the grease—elbow and otherwise. But given what the process entails, I make real fries about as often as I make croissants or pasta from scratch, which is to say almost never.

Most people's alternative to deep-fried fries is oven fries, which are usually less fussy to make, often less greasy—and always a disappointment. OK, that might be a bit harsh, but I think you'll agree that oven fries frequently fall short. The most basic methods call for simply tossing cut potatoes with a few tablespoons of oil, spreading them in a single layer on a rimmed baking sheet, and roasting them in a hot oven for about 30 minutes, turning them a few times so that all sides make contact with the hot surface and brown. More-involved recipes take the time to parcook (either usually by boiling or microwaving) the cut potatoes before the oven phase, which helps the insides turn tender by the time the outsides are brown.

The perks are obvious: No lengthy potato prep work, no grease-splattered stovetop to clean, no vat of hot oil to deal with afterward. But in my experience,

A mere 3 tablespoons of oil is all it takes to produce spuds with a crispy crust—and it's actually the key to their rich "fry" flavor.

oven-fried potatoes rarely cook up with a French fry's evenly golden exterior, instead emerging pale or flabby in spots or shriveled and tough at the edges. Worse still, they lack that unmistakably lush, nutty, subtly savory "fry" flavor of French fries. What do they taste like? Compromise and wasted potential.

But what if you could have it both ways: the flavor and crispiness of deep-fried fries produced with no more work than roasting potatoes? For the sake of French fry lovers everywhere, I had to try.

Oven Obstacles

To understand what goes wrong when you "fry" in the oven, I took a closer look at the aforementioned basic method. I cut 2 pounds of peeled russet potatoes into ½-inch-thick planks; tossed them with 4 tablespoons of vegetable oil, a common amount used in other oven fry recipes; spread them on a heavy-duty rimmed baking sheet that wouldn't warp in the hot oven; and cooked them at 425 degrees for about 30 minutes. (If the oven were any hotter, the oil would smoke and give the fries an acrid flavor.) I flipped the planks a few times during cooking so that they could brown all over.

There were two problems. First, the potatoes weren't tender by the time their exteriors were brown, which explained why some oven fry recipes called for parcooking the potatoes. Second, while each side of the potatoes was at least somewhat brown, only the sides originally in contact with the hot baking sheet were actually crispy; the other surfaces were tough and leathery.

Those flaws made sense when I considered how fried fries are typically made. Most recipes call for frying the potatoes twice. The first fry, often called blanching, cooks the potatoes through and causes the surface starch to gel. You then remove the potatoes and let them cool briefly before frying them again, which rapidly drives the water out of the starch gel at the surface, leaving behind tiny cavities. It's these cavities that lighten the crust during the second fry so that it shatters when you bite through it.

The problem with my oven fries was that the water in the potatoes wasn't heating rapidly. It was heating slowly, because air doesn't conduct heat as quickly as oil does. Consequently, no air pockets are formed and the starch molecules nestle together, leading to a tough crust.

Proof's in the Pudding

To ensure tender fries, parcooking the potatoes was definitely in order. I could blanch them in water, but it would be more efficient to cover the baking sheet tightly with foil for the first part of cooking so that they could steam. After a few trial rounds, I determined that about 12 minutes under cover parcooked the potatoes enough that they would be fully tender by the end of the uncovered phase.

As for creating a crispy exterior, what if I could put a different starchy coating on the outside instead of relying on hot, bubbling oil to crisp the potato starch? Cornstarch is what I had in mind: Like those of potato starch, its particles are quite small, which is why we've had good luck in the past using it as a fry coating on everything from chicken wings to sweet potato wedges. Plus, its starch granules—much finer than those of potatoes—don't hold on to much water and don't hold on to it tightly, so it can easily form a crispy crust. Plus, it's an ingredient that most cooks keep on

---

Don't Skip the Spray

Vegetable oil spray isn't just oil in a can, which is why it's more effective at preventing sticking than oil alone. It contains a surfactant (an ingredient that reduces tension between a surface and a liquid) called lecithin that helps the oil flow to coat the metal evenly, so it forms a thin, complete layer between the baking sheet and the food. As a result, the potatoes in our recipe don't stick and we can use less oil.

SLICK SOLUTION

hand. But instead of simply dusting cornstarch directly on the food, which we've found can leave a chalky film in your mouth, we prefer to mix the cornstarch with water to make a slurry. Doing so hydrates the starch, essentially creating a batter that coats the food.

I spent the next several tests mixing up different ratios of cornstarch and water, but no matter what I tried, I couldn't produce a batter that coated the potatoes evenly. Thinner slurries slid right off the potatoes and pooled on the sheet, while thicker batches formed goopy clumps. What I wanted was that loose, pudding-like consistency you get when cooking cornstarch in a warm liquid, as you would when thickening a sauce. So for the next test I microwaved the slurry (3 tablespoons of cornstarch mixed with ¾ cup of water) for a minute or so, giving it a stir periodically. That helped; the cornstarch absorbed the water and thickened into a smooth pudding that coated the potatoes beautifully. I had, in effect, re-created the starch gel found on the surface of traditional oil-blanched fries.

I arranged the slurry-covered spuds on the oiled baking sheet, covered the sheet tightly with greased aluminum foil (to prevent it from sticking), and cooked the potatoes for 12 minutes before pulling off the cover and letting the potatoes brown for about 10 more minutes. I then flipped the fries and let them brown for another 10 minutes. The results were better than any I'd had to date: On most pieces, the coating was crispy and delicate and gave way to a fluffy, evenly tender interior. The problem was that the oil was pooling on the baking sheet, leaving some of the fries saturated and a tad greasy and others almost dry, meaning that they stuck to the pan and didn't crisp. And they still didn't deliver that rich "fry" flavor.

How Low Can You Go?

One quick change I made was to swap the russet potatoes for Yukon Gold potatoes, since the latter have a naturally buttery flavor that hinted at the richness of real fries. Their skins are also thinner than those of russets, so they didn't require peeling.

Oil pooling on the cooking surface is a problem we've run into before, most notably when we developed a recipe for Thick-Crust Sicilian-Style Pizza (March/April 2015). Our solution there was to spray the baking sheet with vegetable oil spray before coating it with oil. Odd as that sounds—grease held in place with grease—the cooking spray contains a key ingredient that oil doesn't: lecithin, a surfactant (an ingredient that reduces tension between a surface and a liquid) that helps the oil flow to coat the metal evenly and form a thin, complete layer between the baking sheet and the food.

I made another batch of fries, this time spraying the sheet before adding the 4 tablespoons of oil, and the results were much better. No more sticking, and the fries were evenly golden on the two flat sides. But now that the sticking wasn't a problem, did I even need 4 tablespoons of oil? After all, relative leanness is another supposed selling point of oven fries. Maybe I could get away with less, and that would help the greasiness, too.

I made several more batches, coating the potatoes with varying amounts of fat, including an ambitious batch where I used only the spray. I was able to take the oil down to 3 tablespoons and the fries still cooked up crispy; even better, the greasiness was gone and they delivered that rich, savory, from-the-fry-o-lator flavor (for more information, see "What Puts the 'Fry' in These Potatoes?").

These spuds cooked in the oven truly deserved the title of "fries." They were delicately crispy on the outside, fluffy within, and full of fry flavor. In other words, they tasted like victory.

WHAT PUTS THE "FRY" IN THESE POTATOES?

CORNSTARCH SLURRY: Microwaving a mixture of cornstarch and water for a few minutes evenly hydrates the starch molecules, creating a smooth, pudding-like mixture. This batter coats the potatoes evenly, forming a delicately crispy crust as it fries.

The slurry should have a thick, pudding-like texture.

JUST ENOUGH OIL: Coating the baking sheet with 3 tablespoons of oil gives our fries rich, truly fried flavor. More oil was unnecessary, and too little yielded fishy off-flavors since the less oil used, the faster it heats and the more it will break down into unpleasant flavor compounds.

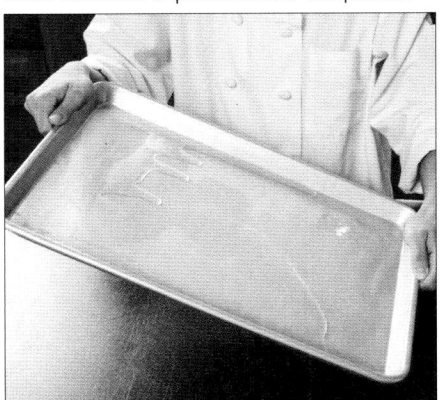
Tilt the baking sheet to evenly coat it with oil.

THICK-CUT OVEN FRIES
SERVES 4

Choose potatoes that are 4 to 6 inches in length to ensure well-proportioned fries. Trimming thin slices from the ends of the potatoes in step 2 ensures that each fry has two flat surfaces for even browning. This recipe's success is dependent on a heavy-duty rimmed baking sheet that will not warp in the heat of the oven. Spraying the sheet with vegetable oil spray will help the oil spread evenly and prevent sticking. The rate at which the potatoes brown is dependent on your baking sheet and oven. After removing the foil from the baking sheet in step 5, monitor the color of the potatoes carefully to prevent scorching. Our recipe for Thick-Cut Oven Fries for Two is available for free for four months at CooksIllustrated.com/feb18.

- 3 tablespoons vegetable oil
- 2 pounds Yukon gold potatoes, unpeeled
- 3 tablespoons cornstarch
- Salt

1. Adjust oven rack to lowest position and heat oven to 425 degrees. Generously spray rimmed baking sheet with vegetable oil spray. Pour oil into prepared sheet and tilt sheet until surface is evenly coated with oil.

2. Halve potatoes lengthwise and turn halves cut sides down on cutting board. Trim thin slice from both long sides of each potato half; discard trimmings. Slice potatoes lengthwise into ⅓- to ½-inch-thick planks.

3. Combine ¾ cup water and cornstarch in large bowl, making sure no lumps of cornstarch remain on bottom of bowl. Microwave, stirring every 20 seconds, until mixture begins to thicken, 1 to 3 minutes. Remove from microwave and continue to stir until mixture thickens to pudding-like consistency. (If necessary, add up to 2 tablespoons water to achieve correct consistency.)

4. Transfer potatoes to bowl with cornstarch mixture and toss until each plank is evenly coated. Arrange planks on prepared sheet, leaving small gaps between planks. (Some cornstarch mixture will remain in bowl.) Cover sheet tightly with lightly greased aluminum foil and bake for 12 minutes.

5. Remove foil from sheet and bake until bottom of each fry is golden brown, 10 to 18 minutes. Remove sheet from oven and, using thin metal spatula, carefully flip each fry. Return sheet to oven and continue to bake until second sides are golden brown, 10 to 18 minutes longer. Sprinkle fries with ½ teaspoon salt. Using spatula, carefully toss fries to distribute salt. Transfer fries to paper towel–lined plate and season with salt to taste. Serve.

▶ Lan "Fries" in the Oven
A step-by-step video is available at CooksIllustrated.com/feb18

Next-Level Chicken Piccata

For a sauce with deep citrus flavor, don't waste any part of the lemon.

≥ BY ANNIE PETITO ≤

Chicken piccata needs little introduction, for better or for worse. A good version—chicken breasts pounded thin, lightly dusted with flour, pan-seared, and bathed in a rich lemon-butter pan sauce, perhaps with scatterings of capers, garlic, shallot, and parsley—deserves nothing but praise. Yet piccata can also be punishingly bad, featuring dry, tough chicken drowning in sauce that's either boring or brash.

I looked first at the preparation of the cutlets themselves. A common approach is to flatten a whole breast with a meat pounder, which can tear the flesh. In the test kitchen, we have a better way: Halve the breast crosswise and then split the thick side horizontally to create three similar-size pieces that require only minimal pounding. To season the meat and help it retain moisture, I tossed the cutlets with salt and pepper and set them aside for 15 minutes.

At this point, the cutlets are normally dredged in flour and seared in batches. The flour helps with browning by absorbing surface moisture; the proteins and starch in the flour also brown. The problem is that in the short time the cutlets are in the pan, the flour doesn't cook through, so the cutlets turn gummy on the surface once the sauce is poured on.

I tried a different approach—I floured the cutlets, pan-seared them, and then transferred them to a placeholder sauce to simmer. Problem solved: Any uncooked flour sloughed off into the sauce, thickening it and leaving the coating thin and silky. Because I had salted the chicken, the additional cooking didn't dry it out.

For the sauce, I sautéed garlic and shallot and then stirred in chicken broth and a few tablespoons of lemon juice. After simmering the cutlets in the sauce, I finished it with capers and butter.

The sauce had nice body, but its lemon flavor was one-dimensional. Zest contributed depth, but something was still missing. I thought about eastern Mediterranean cuisines, in which whole lemons are preserved in salt and then sliced or chopped and incorporated into stews and tagines for incredible complexity. Preserved lemons weren't appropriate here, but what about adding whole lemon pieces to piccata? I quartered thin slices of lemon and simmered them in the sauce until they softened. Bingo: My twist on this classic recipe resulted in a truly complex sauce featuring tartness from the juice, fruity aroma from the zest, and a subtle bitterness from the pith.

The lemon slices soften as they simmer and can be eaten along with the chicken.

▶ See Annie Prepare Piccata
A step-by-step video is available at CooksIllustrated.com/feb18

SCIENCE Lemon Law: For Complexity, Use Every Part

We add lemon slices to our piccata to take advantage of the unique flavor that each part of the fruit provides.

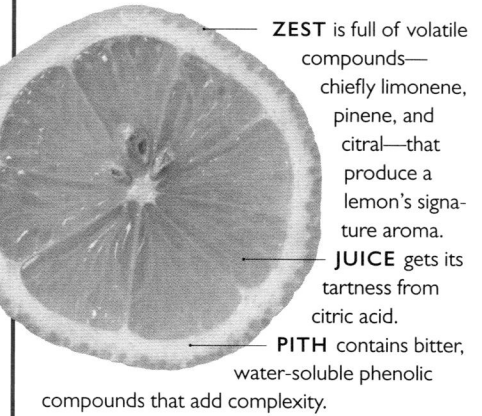

ZEST is full of volatile compounds—chiefly limonene, pinene, and citral—that produce a lemon's signature aroma.

JUICE gets its tartness from citric acid.

PITH contains bitter, water-soluble phenolic compounds that add complexity.

CHICKEN PICCATA
SERVES 4 TO 6

Serve with buttered pasta, white rice, potatoes, or crusty bread and a simple steamed vegetable. Our recipe for Chicken Piccata for Two is available for free for four months at CooksIllustrated.com/feb18.

- 4 (6- to 8-ounce) boneless, skinless chicken breasts, trimmed
- Kosher salt and pepper
- 2 large lemons
- ¾ cup all-purpose flour
- ¼ cup plus 1 teaspoon vegetable oil
- 1 shallot, minced
- 1 garlic clove, minced
- 1 cup chicken broth
- 3 tablespoons unsalted butter, cut into 6 pieces
- 2 tablespoons capers, drained
- 1 tablespoon minced fresh parsley

1. Cut each chicken breast in half crosswise, then cut thick half in half again horizontally, creating 3 cutlets of similar thickness. Place cutlets between sheets of plastic wrap and gently pound to even ½-inch thickness. Place cutlets in bowl and toss with 2 teaspoons salt and ½ teaspoon pepper. Set aside for 15 minutes.

2. Halve 1 lemon lengthwise. Trim ends from 1 half, halve lengthwise again, then cut crosswise ¼-inch-thick slices; set aside. Juice remaining half and whole lemon and set aside 3 tablespoons juice.

3. Spread flour in shallow dish. Working with 1 cutlet at a time, dredge cutlets in flour, shaking gently to remove excess. Place on wire rack set in rimmed baking sheet. Heat 2 tablespoons oil in 12-inch skillet over medium-high heat until smoking. Place 6 cutlets in skillet, reduce heat to medium, and cook until golden brown on 1 side, 2 to 3 minutes. Flip and cook until golden brown on second side, 2 to 3 minutes. Return cutlets to wire rack. Repeat with 2 tablespoons oil and remaining 6 cutlets.

4. Add remaining 1 teaspoon oil and shallot to skillet and cook until softened, 1 minute. Add garlic and cook until fragrant, 30 seconds. Add broth, reserved lemon juice, and reserved lemon slices and bring to simmer, scraping up any browned bits.

5. Add cutlets to sauce and simmer for 4 minutes, flipping halfway through simmering. Transfer cutlets to platter. Sauce should be thickened to consistency of heavy cream; if not, simmer 1 minute longer. Off heat, whisk in butter. Stir in capers and parsley. Season with salt and pepper to taste. Spoon sauce over chicken and serve.

Red Wine Risotto with Beans

Northern Italians put an unexpected spin on risotto for a satisfying one-pot meal.

> BY ANNIE PETITO <

I was skeptical when I first heard of *paniscia*, a specialty from the city of Novara in Piedmont, northern Italy. It is essentially a merger of two dishes: risotto—flavored with cured meats and red wine—and a minestrone-like bean and vegetable soup. Bean, meat, and red wine risotto? Figuring that paniscia must be experienced to be understood, I headed into the kitchen.

I first made a minestrone, simmering dried soaked cranberry beans in chicken broth along with *mirepoix* (chopped carrot, celery, and onion), cabbage, and pancetta. Meanwhile, I started a risotto, first browning Genoa salami (my sub for the traditional but hard-to-find lard-cured salami called *salam d'la duja*) and then toasting Arborio rice in the fat before pouring in red wine. Adhering to the established risotto method, I stirred liquid (here, the soup) into the rice in multiple additions. I finished the dish with a little butter.

I ate every grain. This was pure, soul-satisfying nourishment with deep, layered flavor.

With all hesitations about paniscia cast aside, I started thinking on a practical level. Was it truly necessary to prepare two dishes to make one? Specifically, could I use our Almost Hands-Free Risotto method to combine the minestrone ingredients with the rice?

The trick in that recipe is to add most of the liquid to the rice up front rather than in stages, which helps the grains cook evenly so that you need to stir only a couple of times. We also cover the pot, which helps evenly distribute the heat so that every grain is tender.

I sautéed pancetta and then added the mirepoix. Next, I added the rice, salami, and wine, stirring until the wine was absorbed. I then incorporated hot chicken broth—which I had bubbling on a back burner—all at once. Cabbage went in next, followed by canned pinto beans (our favorite substitution for dried cranberry beans). A cup of hot water thinned the texture, and after a few minutes the rice was beautifully creamy. But the dish didn't taste very meaty. Also, I wondered if I could make one more shortcut by not preheating the broth.

For more savoriness, I added tomato paste and minced garlic and tripled the amount of salami. As for the broth question, the recipe worked seamlessly with room-temperature broth, saving me a pan to wash.

My streamlined recipe boasted tangy salami, just-wilted cabbage, and creamy beans, combined in a luscious risotto. Fresh parsley and red wine vinegar offset its rich flavors. And, though it's not traditional, I couldn't pass up a bit of grated Parmesan as well.

RED WINE RISOTTO WITH BEANS (PANISCIA)
SERVES 6 TO 8

We prefer to use a smaller, individually packaged, dry Italian-style salami such as Genoa or *soppressata*, but unsliced deli salami can be used (see "Common Salamis" on page 28 for more information). See page 31 for tips on chopping the cabbage.

- 2 tablespoons extra-virgin olive oil
- 2 ounces pancetta, chopped fine
- 1 onion, chopped fine
- 1 carrot, chopped fine
- 1 celery rib, chopped fine
  Salt and pepper
- 6 garlic cloves, minced
- 1½ cups Arborio rice
- 6 ounces salami, cut into ¼-inch dice
- 2 tablespoons tomato paste
- 1 cup dry red wine
- 4 cups chicken broth
- 1 small head green cabbage, halved, cored, and cut into ½-inch pieces (4 cups)
- 1 (15-ounce) can pinto beans, rinsed
- 1 cup hot tap water, plus extra as needed
- 1 ounce Parmesan cheese, grated (½ cup), plus extra for serving
- 2 tablespoons unsalted butter
- 2 teaspoons red wine vinegar
- 2 tablespoons chopped fresh parsley

1. Heat oil in Dutch oven over medium heat until shimmering. Add pancetta and cook, stirring occasionally, until beginning to brown, 3 to 5 minutes.

Though it's not traditional to *paniscia*, we stir in grated Parmesan at the end to add salty depth.

Add onion, carrot, celery, ½ teaspoon salt, and ¼ teaspoon pepper and cook, stirring occasionally, until vegetables are softened, 5 to 7 minutes. Add garlic and cook until fragrant, 30 seconds. Add rice and salami and cook, stirring frequently, until rice grains are translucent around edges, about 3 minutes.

2. Stir in tomato paste and cook until fragrant, about 1 minute. Add wine and cook, stirring constantly, until fully absorbed, 2 to 3 minutes. Stir in broth, reduce heat to medium-low, cover, and simmer for 10 minutes, stirring halfway through simmering.

3. Stir in cabbage and continue to cook, covered, until almost all liquid has been absorbed and rice is just al dente, 6 to 9 minutes longer.

4. Add beans and hot water and stir gently and constantly until risotto is creamy, about 3 minutes. Remove from heat, cover, and let stand for 5 minutes. Stir in Parmesan and butter. If desired, add up to 1 cup extra hot water to create fluid, pourable consistency. Stir in vinegar and season with salt and pepper to taste. Sprinkle with parsley and serve immediately, passing extra Parmesan separately.

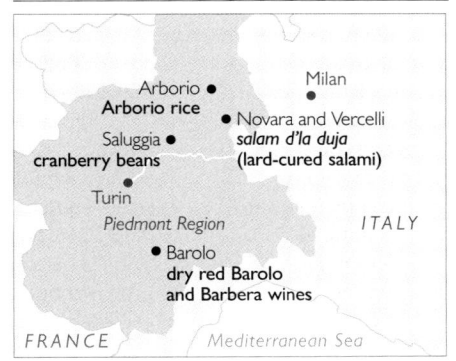

NEIGHBORING FLAVORS

At first blush, the mix of components in *paniscia* may seem odd, but it makes perfect sense from a geographical standpoint: The dish combines ingredients from Italy's Piedmont region in one pot.

◯ See Annie's Risotto Tricks
A step-by-step video is available at CooksIllustrated.com/feb18

Great—Not Grated—Carrot Salads

Forget about your grater, your peeler, and any preconceptions of what carrot salad should be. We've got something better.

⇒ BY ANDREW JANJIGIAN ⇐

I'd spent days scraping pounds of carrots—and my knuckles—against a box grater, but I still wasn't any closer to improving upon the classic shredded carrot salad, which is usually damp and clumpy. Using the shredding disk on my food processor wasn't any help; it produced long, overly thick shreds that were unpleasant to eat. In fact, it wasn't until I stumbled upon an unusual recipe from cookbook author Joan Nathan that I realized I'd been approaching my revamp of this dish all wrong. It wasn't so much the flavors or the ratio of dressing to carrots or even my shredding technique that needed to change. It was the method itself: The grater had to go.

Nathan's recipe, based on an Israeli technique, calls for finely chopping the carrots in a food processor. The resulting texture is entirely different from the damp, clumpy consistency of a shredded carrot salad. The fine bits deliver the vegetable's juicy, earthy sweetness but offer a texture that's more like grains with a pleasant crunch. To lighten things up, Nathan mixes the chopped carrots with lots of fresh herbs, garlic, and nuts and binds the salad together with a bright lemony dressing. The result—something like a vivid orange tabbouleh, with carrots in place of cracked wheat—is a surprising and refreshing take on a too-familiar vegetable and a frustrating technique. Best of all, it takes mere seconds to make, since the food processor does the lion's share of the work.

I was sold on this template and excited to come up with flavor variations of my own. I also had a few ideas for tweaking the technique, starting with exactly how thoroughly to process the carrots and herbs to produce even pieces. Another change on my list was to dial down the garlic flavor, which was rather strong, and mix in other components to add complexity and further lighten the consistency of the salad.

We finely chop carrots in the food processor and then balance their sweetness with fresh herbs, nuts, fruit, and assertive spices.

Due Process

I wanted the bits of carrots and herbs to be fine, not ground. But as anyone who's blitzed vegetables or herbs in the food processor knows, if you process until every last piece is finely chopped, some of the mixture inevitably breaks down into a soupy mush. On the other hand, if you are too conservative and don't process the pieces enough, you're likely to leave large carrot chunks or whole herb leaves in the processor bowl. I found that the best way to avoid uneven pieces was to cut the whole peeled carrots into 1-inch chunks before adding them to the processor bowl; doing so added just minutes to the recipe and helped produce the fine, even bits that I wanted.

The herbs—I started with ½ cup of cilantro leaves—were more challenging. No matter when I added the leaves to the processor bowl (before, with, or after the carrots) or how conservatively I processed them, some inevitably turned to mush, muddying the salad's fresh flavor and sabotaging the delicately crunchy texture I was after. Mincing the cilantro by hand was a bit more work, but it gave me much better control over the final product. And it wasn't as onerous as it sounds, especially once I implemented our efficient mincing method: Gather the leaves into a tight pile with your nonknife hand, slice them thin using a rocking motion, turn the pile 90 degrees, gather them again, and repeat. Using this approach, I sped through the knife work.

The only part of the vegetable prep that was a bit of a drag was peeling all those carrots, and it made me wonder if I could skip peeling altogether and just give the roots a trim and a good scrub instead. I gave it a shot and was pleased to discover that it was actually advantageous: Not only was the skin's slightly tougher texture imperceptible in those tiny pieces but the skin also lent the salad a subtle earthy bitterness that matched well with the vegetable's sweeter core and all those grassy-tasting fresh herbs (for more information, see "The Skinny on Carrot Skin").

Mixing It Up

Circling back to the garlic, I tried mincing it by hand to make sure it was fine enough, along with incrementally reducing the amount. But in both cases, its harsh taste overwhelmed the more subtle flavors of the other components. It was better to leave it out altogether.

Now for some salads with flavors of my own. The first was a nod to Nathan's original: I kept the lemon-based dressing and the pistachios but added a touch of honey, swapped out the cilantro for mint, seasoned the mixture with smoked paprika and a

---

SCIENCE **The Skinny on Carrot Skin**

In most applications, we've found that it's important to peel carrots because the skin can be a little tough and impart a slightly bitter flavor. The source of that flavor is high levels of two bitter-tasting compounds, falcarindiol and dicaffeic acid, which protect the carrot from oxidation and fungi (carrot flesh contains very small amounts of these compounds). But for our chopped carrot salads, we chose to leave the skin on the carrots for three reasons: The texture of the skin is not detectable in the tiny pieces, it saves us the tedious step of peeling, and the faint bitterness complements the bright, sweet, fresh flavors of the other components.

SHOPPING Bunched versus Bagged Carrots

Carrots sold with their feathery green leaves still attached are typically less than three weeks old, the point at which the greens begin to wilt. They're often more expensive than bagged carrots, which may sit in storage for up to six months before they reach the supermarket.

We tasted both types plain in three applications—raw, steamed, and sautéed—as well as finely chopped and dressed with vinaigrette in our carrot salads. In each of the plain applications, tasters thought the green-topped carrots had a "deeper carrot flavor" that we preferred, while the bagged carrots tasted one-dimensional but "undeniably sweeter"; those flavor differences were less obvious in the highly seasoned salads.

The green-topped carrots had deeper flavor because they contain higher concentrations of volatile flavor compounds that are largely responsible for carrot flavor; the compounds dissipate as the carrots age. The bagged ones were sweeter because certain root vegetables, including carrots and potatoes, sweeten over time when refrigerated, as the cool environment encourages the conversion of starch to sugar.

FRESH PICK
Carrots with their green tops attached boast deep carrot flavor.

IN THE BAG
Bagged carrots undergo extended storage, which makes them sweet, but they lack the intense carrot taste of the just-picked vegetable.

---

touch of cayenne, and mixed in pomegranate seeds for bursts of tangy sweetness and vibrant color. I liked the addition of fruit with the carrots, so I mixed up a couple more variations in the same vein: One was a riff on classic American carrot salad, with raisins, celery, and parsley, and the other featured chopped fennel, toasted hazelnuts, orange juice and zest, and chives. The last salad, a kimchi-inspired version, paired a rice vinegar–based dressing with cilantro, plus coarsely chopped radishes and toasted sesame seeds for extra crunch.

Never thought you'd be excited to make—or eat—carrot salad? Give these a whirl.

RECIPE TESTING
WHEN BETTER IS ALSO FASTER

Carrots that are finely chopped in the food processor make a salad that's much lighter and more open-textured than the shredded kind. Best of all, processing the carrots takes mere seconds and keeps your knuckles out of harm's way.

GRATED
Clumpy and damp

PROCESSED
Fine and fluffy

CHOPPED CARROT SALAD WITH MINT, PISTACHIOS, AND POMEGRANATE SEEDS
SERVES 4 TO 6

We prefer the convenience and the hint of bitterness that leaving the carrots unpeeled lends to this salad; just be sure to scrub the carrots well before using them.

- ¾ cup shelled pistachios, toasted
- ¼ cup extra-virgin olive oil
- 3 tablespoons lemon juice
- 1 tablespoon honey
  Salt and pepper
- ½ teaspoon smoked paprika
- ⅛ teaspoon cayenne pepper
- 1 pound carrots, trimmed and cut into 1-inch pieces
- 1 cup pomegranate seeds
- ½ cup minced fresh mint

Pulse pistachios in food processor until coarsely chopped, 10 to 12 pulses; transfer to small bowl. Whisk oil, lemon juice, honey, 1 teaspoon salt, ½ teaspoon pepper, paprika, and cayenne in large bowl until combined. Process carrots in now-empty processor until finely chopped, 10 to 20 seconds, scraping down sides of bowl as needed. Transfer carrots to bowl with dressing; add ½ cup pomegranate seeds, mint, and half of pistachios and toss to combine. Season with salt to taste. Transfer to serving platter, sprinkle with remaining pomegranate seeds and pistachios, and serve.

CHOPPED CARROT SALAD WITH CELERY AND RAISINS

Omit pistachios, paprika, cayenne, and pomegranate seeds. Substitute parsley for mint. Add 3 celery ribs, trimmed and sliced thin, and ¾ cup raisins to dressing with carrots.

CHOPPED CARROT SALAD WITH FENNEL, ORANGE, AND HAZELNUTS

Substitute toasted and skinned hazelnuts for pistachios. Omit paprika, cayenne, and pomegranate seeds. Substitute ¼ teaspoon grated orange zest plus ⅓ cup juice and 2 tablespoons white wine vinegar for lemon juice. Substitute chives for mint, saving ¼ cup to use as garnish. Before processing carrots, pulse 1 fennel bulb, stalks discarded, bulb halved, cored, and cut into 1-inch pieces, in food processor until coarsely chopped, 10 to 12 pulses, then add to dressing.

CHOPPED CARROT SALAD WITH RADISHES AND SESAME SEEDS

Omit pistachios. Substitute 3 tablespoons vegetable oil and 2 teaspoons toasted sesame oil for olive oil. Substitute rice vinegar for lemon juice and 1½ teaspoons Korean red pepper flakes for paprika, cayenne, and pepper. Increase honey to 2 tablespoons and salt to 1¼ teaspoons. Before processing carrots, pulse 8 ounces radishes, trimmed and halved, in food processor until coarsely but evenly chopped, 10 to 12 pulses; add to dressing. Substitute ¼ cup toasted sesame seeds for pomegranate seeds and cilantro for mint.

▶ Watch: Carrot Salad in a Flash
A step-by-step video is available at CooksIllustrated.com/feb18

Bringing Back Gougères

Airy, elegant French cheese puffs, known as *gougères*, deliver toasty flavor within delicately crisp shells. Bonus: Ours are a cinch to make.

⇒ BY LAN LAM ⇐

While some French classics can feel stodgy and old-fashioned (think Mornay sauce or chicken fricassee), I'm willing to bet that *gougères* (and their sweet cousins, profiteroles) will never go out of style. It's not just that their crisp, browned exteriors and airy, popover-like interiors flavored with nutty Gruyère cheese give them huge appeal. These two-bite puffs also look impressive and can be made in advance and reheated.

The foundation for gougères (and profiteroles) is *pâte à choux*, or choux pastry. The most classic versions involve cooking butter, water, and flour in a saucepan until the loose batter stiffens and turns into a dough—this ensures that it's pipeable rather than a runny mess. Eggs then get beaten in, one at a time, for structure and flavor. To make the choux into gougères, the next steps are to stir in grated cheese, pipe the dough into little rounds, and bake. Starting in a hot oven (425 degrees is typical) ensures that the puffs expand dramatically. The temperature is then lowered to 375 degrees or so to finish cooking them through.

Following a few such recipes, I found room for improvement. Fresh out of the oven, the best puffs were crisp outside and just custardy enough inside to provide contrast—but if they sat around for even 20 minutes, they softened. I also found that, depending on the oven, the puffs could overbrown. They weren't nearly cheesy enough, and beating in the eggs by hand was a chore.

Choux Drop

I cooked a paste of ½ cup of water, 5 tablespoons of butter, and ½ cup of flour along with a little salt and cayenne for depth. But instead of beating in the eggs by hand, I worked them into the dough in a food processor, along with an extra egg white. The proteins in the white would boost crispness and provide structure for more airiness. The water in the white would provide steam to help the dough puff.

I also adjusted the baking process. With the help of a probe thermometer, I confirmed that when I turned the dial on my well-insulated oven from 425 to 375 degrees, the temperature didn't always drop much, depending on where the oven was in its heating cycle. When the temperature didn't drop much,

The dough, which comes together in minutes, can be made several hours in advance. Baked *gougères* can be stored for 24 hours and rewarm nicely.

the puffs browned and dried out on their exteriors by the time the interiors were done. But when I pulled them earlier, the interiors were gummy and dense. I wondered if I could get more consistent results by simply shutting off the oven. This would guarantee that the temperature inside the oven, no matter how well insulated, would drop more rapidly. I gave this approach a shot: After 15 minutes at 425 degrees, I turned off the oven and left the puffs inside with the door closed for another 15 minutes. This batch came out just right: perfectly browned with the ideal airy centers.

Stretched to the Limits

With the choux settled, it was time to bring cheese into the picture. I made another batch of choux, but this time after adding the eggs to the processor I added 4 ounces (1 cup) of grated Gruyère—a full ounce more than other recipes—and then piped my rounds and baked them as before.

When I removed my gougères from the oven, I could see that they were overbrowned on the bottoms and a little greasy. But the bigger problem was the interiors, which were dense and doughy. When I inspected them carefully, I noticed that most of the air bubbles had tears in their walls. The addition of such a hefty amount of cheese was preventing the bubbles from expanding fully.

To find a solution, I gave the choux ingredients a closer look. First, I considered the gluten-forming proteins in the flour. Gluten creates a stretchy network that provides structure to baked goods, so it seemed logical that more gluten would provide more strength so that the bubbles could expand properly without tearing. To that end, I switched from using all-purpose flour to higher-protein bread flour. Second, since fat inhibits gluten formation, I reduced the amount of butter from 5 tablespoons to 2; this would mitigate greasiness. To my disappointment, these changes brought only marginal improvement.

Two Tricks to Prevent Burnt Bottoms

Baking the *gougères* on the upper rack of the oven helps mitigate the bottoms' exposure to heat, but so does creating an air gap beneath the puffs. You can do this in either of the following ways:

NEST BAKING SHEETS
Nesting two rimmed baking sheets creates a thin air gap between them that keeps the top sheet cooler.

LINE SHEET WITH CRINKLED FOIL
If you don't have two baking sheets, you can create multiple tiny air gaps by lining the sheet with crinkled foil before covering it with parchment.

Smooth the Way to Perfect Puffs

Use the back of a spoon lightly coated with vegetable oil spray to smooth away any creases and large peaks on each mound of dough.

I wondered if I could do better by manipulating the egg proteins. Raw egg proteins are coiled up in tight bundles. When heated, they uncoil and form strong, springy networks. I ran a series of tests: more whole eggs, more whites, and more yolks in varying amounts. But in all cases, the dough became too wet, making it hard to work with. Was there some way to get the two eggs and one white I'd been using all along to set up and establish some structure more quickly?

Egg proteins unwind not only when heated but also when beaten well (something we've learned from making omelets and baked goods). But after a chat with our science editor, I discovered another way to make them unwind more quickly: Combine them with salt. Up to this point, I'd been adding the salt to the dough, but in my next batch I added it directly to the eggs instead. What an impressive difference one little change made. When I tore open these gougères, I found the airy centers I was after. (See "For Airy Puffs, Salt Is Key" for a full explanation.)

Still, the puffs were browning too much on their bottoms. Baking them on the upper-middle rack helped, but it wasn't enough. The fix was nesting my rimmed baking sheet in a second baking sheet, which created a thin air gap between the two. This gap insulated the pastry bottoms just enough to keep them from overbrowning. (For an alternative solution, see "Two Tricks to Prevent Burnt Bottoms").

Now I took a closer look at portioning the dough. Piping the dough with a pastry bag was of course an option, but two spoons worked almost as well. (With this dough, a zipper-lock bag with the corner snipped off was not a possibility, as the dough was too stiff and came out of the bag in odd shapes.) Whether I used a pastry bag or spoons, I only had to smooth away any creases or large peaks with the back of a spoon coated in vegetable oil spray.

From here, I came up with a few more recipes that varied the cheese and the spices, making sure to pick cheeses that are similar in age and texture—and, thus, moisture content—to Gruyère so as not to alter my puffs' perfect texture. Manchego and black pepper paired well, as did Gouda and smoked paprika.

These luxuriously cheesy, delicately crisp bites are sure to make an appearance at my next party. Though they'll stay perfectly crisp for a full hour, I don't expect they'll last that long.

GOUGÈRES
MAKES 24 PUFFS

Use a Gruyère that has been aged for about one year. The doubled baking sheets prevent the undersides of the puffs from overbrowning. Alternatively, loosely roll up an 18 by 12-inch piece of aluminum foil, unroll it, and set it in a rimmed baking sheet. Cover the foil with a sheet of parchment paper and proceed with the recipe. In step 4, the dough can be piped using a pastry bag fitted with a ½-inch plain tip. For tips on how to use a pastry bag, see page 30.

- 2 large eggs plus 1 large white
- ¼ teaspoon salt
- ½ cup water
- 2 tablespoons unsalted butter, cut into 4 pieces
- Pinch cayenne pepper
- ½ cup (2½ ounces) all-purpose flour
- 4 ounces Gruyère cheese, shredded (1 cup)

1. Adjust oven rack to upper-middle position and heat oven to 425 degrees. Line rimmed baking sheet with parchment paper and nest it in second rimmed baking sheet. In 2-cup liquid measuring cup, beat eggs and white and salt until well combined. (You should have about ½ cup egg mixture. Discard excess.) Set aside.

2. Heat water, butter, and cayenne in small saucepan over medium heat. When mixture begins to simmer, reduce heat to low and immediately stir in flour using wooden spoon. Cook, stirring constantly, using smearing motion, until mixture is very thick, forms ball, and pulls away from sides of saucepan, about 30 seconds.

3. Immediately transfer mixture to food processor and process with feed tube open for 5 seconds to cool slightly. With processor running, gradually add reserved egg mixture in steady stream, then scrape down sides of bowl and add Gruyère. Process until paste is very glossy and flecked with coarse cornmeal–size pieces of cheese, 30 to 40 seconds. (If not using immediately, transfer paste to bowl, press sheet of greased parchment directly on surface, and store at room temperature for up to 2 hours.)

4. Scoop 1 level tablespoon of dough. Using second small spoon, scrape dough onto prepared sheet into 1½-inch-wide, 1-inch-tall mound. Repeat, spacing mounds 1 to 1¼ inches apart. (You should have 24 mounds.) Using back of spoon lightly coated with vegetable oil spray, smooth away any creases and large peaks on each mound.

5. Bake until gougères are puffed and upper two-thirds of each are light golden brown (bottom third will still be pale), 14 to 20 minutes. Turn off oven; leave gougères in oven until uniformly golden brown, 10 to 15 minutes (do not open oven for at least 8 minutes). Transfer gougères to wire rack and let cool for 15 minutes. Serve warm. (Cooled gougères can be stored in airtight container at room temperature for up to 24 hours or frozen in zipper-lock bag for up to 1 month. To serve, crisp gougères in 300-degree oven for about 7 minutes.)

For Airy Puffs, Salt Is Key

Adding a little salt is important in almost all recipes to enhance flavor; the salt in our Gougères also improves their structure, allowing us to make puffs that are airy, not dense. But how the salt is added is critical. Rather than add it to the dough, we beat the salt with the eggs before they are combined with the flour mixture. Why?

Mixing salt with the eggs changes the electrical charges on the egg proteins so they uncoil at a lower temperature, allowing them to set up into a strong network earlier in the baking time. This means they can buttress the dough as it inflates, ensuring that it doesn't collapse under the added weight of the cheese. Bottom line? Our Gougères contain fewer and larger interior bubbles, creating the airy results we were after.

PERFECTLY HOLLOW
Salting the eggs before incorporating them into the dough makes a strong puff that inflates well.

POORLY INFLATED
Mixing salt directly into the dough makes for a weaker puff that doesn't inflate well.

GOUGÈRES WITH AGED GOUDA AND SMOKED PAPRIKA

Substitute aged gouda for Gruyère and ½ teaspoon smoked paprika for cayenne.

GOUGÈRES WITH MANCHEGO AND BLACK PEPPER

Substitute Manchego for Gruyère and ½ teaspoon pepper for cayenne.

▶ Look: Perfect Puffs
Video available free for 4 months at CooksIllustrated.com/feb18

How to Roast a Great Chicken

Whether you need dinner on the table in a hurry or have time to pull out all the stops, we'll guide you to the best results. BY ELIZABETH BOMZE

Be Savvy About the Label

NOT JUST HYPE

➤ **Air-Chilled** means the chickens weren't water-chilled in a chlorinated bath, so they didn't absorb water during processing, which dilutes flavor and makes the skin harder to crisp. Air-chilled meat is typically more tender, possibly because the slower cooling leaves time for enzymes in the meat to tenderize muscle tissue.

➤ **USDA Organic** poultry must eat organic feed that doesn't contain animal byproducts, must be raised without antibiotics, and must have access to the outdoors (how much access, however, isn't regulated).

BUYER BEWARE

➤ **Raised Without Antibiotics** and other claims regarding antibiotic use are important; too bad they're not strictly enforced. (Poultry is randomly monitored for residues, but the only rigorous enforcement is when the claim is subject to the USDA Organic seal.)

➤ **Natural and All Natural** mean only that the bird was minimally processed with no added synthetic ingredients. Producers may thus raise their chickens under the most unnatural circumstances on the most unnatural diets and still put this claim on their packaging.

➤ **Hormone-Free** is empty reassurance, since the USDA does not allow the use of hormones or steroids in poultry production.

➤ **Vegetarian Fed and Vegetarian Diet** may sound healthy, but the terms aren't regulated. That said, the producers of our winning chickens assured us that their definitions mean a diet of corn and soy.

OUR FAVORITE WHOLE CHICKENS

MARY'S Free Range Air Chilled Chicken (also sold as Pitman's)
PRICE: $1.99 per lb
WHY WE LIKE IT: Air chilling plus plenty of fat added up to a bird that tasted "clean," "savory," "chicken-y," "juicy," and "tender."

BELL & EVANS Air Chilled Premium Fresh Chicken
PRICE: $3.29 per lb
WHY WE LIKE IT: This air-chilled bird was "perfectly moist," with "concentrated" flavor. It also had the most fat—more than 15 percent—of any bird in our tasting.

BEST FOR Getting dinner on the table in about an hour.

WEEKNIGHT ROAST CHICKEN

1. SWAP ROASTING PAN FOR SKILLET Adjust oven rack to middle position, place 12-inch ovensafe skillet on rack, and heat oven to 450 degrees. Combine 1 tablespoon kosher salt and ½ teaspoon pepper in bowl. Pat 3½- to 4-pound whole chicken (giblets discarded) dry. Rub surface with 1 tablespoon olive oil. Rub salt mixture over surface to evenly coat. Tie legs together with kitchen twine and tuck wingtips behind back.

WHY Juices pool deeply in a skillet, which prevents them from burning so that they can be used later to make a pan sauce.

2. SEAR THIGHS Transfer chicken, breast side up, to preheated skillet in oven. Roast until breast registers 120 degrees and thighs register 135 degrees, 25 to 35 minutes.

WHY Direct contact with a preheated skillet gives the thighs a head start so that they cook in sync with the delicate breast meat.

3. CUT HEAT Turn off oven and leave chicken in oven until breast registers 160 degrees and thighs register 175 degrees, 25 to 35 minutes. Transfer chicken to carving board and let rest, uncovered, for 20 minutes.

WHY Cutting the heat allows the chicken to finish cooking gently (its temperature will rise 40 degrees).

4. SKIM FAT While chicken rests, remove all but 1 tablespoon fat from skillet, leaving any fond and jus in skillet.

WHY Removing most of the fat prevents the sauce from being greasy.

5. USE FOND Place skillet over medium-high heat. Add 1 minced shallot, 2 minced garlic cloves, and 2 teaspoons chopped fresh thyme and cook until softened, about 2 minutes. Stir in 1 cup chicken broth and 2 teaspoons Dijon mustard, scraping up any browned bits. Cook until reduced to ¾ cup, about 3 minutes. Off heat, whisk in 2 tablespoons unsalted butter and 2 teaspoons sherry vinegar until butter has melted. Season with pepper to taste; cover and keep warm. Carve chicken and serve with sauce.

WHY It takes minutes to transform the savory browned bits of fond into a flavorful pan sauce by stirring in aromatics and other flavorings.

FOUR ROAST CHICKEN RULES

1. Portion Seasonings
To avoid constantly washing and rewashing your hands—and to greatly reduce the risks of cross-contamination—make sure to portion and set aside any seasonings, such as salt and pepper, before you start handling the meat.

2. Don't Rinse Raw Poultry
The United States Department of Agriculture (USDA) advises against rinsing raw poultry under cold running water; this applies to both whole chickens and chicken parts. Doing so will not remove much bacteria, and the splashing of the running water around the sink can spread the bacteria found on the surface of the raw chicken.

BEST FOR When you have time to let the bird rest overnight for supercrispy skin.

CRISP ROAST CHICKEN

How to Carve a Whole Chicken

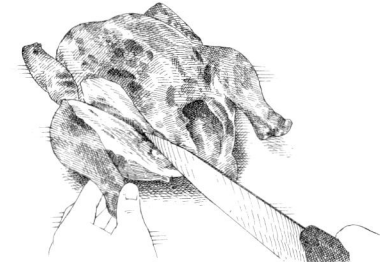

1. EXPOSE LEG JOINT Using chef's knife, make cut through skin to expose where thigh meets breast.

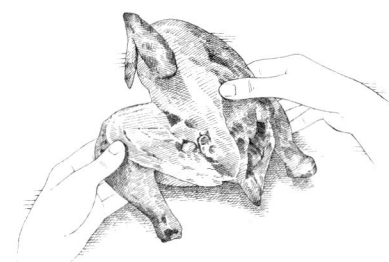

2. SEPARATE JOINT TO REMOVE LEG QUARTER Pull leg quarter away from carcass, gently pull leg out to side, and push up on joint. Cut through joint to remove leg quarter from carcass.

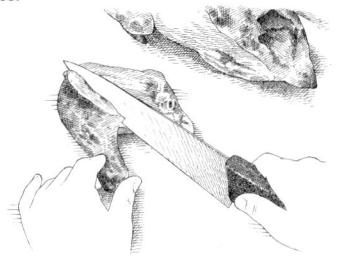

3. SEPARATE DRUMSTICK AND THIGH Cut through joint that connects drumstick to thigh. Repeat steps 1 through 3 on chicken's other side.

4. REMOVE BREAST MEAT Cut down along side of breastbone, pulling breast meat away from breastbone as you cut.

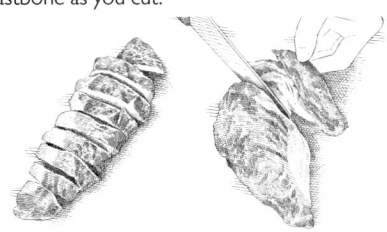

5. SLICE BREAST MEAT Remove wing from breast by cutting through wing joint. Slice breast crosswise. Repeat with other side.

1. CUT CHANNELS, LOOSEN SKIN, POKE HOLES Place 3½- to 4-pound whole chicken (giblets discarded), breast side down, on cutting board. Using tip of paring knife, make four 1-inch incisions along back. Using your fingers, gently loosen skin covering breast and thighs. Using metal skewer, poke 15 to 20 holes in fat deposits on top of breast and thighs. Tuck wings behind back.

WHY These cuts create escape routes for rendered fat and juices, which helps the skin crisp.

2. RUB AND CHILL Combine 1 tablespoon kosher salt, 1 teaspoon baking powder, and ½ teaspoon pepper in bowl. Pat chicken dry with paper towels and sprinkle evenly with salt mixture. Rub in mixture with your hands, evenly coating entire surface. Set chicken, breast side up, in V-rack set on rimmed baking sheet and refrigerate, uncovered, for at least 12 hours or up to 24 hours.

WHY Salt and baking powder, plus air drying, dehydrate the skin so that it will crisp and brown.

3. ROAST HIGH AND FLIP Adjust oven rack to lowest position and heat oven to 450 degrees. Using paring knife, poke 20 holes about 1½ inches apart in 16 by 12-inch piece of aluminum foil. Place foil loosely in roasting pan. Flip chicken so breast side faces down and set V-rack in prepared pan on top of foil. Roast chicken for 25 minutes. Remove pan from oven. Using 2 large wads of paper towels, flip chicken breast side up. Continue to roast until breast registers 135 degrees, 15 to 25 minutes longer.

WHY A hot oven browns the skin quickly so that the meat doesn't have time to dry out; a foil liner prevents any rendered fat from burning and smoking. Flipping the chicken midway through cooking helps it cook evenly.

4. BLAST IT Increase oven temperature to 500 degrees. Continue to roast chicken until skin is golden brown and crispy, breast registers 160 degrees, and thighs register 175 degrees, 10 to 20 minutes longer. Transfer chicken to carving board and let rest for 20 minutes. Carve chicken and serve immediately.

WHY A final high-heat blast deeply browns and crisps the skin.

Science: New Powers for Baking Powder

An overnight rub made with baking powder and salt guarantees supercrispy skin. The process works in two ways. First, it draws moisture out of the skin, concentrating flavor and leaving the skin ready to crisp up fast while it cooks. Second, the alkaline baking powder helps proteins in the chicken skin break down over the course of the overnight rest. Broken-down proteins crisp and brown more readily than intact ones, so the upshot is crackly, flavor-packed skin.

---

3. Let Meat Rest to Maximize Juiciness
When meat cooks, its proteins contract and squeeze out moisture. Carving meat without letting it rest causes it to lose this moisture. Resting before carving allows the contracted proteins to relax and reabsorb some of the expelled moisture. That's why we recommend letting whole chickens rest for 20 minutes.

4. Temp Properly
Inserting the thermometer incorrectly can give you an inaccurate reading. Here's our method:
White Meat: Insert probe low into thickest part of breast, just above bone. Withdraw probe slowly, checking for lowest registered temperature.
Dark Meat: Insert probe down into space between tip of breast and thigh. Slightly angle probe outward so that it pierces meat in lower part of thigh.

Rethinking Coffee Cake

Could we streamline the process for this breakfast treat and still produce a soft, tender crumb crowned with a crunchy, nutty streusel?

≥ BY LAN LAM ≤

The custom of sipping a hot beverage while enjoying a sweet cake or bread goes back to 17th-century Europe when German, Dutch, and Scandinavian cooks were habitual pastry makers and coffee was fast becoming part of the daily routine. Eventually, the practice spread to the United States, and today, three types of coffee cake are common: the yeasted kind, featuring a sweet cheese and/or fruit filling; the rich sour cream Bundt version that shows off elegant bands of crumb filling when sliced; and the streusel-topped type, with a nutty crunch highlighting a moist cake. It is this last cake that appeals to me the most. Instead of drawing attention with graceful swirls of filling or the dramatic curves of a Bundt shape, its focus is on the contrasting textures and complementary flavors of the cake and topping.

The trouble is, many such coffee cake recipes are relatively complicated, requiring multiple bowls and appliances. I wanted a simpler method suitable for off-the-cuff baking—but one that produced the same tender cake and crunchy, flavorful topping.

Adding just a teaspoon of water to the streusel ingredients while pulsing them in the food processor helps the mixture adhere to the cake.

Working in Stages

The cake portion of this treat is commonly made by creaming butter and sugar using a handheld or stand mixer and then alternately incorporating the flour and liquid ingredients. Since I like to use a food processor to chop nuts for streusel and I wanted to avoid dirtying a second appliance, my first instinct was to adapt this method to a food processor. But while the food processor deftly whipped the butter and sugar into a pale, aerated state, its powerful motor was incapable of gently folding in flour and liquids. The result of those aggressively whizzing blades was one seriously tough cake. That's because flour contains proteins, which, in the presence of water, link up to form gluten. As the gluten strands are manipulated by mixing, they link and form a stretchy network. While some gluten is necessary to give baked goods structure, cakes with too much gluten are unpleasantly tough.

Luckily, there was another method to consider. Reverse creaming—what pastry texts refer to as a "two-stage" method—limits gluten formation by "waterproofing" the gluten-forming proteins. Without access to water, gluten can't develop, so the method virtually guarantees a soft, tender crumb. It goes like this: In stage one, you work the butter into the dry ingredients until the flour is mostly coated in fat. In stage two, you mix in the wet ingredients. It seemed like the technique would adapt well to a food processor, so it was definitely worth trying.

From the Top

Since I planned to use the food processor for both components of my coffee cake, I started by making the streusel. I prepared a standard topping by processing toasted pecans (their slightly sweet, buttery flavor makes them a favorite for streusel) and brown sugar until the nuts were finely ground. Then it was a simple matter of incorporating flour, cinnamon, salt, and finally, some melted butter.

After scraping the streusel from the processor bowl and setting it aside, I prepared the cake batter using a recipe I'd cobbled together from my research. First, I whizzed together flour, sugar, baking soda, baking powder, salt, and cinnamon. Then I added softened butter and pulsed until only very small pieces of the butter remained. Finally, I pulsed in milk, an egg, an egg yolk (for extra richness), and vanilla extract to form a thick batter. After scraping the batter into a greased and floured round cake pan, I smoothed the top with a rubber spatula, sprinkled the streusel evenly over the top, and baked the cake in a 350-degree oven.

An hour later, as I was flipping the cake out of the pan and inverting it onto a wire rack to cool, I could see that my streusel—though it was wonderfully nutty and delicately spiced—needed some help. It was sinking into the batter at the edge, losing its crunch and marring the cake's appearance. What's more, it was too fine and rained down from the pan when I inverted the cake. The good news was that the reverse-creaming method had lived up to my expectations: The cake itself was tender as could be.

But back to the streusel. It didn't make sense to invert a cake with a crumbly topping. How about switching from the typical cake pan to a springform pan, which would allow me to remove the collar without dislodging the topping?

RECIPE TESTING **Stabilizing the Streusel**

During testing, we noticed that the streusel at the edges of the cake sometimes appeared to sink into the batter. Eventually, we realized that it was actually the cake batter and not the streusel that was on the move. As the batter at the edges of the pan heats up, it becomes more fluid and rises, eventually flowing over the topping. To solve the problem, we added extra flour to stiffen the batter and prevent it from climbing up and over the streusel.

SINKING STREUSEL
As the thin batter heated, it climbed the pan's sides and flowed over the streusel layer. Some extra flour took care of that problem.

TECHNIQUE | GIVE IT A SHAKE

When checking for doneness, don't just poke a toothpick or skewer into the cake. Give the pan a gentle shake first to make sure the batter has set enough to support the streusel. If the batter still jiggles, the pressure of the skewer on the streusel may cause the center of the cake to sink.

A Better Way to Make Coffee Cake
We rewrote the rule book on coffee cake, changing up both the equipment and the mixing method.

SKIP THE STAND MIXER
With a food processor, we need just one appliance for chopping the nuts, mixing the streusel, and preparing the batter.

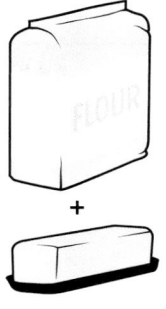
"WATERPROOF" THE FLOUR
Blending the butter into the flour—instead of creaming the butter and sugar—before adding liquids limits gluten formation, so the cake is extra-tender.

DITCH THE CAKE PAN
A springform pan eliminates the tricky prospect of inverting a streusel-topped cake onto a serving platter.

I gave it a go. Once the springform pan was prepared, I set it on a rimmed baking sheet to catch any batter that oozed out. To help the streusel cling together, I added 1 teaspoon of water. After just a couple of pulses, I could see that this seemingly minor addition made this batch much more cohesive. After scattering the topping over the batter, I placed my assembled cake in the oven. When I released the collar on the springform pan and sliced the cooled cake, I was pleased to see that this streusel was just right, boasting a cohesive, lightly clumped texture.

Not-So-Sinking Feeling
Now I just needed to prevent the streusel from disappearing into the edges of the cake. To better understand the problem, I peered into the oven to monitor a batter-filled pan during baking. After a while, I realized that the streusel wasn't actually sinking at all. Rather, the cake batter at the edges, nearest the hot pan, was heating up first and thus thinning out, filling with bubbles from the leavener, and climbing the sides of the pan, where it flowed over onto the streusel.

At first I thought I needed to reduce the amount of leavener in the cake to prevent it from rising so much, but no matter how much I cut back and no matter what combination of baking soda and baking powder I tried, I couldn't stop the cake from rising up and over onto sections of the streusel. Furthermore, in some cases, the reduction in leavening produced a dense, heavy crumb.

What ultimately worked was increasing the viscosity of the batter to make it less prone to climbing. I had been using 1½ cups of flour and decided to bump the amount up to 1⅔ cups. Sure enough, this slight addition thickened and firmed the batter just enough to keep it and the streusel in place at the edges as it heated up. And fortunately, the additional flour wasn't enough to make the crumb noticeably drier.

Each bite of this coffee cake offered an appealing combination of crunchy cinnamon-pecan streusel and rich, tender cake. And I could make it quickly, using a single kitchen appliance.

COFFEE CAKE WITH PECAN-CINNAMON STREUSEL
SERVES 8 TO 10

For the best results, we recommend weighing the flour in this recipe. Do not insert a skewer into this cake to test for doneness until the center appears firm when the pan is shaken. If you do, the weight of the streusel may squeeze out air and the cake may sink. This cake can be stored at room temperature, wrapped in plastic wrap, for up to 24 hours.

Streusel
- 1 cup pecans, toasted
- ⅓ cup packed (2⅓ ounces) brown sugar
- ½ cup (2½ ounces) all-purpose flour
- ¾ teaspoon ground cinnamon
- ¼ teaspoon salt
- 4 tablespoons unsalted butter, melted and cooled
- 1 teaspoon water

Cake
- 1⅔ cups (8⅓ ounces) all-purpose flour
- 1 cup (7 ounces) sugar
- 1 teaspoon ground cinnamon
- 1 teaspoon baking powder
- ½ teaspoon baking soda
- ¾ teaspoon salt
- 7 tablespoons unsalted butter, cut into 7 pieces and softened
- ¾ cup milk
- 1 large egg plus 1 large yolk
- 1 teaspoon vanilla extract

1. Adjust oven rack to lower-middle position and heat oven to 350 degrees. Grease and flour 9-inch springform pan and place on rimmed baking sheet.

2. FOR THE STREUSEL: Process pecans and sugar in food processor until finely ground, about 10 seconds. Add flour, cinnamon, and salt and pulse to combine, about 5 (1-second) pulses. Add melted butter and water and pulse until butter is fully incorporated and mixture begins to form clumps, 8 to 10 (1-second) pulses. Transfer streusel to bowl and set aside.

3. FOR THE CAKE: In now-empty processor, process flour, sugar, cinnamon, baking powder, baking soda, and salt until combined, about 10 seconds. Add butter and pulse until very small but visible pieces of butter remain, 5 to 8 (5-second) pulses. Add milk, egg and yolk, and vanilla; pulse until dry ingredients are moistened, 4 to 5 (1-second) pulses. Scrape down sides of bowl. Pulse until mixture is well combined, 4 to 5 (1-second) pulses (some small pieces of butter will remain). Transfer batter to prepared pan and smooth top with rubber spatula.

4. Starting at edges of pan, sprinkle streusel in even layer over batter. Bake cake on sheet until center is firm and skewer inserted into center of cake comes out clean, 45 to 55 minutes. Transfer pan to wire rack and let cake cool in pan for 15 minutes. Remove side of pan and let cake cool completely, about 2 hours. Using offset spatula, transfer cake to serving platter. Using serrated knife, cut cake into wedges and serve.

Wake and Bake
Our Coffee Cake with Pecan-Cinnamon Streusel is great for a make-ahead breakfast. Wrap the topped but unbaked cake in plastic wrap and refrigerate it overnight. The next morning, transfer the cake to the preheated oven, increasing the baking time by 15 to 20 minutes.

▶ **Lan Makes It Simple**
A step-by-step video is available at CooksIllustrated.com/feb18

Creamy French-Style Scrambled Eggs

For incredibly lush and creamy eggs, the key is to take things slow.

≥ BY ANDREA GEARY ≤

American-style scrambled eggs are the speediest of home-cooked breakfasts: Heat butter or oil in a skillet; add eggs beaten with water or milk; stir, stir, stir; and you're done. The process takes less than 3 minutes and can produce eggs sturdy enough to be tucked inside an English muffin and eaten on the go.

But French cooks, and often British ones, too, employ a more leisurely approach. They cook their eggs slowly over low heat with plenty of butter, stirring constantly until the mixture forms small, delicate curds bound in a velvety sauce. This technique can take five times as long as the American version, but the reward is eggs that are so extravagantly creamy and rich that they linger on the palate, allowing you time to thoroughly appreciate the fullness of their flavor. They're so satisfying that the French often opt to serve them for lunch or dinner.

The American version is undeniably convenient, but a recipe for deluxe slow-cooked scrambled eggs would be ideal for those occasions when I can luxuriate in a laid-back breakfast.

Haste Makes Waste

Starting with Julia Child's recipe, I smeared a skillet with 2 tablespoons of soft butter; added 6 eggs beaten with salt, pepper, and milk; and placed the skillet over low heat. Then I stirred. And stirred. For a while nothing seemed to be happening, but after 18 minutes, the eggs coalesced into a soft mass of small, tender curds that stopped just short of flowing across the skillet. Following Child's guidance, I took the pan off the heat and stirred in another 2 tablespoons of butter before spooning the eggs onto slices of toast.

These eggs were delectable enough to justify the indulgence of time and calories, but I wondered if both were strictly necessary. In the past we've noted that fat coats egg proteins, which prevents them from bonding tightly. Confident that 4 tablespoons of butter would be sufficient to tenderize 8 eggs (I decided to increase the recipe to serve 4) even if they were cooked a bit more quickly, I turned up the heat.

But I found that eggs cooked in less than 10 minutes, though tender, lacked the lush viscosity of the slow-cooked version, no matter how much fat

▶ Andrea Explains It All
A step-by-step video is available at CooksIllustrated.com/feb18

Save the butter for your toast. These creamy eggs require no added fat.

I added. The higher heat transformed every bit of the liquid egg into curds, leaving no sauce. And pulling the skillet off the heat earlier was no solution either. That left me with curds swimming in an unappetizing mixture of thin, raw egg and melted butter.

Fat Loss

Suspecting that I'd overestimated the importance of fat and underestimated the importance of taking it slow, I ran a series of tests in which I incrementally lowered the cooking temperature (which increased the cooking time) while also decreasing the amount of butter. Success: At the 12-minute mark, the eggs were creamy even when cooked in a single tablespoon of butter. The curds were small and tender, and the lush egg "sauce" that united them registered 160 degrees, an indication that the eggs were fully cooked.

Slow cooking was clearly the key, so did I need any added fat? After all, my nonstick skillet would eliminate any risk of sticking. But that tablespoon of butter was handy because its melting signaled that the pan was hot enough to jump-start the heating of the eggs. With no butter, how would I know when the skillet was the right temperature?

Well, I thought, how about using water as my temperature indicator? I put 2 tablespoons of water in the skillet, and when the water started to steam,

I knew the pan was hot enough. I added the eggs and immediately started stirring to help them heat evenly. The water served a second purpose: It diluted the egg proteins so that they didn't begin to coagulate too soon. After about 8 minutes, tiny curds began to form. I began to stir more energetically at that point, eager to keep the curds small and the eggs loose. After 4 more minutes, the eggs mounded gently but were still soft and saucy, all without a bit of added fat.

In fact, the sauce was so thick that it was verging on gluey. Would I need to finish them with a bit of butter or cream after all? No. It turned out that just one more tablespoon of water smoothed them out nicely. Finally, a sprinkle of fresh minced herbs complemented their richness. Now I can save the butter for my toast and the cream for my coffee.

CREAMY FRENCH-STYLE SCRAMBLED EGGS
SERVES 4

For the creamiest, richest-tasting result, be sure to cook these eggs slowly, following the visual cues provided. It should take 12 to 14 minutes total. Though the eggs will be rather loose, their extended cooking time ensures that they reach a safe temperature. You can prepare two servings by halving the amounts of all the ingredients and using an 8-inch skillet. Chives or tarragon can be substituted for the parsley, if desired. Serve with buttered toast.

- 8 large eggs
- ½ teaspoon salt
- 3 tablespoons water
- 1 teaspoon minced fresh parsley

1. Using fork, beat eggs and salt until blended. Heat 2 tablespoons water in 10-inch nonstick skillet over low heat until steaming. Add egg mixture and immediately stir with rubber spatula. Cook, stirring slowly and constantly, scraping edges and bottom of skillet, for 4 minutes. (If egg mixture is not steaming after 4 minutes, increase heat slightly.)

2. Continue to stir slowly until eggs begin to thicken and small curds begin to form, about 4 minutes longer (if curds have not begun to form, increase heat slightly). If any large curds form, mash with spatula. As curds start to form, stir vigorously, scraping edges and bottom of skillet, until eggs are thick enough to hold their shape when pushed to 1 side of skillet, 4 to 6 minutes. Remove skillet from heat. Add remaining 1 tablespoon water and parsley and stir vigorously until incorporated, about 30 seconds. Serve.

Foolproof All-Butter Pie Dough

Our ultimate pie dough. It uses all butter, it's dead easy to roll, and it bakes up tender, crisp, and shatteringly flaky.

➤ BY ANDREA GEARY ≼

Outside the kitchen I'm sometimes a bit of a klutz, but give me a rolling pin and a lump of traditional all-butter pie dough—the kind that's dry and brittle and exhibits an alarming tendency to crack—and I'll dazzle you with my proficiency and grace as I roll it into a flawless circle. It's a skill that's taken me decades to acquire, and practicing it makes me feel like some sort of high priestess of pastry. Happily, that feeling of accomplishment became accessible to even the most inexperienced bakers in 2010 when we developed our Foolproof Pie Dough, which is soft and moist and a dream to roll out and bakes up flaky and tender. But as great as that recipe is, I've never been 100 percent converted from my traditional ways (for reasons that I'll explain).

Upending Pie Tradition

The 2010 recipe controls the ability of the flour in the dough to absorb water, and that's important because water bonds with protein in flour to form gluten, the elastic network that gives baked goods their structure. If there's too little water, the dough will be crumbly and impossible to roll and the baked crust will fall apart; too much water and the dough will roll out easily enough, but it may shrink when it bakes and will certainly be tough.

To appreciate just how revolutionary the 2010 recipe is, it's helpful to recall the way that pie dough has been made for centuries: You start by combining the dry ingredients—flour, salt, and sugar—and you

With our new dough, a fluted edge won't slump in the oven. It will hold its definition for a pie that always looks sharp.

cut in cold butter until it's broken into pea-size nuggets. Then you add water and mix until the dough comes together in a crumbly mass with visible bits of butter strewn throughout.

But our 2010 dough spurns tradition: Using a food processor, you mix 1½ cups of flour with some sugar and salt before adding 1½ sticks of cold butter and ½ cup of shortening (often added to pie doughs to increase flakiness); you continue processing until the fat and the dry ingredients form a smooth paste. Next you pulse in the remaining cup of flour until you have a bunch of flour-covered chunks of dough and a small amount of free flour.

Finally, you transfer the dough to a bowl and stir in ¼ cup of water and ¼ cup of vodka to bring it all together. Why vodka? Because it's 60 percent water and 40 percent alcohol, and alcohol doesn't activate gluten. So replacing some of the water with vodka gives you the freedom to add enough liquid to make a moist, supple dough without the risk of forming excess gluten.

Taking the All-Butter Route

I've made plenty of pies with the 2010 dough, but honestly, I'm not crazy about using vodka and shortening. I don't always have spirits on hand and, purist that I am, I prefer the richer flavor and cleaner mouthfeel of an all-butter pie crust. So I was intrigued when food writer J. Kenji Lopez-Alt, who developed the original recipe while working at *Cook's Illustrated*, went on to create a shortening- and vodka-free version of the dough for the website Serious Eats. How could it work without shortening and vodka?

Quite well, actually. The new recipe called for just 6 tablespoons of water—the ¼ cup (4 tablespoons) called for in the original recipe plus 2 additional tablespoons to replicate the water content in ¼ cup of vodka. Even with less water, I found the dough

---

SCIENCE Why the Mixing Method Matters

Many of the pie dough recipes we consulted during the recipe development process call for a range of added water—which can create anxiety, especially in novice bakers, about adding too much and turning the crust tough. Our recipe reduces the potential anxiety by calling for a specific amount. Here's why we don't need a range: "Waterproofing" two-thirds of the flour by thoroughly mixing it with butter in the food processor ensures that the ½ cup of water we call for goes only toward amply hydrating the remaining flour, consistently producing a dough that is moist and workable. When we used the same quantities of ingredients to create a dough mixed in the traditional way—pulsing the butter into the flour until pea-size pieces form and then folding in the water—the result was dry and crumbly.

SAME INGREDIENTS, DIFFERENT RESULTS

OUR MIXING METHOD
Moist, workable dough

TRADITIONAL MIXING METHOD
Dry, crumbly dough

STEP BY STEP | NOT YOUR TYPICAL PIE DOUGH

Both the flour and the butter in this pie dough are added in two stages. This dough will look wetter than others you may have made, but fear not: As it chills, it will absorb extra moisture and will eventually form a smooth, easy-to-roll dough.

1. MAKE FLOUR-AND-BUTTER PASTE Process most of flour (and sugar and salt) and cubed butter until homogeneous paste forms, about 40 seconds.

2. BREAK IT UP; ADD MORE FLOUR Separate paste into 2-inch chunks and distribute around processor blade, then pulse in remaining flour.

3. TOSS IN GRATED BUTTER Transfer mixture to bowl, add frozen grated butter, and gently toss to coat butter shreds with flour.

4. ADD WATER Using rubber spatula, mix in ice water in 2 additions to form wet, sticky dough. Transfer to plastic wrap, press into disk, and refrigerate.

---

only a little harder to roll out than the original, and it baked up just as tender and flaky.

Turns out that the quirky mixing method was much more important than I'd initially realized. Thoroughly processing a lot of the flour with all the fat effectively waterproofed that portion of the flour, making it difficult for its proteins to hydrate enough to form gluten. Only the remaining cup of flour that was pulsed into the paste was left unprotected and therefore available to be hydrated. The result was a limited gluten network, which produced a very tender crust even without the vodka.

And how did Lopez-Alt's recipe work so well even without shortening? Well, shortening can be valuable in pie dough because it's pliable even when cold, so it flattens into thin sheets under the force of the rolling pin more readily than cold, brittle butter does. But the flour-and-butter paste in this dough also rolls out more easily than butter alone would, so with the paste mixing method there's no shortening required.

A Grate Solution

There's no denying that the mixing method is a real game changer, but the crust it produces has a couple of faults that offend my perfectionist sensibilities. When I make pie dough the old-fashioned way I always get a nice sharp edge and a shatteringly flaky crust, but the edges of crusts made using the paste method usually slump a bit in the oven, even when I'm hypervigilant about chilling and even freezing the formed crust. And that flakiness, which looks so impressive when you break the crust apart, doesn't hold up when you eat it. The crust is a bit too tender, so the flakes disintegrate too readily on the palate.

Luckily, I thought I might know a way to fix both problems with one solution: I made a dough with a full ½ cup of water. My hope was that it would actually produce a little *more* gluten, thus giving the baked crust more structure and true crispness.

With all that water, the dough was as easy to roll as the vodka crust had been, and the slightly increased gluten gave the baked crust a more defined edge. But the crust was still a bit too tender for my taste. Perhaps there was simply too much fat in the mix. Maybe the best way to decrease the tenderizing effect of the butter was simply to decrease the butter.

I had been using two-and-a-half sticks of butter to equal the amount of fat in the vodka pie crust. For my next batch I cut back to an even two sticks of butter, but that crust baked up hard and tough, especially at the edge. It felt stale right out of the oven. It was just too lean; I'd have to bring the butter back up to two-and-a-half sticks.

But something was bugging me: Over the years I'd made plenty of traditionally mixed all-butter pie crusts with an equally high proportion of fat, and though these doughs were challenging to roll out, the finished crusts always boasted just the right balance of crispness and tenderness. Why was this one so infuriatingly delicate?

And then I realized: In the traditional method much of the butter is left in discrete pieces that enrich the dough without compromising gluten development, but in my new crust, every bit of the butter was worked in. Perhaps the answer was to use the same amount of butter overall but to use less butter in the paste and to make sure that some of the butter remained in pieces.

Cutting the butter into very small pieces wasn't feasible, but what if I grated it? I gave it a try, shredding 4 tablespoons of butter on a box grater. To ensure that those pieces stayed firm enough not to mix with the flour, I froze them. Meanwhile, I processed the remaining two sticks into the dry ingredients. After breaking up the paste, I pulsed in the remaining flour, transferred the mixture to a bowl, and tossed in the grated butter. Finally, I folded in ½ cup of ice water, which was absorbed by the dry flour that coated the dough chunks and the grated butter.

After a 2-hour chill, the dough rolled out beautifully, and it looked beautiful, too. The fat-rich paste and the shredded butter–flour mixture swirled together, making a subtly variegated dough overlaid with thin wisps of pure butter. Once baked, the crust held a perfect, crisp edge and was rich-tasting while being both tender and truly flaky.

Now that I have an all-butter pie dough that's a cinch to roll out, I'm ready to adopt a new tradition.

FOOLPROOF ALL-BUTTER DOUGH FOR DOUBLE-CRUST PIE

MAKES ONE 9-INCH DOUBLE CRUST

Be sure to weigh the flour for this recipe. In the mixing stage, this dough will be more moist than most pie doughs, but as it chills it will absorb a lot of excess moisture. Roll the dough on a well-floured counter. For tips on preventing cracks during rolling, see page 31.

- 20 tablespoons (2½ sticks) unsalted butter, chilled
- 2½ cups (12½ ounces) all-purpose flour
- 2 tablespoons sugar
- 1 teaspoon salt
- ½ cup ice water

Pie Dough: A World View

Our rolled-out Foolproof All-Butter Pie Dough looks a lot like an aerial view of the earth: It has wisps of fat and fatty flour strewn across it. A traditionally made dough will be more speckled in appearance.

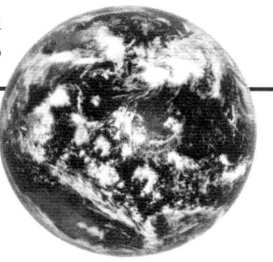
EARTH

OUR PIE DOUGH

1. Grate 4 tablespoons butter on large holes of box grater and place in freezer. Cut remaining 16 tablespoons butter into ½-inch cubes.

2. Pulse 1½ cups flour, sugar, and salt in food processor until combined, 2 pulses. Add cubed butter and process until homogeneous paste forms, 40 to 50 seconds. Using your hands, carefully break paste into 2-inch chunks and redistribute evenly around processor blade. Add remaining 1 cup flour and pulse until mixture is broken into pieces no larger than 1 inch (most pieces will be much smaller), 4 to 5 pulses. Transfer mixture to medium bowl. Add grated butter and toss until butter pieces are separated and coated with flour.

3. Sprinkle ¼ cup ice water over mixture. Toss with rubber spatula until mixture is evenly moistened. Sprinkle remaining ¼ cup ice water over mixture and toss to combine. Press dough with spatula until dough sticks together. Use spatula to divide dough into 2 portions. Transfer each portion to sheet of plastic wrap. Working with 1 portion at a time, draw edges of plastic over dough and press firmly on sides and top to form compact, fissure-free mass. Wrap in plastic and form into 5-inch disk. Repeat with remaining portion; refrigerate dough for at least 2 hours or up to 2 days. Let chilled dough sit on counter to soften slightly, about 10 minutes, before rolling. (Wrapped dough can be frozen for up to 1 month. If frozen, let dough thaw completely on counter before rolling.)

FOOLPROOF ALL-BUTTER DOUGH FOR SINGLE-CRUST PIE
MAKES ONE 9-INCH SINGLE CRUST

Be sure to weigh the flour for this recipe. This dough will be more moist than most pie doughs, but as it chills it will absorb a lot of excess moisture. Roll the dough on a well-floured counter. For tips on preventing cracks during rolling, see page 31.

- 10 tablespoons unsalted butter, chilled
- 1¼ cups (6¼ ounces) all-purpose flour
- 1 tablespoon sugar
- ½ teaspoon salt
- ¼ cup ice water

1. Grate 2 tablespoons butter on large holes of box grater and place in freezer. Cut remaining 8 tablespoons butter into ½-inch cubes.

2. Pulse ¾ cup flour, sugar, and salt in food processor until combined, 2 pulses. Add cubed butter and process until homogeneous paste forms, about 30 seconds. Using your hands, carefully break paste into 2-inch chunks and redistribute evenly around processor blade. Add remaining ½ cup flour and pulse until mixture is broken into pieces no larger than 1 inch (most pieces will be much smaller), 4 to 5 pulses. Transfer mixture to medium bowl. Add grated butter and toss until butter pieces are separated and coated with flour.

3. Sprinkle 2 tablespoons ice water over mixture. Toss with rubber spatula until mixture is evenly moistened. Sprinkle remaining 2 tablespoons ice water over mixture and toss to combine. Press dough with spatula until dough sticks together. Transfer dough to sheet of plastic wrap. Draw edges of plastic over dough and press firmly on sides and top to form compact, fissure-free mass. Wrap in plastic and form into 5-inch disk. Refrigerate dough for at least 2 hours or up to 2 days. Let chilled dough sit on counter to soften slightly, about 10 minutes, before rolling.

A Diner-Style Pie

There's no better match for our tender, flaky pie crust than a chocolate cream filling. For a deeply chocolaty mixture that is not too heavy, we make a milk-based cocoa pudding and then whisk in bittersweet chocolate, along with vanilla for extra depth. A few tablespoons of butter help the filling set up with a silky consistency once it is poured into the prebaked pie shell and refrigerated. Finally, we finish off the pie with a complementary topping of lightly sweetened whipped cream. –A.G.

CHOCOLATE CREAM PIE
SERVES 8 TO 10

We developed this recipe with whole milk, but you can use 2 percent low-fat milk, if desired. Avoid using 1 percent low-fat or skim milk, as the filling will be too thin. Ghirardelli 60% Cacao Bittersweet Chocolate Premium Baking Bar is our favorite dark chocolate.

- 1 recipe Foolproof All-Butter Dough for Single-Crust Pie

Filling
- ⅓ cup (2⅓ ounces) sugar
- ¼ cup (1-ounce) cornstarch
- 2 tablespoons unsweetened cocoa powder
- ¼ teaspoon salt
- 3 cups whole or 2 percent low-fat milk
- 6 ounces bittersweet chocolate, chopped fine
- 3 tablespoons unsalted butter, cut into 3 pieces
- 2 teaspoons vanilla extract

Topping
- 1 cup heavy cream
- 1 tablespoon confectioners' sugar

1. Roll dough into 12-inch circle on well-floured counter. Roll dough loosely around rolling pin and unroll it onto 9-inch pie plate, leaving at least 1-inch overhang around edge. Ease dough into plate by gently lifting edge of dough with your hand while pressing into plate bottom with your other hand.

2. Trim overhang to ½ inch beyond lip of plate. Tuck overhang under itself; folded edge should be flush with edge of plate. Crimp dough evenly around edge of plate using your fingers. Refrigerate dough-lined plate until firm, about 30 minutes. Adjust oven rack to middle position and heat oven to 350 degrees.

3. Line chilled pie shell with aluminum foil, covering edges to prevent burning, and fill with pie weights. Bake until edges are set and just beginning to turn golden, 15 to 20 minutes. Remove foil and weights, rotate plate, and continue to bake until golden brown and crisp, 15 to 20 minutes longer. If crust begins to puff, pierce gently with tip of paring knife. Let crust cool completely in plate on wire rack, about 30 minutes.

4. FOR THE FILLING: Whisk sugar, cornstarch, cocoa, and salt together in large saucepan. Whisk in milk until incorporated, making sure to scrape corners of saucepan. Place saucepan over medium heat; cook, whisking constantly, until mixture is thickened and bubbling over entire surface, 8 to 10 minutes. Cook 30 seconds longer; remove from heat. Add chocolate and butter and whisk until melted and fully incorporated. Whisk in vanilla. Pour filling into cooled pie crust. Press lightly greased parchment paper against surface of filling and let cool completely, about 1 hour. Refrigerate until filling is firmly set, at least 2½ hours or up to 24 hours.

5. FOR THE TOPPING: Using stand mixer fitted with whisk attachment, whip cream and sugar on medium-low speed until foamy, about 1 minute. Increase speed to high and whip until stiff peaks form, 1 to 2 minutes. Spread whipped cream evenly over chilled pie and serve.

Our crust stays crisp beneath the creamy filling.

(Wrapped dough can be frozen for up to 1 month. If frozen, let dough thaw completely on counter before rolling.)

▶ See How Andrea Rolls
A step-by-step video is available at CooksIllustrated.com/feb18

Testing High-End Blenders

We investigate the new crop of pricey blenders to see what you get—and whether it's worth it—when the sky's the limit.

> BY HANNAH CROWLEY <

We're longtime fans of the Vitamix 5200 ($449.00). Given its price, this commercial-turned-consumer luxury item is not for everyone. But for those who want a blender that can pulverize anything and will likely outlast its 7-year warranty, this has been our top recommended model for years.

The Vitamix 5200 is admittedly a stripped-down machine. It has three features on its control panel: a speed dial, an on/off switch, and a switch that ramps up the power to a higher level. But recently, Vitamix and other major manufacturers have released new models with more power and extra bells and whistles. One major difference: preset buttons that run for a fixed amount of time, so you can start your blender, walk away, and trust that it will shut itself off when the cycle is complete.

There are other purported upgrades. One blender we tested offers a fancy LCD touch screen and a "cavitation warning" that tells you when there's an air pocket forming above the blades, inhibiting blending; another has an insulated "thermal control jar" designed to keep hot blends hotter. But these innovations aren't cheap—prices soar to almost $700.00. So we tested the Vitamix 5200 against four newcomers to see if more money gets you a superior blender.

Are Fancy New Features Worth It?

Mostly, no. The LCD touch screen on one blender (particularly its speed dial) wasn't responsive enough to be a practical upgrade. This blender was also the one that featured the unnecessary cavitation warning. When an air pocket forms above the blades—typically when blending thicker foods such as hummus or almond butter—you don't need the machine to tell you; you can hear it, as the blades start whirring faster and sound more high-pitched. All you need to do is use a tamper (included with most models) to poke the food down into the air bubble to get things moving again and prevent the motor from overheating.

All the new models we tested also included preset buttons; the most common ones were for smoothies, crushed ice, cleaning, frozen desserts, hot soup, and juicing. These buttons make certain tasks more hands-off, so you can start your blender and walk away, knowing it will stop on its own. In practice, however, they weren't especially helpful. Making a smoothie or crushing ice takes less than a minute, so the luxury of walking away while the blender works is a bit overstated; the self-cleaning preset is little more than a high-speed button and doesn't clean the top of the jar or the lid; none of the machines contain cooling or heating elements, so settings for frozen desserts and hot soup mostly fell short; and the juice presets couldn't compete with a true extractor.

Overall, we were unimpressed with the presets, especially considering that they can add as much as $200.00 to a blender's price. And we didn't find that these new blenders were capable of replacing other appliances such as ice cream makers or electric juicers.

Is a More Powerful Blender Better?

Just as we found with the preset buttons, more wasn't necessarily better when it came to power. Our five high-end blenders ranged from 1,380 to a whopping 2,800 watts in power (compared with 750 watts in our winning midpriced blender). The most powerful model, the Blendtec Designer 725 ($679.95), wasn't able to make mayonnaise because its lowest speed was too fast, so the ingredients splattered too chaotically inside the jar to emulsify.

The Vitamix 5200, which had the lowest wattage of the bunch, produced finely-textured food, but other blenders produced even finer results. The smoothies made in the Vitamix 5200 had a few barely visible specks of kale while some of the other high-powered blenders made smoothies with no visible specks at all. When we sipped the Vitamix 5200's smoothies, we couldn't feel the particles and the smoothies were velvety and creamy. While speck-free, the other blenders' smoothies tended to be slightly aerated and frothy. This played out in other liquid-y applications such as soup, too.

Jar shape, it turned out, was responsible for these differences in texture. When we studied the blender jars side by side, we discovered that the Vitamix 5200's jar was taller and narrower than the other blenders' jars, with an inner height of 9 inches and interior diameter of 4 inches; the others ranged from 7 to 7.7 inches high and 4.5 to 5.75 inches across inside. As blender blades turn, they move their contents into a vortex, which looks like a small tornado. In shorter, broader jars, the vortexes were far more chaotic; contents ricocheted off the sides of the jars and smashed up against the lids as if a fire hose were loose inside. No wonder their blends were more aerated. Only the Vitamix 5200 kept its food more contained toward the bottom of the jar, where it combined readily without incorporating extra air.

There are drawbacks to the Vitamix 5200, though: It won't fit on a counter beneath a standard 18-inch-tall kitchen cabinet, and its narrower jar is a challenge to completely scrape out. If those are deal breakers, there are other good options to consider. A slightly frothy smoothie can still be a delicious smoothie; we just preferred the Vitamix 5200's creamier, silkier blends overall.

Simplicity and Functionality Win

While we ultimately can recommend three of the four new high-end models in the mix, none of them topped our previous winner. The Vitamix 5200 is still the best high-end blender for the money. Its control panel is simple, but its powerful motor produced superior results. And while it is expensive, it costs hundreds of dollars less than some of its more complex competitors. It was also the quietest blender we tested—a boon for early morning blending. If kitchen-counter storage and a wider jar that's easier to scrape out are priorities, our runner-up, the Vitamix Professional Series 750, is a good choice.

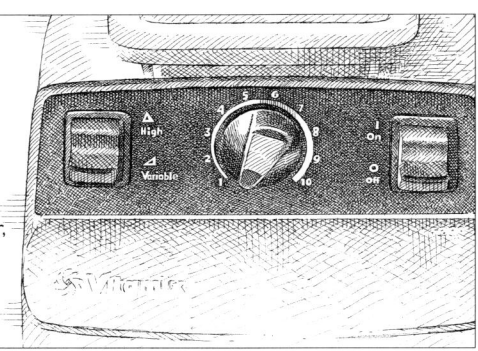

Dial Down the Fuss

Most of the high-end blenders we tested offered preset buttons for specific tasks such as making smoothies and crushing ice. But in most cases, we found them inferior to controlling the blender's motor speed manually and thus not worth the money. In fact, the no-frills control panel on the Vitamix 5200, our longtime top-rated high-end blender, is one of our favorite features. There's an on/off switch, a numbered speed dial, and a switch that can instantly ramp up the power to a higher level—that's it.

▶ Hannah Takes Them for a Spin
A free video is available at CooksIllustrated.com/feb18

TESTING HIGH-END BLENDERS

We tested five blenders, priced from $399.95 to $679.95, rating them on their ability to blend smoothies, puree hummus, crush ice, emulsify mayonnaise, and grind almond butter. We also made ice cream, pureed hot soup, and juiced carrots in each model. We evaluated each blender on how easy it was to operate, clean, and maneuver, as well as how loud it was. We weighed and measured each model's base and jar, used a tachometer to measure how fast its blades turned, and used a decibel meter to measure how loud it was. Prices listed are what we paid online. The blenders appear below in order of preference. To see the full results chart, go to CooksIllustrated.com/feb18.

SMOOTHIES: We made smoothies two ways. First, we blended the ingredients for 60 seconds on high. Second, we followed manufacturer-provided instructions, using the "smoothie" button if a model had one. We awarded points to models that made smooth smoothies with little air incorporated.

HUMMUS: We made hummus, giving highest marks to the models that pureed the ingredients into a smooth dip with minimal scraping.

CRUSHED ICE: We crushed ice, looking for cubes transformed into fluffy white snow with little scraping.

MAYONNAISE: We emulsified eggs and oil to evaluate the lower speeds of each model and the opening in each lid.

ALMOND BUTTER: We ground almonds into almond butter, noting if models produced a smooth paste with minimal scraping and without overheating the motor.

ICE CREAM: We made vanilla ice cream. None of the machines produced acceptable ice cream.

HOT SOUP: We made tomato soup, testing a blender's ability to puree and heat ingredients; the best model got the soup to a piping-hot 160 degrees.

JUICE: We made carrot juice by combining carrots and water; all the blenders made similar, slightly pulpy juice that was not as good as juice from a dedicated juicer.

MANEUVERABILITY: We rated each model on how easy its jar and lid were to attach and detach and how easy it was to move around.

EASE OF USE: We rated models on how logical and intuitive its controls were, how easy it was to use and clean, and how loud its motor was.

HIGHLY RECOMMENDED

VITAMIX 5200
MODEL: 5200   PRICE: $449.00
WARRANTY: 7-year full
WATTS: 1,380   DECIBELS ON HIGH: 96.1
JAR DIAMETER: 4 in
SMOOTHIES: ★★★
HUMMUS: ★★★
CRUSHED ICE: ★★★
MAYONNAISE: ★★★
ALMOND BUTTER: ★★★
ICE CREAM: 0
HOT SOUP: ★★
JUICE: ★ ½
MANEUVERABILITY: ★★★
EASE OF USE: ★★ ½

COMMENTS: This quiet, high-powered blender has simple, intuitive controls. As for its blending capability, it was top-notch. It was able to produce fine-textured foods without incorporating excess air, thanks to its narrow jar. The tamper accessory was helpful when blending thicker foods, and the blender's 7-year warranty insured our investment. It's tall, at 20.25 inches, so it can't be stored on a counter beneath a standard 18-inch-tall cabinet, and its narrow jar made scraping out its contents a minor challenge.

VITAMIX Professional Series 750
MODEL: 750   PRICE: $574.99
WARRANTY: 7-year full
WATTS: 1,440   DECIBELS ON HIGH: 104
JAR DIAMETER: 4.5 in
SMOOTHIES: ★★ ½
HUMMUS: ★★★
CRUSHED ICE: ★★★
MAYONNAISE: ★★★
ALMOND BUTTER: ★★★
ICE CREAM: 0
HOT SOUP: ★★
JUICE: ★ ½
MANEUVERABILITY: ★★★
EASE OF USE: ★★ ½

COMMENTS: With its slightly more powerful motor, this model blended more finely than its sibling, the winning Vitamix 5200, but its wider jar allowed more air to be incorporated into the food, and its motor was louder. We also didn't think presets for tasks such as making smoothies and cleaning warranted its higher price tag. However, it's shorter, so it can be stored on a kitchen counter beneath an 18-inch-tall cabinet, and its wider jar was slightly easier to scrape out.

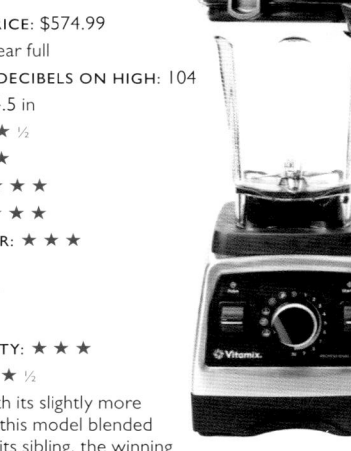

RECOMMENDED

KITCHENAID Pro Line Series Blender with Thermal Control Jar
MODEL: KSB8270CA
PRICE: $524.95
WARRANTY: 10 years
WATTS: 1,800
DECIBELS ON HIGH: 105.7
JAR DIAMETER: 4.5 in
SMOOTHIES: ★★ ½
HUMMUS: ★★★
CRUSHED ICE: ★★★
MAYONNAISE: ★★★
ALMOND BUTTER: ★★★
ICE CREAM: 0
HOT SOUP: ★★
JUICE: ★ ½
MANEUVERABILITY: ★ ½
EASE OF USE: ★★ ½

COMMENTS: This blender made creamy almond butter and great mayonnaise. Smoothies and soups were very smooth but slightly aerated. Its motor was loud, and the blender shimmied and rocked at higher speeds. The thermal control jar didn't keep contents any hotter than regular jars. A warning: At a whopping 20 pounds, this model is cumbersome to move, but at 17.5 inches tall, it can be stored in a fixed spot on your counter beneath a standard 18-inch-tall cabinet.

RECOMMENDED WITH RESERVATIONS

BREVILLE The Boss
MODEL: BBL910XL
PRICE: $399.95
WARRANTY: 7 years
WATTS: 1,500
DECIBELS ON HIGH: 99.1
JAR DIAMETER: 4.5 in
SMOOTHIES: ★★ ½
HUMMUS: ★★★
CRUSHED ICE: ★★★
MAYONNAISE: ★★★
ALMOND BUTTER: ★ ½
ICE CREAM: 0
HOT SOUP: ★
JUICE: ★ ½
MANEUVERABILITY: ★★ ½
EASE OF USE: ★★★

COMMENTS: We liked this blender's bright LCD screen and built-in timer. Smoothies and soups were smooth but slightly aerated. We made almond butter twice; the first time the motor overheated. The second time it smelled like it was burning but powered through. The butter was not as finely ground as samples from other models. Breville also makes our winning midpriced blender, The Hemisphere Control, which turns out slightly less smooth food, can make almond butter, and costs $200.00 less.

NOT RECOMMENDED

BLENDTEC Designer 725
MODEL: CTB3
PRICE: $679.95
WARRANTY: 8 years
WATTS: About 2,800
DECIBELS ON HIGH: 103.2
JAR DIAMETER: 5.75 in
SMOOTHIES: ★★ ½
HUMMUS: ★★ ½
CRUSHED ICE: ★★
MAYONNAISE: 0
ALMOND BUTTER: ★★
ICE CREAM: 0
HOT SOUP: ★★ ½
JUICE: ★ ½
MANEUVERABILITY: ★★ ½
EASE OF USE: ★

COMMENTS: The blade on this loud, powerful blender spun incredibly fast. Unfortunately, its lowest speed was too vigorous to effectively emulsify mayonnaise. The "cavitation warning," which signals the formation of air bubbles, was unnecessary; a tamper (which this model lacks) is better for preventing air pockets. Its LCD screen constantly scrolled messages to us; we counted 12 as we blended a single food item. We don't want to be told "Tweet this!" by an appliance first thing in the morning.

The Best Dark Chocolate Chips

With chocolate chips now coming in different shapes, sizes, and even cacao percentages, how do you choose? We tested 14 options to find a winner.

≥ BY LISA McMANUS ≤

Chocolate chip cookies are America's favorites, according to *The Great American Chocolate Chip Cookie Book* (2013) by Carolyn Wyman. Invented in the 1930s, the recipe called for semisweet chocolate. Today, chocolate chip choices abound, and dark chocolate—which includes "semisweet" and "bittersweet" since there's no legal distinction—has come a long way. Even Nestlé, which in 1940 launched chocolate morsels, now sells four styles of dark chocolate chips (plus quirky varieties including peanut butter, mint, and pumpkin spice). We bought 14 products labeled dark, special dark, bittersweet, or semisweet and sold as chips, oversize "super" chips, morsels, or chunks. In blind tastings, we sampled them plain and in our Perfect Chocolate Chip Cookies (May/June 2009).

Changing Chips

A few years ago, when dark chocolate bars got fancy with cacao percentages and exotic origin stories, chips were left behind. They were also made more cheaply: To scrimp on costly cocoa butter and retard melting, manufacturers made them with less fat, resulting in firmer and grittier chips. Today, most chocolate chips we sampled were just as creamy and rich as bar chocolate, called themselves "premium" or "artisan," and touted cacao percentages. Prices rose, too: When we tasted dark chocolate chips in 2009, prices ranged from $0.19 to $0.30 per ounce, but this time around they cost from $0.27 to $0.74 per ounce.

While we wondered if this premium trend was mere hype, the truth was in our results: Tasters recommended all 14 products, with reservations about three. The top two even earned our highest recommendation.

We had surprising preferences. Since the cookie recipe was invented using so-called semisweet chocolate, we'd worried that darker, more bitter chips might seem out of place—but our tasters actually preferred them. "This is the perfect chocolate chip cookie," a happy taster wrote about the cookie featuring our winning chip.

Why were darker chips more successful? The ratio of sugar to chocolate. A chocolate's cacao percentage tells you how much of the candy comes from the cacao bean. Cacao beans are fermented, dried, roasted, cracked, and winnowed to produce nibs, which are ground into a paste called chocolate liquor. This contains cocoa butter and cocoa solids. In chocolate chips, once you account for the cacao, the rest is primarily sugar. The United States Food and Drug Administration only mandates that dark, bittersweet, or semisweet chocolate have at least 35 percent cacao; beyond that, manufacturers are free to tweak processes, recipes, and nomenclature. So one company's "semisweet" offering can actually have a higher cacao percentage than another company's "bittersweet." Our lineup had a huge range, from 40 percent to 70 percent cacao. While none tasted bad—they're chocolate, after all—when compared side by side, the lower-cacao chips seemed too sweet. All but two of these products contained more sugar than any other ingredient. About our favorite "darker" chip, a taster wrote, "the bitterness of the chocolate complements the cookie dough."

Our top two chocolate chips contain 60 percent and 63 percent cacao; most lower-ranked chips were in the 40 to 50 percent range. The third-place product, which we estimated at 47 percent cacao (its manufacturer withheld details), listed a unique ingredient: Dutch-processed cocoa powder, which is alkali-treated to neutralize acidity. This addition boosted its chocolate flavor.

Fat was also a factor. The total cacao percentage doesn't reveal how much fat comes from cocoa butter and how much from cocoa solids. Two 60-percent-cacao chocolates can have very different ratios of fat to solids, as long as they total 60 percent. Our winning 60-percent-cacao chip contained about 40 percent fat, the highest of the lineup. Lower-ranked chips dipped as low as 25 percent fat. In our top chip, that extra creaminess won tasters' highest praise. Only one other chip contained this much fat—but it suffered from other woes: its proportions. In addition to fat and cacao percentages, we discovered that shape was integral to chips' success in cookies. When chips were too angular, they didn't disperse evenly in cookie dough. This resulted in some virtually chip-free cookies, while others contained so many chips that, without enough dough to protect them, the chocolate scorched in the oven and looked unappealing. Traditional dewdrop-shaped chips or chunks with curved edges distributed more evenly.

Better Chips

While fresh, homemade chocolate chip cookies really can't fail, our winning chips will give yours an advantage. Their high cacao percentage helps guarantee deep, rich chocolaty flavor; their bittersweet profile, with more cacao than sugar, ensures a milder sweetness that balances the sugary cookie; and a generous amount of cocoa butter (plus milk fat for smoother melting) gives them a creamy texture. Our winner, Ghirardelli 60% Premium Baking Chips ($4.39 for 10 ounces), hits all the right notes, and the slightly oversize chips provide just a little more chocolate in every bite. Made with the same ingredients as our favorite dark chocolate bar, also from Ghirardelli, these chips won't let you down.

A Motley Assortment

Our tasters preferred chocolate chips with higher cacao and fat percentages, but we found that shape mattered, too. Chips with traditional dewdrop shapes, including our winner, Ghirardelli 60% Premium Baking Chips, distributed evenly when portioning cookie dough. While tasters raved about the flavor of the two lowest-ranked chips, both by Scharffen Berger, they disliked how the rectangular pieces dispersed in cookies.

IT'S NOT (C)HIP TO BE SQUARE
Angular chips, such as those from Scharffen Berger, didn't distribute evenly when portioning cookie dough, so cookies had too many—or too few—chips.

TASTING DARK CHOCOLATE CHIPS

We purchased 14 products, including those labeled bittersweet, semisweet, dark, extra dark, and special dark, in the shape of chips, oversize "super" chips, morsels, and chunks. We sampled them in two blind tastings, plain and in our Perfect Chocolate Chip Cookies. Most are nationally available in supermarkets; a few were ordered online. Prices shown are what we paid, minus any shipping charges. We obtained total cacao percentages (the total amount of cocoa butter plus cocoa solids from the cacao bean) from the manufacturer when available; otherwise, we used package nutritional information to calculate an estimated cacao percentage. Taste test results were averaged, and products appear below in order of preference. To see the complete results chart, go to CooksIllustrated.com/feb18.

HIGHLY RECOMMENDED

GHIRARDELLI 60% Premium Baking Chips

PRICE: $4.39 for 10 oz ($0.44 per oz)
INGREDIENTS: Bittersweet chocolate (unsweetened chocolate, sugar, cocoa butter, milk fat, soy lecithin-an emulsifier, vanilla)
TOTAL CACAO: 60%
COMMENTS: "Creamy, raisiny, intense," and "cocoa-y" when tasted plain, in cookies these slightly oversize chips were "very rich." Tasters called them "balanced." "This is the perfect chocolate chip cookie," said one taster. "The bitterness of the chocolate complements the cookie dough, and the size of the chips is ideal."

GUITTARD Extra Dark Chocolate Chips 63%

PRICE: $4.49 for 11.5 oz ($0.39 per oz)
INGREDIENTS: Cacao beans, sugar, sunflower lecithin, and real vanilla
TOTAL CACAO: 63%
COMMENTS: This product nearly tied with the top-ranked chips. Its high percentage of cocoa solids made "a more bitter chocolate chip, which I enjoyed," with a "classic chip shape." It was "creamy, full-flavored, deeply cocoa-y. Not overly sweet but intensely chocolaty." Tasters picked up on "coffee/espresso" notes, finding the chips "roasty, not too sweet," with a "mellow brightness and a crumbly texture."

RECOMMENDED

HERSHEY'S KITCHENS Special Dark Mildly Sweet Chocolate Chips

PRICE: $3.29 for 12 oz ($0.27 per oz)
INGREDIENTS: Sugar, chocolate, cocoa butter, cocoa processed with alkali, milk fat. Contains 2% or less of lecithin (soy), natural flavor, milk
ESTIMATED TOTAL CACAO: 46.7%
COMMENTS: Tasters called these "petite" chips "the quintessential chip, smooth and chocolaty."

NESTLÉ TOLL HOUSE Bittersweet Chocolate Morsels 62%

PRICE: $2.99 for 10 oz ($0.30 per oz)
INGREDIENTS: Chocolate, sugar, cocoa butter, milk fat, nonfat milk, natural flavor
TOTAL CACAO: 62%
COMMENTS: These complex, "silky," "luxurious" chips "toe the line between 'about right sweet and too sweet.'" "They taste dark! Like good-quality bar chocolate." Some felt they held their shape "a little too well" when baked.

GUITTARD Super Cookie Chips Semisweet Chocolate Chips 48%

PRICE: $4.49 for 10 oz ($0.45 per oz)
INGREDIENTS: Sugar, cacao beans, cocoa butter, sunflower lecithin, and vanilla
TOTAL CACAO: 48%
COMMENTS: Though some tasters found these chips "too big"—each was about the size of a nickel—they earned points for being "very creamy and rich."

BARRY CALLEBAUT Semisweet Chocolate Chips

PRICE: $9.95 for 16 oz ($0.62 per oz)
INGREDIENTS: Cocoa mass, sugar, anhydrous dextrose, soy lecithin (emulsifier), vanilla extract
TOTAL CACAO: 49.9%
COMMENTS: "Sweet, simple" with "classic" chocolate flavor; tasters enjoyed these chips' complexity, including "dried cherry," "orange peel," and "warm spice" notes.

NESTLÉ TOLL HOUSE Dark Chocolate Morsels 53%

PRICE: $3.29 for 10 oz ($0.33 per oz)
INGREDIENTS: Chocolate, sugar, cocoa butter, milk fat, nonfat milk, natural flavor
TOTAL CACAO: 53%
COMMENTS: These chips came across as "deep, dark," "fancy chocolate," with a "melt in your mouth" texture.

HERSHEY'S KITCHENS Semi-Sweet Chocolate Chips

PRICE: $3.29 for 12 oz ($0.27 per oz)
INGREDIENTS: Semisweet chocolate [sugar, chocolate, cocoa butter, milk fat, lecithin (soy), natural flavor, milk]
ESTIMATED TOTAL CACAO: 40%
COMMENTS: These petite chips tasted "almost like milk chocolate" but held their shape well in cookies.

GHIRARDELLI Semisweet Premium Baking Chips 44%

PRICE: $4.39 for 12 oz ($0.37 per oz)
INGREDIENTS: Sugar, unsweetened chocolate, cocoa butter, whole milk powder, soy lecithin-an emulsifier, vanilla
TOTAL CACAO: 44%
COMMENTS: Tasters called them "caramelly," "with some roasty notes," but these chips lacked "depth." "Perfectly sweet, good texture."

NESTLÉ TOLL HOUSE Semi-Sweet Chocolate Chunks

PRICE: $3.29 for 11.5 oz ($0.29 per oz)
INGREDIENTS: Sugar, chocolate, milk fat, cocoa butter, soy lecithin, natural flavors
ESTIMATED TOTAL CACAO: 41%
COMMENTS: These "chunky" "logs" were a bit "cloying and mild," and tasters noted that "larger chunks means lots of nonchocolate bites."

GUITTARD Semisweet Chocolate Baking Chips 46%

PRICE: $4.49 for 12 oz ($0.37 per oz)
INGREDIENTS: Sugar, cacao beans, cocoa butter, sunflower lecithin, and real vanilla
TOTAL CACAO: 46%
COMMENTS: "Cute and tiny," these chips were "slightly sweet and cocoa-y." However, they were "a bit too sweet" in cookies.

RECOMMENDED WITH RESERVATIONS

NESTLÉ TOLL HOUSE Semi-Sweet Chocolate Morsels

PRICE: $3.29 for 12 oz ($0.27 per oz)
INGREDIENTS: Sugar, chocolate, milk fat, cocoa butter, soy lecithin, natural flavors
ESTIMATED TOTAL CACAO: 43%
COMMENTS: The original Toll House chips were "slightly gritty" eaten plain but had a "creamy texture" in cookies.

SCHARFFEN BERGER 62% Semisweet Baking Chunks

PRICE: $4.44 for 6 oz ($0.74 per oz)
INGREDIENTS: Cacao beans, sugar, cocoa butter, non-GMO soy lecithin, whole vanilla beans
TOTAL CACAO: 62%
COMMENTS: These "dark and rich" "brick-shaped" chunks "didn't disperse evenly," leaving large chip-free areas.

SCHARFFEN BERGER 70% Bittersweet Baking Chunks

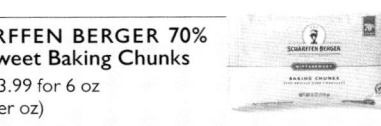

PRICE: $3.99 for 6 oz ($0.67 per oz)
INGREDIENTS: Cacao beans, sugar, cocoa butter, non-GMO soy lecithin, whole vanilla beans
TOTAL CACAO: 70%
COMMENTS: While great plain, these rectangular chunks were "too big for cookies," and the chocolate tasted "burnt around the edges."

INGREDIENT NOTES

BY ELIZABETH BOMZE, STEVE DUNN, ANDREW JANJIGIAN & ANNIE PETITO

Tasting Canned Chickpeas

Chickpeas are incredibly versatile, showing up in Italian pasta dishes and vegetable soups, Indian curries, and Middle Eastern hummus. We also use the starchy bean liquid, known as aquafaba, to add flavor and body to soups and stews; in recent years, this liquid has become a popular vegan egg replacement in foods such as muffins and meringues. We decided to reexamine this pantry staple, tasting six nationally available products plain, in hummus, and in our recipe for Pasta e Ceci. We evaluated the chickpeas' flavor, texture, and overall appeal.

SALT MADE THESE THE WINNER

Salt played a crucial role in determining our favorite products. Those with lower sodium levels (less than 125 milligrams per ½-cup serving including bean liquid) had a hint of "nutty," slightly "sweet" chickpea flavor but were easily overwhelmed by other ingredients. The other four products, which contain between 280 and 470 milligrams of sodium per ½-cup serving, had bolder chickpea flavor that our tasters liked.

We also noticed textural differences among products. Some were "mushy" when tasted plain and in pasta and produced hummus that was "supersmooth" but "thin." On the other hand, "crunchy" chickpeas gave hummus a "gritty" quality. Our favorite products struck a balance, with a firm-tender texture and creamy interiors.

While we can fully recommend four of the products we tested, our winner, Goya Chick Peas/Garbanzos ($0.89 for 15.5-ounce can), earned top marks in all three tastings. With 360 milligrams of sodium per ½-cup serving, these chickpeas tasted "nicely seasoned," "earthy," and "slightly nutty." Tasters also praised their texture, which was "firm with just enough give." As a bonus, we've found that the aquafaba from our winner produces great results when used in desserts and other recipes. For the complete tasting results, go to CooksIllustrated.com/feb18. –Kate Shannon

RECOMMENDED

GOYA Chick Peas/Garbanzos — WINNER
PRICE: $0.89 for 15.5-oz can ($0.06 per oz)
INGREDIENTS: Chick peas, water, salt, and disodium EDTA to promote color retention
SODIUM: 360 mg per ½-cup serving
COMMENTS: Our new winner scored top marks throughout our tastings. Plain, these "plump" chickpeas were "nutty" and, with 360 milligrams of sodium per serving, tasted "nicely seasoned." In both recipes, these chickpeas contributed "more vibrant flavor" than milder samples. We especially liked their texture, which was "firm with just enough give" and had "the perfect consistency" in pasta. Hummus was "buttery"-smooth "yet nicely dense."

PASTENE Chick Peas - Ceci Cotti
PRICE: $1.19 for 14-oz can ($0.09 per oz)
INGREDIENTS: Chick peas, water, salt, antioxidant: ascorbic acid
SODIUM: 330.4 mg per ½-cup serving
COMMENTS: Our old favorite has been reformulated slightly since our last tasting, and we liked this new version nearly as much as our new winner. It had "straightforward chickpea flavor" with slight "vegetal" notes. The chickpeas were quite "buttery" and remained "al dente" even after simmering with pasta. Hummus was thick and creamy.

Subbing Meyer Lemons

MEYER   STANDARD

Meyer lemons were first introduced to the United States from Beijing, China, in the early 20th century by Frank Meyer, a United States Department of Agriculture employee. Typically available from December through May, they are thought to be a natural cross between a standard lemon (Eureka or Lisbon variety) and a mandarin orange. Meyer lemons are smaller and rounder than standard lemons and boast smooth, thin, deep-yellow skin and pale orange pulp. They are also less acidic and sweeter—in a pH test, we found standard lemon juice to be 1.3 times more acidic than Meyer lemon juice (their pH values are 2.23 and 2.33, respectively) —and their rind is more fragrant when zested.

To see how Meyer lemons compare with standard lemons in cooking, we used both in our Lemon Posset and Lemon Pound Cake recipes. In both instances, tasters found the "sweeter, more floral" Meyer lemons to be an appealing substitute for standard lemons. In our Lemon Vinaigrette recipe, however, the Meyer lemons produced a "weak" dressing, lacking the "acidic punch and boldness" to stand up to rich olive oil.

➤ **Bottom line:** For applications that don't depend on the bracing acidity of a standard lemon, a Meyer lemon can be a fine substitute. But where a recipe demands bold, bright flavor for balance, reach for a standard lemon. –S.D.

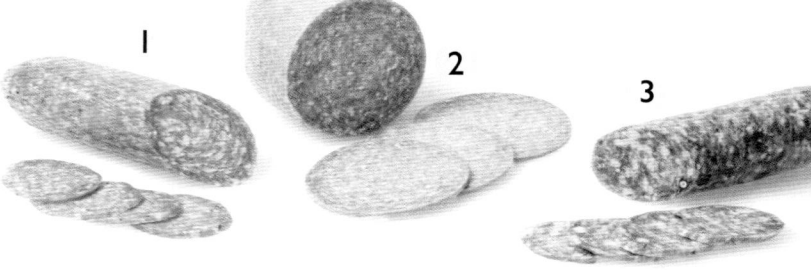

1   2   3

Common Salamis

Panisicia, the inspiration for our Red Wine Risotto with Beans (page 11), is traditionally made with *salam d'la duja*, an Italian salami that's hard to find in the United States. We found three widely available deli salamis that work well as substitutes: Genoa, hard salami, and *soppressata*. Each is made from a mixture of raw ground meat, salt, and seasonings, which is stuffed into a casing and left to ferment and dry until cured. Below are some of their distinguishing features. –A.P.

1. GENOA This red-wine-and-garlic-flavored salami is usually made from pork but may also include veal and even beef. It has a funky, brightly acidic flavor and a softer texture than many other types of salami.

2. HARD SALAMI Often imported from central or eastern Europe and made from pork or a pork-and-beef blend, this salami, which is smoked after being cured, is mild in flavor, with a firm, dry texture.

3. SOPPRESSATA This traditionally all-pork salami is made in numerous regions in Italy; the versions sold in the United States are typically heavily flavored with either black peppercorns or spicy Calabrian chile peppers and feature a coarse grind with a firm, slightly chewy texture.

A Good Reason to Store Spices in Glass

When we developed a recipe for freshly ground five-spice powder, we blitzed whole star anise, cloves, white pepper, cinnamon, and fennel seeds in a spice grinder and then stored the powder in a plastic deli-style container. A week later, we were surprised to find that the plastic appeared to have melted where it made contact with the spices.

It turns out that cloves and star anise contain high concentrations of two chemically similar oils called eugenol and anethole. The chemical structures of these oils are similar to that of the plastic called polystyrene (stamped PS or plastic #6 on the bottom of containers) and are therefore able to soften or dissolve the plastic.

➤ **Bottom line:** We recommend storing ground cloves or star anise (whole spices were not problematic) in glass jars. –S.D.

CONTAINER MELTDOWN
Some ground spices can eat through plastics.

Two Good Ways to Store Ginger

We've had multiple readers reach out to say that the best way to store leftover fresh ginger is to refrigerate peeled chunks submerged in vodka or sherry. We tested these methods against our usual approach (freezing the peeled nubs) as well as against ginger that we refrigerated after submerging it in plain water (to evaluate if simply storing it in liquid was key). After four weeks, we grated the ginger and cooked the samples in a stir-fry.

➤ **The upshot:** All the samples retained equivalent ginger flavor, and the frozen ginger and the ginger stored in sherry and vodka were equally easy to grate. However, the ginger stored in sherry picked up sherry flavor, and the ginger stored in water became mushy, so its fibers got tangled in the grater. That's because fresh ginger contains enzymes that break down its starch and pectin over time. Alcohol inhibits these enzymes, as does freezing, so ginger stored via those methods was able to maintain its firm texture.

➤ **The takeaway:** We now have two good ways to store ginger: freezing the nubs or submerging them in vodka. –A.P.

Get More out of Lemon Grass

When cooking with lemon grass, we use only the tender inner leaves from the bottom 4 or 5 inches of the stalk, which we find more flavorful and less fibrous than the outer leaves or the upper green parts of the stalk. When we recently found ourselves with an excess of lemon grass, we had an idea: **Could we place the stalks in a glass of water and, as we have with scallions, grow tender shoots from the top that would be usable for cooking?** To find out, we removed any loose leaves from the exterior of a lemon grass stalk with the root end intact, placed it in about 3 inches of water in a glass on a sunny windowsill, and changed the water daily. Sure enough, in about two days, shoots sprouted from the top of the stalk. The shoots continued to grow quickly, about 2 inches a day. Plus, the bottom of the stalk remained tender and fresh. When we compared our homegrown shoots with the bottom parts that we usually use in Thai chicken soup, the shoots were less tender than stalks but were no less flavorful and fragrant. –A.J.

SHOOTING UP
Lemon grass stalks placed in water will grow edible shoots.

DIY RECIPE Tart Pomegranate Molasses

Pomegranate molasses is a pantry staple throughout the eastern portion of the Mediterranean. Made by reducing pomegranate juice, this sticky syrup layers astringent, floral, and faintly bitter notes over a sweet-tart, fruity flavor. It can be whisked into vinaigrette, drizzled over vegetables, brushed onto roasted meats, or pureed into dips. Many recipes call for boiling pomegranate juice and a generous amount of sugar (and sometimes lemon juice) in a saucepan. We found that those syrups tasted too jam-like and required at least 20 minutes of cooking. We use only a small amount of sugar and no lemon juice. To speed up evaporation, we use a 12-inch skillet, which offers more surface area. –Lan Lam

TART POMEGRANATE MOLASSES
MAKES ⅓ CUP

Reducing the pomegranate juice at a simmer, rather than at a boil, drives off fewer flavor compounds and results in fresher, more complex flavor.

- 2 cups pomegranate juice
- ½ teaspoon sugar
- Pinch salt

Bring pomegranate juice, sugar, and salt to simmer in 12-inch skillet over high heat. Reduce heat to low and simmer, stirring and scraping thickened juice from sides of skillet occasionally, until mixture is thick and syrupy and measures ⅓ cup, 12 to 15 minutes. Let cool slightly before transferring to container. (Syrup can be refrigerated in airtight container for up to 1 month.)

Understanding Spareribs

A full rack of spareribs contains the brisket bone and surrounding brisket meat and usually weighs about 5 pounds. The brisket bone and meat (which contains tough pieces of cartilage) are often trimmed off to produce a narrower, rectangular rack. These are St. Louis–style spareribs, and each rack weighs 2½ to 3 pounds. We prefer St. Louis–style spareribs in many recipes, including our Chinese-Style Barbecued Spareribs (page 7), for three reasons: They fit side by side in the oven or on the grill's cooking grate (larger regular spareribs may not fit), they cook more quickly and evenly than larger racks, and, without the brisket bone section in the way, they are easier to slice and eat. –E.B.

ST. LOUIS–STYLE SPARERIBS VERSUS A FULL SPARERIB RACK

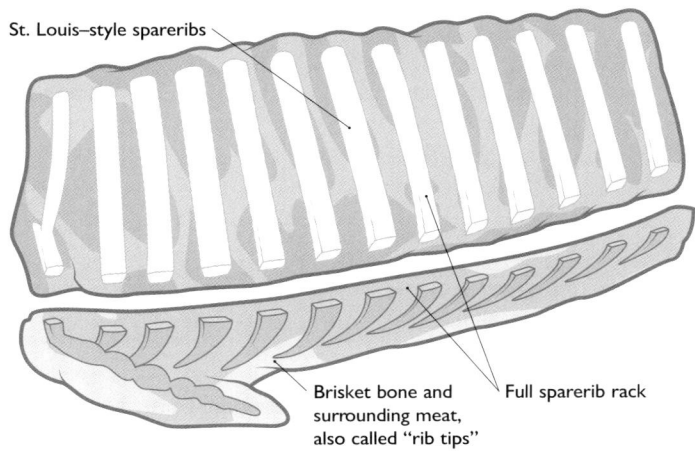

St. Louis–style spareribs

Brisket bone and surrounding meat, also called "rib tips"

Full sparerib rack

KITCHEN NOTES

⇒ BY ANDREA GEARY, STEVE DUNN, LAN LAM & ANNIE PETITO ⇐

WHAT IS IT?

This 1935 ACME Rotary Mincer promised to ease a cook's workload by offering 10 stainless-steel rotary blades that would mince herbs and vegetables with "lightning rapidity." The tool is about 8 inches long, has a bright red wooden handle, and offers a metal finger guard for safety. To use it, herb sprigs or vegetable slices would be placed on a board and the cook would roll the tool over them to mince the food. Is it effective? Sadly, not at all.

In the test kitchen, we found that the mincer did more crushing than cutting, leaving scallions, chives, parsley, oregano, and onion slices smashed rather than neatly chopped. Perhaps the most telling indicator of its performance was the condition of our cutting board after testing. The board was stained green with chlorophyll from where the greens had been crushed to the point of being juiced. It's no wonder that this tool never gained popularity. –S.D.

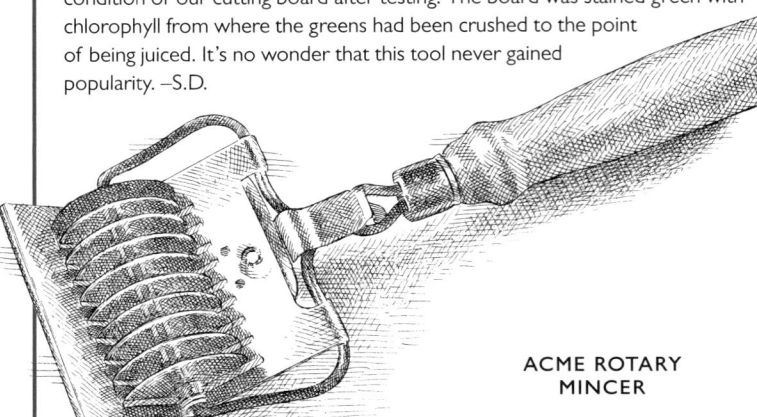

ACME ROTARY MINCER

Carbon-Steel Skillet Care

We love our winning 12-inch carbon-steel skillet, the Matfer Bourgeat Black Steel Round Frying Pan, 11⅞" ($44.38). Just as with a cast-iron skillet, its nonstick coating, or seasoning, develops when oil (flaxseed or sunflower is best, but any vegetable oil will do) is heated in the pan until it smokes and breaks down, polymerizes, and bonds to the surface. Once the initial patina on carbon steel has been established, simply cooking in the pan is generally enough to maintain it. And if the coating chips or is scrubbed off, reseasoning requires minimal work. Here's how to care for a carbon-steel skillet to ensure that it keeps an optimally slick surface.

INITIAL SEASONING
Our favorite method for the initial seasoning of a new skillet is available free online at CooksIllustrated.com/panseasoning.

ROUTINE MAINTENANCE
Rinse with water, scrubbing gently with soft-bristled brush or sponge if necessary; avoid soap or abrasive scrubbers. Dry skillet thoroughly over warm burner. If kitchen is humid or you don't use skillet often, apply very thin coating of oil to surface to prevent rusting.

RESEASONING
If cooking surface feels bumpy or has tacky residue (caused by partially polymerized oil) or patina is chipped, scrub with moderately abrasive sponge (also use a little soap if skillet is tacky) until patina feels even to touch (color does not need to be even).

Next, apply 1 to 2 teaspoons oil (depending on skillet size) over surface of clean skillet. Wipe away as much oil as possible with paper towel (excess oil will lead to tackiness); reserve paper towel. Heat skillet over medium heat, watching for oil to bead. Using tongs, wipe away beaded oil with reserved paper towel. Continue to heat, wiping away beaded oil, if any, as necessary, until skillet smokes (indicating oil breakdown). Let skillet smoke for 2 minutes. Turn off heat and let skillet cool. –L.L.

Ditching the Traditional Rules for Risotto

The classic technique for making risotto calls for near-constant stirring for roughly 25 minutes. This accomplishes two things: It maximizes the release of starch from the rice to create a creamy sauce, and it ensures that every grain cooks evenly. Frequent small additions of hot broth are ladled in from a separate saucepan on the stove, which purportedly helps keep the cooking from slowing down.

In our recipe for Red Wine Risotto with Beans (Paniscia) (page 11), we found that we could achieve the same perfectly cooked grains bound in a creamy sauce by breaking these rules. Here's how we did it. –A.P.

RULE #1
USE HOT BROTH
HOW WE BROKE IT: We don't bother heating the broth before adding it. When room-temperature broth hits the already-hot pot, it quickly comes up to temperature.

RULE #2
ADD BROTH INCREMENTALLY
HOW WE BROKE IT: Simmering the rice in almost all the liquid at the start of cooking agitates the grains much like stirring does, accelerating the release of creamy starch.

RULE #3
STIR CONSTANTLY
HOW WE BROKE IT: We need to stir only occasionally because we cook the rice in a covered heavy-bottomed Dutch oven over medium-low heat, which distributes the heat as evenly as does stirring, making every grain as tender as the next. A brief stir at the end of cooking followed by a 5-minute rest provides additional insurance that the rice will be perfectly al dente, from the top of the pot to the bottom.

Preventing Pastry Bag Leaks

Pastry bags can quickly and neatly deliver beautifully decorated cookies, perfectly portioned pastries, or uniformly filled pastas, but they can be messy to use. Here's a way to prevent the filling from leaking out of the tip as you fill the bag. –L.L.

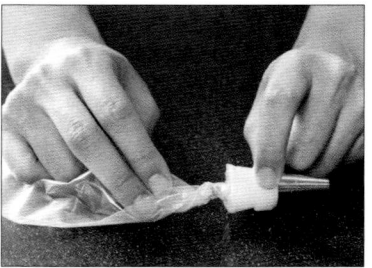
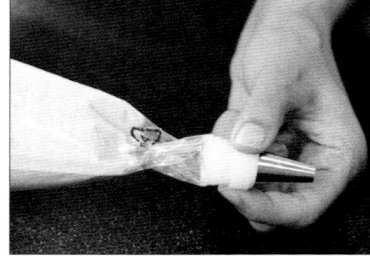

1. Place pastry tip in bag. Twist bag near tip and gently press twisted portion into tip to create temporary barrier. Fill bag.

2. To pipe, pull on tip to release barrier and squeeze bag to push filling down into tip.

Fray-Free Pie Dough

You won't have big cracks forming at the edges of the dough when rolling out our Foolproof All-Butter Pie Dough (page 22). But if you want to be a real perfectionist, here's how to ensure that the edges are entirely fray-free. –A.G.

KEEP IT TIGHT When wrapping the finished dough in plastic wrap, press firmly on the sides and top of the dough to form a compact, fissure-free mass.

SEAL IT UP Before unwrapping the chilled dough, stand it on its edge and roll the edge firmly along the counter to seal any remaining cracks.

Guacamole for a Crowd

The key to our Classic Guacamole (May/June 2017) is to first dice three ripe avocados into ½ inch pieces and then mash them with a whisk for the perfect combination of chunky and smooth consistencies. But if you're making guacamole for a crowd, that dicing step can prove tedious. We wondered if there was a faster way to either dice or partially mash (but not completely pulverize) a big batch of avocados. We tried an array of kitchen implements: potato masher, wire cooling rack, large spoon, mortar and pestle, and pastry cutter.

The best tool for the job, surprisingly, turned out to be the wire cooling rack. Pushing pitted avocado halves through it (leaving the skins on) speedily diced the fruit into chunks that we could then stir and mash with a whisk. (Be sure to use a rack that has wires arranged in a grid.) –L.L.

How to Chop Cabbage

Here's a quick and easy way to cut the cabbage for our Red Wine Risotto with Beans (Paniscia) (page 11) into appropriately sized pieces. –A.P.

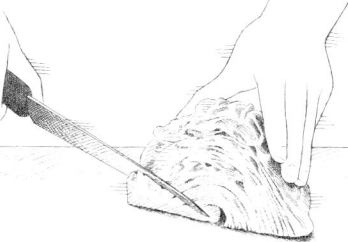

1. Cut cabbage into quarters, then trim and discard hard core.

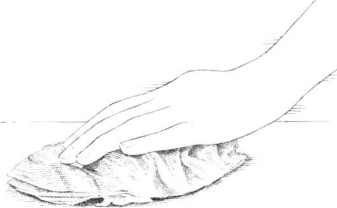

2. Separate leaves into small stacks; press to flatten.

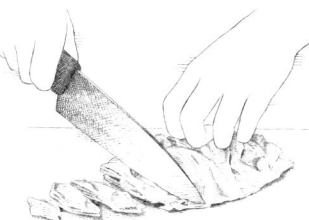

3. Cut each stack into ½-inch strips. Cut strips into ½-inch pieces.

SCIENCE
Salt and Serving Temperature

We've noticed that foods served either hot or chilled need more salt to taste fully seasoned than foods served at room temperature. We designed an experiment to delve into the topic.

EXPERIMENT
We made a large batch of chicken broth, omitting the salt. Then we divided the broth into five batches and seasoned each batch, using no salt and 1, 2, 3, and 4 teaspoons of salt, respectively. Tasters sampled each broth at three different temperatures—180 degrees, 90 degrees, and 45 degrees—and noted which samples seemed properly seasoned.

RESULTS
Tasters preferred the hot broth seasoned with 3 teaspoons of salt. But as the broth cooled, their preferences changed. At 90 degrees, they preferred the broth that contained 2 teaspoons of salt, and at refrigerator temperature they preferred the broth with 4 teaspoons of salt.

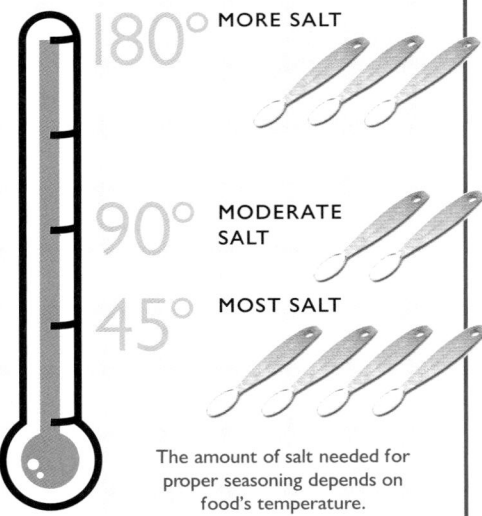

The amount of salt needed for proper seasoning depends on food's temperature.

EXPLANATION
Food with the same amount of salt tastes less salty to us at high or low temperatures than it does when it is lukewarm. This is because the receptors through which tastebuds signal the brain that food tastes salty tend to be the most responsive at temperatures between 85 and 95 degrees—in other words, close to the temperature inside our mouths.

TAKEAWAY
To ensure that food is properly seasoned, we recommend tasting it at serving temperature and adjusting the salt accordingly. –L.L.

EQUIPMENT CORNER

≥ BY MIYE BROMBERG AND EMILY PHARES ≤

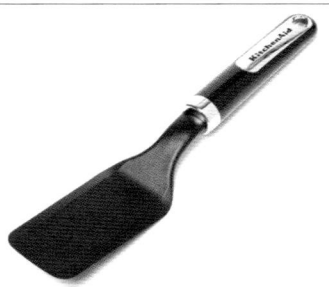

HIGHLY RECOMMENDED
KITCHENAID Cookie/Pastry Lifter
MODEL: KC038OHOBA
PRICE: $8.00

HIGHLY RECOMMENDED
LE CREUSET Table Model Corkpull
MODEL: TM100L-31
PRICE: $19.95

HIGHLY RECOMMENDED
SIMPLEHUMAN Sensor Pump
MODEL: ST1023
PRICE: $39.99

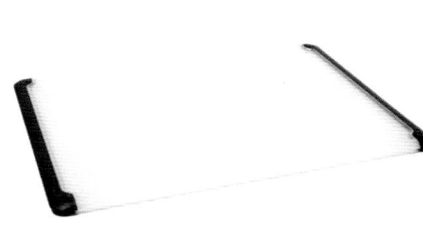

HIGHLY RECOMMENDED
OXO Good Grips Utility Cutting Board
MODEL: 1063790
PRICE: $14.95

Compact Spatulas

Compact spatulas, or cookie spatulas, are designed to deftly navigate tight baking pans and cookie sheets, but they are also handy when cooking food in a skillet, so we set out to find one that was useful for both of those tasks. We selected seven models made from plastic, silicone, or stainless steel and priced from $6.77 to $14.44, including our previous winner, the OXO Good Grips Silicone Cookie Spatula. To test them, we made cookies, brownies, over-easy eggs, and pancakes.

The plastic and silicone spatulas prevented the baked goods from slipping and sliding and performed best overall. The dimensions of the spatulas' heads also made a big difference. Shorter heads couldn't support eggs or pancakes, and wider ones didn't maneuver easily in crowded baking pans. During the egg and pancake tests, we docked points for shorter handles that brought our hands too close to the heat. In the end, the KitchenAid Cookie/Pastry Lifter ($8.00) took the top spot for its plastic head, ideal dimensions, and long, comfortable handle. –E.P.

Twist Corkscrews

There's a bit of a learning curve to using a waiter's corkscrew, so many prefer to open their wine bottles with a twist corkscrew instead. With a continuous-turn corkscrew, you twist the handle to insert the worm into the cork, then continue twisting to remove the cork. With a winged corkscrew, you depress two wings on either side of the handle to remove the inserted worm and the cork. We wanted to know whether either type of corkscrew was worth buying, so we rounded up nine models priced from $8.90 to $24.95: four continuous-turn models and five winged models—and used them to open bottles with both natural and synthetic corks. After opening hundreds of bottles, we found the continuous-turn corkscrews to be more intuitive, less fussy, and easier to use than winged corkscrews. Our favorite continuous-turn corkscrew, the Le Creuset Table Model Corkpull ($19.95), is virtually foolproof, removing corks of all materials both easily and quickly. –M.B.

Automatic Hand Soap Dispensers

Hand-washing is sometimes imperative during cooking and sometimes problematic—such as when you've been handling raw chicken and don't want to touch anything. This is when a hands-free soap dispenser is useful. These battery-operated devices have sensors that, when activated, prompt the dispensers to squirt soap. We selected four models priced from $24.95 to $59.99 and tested them after handling raw chicken and after coating our hands in olive oil. After a series of tests, one was the clear winner. The Simplehuman Sensor Pump ($39.99) was easy to fill and released soap neatly and quickly, dispensing it in less than 1 second. Also, as the shortest dispenser in our lineup, it didn't feel intrusive on our counters. –E.P.

Small Cutting Boards

We love our full-size cutting boards for most tasks, but sometimes we want a more compact board for a small job or if we're working in a cramped space. To find the best small cutting board—one that would be durable, sit securely on the counter, and be easy to maneuver and clean—we selected nine models made from different materials, including plastic, wood, and bamboo, and priced from $9.49 to $38.95. We put them through a taxing series of tests. Although some testers preferred cutting on wood or bamboo boards, we ranked two plastic boards the highest due to their durability, stability, and convenience. Both are dishwasher-safe, don't require maintenance as wood boards do, and are lightweight yet secure on the counter thanks to rubbery sides or feet. Our favorite, the OXO Good Grips Utility Cutting Board ($14.95), is a smaller version of our full-size Best Buy cutting board. Testers liked cutting on its textured plastic surface and appreciated that one side features a small trench for collecting juices from roasts or wet foods. –M.B.

> For complete testing results, go to CooksIllustrated.com/feb18.

U.S. POSTAL SERVICE STATEMENT OF OWNERSHIP, MANAGEMENT AND CIRCULATION

1. Publication Title: *Cook's Illustrated*; 2. Publication No. 1068-2821; 3. Filing date: 10/01/17; 4. Issue frequency: Jan/Feb, Mar/Apr, May/June, Jul/Aug, Sept/Oct, Nov/Dec; 5. Number of issues published annually: 6; 6. The annual subscription price is $41.70; 7. Complete mailing address of known office of publication: 17 Station Street, Brookline, MA 02445; 8. Complete mailing address of headquarters or general business office of publisher: 17 Station Street, Brookline, MA 02445; 9. Full names and complete mailing addresses of publisher, editor, and managing editor. Publisher, David Nussbaum, 17 Station Street, Brookline, MA 02445; Editor, Jack Bishop, 17 Station Street, Brookline, MA 02445; Managing Editor, Todd Meier, 17 Station Street, Brookline, MA 02445; 10. Owner: America's Test Kitchen LP; 17 Station Street, Brookline, MA 02445; 11. Known bondholders, mortgages and other securities: None. 12. Tax status: Has Not Changed During Preceding 12 Months.; 13. Publication title: *Cook's Illustrated*; 14. Issue date for circulation data below: September/October 2017; 15A. Total number of copies: Average number of copies each issue during preceding 12 months: 923,539 (Sept/Oct 2017: 889,948); B. Paid circulation: 1. Mailed outside-county paid subscriptions: 743,612 (Sept/Oct 2017: 723,352); 2. Mailed in-county paid subscriptions: 0 (Sept/Oct 2017: 0); 3. Sales through dealers and carriers, street vendors, and counter sales. Average number of copies each issue during preceding 12 months: 37,019 (Sept/Oct 2017: 41,565); 4. Paid distribution through other classes mailed through the USPS. Average number of copies each issue during preceding 12 months: 0 (Sept/Oct 2017: 0); C. Total paid distribution. Average number of copies each issue during preceding 12 months: 780,631 (Sept/Oct 2017: 764,917); D. Free or nominal rate distribution (by mail and outside mail). 1. Free or nominal Outside-County. Average number of copies each issue during preceding 12 months: 3,392 (Sept/Oct 2017: 3,411). 2. Free or nominal rate in-county copies. Average number of copies each issue during preceding 12 months: 0 (Sept/Oct 2017: 0); 3. Free or nominal rate copies mailed at other Classes through the USPS. Average number of copies each issue during preceding 12 months: 0 (Sept/Oct 2017: 0); 4. Free or nominal rate distribution outside the mail. Average number of copies each issue during preceding 12 months: 1,000 (Sept/Oct 2017: 1,000); E. Total free or nominal rate distribution. Average number of copies each issue during preceding 12 months: 4,392 (Sept/Oct 2017: 4,411); F. Total free distribution. Average number of copies each issue during preceding 12 months: 785,023 (Sept/Oct 2017: 769,328); G. Copies not Distributed. Average number of copies each issue during preceding 12 months: 138,516 (Sept/Oct 2017: 120,620); H. Total. Average number of copies each issue during preceding 12 months: 923,539 (Sept/Oct 2017: 889,948); I. Percent paid. Average percent of copies paid for preceding 12 months: 99.44% (Sept/Oct 2017: 99.43%).

INDEX
January & February 2018

RECIPES
MAIN DISHES
Chicken Piccata 10
Chinese-Style Barbecued Spareribs 7
Crisp Roast Chicken 17
Ground Beef and Cheese Enchiladas 5
Red Wine Risotto with Beans (Paniscia) 11
Weeknight Roast Chicken 16

SIDE DISHES
Chopped Carrot Salad with Mint, Pistachios,
and Pomegranate Seeds 13
    with Celery and Raisins 13
    with Fennel, Orange, and Hazelnuts 13
    with Radishes and Sesame Seeds 13
Thick-Cut Oven Fries 9

HORS D'OEUVRES
Gougères 15
    with Aged Gouda and Smoked
    Paprika 15
    with Manchego and Black Pepper 15

BREAKFAST
Coffee Cake with Pecan-Cinnamon
Streusel 19
Creamy French-Style Scrambled Eggs 20

DESSERTS
Chocolate Cream Pie 23
Foolproof All-Butter Pie Dough for
Double-Crust Pie 22
Foolproof All-Butter Pie Dough for
Single-Crust Pie 23

CONDIMENT
Tart Pomegranate Molasses 29

BONUS ONLINE CONTENT
More recipes, reviews, and videos are available at CooksIllustrated.com/feb18

RECIPES
Chicken Piccata for Two
Thick-Cut Oven Fries for Two

EXPANDED REVIEWS
Tasting Canned Chickpeas
Tasting Dark Chocolate Chips
Testing Automatic Hand Soap Dispensers
Testing Compact Spatulas
Testing High-End Blenders
Testing Small Cutting Boards
Testing Twist Corkscrews

▶ RECIPE VIDEOS
Want to see how to make any of the recipes in this issue? There's a free video for that.

BONUS TECHNIQUE
Seasoning a Carbon-Steel Skillet

FOLLOW US ON SOCIAL MEDIA
facebook.com/CooksIllustrated
twitter.com/TestKitchen
pinterest.com/TestKitchen
instagram.com/CooksIllustrated
youtube.com/AmericasTestKitchen

Foolproof All-Butter Pie Dough, 22

Chicken Piccata, 10

Carrot Salad with Mint and Pomegranate, 13

Creamy French-Style Scrambled Eggs, 20

Thick-Cut Oven Fries, 9

Ground Beef and Cheese Enchiladas, 5

Red Wine Risotto with Beans (Paniscia), 11

Gougères, 15

Chinese-Style Barbecued Spareribs, 7

Coffee Cake with Pecan-Cinnamon Streusel, 19

America's Test Kitchen
COOKING SCHOOL
Visit our online cooking school today, where we offer 180+ online lessons covering a range of recipes and cooking methods. Whether you're a novice just starting out or are already an advanced cook looking for new techniques, our cooking school is designed to give you confidence in the kitchen and make you a better cook.

▸ Start a 14-Day Free Trial at
OnlineCookingSchool.com

Cook's Illustrated on iPad
Enjoy *Cook's* wherever you are whenever you want.

Did you know that *Cook's Illustrated* is available on iPad? Go to CooksIllustrated.com/iPad to download the app through iTunes. You'll be able to start a free trial of the digital edition, which includes bonus features like recipe videos, full-color photos, and step-by-step slide shows of each recipe.

Go to CooksIllustrated.com/iPad to download our app through iTunes.

PHOTOGRAPHY: CARL TREMBLAY; STYLING: KENDRA McKNIGHT

NUMBER 151   MARCH & APRIL 2018

COOK'S
ILLUSTRATED

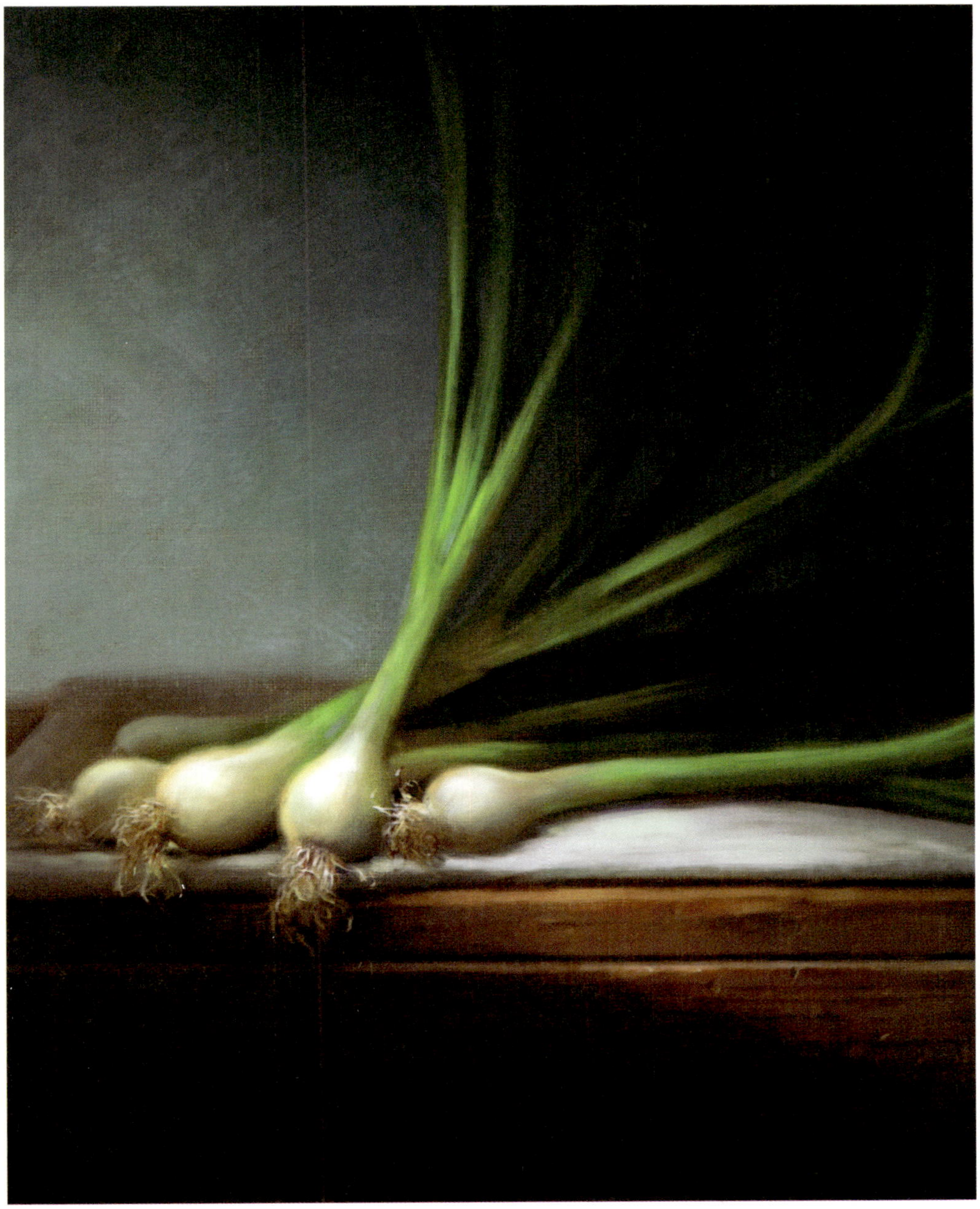

Indoor Pulled Chicken
Real Smoke, Tender Chicken

No-Fear Caramel Sauce

Lemoniest Lemon Bars
Secret Pantry Ingredient

Irish Brown Soda Bread
Authentic and Easy

Pork Tenderloin Steaks
Better Than Chops

Three-Cup Chicken
We Found a Better Formula

Brazilian Shrimp and Fish Stew
Pan-Steamed Broccolini
Testing Parchment Paper

CooksIllustrated.com
$6.95 U.S. & $8.95 CANADA

Display until April 9, 2018

MARCH & APRIL 2018

2 Quick Tips
Quick and easy ways to perform everyday tasks, from storing cutting boards to cleaning a whisk. COMPILED BY ANNIE PETITO

4 Indoor Pulled Chicken
Our stovetop method yields pulled chicken so good—and so quick—that you'll think twice about making the outdoor kind.
BY ANDREW JANJIGIAN

6 Perfect Pork Tenderloin Steaks
How do you cook this lean cut so that it's superjuicy, rosy from edge to edge, and deeply browned? Use two cooking methods. BY LAN LAM

8 One-Hour Pizza
The ultimate challenge for a pizza master with 30 years of experience? Making a good one in just 60 minutes. BY ANDREW JANJIGIAN

10 Brazilian Shrimp and Fish Stew
This coconut milk–based stew has such big flavor yet comes together so quickly that it sounded too good to be true—until we made it for ourselves.
BY ANNIE PETITO

12 Irish Brown Soda Bread
Ireland's everyday bread is so quick, foolproof, and wholesome that you'll want to make it every day, too. BY ANDREA GEARY

14 Moroccan Lentil and Chickpea Soup
Spices play more than just a supporting role in this hearty North African soup. BY STEVE DUNN

PAGE 18

15 Sweeter and Easier Than Broccoli
The trick to cooking slender, verdant broccolini is best illustrated using long division. BY STEVE DUNN

16 Quick Pasta Sauces, Perfected
We retooled a week's worth of classic sauces to keep in our back pockets for busy nights.
BY ELIZABETH BOMZE

18 No-Fear Caramel
Whether you've been burned by caramel in the past or have questions to sort out before making your first batch, we're here to help. BY LAN LAM

20 Three-Cup Chicken
One cup each of soy sauce, sesame oil, and rice wine is easy to remember. Too bad it doesn't work. We figured out a better formula and streamlined the recipe. BY STEVE DUNN

22 The Lemoniest Lemon Bars
What's the secret to bars with bold, multifaceted citrus flavor? Cut back on the lemon juice.
BY LAN LAM

24 Testing Parchment Paper
Parchment paper is simple. Why are so many products hard to use? BY KATE SHANNON

26 In Search of the Best Romano Cheese
Is Pecorino Romano from Italy worth seeking out, or can domestic options do the job?
BY LISA McMANUS

28 Ingredient Notes
BY STEVE DUNN, ANDREA GEARY, ANDREW JANJIGIAN, LAN LAM & KATE SHANNON

30 Kitchen Notes
BY STEVE DUNN, ANDREA GEARY, ANDREW JANJIGIAN, LAN LAM & ANNIE PETITO

32 Equipment Corner
BY MIYE BROMBERG AND KATE SHANNON

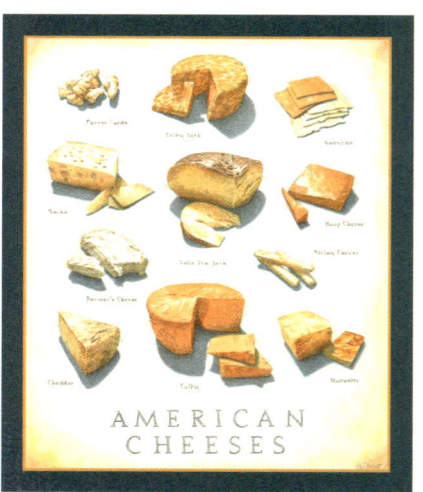

BACK COVER ILLUSTRATED BY JOHN BURGOYNE

American Cheeses

American cheeses are products of both old-world techniques and technological innovations. **AMERICAN** cheese melts beautifully thanks to emulsifying salts that keep its texture smooth when heated. Mellow **MUENSTER**—not to be confused with pungent Alsatian Munster—is known by its rust-colored rind and semisoft interior. Neon orange **COLBY** bends like a pencil eraser and usually tastes more acidic than marbled **COLBY JACK**. Cocoa- and black pepper–rubbed wheels of **VELLA DRY JACK** are sharp like Parmesan but sweeter. The American imitation of Emmentaler is referred to as **SWISS**, but it's milder and waxy. **STRING CHEESE** and **CHEESE CURDS** are made for snacking: The former pulls apart into wispy strands; the latter squeaks between your teeth when chewed. **HOOP CHEESE**, native to the American South, is named for the ring molds used to shape it. Damp, clean-tasting **FARMER'S CHEESE** is the American equivalent of Latin *queso fresco*. Domestic **CHEDDAR** ranges from mild and creamy to craggy and funky like the English original.

America's Test Kitchen is a real test kitchen located in Boston. It is the home of more than 60 test cooks, editors, and cookware specialists. Our mission is to test recipes until we understand exactly how and why they work and eventually arrive at the very best version. We also test kitchen equipment and supermarket ingredients in search of products that offer the best value and performance. You can watch us work by tuning in to *America's Test Kitchen* (AmericasTestKitchen.com) and *Cook's Country from America's Test Kitchen* (CooksCountry.com) on public television and listen to our weekly segments on *The Splendid Table* on public radio. You can also follow us on Facebook, Twitter, Pinterest, and Instagram.

EDITORIAL STAFF

Chief Executive Officer David Nussbaum
Chief Creative Officer Jack Bishop
Editor in Chief Dan Souza
Executive Editor Amanda Agee
Deputy Editor Rebecca Hays
Executive Managing Editor Todd Meier
Executive Food Editor Keith Dresser
Senior Editors Andrea Geary, Andrew Janjigian, Lan Lam
Senior Editors, Features Elizabeth Bomze, Kristin Sargianis
Associate Editor Annie Petito
Lead Cook, Photo Team Dan Cellucci
Test Cook Steve Dunn
Assistant Test Cooks Mady Nichas, Jessica Rudolph
Senior Copy Editor Krista Magnuson
Copy Editor Jillian Campbell
Senior Science Research Editor Paul Adams

Executive Editor, Tastings & Testings Lisa McManus
Deputy Editor, Tastings & Testings Hannah Crowley
Associate Editors, Tastings & Testings
  Miye Bromberg, Lauren Savoie, Kate Shannon
Assistant Editor, Tastings & Testings Emily Phares
Editorial Assistant, Tastings & Testings Carolyn Grillo

Director, Creative Operations Alice Carpenter
Test Kitchen Director Erin McMurrer
Assistant Test Kitchen Director Alexxa Benson
Test Kitchen Manager Meridith Lippard
Test Kitchen Facilities Manager Sophie Clingan-Darack
Senior Kitchen Assistant Receiver Kelly Ryan
Senior Kitchen Assistant Shopper Marissa Bunnewith
Lead Kitchen Assistant Ena Gudiel
Kitchen Assistants Gladis Campos, Blanca Castanza

Creative Director John Torres
Design Director Greg Galvan
Photography Director Julie Cote
Designer Maggie Edgar
Senior Staff Photographer Daniel J. van Ackere
Staff Photographers Steve Klise, Kevin White
Photography Producer Meredith Mulcahy
Styling Kendra McKnight, Elle Simone

Executive Editor, Web Christine Liu
Managing Editor, Web Mari Levine
Senior Editors, Web Roger Metcalf, Briana Palma
Assistant Editor, Web Molly Farrar

BUSINESS STAFF

Chief Financial Officer Jackie McCauley Ford
Director, Customer Support Amy Bootier
Senior Customer Loyalty & Support Specialist
  Rebecca Kowalski
Customer Loyalty & Support Specialist J.P. Dubuque
Production Director Guy Rochford
Imaging Manager Lauren Robbins
Production & Imaging Specialists Heather Dube,
  Dennis Noble, Jessica Voas

Chief Revenue Officer Sara Domville
Director, Special Accounts Erica Nye
Director, Business Partnerships Mehgan Conciatori
Partnership Marketing Manager Pamela Putprush
Director, Sponsorship Marketing & Client Services
  Christine Anagnostis
Client Services Manager Kate Zebrowski
Client Service & Marketing Representative Claire Gambee

Chief Digital Officer Fran Middleton
VP, Marketing Natalie Vinard
**Marketing Director, Social Media & Content
  Strategy** Claire Oliverson
Senior Social Media Coordinators Kelsey Hopper,
  Morgan Mannino

**Senior VP, Human Resources & Organizational
  Development** Colleen Zelina
Human Resources Director Adele Shapiro

Circulation Services ProCirc

Cover Art Robert Papp

PRINTED IN THE USA

ILLUSTRATION: JOHN BURGOYNE

LETTER FROM THE EDITOR

PRACTICE MAKES PIZZA

If you're like me, you can chart your development as a cook by the pizzas you've pulled from your oven over the years. There was the preferred pie of my early days: half an English muffin topped with brick-red jarred pizza sauce and hand-torn string cheese, baked in the toaster oven until cheese drooled from the sides and ignited on the glowing coil below. The middle years could be best described as homemade-ish. A signature technique of this period was to start with a store-bought frozen pizza and patch its sparse coating of freezer-burnt cheese with a fresh layer of pregrated part-skim mozzarella. From there I advanced to hitting up the supermarket—or an accommodating local pizza shop—for premade dough. Back home, I'd assault the dough with a rolling pin and stern language in an attempt to make it thin and round. After failing on both measures, I'd garnish my dough amoebas with up to a dozen (thoughtfully chosen) toppings and cheeses and bake them off for my ever-supportive family.

Make no mistake, I learned a lot about pizza making during these early trials. But most of my advanced pizza development happened right here at *Cook's Illustrated* and as a result of working side by side with senior editor Andrew Janjigian. I've learned that a freshly whirled-together mixture of flour, water, yeast, salt, and a touch of olive oil tastes of remarkably little. Worse still, when stretched, it recoils with stress. However, let that same dough vacation for a few days in the cool climes of your fridge and you'll find its attitude entirely adjusted. Once uptight and inflexible, your dough has, quite literally, relaxed. Give it a poke or a stretch and you'll see. Bake it into a pizza and you'll taste the difference. Andrew has been refining his pizza-making technique for the better part of three decades. If I could sum up his philosophy for him, it would be "Wait." That's because dough that has fermented for three days is easier to stretch, bakes up crispier, and tastes more complex.

Dan Souza

Unfortunately, pizza cravings aren't nearly as amenable to a three-day pause. So, for this issue, I tasked Andrew with the ultimate challenge: Make great pizza in an hour. He spent about eight weeks developing the recipe on page 9. In true form, he discovered creative solutions to the problems that plague all quick-rise doughs. His is deeply flavorful, bakes up crispy, and, best of all, is a cinch to roll out. Dough amoebas and stern language? Mere relics of the past.

Dan Souza
Editor in Chief

FOR INQUIRIES, ORDERS, OR MORE INFORMATION

COOK'S ILLUSTRATED MAGAZINE
Cook's Illustrated magazine (ISSN 1068-2821), number 151, is published bimonthly by America's Test Kitchen Limited Partnership, 2 Drydock Avenue, Suite 210E, Boston, MA 02210. Copyright 2018 America's Test Kitchen Limited Partnership. Periodicals postage paid at Boston, MA, and additional mailing offices, USPS #012487. Publications Mail Agreement No. 40020778 Return undeliverable Canadian addresses to P.O. Box 875, Station A, Windsor, ON N9A 6P2. POSTMASTER: Send address changes to *Cook's Illustrated*, P.O. Box 6018, Harlan, IA 51593-1518. For subscription and gift subscription orders, subscription inquiries, or change of address notices, visit AmericasTestKitchen.com/support, call 800-526-8442 in the U.S. or 515-237-3663 from outside the U.S., or write to us at *Cook's Illustrated*, P.O. Box 6018, Harlan, IA 51593-1518.

CooksIllustrated.com
At the all new CooksIllustrated.com, you can order books and subscriptions, sign up for our free e-newsletter, or renew your magazine subscription. Join the website and gain access to 25 years of *Cook's Illustrated* recipes, equipment tests, and ingredient tastings, as well as companion videos for every recipe in this issue.

COOKBOOKS
We sell more than 50 cookbooks by the editors of *Cook's Illustrated*, including *How to Roast Everything* and *Just Add Sauce*. To order, visit our online bookstore at CooksIllustrated.com/bookstore.

EDITORIAL OFFICE 21 Drydock Avenue, Suite 210E, Boston, MA 02210; 617-232-1000; fax: 617-232-1572. For subscription inquiries, visit AmericasTestKitchen.com/support or call 800-526-8442.

QUICK TIPS

≥ COMPILED BY ANNIE PETITO ≤

Clip—or Stitch—Tacos Closed
To prevent soft tacos from spilling open while she's filling the others, Sue Wallin of Seattle, Wash., uses one of two tricks to keep the stuffed tortillas closed: She pinches each one with a bag clip or threads a toothpick through the top of the tortilla, which holds the taco together much like it would a club sandwich.

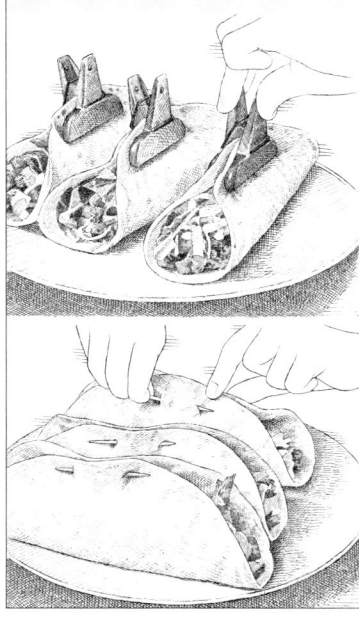

Make Supersmooth Guacamole with a Ricer
To make silky guacamole without wearing out her arm, Rochelle Rougier-Maas of Mahtomedi, Minn., presses peeled and pitted avocado halves through the fine holes of a potato ricer before mixing in other ingredients.

Avoid Coffee Grinder Static
When transferring ground coffee from his burr-style coffee grinder's container to his coffee maker, Jim Forrest of Franconia, N.H., has found that static in the container can cause the grounds to fly all over the counter. His solution: Add a few drops of water (about 1/8 teaspoon) to the hopper with the beans before grinding them.

Whisk a Whisk Clean
To clean a whisk after mixing pancake batter, Diane Scalisi of Aptos, Calif., puts warm soapy water in the dirty mixing bowl and beats it with the whisk. To rinse it, she repeats the process with plain warm water.

Transport Soups and Stews in Your Pressure Cooker
Nathan Lyon of Arlington, Va., uses his pressure cooker not only to cook soups and stews but also to transport them, since the seal ensures that the contents will not spill. The pressure cooker can also be used to reheat the contents.

Stop Cutting Boards from Sliding
To prevent her cutting boards from sliding in the kitchen cabinet, Janyce Turturici of Novato, Calif., glues rubber doorstops to the floor of the cabinet. The angled doorstops are sturdy enough to keep the boards upright so that she can store several of them in the same space.

SEND US YOUR TIPS We will provide a complimentary one-year subscription for each tip we print. Send your tip, name, address, and telephone number to Quick Tips, *Cook's Illustrated*, 21 Drydock Avenue, Suite 210E, Boston, MA 02210, or to QuickTips@AmericasTestKitchen.com.

Steam-Clean Your Panini Press

To thoroughly clean the grooves of their panini press (or waffle iron), John and Denise Goodman of Oak Park, Calif., soak four or five paper towels in water, stack them on the bottom cooking surface of the unplugged-but-still-warm press, and close the lid. The warm, moist towels generate steam that loosens food from the press so that it can be easily wiped clean with the towels.

Easily Separate Coffee Filters

It can be a maddening struggle to pull a paper-thin coffee filter from inside a stack, so Sherry Johnston of Gilbert, Ariz., turns the stack inside out, which makes it a cinch to pull off a filter.

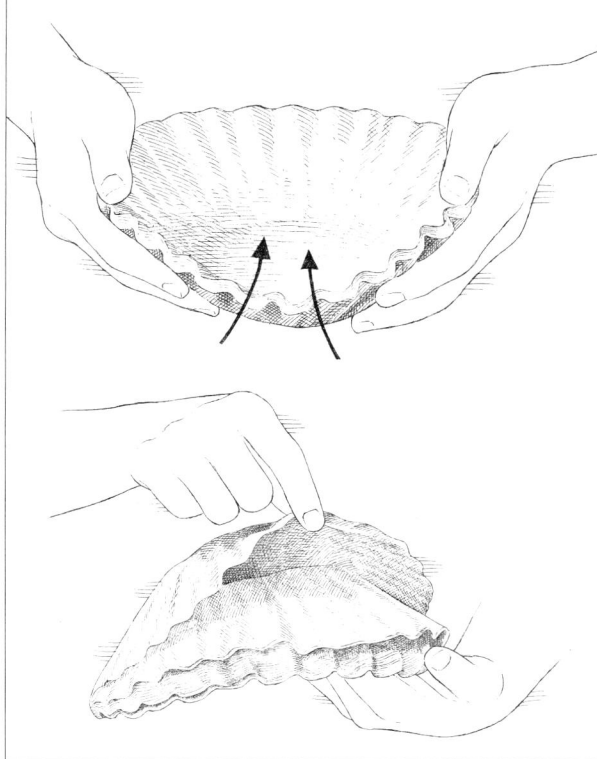

Nifty Egg Holder

To store one egg outside of its space-hogging carton, Milton Zelman of Aiken, S.C., creates a perch for it by cutting a 1-inch piece from a paper towel tube. He stands the tube on one of the cut ends and places the egg on the other so that it sits securely in the opening.

Hollow Out Cupcakes for Filling

Kristin Peek of Charleston, S.C., found that the fastest, most efficient way to hollow out cupcakes for filling is with a strawberry huller.

Dish Rack for Pot Lid Storage

Louise Oates of Grass Valley, Calif., has an effective way of keeping pot lids arranged within easy reach of her pots and pans, which she keeps stacked inside one another: She lines up the lids in a dish-drying rack placed beside the pots.

Steadying Olives for Slicing

By spearing the center of a pitted olive with a small fork, Bette Williams of Nashotah, Wis., finds that she can firmly hold the slippery fruit in place while she slices it with a paring knife.

Indoor Pulled Chicken

Our stovetop method yields pulled chicken so good—and so quick—that you'll think twice about making the outdoor kind.

⋟ BY ANDREW JANJIGIAN ⋞

Traditional pulled chicken is a true labor of love: First you brine bone-in, skin-on parts for an hour or so. Then you cook them slowly over coals and wood chunks until the meat is moist and tender within and kissed with smoke flavor throughout. With the skin burnished to a deep mahogany, smoked chicken is a beautiful thing—making it feel almost like a crime to pull off the skin, shred the richly flavored meat, and douse it in barbecue sauce for sandwiches.

I developed a killer recipe for Smoked Chicken (July/August 2011), and if I make it for friends, you'd better believe I'm going to get full credit for all the work by showing off its burnished parts. But for those times when I need a quick weeknight meal or when my grill is covered with 16 inches of snow, I had a hunch that I could make some really good pulled chicken by simply braising chicken parts in a smoky barbecue sauce. It wouldn't give me burnished skin—but I wouldn't need that anyway.

Smoke and Mirrors

My Smoked Chicken recipe calls for whole breasts and leg quarters; I pull the white meat off the fire early since it cooks faster than the dark meat. But in the interest of keeping things as simple as possible, I decided to use only thighs for my indoor pulled chicken. They are our preferred cut for braising since they have lots of collagen, which turns to gelatin and gives the meat a moist, tender texture. Using the boneless, skinless type was one more way to streamline things.

I arranged 2 pounds of thighs (enough to make 6 to 8 sandwiches) in a Dutch oven along with the makings of a tangy barbecue sauce—ketchup, molasses, Worcestershire sauce, hot sauce, and salt and pepper—and enough water to comfortably cover the chicken. I also stirred in a couple of teaspoons of liquid smoke. I know what you might be thinking, but stick with me: Liquid smoke is an all-natural

▶ Watch: Smoke Without Fire
A step-by-step video is available at CooksIllustrated.com/apr18

Thirty-five minutes is all it takes to put tender, sweet, and smoky pulled chicken sandwiches on the table.

ingredient made from real woodsmoke and would replicate the flavor achieved via wood chips (see "Don't Shy Away from Liquid Smoke").

I brought the pot to a simmer and let it bubble until the thighs were tender, about 25 minutes. To shred the chicken, I found that our usual method of pulling it apart with a pair of forks was overkill for meat so fall-apart tender. It was also slow. Putting the thighs in the bowl of a stand mixer and using the paddle attachment—which we sometimes use to shred large quantities—worked, but it was a big piece of equipment to haul out for 10 seconds of use. In the end, shredding the meat with a pair of tongs was the most efficient way to get the job done.

I stirred some of the braising liquid into the shredded chicken and piled it onto buns. Between bites, my colleagues offered critiques. One was that the meat was washed-out: It lacked seasoning and had none of the concentrated chicken-y taste that you get in real smoked chicken. Also, the sauce was thin.

I changed up my method, this time simmering the thighs in a much smaller amount of liquid, hoping it would produce better-tasting meat. I used only 1 cup of water mixed with sugar, salt, molasses, and liquid smoke. Sugar and salt are common brine components and would flavor the meat, molasses would add bittersweet notes, and liquid smoke would of course contribute the smoky element. I separately prepared a thick barbecue sauce to coat the chicken in before serving.

Sure enough, the salty/sweet braising liquid had infused the meat with the taste of a brined, slowly smoked bird. Still, it was lacking the deep poultry flavor and unctuous meatiness of real smoked chicken. But aside from the cooking method, the only other difference between this recipe and my outdoor recipe was the lack of skin and bones.

Fat Chance

Chicken skin contains fat that renders and bastes the meat as it cooks. Chicken skin, bones, and tendons offer collagen, which breaks down during cooking to form gelatin, giving the meat a rich, luxurious texture. How could I get more of these missing elements—fat and gelatin—into my recipe?

As I prepped my next batch, I thought about how we normally trim and discard the fat attached to boneless, skinless chicken thighs. This time around, I decided to leave it. Once the chicken was cooked, I strained the braising liquid, skimmed off the fat (2 pounds of thighs yielded about

TECHNIQUE

A NEW WAY TO SHRED CHICKEN

Instead of using two forks to shred the chicken, we squeeze it gently with tongs. The meat is so tender that it falls apart easily into bite-size pieces.

Speeding the Way to Pulled Chicken

Cooking untrimmed boneless, skinless thighs with powdered gelatin replicates the fat and gelatin naturally found in bone-in, skin-on parts.

OUTDOOR 2½ hours		INDOOR 35 minutes
Bone-in, skin-on parts	JUICINESS	Boneless, skinless thighs with fat intact; add gelatin
Brine for 1 hour in sugar and salt	SEASONING	Cook in broth, molasses, sugar, and salt
1½ hours	COOKING TIME	35 minutes
Wood chips	SMOKY FLAVOR	Liquid smoke

3 tablespoons), and added it to the chicken. I also swapped the braising water for chicken broth and stirred in some powdered gelatin. The extra fat, along with the broth and gelatin, greatly improved the flavor and overall unctuousness of the meat.

The chicken needed to be reheated after shredding, so I mixed it with some of the braising liquid and a little barbecue sauce and heated it until it absorbed all the liquid and appeared dry, which took about 5 minutes. (Since the liquid smoke flavor seemed to diminish during braising, I added a bit more at this point.) After this step, the chicken was meaty and dense, ready for extra sauce to be added at the table.

For some variety, I mixed up two more sauces: a mustardy South Carolina–style sauce and a vinegary North Carolina–style option. Now when I crave pulled chicken, will I head outside? Maybe, if the sun is shining and I have time to burn. Otherwise, I'm staying in.

Don't Shy Away from Liquid Smoke

Until we did some research years ago, we assumed (as many people do) that there must be some kind of synthetic chemical chicanery going on in the making of liquid smoke. But that's not the case. Liquid smoke is made by channeling smoke from smoldering wood chips through a condenser, which quickly cools the vapors, causing them to liquefy. The water-soluble flavor compounds in the smoke are trapped within this liquid, while the insoluble tars and resins are removed by a series of filters, resulting in a clean, all-natural smoke-flavored liquid. Some manufacturers add other flavorings to liquid smoke, but our top-rated product, Wright's Liquid Smoke, contains nothing but smoke and water.

INDOOR PULLED CHICKEN
SERVES 6 TO 8

Do not trim the fat from the chicken thighs; it contributes to the flavor and texture of the pulled chicken. If you don't have 3 tablespoons of fat to add back to the pot in step 3, add melted butter to make up the difference. We like mild molasses in this recipe; do not use blackstrap. Serve the pulled chicken on white bread or hamburger buns with pickles and coleslaw.

- 1 cup chicken broth
- 2 tablespoons molasses
- 1 tablespoon sugar
- 1 tablespoon liquid smoke
- 1 teaspoon unflavored gelatin
- Salt and pepper
- 2 pounds boneless, skinless chicken thighs, halved crosswise
- 1 recipe barbecue sauce (recipes follow)
- Hot sauce

1. Bring broth, molasses, sugar, 2 teaspoons liquid smoke, gelatin, and 1 teaspoon salt to boil in large Dutch oven over high heat, stirring to dissolve sugar. Add chicken and return to simmer. Reduce heat to medium-low, cover, and cook, stirring occasionally, until chicken is easily shredded with fork, about 25 minutes.

2. Transfer chicken to medium bowl and set aside. Strain cooking liquid through fine-mesh strainer set over bowl (do not wash pot). Let liquid settle for 5 minutes; skim fat from surface. Set aside fat and defatted liquid.

3. Using tongs, squeeze chicken until shredded into bite-size pieces. Transfer chicken, 1 cup barbecue sauce, ½ cup reserved defatted liquid, 3 tablespoons reserved fat, and remaining 1 teaspoon liquid smoke to now-empty pot. Cook mixture over medium heat, stirring frequently, until liquid has been absorbed and exterior of meat appears dry, about 5 minutes. Season with salt, pepper, and hot sauce to taste. Serve, passing remaining barbecue sauce separately.

LEXINGTON VINEGAR BARBECUE SAUCE
MAKES ABOUT 2 CUPS

For a spicier sauce, add hot sauce to taste.

- 1 cup cider vinegar
- ½ cup ketchup
- ½ cup water
- 1 tablespoon sugar
- ¾ teaspoon salt
- ¾ teaspoon red pepper flakes
- ½ teaspoon pepper

Whisk all ingredients together in bowl.

SOUTH CAROLINA MUSTARD BARBECUE SAUCE
MAKES ABOUT 2 CUPS

You can use either light or dark brown sugar in this recipe.

- 1 cup yellow mustard
- ½ cup distilled white vinegar
- ¼ cup packed brown sugar
- ¼ cup Worcestershire sauce
- 2 tablespoons hot sauce
- 1 teaspoon salt
- 1 teaspoon pepper

Whisk all ingredients together in bowl.

SWEET AND TANGY BARBECUE SAUCE
MAKES ABOUT 2 CUPS

We like mild molasses in this recipe.

- 1½ cups ketchup
- ¼ cup molasses
- 2 tablespoons Worcestershire sauce
- 1 tablespoon hot sauce
- ½ teaspoon salt
- ½ teaspoon pepper

Whisk all ingredients together in bowl.

Perfect Pork Tenderloin Steaks

How do you cook this lean cut so that it's superjuicy, rosy from edge to edge, and deeply browned? Use two cooking methods.

⇒ BY LAN LAM ⇐

We've all suffered through dry, chalky, or tough pork tenderloin. That's because traditional techniques such as oven roasting or pan searing use high heat in an attempt to give the mild meat a flavorful browned crust, but these methods typically overcook the lean pork. Lowering the heat can alleviate dryness—but at the expense of browning. What if there were a way to guarantee juicy, flavorful, fork-tender meat?

Chefs in high-end restaurants have been doing just that by cooking food very gently using a technique called *sous vide* that keeps the food from rising above the ideal doneness temperature; afterward meat is typically seared rapidly to produce a browned crust. (In recent years, sous vide machines have gotten far less expensive. See "Sous Vide Circulators" for details.) In the test kitchen, we have learned to produce the same results without special equipment. The key is to use two cooking methods: Slow-roast the meat in a low-temperature oven, and then transfer it to the stovetop for a quick sear.

To put the technique into action, I borrowed a trick a colleague had used when grilling pork tenderloin. I lightly pounded 2 tenderloins to a 1-inch thickness and then halved each one crosswise, creating four pieces total. This would help greatly when it came time to sear the meat: I'd be working with steaks—with large, flat surfaces for browning—instead of cylinders.

My goal was to cook the interiors of the pork to 140 degrees and keep the outer layers as close to that temperature as possible. Cooked to this degree, the meat is faintly pink, superjuicy, and optimally tender. I seasoned the steaks with salt and pepper and arranged them on a wire rack (spritzed with vegetable oil spray) set in a rimmed baking sheet. This would raise the meat off the hot sheet and prevent the undersides from overcooking. I placed the assembly in a 275-degree oven, where the pork took about 30 minutes to reach 140 degrees. I then removed the sheet from the oven and swaddled the steaks in paper towels to wick away moisture. I needed to get the pork as dry as possible because any water on the surface would inhibit browning.

▶ Watch: Perfect Pork
A step-by-step video is available at CooksIllustrated.com/apr18

We pound the pork flat for better browning.

Next, I heated 2 tablespoons of vegetable oil in a 12-inch skillet over medium-high heat, waiting for wisps of smoke to rise. At that point, I knew the pan was ready, so I turned the burner to high and added the steaks, which browned evenly and deeply in just a minute or two per side. The high heat browned the surfaces quickly, so the steaks were in and out of the pan before their interior temperature could rise much above 140 degrees. After letting the meat rest, I sliced into pork tenderloin perfection: juicy, tender, and evenly rosy meat encased in a flavorful mahogany crust. (To learn how to make this recipe using sous vide, see "Want to Try Sous Vide?")

PERFECT PAN-SEARED PORK TENDERLOIN STEAKS
SERVES 4

Choose tenderloins that are equal in size to ensure that the pork cooks at the same rate. We prefer natural pork in this recipe. If using enhanced pork (injected with a salt solution), reduce the salt in step 2 to ¼ teaspoon per steak. Open the oven as infrequently as possible in step 2. If the meat is not yet up to temperature, wait at least 5 minutes before taking its temperature again. Serve the pork with Scallion-Ginger Relish (recipe follows), if desired.

Our recipe for Perfect Pan-Seared Pork Tenderloin Steaks for Two is available for free for four months at CooksIllustrated.com/apr18.

- 2 (1-pound) pork tenderloins, trimmed
- Kosher salt and pepper
- 2 tablespoons vegetable oil

1. Adjust oven rack to middle position and heat oven to 275 degrees. Set wire rack in rimmed baking sheet and lightly spray rack with vegetable oil spray.

2. Pound each tenderloin to 1-inch thickness. Halve each tenderloin crosswise. Sprinkle each steak with ½ teaspoon salt and ⅛ teaspoon pepper. Place steaks on prepared wire rack and cook until meat registers between 137 and 140 degrees, 25 to 35 minutes.

3. Move steaks to 1 side of rack. Line cleared side with double layer of paper towels. Transfer steaks to paper towels, cover with another double layer of paper towels, and let stand for 10 minutes.

4. Pat steaks until surfaces are very dry. Heat oil in 12-inch skillet over medium-high heat until just smoking. Increase heat to high, place steaks in skillet, and sear until well browned on both sides, 1 to 2 minutes per side. Transfer to carving board and let stand for 5 minutes. Slice steaks against grain ¾ inch thick and transfer to serving platter. Season with salt to taste, and serve.

SCALLION-GINGER RELISH
MAKES ABOUT ⅔ CUP

We like the complexity of white pepper in this recipe.

- 6 scallions, white and green parts separated and sliced thin
- 2 teaspoons grated fresh ginger
- ½ teaspoon ground white pepper
- ½ teaspoon grated lime zest plus 2 teaspoons juice
- ¼ cup vegetable oil
- 2 teaspoons soy sauce

Combine scallion whites, ginger, pepper, and lime zest in heatproof bowl. Heat oil in small saucepan over medium heat until shimmering. Pour oil over scallion mixture. (Mixture will bubble.) Stir until well combined. Let cool completely, about 15 minutes. Stir in scallion greens, lime juice, and soy sauce. Let mixture sit for 15 minutes to allow flavors to meld.

SOUS VIDE PORK TENDERLOIN STEAKS
SERVES 4

We prefer natural pork in this recipe. If using enhanced pork (injected with a salt solution), reduce the salt in step 2 to ¼ teaspoon per steak. Serve the pork with Scallion-Ginger Relish (page 6), if desired. Our recipe for Sous Vide Pork Tenderloin Steaks for Two is available for free for four months at CooksIllustrated.com/apr18. Our quick guide to getting started with *sous vide* is available at CooksIllustrated.com/sousvideguide. Two additional sous vide recipes—Butter-Basted Thick-Cut Rib-Eye Steaks and Soft-Poached Eggs—are available at CooksIllustrated.com/sousvide.

Want to Try Sous Vide?
While our oven-to-stovetop method for cooking pork tenderloin steaks (page 6) works very well, the *sous vide* cooking method gives you control over the precise doneness temperature of the meat without having to monitor it (for a comparison of the two methods, see page 31). It also offers the convenience of being able to hold the meat at that temperature for a couple of hours until you're ready to serve it. For this technique, you'll need a sous vide circulator, a 7-quart Dutch oven or similar-size heatproof container, and zipper-lock bags.

TESTING Sous Vide Circulators
Whether or not you're familiar with *sous vide*, chances are you've eaten food prepared this way. In the past decade, sous vide—the method of cooking food in a precise, controlled water bath—has gone from high-end restaurants to home kitchens. Though freestanding machines exist, home cooks typically use immersion circulators—slim, stick-like devices that attach to different vessels and continuously heat the water. We evaluated seven models with prices ranging from $129.99 to $274.95 by cooking eggs, salmon, flank steak, pork loin, and beef short ribs to a range of temperatures.

Our testing revealed flaws in certain models: Some fluctuated more than 1 degree from the target temperature, which resulted in over- or undercooked eggs; a few machines required a confusing sequence of button-pushing to get started; and the two largest circulators, while powerful, didn't leave much room in a 6-quart water bath to add food.

On the other hand, our top-ranked circulators were temperature-stable, slim, lightweight, and easy to use. The Joule ($199.00), made by ChefSteps, was powerful enough to heat quickly and stayed within 0.2 degrees of the target temperature. It also featured 6.5 inches between the minimum and maximum water fill lines, which allowed us to cook uninterrupted without needing to refill (due to water evaporation). Though it can be operated only with an accompanying smartphone app, its lack of buttons and display screens allowed for the larger distance between the water fill lines. We also like the Anova Precision Cooker WI-FI ($199.00), which can be operated with or without a smartphone. To read the full testing, go to CooksIllustrated.com/apr18. —Lauren Savoie

1. HEAT WATER TO PRECISE TEMPERATURE
Using sous vide circulator, bring 4 quarts water (water should be 4 inches deep) to 140°F/60°C in 7-quart Dutch oven or similar-size heatproof container.
WHY? A sous vide circulator brings the water to the exact ideal doneness temperature of the food. Since the food can't exceed the temperature of the water in which it is submerged, there is no risk of overcooking.

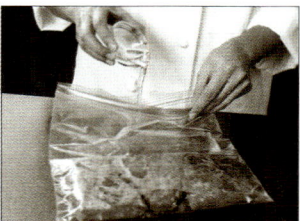

2. PUT MEAT IN BAG WITH OIL Pound two 1-pound pork tenderloins to 1-inch thickness. Halve each tenderloin crosswise to create 4 steaks total. Sprinkle each steak with ½ teaspoon kosher salt and ⅛ teaspoon pepper. Place steaks and 2 tablespoons vegetable oil in 1-gallon zipper-lock freezer bag.
WHY? Oil conducts heat better than air and therefore helps the meat cook evenly. It also keeps the steaks from sticking together.

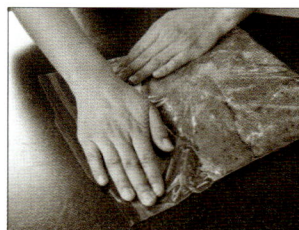

3. REMOVE AIR FROM BAG Seal bag, pressing out as much air as possible.
WHY? Removing air from the bag is critical because air is a poor conductor of heat and slows cooking. In fact, *sous vide* is French for "under vacuum" and references the removal of air from the bag.

4. SUBMERGE BAG Gently lower bag into water bath until pork is submerged, then clip top corner of bag to side of pot, allowing remaining air bubbles to rise to top of bag. Open 1 corner of zipper, release air bubbles, and reseal bag. Cover pot with plastic wrap and cook pork for at least 1 hour or up to 2 hours.
WHY? Properly submerging the food ensures even cooking. Securing the food to the container keeps it away from the circulator's intake/outtake areas.

5. DRY MEAT Line wire rack with double layer of paper towels and place in rimmed baking sheet. Transfer steaks to paper towels, cover with another double layer of paper towels, and let stand for 10 minutes. Pat steaks until surfaces are very dry.
WHY? The meat will be somewhat wet when you remove it from the sous vide bag. Thoroughly drying the pork steaks with double layers of paper towels eliminates moisture that would impede browning.

6. SEAR MEAT Heat 2 tablespoons vegetable oil in 12-inch skillet over medium-high heat until just smoking. Increase heat to high, place steaks in skillet, and sear until well browned on both sides, 1 to 2 minutes per side. Transfer to carving board and let stand for 5 minutes. Slice steaks against grain ¾ inch thick and transfer to serving platter. Season with salt to taste, and serve.
WHY? Searing creates the deeply flavorful browned crust that sous vide cooking doesn't produce.

HIGHLY RECOMMENDED
JOULE
MODEL: Stainless Steel
PRICE: $199.00
COMMENTS: This slim, lightweight machine heated water almost as fast as the biggest circulators and was the most accurate model in our lineup. It requires a smartphone to operate, but the app is intuitive and simple. Testers loved its magnetic bottom, which allowed it to stand stably in the center of metal pots.

RECOMMENDED
ANOVA Precision Cooker WI-FI
MODEL: A3.2
PRICE: $199.00
COMMENTS: We liked that we could set this model's temperature and time on the circulator or with an app. However, it lagged behind our winner on heating speed and accuracy and was a little too bulky to be stored in a standard drawer.

MARCH & APRIL 2018

One-Hour Pizza

The ultimate challenge for a pizza master with 30 years of experience? Making a good one in just 60 minutes.

⇒ BY ANDREW JANJIGIAN ⇐

If there is anything in life I can claim to have mastered, it's making pizza: It was the first food I learned to cook, at age 15. Since then, I've developed nine pizza recipes. I've built two outdoor pizza ovens. Heck, I even teach pizza-making classes in my free time. But mastery can turn to complacency, so I was intrigued when editor in chief Dan Souza tasked me with the following challenge: Make really good pizza from scratch in just 1 hour, start to finish.

It would be the ultimate test, as it went against the gospel I've been preaching for years, which says that for superlative pizza—a mildly yeasty, slightly tangy crust that's crisp on the outside and pleasantly chewy within—you must let the dough proof in the refrigerator for at least one day or up to three days.

Burden of Proof

Time is so important because it significantly affects both flavor and texture. During a slow, cold rise, yeast creates fermented and acidic flavor compounds. Meanwhile, enzymes in the flour go to work on the gluten, snipping some bonds to make a supremely extensible dough. I'd have to find speedy ways to accomplish both effects. It would be no easy feat.

I started with a test run using my Thin-Crust Pizza recipe (January/February 2011): Combine bread flour, a little sugar, and a small amount of yeast in a food processor with water, and then let it sit for 10 minutes; this lets the flour absorb the water, which allows gluten to form. Next, add salt and oil and run the machine until the dough is smooth. After that, you'd normally refrigerate the dough and wait a few days for fermentation to happen. But the clock was ticking, so I divided the dough into two balls and let them proof at room temperature for just 30 minutes. As I expected, when I tried to shape a ball into a round, it stubbornly sprang back. The only way to get the dough near 12 inches in diameter was to strong-arm it with a rolling pin. It baked up flat, bland, and tough.

Clearly, the few pinches of yeast in my original recipe (which do a great job of leavening in 24 hours) weren't enough to make the dough rise much in 30 minutes—not to mention that the rolling pin was pushing out what little air there was. Increasing the yeast was the obvious answer, but it's also the adjustment where most quick pizza recipes fail. Good pizza dough should taste subtly fermented, not just yeasty. So how much more yeast could I add? I ended up with 2 teaspoons, enough to give the dough lift but not so much that it tasted too yeasty. I also started with warm tap water, which activated the yeast more quickly.

The rise was better, but I still needed a rolling pin to shape the highly elastic dough. Furthermore, while the pizza didn't taste overly yeasty, it didn't taste like much else either. Fortunately, for the latter issue I knew of a trick from our Almost No-Knead Bread (January/February 2008): Mix in vinegar and beer. Beer includes many

For a supercrisp crust, we preheat the baking stone at 500 degrees; then, for a blast of heat before baking, we turn on the broiler for 10 minutes.

Ensuring Extensibility in One-Hour Pizza

Most of our pizza recipes allow ample time to let the gluten relax, which makes the dough easy to shape and prevents springback. Without the luxury of time, we found other ways to make the dough workable.

ADD EXTRA LIQUID A high hydration level (we use about 7 ounces of liquid for about 10 ounces of flour) makes the dough more extensible.

USE PART SEMOLINA FLOUR The gluten network that semolina forms is less elastic, so the dough doesn't snap back as much.

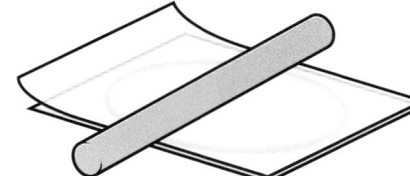
ROLL; THEN PROOF Immediately rolling the dough means no wrestling it into shape after proofing—or pushing out any precious air bubbles.

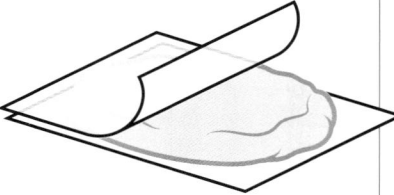
PROOF PRESHAPED ROUNDS After 30 minutes, the dough will be puffy and ready to top and bake (the parchment will keep the dough moist).

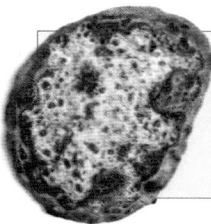
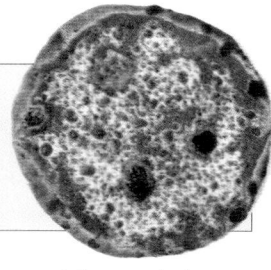

A Tale of Two Doughs

Quick pizza dough is particularly hard to shape. Anyone who has tried it is familiar with the misshapen pizza on the left. Our formula and method make it easy to shape the perfect pizza on the right.

of the same flavorful compounds that are created by yeast during bread fermentation—alcohols, aldehydes, and esters—and vinegar adds the acidity that yeast and bacteria create in slow-fermented dough.

Upper Crust

The two quickest ways to improve my dough's extensibility were to increase its moisture and to take a close look at the type of flour I was using. I was only able to increase the liquid from 6.5 to 7 ounces before the dough became too wet to handle. It was a little more yielding, but not enough.

As for the flour, the bread flour that my Thin-Crust Pizza recipe calls for is high in protein. Generally speaking, the more protein a flour has, the more gluten it forms. That's great if you can use a long proof to let that gluten relax. But without the luxury of time, I wondered if lower-protein (less gluten-forming) all-purpose or cake flour might help. Sure enough, doughs made with these flours were easier to work with. But gluten formation is not the only reason bread bakers use bread flour. High-protein flour also helps a dough bake up crisp and light. It holds more water, which forms bubbles throughout the crust when it turns to steam, and an airier crust crisps up much better than a dense one. Without enough protein, these crusts were anything but crisp.

How about using semolina flour? It's unusual in that it's high in protein but forms a dough that's easier to stretch than typical bread doughs. In other words, it was just what my dough needed: A high protein level would help create crispness, and more stretch would make for a more workable dough.

Indeed, when I swapped a portion of the bread flour for semolina, the crust was transformed, with greater extensibility along with the crispness that is a hallmark of a great pizza. But there was a limit to how much semolina I could use: Beyond 50 percent of the total by weight, the dough didn't have enough structure to hold air bubbles. Even with my modest ½ cup of semolina, it was still too tight to shape without a rolling pin.

Rolling in Dough

At this point, I'd questioned almost everything about the pizza-making process. But there was one question I'd yet to ask: Why proof the dough and *then* roll it (and push out all those valuable air bubbles)? If I rolled the dough as soon as it was mixed, it could proof in its round shape.

With an eye on the clock, I rolled a ball of dough between sheets of oiled parchment and then let it proof for 30 minutes. I removed the top sheet, sprinkled the puffy round with flour, flipped it onto a peel, and removed the second sheet before topping it with sauce and cheese and baking it on a preheated stone.

Sixty minutes after I'd started, I was enjoying my best quick pizza yet. It had been easy to shape, and the crust was chewy but light since the air bubbles that developed during proofing hadn't been knocked out by shaping. Will it be replacing my three-day pizza recipe? No chance. Will I be making this dough every time I want same-day pizza? Without a doubt.

ONE-HOUR PIZZA
MAKES TWO 11½-INCH PIZZAS

For the best results, weigh your ingredients. We like the depth anchovies add to the sauce, but you can omit them, if desired. For the mild lager, we recommend Budweiser or Stella Artois. Extra sauce can be refrigerated for up to a week or frozen for up to a month. Some baking stones can crack under the intense heat of the broiler. Our recommended stone from Old Stone Oven won't, but if you're using another stone, check the manufacturer's website. If you don't have a pizza peel, use an overturned rimmed baking sheet instead.

Dough
- 1⅓ cups (7⅓ ounces) bread flour
- ½ cup (3 ounces) semolina flour
- 2 teaspoons instant or rapid-rise yeast
- 2 teaspoons sugar
- ½ cup plus 2 tablespoons (5 ounces) warm water (115 degrees)
- ¼ cup (2 ounces) mild lager
- 2 teaspoons distilled white vinegar
- 1½ teaspoons extra-virgin olive oil
- 1 teaspoon salt
-   Vegetable oil spray
-   All-purpose flour

Sauce
- 1 (28-ounce) can whole peeled tomatoes, drained
- 1 tablespoon extra-virgin olive oil
- 3 anchovy fillets, rinsed and patted dry (optional)
- 1 teaspoon salt
- 1 teaspoon dried oregano
- ½ teaspoon sugar
- ¼ teaspoon pepper
- ⅛ teaspoon red pepper flakes

Pizza
- 1 ounce Parmesan cheese, grated fine (½ cup)
- 6 ounces whole-milk mozzarella, shredded (1½ cups)

1. FOR THE DOUGH: Adjust oven rack 4 to 5 inches from broiler element, set pizza stone on rack, and heat oven to 500 degrees.

2. While oven heats, process bread flour, semolina flour, yeast, and sugar in food processor until combined, about 2 seconds. With processor running, slowly pour warm water, lager, vinegar, and oil through feed tube; process until dough is just combined and no dry flour remains, about 10 seconds. Let dough stand for 10 minutes.

3. Add salt to dough and process until dough forms satiny, sticky ball that clears sides of workbowl, 30 to 60 seconds. Transfer dough to lightly floured counter and gently knead until smooth, about 15 seconds. Divide dough into 2 equal pieces and shape each into smooth ball.

4. Spray 11-inch circle in center of large sheet of parchment paper with oil spray. Place 1 ball of dough in center of parchment. Spray top of dough with oil spray. Using rolling pin, roll dough into 10-inch circle. Cover with second sheet of parchment. Using rolling pin and your hands, continue to roll and press dough into 11½-inch circle. Set aside and repeat rolling with second ball of dough. Let dough stand at room temperature until slightly puffy, 30 minutes.

5. FOR THE SAUCE: Process all ingredients in food processor until smooth, about 30 seconds. Transfer to medium bowl.

6. FOR THE PIZZA: When dough has rested for 20 minutes, heat broiler for 10 minutes. Remove top piece of parchment from 1 disk of dough and dust top of dough lightly with all-purpose flour. Using your hands or pastry brush, spread flour evenly over dough, brushing off any excess. Liberally dust pizza peel with all-purpose flour. Flip dough onto peel, parchment side up. Carefully remove parchment and discard.

7. Using back of spoon or ladle, spread ½ cup sauce in thin layer over surface of dough, leaving ¾-inch border around edge. Sprinkle ¼ cup Parmesan evenly over sauce, followed by ¾ cup mozzarella. Slide pizza carefully onto stone and return oven to 500 degrees. Bake until crust is well browned and cheese is bubbly and beginning to brown, 8 to 12 minutes, rotating pizza halfway through baking.

8. Transfer pizza to wire rack and let cool for 5 minutes before slicing and serving. Repeat steps 6 and 7 to top and bake second pizza.

SHORTCUTTING FERMENTED FLAVOR

Since the yeast in our dough doesn't have enough time to create rich flavors, we add beer, which contains flavor compounds created by yeast fermentation. We also add vinegar, which provides the acetic acid that yeast produces during a slow rise.

▶ See Andrew Beat the Clock
A step-by-step video is available at CooksIllustrated.com/apr18

Brazilian Shrimp and Fish Stew

This coconut milk–based stew has such big flavor yet comes together so quickly that it sounded too good to be true—until we made it for ourselves.

≽ BY ANNIE PETITO ≼

Adding the seafood to the boiling coconut milk mixture and then turning off the heat guarantees perfectly cooked shrimp and fish.

Every region with a coastline seems to boast its own version of seafood stew—bouillabaisse, cioppino, gumbo, and chowder, to name a few. But I'd argue that Brazil's take, called *moqueca* (mo-KAY-kah), particularly the version popular in the country's northeastern region, known as Moqueca Baiana, is a standout among the rest. To make it, cooks typically marinate fish and/or shellfish in lime juice, salt, and garlic; stew the mixture in a clay pot with coconut milk and a few aromatic vegetables and herbs; drizzle the dish with sweet, nutty African *dendé* (palm) oil and a creamy, tangy hot pepper sauce made from local *malagueta* chiles; and serve it with rice alongside. That combination of rich coconut milk, briny seafood, bright citrus, and savory vegetables produces a broth that's full-bodied, lush, and vibrant—a particularly complex concoction compared with stews based solely on dairy, tomatoes, or broth.

But here's an even bigger selling point: Moqueca is fast and easy to make, and except for the fish and condiments, you might even have most of the ingredients on hand already. Dare I say it's one of the most impressive dinners you can throw together on a weeknight, not to mention serve to company?

That doesn't mean you can't make a bad batch. As with any seafood stew, I found that the fish could go from delicately tender to tough and chewy in a flash. And the broth could be either thin and lackluster or exceedingly rich. My goal: a well-balanced, satisfying stew teeming with pristine, perfectly cooked seafood.

Gone Fishin'

In Brazil, moqueca is made with just about any type and combination of seafood. For simplicity's sake, I settled on just two kinds: shrimp and cod. Both are widely available and would provide great texture: plump-but-tender snap from the shrimp and firm, delicate meatiness from the cod.

▶ **See Annie Make Stew**
A step-by-step video is available at CooksIllustrated.com/apr18

I'll be honest: I had a feeling that the marinade, or at least the lime juice, might do more harm than good. Soaking seafood in an acidic liquid such as lime juice causes its proteins to denature and its flesh to turn opaque and firm, much like it does when heated. That's a good thing if you're making ceviche, but what benefit would it provide to seafood I then planned to cook? Would it give the fish and shrimp more acidic punch?

I set up a side-by-side test to find out. For each batch, I combined a pound each of large shrimp (a reasonably meaty size that wouldn't cook too fast) and cod that I'd cut into chunks. I marinated the first batch of seafood in garlic, salt, and a few tablespoons of lime juice and simply tossed the second batch with garlic and salt (both of which, we've proven in experiments, penetrate foods during marinating). Then I prepared two batches of stew, softening chopped onion, red and green bell peppers, and cilantro in two Dutch ovens (the best alternative to the traditional clay pot). I followed with canned tomatoes (a year-round alternative to the traditional fresh tomatoes) and coconut milk and then the seafood—the batch marinated with lime juice in one pot and the batch without lime juice in the other. I covered the pots and let them simmer for just 5 minutes, hoping that would give the flavors enough time to meld without overcooking the seafood.

I'd guessed right: There was nary a trace of bright citrus flavor in the seafood that had been marinated with lime juice, and its texture was rather chewy and dry. But, admittedly, the seafood in the other stew was also overcooked, and in both cases the broth was thin and overwhelmed by coconutty sweetness.

Thickening the broth was as simple as pureeing the canned tomatoes, the onion, and some of the cilantro in the food processor and then sautéing the

Multifaceted Flavor
By hitting a range of different flavor notes, our *moqueca* delivers surprising complexity with little effort and a short ingredient list (including many staples you may already have in your pantry).

CREAMY RICHNESS
Coconut milk and extra-virgin olive oil

BRIGHTNESS
Lime juice and tomatoes

AROMATIC DEPTH
Cilantro, onion, bell peppers, and garlic

TANGY HEAT
Pickled hot cherry peppers

mixture briefly with the softened bell peppers to allow some of the puree's excess moisture to evaporate. Even though I hadn't increased the amount of tomato, onion, or cilantro, the thoroughly processed mixture ably tempered the coconut milk's sweetness; I also added lime juice directly to the pot with the seafood to make up for the lime juice I'd ditched as a marinade. Now the stew had the rich but vibrant flavor profile I was trying to achieve. But could I find a way to cook the seafood even more gently so it would stay moist and tender?

> "Delicious broth and tender seafood. The plates were beautiful—and pretty much licked clean."
> —Home recipe tester

Shut It Down

The answer was to shut off the stove. We've had good luck in the past poaching delicate proteins such as chicken breasts by heating the cooking liquid, adding the food, covering the pot, removing the pot from the heat, and allowing the liquid's residual heat to cook the food very gently.

Shrimp and cod are easy to overcook, so I wanted to be conservative with the temperature of the liquid. For my first test I let the broth come to just a simmer before adding the seafood to the pot and cutting the heat. But when I checked the seafood after several minutes, the fish and shrimp were still translucent. I realized that the simmering liquid just didn't have enough residual heat to fully cook the 2 pounds of seafood. I tried again, this time bringing the stew to a full boil, gently stirring in the seafood so it was evenly submerged, and then removing the covered pot from the heat. After a 15-minute wait, I had perfectly moist, tender shrimp and cod.

Fiery Finish

Back to the accompaniments. We tracked down some dendê oil and realized that its distinctively nutty character would be impossible to replicate, so we decided to leave it out. If you can find it, you can season individual bowls to taste. But start small, as its flavor is quite strong. The thin, spicy malagueta chiles used to make the tangy pepper sauce weren't easy to find either, but I was able to approximate them with vinegar-packed hot cherry peppers. I pulsed these in a food processor with a little onion and a bit of sugar to temper the heat plus extra-virgin olive oil to add creamy body. The sauce brought such tang and brightness to the stew that I decided to stir some of it directly into the pot right before serving, as well as pass it at the table. If there were any leftovers, I'd stash the sauce in the fridge to punch up other soups and stews—and even eggs, meats, and grains.

When all was said and done, I'd made one of the most complex, satisfying stews I'd ever tasted from (mostly) pantry staples—and in just about 45 minutes.

BRAZILIAN SHRIMP AND FISH STEW (MOQUECA)
SERVES 6

Pickled hot cherry peppers are usually sold jarred, next to the pickles or jarred roasted red peppers at the supermarket. Haddock or other firm-fleshed, flaky whitefish may be substituted for cod. We prefer untreated shrimp, but if your shrimp are treated with sodium, do not add salt to the shrimp in step 2. Our favorite coconut milk is made by Aroy-D. Serve with steamed white rice.

Pepper Sauce
- 4 pickled hot cherry peppers (3 ounces)
- ½ onion, chopped coarse
- ¼ cup extra-virgin olive oil
- ⅛ teaspoon sugar
- Salt

Stew
- 1 pound large shrimp (26 to 30 per pound), peeled, deveined, and tails removed

A FULL BOIL IS KEY
Once the entire surface is bubbling, it's time to add the seafood.

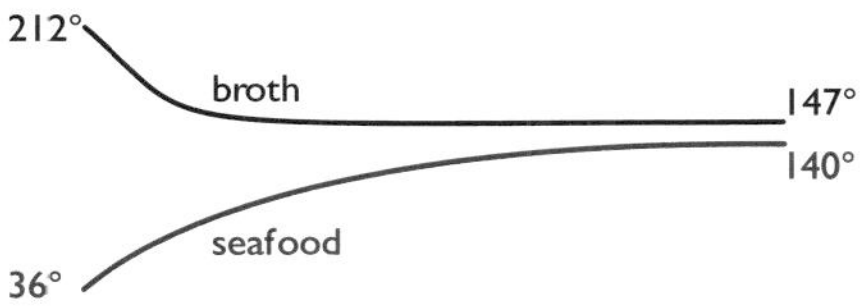

212° broth 147°
140°
36° seafood

AS THE STEW COOLS, THE SEAFOOD COOKS

TECHNIQUE

COOKING WITH RESIDUAL HEAT

To gently and evenly cook the delicate fish and shrimp in our *moqueca*, bring the stew to a full boil, and then add the seafood and remove the pot from the heat. Letting food cook in residual heat—a technique we've used in several other recipes, such as Weeknight Roast Chicken, Shrimp Salad, and even Foolproof Boiled Corn—provides insurance against overcooking. After 15 minutes off the heat, the temperatures of the seafood and the cooking liquid equalize at about 140 degrees, our preferred doneness temperature for whitefish such as cod.

Making sure the stew is at a full boil before adding the cold seafood is key for proper cooking—note the significant drop in temperature at the outset. If the stew wasn't at 212 degrees, the seafood would be undercooked.

Best-Ever Hot Sauce?

The tangy, creamy hot pepper sauce for our *moqueca*—made with pickled cherry peppers, onion, olive oil, and a pinch of sugar—is so good that we guarantee you're going to want to make more to put on everything from eggs to tacos to rice.

- 1 pound skinless cod fillets (¾ to 1 inch thick), cut into 1½-inch pieces
- 3 garlic cloves, minced
- Salt and pepper
- 1 onion, chopped coarse
- 1 (14.5-ounce) can whole peeled tomatoes
- ¾ cup chopped fresh cilantro
- 2 tablespoons extra-virgin olive oil
- 1 red bell pepper, stemmed, seeded, and cut into ½-inch pieces
- 1 green bell pepper, stemmed, seeded, and cut into ½-inch pieces
- 1 (14-ounce) can coconut milk
- 2 tablespoons lime juice

1. FOR THE PEPPER SAUCE: Process all ingredients in food processor until smooth, about 30 seconds, scraping down sides of bowl as needed. Season with salt to taste and transfer to separate bowl. Rinse out processor bowl.

2. FOR THE STEW: Toss shrimp and cod with garlic, ½ teaspoon salt, and ¼ teaspoon pepper in bowl. Set aside.

3. Process onion, tomatoes and their juice, and ¼ cup cilantro in food processor until finely chopped and mixture has texture of pureed salsa, about 30 seconds.

4. Heat oil in large Dutch oven over medium-high heat until shimmering. Add red and green bell peppers and ½ teaspoon salt and cook, stirring frequently, until softened, 5 to 7 minutes. Add onion-tomato mixture and ½ teaspoon salt. Reduce heat to medium and cook, stirring frequently, until puree has reduced and thickened slightly, 3 to 5 minutes (pot should not be dry).

5. Increase heat to high, stir in coconut milk, and bring to boil (mixture should be bubbling across entire surface). Add seafood mixture and lime juice and stir to evenly distribute seafood, making sure all pieces are submerged in liquid. Cover pot and remove from heat. Let stand until shrimp and cod are opaque and just cooked through, 15 minutes.

6. Gently stir in 2 tablespoons pepper sauce and remaining ½ cup cilantro, being careful not to break up cod too much. Season with salt and pepper to taste. Serve, passing remaining pepper sauce separately.

Irish Brown Soda Bread

Ireland's everyday bread is so quick, foolproof, and wholesome that you'll want to make it every day, too.

⇒ BY ANDREA GEARY ⇐

Compared with the white soda bread strewn with raisins and caraway seeds that makes its annual appearance in the United States around St. Patrick's Day, Ireland's rustic brown soda bread might seem austere. It's traditionally made with just four ingredients: wholemeal flour (more about that later), baking soda, salt, and buttermilk. But those minimal ingredients make a crusty bread with a savory, nutty flavor that pairs well with a wide variety of foods. Soups, cheese, cured fish, beer, and hard cider all make excellent accompaniments, and it's equally good with a smear of salted butter. Considering its versatility, it's little wonder that brown soda bread is the preferred version in Ireland.

The other appeal of soda bread—both white and brown versions—is that it's dead simple to make. In fact, it's even easier and faster to make than so-called quick breads such as banana bread, because it contains fewer ingredients (there are no eggs, for instance) and they can all be mixed by hand in a single bowl. The mixture forms a thick dough, not a batter, which immediately gets shaped into a round: There's no kneading or proofing. Then it's scored on the top and baked, either free-form or in a pan, until it's risen, brown, and crusty.

You can serve brown soda bread alongside soup, cheese, or cured fish or simply slathered with good butter or marmalade.

What you get is a homemade whole-grain, multipurpose bread in less than an hour. I ate it often when I was in Ireland and returned home planning to make it just as regularly. But, as I discovered, the main ingredient, Irish wholemeal flour, is hard to come by in the States. I hoped that the closest equivalent, American whole-wheat flour, would suffice.

The Whole (Wheat) Story

I was optimistic that it would, since both domestic whole-wheat and Irish wholemeal flours consist of entire wheat kernels that have been dried and ground to a powder. So I followed a traditional recipe, combining 3 cups of whole-wheat flour (a straight substitution for wholemeal), 1½ teaspoons of baking soda, and 1 teaspoon of salt in a bowl. Then I stirred in 2 cups of buttermilk to make a shaggy dough. I turned it out onto the counter, shaped it into a round, and, as most recipes instruct, cut a shallow cross in the top to allow for expansion in the oven before baking it on a baking sheet for about 45 minutes. The process was indeed simple, but the loaf was disappointing.

Granted, lightness is not a characteristic attribute of brown soda bread, but this loaf hardly rose at all in the oven, so it was dense—real doorstop material. It also lacked the rustic crumb of authentic Irish breads, and it spread too much, so it was quite flat. Wondering if I had underestimated the importance of using that authentic Irish flour, I ordered some.

Side by side, the two flours actually looked quite different. The American whole-wheat flour, which does contain bran and germ, was uniformly ground very fine and had a monochrome deep-tan hue. The Irish flour was lighter in color, but it contained discrete pieces of bran and germ and felt rough when I rubbed it between my fingers. Those distinct bits, I guessed, were necessary to produce the coarser crumb I was after, and I proved it by making the same recipe again using the Irish flour. This bread was still as dense and flat as the previous loaf, but it had a nicely rustic texture that made it more like the bread I had eaten in Ireland.

The obvious way to replicate the bran and germ presence of the Irish flour? Add bran and germ to domestic whole-wheat flour. Doing so didn't make the loaf any less dense or flat, but it did interrupt the uniformity of the American flour, creating the rustic consistency I was after.

I tend to scoff when people talk in terms of anything more than 100 percent. But as I did the math, I realized that by adding bran and germ to whole-wheat flour, I had created a loaf that was roughly 150 percent whole wheat. That extra jolt actually made the bread taste too wheaty, but I'd worry about that later and stay focused on the texture for now.

Liftoff

In this bare-bones recipe, the lift is dependent upon the acidic buttermilk reacting with the alkaline baking soda to create carbon dioxide gas, which gets trapped in the dough. When the dough heats up in the oven, the trapped gas expands and the bread rises. At least, that's what is supposed to happen.

But that reaction between buttermilk and baking soda is both instant and fleeting. Lacking the deftness and muscle memory of a lifelong soda bread baker, I was probably taking too long to get the

The Other Irish Soda Bread

The white-flour version of Irish soda bread shares a name and a basic round shape with the more rustic brown version, but that's about it. Whereas brown bread is craggy, coarse, and savory, the white kind tends to have a finer, tighter, sweeter crumb and is typically strewn with either currants or raisins and/or caraway seeds.

Soda Makes the Flavor Pop

You don't need baking soda to leaven Irish soda bread. We discovered that baking powder is actually a more practical rising agent here because its chemical reaction that causes the bread to rise is not as time-sensitive or fleeting as that of baking soda.

But you do need baking soda for flavor. The loaf we made without it lacked this bread's mineral-y tang and salinity—and frankly, its identity. So we added back the soda for its flavor contribution (and for improved browning).

BLAND WITHOUT IT
Baking soda isn't crucial for leavening, but it is for flavor.

bread into the oven and possibly also knocking air out of the dough as I shaped it. Either way, there wasn't enough air left to lighten the loaf. Luckily, I found salvation in the pantry. Actually, I found baking powder, but it amounted to the same thing.

Baking powder came late to Ireland, so really old soda bread recipes don't call for it, but it's a far more reliable leavener than baking soda. It contains both acid and alkaline components, so it's a complete leavening system, but here's the really clever bit: Some of the acids don't dissolve until they warm up, so the chemical reaction is delayed until the dough is safely in the oven. The upshot: When you have baking powder in your recipe, you don't have to be as speedy or as gentle when handling the dough.

Flavor Makers

I made another loaf with American whole-wheat flour, wheat germ, and bran, this time substituting baking powder for the baking soda. I still mixed and shaped the dough minimally to preserve its craggy, rustic look. I slashed the top, and into the oven it went.

The baking powder did the trick, as I finally produced a risen loaf with the nubbly, coarse, tender crumb I was after. But while I no longer needed the baking soda for lift, I was surprised to discover that I missed its flavor. When I tried the loaf without the baking soda, my tastebuds were confused: It didn't have the tang of a yeast bread or the distinctive flavor of a soda bread (see "Soda Makes the Flavor Pop"). What's more, the crust looked a bit wan, since alkaline baking soda raises the pH of the dough and encourages browning. I'd add baking soda back to the recipe.

Since the wheat bran and germ were making the loaf too wheaty, I made some adjustments to my next loaf: I combined whole-wheat and white flour in a ratio of 2 to 1, and I added 2 teaspoons of sugar. I mixed in bran and germ for texture and baking powder for leavening. After adding baking soda and salt for flavor, I stirred in the buttermilk. This time I baked the dough in a cake pan instead of on a baking sheet. The pan gently corralled the soft dough in the oven, preventing too much spread, so the loaf expanded up as well as out.

Crusty and risen, with a coarse, tender crumb and slightly tangy flavor, this loaf finally checked all the boxes. Like the people of Ireland, I now had a quick and versatile soda bread I could enjoy every day.

IRISH BROWN SODA BREAD
MAKES ONE 8-INCH LOAF

Our favorite whole-wheat flour is King Arthur Premium. To ensure the best flavor, use fresh whole-wheat flour. Wheat bran can be found at natural foods stores or in the baking aisle of your supermarket. This bread is best when served on the day it is made, but leftovers can be wrapped in plastic wrap for up to 2 days.

- 2 cups (11 ounces) whole-wheat flour
- 1 cup (5 ounces) all-purpose flour
- 1 cup wheat bran
- ¼ cup wheat germ
- 2 teaspoons sugar
- 1½ teaspoons baking powder
- 1½ teaspoons baking soda
- 1 teaspoon salt
- 2 cups buttermilk

1. Adjust oven rack to middle position and heat oven to 375 degrees. Lightly grease 8-inch round cake pan. Whisk whole-wheat flour, all-purpose flour, wheat bran, wheat germ, sugar, baking powder, baking soda, and salt together in medium bowl.

2. Add buttermilk and stir with rubber spatula until all flour is moistened and dough forms soft, ragged mass. Transfer dough to counter and gently shape into 6-inch round (surface will be craggy). Using serrated knife, cut ½-inch-deep cross about 5 inches long on top of loaf. Transfer to prepared pan. Bake until loaf is lightly browned and center registers 185 degrees, 40 to 45 minutes, rotating pan halfway through baking.

3. Invert loaf onto wire rack. Reinvert loaf and let cool for at least 1 hour. Slice and serve.

Making Ireland's Bread Without Ireland's Flour

The main ingredient in Irish brown bread, wholemeal flour, is responsible not only for the loaf's nutty flavor but also for its craggy crumb. But that product isn't easily found in the States, and we discovered that the domestic equivalent, whole-wheat flour, doesn't deliver the same coarse consistency. What's the difference? The size of the grind. Whereas whole-wheat flour is ground uniformly fine, wholemeal contains distinct bits of bran and germ that produce a coarse crumb. To mimic that texture, we supplement whole-wheat flour with additional bran and germ, which disrupt the uniform consistency of domestic flour.

Hearth-Baked Original

The first Irish soda bread would have been made in an open hearth over a turf fire. The cook would have heated a footed cast-iron pot called a bastable in the glowing coals, placed the shaped loaf inside, put the lid on concave side up, and filled the lid's cavity with coals so that the loaf would bake evenly. Just for fun, we simulated this setup with a similar lidded cast-iron vessel, which we set on bricks over the coals to raise the pan as feet would.

POT O' BROWN BREAD
Baking our brown soda bread in a covered cast-iron pot that we set over coals produced a loaf with a particularly thick, well-browned crust.

The Quickest Bread, Even Quicker

Since all the wheat components in this bread are best stored in the freezer, we made up a mix that can be frozen and used to make fresh bread in a flash. You can even take the mix with you on vacation.

➤ **Here's how to do it:** Combine one batch of dry ingredients with ½ cup of powdered buttermilk and freeze the mixture in a zipper-lock bag for up to six months. When ready to use, simply transfer the mix to a bowl, stir in 2 cups of water, and proceed with the recipe as directed.

▶ Watch: Bread in 1 Hour
A step-by-step video is available at CooksIllustrated.com/apr18

Moroccan Lentil and Chickpea Soup

Spices play more than just a supporting role in this hearty North African soup.

≥ BY STEVE DUNN ≤

If you only know lentil soup as a plain and rather homogeneous dish, prepare to be wowed by the Moroccan version known as *harira*. Not only is this soup, which is native to the Maghreb region of North Africa, full of warm spices and fresh herbs, but it's usually bulked up with chickpeas or fava beans, pasta or rice, tomatoes, hearty greens, and sometimes even lamb, beef, or chicken. The hearty base is usually brightened with a good bit of lemon juice and maybe a spoonful of the spicy North African chili paste, harissa. No wonder it's often the first dish Muslims eat when they break their daily fast during Ramadan.

Like countless other regional dishes, harira's exact ingredients vary from region to region and even from family to family. I wanted my version to be doable on a weeknight and ideally call mainly for staples I already had on hand. I also decided to omit any meat—with all the other robust flavors and textures in the mix, I wasn't sure what more it could offer.

Happily, dried lentils take only about 20 minutes to cook. Since fava beans in any form are hard to find, I opted for chickpeas—canned was a must. Harira recipes can call for a dozen or more spices, but I pared down the list to five that would contribute different flavor notes: cumin and cinnamon for warmth; smoked paprika for depth; coriander for nutty, floral notes; and a tiny bit of crushed red pepper for a hint of heat. Instead of the dried ginger I saw in some recipes, I opted for the brighter zing of fresh ginger. I decided to limit the fresh herbs to cilantro and parsley, and to use an abundance of them, a total of more than 1 cup. I began by sautéing onion, celery, garlic, and ginger in oil and then added tomato paste, my dried spices, and the fresh herbs. Dried lentils, canned chickpeas, and water went in next, followed by crushed tomatoes and a handful of orzo, a common choice. When the pasta was halfway cooked, I added some chopped Swiss chard before finishing the soup with lemon juice. The result? My soup tasted more like Italian minestrone than North African harira.

In my next batch, I eliminated the tomato paste and increased the smoked paprika and coriander, two of the most distinctive spices in the mix. For more depth, I also replaced half the water with chicken broth (any more and the soup tasted too chicken-y)

My soup was just about there, but it lacked the freshness of some versions I'd tried. The solution: I reserved ¼ cup each of the parsley and cilantro to add off the heat before serving.

My tasters certainly agreed: This wonderfully complex-tasting, spice-filled soup, made almost entirely from pantry ingredients, brings humble lentils to a whole new level.

Lemon and herbs balance the soup's warm spices.

Spice Cabinet Need a Refresh? Now's the Time.

Our soup calls for more than 5 teaspoons of dried spices—so make sure yours are fresh. How to tell? Give them a sniff. If they've lost their pungent aroma, it's time to replace them. In general, ground spices retain their flavor and aroma for about a year when stored in a cool, dark place.

▶ **Steve Makes the Soup**
A step-by-step video is available at CooksIllustrated.com/apr18

MOROCCAN LENTIL AND CHICKPEA SOUP (HARIRA)
SERVES 6 TO 8

For a vegetarian version, substitute vegetable broth for the chicken broth and water. We like to garnish this soup with a small amount of harissa, a fiery North African chili paste, which is available at some supermarkets. For our DIY version, see page 29.

- ⅓ cup extra-virgin olive oil
- 1 large onion, chopped fine
- 2 celery ribs, chopped fine
- 5 garlic cloves, minced
- 1 tablespoon grated fresh ginger
- 2 teaspoons ground coriander
- 2 teaspoons smoked paprika
- 1 teaspoon ground cumin
- ½ teaspoon ground cinnamon
- ⅛ teaspoon red pepper flakes
- ¾ cup minced fresh cilantro
- ½ cup minced fresh parsley
- 4 cups chicken broth
- 4 cups water
- 1 (15-ounce) can chickpeas, rinsed
- 1 cup brown lentils, picked over and rinsed
- 1 (28-ounce) can crushed tomatoes
- ½ cup orzo
- 4 ounces Swiss chard, stemmed and cut into ½-inch pieces
- 2 tablespoons lemon juice
- Salt and pepper
- Lemon wedges

1. Heat oil in large Dutch oven over medium-high heat until shimmering. Add onion and celery and cook, stirring frequently, until translucent and starting to brown, 7 to 8 minutes. Reduce heat to medium, add garlic and ginger, and cook until fragrant, 1 minute. Stir in coriander, paprika, cumin, cinnamon, and pepper flakes and cook for 1 minute. Stir in ½ cup cilantro and ¼ cup parsley and cook for 1 minute.

2. Stir in broth, water, chickpeas, and lentils; increase heat to high and bring to simmer. Reduce heat to medium-low, partially cover, and gently simmer until lentils are just tender, about 20 minutes.

3. Stir in tomatoes and pasta and simmer, partially covered, for 7 minutes, stirring occasionally. Stir in chard and continue to cook, partially covered, until pasta is tender, about 5 minutes longer. Off heat, stir in lemon juice, remaining ¼ cup cilantro, and remaining ¼ cup parsley. Season with salt and pepper to taste. Serve, passing lemon wedges separately.

Sweeter and Easier Than Broccoli

The trick to cooking slender, verdant broccolini is best illustrated using long division.

≥ BY STEVE DUNN ≤

You have to hand it to the botanists at Sakata Seed Corporation. When they crossbred conventional broccoli and Chinese broccoli in the early 1990s, the resulting broccolini plant combined the best traits of the two parents with virtually none of their flaws. Whereas broccoli is thick and sturdy and its flavor can be slightly bitter, broccolini is svelte, with the asparagus-like crunch and sweetness of Chinese broccoli. Broccolini also trades broccoli's densely packed crowns and the Chinese version's abundance of cabbagey leaves for just a few delicate, mild-tasting florets and greens. These traits make broccolini easy to prepare, too. There's no fibrous skin to strip away, no shrub-like crowns to break down, and no floret debris to sweep from the cutting board.

A lot of recipes call for treating broccolini like broccoli, searing or roasting it so that it develops flavorful browning. I did the same initially, but browning the vegetable overwhelmed its sweetness, and by the time color had developed, the once-crisp stalks were limp. So I decided to skip the sear and find a method that would preserve broccolini's delicate profile while allowing me to season it simply.

One way would be to blanch and shock the vegetable before sautéing it, plunging the whole stalks into boiling salted water and then submerging them in ice water to stop the cooking. The upshot is that the vegetable turns bright green, loses its raw crunch, and needs only a few minutes in a skillet to turn tender, thus minimizing browning. But I took a shortcut, a combined steam-sauté method that employs a covered skillet and just enough salted water to provide ample steam. Once the water was boiling, I added two trimmed broccolini bunches, threw on a lid, and lowered the heat. When I uncovered

Broccolini is an elegant alternative to broccoli.

the skillet a few minutes later, the water had mostly evaporated (that happens, even with a lid on) and the stalks and florets were vibrant green. But they weren't as perfectly cooked as they appeared; the thinner stems were crisp-tender, but the thicker pieces hid still-crunchy cores.

To equalize the cooking, I chopped the thicker ends into pieces and added them first to give them a head start, which worked fine. But in the same way that I'm hesitant to solve the age-old Thanksgiving problem—white and dark meat cook at different rates—by cooking turkey parts instead of a whole bird, I didn't want to forgo the vegetable's elegant length if I could help it. So instead of chopping the stems, I divided them lengthwise: the widest pieces from floret to base and the moderately thick pieces into two thinner "legs" that remained attached at the base of the florets. I left thinner lengths whole.

This quick knife work made all the difference, except that the stems no longer fit in a single layer in the skillet and those in direct contact with the pan cooked through more quickly. The solution was as simple as rearranging the stems midsteam so that each piece spent time on the skillet bottom.

I continued to cook the stalks until any excess liquid had evaporated and then, off the heat, tossed in some butter and various combinations of seasonings that complemented the broccolini's sweet flavor. I now had a side dish I could serve with, well, anything.

Split Decision

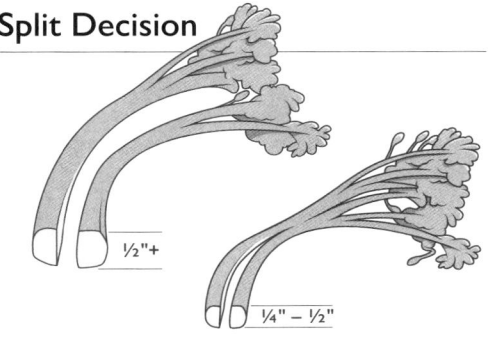

Cut stalks thicker than ½ inch in half lengthwise; for stalks between ¼ inch and ½ inch thick, slice the stalks only up to the florets, leaving the florets intact.

PAN-STEAMED BROCCOLINI WITH SHALLOT
SERVES 4 TO 6

Shake the rinsed broccolini over the sink to rid it of excess water before slicing the stems. If your skillet lid does not fit securely and allows too much steam to escape, add a bit more water in step 2 to keep the skillet from drying out. Our recipes for Pan-Steamed Broccolini with Lemon and Capers and Pan-Steamed Broccolini with Garlic and Mustard are available for free for four months at CooksIllustrated.com/apr18.

- 1 pound broccolini, trimmed and rinsed
- ⅓ cup water
- ½ teaspoon salt
- 2 tablespoons unsalted butter
- 2 teaspoons minced shallot
- 1 teaspoon grated lemon zest
- 1 teaspoon minced fresh thyme
- ¼ teaspoon pepper

1. Cut broccolini stalks measuring more than ½ inch in diameter at base in half lengthwise. Cut stalks measuring ¼ to ½ inch in diameter at base in half lengthwise, starting below where florets begin and keeping florets intact. Leave stalks measuring less than ¼ inch in diameter at base whole.

2. Bring water to boil in 12-inch skillet over high heat. Add broccolini and sprinkle with salt. Cover, reduce heat to medium-low, and cook for 3 minutes. Uncover and gently toss broccolini with tongs; cover and continue to cook until broccolini is bright green and crisp-tender, 3 to 5 minutes longer. Uncover and cook until any remaining liquid evaporates, about 30 seconds. Remove skillet from heat.

3. Push broccolini to 1 side of skillet. Add butter, shallot, lemon zest, thyme, and pepper to cleared side of skillet and stir to combine. Using tongs, toss broccolini with butter mixture until evenly coated, transfer to platter, and serve.

PAN-STEAMED BROCCOLINI WITH GINGER

Reduce lemon zest to ½ teaspoon. Substitute 2 teaspoons grated fresh ginger and ¼ teaspoon honey for shallot and thyme.

▶ Watch: Better Than Broccoli
A step-by-step video is available at CooksIllustrated.com/apr18

Quick Pasta Sauces, Perfected

We retooled a week's worth of classic sauces to keep in our back pockets for busy nights. BY ELIZABETH BOMZE

QUICK TOMATO SAUCE

What Can Go Wrong: With little time to simmer and meld flavors, quick tomato sauces can taste dull or, worse, like you simply dumped a can of tomatoes on the pasta.

How We Fix It: Minimally processed crushed tomatoes offer bright, fresh flavor and preclude the need to puree whole canned tomatoes ourselves. Grating the onion releases a lot of its flavor quickly. Sautéing the onion in butter, versus oil, contributes rich meatiness from the browned milk solids. Garlic; oregano; and a touch of sugar; plus basil and olive oil further ramp up the flavor.

Cooking Time: 15 minutes

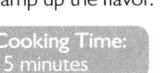

GRATE ONION
Efficiently creates more of the compounds that give cooked onion complex flavor

- 2 tablespoons unsalted butter
- ¼ cup grated onion
- 1 teaspoon minced fresh oregano or ¼ teaspoon dried
- Salt and pepper
- 2 garlic cloves, minced
- 1 (28-ounce) can crushed tomatoes
- ¼ teaspoon sugar
- 2 tablespoons chopped fresh basil
- 1 tablespoon extra-virgin olive oil

Melt butter in medium saucepan over medium heat. Add onion, oregano, and ½ teaspoon salt and cook, stirring occasionally, until onion is softened and lightly browned, 5 to 7 minutes. Stir in garlic and cook until fragrant, about 30 seconds. Stir in tomatoes and sugar, bring to simmer, and cook until slightly thickened, about 10 minutes. Off heat, stir in basil and oil and season with salt and pepper to taste. Add sauce to pasta and toss well to coat, adjusting consistency with pasta cooking water as needed.

PUTTANESCA

What Can Go Wrong: Assertive flavors such as anchovies, garlic, olives, capers, and pepper flakes can overwhelm a sauce.

How We Fix It: Gently sautéing the garlic, anchovies, and pepper flakes in oil mellows and blends their flavors. We use diced tomatoes, since they retain their shape better than whole or crushed products; the bright, sweet-tasting tomato pieces balance the other flavors and yield a sauce with a chunky texture. Drizzling olive oil over each portion adds richness.

SAUTÉ AROMATICS
Mellows and melds assertive anchovy and garlic flavors

Cooking Time: 15 minutes

- 2 tablespoons extra-virgin olive oil, plus extra for drizzling
- 8 anchovy fillets, rinsed, patted dry, and minced
- 4 garlic cloves, minced
- 1 teaspoon red pepper flakes
- 1 (28-ounce) can diced tomatoes, drained
- ½ cup pitted kalamata olives, chopped coarse
- ¼ cup minced fresh parsley
- 3 tablespoons capers, rinsed
- Salt

1. Heat oil, anchovies, garlic, and pepper flakes in 12-inch skillet over medium heat. Cook, stirring often, until garlic turns golden but not brown, about 3 minutes. Stir in tomatoes and cook until slightly thickened, about 8 minutes.

2. Stir in olives, parsley, and capers. Add sauce to pasta and toss well to coat, adjusting consistency with pasta cooking water as needed. Season with salt to taste. Drizzle extra oil over individual portions and serve immediately.

CLASSIC BASIL PESTO

What Can Go Wrong: Sharp raw garlic can overpower delicate, aromatic basil. The basil can also turn a drab, unappealing dark green.

How We Fix It: To mellow the garlic, we toast unpeeled cloves in a dry skillet before processing. Adding parsley (which doesn't discolor as easily as basil) helps keep the pesto green. Pounding the herbs before pureeing them releases their flavorful oils.

TOAST UNPEELED GARLIC CLOVES
Softens and sweetens garlic's harsh bite

Prep Time: 10 minutes

- 3 garlic cloves, unpeeled
- 2 cups fresh basil leaves
- 2 tablespoons fresh parsley leaves
- 7 tablespoons extra-virgin olive oil
- ¼ cup pine nuts, toasted
- Salt and pepper
- ¼ cup grated Parmesan cheese, plus extra for serving

1. Toast garlic in small, heavy skillet over medium heat, shaking skillet occasionally, until fragrant and color of cloves deepens slightly, about 7 minutes. Let garlic cool slightly, then peel and chop.

2. Place basil and parsley in heavy-duty 1-gallon zipper-lock bag. Pound bag with flat side of meat pounder or rolling pin until all leaves are bruised.

3. Process oil, pine nuts, ½ teaspoon salt, garlic, and basil-parsley mixture in food processor until smooth, about 1 minute, scraping down sides of bowl as needed. Stir in Parmesan and season with salt and pepper to taste. Add sauce to pasta and toss well to coat, adjusting consistency with pasta cooking water as needed. Serve, passing extra Parmesan separately.

Pasta Sauce Pantry Staples

High-quality ingredients make a big difference in any sauce. Here are our favorites.

Muir Glen Organic Whole Peeled Tomatoes

Hunt's Diced Tomatoes

SMT Crushed Tomatoes

Goya Tomato Paste

King Oscar Anchovies— Flat Fillets in Olive Oil

California Olive Ranch Extra Virgin Olive Oil

CHOOSE YOUR NOODLE
Each recipe will sauce 1 pound of pasta, serving 4 to 6, and the sauces pair well with any pasta shape.

DON'T DUMP THE WATER!
Each sauce relies on the addition of pasta cooking water, so be sure to reserve at least ½ cup before draining. Set a measuring cup in the colander to remind yourself.

GARLIC AND OIL SAUCE (AGLIO E OLIO)

What Can Go Wrong: The garlic tastes harsh, and the oil-based sauce doesn't cling to the pasta.
How We Fix It: Treating the minced garlic two different ways—gently sautéing some of it until pale golden brown and then stirring in the rest raw—yields garlic flavor that is nutty, mellow, and sweet, with a pleasantly sharp finish. We use the pasta cooking water as the sauce's base, not just to adjust its consistency. The starchy liquid helps the sauce cling to the noodles and helps evenly distribute the garlicky oil.

BUILD SAUCE WITH PASTA COOKING WATER
Helps sauce cling to pasta; evenly distributes garlic flavor

Cooking Time: 15 minutes

- 6 tablespoons extra-virgin olive oil
- 12 garlic cloves, minced
- Salt
- 3 tablespoons chopped fresh parsley
- 2 teaspoons lemon juice
- ¾ teaspoon red pepper flakes
- Grated Parmesan cheese

1. Heat 3 tablespoons oil, two-thirds of garlic, and ½ teaspoon salt in 10-inch nonstick skillet over low heat. Cook, stirring constantly, until garlic foams and is sticky and straw-colored, about 10 minutes. Off heat, add parsley, lemon juice, pepper flakes, remaining garlic, and 2 tablespoons reserved pasta cooking water.

2. Add garlic mixture and remaining 3 tablespoons oil to pasta and toss well to coat, adjusting consistency with pasta cooking water as needed. Season with salt to taste, and serve immediately, passing Parmesan separately.

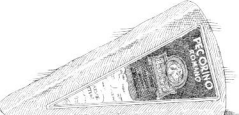

Boar's Head Parmigiano-Reggiano | Boar's Head Pecorino Romano (see page 27)

SIMPLE ITALIAN-STYLE MEAT SAUCE

What Can Go Wrong: The ground meat dries out. The meaty flavor is only superficial.
How We Fix It: We brown mushrooms, onion, and tomato paste to develop meaty flavor without browning (and drying out) the beef. Blending bread and milk into the meat keeps it tender. Crushed and diced tomatoes add body and bright flavor.

BROWN VEGETABLES, NOT MEAT
Develops meaty flavor without drying out meat

Cooking Time: 45 minutes

- 4 ounces white mushrooms, trimmed
- 1 slice hearty white sandwich bread, torn into quarters
- 2 tablespoons whole milk
- Salt and pepper
- 1 pound 85 percent lean ground beef
- 1 tablespoon olive oil
- 1 large onion, chopped fine
- 6 garlic cloves, minced
- 1 tablespoon tomato paste
- ¼ teaspoon red pepper flakes
- 1 (14.5-ounce) can diced tomatoes, drained with ¼ cup juice reserved
- 1 teaspoon dried oregano
- 1 (28-ounce) can crushed tomatoes
- ¼ cup grated Parmesan cheese, plus extra for serving

1. Process mushrooms in food processor until finely chopped, about 8 pulses, scraping down sides of bowl as needed; transfer mushrooms to bowl. Process bread, milk, ½ teaspoon salt, and ½ teaspoon pepper in now-empty processor until paste forms, about 8 pulses. Add beef and pulse until mixture is well combined, about 6 pulses.

2. Heat oil in large saucepan over medium-high heat until just smoking. Add onion and mushrooms and cook, stirring frequently, until vegetables are browned and dark bits form on saucepan bottom, 6 to 12 minutes. Stir in garlic, tomato paste, and pepper flakes; cook until fragrant, about 1 minute. Add reserved tomato juice and oregano, scraping up any browned bits. Add beef mixture and cook, breaking meat into small pieces, until beef is no longer pink, 2 to 4 minutes.

3. Stir in crushed tomatoes and diced tomatoes and bring to simmer. Reduce heat to low and gently simmer until sauce has thickened and flavors have blended, about 30 minutes. Stir in Parmesan and season with salt and pepper to taste. Add sauce to pasta and toss well to coat, adjusting consistency with pasta cooking water as needed. Serve, passing extra Parmesan separately.

AMATRICIANA

What Can Go Wrong: *Guanciale*, which is made by salting and drying hog jowls, is hard to find in the States. Stirring grated Pecorino Romano into the hot pasta causes the cheese to clump.
How We Fix It: We swap guanciale for easy-to-find salt pork (salt-cured, unsmoked pork belly). Simmering it first renders its fat, which allows the meat to quickly brown once the water evaporates. Mixing the cheese with rendered pork fat prevents it from clumping (the fat keeps the cheese proteins dispersed so they don't bond to each other in clumps) and adds extra pork flavor to the dish.

MIX CHEESE WITH PORK FAT
Prevents cheese from clumping; distributes rich pork flavor

Cooking Time: 30 minutes

Use salt pork that is 70 percent fat and freeze it for 15 minutes to make it easier to slice. Use imported Pecorino Romano cheese, not domestic cheese labeled "Romano."

- 8 ounces salt pork, rind removed, rinsed thoroughly and patted dry
- ½ cup water
- 2 tablespoons tomato paste
- ½ teaspoon red pepper flakes
- ¼ cup red wine
- 1 (28-ounce) can diced tomatoes
- 2 ounces Pecorino Romano cheese, grated fine (1 cup)

1. Slice pork into ¼-inch-thick strips, then cut each strip crosswise into ¼-inch pieces. Bring pork and water to simmer in 10-inch nonstick skillet over medium heat; cook until water evaporates and pork begins to sizzle, 5 to 8 minutes. Reduce heat to medium-low and continue to cook, stirring frequently, until fat renders and pork turns golden, 5 to 8 minutes longer. Using slotted spoon, transfer pork to bowl. Pour off fat from skillet and set aside.

2. Return skillet to medium heat and add 1 tablespoon reserved fat, tomato paste, and pepper flakes; cook, stirring constantly, for 20 seconds. Stir in wine and cook for 30 seconds. Stir in tomatoes and their juice and pork and bring to simmer. Cook, stirring frequently, until thickened, 12 to 16 minutes. While sauce simmers, smear 2 tablespoons reserved fat and ½ cup Pecorino together in bowl to form paste.

3. Add sauce, ⅓ cup pasta cooking water, and Pecorino-fat mixture to pasta and toss well to coat, adjusting consistency with remaining cooking water as needed. Serve, passing remaining ½ cup Pecorino separately.

No-Fear Caramel

Whether you've been burned by caramel in the past or have questions to sort out before making your first batch, we're here to help.

> BY LAN LAM <

I've had plenty of trials with fancy layer cakes and macarons—dishes that challenge even the most experienced chefs—but if you ask me, the task with the real intimidation factor is caramel. It's something I've been making for more than 30 years but have only recently mastered, let alone understood.

That's because the process of making caramel is riddled with pitfalls. Sugar can melt unevenly and burn or crystallize, leaving you with a gritty mess. Many recipes offer tweaks to prevent these mishaps, but there's little agreement on what actually works.

I tested every variable and question I could think of until I had a firm grip on what makes caramel succeed and fail (keep reading—I'll walk you through everything I learned) and a technique that even novice cooks will feel confident about.

What exactly is caramel?
"Caramelization" is the term used to describe the chain of chemical reactions that occurs when sugar is heated to the point at which its molecules break down and create hundreds of new compounds. Some of these compounds give caramel its rich color while others are aromatic and flavorful. The longer a caramel is cooked, the more sugar breaks down into these compounds, and the less sweet a caramel will taste.

How does the basic process work?
You melt sugar and cook it until it browns. This action forms a basic caramel.

Do I need to add water to the sugar?
Definitely. If you cook sugar alone—a "dry caramel"—you run the risk that some will burn before the rest caramelizes. Adding water, which makes a "wet caramel," helps the sugar melt evenly.

Is a thermometer necessary?
Yes. Judging caramel's doneness by visual cues

▶ Watch: Worry-Free Caramel
A step-by-step video is available at CooksIllustrated.com/apr18

Once you've caramelized sugar, you add butter or liquid (cream, broth, or vinegar) to make everything from a fluid sauce to candy to a savory glaze.

such as its color isn't foolproof (see "Don't Judge Caramel by Color Alone" on page 30). The only reliable way to assess its doneness is to take its temperature.

What about heavy-bottomed cookware?
You do need a heavy-bottomed pot. Lightweight cookware heats unevenly and creates hot spots where the sugar can burn.

Does burner temperature matter?
It does. The key to caramelizing sugar so that it's flavorful but not burnt is cooking it to a specific temperature (see "When should I stop cooking?"), which can be tricky. Sugar burns easily over high heat, but the process can be tediously long over low heat. That's why we use two heat levels: We melt the sugar over medium-high heat and then reduce the heat to low when the caramel is straw-colored to provide a wider window for nailing the temperature.

When should I stop cooking?
It depends on the type of flavor you want. The degree to which you cook the sugar determines the caramel's flavor: the higher the temperature, the more complex and bitter it will taste. For our recipes, we cook the sugar to between 360 and 375 degrees.

How do I prevent crystallization?
When all the sugar molecules in a pan of melted sugar are identical sucrose molecules, they all fit neatly together side by side like bricks and form crystals. These crystals build up on the sides of the pan or at the surface of the caramel, making it grainy.

The best way to prevent crystallization is to make sure that other shapes of sugar molecules—not only sucrose—are present. The effect is like mixing round rocks into a box full of rectangular bricks: The bricks can no longer fit together neatly. There are two common approaches. The first is to add an acidic ingredient such as lemon juice to the sugar, which causes some of the sucrose molecules to break down into different sugar molecules (fructose and glucose), which interfere with sucrose crystallization. Or there's our preferred method: Replace some of the sucrose with glucose in the form of corn syrup. In addition to diluting the sucrose, corn syrup contains small carbohydrate

---

It Will Bubble, but Don't Worry!
Prepare yourself for some drama—a puff of steam and some vigorous bubbling—when you add the liquid to the caramelized sugar. It can look impressive, but it's merely a visual cue that the liquid is absorbing a lot of the heat from the caramel and essentially arresting the cooking process, which prevents the caramel from burning. There is nothing to fear: Once you stir the caramel, the theatrics will quickly die down.

Stirring ensures that no hot pockets of caramel remain.

Caramelizing Sugar the Foolproof Way
Follow these simple guidelines and you'll produce perfect caramel every time.

1. **USE HEAVY COOKWARE** to help prevent the sugar from burning.

2. **ADD WATER AND CORN SYRUP** to prevent crystallization.

3. **USE TWO HEAT LEVELS** to cook the caramel carefully but efficiently.

4. **TAKE THE CARAMEL'S TEMPERATURE** to know exactly when it is done.

HOW TO ACCURATELY TAKE THE TEMPERATURE OF CARAMEL

It's crucial to use a digital instant-read thermometer to measure the caramel's temperature.
1. To ensure an accurate reading, swirl the caramel to even out any hot spots.
2. Tilt the pan so that the caramel pools 1 to 2 inches deep.
3. Move the thermometer back and forth in the caramel for about 5 seconds before taking a reading.

---

molecules that slow the movement of the sugar molecules, reducing their chances of forming crystals.

How do I prevent caramel from burning?
Even if you nail the temperature of the caramel, the residual heat of the pan will continue to cook—and can burn—it. The key is to quickly stir in the liquid ingredient(s) or butter, which will rapidly absorb some of the heat and slow the cooking process. Note: The caramel will bubble vigorously when you add the liquid (see "It Will Bubble, but Don't Worry!").

How do I clean up a sticky pan?
The fastest way: Fill the pan about 1/3 full of water and bring it to a simmer over medium heat, stirring frequently. Do not use high heat: Caramel at the bottom of the pan will heat quickly, and any water in contact with it will turn to steam and splatter as it escapes.
The easiest way: Fill the pan with water and let it soak overnight. Wipe away sticky bits with a soapy sponge.

ALL-PURPOSE CARAMEL SAUCE
MAKES 2 CUPS

Serve this sauce over ice cream, cakes, or fresh fruit.

- 1¾ cups (12¼ ounces) granulated sugar
- ½ cup water
- ¼ cup light corn syrup
- 1 cup heavy cream
- 1 teaspoon vanilla extract
- ¼ teaspoon salt

1. Bring sugar, water, and corn syrup to boil in large heavy-bottomed saucepan over medium-high heat. Cook, without stirring, until mixture is straw-colored, 6 to 8 minutes. Reduce heat to low and continue to cook, swirling saucepan occasionally, until mixture is amber-colored and registers between 360 and 370 degrees, 2 to 5 minutes longer.

2. Off heat, quickly but carefully stir in cream, vanilla, and salt (mixture will bubble and steam). Continue to stir until sauce is smooth. (Sauce can be refrigerated for up to 2 weeks. Reheat in microwave, stirring frequently, until warm and smooth.)

SPICY CARAMEL POPCORN
MAKES ABOUT 3½ QUARTS

If using salted popcorn, decrease the salt to ¼ teaspoon. For spicier popcorn, use the greater amount of cayenne pepper. Salted roasted almonds can be used in place of the smoked almonds, if desired.

- 10 cups popped popcorn
- 1¼ cups granulated sugar
- ½ cup water
- ⅓ cup light corn syrup
- 6 tablespoons unsalted butter
- ½ teaspoon salt
- ⅛–¼ teaspoon cayenne pepper
- ½ teaspoon baking soda
- ⅔ cup smoked almonds, chopped coarse

1. Lightly spray large bowl and rimmed baking sheet with vegetable oil spray. Place popcorn in prepared bowl. Bring sugar, water, and corn syrup to boil in medium heavy-bottomed saucepan over medium-high heat. Cook, without stirring, until mixture is straw-colored, 6 to 8 minutes. Reduce heat to medium-low and continue to cook, swirling saucepan occasionally, until mixture is dark amber and registers between 365 and 375 degrees, 2 to 5 minutes longer.

2. Off heat, quickly but carefully add butter, salt, and cayenne; stir until fully combined (mixture will bubble and steam). Return saucepan to low heat, stir in baking soda, and cook, stirring constantly, until mixture is uniform in color. Pour caramel over popcorn and, working quickly, stir until well coated. (Use towel or oven mitt to hold bowl, and avoid touching hot caramel.) Stir in almonds. Transfer mixture to prepared sheet and spread into even layer. Let cool for 15 minutes. Break cooled popcorn into pieces of desired size. (Popcorn can be stored in airtight container at room temperature for up to 5 days.)

CARAMEL-BRAISED SHALLOTS WITH BLACK PEPPER
SERVES 4

For the best results, we recommend buying shallots that measure 1½ to 2 inches long and 1½ inches in diameter for this recipe. Halve large shallots through the root end so that the root keeps each half intact. Serve the braised shallots alongside roasted or grilled meats, or chop them to use as a spread for sandwiches or burgers. Laurent du Clos Red Wine Vinegar is the test kitchen's favorite.

- ½ cup water
- ⅓ cup granulated sugar
- 2 tablespoons light corn syrup
- 1½ cups chicken broth
- 2 tablespoons unsalted butter
- 1½ pounds small shallots, peeled
- 1 teaspoon minced fresh thyme
- Salt and pepper
- ⅓ cup red wine vinegar
- 2 tablespoons chopped fresh parsley

1. Bring water, sugar, and corn syrup to boil in 10-inch skillet over medium-high heat. Cook, without stirring, until sugar at edges of skillet is straw-colored, 5 to 8 minutes. Reduce heat to medium-low and cook, swirling skillet occasionally, until mixture is dark amber and registers between 365 and 375 degrees, 1 to 3 minutes.

2. Off heat, quickly but carefully stir in broth and butter (mixture will bubble and steam). Stir in shallots, thyme, 1 teaspoon pepper, and ½ teaspoon salt. (Salt does not need to be fully dissolved.) Return skillet to heat and bring to boil. Reduce heat to medium, cover, and cook until shallots are tender, 12 to 14 minutes.

3. Uncover and gently boil until sauce has consistency of maple syrup, 9 to 12 minutes. Add vinegar and continue to cook, swirling occasionally, until sauce has returned to consistency of maple syrup, 3 to 5 minutes longer. Off heat, stir in parsley and season with salt and pepper to taste. Serve.

Three-Cup Chicken

One cup each of soy sauce, sesame oil, and rice wine is easy to remember. Too bad it doesn't work. We figured out a better formula and streamlined the recipe.

≥ BY STEVE DUNN ≤

Long ago—in 1283, to be exact, if stories are to be believed—the warden of a military prison in Dadu (modern Beijing) prepared the final meal for Wen Tianxiang, a Song dynasty patriot. Legend has it that on the eve of the execution, with just a handful of ingredients at his disposal—soy sauce, sesame oil, and rice wine—the warden invented a chicken recipe by combining 1 cup of each ingredient. *San bei ji*, or three-cup chicken, as it has come to be known, must have been well received, for in the ensuing years, the recipe was adopted by neighboring Taiwan and has since evolved into a national dish of sorts. These days, chiles are included for heat, along with generous amounts of fresh ginger, garlic, scallions, and Thai basil. Intrigued by the robust, aromatic flavors, I got to work on creating my own version of the dish.

Breaking It Down

Many recipes start with instructions for butchering a whole bird into 2- to 3-inch pieces, a job requiring a heavy cleaver and more than a little bit of nerve. Even in the loud, busy test kitchen, the violent sounds produced as I hacked thighs and legs into bite-size chunks raised a few eyebrows. In addition, tasters struggled to eat the small, bone-in, skin-on chicken pieces—a common preparation in Taiwan but one that runs counter to our expectations here. Looking for alternatives, I ruled out whole bone-in parts—if I was veering from tradition, I might as well try to make the dish as speedy as possible. Instead, I settled on boneless, skinless thighs; their rich flavor would stand up to the potent sauce better than that of milder breasts. I cut them into 2-inch pieces that would cook in well under 30 minutes.

Many modern recipes call for stir-frying the chicken and aromatics in untoasted sesame oil in a wok before adding the soy sauce and wine. I got my skillet good and hot and browned the chicken,

Thinly sliced scallions, fresh Thai basil, and plenty of garlic and ginger complement the savory elements of the dish.

which took a bit of time because I had to do it in batches to avoid crowding. As I worked, I began to question why I was bothering with this step at all. Browning is normally used to build deep flavor, but here, where a sauce rich in soy sauce, wine, sesame, ginger, chiles, and garlic would dress the chicken, was it even necessary?

I quite literally put the chicken on the back burner to do more research, ultimately learning that history was on my side: In 13th-century China, the chicken for this dish wasn't browned at all. Instead, it was cooked in an earthenware pot until the sauce reduced to a glaze. Inspired by this finding, I eliminated the browning step and moved on to developing an efficient process whereby I would briefly marinate the chicken in what would become the cooking liquid. (Marinating is not traditional, but it would be an easy way to enhance the chicken's flavor.) I combined placeholder amounts of soy sauce and Chinese rice wine, added the chicken, and set it aside while I sautéed the aromatics (also placeholders) in the sesame oil. I then added the chicken and the marinade and brought it all to a simmer. It worked beautifully: Tasters didn't miss the browned flavor at all.

As we have found in other recipes, cooking the dark chicken meat until it registered 200 degrees (well beyond its food-safe point of 165 degrees) not only fully rendered any fat but also melted tough connective tissue into rich gelatin, which coats the meat's protein fibers, enhancing tenderness.

Matters of Taste

Having found a fuss-free method for tender chicken, I shifted my focus to the big, bold flavors that characterize this dish. Dealing with the aromatics turned out to be largely an exercise in how to prep them. Cutting the scallions into 2-inch lengths resulted in flabby pieces by the end of cooking, but slicing them thin on the bias delivered a pleasant texture. Grated ginger clouded the translucent sauce, so I sliced it into thin half-moons instead. Tasters praised these larger pieces for the spicy pop they

▶ See What "3-Cup" Means
A step-by-step video is available at CooksIllustrated.com/apr18.

Three Cups? Not So Much

Few modern recipes for three-cup chicken actually use the original formula of 1 cup each of untoasted sesame oil, soy sauce, and rice wine; a full cup of oil makes the dish greasy, and 1 cup each of soy sauce and rice wine take too long to reduce. We use just ⅓ cup each of soy sauce and dry sherry (our substitute for rice wine) and season the dish with a mere tablespoon of deeply aromatic toasted sesame oil.

TECHNIQUE | PEELING GINGER

Using a paring knife or a peeler on ginger is overkill since it removes too much of the flesh. Simply scrape the edge of a spoon along the ginger to remove the skin. Unlike the straight blade of a knife, the curved spoon is easy to maneuver around the root's irregular shape.

provided. As for the garlic, simply halving cloves lengthwise provided a sweet, mellow counterpoint to the spicy ginger. Instead of traditional Thai bird chiles, which can be hard to find, I opted for red pepper flakes, which are available everywhere. Finally, most recipes call for sautéing the aromatics in untoasted sesame oil, but since American cooks typically have only the toasted kind, which is not for cooking but rather for seasoning, I decided to sauté in vegetable oil and finish with a small amount of the potent toasted sesame oil.

As for the sauce, some recipes specify a large volume of ingredients (one even called for the original 1 cup each of soy sauce and wine) that takes a long time to reduce. In the end, I cut the total amount of liquid to only about ⅔ cup, tossing in a touch of sugar to balance the acidic sherry. Finally, for a silky consistency, I finished the sauce with a simple cornstarch slurry. A handful each of scallion greens and fragrant Thai basil contributed fresh elements.

In less than an hour and without having to wield a heavy cleaver, I had produced san bei ji that stayed true to its roots.

THREE-CUP CHICKEN
SERVES 4

We prefer the flavor of Thai basil in this recipe, but you can substitute sweet Italian basil, if desired (see page 29 for more information). For a spicier dish, use the larger amount of red pepper flakes. Serve with white rice. Our recipe for Three-Cup Chicken for Two is available for free for four months at CooksIllustrated.com/apr18.

- ⅓ cup soy sauce
- ⅓ cup Shaoxing wine or dry sherry
- 1 tablespoon packed brown sugar
- 1½ pounds boneless, skinless chicken thighs, trimmed and cut into 2-inch pieces
- 3 tablespoons vegetable oil
- 1 (2-inch) piece ginger, peeled, halved lengthwise, and sliced into thin half-rounds
- 12 garlic cloves, peeled and halved lengthwise
- ½–¾ teaspoon red pepper flakes
- 6 scallions, white and green parts separated and sliced thin on bias
- 1 tablespoon water
- 1 teaspoon cornstarch
- 1 cup Thai basil leaves, large leaves sliced in half lengthwise
- 1 tablespoon toasted sesame oil

1. Place rice in fine-mesh strainer set over bowl. Rinse under running water, swishing with your hands, until water runs clear. Drain thoroughly.
2. Bring rice and water to boil in saucepan over medium-high heat. Cook, uncovered, until water level drops below surface of rice and small holes form, about 5 minutes.
3. Reduce heat to low, cover, and cook until rice is tender and water is fully absorbed, about 15 minutes. Serve.

1. Whisk soy sauce, wine, and sugar together in medium bowl. Add chicken and toss to coat; set aside.
2. Heat vegetable oil, ginger, garlic, and pepper flakes in 12-inch nonstick skillet over medium-low heat. Cook, stirring frequently, until garlic is golden brown and beginning to soften, 8 to 10 minutes.
3. Add chicken and marinade to skillet, increase heat to medium-high, and bring to simmer. Reduce heat to medium-low and simmer for 10 minutes, stirring occasionally. Stir in scallion whites and continue to cook until chicken registers about 200 degrees, 8 to 10 minutes longer.
4. Whisk water and cornstarch together in small bowl, then stir into sauce; simmer until sauce is slightly thickened, about 1 minute. Remove skillet from heat. Stir in basil, sesame oil, and scallion greens. Transfer to platter and serve.

SHOPPING
Chinese Cooking Wines

Many Chinese recipes (ours included) call for Shaoxing rice wine, an amber-colored specialty of Shaoxing, China, that contributes distinctive savory, nutty flavors. But shopping for Shaoxing wine in the United States can be confusing because there are multiple products with similar names: authentic Shaoxing wine and Shaoxing cooking wine.

To see how each functioned in a recipe, we tasted them, as well as dry sherry (a common substitute for Shaoxing), in a beef stir-fry. All the products were acceptable, but we preferred the more complex, less salty flavors of the authentic Shaoxing wine and the dry sherry. –S.D.

Best choice: Authentic Shaoxing wine
Tip: This is sold in an elaborate bottle and only in liquor stores.

Good alternative: Dry sherry
Tip: Our favorite option, Lustau Palo Cortado Península Sherry ($19.99), delivered nutty, complex flavor. Avoid "sherry cooking wine," which lacks complexity and contains salt that we could taste.

Only in a pinch: Shaoxing cooking wines
Tip: These are made by adding salt (you'll see it listed on the label) to lower-quality wines so they become "undrinkable" and can therefore be sold in markets that aren't licensed to sell alcohol. We could taste the salinity, even in a stir-fry.

Chinese Restaurant–Style Rice

The rice served in Chinese restaurants is soft enough to soak up savory sauces and sticky enough to be picked up with chopsticks. Chinese cooks never salt their rice, making it an ideal accompaniment to highly flavorful and/or soy-heavy dishes such as three-cup chicken. We found that rinsing the grains removed some of their surface starch and that starting them in boiling water provided enough agitation to release the remaining starch, resulting in just the right amount of stickiness.

CHINESE RESTAURANT–STYLE RICE
SERVES 4 TO 6

Do not stir the rice as it cooks. The finished rice can stand off the heat, covered, for up to 15 minutes. Medium-grain or jasmine rice can also be used.

- 2 cups long-grain white rice
- 3 cups water

The Lemoniest Lemon Bars

What's the secret to bars with bold, multifaceted citrus flavor?
Cut back on the lemon juice.

≽ BY LAN LAM ≼

If tart, citrusy flavors are the rays of sunshine that brighten lemon bars, then thickeners are the storm clouds that cover them up. And therein lies a culinary catch-22: For bars with lots of lemon zing, you need lots of lemon juice. But the more juice you use, the more flavor-dulling binders—such as eggs and starch—are required to keep the filling firm and sliceable. My task was to find a way around this problem.

Laying the Foundation

With lemon bars, it's easy to overlook the crust and focus on the wobbly, creamy, lemony layer. And that's exactly what most recipes do. But not mine. Instead of a nondescript platform for the filling, I wanted a crisp crumb with buttery sweetness.

The typical crust is modeled on a British shortbread cookie. I made a classic version, using the food processor to cut cold butter into a mixture of flour, confectioners' sugar, and salt. To ensure that every bite would have the same ratio of crust to filling, I did my best to evenly press the crumbly mixture into an aluminum foil–lined 8-inch square pan. (The foil would facilitate removing the baked bars from the pan.) I had to work carefully because, once compressed, the mixture stayed put, and it became difficult to fill in thinner areas or level out thicker spots. I popped the pan into a 350-degree oven and let the crust bake for 25 minutes. This is longer than most recipes specify, but I hoped that deeper browning would produce an especially crisp, full-flavored crust.

When a buttery scent filled the kitchen, the crust was dark brown, so I pulled the pan from the oven. I topped the baked crust with a placeholder filling made by whisking lemon juice and eggs together with sugar and salt before returning the pan to the oven for 30 more minutes.

The longer baking time had indeed helped develop a rich taste. Unfortunately, it didn't make the crust any crispier. After brainstorming with my colleagues,

▶ **Lan Raises the Bar**
A step-by-step video is available at CooksIllustrated.com/apr18

For a silky-smooth texture, we parcook the filling on the stovetop, pour it onto a parbaked crust, and then bake the bars for just 10 minutes.

I realized why: The powdery sugar was producing a fine, delicate crumb that melted on my tongue. For a coarser, crunchier consistency, I needed coarser, crunchier granulated sugar. A side-by-side comparison of crusts made with both types of sugar confirmed it.

Finally, to make the dough easier to work with, I melted the butter in the microwave and stirred it into the flour. This created a pliable mass that was much easier to distribute evenly—with no adverse effect on the finished product. As a bonus, I no longer needed a food processor.

Flawless Filling

I now had a good base on which to showcase a bright, sweet-tart lemon filling. After my initial tests, I concluded that a filling that was twice as deep as the crust was most pleasant to eat (see "A Question of Proportions"); now I just needed to perfect the filling itself. I'd already fiddled with the simplest approach: whisking together lemon juice, sugar, salt, and a thickener—some combination of eggs, flour, and/or cornstarch—and baking until set. Unfortunately, by the time this filling was cooked at the center, its edges were curdled, as evidenced by pockmarks. A liberal dusting of confectioners' sugar, the baker's Band-Aid, disguised the unevenness, but nothing could camouflage the lumpy consistency. No matter how I tweaked the ingredients, oven temperature, and baking time, I couldn't fix this style of filling.

A more promising method required only marginally more work—the filling is precooked, poured over the crust, and baked until set. I gave it a try, cooking ⅔ cup of lemon juice, six eggs, 1 cup of sugar, and ¼ teaspoon of salt over medium heat. As soon as it reached a pudding-like consistency, I stirred in 4 tablespoons of butter for richness. I poured the filling over my baked crust and returned the pan to the oven. After 10 minutes, the curd barely jiggled when I shook the pan.

Less time in the oven had solved the textural issues since the edges and center of the filling now finished cooking at the same time: These bars boasted an incredibly smooth surface. However, their flavor was marred by egginess, and they lacked the requisite lemony punch. The former problem was relatively easy to solve. While developing Greek Chicken and Rice Soup with Egg and Lemon (March/April 2017), I learned that the sulfur compounds in egg whites are

What Is Cream of Tartar, Anyway?

The white, odorless powder known as cream of tartar is a product of grape fermentation. It is said to have been first isolated from the bottom of wine barrels by the Persian alchemist Jabir ibn Hayyan around 800 AD. Today, we know that tartaric acid, the acid component of cream of tartar, is found in the greatest concentration in grapes but is also present in bananas and tamarind. To make cream of tartar, the grape sediment, called beeswing, is scraped from wine barrels, purified, and ground. Using cream of tartar to boost acidic flavor as we do in our Best Lemon Bars is novel; it is most often incorporated into beaten egg whites for stability or into sugar syrup to help prevent crystallization.

SOUR NOTE
Cream of tartar enhances the tart taste of lemon bars.

TECHNIQUE
PAT-IN-THE-PAN CRUST

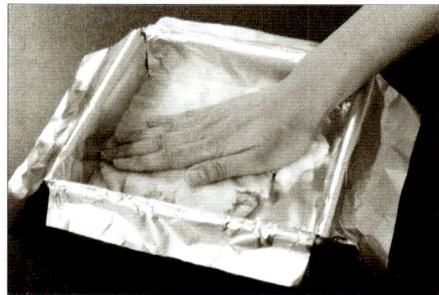

Most lemon bar crust recipes call for using a food processor to cut cold butter into flour. Our stripped-down approach calls for simply stirring melted butter into a mixture of flour, sugar, and salt. The upshot: a no-fuss, pliable dough that's easy to press into an even layer.

Incorporating lemony aroma would be easy: I could add lemon zest. Zest has even more volatile flavor chemicals than the juice, which is why it is so often added to foods to enhance lemony flavor. I found that 2 teaspoons of grated zest cooked into the filling (and later strained out) boosted its fruity flavor significantly. The trickier task was increasing that acidic punch in the filling without adding more liquid. What ingredient would help with that?

I flirted with the idea of purchasing powdered citric acid or grinding up vitamin C tablets (ascorbic acid). But then I realized I already had a truly sour-tasting powder in my pantry: cream of tartar. I whipped up two more batches of bars, one of which contained 2 teaspoons of cream of tartar. This was the magic ingredient: Tasters loved the bold sharpness of the bars containing cream of tartar, claiming they were unlike any others they'd tasted. And when they raved about the interplay of the tart, silky filling and the crisp, buttery crust, I knew I had a winner.

SCIENCE
Lemon Flavor That Lingers

To make our bars more lemony without adding more liquid, which would require a flavor-muting thickener, we turned to the science of flavor. When we chew, our brains register the five tastes (sweet, sour, salty, bitter, and umami) on the tongue and potentially a trillion aromas through a pathway in the back of the mouth that leads to the nasal passages. The dominant taste chemical in lemon juice, citric acid, is nonvolatile and registers only on the tongue. But lemon juice also contains a small amount of volatile compounds that give it subtle fruity-floral flavors as well.

With that in mind, we looked to lemon zest, which is full of the aromatic oils limonene, pinene, citral, neral, geranial, and linalool and would enhance the experience of lemon flavor in the nose. For a tangy boost from a nonliquid ingredient that would register on the tongue, we incorporated cream of tartar.

Together, these ingredients gave our lemon bars a complex lemony punch that was even better than if we'd added plain lemon juice.

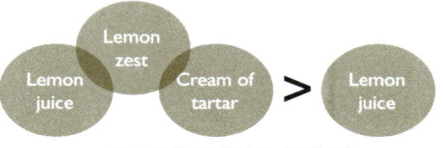

THREE TART FLAVORS TASTE BETTER THAN ONE

the source of eggy flavor. Reducing the number of whites by three took care of any egginess, but it also left the filling runny. That's because the proteins in the egg whites were providing structure when they set. After some experimentation, I found that I could replace that protein with the starch in 2 tablespoons of flour. This would dull the lemon flavor, but I'd get to that next.

Leaving a Sour Taste

As I'd known from the start, the flavor issue would be a challenge. Increasing the lemon juice was out of the question—I'd have to add even more flavor-dulling thickeners, which would defeat the purpose.

I took a step back to consider how flavor in lemon juice (and all foods) works: When you take a bite, you encounter taste with your tongue and aroma through a channel in the back of your mouth that leads directly to your nose. With lemon juice specifically, you taste only the tartness of its citric and malic acids on the tongue, while all the fruity, lemony flavors come from volatile compounds that shoot into that back door to your nasal passage when you exhale. So to add more lemon flavor without more lemon juice, I'd have to consider both taste and aroma.

BEST LEMON BARS
MAKES 12 BARS

Do not substitute bottled lemon juice for fresh here.

Crust
- 1 cup (5 ounces) all-purpose flour
- ¼ cup (1¾ ounces) granulated sugar
- ½ teaspoon salt
- 8 tablespoons unsalted butter, melted

Filling
- 1 cup (7 ounces) granulated sugar
- 2 tablespoons all-purpose flour
- 2 teaspoons cream of tartar
- ¼ teaspoon salt
- 3 large eggs plus 3 large yolks
- 2 teaspoons grated lemon zest plus ⅔ cup juice (4 lemons)
- 4 tablespoons unsalted butter, cut into 8 pieces

Confectioners' sugar (optional)

1. FOR THE CRUST: Adjust oven rack to middle position and heat oven to 350 degrees. Make foil sling for 8-inch square baking pan by folding 2 long sheets of aluminum foil so each is 8 inches wide. Lay sheets of foil in pan perpendicular to each other, with extra foil hanging over edges of pan. Push foil into corners and up sides of pan, smoothing foil flush to pan.

2. Whisk flour, sugar, and salt together in bowl. Add melted butter and stir until combined. Transfer mixture to prepared pan and press into even layer over entire bottom of pan (do not wash bowl). Bake crust until dark golden brown, 19 to 24 minutes, rotating pan halfway through baking.

3. FOR THE FILLING: While crust bakes, whisk sugar, flour, cream of tartar, and salt together in now-empty bowl. Whisk in eggs and yolks until no streaks of egg remain. Whisk in lemon zest and juice. Transfer mixture to saucepan and cook over medium-low heat, stirring constantly, until mixture thickens and registers 160 degrees, 5 to 8 minutes. Off heat, stir in butter. Strain filling through fine-mesh strainer set over bowl.

4. Pour filling over hot crust and tilt pan to spread evenly. Bake until filling is set and barely jiggles when pan is shaken, 8 to 12 minutes. (Filling around perimeter of pan may be slightly raised.) Let bars cool completely, at least 1½ hours. Using foil overhang, lift bars out of pan and transfer to cutting board. Cut into bars, wiping knife clean between cuts as necessary. Before serving, dust bars with confectioners' sugar, if using.

A Question of Proportions
After sampling unbalanced bars like the ones below, we experimented to find the ideal filling-to-crust ratio.

EQUAL—BUT BETTER?
In a 1:1 ratio, the buttery crust overwhelmed the lemony filling.

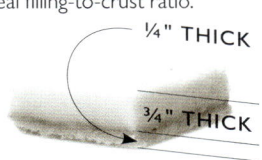

TOP-HEAVY
A superthick filling made the dessert seem more like a tart than a bar.

PROPER PROPORTIONS
The filling for our bars is twice as thick as the crust.

Testing Parchment Paper

Parchment paper is simple. Why are so many products hard to use?

> BY KATE SHANNON <

Whenever a piece of restaurant equipment becomes available to home cooks, we take notice. Replacing flimsy jelly roll pans with sturdy rimmed baking sheets changed the way we cook. Using bench scrapers and Y-shaped vegetable peelers made our prep work easier and more efficient. More expensive and esoteric tools, such as high-powered blenders, *sous vide* machines, and carbon-steel skillets, have also transitioned from restaurant to home kitchens.

Recently, a low-frills restaurant product appeared on supermarket shelves: parchment paper sheets, a precut version of the rolls that we have long used to line baking sheets. Since the sheets are cut to the dimensions of a standard rimmed baking sheet, no trimming is necessary, which saves time and waste. And unlike rolled parchment, which needs to be wrestled out of its box and smoothed, some parchment sheets store completely flat.

Given that not every restaurant product successfully transitions to home kitchens, we were curious how these new commercially inspired products would compare with traditional parchment paper rolls. To find out, we purchased 10 parchment paper products: seven rolls and three packages of precut sheets.

Parchment Performance

The primary function of parchment paper is to keep food from sticking to baking sheets. Happily, all the papers we tested produced cakes, cookies, and pizzas that were evenly baked and that released cleanly. The papers also performed well outside the oven. None tore under heavy pizzas or pie weights or caught fire in a 500-degree oven. (Even if products list lower maximum temperatures, we've learned from manufacturers that they're still safe to use in a hot oven.) When we sandwiched and rolled out disks of cookie dough between two sheets of each paper, none of them stuck to the dough, tore, or crumpled. So we turned our attention to how easy they were to use. In these evaluations, scores were anything but even.

For Parchment Rolls, Two Things Mattered

The user-friendliness of the rolls boiled down to two factors: size and cutting mechanism. We found that the dimensions of most of the rolls were too wide. The cooking surface of a standard rimmed baking sheet measures 16½ by 11½ inches, yet most of the rolls were between 13 and 15 inches wide. Positioning them in a baking sheet widthwise left a wide swath of the baking sheet exposed; positioning them lengthwise forced us to trim 1 to 3 inches of paper. On the widest rolls, about 15 inches across, that trimming resulted in 20 percent waste. Only one roll measured 12 inches across, almost the same width as our baking sheets.

We rolled multiple jelly roll cakes into coils to test the strength and flexibility of the parchment papers.

We preferred rolls that were easy to tear into sheets with straight, clean edges. Success was due to both the cutting mechanism and the packaging. Some products have simple designs: The user tears the paper against the front edge of the container. Boxes that weren't sturdy were a pain to use: The cutting edge folded over and became ineffective, meaning the parchment crumpled in the corners and tore jaggedly or jumped out of the widened opening and unspooled on the floor. Our favorite parchment roll products relied on tension: The front edge of the lid tucks inside the box (like a takeout pizza box), which holds the roll in place and provides a firm, blunt edge that facilitates straight, clean tears.

Were Precut Sheets Better?

All the precut sheets we tested fit in a standard rimmed baking sheet without trimming, and were big enough to use when rolling out disks of cookie dough, lifting pie weights, and maneuvering pizzas around the kitchen. They were too short by a few inches to use for rolling jelly roll cakes into coils, but using two overlapping sheets was an easy work-around.

And just as with the parchment rolls, packaging influenced which products we preferred. Two had compact boxes. In one of these, the sheets were rolled together in a way that allowed us to pull out a single sheet without unspooling the whole roll. Though it was easy to separate the sheets, it was a struggle to flatten them. Even when we positioned the curled edges down, the sheets often rerolled into a tight scroll. The other product was also frustrating; it was folded in quarters and packaged in a roughly 8 by 6-inch box. The sheets were so tightly creased that even the weight of cake batter or pizza dough wasn't enough to flatten the peaks and valleys. As a result, baked goods were marked with deep lines and Xs (see "Foiled by the Fold").

Our favorite parchment sheets were stored flat in a large zipper-lock bag, so they never got wrinkled, curled, or creased. Sized just right and perfectly smooth, they practically floated into baking sheets.

The Most Practical Paper

After weeks of tearing, trimming, and flattening parchment paper, we had a newfound appreciation for products that didn't require so much fuss. King Arthur Flour Parchment Paper 100 Half-Sheets ($19.95 for 100 sheets, plus shipping) is the only one that combines precut sheets—which eliminate the need to trim and tear—with packaging that allows them to be stored flat. This parchment slid neatly into a rimmed baking sheet and fit it well. At $0.20 per sheet (shipping not included), our runaway favorite is priced similarly to the other products in our lineup and is well worth the cost. It's the latest commercial-inspired home product that will have you wondering how you ever got by without it.

Foiled by the Fold

Sharply creased or curled sheets of parchment paper can lead to misshapen baked goods.

CREASED
Folded paper printed lines on cookies.

WAVY
Curled paper turned out uneven cookies.

TESTING PARCHMENT PAPER

We tested 10 parchment papers, with our lineup including a mix of rolls and precut sheets. We baked a variety of foods on each product (including some in a 500-degree oven) and used sheets of each to roll out disks of cookie dough and roll jelly roll cakes. We also tested the papers' strength. Throughout, we evaluated how cleanly the baked foods released from the papers and checked the foods for even, consistent browning. Several users took the papers home, where they evaluated their performance and ease of use and noted how easy they were to store in kitchen cabinets and drawers. For parchment rolls, we calculated the approximate number of sheets per container by roughly dividing the total length by 16 inches (the approximate length of the cooking surface of a standard-size rimmed baking sheet). Scores from testing were averaged. Prices listed are what we paid online, and products appear below in order of preference.

PERFORMANCE: We baked two kinds of cookies, jelly roll cake, and pizza on each paper, checking to see how easily foods released and if they had even, consistent browning.

SIZE: We used each parchment paper to line a standard-size rimmed baking sheet, whose cooking surface measures 16½ by 11½ inches. Papers rated best if they fit in the baking sheet straight from the package or with minimal trimming.

HANDLING: Sheets of perfectly flat parchment paper were easy to use and ensured that foods baked evenly with smooth surfaces. We docked points from papers that curled, were creased, or were generally difficult to lay flat. Products that negatively affected the appearance of our baked goods lost points.

PACKAGING: We evaluated the design and construction of the packaging. For sheets, the best packaging allowed the paper to be stored flat. For rolls, good packaging had firm, rigid edges or sharp teeth that facilitated clean, neat tears. Products lost points if their packaging fell apart or became misshapen during testing.

▶ **Lisa Tears It Up**
A free video is available at CooksIllustrated.com/apr18

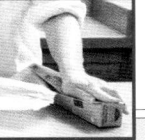

HIGHLY RECOMMENDED

KING ARTHUR FLOUR Parchment Paper 100 Half-Sheets
PRICE: $19.95 per package ($0.20 per sheet), plus shipping
STYLE: Precut sheets **DIMENSIONS:** 16½ x 12¼ in
SHEETS PER PACKAGE: 100
PERFORMANCE ★★★ **SIZE:** ★★ ½
HANDLING: ★★★ **PACKAGING:** ★★★

TESTERS' COMMENTS: These precut parchment sheets, are the only ones in our lineup that are stored completely flat. They're also sized just right to slide easily into a standard rimmed baking sheet. Their superior convenience made them the runaway favorite. Don't let the purchase price distract you: The per-sheet cost falls squarely in the middle of our lineup.

RECOMMENDED

PAPERCHEF Parchment Rolls
PRICE: $12.95 per package (approximately $0.18 per sheet)
STYLE: Roll **DIMENSIONS:** 15 in x 98.4 ft
SHEETS PER PACKAGE: Approximately 73
PERFORMANCE: ★★★ **SIZE:** ★★ **HANDLING:** ★★ ½ **PACKAGING:** ★★★

The lid on our favorite rolled paper fits inside the box and holds the roll in place, providing tension for neat, even tears. However, we had to trim a few inches to fit the paper in a rimmed baking sheet.

REYNOLDS Parchment Paper
PRICE: $5.33 per package (approximately $0.20 per sheet)
STYLE: Roll **DIMENSIONS:** 15 in x 36 ft
SHEETS PER PACKAGE: Approximately 27
PERFORMANCE: ★★★ **SIZE:** ★★ **HANDLING:** ★★ **PACKAGING:** ★★★

Cleanly tearing sheets from this roll was easy, but they had to be trimmed significantly to fit into a baking sheet. The edges curled, especially when the paper was near the end of the roll.

RECOMMENDED WITH RESERVATIONS

REYNOLDS Cookie Baking Sheets
PRICE: $3.48 per package ($0.16 per sheet) **STYLE:** Precut sheets
DIMENSIONS: 12 x 16 in **SHEETS PER PACKAGE:** 22
PERFORMANCE: ★★ **SIZE:** ★★ ½ **HANDLING:** ★★ **PACKAGING:** ★★★

TESTERS' COMMENTS: Folded into quarters, these precut sheets were easy to store. The downside: The tight creases did not flatten out and imprinted lines on cookie dough when we rolled it between two sheets.

GOOD COOK Parchment Paper
PRICE: $5.27 per package (approximately $0.35 per sheet) **STYLE:** Roll
DIMENSIONS: 12 in x 20 ft **SHEETS PER PACKAGE:** Approximately 15
PERFORMANCE: ★★★ **SIZE:** ★★ ½ **HANDLING:** ★★ ½ **PACKAGING:** ★ ½

The only roll in our lineup that fit in a rimmed baking sheet—a huge perk—was sold in flimsy packaging that came completely unglued by the end of testing. Per sheet, it was the most expensive product in our lineup.

NORPRO Unbleached Baking Paper
PRICE: $7.04 per package (approximately $0.16 per sheet) **STYLE:** Roll
DIMENSIONS: 15 in x 59 ft **SHEETS PER PACKAGE:** Approximately 44
PERFORMANCE: ★★★ **SIZE:** ★★ **HANDLING:** ★★ **PACKAGING:** ★★

We thought that the sharp serrations on the box would guarantee a clean tear, but many sheets had uneven or jagged edges—and still had to be trimmed to fit in a baking sheet. Though sturdy, the box lacked a closure and stayed slightly ajar.

WILTON Parchment Paper
PRICE: $12.98 per 2-box package (approximately $0.27 per sheet) **STYLE:** Roll
DIMENSIONS: 14.9 in x 32.8 ft **SHEETS PER PACKAGE:** Approximately 48
PERFORMANCE: ★★★ **SIZE:** ★★ **HANDLING:** ★★ **PACKAGING:** ★★

Even with the box's plastic serrated teeth, this paper routinely tore jaggedly. It also required trimming to fit into a baking sheet. The only plus was that the paper remained fairly flat, even near the end of the roll.

PAPERCHEF Parchment Sheets 12" x 16"
PRICE: $6.00 per package ($0.25 per sheet) **STYLE:** Precut sheets
DIMENSIONS: 12 x 16 in **SHEETS PER PACKAGE:** 24
PERFORMANCE: ★★★ **SIZE:** ★★ ½ **HANDLING:** ½ **PACKAGING:** ★★★

Rolling these precut sheets inside a standard rectangular cardboard box seemed like a clever idea, but they were hard to flatten. Even when we pointed the curled sides down, some sheets sprung up and rerolled themselves.

NOT RECOMMENDED

BEYOND GOURMET Unbleached Parchment Paper
PRICE: $10.25 per package (approximately $0.21 per sheet) **STYLE:** Roll
DIMENSIONS: 13 in x 65.6 ft **SHEETS PER PACKAGE:** Approximately 49
PERFORMANCE: ★★★ **SIZE:** ★★ **HANDLING:** ★ **PACKAGING:** ½

We had to wrestle this paper into a baking sheet. Worse, the soft cardboard box lacks a cutting edge and stretched out after just a few uses. Because it was difficult to tear the paper, the sheets became wrinkled and had uneven edges.

IF YOU CARE Unbleached Parchment Baking Paper
PRICE: $7.99 per package (approximately $0.17 per sheet) **STYLE:** Roll
DIMENSIONS: 13 in x 65 ft **SHEETS PER PACKAGE:** Approximately 48
PERFORMANCE: ★★★ **SIZE:** ★★ **HANDLING:** ★ **PACKAGING:** ½

The flimsy cardboard box came unglued shortly after testing started. The soft tearing edge produced sheets so jagged and uneven that we couldn't use them.

In Search of the Best Romano Cheese

Is Pecorino Romano from Italy worth seeking out, or can domestic options do the job?

> BY LISA McMANUS <

Pecorino Romano is like the seasoned character actor who improves dozens of movies but never gets recognition. It's one of the world's oldest cheeses, named for its origins in ancient Rome, and its firm, slightly oily, crystalline texture and salty, funky flavor deserve fresh consideration out of the shadow of its more famous cousin, Parmigiano-Reggiano. In the test kitchen, we use Pecorino in salads, soups, and frittatas, as well as in classic Italian pasta dishes such as *cacio e pepe*, *pasta all'amatriciana*, and lasagna, where its complex flavor is a quiet powerhouse.

But does it matter which cheese you bring home? We chose seven nationally available versions priced from $0.67 to $1.33 per ounce. In supermarkets, you'll find cheeses labeled Pecorino Romano and Romano sold side by side, so we included both. In blind tastings, we asked panels to evaluate the cheeses both plain and cooked in our recipe for Spaghetti with Pecorino and Black Pepper (Cacio e Pepe). To help us understand our preferences, we sent samples to an independent laboratory to measure their pH and compared the nutrition content provided on product labels.

Pecorino Romano versus Romano

With *Denominazione di Origine Protetta* (DOP) status in the European Union, the cheese called Pecorino Romano can be made only in Lazio (the province that includes Rome), in Grosseto in Tuscany, and on the island of Sardinia, where most of it is produced today. It's made with sheep's milk (*pecora* means "sheep" in Italian) from local flocks that is heated and curdled with rennet from local lambs. Then the cheese is pressed, rubbed repeatedly with salt, stamped with identifying marks, and aged, all according to the standards of a consortium that oversees its production. This results in a unique cheese important in central and southern Italian and Italian American cooking. Today, Italy produces 25,000 tons per year; 60 percent of that is exported, and the top buyer is the United States—Pecorino Romano accounts for one-third of all Italian cheese exported to America. American cheesemakers, however, lacking access to sheep's milk on an industrial scale, make the cheese with cow's milk.

Whether plain or in pasta, our tasters preferred imported Pecorino Romano over domestic Romano, which we found milder, less aromatic, and more like Swiss than sharper, funkier, more crystalline Pecorino Romano. Cheese becomes firmer and its flavor more complex the longer it is aged, and it turns out that our domestic Romanos were aged for as little as five months, compared with more than eight months for the imports. And the two lowest-ranked domestic cheeses had the lowest pH in the lineup, indicating a higher acidity that was likely the cause of the slightly sour flavor and pebbly texture we noticed when we sampled these cheeses plain. The imports contained more sodium, providing a deeply savory taste, and our winner had the most sodium of all. Finally, the basic flavor profiles of the domestic and imported cheeses didn't match up.

Cow's-Milk versus Sheep's-Milk Cheese

Simply put, cow's milk and sheep's milk make different cheeses. Sheep's milk has many short-chain and medium-chain fatty acids, while cow's milk contains long-chain fatty acids, so they break down into different aroma compounds, explained Sarah Hoffmann, founder of Green Dirt Farm in Weston, Missouri, which produces small-batch sheep's-milk cheeses. Certain fatty acids that create the gamy, funky taste of goat cheese appear in very small concentrations in sheep's milk, too, but they're absent from cow's milk, she said.

Domestic Romano cheesemakers try to re-create some of the pungency of Pecorino Romano by adding lipase to the cow's milk, explained Dean Sommer, senior food technologist for the Center for Dairy Research at the University of Wisconsin–Madison. This enzyme digests and breaks down dairy fat into fatty acids and glycerol, and in the process, it lends flavor and aroma to the cheese. In Sommer's opinion, while this does create "strong" flavors, it doesn't quite succeed in making cow's-milk Romano taste like Pecorino Romano. Instead, he said, the result is "very similar to aged provolone cheese." Anna Thomas Bates, co-owner of sheep's-milk cheese producer Landmark Creamery in Albany, Wisconsin, agreed: "You just can't duplicate the chemical makeup of sheep's milk."

Sheep's milk is renowned for its excellent composition for cheese making, with nearly twice the protein, fat, calcium, and solids of cow's milk and an ability to develop complex, rich, fruity, toasted-nut, caramel, toffee, and even browned butter–like flavors as the cheese ages. So why don't domestic cheesemakers make an effort to produce more sheep's milk and age it more to make firmer, more flavorful Romano?

There are a few reasons. First, since a sheep produces about one-tenth the volume of milk that a cow does, Hoffmann explained, it's much more expensive. Basic "commodity" cow's milk costs about $0.15 per pound in the United States, while organic, grass-fed versions sell for $0.35 per pound. Sheep's milk, meanwhile, ranges from $0.80 to $1.20 per pound. Second, American sheep breeds produce even less milk than those in Europe. (Federal bans on importing higher-yield breeds were lifted in 2017, so this may change.) Third, "aging is an expensive undertaking for producers, as it ties up inventory," said Nora Weiser, executive director of the American Cheese Society.

We recommend all the imported Italian Pecorino Romano cheeses in our lineup, but our top choice was the "pungent, salty, and sharp" Boar's Head Pecorino Romano ($1.00 per ounce), which is widely available and moderately priced. (Note: This cheese is made in Italy following DOP guidelines, but because the wheels are cut and repackaged in the United States, they are considered non-DOP, a Boar's Head spokesperson confirmed.) In a pinch, a domestic Romano will do, but we think you'll miss the extra richness and complexity that Pecorino Romano brings to the table.

If It Doesn't Say "Pecorino," It's Not the Right Romano

Domestic cheeses labeled "Romano" are an entirely different breed than the Italian imports bearing the name "Pecorino Romano." The two differ in many ways, from raw ingredients to flavor, texture, salt content, and even how long they are aged. Here's a quick rundown:

PECORINO ROMANO
- Made from sheep's milk
- Sharp, funky flavor
- Crumbly texture
- More salt
- DOP designation

ROMANO
- Made from cow's milk
- Mild flavor
- Soft texture
- Less salt
- No DOP designation

Sheep's milk is renowned for its excellent composition for cheese making, with nearly twice the protein, fat, calcium, and solids of cow's milk and an ability to develop complex, rich, fruity, toasted-nut, caramel, toffee, and even browned butter–like flavors as the cheese ages.

TASTING PECORINO ROMANO AND ROMANO CHEESES

Twenty-one editors and cooks at America's Test Kitchen sampled seven Pecorino Romano and Romano cheese products plain at room temperature and in our recipe for Spaghetti with Pecorino and Black Pepper (Cacio e Pepe). Scores were averaged, with the cooked application's scores weighted more heavily since this cheese is more frequently used for cooking than as a table cheese. Products are listed below in order of preference. Nutrition data is from product labels, standardized for comparison, using a serving size of 1 ounce (28 grams). An independent laboratory analyzed pH. Prices were paid in Boston-area supermarkets and online (not including shipping). To see the full tasting results, go to CooksIllustrated.com/apr18.

RECOMMENDED

BOAR'S HEAD Pecorino Romano

PRICE: $6.99 for 7 oz ($1.00 per oz)
ORIGIN: Sardinia, Italy (non-DOP)
MILK: Sheep
AGED: More than 8 months
INGREDIENTS: Pasteurized sheep's milk, cultures, rennet, salt
pH: 5.3 FAT: 8.4 g
SODIUM: 672 mg

COMMENTS: "Delicious! Rich, complex, deeply savory, with a long finish" and a "crystalline" crunch, this imported sheep's-milk Pecorino Romano sold under the Boar's Head banner was "dense, nicely dry, salty in a fruity, fatty kind of way" and was our tasters' overall favorite. It also had by far the highest sodium level in our lineup, adding to its savory appeal. In pasta, it was "smooth," "pungent, salty, and sharp," with "the perfect taste and creamy texture I've been looking for! Silky, tangy, cheesy, creamy, assertive."

Pecorino Romano by ZERTO

BEST BUY

PRICE: $4.99 for 7.5 oz ($0.67 per oz)
ORIGIN: Sardinia, Italy (DOP)
MILK: Sheep
AGED: 9 months
INGREDIENTS: 100% sheep's milk, rennet, salt
pH: 5.4 FAT: 8 g
SODIUM: 550 mg

COMMENTS: With "lots of crystals," this "salty, rich, funky" cheese was "almost crunchy" and "pleasingly pungent" when nibbled plain, coming across as "creamy and milky and salty without being overbearing." Its "coarse texture" was described as "perfect for grating." "It's like the other great Pecorinos but a touch more subdued instead of knock-you-out salty/funky." In spaghetti, the cheese's flavor was "a little mild" compared with those of other samples, but it helped achieve a "good balance of salt and cheese and pepper, all working in harmony."

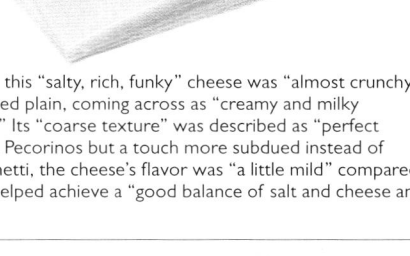

LOCATELLI Pecorino Romano

PRICE: $9.99 for 7.5 oz ($1.33 per oz)
ORIGIN: Sardinia, Italy (DOP)
MILK: Sheep
AGED: Minimum 9 months
INGREDIENTS: 100% pure pasteurized sheep's milk, cultures, rennet, salt
pH: 5.3 FAT: 9 g
SODIUM: 550 mg

COMMENTS: "Full-flavored, complex, crystalline, crumbly, pungent, salty; just right," this imported sheep's-milk Pecorino Romano had a "lovely sheepy, briny flavor" that was "Robust! Salty! Addictive!" and "deeply savory, almost meaty, with a fatty richness" and a "slightly crumbly texture." Tasters found it "funky, but in a good way." In spaghetti, it was "silky," "velvety," "creamy and buttery"—the "strong, lovely cheese flavor makes this dish sing."

GENUINE FULVI Pecorino Romano

PRICE: $7.99 for 7.5 oz ($1.07 per oz)
ORIGIN: Nepi, Lazio, Italy (DOP)
MILK: Sheep
AGED: 10 months to 1 year
INGREDIENTS: Pasteurized sheep's milk, rennet, salt.
pH: 5.6 FAT: 11.2 g
SODIUM: 560 mg

COMMENTS: With "a little kick!" and "some funk on the finish," this imported Pecorino Romano won fans. "Oh, this is just lovely," wrote one taster. "Firm and crumbly yet also creamy. It's grassy and fruity, with sweet winey notes and some crystalline crunch." On spaghetti, the fruity notes came through in a "velvety," "nutty" sauce.

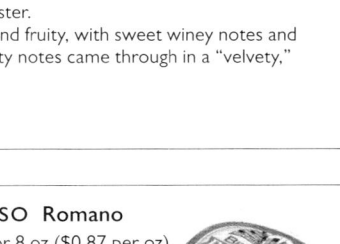

RECOMMENDED WITH RESERVATIONS

SARTORI Cheese Romano

PRICE: $4.19 for 5 oz ($0.84 per oz)
ORIGIN: Wisconsin, USA
MILK: Cow
AGED: 8 months
INGREDIENTS: Pasteurized milk, cheese cultures, salt, enzymes
pH: 5.3 FAT: 7 g
SODIUM: 280 mg

COMMENTS: With "pleasant," "mild," "sweet," "nutty" flavor, this domestic cow's-milk Romano was "very soft" and "not as pungent as it should be," "very buttery and Parmesan-like," like "unhole-y Swiss." "This isn't a bad cheese," wrote a taster. "It's mild, creamy, and toothsome, with good milkiness." But others noted that it "could stand to be saltier." In pasta, it had "nice saucy-ness" and was "smooth, creamy," making for "kid-friendly noodles, for sure," but was "really overwhelmed by the pepper."

STELLA Romano Cheese

PRICE: $5.99 for 8 oz ($0.75 per oz)
ORIGIN: Wisconsin, USA
MILK: Cow
AGED: 5 months
INGREDIENTS: Romano Cheese (Pasteurized part-skim cow's milk, cheese cultures, salt, enzymes)
pH: 5.1 FAT: 8 g
SODIUM: 390 mg

COMMENTS: This cheese was a bit too "mild overall," reminiscent of "gouda," "Gruyère," or "cheddar." It was "buttery, creamy, but missing the funk and crumbliness" tasters sought. "I miss the salty bite!" wrote one. "Lacks the intensity I expect, but I don't dislike the sweet, nutty, caramel-y flavor." A few complained about the texture, noting that it "breaks into pellets." In pasta, it was "perfectly creamy" and "light," but its flavor was "muted."

BEL GIOIOSO Romano

PRICE: $6.99 for 8 oz ($0.87 per oz)
ORIGIN: Wisconsin, USA
MILK: Raw cow's milk, rBst-free
AGED: 5 months
INGREDIENTS: Cultured milk, enzymes, salt
pH: 5.1 FAT: 7 g
SODIUM: 330 mg

COMMENTS: "Mildly salty," "fruity," "soft and slightly creamy," with a "pebbly" texture when broken and a slightly "sour" flavor with "some tanginess to the finish," this domestic cow's-milk Romano "eats like cheddar," "provolone," or "Swiss cheese." "This is missing that gritty saltiness I crave," one taster noted. Others summed it up: "Inoffensive but not beguiling." In spaghetti, it had "no bite or much saltiness" and "could be more flavorful."

INGREDIENT NOTES

BY STEVE DUNN, ANDREA GEARY, ANDREW JANJIGIAN, LAN LAM & KATE SHANNON

Tasting Turkey Bacon

Whether you're intrigued by its purported healthfulness or you prefer turkey to pork products, turkey bacon can be appealing. It's made in two main styles. One is created by grinding white and dark meat separately and extruding the resulting pastes into molds. When the contents are sliced vertically, the strips have a faux-marbled appearance that mimics that of pork bacon. The second style is usually made exclusively with thigh meat that's "chunked" into larger pieces and tumbled until its proteins bind together. The meat is then pressed before being sliced into strips to create a style reminiscent of Canadian bacon or ham.

We purchased five products in a mix of both styles, priced from $1.99 to $6.99 per package. Tasters sampled the pan-fried strips plain and in BLT sandwiches. The verdict: We didn't prefer one style to the other. But several products had artificial or off-flavors, and none crisped up like pork bacon. (But a good cooking method can help. See "The Best Way to Cook Turkey Bacon" on page 30.)

We think there's room for improvement in turkey bacon. Our top scorer, Wellshire All Natural Uncured Turkey Bacon ($6.99 for a 12-ounce package), earned only a lukewarm recommendation. That said, we liked its "good chewy texture" and thought it had the best balance of smoky, sweet, and salty flavors. For the complete tasting results, go to CooksIllustrated.com/apr18. –Kate Shannon

RECOMMENDED WITH RESERVATIONS

WELLSHIRE All Natural Uncured Turkey Bacon
PRICE: $6.99 for 12-oz package ($0.58 per oz)
INGREDIENTS: Turkey, water, sea salt, raw sugar, celery powder, paprika, onion powder, spice
COMMENTS: Made with large chunks of thigh meat, our top scorer resembled Canadian bacon. It had some of the big smoky, salty, sweet flavors we associate with pork bacon. It had a pleasantly "chewy" texture and crisped up more than other products in our lineup.

JENNIE-O Turkey Bacon
PRICE: $1.99 for 12-oz package ($0.17 per oz)
INGREDIENTS: Mechanically separated turkey, turkey, water, sugar, contains 2% or less salt, potassium lactate, natural smoke flavor, flavor (canola oil, natural smoke, natural flavoring), sodium diacetate, sodium phosphate, rosemary extract, sodium erythorbate, sodium nitrite
COMMENTS: The intense flavor of this striated bacon, which came in second, made it stand out. Some tasters thought that flavor was slightly "artificial" and "hot dog"-like, but the bacon stood up to the other ingredients in a BLT sandwich. The strips toed the line between "crisp" and a little "leathery."

OSCAR MAYER Turkey Bacon
PRICE: $4.29 for 12-oz package ($0.36 per oz)
INGREDIENTS: Turkey, sugar, salt, contains less than 2% of potassium lactate, water, potassium chloride, sodium diacetate, sodium phosphates, smoke flavor, sodium ascorbate, autolyzed yeast extract, sodium nitrite, soy lecithin
COMMENTS: Our third-place bacon didn't get very crispy, and we found it a little too "chewy." Sampled plain, it had some "metallic" and "mustard"-y off-notes. When we layered it into a BLT, those funky flavors were much less noticeable and the prominent "smoky" flavor took center stage.

Shishito Peppers at Home

Until recently, Japanese shishito peppers were mostly enjoyed in restaurants as a trendy bar snack or appetizer that you pick up by the stems and eat whole. But these days, they are increasingly available at farmers' markets and supermarkets, so you can prepare them at home. Slender, 3- to 4-inch-long shishitos boast thin skins, delicate flesh, and an addictive fruity, grassy flavor reminiscent of jalapeño or serrano chiles, minus the heat. Restaurants often deep-fry whole shishitos until they blister, but we have found that cooking them in a small amount of oil works just as well.

Here's our method: Heat 2 tablespoons vegetable oil in 12-inch skillet over medium-high heat until just beginning to smoke. Add 8 ounces shishito peppers and cook, without stirring, until skins are blistered, 3 to 5 minutes. Using tongs, flip peppers and continue to cook until blistered on second side, 3 to 5 minutes longer. Transfer to bowl, toss with ½ teaspoon kosher salt, and serve. –A.J.

Dipping in Chocolate Made Easier

Tempering chocolate for dipping fruit or cookies takes patience and care to create a shiny, snappy coating—even when using our foolproof microwave technique. So we were intrigued when the producer of our favorite chocolate baking bar came out with Ghirardelli Chocolate Melting Wafers (available in white, milk, and dark chocolate), which substitute palm oil for the cocoa butter in premium chocolate, allowing them to be melted in the microwave with no fuss whatsoever. We melted a batch of Ghirardelli wafers and used it to dip cookies, pretzels, and strawberries, comparing these with the same items dipped in tempered chocolate.

WORKS IN A PINCH

BEST TO AVOID

The verdict: The Ghirardelli wafers set up shiny and snappy, but they tasted a bit waxy and lacked the robust flavor of the tempered premium samples. That said, if you don't have the time or patience to temper real chocolate, the Ghirardelli wafers will do in a pinch. (Avoid the "candy melts" that are available in craft stores. These contain almost no real cocoa and barely taste of chocolate.) –A.G.

Shelf Life of Dry Vermouth

Dry vermouth is similar enough in flavor to white wine that we've found it to be a good and more shelf-stable substitute. We know that it can be stored for months at room temperature and still make an acceptable pan sauce or risotto. But we wondered how long an open bottle would retain enough aroma and flavor for sipping and cocktails and whether chilling prolonged its quality.

We stored open bottles of two different vermouths at room temperature and in the fridge. Tasters sampled them every other week. After a month, most tasters found that both vermouths stored in the pantry had lost their citrusy aroma and tasted flat. The vermouths stored in the refrigerator remained suitable for sipping for two months before they started tasting medicinal and somewhat bitter. Refrigeration does a better job of preserving flavor because low temperatures slow down the loss of aromatic compounds and the lack of light slows oxidation.

The upshot: If you're cooking with vermouth, it's fine to store it at room temperature for several months. For the best flavor in cocktails, keep the bottle in the refrigerator for no longer than two months. –L.L.

KEEP IT COLD
For better cocktails, store opened bottles of vermouth in the refrigerator and use them within two months.

Does Rinsing Canned Beans Remove Sodium?

A ½-cup serving of canned chickpeas or beans often contains more than 400 milligrams of sodium. That's a sizeable portion of the 2,300-milligram daily limit recommended for adults in the Dietary Guidelines for Americans. Given that we often drain and rinse beans before use, we were curious: Exactly how much sodium does that wash away? To find out, we sent cans of chickpeas, cannellini beans, pinto beans, and black beans to a lab for analysis.

With one set of cans, the lab measured the sodium in a combination of the beans and their liquid. With the second set, the lab carefully drained and rinsed the beans, as we do before using chickpeas to make hummus or stirring black beans into chili.

If you're watching your sodium intake, we have good news. In each case, draining and rinsing beans lowered the sodium by about 100 milligrams per ½-cup serving—or 20.7 to 26.5 percent. –K.S.

RINSED BEANS:

Goya chickpeas	24.7% less sodium
Goya cannellini beans	21.4% less sodium
Bush's pinto beans	26.5% less sodium
Bush's black beans	20.7% less sodium

Thai versus Italian Basil

A variety of the sweet Italian basil used widely in American and European cooking, Thai basil brings slightly savory, spicy, anise-like notes to many Southeast Asian and Chinese dishes. Its leaves are sturdier and stand up to heat better than those of Italian basil, so it can be added during cooking versus as a finishing touch. Italian basil is an acceptable substitute in dishes with many other strong flavors, such as our Three-Cup Chicken (page 21), but Thai basil is worth seeking out for dishes such as Vietnamese spring rolls, where spicy flavor and sturdy texture are key elements. –L.L.

THAI BASIL
Sturdy leaves; purple stems; slightly savory, spicy, licorice-like flavor

ITALIAN BASIL
Delicate leaves, green stems, peppery-sweet taste

DIY RECIPE Harissa

Harissa is a potent paste used both as an ingredient and as a condiment in North African cooking. The backbone of harissa—chiles—can vary greatly from recipe to recipe. For a condiment that we could make on the fly, we chose a mix of ground dried chiles. Paprika gave the paste a mild, sweet flavor, and Aleppo pepper added a complex fruity flavor with a more slowly building heat than that of ordinary red pepper flakes. To the ground chiles we added plenty of garlic and olive oil as well as aromatic spices including coriander, cumin, and anise-like caraway seeds. A dollop of this bright, spicy paste can enliven vegetables, eggs, lamb, and soups such as our Moroccan Chickpea and Lentil Soup (Harira) (page 14). –Anne Wolf

HARISSA
MAKES ABOUT ½ CUP

If you can't find Aleppo pepper, you can substitute ¾ teaspoon of paprika and ¾ teaspoon of finely chopped red pepper flakes.

- 6 tablespoons extra-virgin olive oil
- 6 garlic cloves, minced
- 2 tablespoons paprika
- 1 tablespoon ground coriander
- 1 tablespoon ground dried Aleppo pepper
- 1 teaspoon ground cumin
- ¾ teaspoon caraway seeds
- ½ teaspoon salt

Combine all ingredients in bowl and microwave until bubbling and very fragrant, about 1 minute, stirring halfway through microwaving; let cool completely. (Harissa can be refrigerated for up to 4 days.)

Don't Grate Cheese Too Far in Advance

It can be tempting to grate a wedge of Parmesan or Pecorino Romano ahead of time, but does grating cheese in advance affect its flavor? To find out, we bought a large wedge each of our winning Parmesan and Pecorino Romano cheeses and split each into thirds. We grated one wedge of each type of cheese and refrigerated the samples in airtight containers; we vacuum-packed the remaining wedges. After one week, we repeated the process, grating one wedge of each type of cheese and refrigerating the samples.

Grated Parmesan and Pecorino Romano start to lose flavor after just one week.

At the two-week mark, we grated the remaining wedges and compared them with the one- and two-week-old grated cheeses. Every taster could identify the freshly grated cheeses. The week-old cheeses had slightly muted flavors but were still acceptable. The two-week-old cheeses had lost so much complexity that they were deemed unacceptable. This is because much of the flavor of aged cheese resides in volatile esters, aldehydes, and other flavor compounds that start to degrade when they're exposed to air by grating. In sum: For the best flavor, Parmesan and Pecorino Romano should be consumed within a week of grating. –S.D.

KITCHEN NOTES

BY STEVE DUNN, ANDREA GEARY, ANDREW JANJIGIAN, LAN LAM & ANNIE PETITO

WHAT IS IT?

Back in the days before boutique coffee shops occupied every street corner, many folks not only brewed their own coffee but also roasted their own beans. To do so, they would have used a stovetop roaster such as this one made in Germany around the turn of the century. Weighing in at a hefty 8 pounds, this 8 by 4-inch cast-iron roaster could be used to roast up to 1 pound of beans at a time. Like a stovetop corn popper, the roaster is set over a flame. The user then constantly rotates its handle, which turns a paddle inside the roaster to keep the beans in motion. When we tested this model, we found that it worked well. Over medium heat, it took about 14 minutes to roast ½ pound of green coffee beans to a light roast and about 16 minutes to roast another batch to medium. The only challenge? Gauging the color of the roasted beans, as the roaster's black interior and the light smoke given off by roasting made them a bit hard to see. –S.D.

ANTIQUE GERMAN COFFEE ROASTER

For the Hottest Coffee, Preheat Your Mug

If you like your coffee piping hot, it's a good idea to preheat your mug: Fill it with boiling water, let it sit for a few minutes, dump the water, and fill 'er up. Preheating ensures that most of the heat stays in your drink instead of being absorbed by the mug.

To prove the point, we monitored the temperature of freshly boiled water (212 degrees) that we poured into two identical ceramic mugs, one preheated and the other not. After 1 minute, the water in the preheated mug was 15 degrees hotter than the water in the unheated mug. After 10 minutes it was still 10 degrees warmer, and even after 25 minutes, it was still 5 degrees warmer. Preheating works well because ceramic has a significant amount of mass that can absorb and retain lots of heat. (Note: Don't bother preheating a double-walled carafe. The airless layer between its two walls prevents the transfer of energy, so hot liquids stay hot without any extra help.) –A.G.

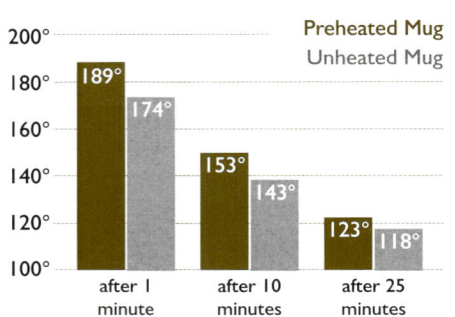

Preheated Mug / Unheated Mug
- after 1 minute: 189° / 174°
- after 10 minutes: 153° / 143°
- after 25 minutes: 123° / 118°

The Best Way to Cook Turkey Bacon

When preparing turkey bacon for our tasting (page 28), we found that the package instructions either were vague and inconsistent or called for cooking the strips in a dry (no fat) skillet, which didn't produce the nicely browned, crisp-tender texture we were after. So we experimented to come up with a method that we liked. We tried cooking the strips on an aluminum foil–lined baking sheet in a 400-degree oven, a method we often use when cooking pork bacon, but the results were leathery. The better approach was to pan-fry them in 2 tablespoons of vegetable oil. The oil ensured that the turkey bacon made full, even contact with the heat, but the results weren't greasy; in fact, when we poured out the spent fat, we collected nearly the full 2 tablespoons we'd started with. The browned, crisp-tender results rivaled pork bacon enough that by the end of testing, we made a couple of turkey bacon converts.

Method for four strips of turkey bacon: Preheat 2 tablespoons vegetable oil in 12-inch skillet (traditional or nonstick) over medium heat until shimmering. Place strips in skillet and cook, turning strips every 2 to 3 minutes and adjusting heat as necessary, until bacon is deeply browned and crispy, 8 to 10 minutes. Transfer strips to paper towel–lined plate and serve. –A.P.

Cook Your Pie Weights?

Dried beans are a great alternative to ceramic pie weights when blind-baking a pie crust, but can you push their utility one step further by cooking and eating them afterward? To find out, we baked three pie crusts, using the same batch of dried small red beans to weigh down each crust as it baked.

When we cooked the thrice-baked beans alongside a pot of never-baked beans and tasted the two side by side, we were surprised to find little difference. The pie-weight beans were a bit firmer than the never-cooked beans and might have benefited from 10 more minutes of cooking, but they were creamy, intact, and entirely acceptable. That's because beans lose some—but not much—of their 12 percent moisture when baked, since the bean is protected by skin and moisture can pass through only two tiny openings where the bean was once attached to the pod. **Our takeaway:** If you're housebound and hungry, go ahead and reach for the pie beans. –A.G.

Don't Judge Caramel by Color Alone

When making caramel (page 19), we recommend using an instant-read thermometer to gauge when the sugar has reached the appropriate degree of caramelization called for in the recipe instead of simply eyeballing it to evaluate if it's dark enough. That's because the color of your cookware, the lighting in your kitchen, and especially the amount and depth of caramel you have in the pan will affect its appearance.

To prove the point, we caramelized two batches of sugar according to our recipe, taking both to 370 degrees. We made one batch in a wide skillet and the other in a small saucepan. Just as water at the shallow end of a pool appears lighter in color, the thinner layer of caramel in the skillet appeared lighter compared with the deeper layer in the saucepan, even though both vessels contained the same volume of identical caramel.

Bottom line: For the best results when making caramel, don't rely on color alone. Use a thermometer to determine how much the sugar has caramelized. –L.L.

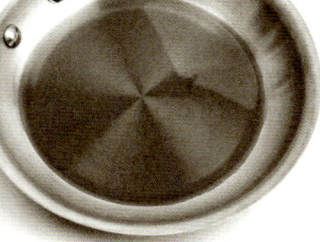

SHALLOW SKILLET
Caramel appears lighter.

DEEP SAUCEPAN
Caramel appears darker.

Low Oven versus Sous Vide

On pages 6 and 7, we offer two cooking methods for pork tenderloin steaks, both of which ensure well-browned exteriors and rosy interiors: a *sous vide* method and a low-oven method. The former gently cooks the pork (first sealed in plastic bags) in a water bath kept at the desired serving temperature of 140 degrees via an immersion circulator; the latter mimics the sous vide method by slowly bringing the meat to 140 degrees in a 275-degree oven. In both cases, we briefly sear the meat afterward in a hot skillet to create nicely browned crusts.

To compare the two methods, we cooked a 1-pound pork tenderloin each way and took each roast's temperature at three locations: the center of the thickest part (where we normally take the temperature of meat), just below the surface at the thickest part, and in the center of the tapered end, the area most likely to overcook.

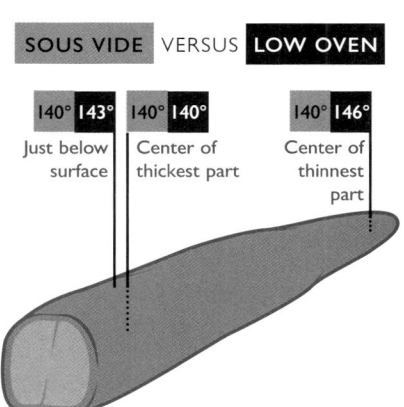

SOUS VIDE VERSUS LOW OVEN

140° / 143° — Just below surface
140° / 140° — Center of thickest part
140° / 146° — Center of thinnest part

Here's how the two approaches measured up.
Sous vide method: Meat registered precisely 140 degrees at all three points.
Oven method: Meat registered 140 at the center of the thickest part but was a few degrees higher closer to the surface and at the tapered end; also had a slight color difference just below the surface.
Bottom line: Using an immersion circulator is the only way to guarantee perfectly even temperature in food, inside to out, but our more conventional method gets you very close. (For more information on sous vide cookery and our testing of immersion circulators, see page 7.) –L.L.

Bake with Parchment; Otherwise, Use Waxed Paper

Parchment and waxed papers are both designed to help keep food from sticking. Because parchment is manufactured to resist relatively high heat, it's indispensable for preventing food from sticking during baking, but it's pricey—our favorite product costs $0.20 per sheet (plus shipping). So for tasks other than baking, we turn to waxed paper. It costs only about $0.05 per sheet and works just as well as parchment, if not better. When we asked readers to tell us how they use waxed paper, the response was overwhelming. Here are some of readers'—and our—favorite uses. –A.J.

Wrapping: It holds creases well, so it's great for wrapping sandwiches, candies, caramels, or cheese (loosely wrap cheese in a second layer of foil).

Layering: Its nonstick coating keeps moist foods, such as fresh tortillas, cookies, burger patties, chops, or steaks, separated for storage or freezing.

Cushioning: Since it doesn't compress easily, waxed paper works well for lining a cookie tin so that pieces don't break.

Microwaving: The material is microwave-safe and won't sag like plastic wrap can when exposed to steam, making it an ideal choice for covering foods to prevent splattering and contain moisture.

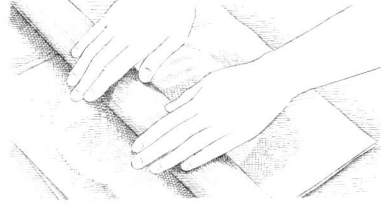

Rolling: The slick surface prevents sticking and functions well as a barrier between cookie or pie dough and the counter or rolling pin.

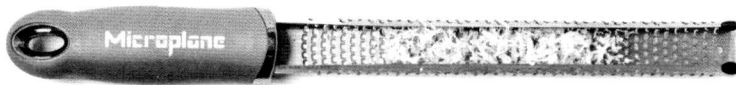

FINE TO KEEP
Zest is fluffy and dry.

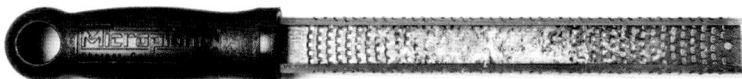

TIME TO REPLACE
Zest forms wet, oily paste.

When to Retire Your Rasp-Style Grater

You're trying to whip up a quick stir-fry, but grating the amount of ginger called for in the recipe is taking forever. Is it possible that your trusty grater has finally lost its edge?

Though they're impressively sharp when new, the teeth of even our favorite rasp-style grater can dull over time. To determine whether it's time to replace your tool, grab a lemon (try to find a really bumpy-skinned one) and run your grater over it. If the resulting zest is fluffy and dry, your grater is fine. But if the zest forms a wet, oily paste, it's time for a new grater. –A.G.

SCIENCE Season the Meat—or the Stew?

Many stew recipes call for seasoning chunks of meat with salt before searing them or adding them unseared to the pot. We wondered if this was truly necessary or if most of that salt simply dissolves into the cooking liquid. Could you save a plate or bowl and simultaneously add the meat and salt directly to the pot? We set up an experiment to find out.

EXPERIMENT

To focus on the seasoning of the meat, we omitted the aromatics, broth, wine, and other flavorings typically found in a stew. In each test we used 1 pound of beef cubes, 2 teaspoons of kosher salt, and 2 cups of water. We varied whether the meat was seared before the water was added to the pot and whether we salted the meat directly or added the salt and meat to the pot simultaneously. All batches were covered and simmered for 1½ hours to mimic a stew's cooking time. Tasters sampled the beef and broth from each batch and rated their saltiness. We repeated the test three times.

RESULTS

Tasters reported that the beef and broth in all batches were appropriately seasoned and that each batch was similarly salty.

EXPLANATION

When salt and meat are added to the pot at the beginning of cooking, the salt dissolves into the stewing liquid. Over time, some of that dissolved salt diffuses into the meat, seasoning it beyond just the surface. In the past, we've found that if you wait to salt beef stew until the end of cooking, the broth becomes unpleasantly salty, while the meat is underseasoned because the salt did not have time to permeate the meat.

TAKEAWAY

Since any salt sprinkled on meat just before stewing it dissolves into the cooking liquid, from a seasoning perspective it doesn't matter if you sprinkle the salt directly on the meat or add it to the stewing liquid. What's critical is adding the salt to the pot early in the process so it has time to permeate the meat over the course of stewing. We'll rely on this knowledge when tackling stew recipes in the future to save ourselves a little bit of time and a dirty dish or two. –L.L.

EQUIPMENT CORNER

> BY MIYE BROMBERG AND KATE SHANNON

RECOMMENDED

DEXAS Heavy Duty Grippmats
MODEL: 6554PK2
PRICE: $19.99 for set of 4

HIGHLY RECOMMENDED

DEMARLE SILPAT U.S. Half-Size Non-Stick Silicone Baking Mat
MODEL: AE420295-07
PRICE: $22.35

HIGHLY RECOMMENDED

MICROPLANE Home Series Fine Grater
MODEL: 44002
PRICE: $14.95

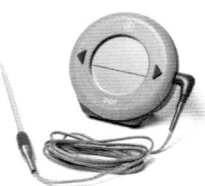

RECOMMENDED

THERMOWORKS DOT
MODEL: TX-1200-OR (orange)
PRICE: $39.00 ($4.00 for pot clip)

RECOMMENDED

LODGE NOKONA Leather Handle Holder
MODEL: ALHHNS85
PRICE: $13.43

Flexible Cutting Mats

Lightweight and flexible, plastic cutting mats are dishwasher-safe and generally flexible enough to be rolled up for funneling ingredients into a skillet or bowl. We put eight models, priced from $2.00 to $8.00 per mat, through a slew of cutting and chopping tasks to evaluate how well they stood up to stains, odors, repeated knife strokes, and washing. Mats that were textured on both sides provided stability on the counter and held slick foods such as halved onions and raw chicken in place. The textured surfaces also concealed knife marks, making the mats more durable. Our favorite models combined sturdiness with flexibility; mats that were too thick or stiff couldn't be curled to funnel ingredients. Our winner, Dexas Heavy Duty Grippmats ($19.99 for a set of four), are strong yet flexible, textured on both sides, and sized just right to contain food while still being maneuverable. –K.S.

Silicone Baking Mats

Made of silicone embedded with heat-conducting fiberglass or nylon fiber mesh, silicone baking mats can be popped into a baking sheet to provide a nonstick surface. Though they were originally used in professional kitchens, these reusable mats have become more popular with home cooks, so we decided to take a fresh look. We tested five mats priced from $8.99 to $24.39, including our former winner, the DeMarle Silpat U.S. Half-Size Non-Stick Silicone Baking Mat ($22.35), and compared each to parchment paper and a bare rimmed baking sheet in a series of tests. All the mats performed similarly when we used them to bake cookies and make roasted salmon and potatoes, but a few details helped our old winner defeat the competition again: The mat fit perfectly inside our winning rimmed baking sheet, was heavy enough to stay put even when we worked with sticky batters, and was dishwasher-safe, so residual oils and odors were reduced. –M.B.

Ginger Graters

To grate ginger, we usually reach for our favorite rasp-style or box grater. But with many tools on the market specifically designed for grating ginger, we wanted to know if we were using the best tool for the job. So we rounded up 10 graters priced from $8.00 to $35.64, including a range of sizes, shapes, materials, and grating styles. After grating more than 6 pounds of ginger, we realized that a grater's style determined its speed, efficiency, and ease of use. The best performers had a generous grating surface area and small etched holes that efficiently separated the puree from the fibrous waste. Surprisingly, many of the products billed as ginger graters fell short due to cramped grating areas or designs that made it difficult to extract the usable puree. We still like our favorite box grater, the Microplane Specialty Series 4-Sided Box Grater ($34.95)—it made speedy work of grating ginger when we used its big plane of fine etched holes. But if you grate ginger frequently, our top choice is the Microplane Home Series Fine Grater ($14.95). For grating ginger, it was the fastest and most efficient tool we tested, and it was easy to handle. –M.B.

UPDATE Probe Thermometer

Recently, the manufacturer of our winning clip-on probe thermometer, the ThermoWorks ChefAlarm ($59.00), released a new, stripped-down model, the ThermoWorks DOT ($39.00), which performs just one function: alerting you when your food has risen to the temperature you set. When we compared the two models, we found that the DOT is just as accurate, fits on just as many pots and pans as long as you buy a pot clip (available separately for $4.00), can monitor the same range of temperatures, and is compatible with six of ThermoWorks's accessory probes. We also liked its intuitive interface. That said, we think the feature-rich ChefAlarm—it includes a low-temperature alarm, a timer, a tracker that monitors the time elapsed since the target temperature was reached, a storage case, and a pot clip, and it's the only model we tested that can be recalibrated—is worth the extra money. –M.B.

Cast-Iron Skillet Handle Covers

Cast-iron skillets offer superior heat retention, but because they get—and stay—so hot, they are hard to move. Skillet handle covers promise to protect your hands while you maneuver the skillet. We used five models (priced from $6.87 to $16.00) to move hot skillets off the stovetop and from a 450-degree oven to a cooling rack. (Keeping the covers on the skillet handles throughout use was not an option for any model; they continued to absorb heat and offered less protection over time.) We found that material and fit separated our winner from the pack. The Lodge Nokona Leather Handle Holder ($13.43) features a liner made from a heat-resistant fiber called aramid that helped the cover stay cool enough to touch for 6½ minutes (our runner-up protected our hands for just 2½ minutes). And while other models were too loose or too tight, the fit on our favorite was perfectly snug. –M.B.

Fire Extinguisher Recall

Kidde has issued a recall of all its fire extinguishers with plastic handles, including our winning model FA110 (or FA110G) and our not-recommended model RESSP. Go to Kidde.com for more information or call the Kidde Customer Support Line at 855-271-0773. We still recommend our second- and third-place models, the First Alert Tundra Fire Extinguishing Spray and the Amerex 2.5 lb ABC Dry Chemical Fire Extinguisher.

For complete testing results, go to CooksIllustrated.com/apr18.

INDEX
March & April 2018

RECIPES

MAIN DISHES
Indoor Pulled Chicken 5
One-Hour Pizza 9
Perfect Pan-Seared Pork Tenderloin Steaks 6
Sous Vide Pork Tenderloin Steaks 7
Three-Cup Chicken 21

SIDE DISHES
Chinese Restaurant–Style Rice 21
Pan-Steamed Broccolini with Shallot 15
   with Ginger 15

BREAD
Irish Brown Soda Bread 13

SOUP AND STEW
Brazilian Shrimp and Fish Stew (Moqueca) 11
Moroccan Lentil and Chickpea Soup (Harira) 14

DESSERT AND SNACK
Best Lemon Bars 23
Spicy Caramel Popcorn 19

SAUCES AND CONDIMENTS
All-Purpose Caramel Sauce 19
Amatriciana 17
Caramel-Braised Shallots with Black Pepper 19
Classic Basil Pesto 16
Garlic and Oil Sauce (Aglio e Olio) 17
Harissa 29
Lexington Vinegar Barbecue Sauce 5
Puttanesca 16
Quick Tomato Sauce 16
Scallion-Ginger Relish 6
Simple Italian-Style Meat Sauce 17
South Carolina Mustard Barbecue Sauce 5
Sweet and Tangy Barbecue Sauce 5

BONUS ONLINE CONTENT
More recipes, reviews, and videos are available at **CooksIllustrated.com/apr18**

RECIPES
Pan-Steamed Broccolini with Garlic and Mustard
Pan-Steamed Broccolini with Lemon and Capers
Perfect Pan-Seared Pork Tenderloin Steaks for Two
Sous Vide Butter-Basted Thick-Cut Rib-Eye Steaks
Sous Vide Pork Tenderloin Steaks for Two
Sous Vide Soft-Poached Eggs
Three-Cup Chicken for Two

EXPANDED REVIEWS
Tasting Pecorino Romano and Romano Cheeses
Tasting Turkey Bacon
Testing Cast-Iron Skillet Handle Covers
Testing Flexible Cutting Mats
Testing Ginger Graters
Testing Parchment Paper
Testing Silicone Baking Mats
Testing Sous Vide Circulators

BONUS TECHNIQUES
Sous Vide Guide

▶ **RECIPE VIDEOS**
Want to see how to make any of the recipes in this issue? There's a free video for that.

FOLLOW US ON SOCIAL MEDIA
facebook.com/CooksIllustrated
twitter.com/TestKitchen
pinterest.com/TestKitchen
instagram.com/CooksIllustrated
youtube.com/AmericasTestKitchen

America's Test Kitchen
COOKING SCHOOL

Visit our online cooking school today, where we offer 180+ online lessons covering a range of recipes and cooking methods. Whether you're a novice just starting out or are already an advanced cook looking for new techniques, our cooking school is designed to give you confidence in the kitchen and make you a better cook.

▶ **Start a 14-Day Free Trial at** OnlineCookingSchool.com

Cook's Illustrated on iPad
Enjoy *Cook's* wherever you are, whenever you want.

Did you know that *Cook's Illustrated* is available on iPad? Go to **CooksIllustrated.com/iPad** to download the app through iTunes. You'll be able to start a free trial of the digital edition, which includes bonus features such as recipe videos, full-color photos, and step-by-step slide shows of each recipe.

Go to CooksIllustrated.com/iPad to download our app through iTunes.

All-Purpose Caramel Sauce, 19

Three-Cup Chicken, 21

Irish Brown Soda Bread, 13

Perfect Pan-Seared Pork Tenderloin Steaks, 6

Moroccan Lentil and Chickpea Soup (Harira), 14

Best Lemon Bars, 23

Pan-Steamed Broccolini with Shallot, 15

Brazilian Shrimp and Fish Stew (Moqueca), 11

One-Hour Pizza, 9

Indoor Pulled Chicken, 5

PHOTOGRAPHY: CARL TREMBLAY, STEVE KLISE; STYLING: KENDRA McKNIGHT, ELLE SIMONE

NUMBER 152   MAY & JUNE 2018

COOK'S
ILLUSTRATED

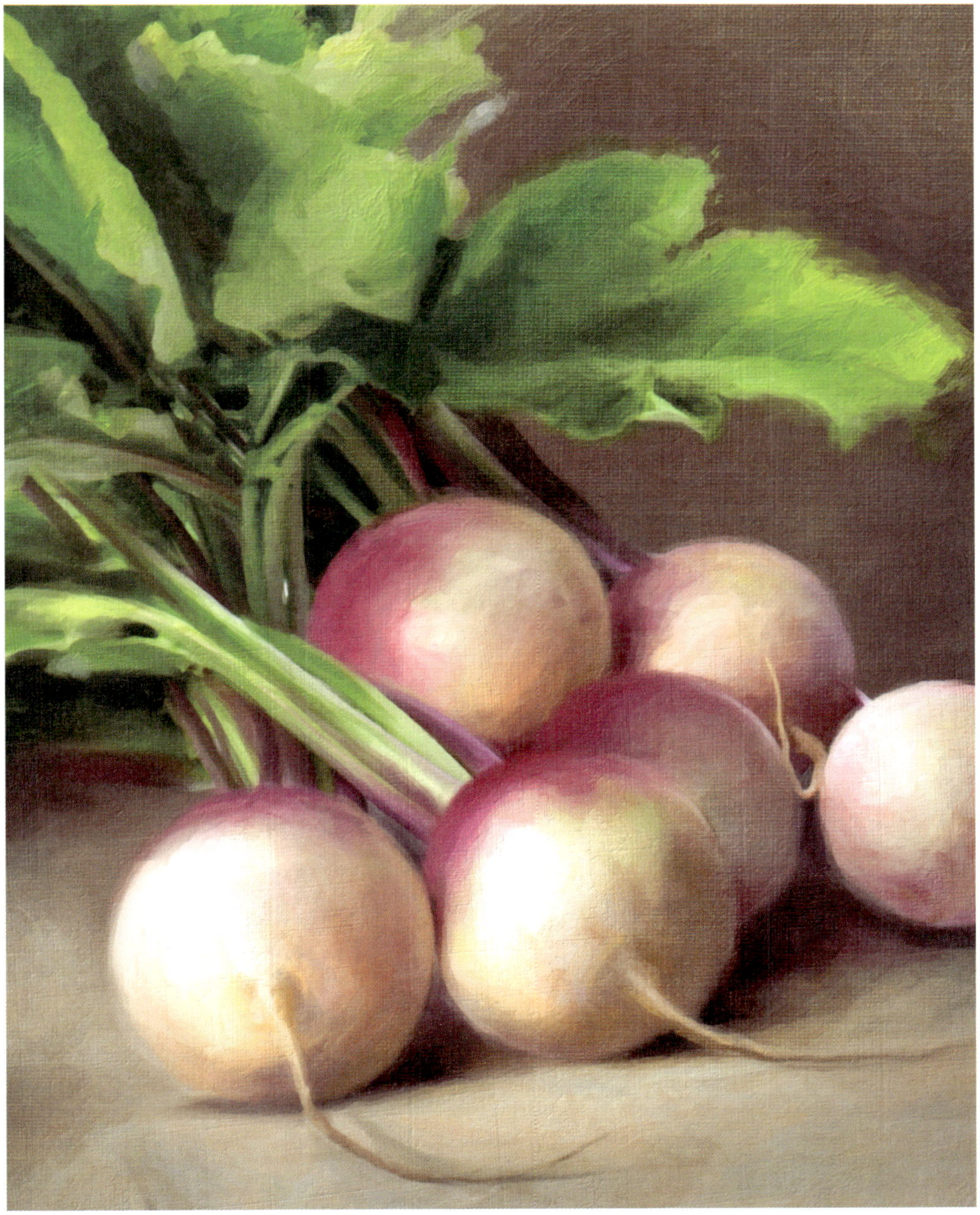

Roast Chicken with
Warm Bread Salad
Ultimate Skillet Dinner

The Best Steak
for Grilling

Roasted Salmon
New Approach, Perfect Results

Buttery Spring
Vegetables

Everyday Pancakes
Put Down the Box Mix

Quick Salads with
Chicken

Best Cocoa Powder
Does It Have to Be Dutched?

Chocolate Semifreddo
Testing Air Fryers
Slow-Roasted Pork Chops

CooksIllustrated.com
$6.95 U.S./$8.95 CANADA

Display until June 4, 2018

MAY & JUNE 2018

PAGE 20

2 Quick Tips
Quick and easy ways to perform everyday tasks, from grating garlic to proofing pizza dough.
COMPILED BY ANNIE PETITO

4 Why You Should Be Grilling Skirt Steak
If you're not grilling skirt steak, you should be: It's a great cut for marinating, it cooks in minutes, and it's especially beefy, tender, and juicy—as long as you buy the right kind. BY LAN LAM

6 Roasted Salmon for a Crowd
When it comes to serving a crowd, most cooks turn to a large roast or bird. But wouldn't it be nice to serve fish? BY ANDREW JANJIGIAN

8 Roast Chicken with Bread Salad
San Francisco's Zuni Café serves perfect roast chicken with a chewy-crisp, warm bread salad that has a cultlike following. We pay homage to the dish with a streamlined take. BY ANNIE PETITO

10 Slow-Roasted Deviled Pork Chops
A punchy mustard-based paste is an age-old cover-up for mild-mannered cuts. But it can't hide meat that's dry and tough below the surface.
BY ANNIE PETITO

12 Anytime Pancakes
Put down the box mix. You've got everything you need to make tall, fluffy pancakes in minutes.
BY LAN LAM

14 Revamping Chicken Salads
Throwing together leftover cooked chicken, dressing, and greens is a way to put dinner on the table without much thought. Maybe that's exactly the problem. BY STEVE DUNN

16 Make the Most of Your Microwave
A microwave oven can do so much more than reheat leftovers. It can save time and prevent messes, all without heating up your kitchen.
BY KRISTIN SARGIANIS

18 Great Barley Side Dishes
Producing distinct, perfectly textured grains is as easy as boiling water. BY STEVE DUNN

19 Beijing-Style Meat Sauce and Noodles
Meet *zha jiang mian*, the most popular Chinese dish you've never heard of.
BY ANDREW JANJIGIAN

20 Chocolate Semifreddo
Italy's elegant alternative to gelato (and ice cream) is rich and decadently creamy—and requires no special equipment to make.
BY ANNIE PETITO

22 Buttery Spring Vegetables
No disrespect to dessert, but perfectly cooked vegetables can dazzle, too. BY ANDREA GEARY

23 The Best Cocoa Powder
The big debate in cocoa powder has always been Dutch-processed versus natural. Is that really the most important factor? BY KATE SHANNON

26 Testing Plastic Food Storage Containers
Could we find a well-made, easy-to-use container that wouldn't warp, stain, leak, or wear out too soon? BY LISA McMANUS

28 Ingredient Notes
BY STEVE DUNN, ANDREW JANJIGIAN, LAN LAM, ANNIE PETITO & KRISTIN SARGIANIS

30 Kitchen Notes
BY STEVE DUNN, ANDREA GEARY, ANDREW JANJIGIAN, LAN LAM & ANNIE PETITO

32 Equipment Corner
BY MIYE BROMBERG, LISA McMANUS & LAUREN SAVOIE

BACK COVER ILLUSTRATED BY JOHN BURGOYNE

Bitter Greens

The bristly, chartreuse leaves of **CURLY ENDIVE** taste relatively mellow, with earthy hints of mushroom and green beans. The light, clean flavor of feathery-yet-crisp **FRISÉE** is the perfect foil to crispy-chewy bacon and runny egg in the classic bistro salad *frisée aux lardons*. Raw **ESCAROLE** is pea-sweet and juicy, but wilting brings out its mineral-y flavor and dense, satisfying chew. Meaty **DANDELION GREENS** taste like spinach but more vegetal. Mature **ARUGULA** packs a fierce, peppery burn, as does deceptively dainty **WATERCRESS**. Shaggy **MUSTARD GREENS** deliver tingly, wasabi-like heat that's also savory. Pungent and leathery, burgundy **RADICCHIO** leaves soften when heated, but their creamy white ribs retain substantial crunch. Those traits are exaggerated in bullet-shaped **TREVISO**, a variety of radicchio. Oblong Belgian **ENDIVE** leaves deliver thirst-quenching crispness and flavor that's both bitter and buttery; their stiff, deep cups make them ideal for scooping up rich dips.

America's Test Kitchen, a real test kitchen located in Boston, is the home of more than 60 test cooks and editors. Our mission is to test recipes until we understand exactly how and why they work and eventually arrive at the very best version. We also test kitchen equipment and taste supermarket ingredients in search of products that offer the best value and flavor. You can watch us work by tuning in to *America's Test Kitchen* (AmericasTestKitchen.com) and *Cook's Country from America's Test Kitchen* (CooksCountry.com) on public television and listen to our weekly segments on *The Splendid Table* on public radio. You can also follow us on Facebook, Twitter, Pinterest, and Instagram.

EDITORIAL STAFF

Chief Executive Officer David Nussbaum
Chief Creative Officer Jack Bishop
Editor in Chief Dan Souza
Executive Editor Amanda Agee
Deputy Editor Rebecca Hays
Executive Managing Editor Todd Meier
Executive Food Editor Keith Dresser
Senior Editors Andrea Geary, Andrew Janjigian, Lan Lam
Senior Editors, Features Elizabeth Bomze, Kristin Sargianis
Associate Editor Annie Petito
Lead Cook, Photo Team Dan Cellucci
Test Cook Steve Dunn
Assistant Test Cooks Mady Nichas, Jessica Rudolph
Senior Copy Editor Krista Magnuson
Copy Editor Jillian Campbell
Senior Science Research Editor Paul Adams

Executive Editor, Tastings & Testings Lisa McManus
Deputy Editor, Tastings & Testings Hannah Crowley
Associate Editors, Tastings & Testings
  Miye Bromberg, Lauren Savoie, Kate Shannon
Assistant Editor, Tastings & Testings Emily Phares
Editorial Assistant, Tastings & Testings Carolyn Grillo

Director, Creative Operations Alice Carpenter
Test Kitchen Director Erin McMurrer
Assistant Test Kitchen Director Alexxa Benson
Test Kitchen Manager Meridith Lippard
Test Kitchen Facilities Manager Sophie Clingan-Darack
Senior Kitchen Assistant Receiver Kelly Ryan
Senior Kitchen Assistant Shopper Marissa Bunnewith
Lead Kitchen Assistant Ena Gudiel
Kitchen Assistants Gladis Campos, Blanca Castanza,
  Amarilys Merced, Sujeila Trujillo

Creative Director John Torres
Design Director Greg Galvan
Photography Director Julie Cote
Designer Maggie Edgar
Senior Staff Photographer Daniel J. van Ackere
Staff Photographers Steve Klise, Kevin White
Photography Producer Meredith Mulcahy
Styling Kendra McKnight

Executive Editor, Web Christine Liu
Managing Editor, Web Mari Levine
Senior Editors, Web Roger Metcalf, Briana Palma
Assistant Editor, Web Molly Farrar

BUSINESS STAFF

Chief Financial Officer Jackie McCauley Ford
Senior Manager, Customer Support Tim Quinn
Senior Customer Loyalty & Support Specialist
  Rebecca Kowalski
Customer Loyalty & Support Specialist J.P. Dubuque
Imaging Manager Lauren Robbins
Production & Imaging Specialists Heather Dube,
  Dennis Noble, Jessica Voas

Chief Revenue Officer Sara Domville
Senior Director, Events & Special Projects
  Mehgan Conciatori
Partnership Marketing Manager Pamela Putprush
Director, Special Accounts Erica Nye
Director, Sponsorship Marketing & Client Services
  Christine Anagnostis
Client Services Manager Kate Zebrowski
Client Service & Marketing Representative Claire Gambee

Chief Digital Officer Fran Middleton
VP, Marketing Natalie Vinard
**Marketing Director, Social Media & Content
  Strategy** Claire Oliverson
Senior Social Media Coordinators Kelsey Hopper,
  Morgan Mannino

**Senior VP, Human Resources & Organizational
  Development** Colleen Zelina
Human Resources Director Adele Shapiro

Circulation Services ProCirc

Cover Art Robert Papp

PRINTED IN THE USA

ILLUSTRATION: JOHN BURGOYNE

LETTER FROM THE EDITOR

HOW DO YOU SAY "FAILURE" IN FRENCH?

Macarons are the beloved French confection featuring two brightly colored, light-as-air almond flour meringue cookies sandwiched around decadent fillings such as pistachio buttercream, chocolate ganache, and lemon curd. They are at once refined yet playful, delicate yet satisfying.

And I hate them.

Let me explain. Years ago, while I was a test cook for this magazine, I was assigned the weighty task of developing a recipe for macarons. I eagerly jumped in. I visited big-name French bakeries in New York City to sample the epitome of the form. I enrolled in a weekend macaron class. I read journal articles with titles such as "Effect of Sugar, Citric Acid and Egg White Type on the Microstructural and Mechanical Properties of Meringues." I considered learning French (but got busy). And here's the key bit: I made almost 120 batches of macarons in the test kitchen over the span of weeks. I lived macarons. And the recipe? It never made it to print.

The term "foolproof" gets bandied about a fair amount in the food world these days. It's such a compelling concept—who doesn't want a recipe that can't be messed up? Well, *Cook's Illustrated* realized years ago that the only way we feel comfortable putting that word in front of one of our recipes is if you tell us it should be there. So, many years ago we started something completely unheard of. We asked readers to make our not-quite-final recipes at home and give us honest feedback. Today, we have more than 31,000 home recipe testers (and another 17,000 home shoppers) peppered across the country. You tell us when our instructions don't work or are hard to follow (or when an ingredient isn't available in your neighborhood). In short, you tell us whether or not a recipe is foolproof. And we listen. We keeping working on every recipe until at least 80 percent (and often more than 90 percent) of those who make it tell us they would make it again. Know where I'm going with this? That's right: My macarons recipe never hit that mark.

Dan Souza

Around the office we call this cadre of volunteers "friends of *Cook's Illustrated*." If you're such a friend, I would like to express our sincere gratitude for your support. You help make this magazine great. Thank you. If you'd like to join in on the home testing fun, we'd love to have you. You can sign up at AmericasTestKitchen.com/recipe_testing. There's zero obligation to make any of the recipes we send you. And who knows? You might just get a sneak peek at that macarons recipe if it ever comes back to life.

Dan Souza
Editor in Chief

FOR INQUIRIES, ORDERS, OR MORE INFORMATION

COOK'S ILLUSTRATED MAGAZINE
Cook's Illustrated magazine (ISSN 1068-2821), number 152, is published bimonthly by America's Test Kitchen Limited Partnership, 21 Drydock Avenue, Suite 210E, Boston, MA 02210. Copyright 2018 America's Test Kitchen Limited Partnership. Periodicals postage paid at Boston, MA, and additional mailing offices, USPS #012487. Publications Mail Agreement No. 40020778. Return undeliverable Canadian addresses to P.O. Box 875, Station A, Windsor, ON N9A 6P2. POSTMASTER: Send address changes to *Cook's Illustrated*, P.O. Box 6018, Harlan, A 51593-1518. For subscription and gift subscription orders, subscription inquiries, or change of address notices, visit AmericasTestKitchen.com/support, call 800-526-8442 in the U.S. or 515-237-3663 from outside the U.S., or write to us at *Cook's Illustrated*, P.O. Box 6018, Harlan, IA 51593-1518.

CooksIllustrated.com
At the all new CooksIllustrated.com, you can order books and subscriptions, sign up for our free e-newsletter, or renew your magazine subscription. Join the website and gain access to 25 years of *Cook's Illustrated* recipes, equipment tests, and ingredient tastings, as well as companion videos for every recipe in this issue.

COOKBOOKS
We sell more than 50 cookbooks, including *All-Time Best Appetizers* and *Kitchen Smarts*. To order, visit our bookstore at CooksIllustrated.com/bookstore.

EDITORIAL OFFICE 21 Drydock Avenue, Suite 210E, Boston, MA 02210; 617-232-1000; fax: 617-232-1572.
For subscription inquiries, visit AmericasTestKitchen.com/support or call 800-526-8442.

QUICK TIPS

≥ COMPILED BY ANNIE PETITO ≤

Buffer for Wine Bottles
Bill Lewis of Mount Kisco, N.Y., found a way to safely transport multiple bottles of wine without a divided cardboard box. He packs two rolls of paper towels next to each other in a sturdy bag and slips the bottles on either side of them. The snug, cushioned fit prevents the bottles from moving.

How to Handle Garlic for Grating
Rather than peel garlic cloves before grating them—and then inadvertently skin his fingers on the blade as he gets down to the nub—David Sokol of Shelburne, Vt., cuts the unpeeled clove in half crosswise and uses the skin as a handle while he grates.

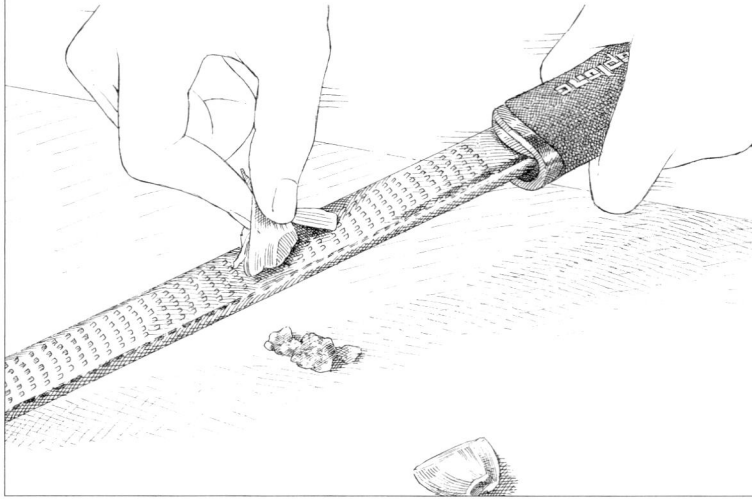

Another Way to Freeze and Prep Chipotles
Rachel Delany of Charleston, S.C., finds that freezing leftover canned chipotle chiles in adobo sauce in ice cube trays makes for easy portioning. Instead of defrosting the chiles, she prefers to mince them when they're still frozen and stiff.

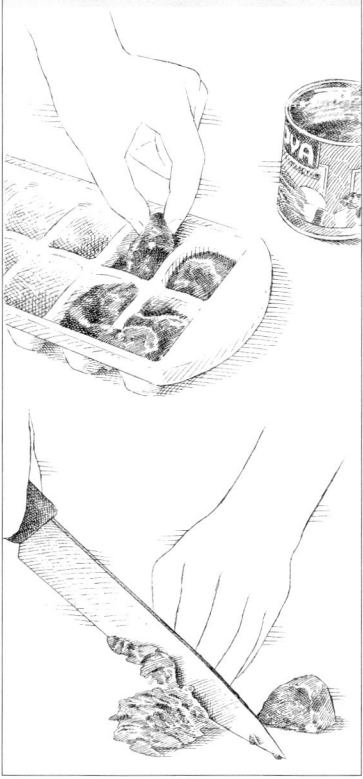

Reminder About Surplus Spices
When Carrie Andersson of Stillwater, Minn., buys bulk spices and ends up with more than will fit in her small spice jar, she places a sticker marked with a "plus" symbol on the lid to remind herself that she has more in the cupboard.

Nonstick Cover for Casseroles
When baking cheese-topped casseroles such as lasagna or enchiladas, Benjamin Harvey of Swannanoa, N.C., covers the dish with an overturned rimmed baking sheet (or a disposable aluminum baking pan) instead of aluminum foil. Since the sheet doesn't directly touch the cheese, sticking isn't a problem.

Spill-Proof Cardboard Containers
Kate Regan of Duluth, Minn., uses binder clips to clamp shut cardboard containers of cream, milk, or juice that don't have resealable caps.

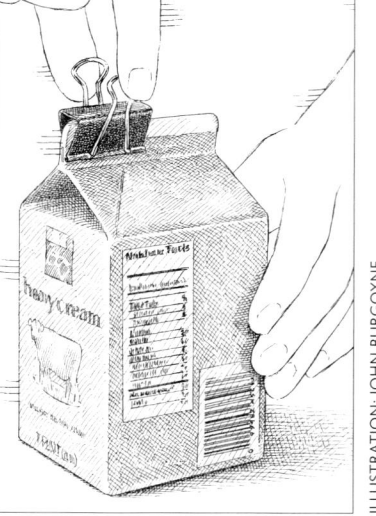

SEND US YOUR TIPS We will provide a complimentary one-year subscription for each tip we print. Send your tip, name, address, and telephone number to Quick Tips, *Cook's Illustrated*, 21 Drydock Avenue, Suite 210E, Boston, MA 02210, or to QuickTips@AmericasTestKitchen.com.

Proof Pizza Dough in Takeout Containers
Geoff Poulet of Cambridge, Mass., uses round plastic takeout containers to proof pizza dough in the refrigerator. They're the perfect shape to hold a flattened dough disk and tall enough to allow the dough to rise before it's turned out for shaping.

Rubber-Glove Rubber Bands
Eleanor Hammonds of Austin, Texas, has found a way to reuse part of her old pairs of rubber gloves. She turns them into rubber bands by cutting narrow rings from the cuffs.

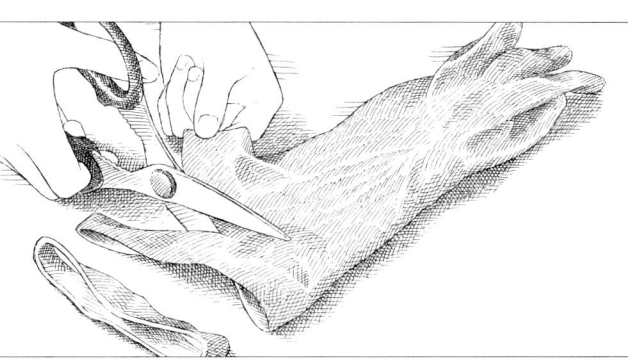

Quick-Soften Butter for a Baking Pan
If she's forgotten to soften butter for greasing a baking pan, Sandra Fried of Seattle, Wash., melts some in the pan while the oven preheats. Once the butter has softened or is just melted, she spreads it evenly over the pan with a pastry brush and then lets the pan cool before adding the dough or batter.

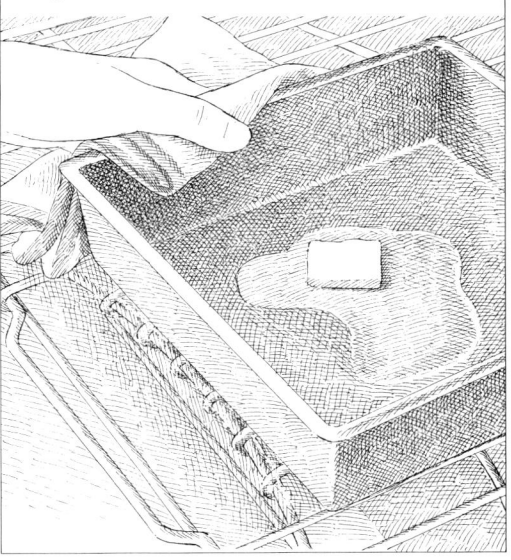

Rinsing Fruit on the Go
Jaime Kriss of New York, N.Y., knows it's best to wash fruits such as berries just before you eat them to prevent molding. To rinse them on the go, she packs them in a zipper-lock bag and then cuts or pokes some small holes in the bottom with scissors to make a tiny "colander." When she's ready to eat, she simply fills the bag with water and then lets it drain out.

Easy-Open Zipper-Lock Bags
To facilitate opening his zipper-lock bags, Jerry Kirk of New Bern, N.C., cuts small notches into all the flaps just above the zippers, which makes it easy to grab the two flaps and pull open the bags.

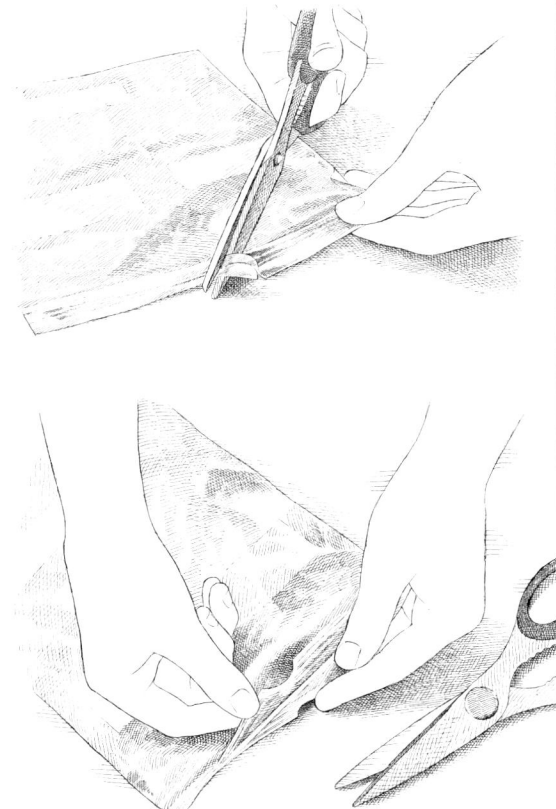

A Sponge for Cleaning Narrow Bottles
When she needs to clean a narrow coffee mug or water bottle, Ashlyn Anderson of Wauwatosa, Wis., uses rubber bands to attach a sponge to a clean wooden spoon, creating a long-handled sponge that can reach all the way down to the bottom of the vessel.

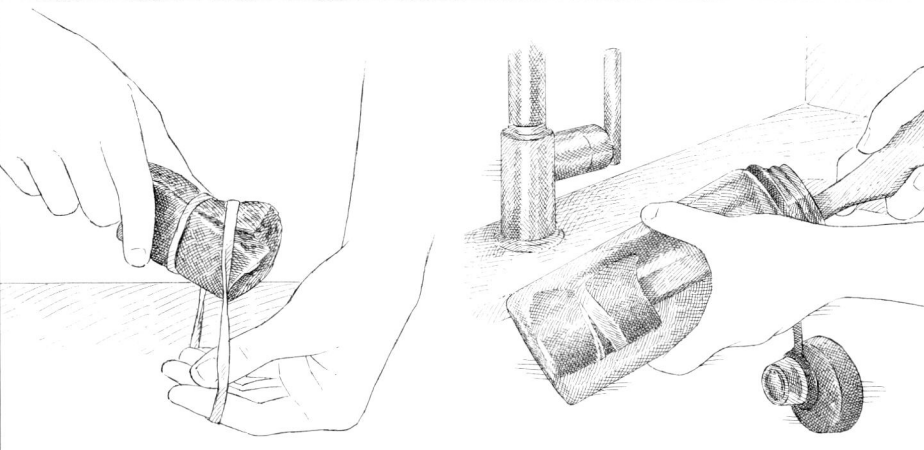

Why You Should Be Grilling Skirt Steak

If you're not grilling skirt steak, you should be: It's a great cut for marinating, it cooks in minutes, and it's especially beefy, tender, and juicy—as long as you buy the right kind.

⋺ BY LAN LAM ⋹

Back when I was a line cook at Craigie Street Bistrot in Cambridge, Massachusetts, we had a nightly routine involving skirt steak. The end pieces were never plated because they were too small to show off the beautifully cooked beef, so the chef habitually tossed them into a "meat bucket." At the end of the night, the tidbits were heated up under the broiler for a postshift snack. Trust me when I tell you (after many, many bites) that this fatty cut is intensely beefy, tender, and juicy—a true cook's treat.

Finding My Mojo

Skirt steak is long, narrow, and only ½ to 1 inch thick. Because it's so thin, you need to cook it over high heat to ensure that the outside is well browned by the time the interior is tender and juicy. That makes a grill, which is easy to get blisteringly hot, the best tool for the job. As a bonus, a large grill grate can accommodate all the ribbon-like steaks at the same time instead of in batches.

Skirt steak is also a great candidate for a marinade. In the test kitchen, we often shy away from marinating meat because the flavorings don't penetrate much beyond the surface of a thick, smooth cut. But because skirt steak is so thin, with loose, open fibers and lots of nooks and crannies, a marinade can have a big effect (see "A Steak Tailor-Made for Marinating").

I knew exactly what I wanted to bathe my steaks in: a garlicky, citrusy, Cuban-style *mojo* that would really stand up to the rich, buttery beef. Once I'd perfected the marinade and the steak cookery, I planned on whipping up a complementary sauce to drizzle onto the meat.

Raising the Steaks

Skirt steaks are often rolled up for packaging because when they are unrolled, they can be nearly 2 feet long. I divided 2 pounds of steak (enough to serve four to six people) into 6- to 8-inch lengths.

▶ **Look: Lan Finds Her Mojo**
A step-by-step video is available at CooksIllustrated.com/jun18

Skirt steak's long, narrow shape makes it unwieldy on the plate, so it is typically sliced before serving.

Then came the marinade: I stirred together ½ cup of orange juice and 2 tablespoons of lime juice (my substitute for the difficult-to-find sour orange juice traditionally used in mojo) and added the usual seasonings: ground cumin, dried oregano, plenty of minced garlic, and a few red pepper flakes. I also made sure to add a good amount of salt—1½ teaspoons for the 2 pounds of meat. The salt would not only season the meat—it would also dissolve some proteins and loosen the bundles of muscle fibers, making the steak more tender, and hold in water to keep the meat moist.

I pulled out a 13 by 9-inch baking dish, which would be a good vessel for soaking the steaks with minimal overlapping. I refrigerated the steaks for an hour, flipping them at the 30-minute mark to make sure both sides got coated with marinade.

When I removed the steaks from the marinade, I thoroughly patted them dry with paper towels since any excess moisture would inhibit browning; I then rubbed them with a light coating of oil. Over a hot fire (created by distributing 6 quarts of lit coals evenly over half the grill) the steaks cooked to medium (130 degrees) in 6 to 8 minutes. Although we bring most steaks to medium-rare (125 degrees), we have found that the tougher muscle fibers of skirt steak need to hit 130 degrees before they shrink and loosen enough to turn perfectly tender.

I gathered my colleagues grillside to have a taste, and the feedback rolled in: The mojo flavor was coming through beautifully, but the steaks could taste even beefier. Also, the browning was good but not great.

Taking It Outside

I had ideas about how to address both problems, so I reached for the two skirt steaks that had arrived in that morning's delivery. I was surprised to see that one was almost twice as wide as the other. But they looked similar otherwise, so I carried on.

This time I added a little soy sauce to the mojo marinade (to compensate, I halved the amount of salt). Soy sauce can be a secret weapon in marinades: Its salt seasons, and its glutamates enhance savory flavor.

Once the steaks were out of the marinade and patted dry, I incorporated an ingredient for better browning: baking soda. Added to the oil I had been rubbing onto the steaks, baking soda would help create more substantial browning by raising the meat's pH. The higher its pH, the better meat is able to hold on to water, so it browns instead of releasing the moisture onto the grill grates and creating steam. A higher pH also speeds up the Maillard reaction, making the treated meat brown even better and more quickly.

I was pleased to see the steaks rapidly develop a deep sear on the grill. This was a signal that they were likely done cooking, so I slid them to the cooler side of the grill to take their temperature (their thinness made temping them on the hotter side risky because they could easily overcook). Sure enough, they registered 130 degrees, so I gave them a 10-minute rest to allow the juices to redistribute throughout the meat. As I sampled a few slices, I was happy to find that the meat was not just deeply seasoned but also had an even beefier flavor than before, thanks to the umami-rich soy sauce.

However, the steaks' texture was a different story: Even though I'd soaked both the narrow and the wide steaks in the same marinade and cooked them

Skirt (Steak) Shopping

There are two types of skirt steak: inside and outside. The inside skirt comes from the transverse abdominal muscle and is rather tough; the more desirable outside skirt comes from the diaphragm and is quite tender.

BUY THE OUTSIDE SKIRT
3 to 4 inches wide, ½ to 1 inch thick, quite tender

AVOID THE INSIDE SKIRT
5 to 7 inches wide, ¼ to ½ inch thick, very chewy

WHY SKIRT STEAK IS HARD TO FIND
If you have trouble finding skirt steak, that's because it's a hot commodity: There are only four skirt steaks (two outside, two inside) on each cow.

ONLY FOUR PER ANIMAL

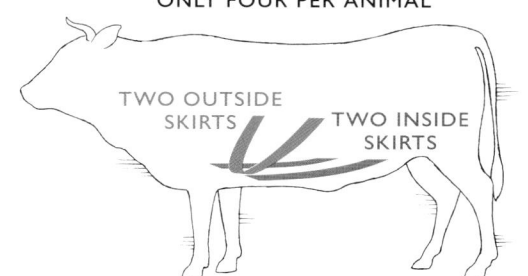

TWO OUTSIDE SKIRTS / TWO INSIDE SKIRTS

---

on the same grill to precisely 130 degrees, the narrow steak was much more tender than the wide one. It was only after speaking to several butchers that I understood why: It turns out that there are two types of skirt steak—the inside skirt and the outside skirt—that come from separate parts of the cow and therefore have markedly different textures (for more information, see "Skirt (Steak) Shopping").

Recycle, Reuse

I prepared one more batch, making sure to use outside skirt steaks. While the meat marinated, I started gathering citrus, garlic, and spices for the mojo sauce I'd been planning. But wait: All the ingredients I needed were already in the leftover marinade. Why not reuse it? I poured it from the baking pan into a saucepan, brought it to a boil to make it food-safe, and took a taste. It needed richness and a little extra acidity to become a sauce, so I stirred in a little lime juice and extra-virgin olive oil. I also tossed in orange and lime zests to give the sauce more of the bright, tropical flavor typical of sour oranges.

Once the steaks were off the grill and had rested, I carefully sliced them against the grain and at an angle (see "How to Slice Tough, Thin Steaks" on page 31) before drizzling on the mojo sauce. My favorite steak had now realized its full potential: The beautifully seared meat was rich, well seasoned, juicy, and tender, and the vibrant sauce played off of it beautifully.

GRILLED MOJO-MARINATED SKIRT STEAK
SERVES 4 TO 6

Skirt steaks come from two different muscles and are sometimes labeled as inside skirt steak or outside skirt steak. The more desirable outside skirt steak measures 3 to 4 inches wide and ½ to 1 inch thick. Avoid the inside skirt steak, which typically measures 5 to 7 inches wide and ¼ to ½ inch thick, as it is very chewy. Skirt steak is most tender when cooked to medium (130 to 135 degrees). Thin steaks cook very quickly, so we recommend using an instant-read thermometer for a quick and accurate measurement. See page 31 for slicing instructions.

- 6 garlic cloves, minced
- 2 tablespoons soy sauce
- 1 teaspoon grated lime zest plus ¼ cup juice (2 limes)
- 1 teaspoon ground cumin
- 1 teaspoon dried oregano
- Salt
- ½ teaspoon grated orange zest plus ½ cup juice
- ¼ teaspoon red pepper flakes
- 2 pounds skirt steak, trimmed and cut with grain into 6- to 8-inch-long steaks
- 2 tablespoons extra-virgin olive oil
- 1 teaspoon baking soda

1. Combine garlic, soy sauce, 2 tablespoons lime juice, cumin, oregano, ¾ teaspoon salt, orange juice, and pepper flakes in 13 by 9-inch baking dish. Place steaks in dish. Flip steaks to coat both sides with marinade. Cover and refrigerate for 1 hour, flipping steaks halfway through refrigerating.

2. Remove steaks from marinade and transfer marinade to small saucepan. Pat steaks dry with paper towels. Combine 1 tablespoon oil and baking soda in small bowl. Rub oil mixture evenly onto both sides of each steak.

3. Bring marinade to boil over high heat and boil for 30 seconds. Transfer to bowl and stir in lime zest, orange zest, remaining 2 tablespoons lime juice, and remaining 1 tablespoon oil. Set aside sauce.

4A. FOR A CHARCOAL GRILL: About 25 minutes before grilling, open bottom vent completely. Light large chimney starter filled with charcoal briquettes (6 quarts). When top coals are partially covered with ash, pour evenly over half of grill. Set cooking grate in place, cover, and open lid vent completely. Heat grill until hot, about 5 minutes.

4B. FOR A GAS GRILL: Turn all burners to high, cover, and heat grill until hot, about 15 minutes. Turn off 1 burner (if using grill with more than 2 burners, turn off burner farthest from primary burner) and leave other burner(s) on high.

5. Clean and oil cooking grate. Cook steaks on hotter side of grill until well browned and meat registers 130 to 135 degrees (for medium), 2 to 4 minutes per side. (Move steaks to cooler side of grill before taking temperature to prevent them from overcooking.) Transfer steaks to cutting board, tent with aluminum foil, and let rest for 10 minutes. Cut steaks on bias against grain into ½-inch-thick slices. Arrange slices on serving platter, drizzle with 2 tablespoons sauce, and serve, passing extra sauce separately.

SCIENCE A Steak Tailor-Made for Marinating

We don't typically marinate steak since we have found that marinades don't penetrate more than a few millimeters beyond its surface. For a thick-cut steak, that means minimal flavor impact. But skirt steak is different: It has much more surface area than other cuts. And because it's so thin, the ratio of surface area to volume is quite large. That means there is a lot of exterior space for a marinade to flavor. If you look carefully, the grain of a skirt steak forms peaks and valleys like, well, a pleated skirt: The amount of fabric required to make a pleated skirt is much greater than the amount required to make a straight skirt. To illustrate this, we placed a measuring tape on a skirt steak and carefully pressed it into the valleys. When we removed the measuring tape, we found that the surface area for a skirt steak was three times that of a strip steak of the same weight.

SKIRT MODEL
Much like a pleated skirt, the surface of a skirt steak has lots of nooks and crannies. That means it has a large surface area for a marinade to flavor.

Roasted Salmon for a Crowd

When it comes to serving a crowd, most cooks turn to a large roast or bird. But wouldn't it be nice to serve fish?

→ BY ANDREW JANJIGIAN ←

The vast majority of the time when I cook salmon, I buy individual fillets for quick weeknight meals. They're easy to pan-sear, poach, roast, or grill, and their uniform shape means they cook evenly. But salmon is ideal for entertaining, too. It requires little prep work; cooks faster than a roast or stew; dresses up beautifully with countless sauces, glazes, and rubs; and makes a striking centerpiece.

But cooking a whole side of salmon—a single fillet that weighs 4 to 5 pounds and serves upwards of eight people—demands different considerations than cooking individual fillets does. The large fillet doesn't fit in a skillet, so you can't cook it on the stovetop. But cooking it in the oven comes with hurdles; namely, browning is more difficult without the stove's intense heat.

I wanted to come up with an approach for a whole roasted fillet that would be evenly moist inside and gorgeously browned on top. And since this salmon would be a for-company dish, I wanted bulletproof methods for shuttling the cooked fillet from pan to platter and for cutting tidy portions.

Embroiled in Problems

I tried one recipe that actually called for flipping the fish halfway through cooking, which was a cruel proposition. I knew I could come up with a more straightforward approach that would deliver the results I sought. I was interested in experimenting with the broiler, which would be the surest way to apply concentrated heat to the fish's surface.

I placed a 5-pound (average weight for a whole side) salmon fillet on a rimmed baking sheet, slid it onto an oven rack placed about 7 inches beneath a preheated broiler (which I hoped was enough distance from the element that the fish wouldn't burn before it was cooked through), and cooked it until the thickest portion registered 125 degrees. That took about 20 minutes, by which time the surface had quite a bit of uneven color. A whole side of salmon slopes considerably on the tail end, so the browning was mostly isolated to the thicker portion that was closest to the broiler element. Meanwhile, the fierce heat had overcooked the top 1/2 inch of the thicker part and all of the thinner ends and caused the fish to shed loads of albumin, the unsightly white protein that seeps out of overcooked fish.

Once the fish is done salting, it can be on the table in 30 minutes. And either of our no-cook accompaniments can be prepared while it roasts.

▶ Watch: Salmon for Company
A step-by-step video is available at CooksIllustrated.com/jun18

Honey-Do

The easiest way to prevent the tapered portions from overcooking was to do away with them. I had the fishmonger lop off the tail portion and belly flap, leaving me with a uniformly thick fillet that weighed about 4 pounds, which was still plenty for at least eight guests. (If you do buy a whole side, see "Buying and Trimming a Side of Salmon" on page 28 for tips on trimming the tail and belly flap.)

Next, I salted the fish, which we've found helps it retain moisture and prevents the albumin from seeping out during cooking. After 1 hour, I patted it dry and repeated the broiler experiment. This time, the albumin stayed inside the fish and the flesh was nicely seasoned. But the uppermost part of the fish was still parched.

What I needed was a way to help the fish brown as quickly as possible under the broiler so that I could lower the oven temperature and the salmon could cook gently for the bulk of the time. Sprinkling sugar over the top of the fish helped, but the color was still spotty—it was hard to evenly distribute the crystals—and rather pale. But what about honey? The sugars it contains caramelize more readily than white sugar. I used 2 tablespoons, which was enough to coat the entire fillet but not so much that the fish tasted sweet, and it was easy to brush on in an even layer (for more information, see "The Sweet Spot for Even Browning").

This time, the surface began to caramelize in 5 minutes and was nicely browned after 15, at which point I turned the oven to 250 degrees and slow-roasted the fish until done. The flesh was almost uniformly cooked from top to bottom, and it was better still when I tried again and turned down the oven temperature after 10 minutes (doing so accounted for any carryover cooking that occurred while the broiler cooled).

TECHNIQUE | CUTTING PERFECT PORTIONS

Don't mar your perfectly cooked side of salmon with sloppy portioning. Here's how to divvy up the fillet into tidy pieces.

1. Use thin metal spatula to cut down center seam of fillet to halve fish lengthwise.

2. Insert spatula into fillet at 45-degree angle, following grain, to cut 8 to 10 equal portions.

RECIPE TESTING The Sweet Spot for Even Browning

To find the best way to brown the salmon as quickly as possible, we coated one portion of the fillet with granulated sugar and another portion with honey and left the remaining portion uncoated. After broiling the fillet, we compared the results. The sugar-coated portion was spotty and almost as pale as the uncoated portion, but the honey-coated portion was deeply and evenly browned. Why? The sugars in honey caramelize more rapidly than does white sugar (sucrose), which must first break down into fructose and glucose before it can caramelize.

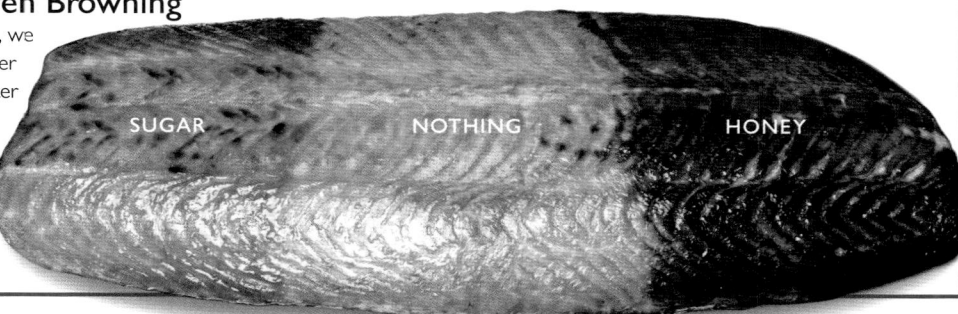

But here's a quirky thing about broilers: While they fiercely heat the upper half of the oven, they leave the bottom half surprisingly cool, particularly when the bottom is blocked by a side of salmon and a baking sheet. In fact, I found that the salmon needed a good 25 minutes to cook through after the broiling step, presumably because the lower portion of the oven took a while to heat up. That made me wonder if I couldn't speed up the cooking by preheating the oven before turning on the broiler. Sure enough, preheating the oven to 250 degrees before broiling the fish raised the temperature of the oven's top portion by 50 degrees and the bottom portion by 125 degrees. This shaved 10 minutes off the cooking time. (Some broilers also don't heat evenly from edge to edge; in those cases, it helps to cover the browned portions of salmon with a piece of aluminum foil to shield them while the paler sections catch up.) I also moved the fish onto a wire rack to raise it off the baking sheet, allowing for better air circulation, which helped it cook more evenly.

Foiling the Fumble

A side of salmon is quite sturdy when raw but very fragile once cooked, which meant I had to be strategic about getting it to the table in one piece. So I made a long foil sling, coated it with vegetable oil spray, and placed it on the wire rack before loading on the raw salmon. Once the salmon was done, I grabbed the ends of the sling, transferred it to the serving platter, and gently slid the foil out from underneath the fish. I then experimented with a few ways to portion the fish (see "Cutting Perfect Portions").

A squeeze of fresh lemon juice was all it took to temper the richness of my salmon, but a pair of vibrant, no-cook condiments—an arugula-based pesto and a crisp cucumber relish—offered even more dress-up potential.

Going to Extremes For Perfection

Broiling can deeply brown a large piece of salmon, but it's not a good method for cooking the fish from start to finish because the intense heat overcooks the outermost layer. To achieve a deeply browned exterior and a silky interior, we used the broiler to jump-start browning and then used very low (250-degree) heat to bake the fish gently.

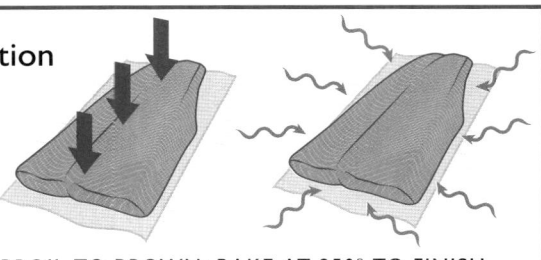

BROIL TO BROWN; BAKE AT 250° TO FINISH
A high-low cooking method guarantees perfectly cooked fish.

ROASTED WHOLE SIDE OF SALMON
SERVES 8 TO 10

This recipe requires salting the fish for at least 1 hour. Look for a fillet that is uniformly thick from end to end. The surface will continue to brown after the oven temperature is reduced in step 4; if the surface starts to darken too much before the fillet's center registers 125 degrees, shield the dark portion with aluminum foil. If using wild salmon, which contains less fat than farmed salmon, remove it from the oven when the center of the fillet registers 120 degrees. Serve as is or with Arugula and Almond Pesto or Cucumber-Ginger Relish (recipes follow).

- 1 (4-pound) skin-on side of salmon, pinbones removed and belly fat trimmed
  Kosher salt
- 2 tablespoons honey
  Lemon wedges

1. Sprinkle flesh side of salmon evenly with 1 tablespoon salt and refrigerate, uncovered, for at least 1 hour or up to 4 hours.

2. Adjust oven rack 7 inches from broiler element and heat oven to 250 degrees. Line rimmed baking sheet with aluminum foil and place wire rack in sheet. Fold 18 by 12-inch piece of foil lengthwise to create 18 by 6-inch sling. Place sling on wire rack and spray with vegetable oil spray.

3. Heat broiler. Pat salmon dry with paper towels and place, skin side down, on foil sling. Brush salmon evenly with honey and broil until surface is lightly but evenly browned, 8 to 12 minutes, rotating sheet halfway through broiling.

4. Return oven temperature to 250 degrees and continue to cook until center of fillet registers 125 degrees, 10 to 15 minutes longer, rotating sheet halfway through cooking. Using foil sling, transfer salmon to serving platter, then carefully remove foil. Serve, passing lemon wedges separately.

ARUGULA AND ALMOND PESTO
MAKES ABOUT 1½ CUPS

For a spicier pesto, reserve, mince, and add the ribs and seeds from the chile. The pesto can be refrigerated for up to 24 hours. If refrigerated, let the pesto sit at room temperature for 30 minutes before serving.

- ¼ cup almonds, lightly toasted
- 4 garlic cloves, peeled
- 4 anchovy fillets, rinsed and patted dry
- 1 serrano chile, stemmed, seeded, and halved lengthwise
- 6 ounces (6 cups) arugula
- ¼ cup lemon juice (2 lemons)
- ¼ cup extra-virgin olive oil
- 1½ teaspoons kosher salt

Process almonds, garlic, anchovies, and serrano in food processor until finely chopped, about 15 seconds, scraping down sides of bowl as needed. Add arugula, lemon juice, oil, and salt and process until smooth, about 30 seconds.

CUCUMBER-GINGER RELISH
MAKES ABOUT 2 CUPS

For a spicier relish, reserve, mince, and add the ribs and seeds from the chile. To keep the cucumbers crisp, serve this relish within 30 minutes of assembling it.

- ½ cup rice vinegar
- 6 tablespoons extra-virgin olive oil
- ¼ cup lime juice (2 limes)
- 2 tablespoons whole-grain mustard
- 1 tablespoon grated fresh ginger
- ½ teaspoon kosher salt
- 1 English cucumber, seeded and cut into ¼-inch dice
- 1 cup minced fresh mint
- 1 cup minced fresh cilantro
- 1 serrano chile, stemmed, seeded, and minced

Whisk vinegar, oil, lime juice, mustard, ginger, and salt in bowl until smooth. Add cucumber, mint, cilantro, and serrano and stir to combine.

Roast Chicken with Bread Salad

San Francisco's Zuni Café serves perfect roast chicken with a chewy-crisp, warm bread salad that has a cultlike following. We pay homage to the dish with a streamlined take.

≥ BY ANNIE PETITO ≤

Few dishes are as beloved and crowd-pleasing as roast chicken. Perhaps no one knew this better than the late, renowned chef Judy Rodgers of Zuni Café in San Francisco. When she put her roast chicken with warm bread salad on the menu in the late '80s, it was a real hit. Now, some 30 years later, it still is.

I recently prepared Rodgers's recipe from *The Zuni Café Cookbook* (2002). The chicken was beautifully executed: the skin deeply bronzed, the meat juicy and well seasoned. And the salad? The bread itself was a lovely mix of crunchy, fried, chewy, and moist pieces, all tossed with savory chicken drippings. Currants, pine nuts, just-softened scallions and garlic, salad greens, and a sharp vinaigrette completed the salad. Served with the chicken, it was a perfect meal.

But the recipe for this rustic dish is anything but simple. It's a meticulously detailed four-page essay that calls for preparing the chicken and bread separately (the latter in two stages), so their cooking has to be coordinated, as do the salad's many components, including vinegar-soaked currants, sautéed aromatics, and toasted nuts. This could all be tackled easily in a professional kitchen, but at home it seemed taxing.

Roast Chicken Rules

Before I did anything else, I wanted to nail the chicken cookery. I butterflied a chicken by snipping out the backbone and then pressing down on its breastbone to help the bird lie flat.

Rodgers called for salting her chicken overnight, which is a trick we often use as well. The salt draws moisture from the flesh, forming a concentrated brine that is eventually reabsorbed, seasoning the meat and keeping it juicy. I lifted up the skin and rubbed kosher salt onto the flesh; I then refrigerated the bird for 24 hours. This would give the salt time to penetrate the flesh as well as dry the skin so it would brown and crisp more readily.

▶ **Watch: Chicken, Zuni-Style**
A step-by-step video is available at CooksIllustrated.com/jun18

This salad is saturated with chicken flavor, from the bread pieces that are cooked under the chicken to the dressing, which also contains drippings.

The next day, I placed the bird skin side up in a 12-inch skillet (rather than a large roasting pan, so the juices could pool without risk of scorching) and slid it, brushed with oil to encourage deep browning, into a 475-degree oven. Because the chicken was butterflied, I was pretty sure I could roast it at a high temperature without the breast and thigh meat cooking unevenly. Sure enough, 45 minutes later I had a mahogany brown, crispy-skinned, succulent chicken.

Breaking Bread

On to my favorite part: the bread. What makes Rodgers's bread salad unique is its mix of crispy-chewy textures, achieved by removing the crusts from a rustic loaf, cutting the bread into large chunks, coating the chunks with oil, and broiling them. The bread chunks are then torn into smaller pieces and tossed with currants, pine nuts, cooked scallions and garlic, broth, and vinaigrette. Finally, the mixture is baked in a covered dish so that the bread emerges, as Rodgers described it, "steamy-hot, a mixture of soft, moist wads, crispy-on-the-outside-but-moist-in-the-middle wads, and a few downright crispy ones."

I wondered if I could streamline things by cooking the bread with the chicken, which would also allow the bread to directly soak up all the bird's juices and fat. The test kitchen has recipes that call for butterflying poultry and draping it over stuffing prior to roasting, and I thought a similar technique could work well here. The pieces touching the skillet would crisp just like Rodgers's broiled bread, and the chicken juices would keep the remaining pieces moist.

Rodgers called for an open-crumbed loaf such as ciabatta; I wanted something sturdier to hold up under the chicken, so I opted for a denser country-style loaf, which I cut into 1-inch pieces and placed in the skillet before arranging the butterflied bird on top. When I removed it from the oven, I was pleased: The bread beneath the chicken was saturated with savory chicken juices on one side and was deeply golden, crispy, and fried on the other side where it had been in contact with the pan. The only problem was that the pieces around the edges of the pan that had not been tucked under the chicken had dried out and burned slightly. Plus, a lot of the bread had stuck to the pan.

For my next batch, I moistened the bread with ¼ cup of chicken broth. I also spritzed the skillet with vegetable oil spray and stirred a little olive oil into the bread before arranging it in the skillet. I hoped this would help the edge pieces fry and crisp without sticking. Finally, I didn't trim away any of

Zuni Café opened its doors in 1979; in 1987, the late Judy Rodgers became the head chef. On an average day, the restaurant serves about 100 of its whole chickens with warm bread salad.

Making the Most of the Star Ingredient

We think the roast chicken in this recipe is terrific, but the crispy, chewy, ultrasavory bread is our favorite part of the dish. Here's how we make it so great.

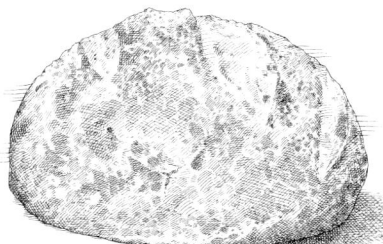

Choose a Sturdy Loaf: Use country-style bread, which has heft and can stand up to cooking. Remove bottom crust but leave top crust attached for some chew.

Stack It Up: Roast untrimmed butterflied chicken on top of bread so juices and fat can be absorbed.

Position It Right: Arrange bread with crust side up so tougher parts are beneath moist chicken.

Avoid the Burn: Add oil and broth to bread so it stays moist and crisps nicely without drying, burning, or sticking.

---

the bird's excess fat or skin. This way, I would be capturing every last drop of the drippings—arguably the most flavorful element a chicken has to offer. These were good moves: The bread boasted a mix of textures and tasted intensely chicken-y, and nothing burned or dried out. That said, the crusted pieces were still tough.

I started anew, this time removing all the crust so I was left with only the soft inner crumb. This eliminated the tough parts, but now the bread had no structure and collapsed into a single mass.

I prepared another loaf but this time removed only the thick bottom crust. So they would be sure to soften, I arranged the remaining crusted pieces directly under the bird, crust side up. To say it worked well would be an understatement: This bread offered a little of everything: crunchy, fried, chewy, and moist pieces. There wasn't a tough piece in the mix. It was time to pull the dish together.

Salad Days

As I examined the salad components, I decided to make a couple of adjustments: Instead of sautéing thinly sliced scallions with garlic, I decided to skip the garlic and keep the scallions raw, which I mixed, along with sweet currants, into a sharp dressing of champagne vinegar (Rodgers called for this type, and I liked its bright, balanced flavor) and extra-virgin olive oil. For body and more punch to cut the dish's richness, I added a spoonful of Dijon mustard. And because the bread would provide plenty of crunch and richness, I left out the pine nuts, too. Finally, I poured the accumulated chicken juices into the dressing before tossing it with the bread and a heap of peppery arugula. Instead of arranging the carved chicken on top of the salad, which caused the greens to wilt, I served it alongside.

My streamlined rendition of the Zuni chicken and bread salad hit all the right notes: salty, savory, sweet, fresh, and bright. I only hope that it will be as memorable and enduring as the original.

ROAST CHICKEN WITH WARM BREAD SALAD
SERVES 4 TO 6

Note that this recipe requires refrigerating the seasoned chicken for 24 hours. This recipe was developed and tested using Diamond Crystal Kosher Salt. If you have Morton Kosher Salt, which is denser than Diamond Crystal, put only ½ teaspoon of salt onto the cavity. Red wine or white wine vinegar may be substituted for champagne vinegar, if desired. For the bread, we prefer a round rustic loaf with a chewy, open crumb and a sturdy outer crust.

- 1 (4-pound) whole chicken, giblets discarded
- Kosher salt and pepper
- 4 (1-inch-thick) slices country-style bread (8 ounces), bottom crust removed, cut into ¾- to 1-inch pieces (5 cups)
- ¼ cup chicken broth
- 6 tablespoons plus 2 teaspoons extra-virgin olive oil
- 2 tablespoons champagne vinegar
- 1 teaspoon Dijon mustard
- 3 scallions, sliced thin
- 2 tablespoons dried currants
- 5 ounces (5 cups) baby arugula

1. Place chicken, breast side down, on cutting board. Using kitchen shears, cut through bones on either side of backbone; discard backbone. Do not trim off any excess fat or skin. Flip chicken over and press on breastbone to flatten.

2. Using your fingers, carefully loosen skin covering breast and legs. Rub ½ teaspoon salt under skin of each breast, ½ teaspoon under skin of each leg, and 1 teaspoon salt onto bird's cavity. Tuck wings behind back and turn legs so drumsticks face inward toward breasts. Place chicken on wire rack set in rimmed baking sheet or on large plate and refrigerate, uncovered, for 24 hours.

3. Adjust oven rack to middle position and heat oven to 475 degrees. Spray 12-inch skillet with vegetable oil spray. Toss bread with broth and 2 tablespoons oil until pieces are evenly moistened. Arrange bread in skillet in single layer, with majority of crusted pieces near center, crust side up.

4. Pat chicken dry with paper towels and place, skin side up, on top of bread. Brush 2 teaspoons oil over chicken skin and sprinkle with ¼ teaspoon salt and ¼ teaspoon pepper. Roast chicken until skin is deep golden brown and thickest part of breast registers 160 degrees and thighs register 175 degrees, 45 to 50 minutes, rotating skillet halfway through roasting.

5. While chicken roasts, whisk vinegar, mustard, ¼ teaspoon salt, and ¼ teaspoon pepper together in small bowl. Slowly whisk in remaining ¼ cup oil. Stir in scallions and currants and set aside. Place arugula in large bowl.

6. Transfer chicken to carving board and let rest, uncovered, for 15 minutes. Run thin metal spatula under bread to loosen from bottom of skillet. (Bread should be mix of softened, golden-brown, and crunchy pieces.) Carve chicken and whisk any accumulated juices into vinaigrette. Add bread and vinaigrette to arugula and toss to evenly coat. Transfer salad to serving platter and serve with chicken.

Skip the Trimming

Most of our chicken recipes call for trimming away any excess fat and skin. But since those elements produce hugely flavorful drippings, we decided to leave them intact for this recipe. This meant that more savory, chicken-y drippings would be available for the bread to absorb.

LIQUID GOLD
An untrimmed 4-pound chicken exudes ½ cup of drippings.

Slow-Roasted Deviled Pork Chops

A punchy mustard-based paste is an age-old cover-up for mild-mannered cuts. But it can't hide meat that's dry and tough below the surface.

≥ BY ANNIE PETITO ≤

You wouldn't usually call upon the devil to save a weeknight dinner, but that's exactly what Mr. Micawber does in Charles Dickens's novel *David Copperfield* (1850) when he covers undercooked mutton with mustard, salt, and black and cayenne peppers. It is a classic example of "deviling," the practice of seasoning food with some combination of mustard, pepper, and/or vinegar, which dates back to at least the 18th century. Nowadays, the term refers to any treatment that uses those components to punch up mild-mannered foods such as hard-cooked eggs, deli ham, or bland chicken breasts and pork chops.

The ease and bold flavors of deviling appeal to me, particularly when applied to boneless pork chops, which I often make for weeknight dinners. But recipes vary widely when it comes to the type and intensity of heat—from a weak sprinkle of black pepper to a thick slather of sharp mustard, neither of which offers the complex, balanced spiciness and acidity that I would want in this dish. Plus, mustard-coated pork chops are often covered in bread crumbs, but I've found that the fine crumbs soak up moisture from the mustard and turn soggy.

But those are just the surface issues related to deviling, and they would be relatively simple to fix. The bigger problem with most deviled pork chops is how they're cooked: They're usually coated with mustard and then seared or broiled, the goal being to develop a deeply browned, flavorful crust. But inevitably, the lean meat dries out and toughens.

To fix these issues, I would start by finding a cooking technique that produced tender, juicy chops. Then I would need to fine-tune a mustard-based deviling paste that would be assertive and vibrant enough to perk up the pork without overwhelming it. Once those elements were in place, I'd see about adding a bread-crumb crust.

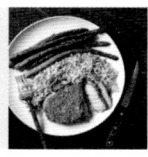

● See Annie's Devilish Side
A step-by-step video is available at CooksIllustrated.com/jun18

In addition to providing bold flavor, our mustard paste glues crisp panko bread crumbs to the chops' exteriors.

The Lowdown

The more I thought about the role of well-browned meat on deviled pork chops, the more I wondered if it was necessary. Once the chops were covered with the punchy mustard paste and, potentially, a crunchy bread-crumb coating, would you really miss the flavor and texture of the seared meat? I did a quick test and confirmed that the answer was no; the mustard-based paste I'd used to coat the meat more or less camouflaged the flavor of the sear. Searing was out.

Instead, I would try to slow-roast the chops, as we often do with large roasts and thick steaks. The benefit is twofold: Lower heat keeps the temperature of the meat's outermost layers low; this prevents them from squeezing out moisture and promotes more-even cooking by reducing the temperature differential between the meat's exterior and interior. Lower heat also encourages enzymes within the pork to break down some of the muscle protein, leading to more-tender meat.

> Searing was out... I would try to slow-roast the chops, as we often do with large roasts and thick steaks.

I placed four boneless, 1-inch-thick chops on a wire rack set in a rimmed baking sheet so that air could circulate around them for even cooking. Then I slid the sheet into a 275-degree oven and left them alone until they hit 140 degrees. That took about 40 minutes, which was longer than I'd ever waited for pork chops to cook. But the juicy, tender results were worth it. The only hiccup was that the chops stuck to the rack, so the next time I coated it with vegetable oil spray to ensure that the meat released cleanly.

The Devil Is in the Details

On to the mustard paste. I followed the lead of other recipes and started with Dijon, which offered an assertive punch of clean heat and acidity along with a creamy texture that clung well to the chops. Then I took a cue from the Dickensian formula and seasoned the mustard with salt as well as black and cayenne peppers; each type of pepper lent its own distinct heat, and both enhanced the mustard's burn. For savory flavor, I worked in a small amount of garlic that I had minced to a paste (which resulted in even flavor distribution) and balanced the fiery concoction with a couple of teaspoons of brown sugar. After patting a new batch of chops dry, I brushed the entire surface of each one with the paste, set them on the rack, and popped them into the oven.

The paste was nicely seasoned and packed decent punch, but now that I was tasting it with the pork, I wanted even more of that nasal bite. A heavier coat of the paste wasn't the way to go; for one thing, I wanted more heat but not more acidity. Plus, it would be messy to both slather more paste on the meat and clean it off the wire rack after cooking; the baked-on coating from the underside of the chops was already sticking to the rack. Instead, I tried adding dry (also known as English) mustard, a variety of hot mustard that's sold in powdered form. In many cases, the powder is reconstituted in a little water before being used, but that wouldn't be necessary here since the Dijon contained plenty of moisture. I ran a few tests and worked my way up to a hefty 1½ teaspoons of dry

SCIENCE Calibrating the Best Burn

Our "deviled" paste draws its complex fiery flavor from a combination of spicy components: Dijon mustard, dry mustard, and cayenne and black peppers. Each of these ingredients activates pain receptors in your mouth—TRPV1, which is the same nerve channel that responds to the pain of piping-hot liquid, and TRPA1, a close relative. But the different ingredients stimulate the nerves in different ways, so the combination adds up to a much more complex experience of spiciness. The stimulation of pain and other tactile nerves in the mouth, called chemesthesis, can take many forms—a quick jolt of heat, a lingering burn, the sensation of a pinprick—and can even affect different parts of your mouth and nose. Here's what each deviling component brings to the mix.

DIJON MUSTARD
COMPOUND: Allyl isothiocyanate
SENSORY EFFECT: Sharp nasal sting

DRY MUSTARD
COMPOUND: Allyl isothiocyanate
SENSORY EFFECT: Sharp nasal sting

CAYENNE PEPPER
COMPOUND: Capsaicin
SENSORY EFFECT: Burning on the tongue and in the throat

BLACK PEPPER
COMPOUND: Piperine
SENSORY EFFECT: Burning and tingling on the tongue

mustard, so that the paste's heat was potent but still layered—a sharp punch that tingled on the tongue and tapered off into a slow, satisfying burn.

I ran two more quick tests. The first was to see if I could get away with coating just the top and sides of the chops now that the paste was so potent. I could, which cut back considerably on the mess before and after roasting. The second test—whether to brush the chops with the paste before or after cooking—confirmed that we preferred the drier consistency and more rounded flavor of the cooked paste. The only downside was the visual: a dull, mottled, ocher coating. It was time to consider that bread-crumb crust.

Crunch Factor

Besides visual appeal, a crust would offer nice textural contrast to the meat, and the mustard paste would be the glue I'd need to help the crumbs adhere to the chops. To keep the coating process simple, I decided to cover just the top surfaces.

To prevent the crumbs from soaking up moisture from the paste and turning mushy, I employed a two-pronged solution. First, I used panko: pre-toasted coarse bread crumbs that we always turn to when we want a craggy texture and great crunch. Second, I sautéed the panko crumbs in butter so that they would turn golden brown; they wouldn't get any color in the low oven. I pressed about 2 tablespoons of crumbs onto the top of each chop and slid them into the oven.

This batch was golden and crispy on top and moist and juicy throughout and boasted a fiery but balanced flavor that kept you going back for more. Best of all, the method was dead simple; once the chops were in the oven, I didn't have to flip them or tend to them in any way until they were done.

I never thought I'd get so excited about a boneless pork chop. I guess you could say the devil made me do it.

DEVILED PORK CHOPS
SERVES 4

For the best results, be sure to buy chops of similar size. This recipe was developed using natural pork; if using enhanced pork (injected with a salt solution), do not add salt to the mustard paste in step 2. Serve the pork chops with mashed potatoes, rice, or buttered egg noodles. Our recipe for Deviled Pork Chops for Two is available for free for four months at CocksIllustrated.com/jun18.

- 2 tablespoons unsalted butter
- ½ cup panko bread crumbs
- Kosher salt and pepper
- ¼ cup Dijon mustard
- 2 teaspoons packed brown sugar
- 1½ teaspoons dry mustard
- ½ teaspoon garlic, minced to paste
- ¼ teaspoon cayenne pepper
- 4 (6- to 8-ounce) boneless pork chops, ¾ to 1 inch thick

1. Adjust oven rack to middle position and heat oven to 275 degrees.

2. Melt butter in 10-inch skillet over medium heat. Add panko and cook, stirring frequently, until golden brown, 3 to 5 minutes. Transfer to bowl and sprinkle with ⅛ teaspoon salt. Stir Dijon, sugar, dry mustard, garlic, cayenne, 1 teaspoon salt, and 1 teaspoon pepper in second bowl until smooth.

3. Set wire rack in rimmed baking sheet and spray with vegetable oil spray. Pat chops dry with paper towels. Transfer chops to prepared wire rack, spacing them 1 inch apart. Brush 1 tablespoon mustard mixture over top and sides of each chop (leave bottoms uncoated). Spoon 2 tablespoons toasted panko evenly over top of each chop and press lightly to adhere.

4. Roast until meat registers 140 degrees, 40 to 50 minutes. Remove from oven and let rest on rack for 10 minutes before serving.

Speak of the Devil

In his 1797 *The Romish Priest. A Tale*, British author John Wolcot used the term "devil" to refer to "a red-hot bit of meat" that was "loaded with kian" (cayenne). The spicy snack was savored in the wee hours by 18th-century gentlemen who found themselves hungry after a night of carousing.

The definition of the term has broadened over the years to encompass any spicy, pungent treatment, but its purpose—to revive jaded appetites and even to strengthen character—remains much the same.

Apply Side and Top Coats

Be strategic about applying the mustard paste and bread crumbs to the chops. That way, you'll produce flavor-packed results with great crunch—and minimal mess.

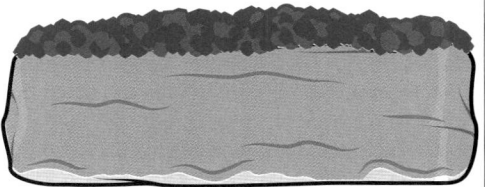

PASTE GOES ON TOP AND SIDES
It's potent enough that coating just the top and sides of the meat delivers plenty of flavor, so you can avoid getting the paste on the rack.

CRUMBS GO JUST ON TOP
The paste will glue the panko crumbs to the chops' top surfaces; there's no need to press them onto the sides.

Anytime Pancakes

Put down the box mix. You've got everything you need to make tall, fluffy pancakes in minutes.

> BY LAN LAM <

Everyone loves sitting down to a plate of fluffy, golden, flavorful pancakes, but making them is another matter. Nobody wants to run out for buttermilk or sour cream before the first meal of the day, never mind haul out (and then clean) their stand mixer to whip egg whites. That's where box mixes come in, but their convenience is hardly worth the results they deliver: rubbery pancakes with a Styrofoam-like flavor that no amount of butter or syrup can hide. Besides, most prefab products still require you to add milk and eggs to the dry mix, so at that point, why not throw together a batter of your own?

So that's exactly what I set out to do. I limited myself to basic ingredients—no buttermilk or sour cream—and no appliances and spent a few weeks as a short-order cook.

Blandcakes

I started with an approach that was as simple and pantry-friendly as possible. Dry ingredients (flour, sugar, baking powder, and salt) went in one bowl, wet (eggs, milk, and vegetable oil) in another. Then I stirred together the wet and dry components. I didn't bother to leave lumps, as almost all pancake recipes instruct, since we found while developing a crêpe recipe that the batter is liquid-y enough that thorough mixing won't develop too much gluten and make the pancakes tough.

I portioned the batter into an oiled, preheated skillet. When bubbles appeared on the surface of the pancakes, I flipped them and cooked them until golden brown. But they weren't good. In fact, they weren't much better than the box-mix kind—thin, splotchy, and, without the tang of buttermilk or sour cream, somewhat bland.

At least the flavors would be easy to fix, I thought as I mixed up another batch with vanilla extract and a dash more salt. I also made a point of beating the eggs

▶ **Look: Lan Flips for Pancakes**
A step-by-step video is available at CooksIllustrated.com/jun18

Flip the pancakes when the edges are set and the surface bubbles are just beginning to break.

with the oil before combining them with the milk and vanilla, which was less messy than whisking all the liquid ingredients together at once. These pancakes tasted more complex, but there was still room for improvement. So for the next round I upped the amount of sugar from 2 tablespoons to three. I also added a little baking soda, which plays a more important role in the flavor of baked goods than you might think: Many pancakes, biscuits, and quick breads rely on its saline tang and are noticeably flat-tasting without it. A mere ½ teaspoon did the trick here; it also helped the pancakes brown more deeply (baking soda increases the pH of the batter, which speeds browning reactions) and rise higher. But they were by no means tall or fluffy.

Soda versus Powder

A quick baking soda and baking powder refresher: Baking powder reacts and creates carbon dioxide both when it comes into contact with moisture and when it's heated, making it a more reliable and forgiving leavener than baking soda, which reacts only when it comes into contact with acid. Many pancake recipes, including ours, call for both.

Through Thick and Thin

One way to increase lift was to add more leavener. I tested increasing amounts of baking powder until I settled on 4 teaspoons—at least double the amount per cup of flour compared with other recipes—but the pancakes were still thin. Next, I thickened the batter by reducing the milk from 2 cups to 1½ cups. This improved the rise—but not enough.

I couldn't further increase the leavener without making the pancakes taste soapy, nor could I further reduce the liquid without producing dry, cottony results. But there was one more variable: the mixing method. A lumpy batter is thicker than a smooth batter since the lumps prevent water from flowing and the mixture from spreading. What if I went back and followed the usual pancake protocol and barely mixed the batter so that lots of lumps remained?

I gently stirred together another batch so that there were still lumpy pockets of flour. I also let the batter rest briefly, another common step that allows the unmixed flour pockets to hydrate slightly. The batter now fell from my whisk in clumps rather than streaming down in thin ribbons. And the pancakes themselves—even when raw in the skillet—were gorgeously tall (see "Leave It Lumpy—but Not for the Reason You Think").

Lesson learned: If I wanted tall, fluffy pancakes, leaving lumps in the batter was key. I also realized that the amount of oil I added to the skillet and even the method I used to flip the pancakes affected their appearance (see "Troubleshooting Pancakes").

Butter Up

The pancakes now looked and tasted so good that folks were grabbing them off the griddle and eating them plain out of hand. But for the occasions that they did make it to the table, I wanted to jazz them up a bit. Stirring blueberries or chocolate chips directly into the batter didn't work well because that required mixing the batter more thoroughly—counterproductive to creating a thick batter. (For tips on adding mix-ins, see "Pancake Mix-In Strategy" on page 28.) Instead, I mixed up some simple flavored butters while the batter rested. I even figured out a way to make them perfectly soft for spreading: Stir cold butter and flavorings—such as citrus zest, honey, grated ginger, or warm spices—into a smaller portion of melted butter. *Voilà*: a spreadable topping with no need to wait for butter to soften on the counter.

I was really happy with where things stood, but I wanted to run one more test, pitting my easy recipe against a more complicated one. Good news: Tasters were unable to distinguish these pancakes from a more traditional buttermilk type. That means you can now make and enjoy a great pancake breakfast even before your morning coffee wakes you up.

Leave It Lumpy—but Not for the Reason You Think

WHISKED UNTIL TOTALLY SMOOTH

LEFT LUMPY

Whisking two batters made with the same ingredients to different degrees dramatically impacted their consistencies. With less stirring, the lumpy batter on the right was noticeably thicker because lumps obstructed the flow of free water. The lumpy batter was also better able to hold on to the air bubbles formed during cooking, producing taller, more leavened pancakes.

EASY PANCAKES
MAKES SIXTEEN 4-INCH PANCAKES; SERVES 4 TO 6

The pancakes can be cooked on an electric griddle set to 350 degrees. They can be held in a preheated 200-degree oven on a wire rack set in a rimmed baking sheet. Serve with salted butter and maple syrup or with one of our flavored butters (recipes follow). For tips on reheating leftover pancakes, see page 31. Our recipe for Pumpkin Spice Butter is available for free for four months at CooksIllustrated.com/jun18.

- 2 cups (10 ounces) all-purpose flour
- 3 tablespoons sugar
- 4 teaspoons baking powder
- ½ teaspoon baking soda
- 1 teaspoon salt
- 2 large eggs
- ¼ cup plus 1 teaspoon vegetable oil
- 1½ cups milk
- ½ teaspoon vanilla extract

1. Whisk flour, sugar, baking powder, baking soda, and salt together in large bowl. Whisk eggs and ¼ cup oil in second medium bowl until well combined. Whisk milk and vanilla into egg mixture. Add egg mixture to flour mixture and stir gently until just combined (batter should remain lumpy with few streaks of flour). Let batter sit for 10 minutes before cooking.

2. Heat ½ teaspoon oil in 12-inch nonstick skillet over medium-low heat until shimmering. Using paper towels, carefully wipe out oil, leaving thin film on bottom and sides of skillet. Drop 1 tablespoon batter in center of skillet. If pancake is pale golden brown after 1 minute, skillet is ready. If it is too light or too dark, adjust heat accordingly.

3. Using ¼-cup dry measuring cup, portion batter into skillet in 3 places, leaving 2 inches between portions. If necessary, gently spread batter into 4-inch round. Cook until edges are set, first sides are golden brown, and bubbles on surface are just beginning to break, 2 to 3 minutes. Using thin, wide spatula, flip pancakes and continue to cook until second sides are golden brown, 1 to 2 minutes longer. Serve. Repeat with remaining batter, using remaining ½ teaspoon oil as necessary.

GINGER-MOLASSES BUTTER
MAKES ½ CUP

Do not use blackstrap molasses; its intense flavor will overwhelm the other flavors. Our favorite is Brer Rabbit All Natural Unsulphured Molasses Mild Flavor

- 8 tablespoons unsalted butter, cut into ¼-inch pieces
- 2 teaspoons molasses
- 1 teaspoon grated fresh ginger
- ⅛ teaspoon salt

Microwave 2 tablespoons butter in medium bowl until melted, about 1 minute. Stir in molasses, ginger, salt, and remaining 6 tablespoons butter. Let mixture stand for 2 minutes. Whisk until smooth. (Butter can be refrigerated for up to 3 days.)

ORANGE-ALMOND BUTTER
MAKES ½ CUP

Do not use buckwheat honey; its intense flavor will overwhelm the other flavors.

- 8 tablespoons unsalted butter, cut into ¼-inch pieces
- 2 teaspoons grated orange zest
- 2 teaspoons honey
- ¼ teaspoon almond extract
- ⅛ teaspoon salt

Microwave 2 tablespoons butter in medium bowl until melted, about 1 minute. Stir in orange zest, honey, almond extract, salt, and remaining 6 tablespoons butter. Let mixture stand for 2 minutes. Whisk until smooth. (Butter can be refrigerated for up to 3 days.)

Troubleshooting Pancakes
To produce consistently round, golden-brown pancakes, follow these three tips.

Problem: Surface is too pale/too dark
Solution: Make tester pancake
Method: To determine if the temperature of your skillet is correct, drop 1 tablespoon of batter onto the heated surface. If it is golden brown after 1 minute, you're ready to cook. If not, adjust the heat as necessary.

Problem: Spotty browning
Solution: Wipe away excess oil
Method: After adding oil to the skillet, wipe it out until there is just a bare sheen remaining. (Metal transfers heat better than oil, so places where oil pools under the pancake will cook more slowly and be relatively pale.)

Problem: Messy flipping
Solution: Flip low and quickly
Method: Slide a thin spatula underneath the pancake and flip it in a smooth, quick motion, keeping the spatula close to the cooking surface.

Revamping Chicken Salads

Throwing together leftover cooked chicken, dressing, and greens is a way to put dinner on the table without much thought. Maybe that's exactly the problem.

≥ BY STEVE DUNN ≤

Our poached chicken delivers ultramoist meat, which we use in our Chicken Caesar Salad, Sichuan-Style Chicken Salad, and Thai-Style Chicken Salad with Mango.

Every time I throw together a salad with chicken using whatever leftover meat I have on hand, I think of what Rodney Dangerfield would say: The chicken don't get no respect.

Corny as that sounds, the chicken tastes exactly like what it is: an afterthought. Straight from the refrigerator, the once flavorful, juicy meat seems dry and dull as cotton (see "Give Cold Chicken the Cold Shoulder" to understand why). Allowing the chicken to come up to room temperature helps, but unless you're using poached chicken, it's never going to be optimally moist.

Here's why: Poaching is much gentler than dry-heat methods such as searing, roasting, and grilling. While the cooler cooking temperature doesn't create a browned crust, it does let the meat retain moisture and fat that would be squeezed out by other cooking methods. And when done well, the results are incredibly succulent and clean-tasting, providing the ideal blank slate for tossing with greens and a flavorful dressing.

The Poach Approach

A while back, we came up with a simple approach to poaching that reliably produces flavorful, succulent meat. It's based on the principles of *sous vide*

▶ Steve Shows You How
A step-by-step video is available at CooksIllustrated.com/jun18

cooking, a technique in which vacuum-sealed foods are submerged in a water bath that's been preset to the food's ideal cooked temperature. But here, we place the chicken in a steamer basket set in a pot of water, bring the water to a subsimmer temperature of 175 degrees, and remove the pot from the burner so that the water's residual heat gently cooks the meat.

I gave it a try with four boneless, skinless breasts and salted water. It took about 15 minutes to bring the liquid up to 175 degrees, at which point I shut off the heat and let the chicken linger in the steamy water until the meat registered 160 degrees.

Dressed for Success

One of the cardinal rules of meat cookery is letting the cooked meat rest before cutting into it. This allows the muscle fibers to relax and reabsorb the flavorful juices. Typically, I would let boneless, skinless breasts rest for about 5 minutes, which would give some of the juices time to redistribute before the chicken gets cold. But since my goal was exceptionally moist meat, and because I intended

Ensuring Maximum Flavor in Chicken Salad
- Poach chicken for juiciest meat.
- Use room-temperature, not chilled, chicken.
- Shred or slice chicken to create lots of surface area for dressing to cling to.
- Toss chicken, not just salad, with some of dressing.

my salads to be served at room temperature, I let the meat rest longer. Why? Picture slicing into hot chicken that has rested for just a few minutes: What you see is a stream of vapor escaping from the cut side, which is moisture. Giving the chicken a good 10 to 15 minutes to cool ensured that more of the moisture would stay locked in the meat.

I was now ready to use the chicken in salad. I'd been eager to work up a version of the classic Sichuan dish called bang bang chicken, a staff favorite in which finely shredded meat is tossed with a dressing made of chili oil, garlic, ginger, Sichuan peppercorns, soy sauce, and black vinegar and then combined with napa cabbage, scallions, celery, and cilantro. When I tossed the fragrant dressing with the chicken, I realized that there were two subtle but significant techniques built into this dish that guaranteed bold flavor: First, shredding the meat instead of cutting it into chunks, as I typically would for chicken salad, created loads of surface area that allowed the dressing to thoroughly soak into the meat and give every bite maximum flavor. Second, dressing the meat by itself before pairing it with the other components ensured that every piece was completely coated.

I applied those lessons to two other bold-tasting salads: a shredded Thai-style chicken-mango version freshened with lots of herbs and spooned into lettuce cups, and a quick chicken Caesar salad, for which I thinly sliced the meat to maximize its surface area.

It didn't take much to give chicken the respect it deserves, and I could taste the difference.

PERFECT POACHED CHICKEN FOR SALAD
MAKES 4 CHICKEN BREASTS

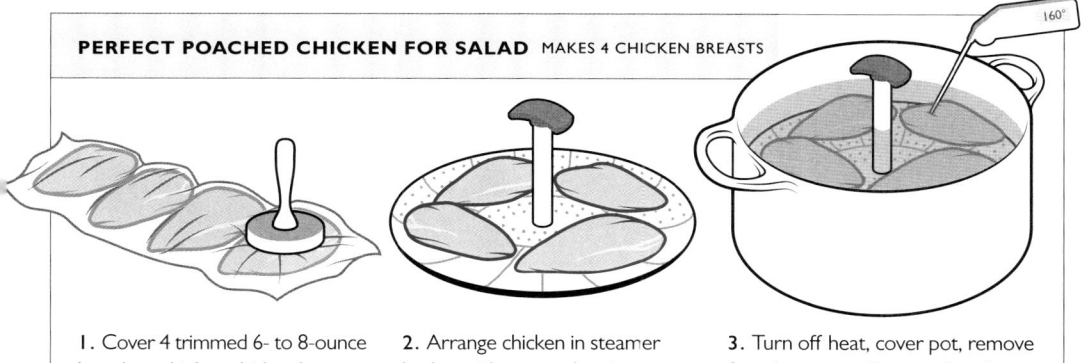

1. Cover 4 trimmed 6- to 8-ounce boneless, skinless chicken breasts with plastic wrap and pound thick ends gently until ¾ inch thick. Whisk 4 quarts cool water with 2 tablespoons salt in large Dutch oven.

2. Arrange chicken in steamer basket without overlapping. Submerge in pot. Heat over medium heat, stirring occasionally, until water registers 175 degrees, 15 to 20 minutes.

3. Turn off heat, cover pot, remove from burner, and let stand until chicken registers 160 degrees, 17 to 22 minutes. Transfer chicken to cutting board and let cool for 10 to 15 minutes.

Give Cold Chicken the Cold Shoulder
If you poach the chicken ahead of time and chill it, be sure to let it come to room temperature before using it in one of our salads. That's because cold meat tastes less juicy and flavorful than meat that's warm or at room temperature.

➤ **Here's Why:** Juiciness and flavor in meat are not just a function of moisture but also of fat and of salivation. When meat is cold, the moisture is gelled and the fat is firm, so neither flows as freely. Less flavor is released, so you also salivate less. In addition, the solidification of the juices means that the muscle fibers don't slide against each other as easily during chewing, which gives the meat a tougher, stringier texture.

SICHUAN-STYLE CHICKEN SALAD (BANG BANG JI SI)
SERVES 4 TO 6

We prefer Sichuan chili powder, but Korean red pepper flakes, called *gochugaru*, are a good alternative. Rice vinegar can be substituted for black vinegar, if desired. Vary the amount of Sichuan peppercorns to suit your taste.

Dressing
- ¼ cup vegetable oil
- 1 garlic clove, peeled and smashed
- 1 (½-inch) piece ginger, peeled and sliced in half
- 2 tablespoons Sichuan chili powder
- 2 tablespoons soy sauce
- 1 tablespoon Chinese black vinegar
- 1 tablespoon toasted sesame oil
- 1 tablespoon Sichuan peppercorns, toasted and ground
- 2 teaspoons sugar

Salad
- 1 recipe Perfect Poached Chicken for Salad, shredded into thin strips
- Salt
- ½ head napa cabbage, sliced thin (6 cups)
- 1½ cups coarsely chopped fresh cilantro leaves and stems
- 6 scallions, sliced in half lengthwise, then sliced thin on bias
- 1 celery rib, sliced thin on bias
- 2 teaspoons toasted sesame seeds (optional)

1. FOR THE DRESSING: Combine vegetable oil, garlic, and ginger in bowl. Microwave until oil is hot and bubbling, about 2 minutes. Stir in chili powder and let cool for 10 minutes.

2. Strain oil mixture through fine-mesh strainer into large bowl; discard solids. Whisk soy sauce, vinegar, sesame oil, 1 teaspoon peppercorns, and sugar into strained oil. Add up to 1 teaspoon additional peppercorns to taste.

3. FOR THE SALAD: Add chicken to bowl with dressing and toss to coat. Season with salt to taste. Toss cabbage, 1 cup cilantro, two-thirds of scallions, celery, and pinch salt in second large bowl. Arrange cabbage mixture in even layer on large platter. Mound chicken on top of cabbage mixture and sprinkle with remaining ½ cup cilantro, remaining scallions, and sesame seeds, if using. Serve.

THAI-STYLE CHICKEN SALAD WITH MANGO
SERVES 4 TO 6

We like to serve this salad in leaves of Bibb lettuce to form lettuce cups, but it can also be served on a bed of greens. Toss 6 to 8 cups of greens with 2 teaspoons of lime juice, 1 teaspoon of toasted sesame oil, 1 teaspoon of vegetable oil, and a pinch of salt before spooning the chicken on top.

Dressing
- 3 tablespoons lime juice (2 limes)
- 1 shallot, minced
- 2 tablespoons fish sauce, plus extra for serving
- 1 tablespoon packed brown sugar
- 1 garlic clove, minced
- ¼ teaspoon red pepper flakes

Salad
- 1 recipe Perfect Poached Chicken for Salad, shredded into thin strips
- 1 mango, peeled, pitted, and cut into ¼-inch pieces
- ½ cup chopped fresh mint
- ½ cup chopped fresh cilantro
- ½ cup chopped fresh Thai basil
- Salt
- 1 head Bibb lettuce (8 ounces), leaves separated
- 2 Thai chiles, sliced thin

1. FOR THE DRESSING: Whisk all ingredients together in large bowl.

2. FOR THE SALAD: Add chicken to bowl with dressing and toss to coat. Add mango, mint, cilantro, and basil and toss to coat. Season with salt to taste. Serve salad in lettuce cups, passing Thai chiles and extra fish sauce separately.

CHICKEN CAESAR SALAD
SERVES 6

We recommend using homemade croutons, but store-bought are fine as well. Adjust the amount of anchovies to suit your taste.

Dressing
- ⅔ cup mayonnaise
- 3 tablespoons lemon juice
- 1 tablespoon Dijon mustard
- 1 tablespoon extra-virgin olive oil
- 2 teaspoons Worcestershire sauce
- 2 garlic cloves, minced
- 3–4 anchovy fillets, rinsed, patted dry, and minced
- ½ teaspoon pepper
- ⅛ teaspoon salt

Salad
- 2 heads romaine lettuce (12 ounces each) (large outer leaves discarded), washed, dried, and cut into 1-inch pieces (16 cups)
- 2 cups croutons
- 2 ounces Parmesan cheese, grated (1 cup)
- 1 recipe Perfect Poached Chicken for Salad, sliced crosswise ¼ inch thick
- Pepper

1. FOR THE DRESSING: Whisk all ingredients together in bowl.

2. FOR THE SALAD: Toss lettuce with croutons, ¾ cup Parmesan, and two-thirds of dressing in large bowl until well combined. Divide dressed lettuce among 6 plates. Toss chicken with remaining dressing. Divide chicken equally among plates and season with pepper. Serve immediately, passing remaining ¼ cup Parmesan separately.

Make the Most of Your Microwave

A microwave oven can do so much more than reheat leftovers. It can save time and prevent messes, all without heating up your kitchen. BY KRISTIN SARGIANIS

HOW MICROWAVE OVENS WORK

Microwave ovens use electric current and magnets to generate electromagnetic waves called "microwaves" (similar to radio and light waves), which create a field with a positive and negative charge. These charges reverse direction an astounding 4.9 billion times per second.

How do microwaves heat food?
Microwaves interact with water molecules and, to a lesser extent, oil. When water molecules, which have positive and negative charges, are exposed to the oscillating positive and negative charges of microwaves, they move at the same incredibly fast rate, bumping into one another (and into nearby molecules, such as fats and proteins) and increasing their temperature.

Why is there mesh on the door?
The holes allow users to see into the oven, and the metal reflects some microwaves back toward the food. The holes are small enough that microwaves can't fit through.

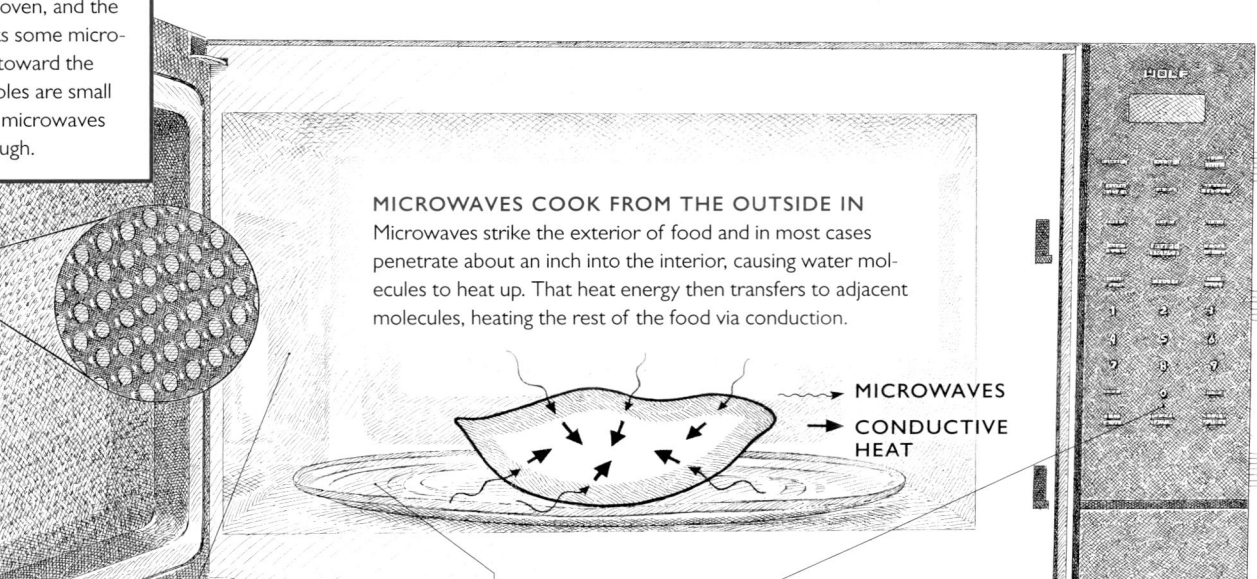

MICROWAVES COOK FROM THE OUTSIDE IN
Microwaves strike the exterior of food and in most cases penetrate about an inch into the interior, causing water molecules to heat up. That heat energy then transfers to adjacent molecules, heating the rest of the food via conduction.

→ MICROWAVES
→ CONDUCTIVE HEAT

Why is the interior metal?
Microwaves bounce off the metal surfaces, back toward the center of the oven.

Why do microwave ovens have turntables?
By rotating the food, the turntable helps microwaves reach—and heat—more of a food's surface.

How does the power level work?
The power level indicates the ratio of time that the power is on to total cooking time. So, 50 percent power means the microwave is emitting electromagnetic waves for 30 seconds out of a 1-minute cooking time by rapidly pulsing on and off.

EASY MICROWAVE CLEANUP: JUST ADD WATER

Microwave 2 cups water at full power until steaming but not boiling, about 2 minutes. Let sit for 5 minutes. Steam will loosen dried, stuck-on food. Wipe clean.

TIPS FOR HEATING FOOD EFFICIENTLY IN THE MICROWAVE

Stir or flip often: Movement allows the microwaves to hit new parts of the food and promotes heat transfer via conduction.

Cover food: Using a plate or an inverted bowl to cover the food traps steam, which provides more cooking via conduction.

Let food rest: Letting food rest for a few minutes after cooking it allows hot and cool spots to even out through conduction.

10 UNEXPECTED WAYS TO USE THE MICROWAVE OVEN

1. TOAST NUTS, COCONUT, WHOLE SPICES, OR BREAD CRUMBS
➤ PRECISE CONTROL = NO BURNING

Place ingredient in shallow bowl or glass pie plate in thin, even layer. Microwave, stirring and checking color every minute. When ingredient starts to color, microwave in 30-second increments until golden brown.

2. MELT OR TEMPER CHOCOLATE
➤ FASTER AND LESS FUSSY THAN DOUBLE BOILER

To melt 4 ounces chocolate: Microwave finely chopped chocolate in bowl at 50 percent power, stirring occasionally, until melted, 2 to 4 minutes.

MELTING CHOCOLATE

5 MINUTES
MICROWAVE

15 MINUTES
DOUBLE BOILER

To temper chocolate: Place three-quarters of chocolate, chopped fine, in bowl. Microwave at 50 percent power, stirring every 15 seconds, until melted but not much warmer than body temperature, about 93 degrees. Add remaining one-quarter of chocolate, grated, and stir until smooth, microwaving for no more than 5 seconds at a time, if necessary, to finish melting.

3. MELLOW RAW GARLIC
➤ EASY WAY TO EASE GARLIC'S EDGE

Place unpeeled garlic cloves in small bowl. Microwave at full power for 15 seconds or until cloves are warm to touch but not cooked. Warming garlic prevents formation of allicin (a sulfur compound that gives raw garlic its bite). Mince or otherwise prep garlic as called for in cooked applications such as pesto, hummus, and dressings. **Bonus:** The quick spin in the microwave makes the cloves a cinch to peel.

RAW AT 70°:
LOADS OF ALLICIN,
SHARP BITE

HEATED TO 140°:
NOT MUCH ALLICIN,
MELLOW FLAVOR

4. SHUCK CORN
➤ NO MORE MESS OF HUSKS AND SILK

Cut off stalk end of cob just above first row of kernels. Place up to 4 ears at a time on plate. Microwave at full power for 1 to 2 minutes or until warm to touch. Hold each ear by uncut end in 1 hand. Shake ear up and down until cob slips free. If cob doesn't slide out easily, continue microwaving in 30-second increments.

5. DRY FRESH HERBS
➤ READY IN MINUTES VERSUS WEEKS

Place hardy herbs (sage, rosemary, thyme, oregano, mint, or marjoram) in single layer between 2 paper towels on microwave turntable. Microwave at full power for 1 to 3 minutes until leaves turn brittle and fall easily from stems—sure signs of dryness.

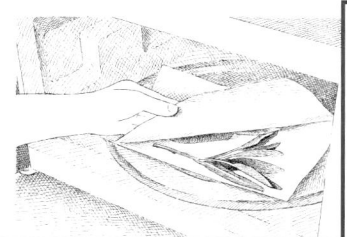

> Not all inks used on printed paper towels are food-safe. We recommend plain paper towels without any printing for use in the microwave.

6. DEHYDRATE CITRUS ZEST
➤ SPEEDY WAY TO ALWAYS HAVE THIS VERSATILE FLAVORING ON HAND

Use vegetable peeler to remove strips of citrus zest, avoiding bitter pith. Place strips on paper towel–lined plate. Microwave at full power for 2 to 3 minutes, let cool, then store in airtight container. Steep in tea, pan sauces, custards, or cooking water for grains to add subtle citrus flavor.

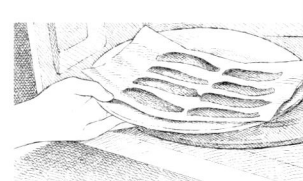

7. CARAMELIZE SUGAR
➤ QUICK AND FOOLPROOF METHOD FOR MAKING CARAMEL

FRESH FROM THE
MICROWAVE

AFTER 5 MINUTES ON
THE COUNTER

Stir 1 cup sugar, 2 tablespoons corn syrup (prevents crystallization), 2 tablespoons water, and ⅛ teaspoon lemon juice together in 2-cup liquid measuring cup. Microwave at full power until mixture is just starting to brown, 5 to 8 minutes. Remove from microwave and let measuring cup sit on dry surface until caramel darkens to rich honey brown, about 5 minutes.

To make caramel sauce: Stir ½ cup hot heavy cream into caramel few tablespoons at a time, followed by 1 tablespoon unsalted butter and pinch salt.

8. MAKE AN EMERGENCY ROUX
➤ NO WHISKING OR SAUCEPAN REQUIRED

Mix 2 tablespoons flour with 2 tablespoons oil. Microwave at full power for 1½ minutes. Stir, then microwave for 45 seconds. Stir, microwave for another 45 seconds, and stir again. For darker roux, continue microwaving and stirring in 15-second increments. Stir roux, 1 tablespoon at a time, into hot stew or gravy base until desired consistency is reached.

9. FRY SHALLOTS
➤ NO SPLATTER AND LESS STIRRING THAN ON STOVETOP

Place 3 shallots, peeled and sliced thin, in medium bowl with ½ cup vegetable oil. Microwave at full power for 5 minutes. Stir, then microwave for 2 minutes. Repeat stirring and microwaving in 2-minute increments until shallots begin to brown (4 to 6 minutes), then stir and microwave in 30-second increments until shallots are deep golden (30 seconds to 2 minutes). Using slotted spoon, transfer shallots to paper towel–lined plate; season with salt. Let drain and turn crisp, about 5 minutes, before serving. Sprinkle on salads and sandwiches; use cooked oil in dressing.

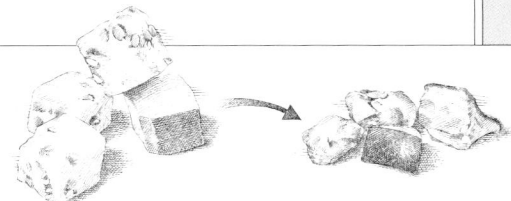

10. DRY EGGPLANT FOR FRYING OR SAUTÉING
➤ SPEEDIER AND MORE EFFECTIVE THAN SALTING ALONE

Toss cubed eggplant with salt in bowl. Line large plate with double layer of paper towels and lightly spray with vegetable oil spray. Spread eggplant in even layer on paper towels. Microwave until dry and shriveled to about one-third of original size, 8 to 15 minutes (it should not brown). Transfer immediately to paper towel–lined plate. This technique eliminates much of eggplant's air and moisture, allowing it to easily brown and absorb less oil during cooking.

Great Barley Side Dishes

Producing distinct, perfectly textured grains is as easy as boiling water.

> BY STEVE DUNN <

If you've only ever used barley to bulk up a brothy soup, consider this your introduction to another hearty grain with great versatility. Like farro, wheat berries, and brown rice, barley is nutty but neutral, so it pairs well with most seasonings and can deliver satisfying chew.

I wanted to feature barley in a handful of simple sides, so I cooked a batch using the absorption method that we commonly use for rice. I soon realized why barley is typically relegated to soup: After I'd simmered 1 cup of barley in 3 cups of water in a covered pot until the grains were tender and had absorbed all the liquid, the barley clumped together, bound by a starchy paste—think gluey oatmeal. Undeterred, I cooked more batches with all the different barleys I could find at the supermarket, and the results were all over the place: Depending on the barley product, the grains took anywhere from 20 minutes to 1 hour to cook and soaked up between 2½ and 4 cups of water.

It turns out that barley has two big strikes against it. Most barley sold in the United States is "pearled"—meaning that the inedible hull has been removed and that the grain has been pearled, or polished. The problem is that depending on the amount of abrasion used during pearling, different amounts of bran (or germ or endosperm) may be left intact. The more bran that is left intact, the more liquid and time barley needs to cook. What's more, barley is prone to releasing starch and clumping (see "Treat Barley Like Pasta").

Treat Barley Like Pasta

Barley is prone to clumping for two reasons: First, its starch granules burst relatively early in the cooking time. Second, the starch is sticky because it's loaded with amylopectin, the branching molecule that's responsible for the stickiness of short-grain rices. Boiling barley in a large volume of water, just as you would when cooking pasta, and then draining it prevents clumping because it dilutes the starch in abundant water, which we then drain away.

○ Look: Barley on the Side
A step-by-step video is available at CooksIllustrated.com/jun18

With this in mind, I turned to the pasta cooking method, in which the barley grains are cooked in a large volume of water and then drained. The cooking times still varied from product to product, but since I could periodically test the grains for doneness, that no longer mattered. Plus, draining the cooking water rid the grains of most of their surface starch, so they remained separate.

Before tossing the cooked barley with bold dressings, I spread the grains on a rimmed baking sheet to cool a bit. The cooled barley would be drier and thus less sticky and wouldn't wilt the fresh herbs I planned to combine it with. Once the grains were no longer steaming, I tossed them with a punchy lemon vinaigrette—a 1:1 ratio of oil to lemon juice rather than the typical 3:1 oil-to-acid ratio—to complement their earthy, nutty flavor, and I further brightened the mix with lemon zest, scallions, and generous amounts of fresh mint and cilantro. I flavored a second batch with a ginger-miso dressing to which I added celery and carrots for crunch; a third version included fresh fennel and dried apricots and was dressed with an orange juice–based vinaigrette. See? Barley's not just for soup anymore.

For distinct grains, let the barley cool before dressing it.

BARLEY WITH LEMON AND HERBS
SERVES 6 TO 8

The cooking time will vary from product to product, so start checking for doneness after 25 minutes.

- 1½ cups pearled barley
- Salt and pepper
- 3 tablespoons extra-virgin olive oil
- 2 tablespoons minced shallot
- 1 teaspoon grated lemon zest plus 3 tablespoons juice
- 1 teaspoon Dijon mustard
- 6 scallions, sliced thin on bias
- ¼ cup minced fresh mint
- ¼ cup minced fresh cilantro

1. Line rimmed baking sheet with parchment paper and set aside. Bring 4 quarts water to boil in Dutch oven. Add barley and 1 tablespoon salt and cook, adjusting heat to maintain gentle boil, until barley is tender with slight chew, 25 to 45 minutes.

2. While barley cooks, whisk oil, shallot, lemon zest and juice, mustard, ½ teaspoon salt, and ¼ teaspoon pepper together in large bowl.

3. Drain barley. Transfer to prepared sheet and spread into even layer. Let stand until no longer steaming, 5 to 7 minutes. Add barley to bowl with dressing and toss to coat. Add scallions, mint, and cilantro and stir to combine. Season with salt and pepper to taste. Serve.

BARLEY WITH CELERY AND MISO DRESSING

Substitute 3 tablespoons seasoned rice vinegar, 1 tablespoon white miso paste, 1 tablespoon soy sauce, 1 tablespoon toasted sesame oil, 1 tablespoon vegetable oil, 2 teaspoons grated fresh ginger, 1 minced garlic clove, 1 teaspoon packed brown sugar, and ¼ to ½ teaspoon red pepper flakes for olive oil, shallot, lemon zest and juice, mustard, salt, and pepper in step 2. Substitute 2 celery ribs, sliced thin on bias, and 2 peeled and grated carrots for scallions. Omit mint and increase cilantro to ½ cup.

BARLEY WITH FENNEL, DRIED APRICOTS, AND ORANGE

Substitute 3 tablespoons red wine vinegar and ½ teaspoon grated orange zest plus 2 tablespoons juice for lemon zest and juice. Omit mustard. Reduce olive oil to 2 tablespoons and add 1 minced garlic clove to dressing in step 2. Substitute 20 chopped dried California apricots and 1 small fennel bulb, 2 tablespoons fronds minced, stalks discarded, bulb halved, cored, and chopped fine, for scallions. Omit mint and substitute parsley for cilantro.

Beijing-Style Meat Sauce and Noodles

Meet *zha jiang mian*, the most popular Chinese dish you've never heard of.

> BY ANDREW JANJIGIAN <

Have you ever "discovered" something new only to find that it's everywhere you turn? That was my experience with the meaty Chinese noodle dish *zha jiang mian* ("ja jang mee-AN"), and I've never been so glad to find a new favorite that I can get in most any Chinese restaurant. This dish has many aliases—fried sauce noodles, Beijing meat sauce, and Old Beijing noodles, to name a few. But what's even better is that it's a good dish to make at home: simple, quick, and flavor-packed.

It starts with a sauce akin to a long-simmered, deeply flavored Italian meat ragu. The difference is that it simmers for just 20 minutes and calls for only ½ pound of ground meat. The savory secret? Two fermented products: sweet bean sauce (*tián miàn jiàng*) and ground bean sauce (*huáng jiàng*).

Most recipes begin by sautéing ground pork, minced mushrooms, garlic, ginger, and scallions. The bean sauces go into the pot next, along with some water. The sauce simmers until it develops a thick consistency and a mahogany color and the flavors meld. It's then spooned over a mound of chewy lo mein noodles and topped with nests of colorful slivered raw vegetables. As the dish is stirred, the vegetables wilt from the heat but retain a refreshing crispness that's an ideal foil for the deep, dark sauce.

Developing a zha jiang mian recipe for home cooks would require finding substitutes for the sweet bean and ground bean sauces, which are hard to source outside of Asian markets. Thick, dark sweet bean sauce has a salty-sweet-umami flavor reminiscent of hoisin, but it's saltier, with an underlying bitter smokiness. It reminded me of molasses, which inspired my first substitution attempt: hoisin and molasses in a 3:1 ratio. The flavor was close but lacked the salty depth of the original. Adding soy sauce did the trick.

Ground bean sauce packs a savory-salty punch. Red miso paste, another long-fermented product, was a solid swap once I added a little more soy sauce.

When I used both substitutes, the flavors of the sauce were spot-on, but the dish was far too salty. Not wanting to upset the savory-salty-sweet balance by adjusting the ingredients, I tried a different approach: What if I simply used less sauce? It worked. The flavors were already so concentrated that reducing the quantity produced a balanced dish.

A few final tweaks: Mixing a baking soda solution into the ground pork kept the meat tender and moist. As for the vegetables, three provided variety and kept knife work to a minimum: Cucumber matchsticks and bean sprouts, along with scallion greens, provided freshness and crunch.

This one-pot meal comes together in just 30 minutes.

BEIJING-STYLE MEAT SAUCE AND NOODLES (ZHA JIANG MIAN)
SERVES 6

We prefer red miso in this recipe. You can use white miso, but the color will be lighter and the flavor milder. You can substitute 8 ounces of dried linguine for the lo mein noodles, if desired (see "Shopping for Lo Mein" on page 29), but be sure to follow the cooking time listed on the package. For an authentic presentation, bring the bowl to the table before tossing the noodles in step 5. Our recipe for Beijing-Style Meat Sauce and Noodles for Two is available for free for four months at CooksIllustrated.com/jun18.

- 8 ounces ground pork
- ⅛ teaspoon baking soda
- 5 tablespoons red miso paste
- 5 tablespoons soy sauce
- 3 tablespoons hoisin sauce
- 1 tablespoon molasses
- 8 scallions, white and light green parts cut into ½-inch pieces, dark green parts sliced thin on bias
- 2 garlic cloves, peeled
- 1 (½-inch) piece ginger, peeled and sliced into ⅛-inch rounds
- 4 ounces shiitake mushrooms, stemmed and sliced ½ inch thick
- 1 tablespoon vegetable oil
- 1 pound fresh lo mein noodles
- ½ English cucumber, unpeeled, cut into 2½-inch-long matchsticks (2 cups)
- 6 ounces (3 cups) bean sprouts

1. Toss pork, 2 teaspoons water, and baking soda in bowl until thoroughly combined. Let stand for 5 minutes. Whisk ½ cup water, miso paste, soy sauce, hoisin, and molasses together in second bowl.

2. Pulse white and light green scallion parts, garlic, and ginger in food processor until coarsely chopped, 5 to 10 pulses, scraping down sides of bowl as needed. Add mushrooms and pulse until mixture is finely chopped, 5 to 10 pulses.

3. Heat oil and pork mixture in large saucepan over medium heat for 1 minute, breaking up meat with wooden spoon. Add mushroom mixture and cook, stirring frequently, until mixture is dry and just begins to stick to saucepan, 5 to 7 minutes. Add miso mixture to saucepan and bring to simmer. Cook, stirring occasionally, until mixture thickens, 8 to 10 minutes. Cover and keep warm while noodles cook.

4. Bring 4 quarts water to boil in large pot. Add noodles and cook, stirring often, until almost tender (center should still be firm with slightly opaque dot), 3 to 5 minutes. Drain noodles and transfer to wide, shallow serving bowl.

5. Ladle sauce over center of noodles and sprinkle with cucumber, sprouts, and dark green scallion parts. Toss well and serve.

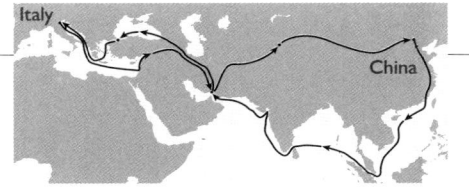

From China to Italy?
Though most food historians no longer believe Marco Polo was the first to introduce pasta to Italy after his travels to China in the 13th century, perhaps he was still the first to introduce *zha jiang mian*; the rich, savory meat sauce in the dish bears an uncanny resemblance to Italian ragu.

▶ **Chinese Favorite at Home**
A step-by-step video is available at CooksIllustrated.com/jun18

Chocolate Semifreddo

Italy's elegant alternative to gelato (and ice cream) is rich and decadently creamy—and requires no special equipment to make.

> BY ANNIE PETITO <

I love ice cream, but it isn't the most elegant way to cap off an evening. Serving a scoop (even homemade) at a dinner party always feels a little too casual. Enter *semifreddo*, a classic Italian dessert that's often described as a frozen mousse. (Though it's fully frozen, its name roughly translates as "half-frozen.") There are many styles, but like ice cream (or gelato), semifreddo typically starts with a custard base. However, instead of being churned in an ice cream maker, semifreddo is lightened with whipped cream and/or beaten egg whites. Then it's frozen in a loaf pan until solid, unmolded, and cut into neat slices. But instead of being hard and densely packed, semifreddo is soft enough that it easily caves to the pressure of a spoon. Better yet, unlike ice cream, it can sit out of the freezer for an extended period of time without melting, which makes it ideal for serving to company. An elegant frozen dessert that doesn't require an ice cream maker, doesn't melt easily, and is make-ahead by design? That checks a lot of boxes for me, so I tried a bunch of chocolate versions (my favorite flavor) that looked appealing.

The *semifreddo*, cherry sauce, and candied nuts can all be prepared well in advance of serving time, making this an ideal dessert for company.

Soft Serve

I immediately ruled out using whipped egg whites to lighten the custard, as they tended to produce a chewy, marshmallow-like semifreddo. I wanted a version that was lush and rich, so whipped cream would be my aerator of choice.

I started with a particularly rich custard from my research: I heated ¾ cup of heavy cream in a saucepan, thoroughly whisked it into five beaten egg yolks mixed with a few tablespoons of sugar, and poured the custard back into the saucepan to cook gently until it reached 160 degrees. I then introduced a nifty trick: I quickly poured the hot custard over 8 ounces of chopped bittersweet chocolate so that the chocolate melted, which saved me the extra step of melting it beforehand. Once the custard cooled, I gently folded in softly whipped cream. Finally, I poured the custard into a plastic wrap–lined loaf pan (that way, it would detach more easily from the pan) and froze it until solid, which took about 6 hours.

But I had gone overboard: While the semifreddo had deep chocolate flavor, it was so rich that I couldn't eat more than a few bites. Also, despite the fact that it had just come out of the freezer, it seemed to lack a certain refreshing coldness. I decided to cut some richness from the next batch of custard by replacing the heavy cream with an equal amount of milk. The dessert tasted lighter for sure—too lean, in fact. And in contrast to the fattier semifreddo, this one seemed overly cold, almost like a popsicle. It also melted a lot faster. (For more information, see "Keeping Semifreddo in Shape.")

I would obviously need to add back some fat, so for my next batch, I used heavy cream cut with ¼ cup water (this combo still had more fat than milk alone). This time I nailed it: The semifreddo was lush, sliced neatly, and—interestingly—tasted cold without feeling numbingly so. The only drawback was the fussy step of separating all those eggs, so I tried again with a combination of heavy cream, water, and three whole eggs instead of five yolks. The results were even better—the perfect balance of decadent and refreshing, thanks to the extra water in the egg whites—and the method was easier and less wasteful.

But I was curious to learn why the dessert had seemed more or less cold, depending on how much fat was in it. After a conversation with our science editor, I understood: When you put a spoonful of frozen dessert on your tongue and you feel its coldness, that's because heat energy is transferring from your tongue into the dessert, making your tongue colder. The extent to which that happens—and hence the amount of coldness you feel—depends not only on the temperature of the dessert but also on its ingredients, such as the amount of fat versus water.

Try this little experiment: Reach into your freezer, pull out an ice cube and a stick of butter, and grasp them for a minute. They're both the same temperature, but the ice cube feels colder. That's because frozen water can take in more heat from your body (and more quickly) than frozen fat, so your hand loses more heat and feels colder. For the same reason, at equal serving temperatures, an ice cream with more fat in it will seem less cold in your mouth than a leaner recipe.

▶ **See Annie Chill Out**
A step-by-step video is available at CooksIllustrated.com/jun18

TECHNIQUE | SMOOTH THE SIDES AND TOP

Before slicing, use an offset spatula to smooth any wrinkles on the surface of the *semifreddo*.

All Dressed Up

Though some semifreddo recipes call for mixing candied fruit, nuts, or cookies into the custard, I enjoyed my version's smooth, creamy texture and was hesitant to change it. But a garnish would offer textural contrast and make the dessert look more festive.

In my research I'd seen a chocolate semifreddo with a deep red cherry sauce spooned over each slice, so I put together my own version made with frozen sweet cherries, sugar, kirsch (cherry brandy), and a little cornstarch for body. The color and flavor were vivid, and the plump fruit nicely complemented the satiny semifreddo. For a bit of crunch, I made a batch of candied nuts with a pinch of salt to contrast with the dessert's sweetness.

Rich and satiny. Elegant. Deeply chocolaty. Make-ahead (you can even slice off a portion and freeze the rest for later). No ice cream maker required. Time to plan another dinner party.

CHOCOLATE SEMIFREDDO
SERVES 12

The *semifreddo* needs to be frozen for at least 6 hours before serving. We developed this recipe with our favorite dark chocolate, Ghirardelli 60% Cacao Bittersweet Chocolate Premium Baking Bar. Do not whip the heavy cream until the chocolate mixture has cooled. If the semifreddo is difficult to release from the pan, run a thin offset spatula around the edges of the pan or carefully run the sides of the pan under hot water for 5 to 10 seconds. For tips on folding in the whipped cream, see "The Best Way to Fold" on page 30. If frozen overnight, the semifreddo should be tempered before serving for the best texture. To temper, place slices on individual plates or a large tray, and refrigerate for 30 minutes. Serve the semifreddo as is or with our Cherry Sauce (recipe follows). For some crunch, sprinkle each serving with Quick Candied Nuts (page 29).

- 8 ounces bittersweet chocolate, chopped fine
- 1 tablespoon vanilla extract
- ½ teaspoon instant espresso powder
- 3 large eggs
- 5 tablespoons sugar
- ¼ teaspoon salt
- 2 cups heavy cream, chilled
- ¼ cup water

1. Lightly spray loaf pan with vegetable oil spray and line with plastic wrap, leaving 3-inch overhang on all sides. Place chocolate in large heatproof bowl; set fine-mesh strainer over bowl and set aside. Stir vanilla and espresso powder in small bowl until espresso powder is dissolved.

2. Whisk eggs, sugar, and salt in medium bowl until combined. Heat ½ cup cream (keep remaining 1½ cups chilled) and water in medium saucepan over medium heat until simmering. Slowly whisk hot cream mixture into egg mixture until combined. Return mixture to saucepan and cook over medium-low heat, stirring constantly and scraping bottom of saucepan with rubber spatula, until mixture is very slightly thickened and registers 160 to 165 degrees, about 5 minutes. Do not let mixture simmer.

3. Immediately pour mixture through strainer set over chocolate. Let mixture stand to melt chocolate, about 5 minutes. Whisk until chocolate is melted and smooth, then whisk in vanilla-espresso mixture. Let chocolate mixture cool completely, about 15 minutes.

4. Using stand mixer fitted with whisk attachment, beat remaining 1½ cups cream on low speed until bubbles form, about 30 seconds. Increase speed to medium and beat until whisk leaves trail, about 30 seconds. Increase speed to high and continue to beat until nearly doubled in volume and whipped cream forms soft peaks, 30 to 45 seconds longer.

5. Whisk one-third of whipped cream into chocolate mixture. Using rubber spatula, gently fold remaining whipped cream into chocolate mixture until incorporated and no streaks of whipped cream remain. Transfer mixture to prepared pan and spread evenly with rubber spatula. Fold overhanging plastic over surface. Freeze until firm, at least 6 hours.

6. When ready to serve, remove plastic from surface and invert pan onto serving plate. Remove plastic and smooth surface with spatula as necessary. Dip slicing knife in very hot water and wipe dry. Slice semifreddo ¾ inch thick, transferring slices to individual plates and dipping and wiping knife after each slice. Serve immediately. (Semifreddo can be wrapped tightly in plastic wrap and frozen for up to 2 weeks.)

CHERRY SAUCE
MAKES ABOUT 2 CUPS

This recipe was developed with frozen cherries. Do not thaw the cherries before using. Water can be substituted for the kirsch, if desired.

- 12 ounces frozen sweet cherries
- ¼ cup sugar
- 2 tablespoons kirsch
- 1½ teaspoons cornstarch
- 1 tablespoon lemon juice

1. Combine cherries and sugar in bowl and microwave for 1½ minutes. Stir, then continue to microwave until sugar is mostly dissolved, about 1 minute longer. Combine kirsch and cornstarch in small bowl.

2. Drain cherries in fine-mesh strainer set over small saucepan. Return cherries to bowl and set aside.

3. Bring juice in saucepan to simmer over medium-high heat. Stir in kirsch mixture and bring to boil. Boil, stirring occasionally, until mixture has thickened and appears syrupy, 1 to 2 minutes. Remove saucepan from heat and stir in cherries and lemon juice. Let sauce cool completely before serving. (Sauce can be refrigerated for up to 1 week.)

You Need Just a Mixer, Not an Ice Cream Maker

Airy whipped cream gives semifreddo its signature light, frozen mousse–like texture, with no churning in an ice cream maker required.

Keeping Semifreddo in Shape

Fat and air help *semifreddo* resist melting and keep its shape once it's out of the freezer. Our semifreddo has an abundance of butterfat, and butterfat melts well above room temperature. Even more important, the air from the whipped cream acts as an insulator, slowing the transfer of ambient heat much like the fluffy feathers in a down jacket. It's this latter factor that allows our semifreddo to retain its shape longer than most ice creams, since whipped cream contains more trapped air than what's introduced into ice cream during churning.

To demonstrate how air acts as an insulator, we compared how quickly 1 cup of frozen unwhipped heavy cream would melt versus 1 cup of heavy cream that we whipped before freezing. The frozen unwhipped heavy cream began to slump and soften after about 15 minutes and was ringed by a puddle of liquid after 45 minutes; meanwhile, the frozen whipped cream remained comparatively firm and exhibited little melting.

NO AIR = MORE MELTING

AIR = LESS MELTING

The frozen unwhipped cream (above left) began to melt after about 15 minutes at room temperature. The trapped air in frozen whipped cream (above right) helped it resist melting, even after 45 minutes at room temperature.

Buttery Spring Vegetables

No disrespect to dessert, but perfectly cooked vegetables can dazzle, too.

⋺ BY ANDREA GEARY ⋲

Recipes for butter-braised spring vegetables abound, but don't let them lead you astray. Braising simply doesn't work for tender spring produce.

Winter vegetables are another story: If you slowly braise sturdy carrots, parsnips, and potatoes in butter over low heat in a covered pot, they stew in their own juices, turning perfectly tender with an earthy sweetness. But do the same with delicate asparagus and peas and you get sodden, drab mush.

That's why most so-called butter-braised spring vegetables aren't technically braised. Instead they're cooked rapidly in a covered skillet with a small amount of butter and water or broth. But I reject those recipes, too. Because the vegetables cook directly in the buttery liquid, they become dull and waterlogged and the buttery richness is lost. For spring vegetables that retained their vibrant colors and crisp textures and butter that clung to their surfaces, I'd have to find another way.

But first, which vegetables to cook? Asparagus, emblematic of spring, was a must. Sugar snap peas would provide the sweetness of their shelled cousins but with extra, well, snap. And I confess I chose radishes mostly for their dazzling color. Turnips' hint of bitterness rounded out my medley.

To prevent the vegetables from becoming soggy, I decided to cook them in a steamer basket over a small amount of water. I halved the radishes and cut the asparagus and turnips to match the size of the whole sugar snap peas, hoping similar dimensions

An emulsified sauce coats crisp-tender vegetables.

would help the vegetables cook at the same rate.

It didn't quite work out, though. The asparagus and turnips were perfectly crisp-tender after 5 minutes, but by that time the peas had long lost their snap. Much of the radishes' color had leached into the water below, and their crisp pepperiness had given way to a vaguely cabbage-like flavor.

For my next batch, I gave the asparagus and turnips a 2-minute head start before adding the peas. And I added the radishes, cut into slim half-moons, just for the last minute to warm through. I lifted the steamer basket out of the saucepan, discarded the water, and tumbled the vegetables back into the saucepan. I stirred in some butter and a bit of salt and transferred everything to a platter.

The colors were beautiful and the vegetables nearly perfectly cooked. However, the butter had slipped right off the food and pooled on the platter.

For my next batch, I spread the vegetables on the platter right after steaming to let excess heat escape and prevent them from overcooking while I made a quick version of the French butter sauce called beurre blanc. An emulsion of flavorful liquid and butter, a beurre blanc coats food much better than butter alone (see "Another Reason to Emulsify" on page 31).

I poured off most of the water from the saucepan and added minced shallot, white wine vinegar, salt, and a bit of sugar. Once the shallot softened, I whisked in chilled butter, tablespoon by tablespoon, until the sauce had the viscosity of heavy cream. I added the vegetables to the sauce, gave them a stir, and returned everything to the platter, finishing with a light sprinkle of minced chives.

The result was a platter of buttery, vibrant, perfectly cooked vegetables worthy of a spring celebration—and certainly worth celebrating.

BUTTERY SPRING VEGETABLES
SERVES 6

To ensure that the turnips are tender, peel them thoroughly to remove not only the tough outer skin but also the fibrous layer of flesh just beneath. This recipe works best with thick asparagus spears that are between ½ and ¾ inch in diameter.

- 1 pound turnips, peeled and cut into ½-inch by ½-inch by 2-inch batons
- 1 pound asparagus, trimmed and cut on bias into 2-inch lengths
- 8 ounces sugar snap peas, strings removed, trimmed
- 4 large radishes, halved and sliced thin
- 1 tablespoon minced shallot
- 1½ teaspoons white wine vinegar
- ¾ teaspoon salt
- ¼ teaspoon sugar
- 6 tablespoons unsalted butter, cut into 6 pieces and chilled
- 1 tablespoon minced fresh chives

1. Bring 1 cup water to boil in large saucepan over high heat. Place steamer basket over boiling water. Add turnips and asparagus to basket, cover saucepan, and reduce heat to medium. Cook until vegetables are slightly softened, about 2 minutes. Add snap peas, cover, and cook until snap peas are crisp-tender, about 2 minutes. Add radishes, cover, and cook for 1 minute. Lift basket out of saucepan and transfer vegetables to platter. Spread into even layer to allow steam to dissipate. Discard all but 3 tablespoons liquid from saucepan.

2. Return saucepan to medium heat. Add shallot, vinegar, salt, and sugar and cook until mixture is reduced to 1½ tablespoons (it will barely cover bottom of saucepan), about 2 minutes. Reduce heat to low. Add butter, 1 piece at a time, whisking vigorously after each addition, until butter is incorporated and sauce has consistency of heavy cream, 4 to 5 minutes. Remove saucepan from heat. Add vegetables and stir to coat. Dry platter and return vegetables to platter. Sprinkle with chives and serve.

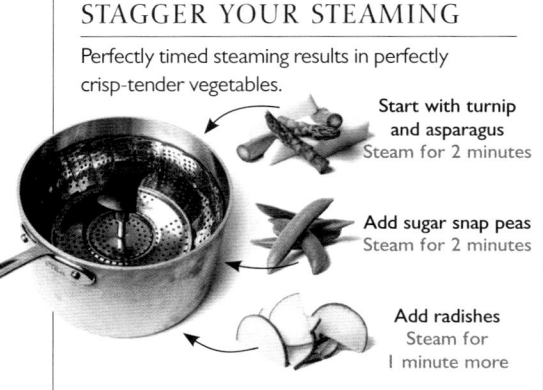

STAGGER YOUR STEAMING
Perfectly timed steaming results in perfectly crisp-tender vegetables.

- **Start with turnip and asparagus** — Steam for 2 minutes
- **Add sugar snap peas** — Steam for 2 minutes
- **Add radishes** — Steam for 1 minute more

▶ See: A Celebration of Spring
A step-by-step video is available at CooksIllustrated.com/jun18

PHOTOGRAPHY: CARL TREMBLAY

The Best Cocoa Powder

The big debate in cocoa powder has always been Dutch-processed versus natural. Is that really the most important factor?

> BY KATE SHANNON <

When we want big chocolate flavor in everything from cookies and cakes to puddings and pies, we turn to cocoa powder. It has a higher proportion of flavorful cocoa solids than any other form of chocolate, so ounce for ounce, it tastes more intensely chocolaty. It's made in two styles—Dutch-processed and natural—and there's fierce debate in the baking world about which is best. Both styles have staunch supporters who are convinced that using the wrong type will ruin a dessert. For years, we also viewed Dutched and natural cocoa powders as distinctly different products. But when we last evaluated cocoa powder, something surprising happened: A natural powder won, a Dutched powder came in second, and the rest of the lineup was a jumble.

In the years since, we've remained curious about cocoa powder. Some of our test cooks prefer the dark color of Dutched powder and swear that it has richer, deeper chocolate flavor to match. Are they onto something? Is choosing between Dutched and natural the most important decision you can make when buying cocoa powder, or is there more to it than that?

To find out, we sampled eight nationally available cocoa powders (priced from $0.34 to $1.70 per ounce): four Dutched and four natural. To zero in on how much Dutch processing matters, we carefully selected recipes for testing: two different sheet cake recipes—one that calls for natural cocoa powder and another that uses Dutched—and a cookie recipe that doesn't specify which style to use.

The results were mixed. While some desserts were simply acceptable, others were excellent. The

We sampled each cocoa powder in two chocolate sheet cake recipes—one calling for Dutched cocoa powder and the other calling for natural. We preferred the Dutched cocoa powders in both recipes.

good-enough cakes and cookies were tall and "airy" with a "crumbly" structure, but a little "dry." Across the board, we preferred "moist" and "fudgy" desserts. Our favorite cakes had a "plush" texture, and cookies toed the line between chewy and tender. As for flavor, samples ranged from "mild" and "slightly fruity" to "intense," "complex," and "earthy," with the slight bitterness of good espresso or dark chocolate. Why had some desserts been dry, mild, and lean, while others were so rich, flavorful, and decadent?

From Pod to Powder

Cocoa powder—and all real chocolate—starts with cacao pods, the fruit of the tropical evergreen tree *Theobroma cacao*. Each pod contains between 20 and 50 beans (also called seeds). The beans generally taste bitter and are surrounded by a fruity-tasting, milky-white pulp, according to Gregory Ziegler, a chocolate expert and professor of food science at Penn State University. The beans are fermented, a critical process that develops their dark brown color, before being roasted. The fermented beans are either roasted whole or are shelled and roasted as nibs. Next, the nibs are ground into a paste called chocolate liquor, which contains a mix of cocoa solids and cocoa butter. Some of the chocolate liquor is used to make candy and chocolate products. The rest is pressed to remove most of the cocoa butter, which is also used to make chocolate. The cocoa solids that remain are ground into small particles and become cocoa powder.

In the 19th century, a Dutch chemist and chocolatier named Conrad Van Houten developed an optional step for the above process, known as Dutching, Dutch processing, or alkalizing. Chocolate is naturally slightly acidic, and so is cocoa powder. Treating the cocoa with an alkalizing agent neutralizes the acid, raising the powder's pH from about 5 to about 7. Natural cocoa powder is usually sandy brown with a reddish tint and tastes bright and fruity; Dutch processing darkens the color to velvety brown or near-black and mellows the cocoa's more astringent notes so that its deeper, earthy notes come to the forefront.

Dutching is not a one-size-fits-all process. Ziegler told us that manufacturers use a variety of alkalizing

The Journey from Pod to Powder

To deliver rich-tasting cocoa powder, producers must perfect every step of the process.

DUTCHING PROCESS
An alkalizing agent such as potassium carbonate or sodium carbonate is added to the nibs, the cocoa liquor, or the final pressed powder. This optional step darkens the powder's color and mellows its astringent notes.

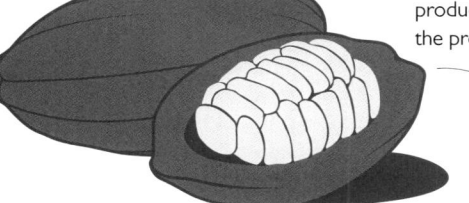

HARVEST PODS
Football-shaped pods are collected from tropical cacao trees. Each pod contains from 20 to 50 beans (seeds), which are surrounded by fruity pulp.

DRY BEANS
Cacao beans are fermented for two to nine days and then dried for up to several weeks before being bagged and sent to processing facilities.

ROAST BEANS OR NIBS
Cacao beans are either roasted whole and then shelled or shelled first, leaving just the meaty center—the nib—to roast.

GRIND POWDER
The roasted nibs are ground into a paste called chocolate liquor, which is pressed to extract cocoa butter. The remainder is then dried and ground into a powder.

agents, such as potassium carbonate or sodium carbonate. They can also adjust the temperature and time of the process and may opt to alkalize the nibs, the cocoa liquor, or the final pressed powder.

Given the potential variation in processing, we were curious about how our powders compared with each other, so we asked an independent laboratory to measure the pH of each cocoa. The lab reported that the pH of the natural powders ranged from 5.36 to 5.73 and the pH of the Dutched powders ranged from 6.88 to 7.90. It doesn't sound like much, but one point indicates a tenfold difference in acidity.

When we reviewed the results of our recipe tests, we saw that some trends fell in line with the Dutched versus natural division. The more acidic natural powders produced some of the tallest, airiest, and crumbliest cookies and cakes. On the other hand, most of the Dutched powders produced baked goods that hadn't risen quite as tall. This makes sense: Baking soda, a common chemical leavener that was in all three of the recipes we tested, releases carbon dioxide bubbles when it reacts with acid and moisture; this is one of the reasons that doughs and batters rise in the oven. The acidity level affected how our cocoa powders interacted with the baking soda and seemed to have played a role in how high our baked goods rose.

In general, the tall, airy cakes and cookies made with natural cocoa powder were perceived as much drier. Our tasters preferred the fudgier, moist desserts made with less-acidic Dutched powders. In fact, a Dutch-processed cocoa powder won every tasting—even when used in a recipe that was specifically designed using natural cocoa powder—and Dutched products took the top three spots overall. But one Dutched powder consistently landed at the bottom of the rankings; baked goods made with it were slightly dry instead of tender and rich. Dutching is clearly an important variable, but it wasn't the whole story.

Fat Is Another Major Factor

There's another big divide in the world of cocoa powder: fat content. When the cocoa liquor is pressed, some cocoa butter remains with the solids, so commercial cocoa powders generally contain between 10 and 24 percent fat. While that full range is technically achievable, cocoa powders don't run the full spectrum. Instead, they're manufactured in two levels: low fat and high fat. An independent lab analyzed the samples and reported that three products in our lineup contained about 11 to 12 percent fat; the rest had nearly double that, about 20 to 22 percent.

Suddenly, things started to come into focus. Most of those high-fat powders scored high in our tastings. Why? Fat adds richness and flavor. It can also help ensure that cookies and cakes bake up moist and tender. The flip side is that desserts made with the low-fat powders, though still acceptable, tended to be dry. The only low-fat cocoa powder to land in the top half of our rankings was Hershey's, which may owe its high score to its familiar flavor. Our other favorites contained at least 20 percent fat, for rich, moist, flavorful cakes and cookies.

The Opposite of Fat Is . . . Starch?

Baking with a low-fat cocoa powder means risking dry baked goods—but not just because fat adds richness and helps prevent baked goods from drying out. Starch is a natural component of all chocolate and cocoa powders, and the less fat cocoa powder has, the more starch it contains. These starches are very absorbent; they're able to soak up 100 percent of their weight in moisture. By comparison, flour can absorb 60 percent of its weight. Like excess flour in a recipe, the extra cocoa starch present in low-fat powders traps moisture and makes for dry cakes and cookies. It's especially noticeable when recipes call for a high ratio of cocoa powder to flour, as with one of the chocolate sheet cakes we made.

To isolate the role of starch, we performed a simple experiment with all eight cocoas. We whisked together precise amounts of cocoa powder and water, transferred the slurries to bags and vacuum-sealed them, and heated the mixtures in a *sous vide* water bath to exactly 180 degrees, the temperature at which the starches in cocoa powder gel, or thicken. The differences were striking. Some were very firm and bouncy, like a memory foam pillow, and others were almost runny.

Of course, none of our desserts had been liquid-y or pillowy, but the results lined up nearly perfectly with the textural differences we'd noticed in the cookies and cakes. The cocoa powders that were the firmest in our experiment had lots of moisture-absorbing starch and made tall, airy cakes that tended to be dry; those that produced the runnier slurries had less starch and resulted in moist, fudgy cake. The pattern was even more evident when we looked at the cookies. Using high-starch powders gave us cookies that rose and had crumbly, cakey textures. Cookies made with low-starch powders spread more, and the available moisture in the dough helped keep them chewy and fudgy. The difference in how much the cookies spread was dramatic. The cookies with the most starch averaged about 3.2 inches in diameter, compared with almost 3.8 inches for those

Take Your Desserts from Good to Great

How cocoa powder is processed and how much fat it contains can have a big impact on your results. Only a Dutched cocoa powder that's also high in fat will ensure the most deeply chocolaty, moist, and fudgy results.

Dutched = Better Flavor, Darker Color
The process of Dutching neutralizes the acidity in cocoa, removing its harsher notes and allowing deeper, earthy notes to shine. Bonus: The Dutching process also darkens the cocoa powder, which in turn leads to baked goods with a darker, richer color.

CAKE MADE WITH NATURAL COCOA POWDER

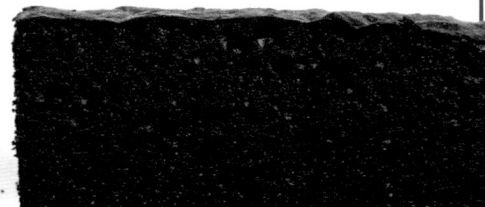
CAKE MADE WITH DUTCHED COCOA POWDER

High Fat = More Moistness and Richness
For richer baked goods, look for cocoa with at least 1 gram of fat per 5-gram serving. A high-fat cocoa powder will have less starch, which is a good thing—starch can suck up moisture and dry out cakes and cookies. To show how much of an effect starch has on baked goods, we combined a small sample of each cocoa powder in our lineup with a precise amount of water and heated the slurries to 180 degrees, the temperature at which the starches in the cocoa powder gel or thicken. Here's what happened:

LOW-FAT, HIGH-STARCH COCOA SLURRIES FORMED A GEL

HIGH-FAT, LOW-STARCH COCOA SLURRIES STAYED MOIST

TASTING COCOA POWDERS

We tested eight cocoa powders, including a mix of Dutched and natural products, all available at supermarkets. Panels of 21 tasters sampled them in three blind tastings: in chocolate sugar cookies and two kinds of chocolate sheet cake. An independent laboratory analyzed the fat content and pH of the cocoa powders; a lower pH indicates higher acidity. Prices were paid in Boston-area supermarkets, and products appear below in order of preference.

RECOMMENDED

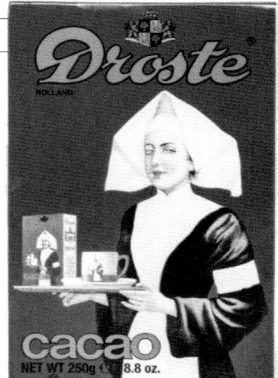

DROSTE Cacao
PRICE: $9.99 for 8.8-oz package ($1.14 per oz)
STYLE: Dutched   **pH:** 7.90   **FAT:** 20.14%
COMMENTS: Our longtime favorite Dutched supermarket cocoa powder was the clear overall winner. It has a high fat content and therefore has less starch, so cookies were "perfectly chewy and moist." Cakes were very "moist," "rich," and "fudgy." We also loved its dark color and "earthy," "woodsy" chocolate flavor.

GUITTARD Cocoa Rouge Cocoa Powder
PRICE: $7.99 for 8-oz package ($1.00 per oz)
STYLE: Dutched   **pH:** 7.22   **FAT:** 22.09%
COMMENTS: Because this cocoa powder contains the most fat in our lineup, it also contains the least starch. As a result, it trapped less moisture than other powders and baked goods were delightfully decadent and "fudgy." With less starch to absorb moisture and no acidity to react with the baking soda, it produced the widest and flattest cookies in our lineup. Cookies and cakes had "deeper chocolate flavor" that was reminiscent of good "espresso" and "molasses."

VALRHONA Cocoa Powder
PRICE: $14.99 for 8.82-oz package ($1.70 per oz)
STYLE: Dutched   **pH:** 6.91   **FAT:** 20.73%
COMMENTS: The priciest cocoa powder in our lineup delivered "intense," "rich chocolate flavor" in all three recipes. Some tasters even detected slightly "smoky," "bitter" notes, which added complexity. Cookies were pleasantly tender and chewy, and cakes had a "brownie-like" and "velvety crumb."

RECOMMENDED (CONTINUED)

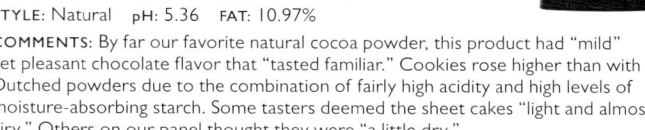

HERSHEY'S Natural Unsweetened Cocoa
PRICE: $3.99 for 8-oz package ($0.50 per oz)
STYLE: Natural   **pH:** 5.36   **FAT:** 10.97%
COMMENTS: By far our favorite natural cocoa powder, this product had "mild" yet pleasant chocolate flavor that "tasted familiar." Cookies rose higher than with Dutched powders due to the combination of fairly high acidity and high levels of moisture-absorbing starch. Some tasters deemed the sheet cakes "light and almost airy." Others on our panel thought they were "a little dry."

SCHARFFEN BERGER Unsweetened Natural Cocoa Powder
PRICE: $7.99 for 6-oz package ($1.33 per oz)
STYLE: Natural   **pH:** 5.51   **FAT:** 21.54%
COMMENTS: Although it's high in fat, this natural cocoa powder couldn't compete with the high-fat Dutched cocoa powders. Its flavor was distinctly "bright" and "fruity," and some tasters wanted "a bit more bitterness." Desserts were "fluffy" and "light" and tended toward dryness.

NESTLÉ Toll House Baking Cocoa
PRICE: $2.69 for 8-oz package ($0.34 per oz)
STYLE: Natural   **pH:** 5.73   **FAT:** 11.46%
COMMENTS: Alongside boldly flavored samples, this inexpensive, low-fat cocoa powder tasted "mild," "like milk chocolate." Throughout our tastings, it produced "tall," light-colored desserts that were a little more "crumbly" than our favorites.

GHIRARDELLI 100% Unsweetened Cocoa
PRICE: $4.99 for 8-oz package ($0.62 per oz)
STYLE: Natural   **pH:** 5.57   **FAT:** 20.51%
COMMENTS: Cakes and cookies made with this natural powder tasted "sweet" and "bright" but weren't as deeply chocolaty or intense as those made with higher-ranked products. Although the textures of the cakes and cookies were "perfectly OK," we preferred products that combined big chocolate flavor and fudgy consistency.

EQUAL EXCHANGE Organic Baking Cocoa
PRICE: $7.99 for 8-oz package ($1.00 per oz)
STYLE: Dutched   **pH:** 6.88   **FAT:** 11.95%
COMMENTS: This was the only low-fat Dutch-processed cocoa in our lineup, and we missed the extra fat. Its "dark," "deep," almost "bitter" flavor earned mixed scores. While cookies made with it had "nice height" and tasters approved of one cake, the other cake was a little too dry.

---

with the least amount of starch—a difference of more than ½ inch. That's a big variation for a chocolate sugar cookie.

Buying the Best Cocoa Powder

By the end of testing, we realized that the old Dutched versus natural debate wasn't wrong but it also wasn't the whole story. The performance of cocoa powder is determined by a complex system of factors including pH, fat, and starch content. For moist and tender baked goods, we recommend buying a Dutch-processed cocoa powder that's high in fat and therefore low in moisture-absorbing starch. (If the nutrition label is all you have to go by, seek out a product with at least 1 gram of fat per 5-gram serving.)

Our top three scorers fell into this category. Each produced "moist" and "fudgy" cakes and cookies that struck the right balance between "chewy" and "tender." The best of the bunch was our former runner-up (and longtime favorite Dutched product), Droste Cacao ($9.99 for 8.8 ounces), which has the right combination of factors to ensure decadent chocolate desserts with perfectly moist textures and the "sophisticated," "complex" flavors of good espresso and fancy chocolate. It's well worth seeking out.

Testing Plastic Food Storage Containers

Could we find a well-made, easy-to-use container that wouldn't warp, stain, leak, or wear out too soon?

⊰ BY LISA McMANUS ⊱

Whether you're storing leftovers, preparing a make-ahead meal, or taking lunch to work, you need a food storage container to keep food fresh, intact, and ready to eat. But the containers most of us have at home are pathetic: a motley pile of warped, stained bottoms and cracked, mismatched lids. Stores are brimming with containers claiming to be leakproof, airtight, microwave-safe, and more, but which ones function as promised—and hold up to serious use over time?

In our last testing, we chose the Snapware Airtight 8 Cup Rectangular Container as our favorite plastic model, but we've heard complaints about the performance of recently purchased copies; plus, new competitors have emerged. We like having both plastic and glass containers on hand since each has advantages: Plastic is light and less fragile, whereas heavier glass won't warp and resists stains. Many glass containers are also ovensafe.

We purchased six plastic containers, including our former winner, and five glass containers (see our testing results for the glass containers on page 32) to find out which functioned best without warping, staining, shattering, or failing to keep a tight seal. We didn't include disposable supermarket versions, which aren't designed for durability.

Keep Air Out; Keep Contents In

We've all tucked a container of lunch into a tote only to discover later that it has dripped all over the inside of the bag. The products in our lineup made plenty of promises to be leakproof and/or airtight. To check, we filled each container with 2 cups of water tinted with food coloring to make drips easy to spot and then shook them hard over white paper towels for 15 seconds. One didn't last 5 seconds before the lid opened and water gushed out. Two—including our former winner—allowed a steady, thin stream or a few drops to escape, but three kept the towels dry.

To test if the containers were truly airtight, we sealed a spoonful of moisture-detecting crystals in each and then submerged them in water for 2 minutes. These crystals change from blue to pink if the slightest moisture reaches them. A few containers

▶ Watch Lisa in Action
See how the testing was done at CooksIllustrated.com/jun18

To test durability, we froze water in the containers and then shoved them off the counter.

kept the crystals uniformly blue, indicating that the interior stayed dry as a bone. But some containers instantly began filling with water; others revealed a smattering of pink crystals among the blue. If moisture can penetrate, so can air, which lets food stale. Additionally, food odors might not stay in the container and could spread through your refrigerator.

Just Say No to Odors and Stains

The most leakproof container is still a poor choice if it's hard to keep clean and odor-free. Most container lids are fitted with a silicone gasket for a tight seal and flaps or extended rims that snap down to hold the lid in place. The problem is, gaskets and lid hardware can trap food, moisture, and odors. We filled the containers with pungent oil-packed tuna and anchovies, refrigerated them overnight, and then removed the fish and ran the containers through the dishwasher. Staffers sniffed the clean containers, noting any lingering fishy odors. The bad news: Most did trap smells and oily residue around their gaskets. But some gaskets were much easier to clean than others. Our front-runner's gasket was not stuffed into the usual narrow channel but simply built into the lid so you could clean under it; another model had a 3/8-inch-wide, soft, square gasket that was easy to remove and replace in a channel broad enough for a cloth-covered fingertip to dry it.

Staining is the plague of plastic containers. They might still function, but they look terrible. We stored chili full of tomatoes and colorful spices in the containers over a weekend. We then microwaved them until the chili hit 160 degrees, a piping-hot serving temperature. Even after we ran them through the dishwasher, most containers were deeply stained. The type of plastic determined the outcome: Five of the six containers were made of polypropylene and kept a cloudy-orange tint. The sixth, made of a clear plastic called Tritan, stayed stain-free.

Used and Abused

A container that works for only a few months is a waste of money. After our first microwave test, the gasket on our former winner broke, leaving a small gap in the channel where the gasket had split and shrunk. (Since our last testing, the manufacturer was sold, which may have affected production methods.) With just weeks to assess long-term durability, we deployed abuse testing: We opened and closed each container 100 times. Next we ran them through 50 dishwasher cycles, simulating a year of use. Then we repeated every previous test: shaking and submerging, storing fish and checking odors, and storing and heating chili. Finally, we filled the containers with water and knocked them off the counter and then froze water in them and dropped them onto the floor. Some burst open and one lid's protruding corner tab (to help open the lid) snapped off, but three models stayed intact and watertight. You might never drop your container, but knowing yours is unlikely to pop open and make a mess gives you peace of mind.

And the Winner Is . . .

After container boot camp, we had a winner: the Rubbermaid Brilliance Food Storage Container, Large, 9.6 Cup ($12.99). We loved its roomy, flat shape that was easy to stack and helped food heat faster and more evenly than in deeper containers. We appreciated that its gasket was attached to the lid for cleaning without the fuss of removing a slippery bit of silicone, and we liked its pair of lid clips that doubled down on its already-tight seal. When open, the clips created small vents so we could microwave with the lid on, reducing splatter. An extended rim stayed cool for easy handling when food was hot. Best of all, it didn't leak, and it emerged from extensive testing still looking clear, clean, and good as new. While we tested the 9.6-cup container, Rubbermaid offers a variety of sizes in this line.

TESTING PLASTIC FOOD STORAGE CONTAINERS

We tested six plastic containers (all BPA-free, according to manufacturers), choosing those as close as possible to an 8-cup capacity (the capacities of the models in our lineup ranged from 6 to 10 cups). All containers were purchased online, and they appear below in order of preference.

LEAKS

We filled the containers with water tinted with blue food coloring and shook them vigorously for 15 seconds. We also filled them with moisture-detecting color-changing crystals and submerged them in water for 2 minutes. Containers that didn't leak when shaken and that kept their contents dry when submerged received high marks.

ODORS

We refrigerated oil-packed tuna and anchovies in each container overnight and ran the containers through a home dishwasher and checked for odors. Containers that resisted odors and cleaned up more easily were preferred.

DESIGN

We considered features that made the containers easier to use, including simple, intuitive seals and shapes that stack well and make cooling and heating more efficient.

STORAGE AND MICROWAVE HEATING

We filled containers with chili, refrigerated them over a weekend, and microwaved them, checking for warping, staining, and other damage. Containers that didn't leak or spill, held plenty of chili, and resisted warping, staining, and other damage rated highest.

DURABILITY

We opened and closed each container 100 times, washed the containers 50 times in a home dishwasher, and repeated all the previous tests (leaking, odors, opening and closing, microwaving). Then we filled containers with water and knocked them off a kitchen counter and froze water in them and dropped them from 3 feet above the floor. Finally, we checked for stains, warping, breakage, and general wear and tear, giving high marks to those still in good condition.

HIGHLY RECOMMENDED

RUBBERMAID Brilliance Food Storage Container, Large, 9.6 Cup
MODEL: 1991158
PRICE: $12.99
MATERIAL: Tritan
CAPACITY: 9.6 cups

LEAKS: ★★★
ODORS: ★★½
DESIGN: ★★★
STORAGE AND MICROWAVE HEATING: ★★★
DURABILITY: ★★★

Our new favorite passed every test and looked good doing it, thanks to its lightweight Tritan plastic material that stayed as stain-free as glass. Microwaving chili was a breeze, with lid vents that let you leave the container fully sealed and extended rims that stayed cool for easy handling. One quibble: While we like that the gasket is attached so we don't have to fuss with removing it, you do need to clean carefully under its open side, as some testers detected slight fishy odors.

RECOMMENDED

KINETIC Fresh Series 54-Ounce Rectangular Food Storage Container with Lid
MODEL: 49014
PRICE: $10.99
MATERIAL: Polypropylene
CAPACITY: 6.75 cups

LEAKS: ★★★
ODORS: ★★
DESIGN: ★★
STORAGE AND MICROWAVE HEATING: ★★½
DURABILITY: ★★½

This container acquired a slightly orange, cloudy look from the microwaved chili, but it didn't warp or sustain other damage during testing and it didn't spill—even when we filled it with water, pushed it off the counter, and two lid flaps popped open as it hit the floor, upside down. Its 6.75-cup capacity seemed a bit cramped, though, and its teensy silicone gasket is nearly impossible to remove for cleaning. Also, its lid is not microwave-safe.

LOCK & LOCK Easy Match, 10.1 Cup
MODEL: HPL341EM
PRICE: $25.97
MATERIAL: Polypropylene
CAPACITY: 10.1 cups

LEAKS: ★★
ODORS: ★★
DESIGN: ★★
STORAGE AND MICROWAVE HEATING: ★★½
DURABILITY: ★★★

This roomy container was a front-runner. It's solidly built and its flaps sealed firmly, but the seal wasn't bulletproof. It leaked a little and admitted some moisture. We liked that a colored dot on the base matches the trim of the lid for easy organization, but other features, notably the thin, hard-to-remove gasket, were less successful.

RECOMMENDED WITH RESERVATIONS

OXO GOOD GRIPS 9.6 Cup Smart Seal Container
MODEL: 11174900
PRICE: $12.99
MATERIAL: Polypropylene
CAPACITY: 9.6 cups

LEAKS: ★★★
ODORS: ★½
DESIGN: ★★½
STORAGE AND MICROWAVE HEATING: ★★
DURABILITY: ★½

This container displayed some good design elements, such as its soft, easy-to-remove gasket—but we really did have to remove, wash, and dry that gasket or it would trap odors. The container's tall, narrow shape meant foods took slightly longer to heat or chill than when in flatter containers. The plastic stained faint orange in our chili test, and when we filled the container with water and pushed it onto the floor, the flaps flew open and water gushed out.

NOT RECOMMENDED

SNAPWARE Airtight Food Storage 8 Cup Rectangular Container
MODEL: 1098434
PRICE: $7.99
MATERIAL: Polypropylene
CAPACITY: 8 cups

LEAKS: ★
ODORS: ★½
DESIGN: ★★
STORAGE AND MICROWAVE HEATING: ★★½
DURABILITY: ★

Our former winner didn't hold up this time. It leaked, held onto stains, retained slight fishy odors, and worst of all, the gasket darkened and split in our first round of testing and then continued to degrade and crack as we completed testing. We have learned that the company was sold since our previous testing, which may have affected production methods. While we still like its flat stackable lid and low profile, the failure of the gasket means we no longer recommend it.

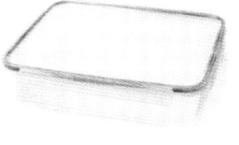

JOSEPH JOSEPH Nest Storage Plastic Food Storage Containers Set
MODEL: 81009
PRICE: $35.00 for set of six graduated sizes (we tested the 3-liter model)
MATERIAL: Polypropylene
CAPACITY: 12.6 cups

LEAKS: ★
ODORS: ★½
DESIGN: ★½
STORAGE AND MICROWAVE HEATING: ★★
DURABILITY: ★★

"This closing system doesn't feel secure," one tester complained of this container, the second largest in a set of six. The lid leaked when the container was shaken, and the container filled with water when submerged. Expanding ice pushed the lid up and nearly off in the freezer, and the lid slightly warped over the course of testing. The container retained odors, and its depth meant food chilled and heated unevenly.

INGREDIENT NOTES

> BY STEVE DUNN, ANDREW JANJIGIAN, LAN LAM, ANNIE PETITO & KRISTIN SARGIANIS

Tasting Ground Turmeric

We've always used turmeric in Indian-inspired curries, rice, and vegetables, but now this vibrant orange spice is showing up in all sorts of foods and drinks. The uptick in popularity is due in large part to curcumin, a compound in turmeric that has gotten a lot of attention for its antioxidant properties, although no scientific studies have proven that eating it confers any health benefits.

Does it matter which ground turmeric you buy? To find out, we purchased five products priced from $2.10 to $3.46 per ounce and sampled them in warm milk and in our Turmeric Chicken Salad.

Our tastings gave us a newfound appreciation for turmeric. In recipes, we typically combine it with other bold spices, but when we were able to home in on just the turmeric, we found that many samples were warm and "zippy," some had a "piney" flavor, and others were "vegetal" and "grassy."

We also took a closer look at curcumin, which, in addition to being responsible for turmeric's purported health benefits, is the source of its bright orange hue. (It has little bearing on flavor.) Three manufacturers told us that their turmeric contains between 3.6 and 5 percent curcumin; the others declined to comment. Our top two products contain about 5 percent curcumin. The winner of our tasting, Frontier Co-Op Ground Turmeric, stood out in a crowd of good options thanks to its strong "floral," "earthy," and "gingery" notes. For the complete tasting results, go to CooksIllustrated.com/jun18. –Kate Shannon

RECOMMENDED

FRONTIER CO-OP Ground Turmeric
PRICE: $3.99 for 1.9-oz jar ($2.10 per oz)
CURCUMIN: Minimum of 5%
COMMENTS: Our winner had a hint of the "warm," moderate heat that we associate with ginger and cinnamon. Both in warm milk and in turmeric chicken salad, it was "aromatic" and "earthy."

MORTON & BASSETT Turmeric
PRICE: $6.19 for 2.4-oz jar ($2.58 per oz)
CURCUMIN: 5%
COMMENTS: Our second-place turmeric had a pronounced "woodsy," "earthy" flavor with a pleasant "bitter" finish. That bitterness was balanced nicely with a strong "aromatic" and "floral" quality.

Cilantro: More than Just Leaves

Coriandrum sativum—better known as cilantro or coriander—is an entirely edible plant. The leaves and stems are used widely in Asian and South American cuisines. Coriander "seeds" are the dried fruit of the plant (and inside each fruit is a seed). They're used whole, crushed, or ground and are a common ingredient in Indian and Middle Eastern dishes and in vegetable pickling. The plant's roots, while not as widely used as the leaves and seeds, are sometimes found in Asian curries and soups, particularly in Thailand. In general, delicate cilantro leaves are used as a garnish before serving or added late in the cooking process because they quickly lose their aroma when heated, whereas the heartier roots and seeds are typically added earlier to contribute to the foundational flavor of a dish. Interestingly, around 12 percent of the global population are able to detect particular fatty aldehyde compounds in cilantro that give it an unpleasant "soapy" flavor. –S.D.

Seeds: Toasty, soft, citrus flavor reminiscent of leaves but with more "perfumy" hints of peppery spice

Leaves: Floral, herbal, bright, grassy, slightly peppery

Roots: Slightly sweet, citrusy, and vegetal

Stems: Similar in flavor to leaves but more potent

Pancake Mix-In Strategy

We don't suggest stirring fruit, chocolate chips, or nuts directly into thick pancake batters, such as that for our Easy Pancakes (page 13). This will overmix the batter, compromising the pancakes' height and texture. Instead, add items (cut into ½-inch pieces) immediately after portioning the batter into the skillet. The batter will partially surround the add-ins during cooking. –L.L.

DON'T MIX THE MIX-INS
Add them in the skillet.

Buying and Trimming a Side of Salmon

A side of salmon—that is, a single fillet that runs the length of the fish—typically weighs between 4 and 5 pounds. Most of the fillet is uniformly thick and will cook evenly; however, the tail end tapers, so we prefer to trim off that portion if the fillet weighs more than the recipe calls for. For our Roasted Whole Side of Salmon recipe on page 7, look for a 4-pound piece that is relatively uniform in thickness.

Ideally, your fishmonger will remove the tail portion for you, but you can easily do it yourself with a sharp knife. We also recommend trimming off the belly fat, which is a heavily marbled strip that runs most of the length of the fillet. If you trim the salmon yourself, save the excess for making salmon cakes or gravlax. –A.J.

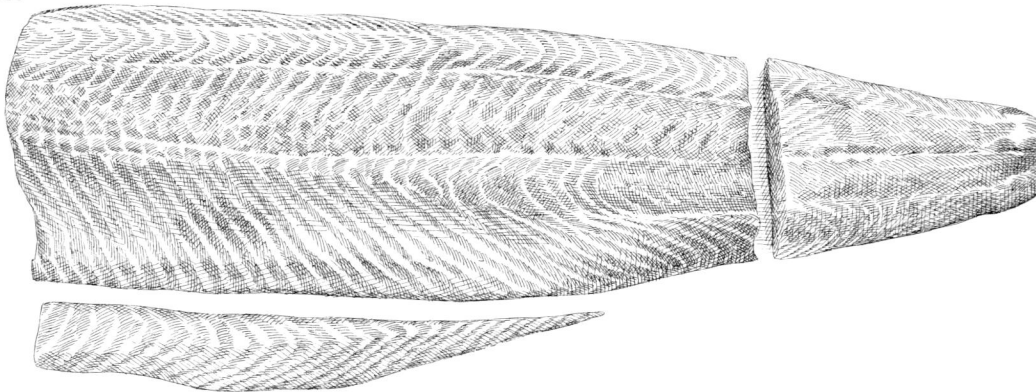

Purple Potatoes

These days, many supermarkets and farmers' markets offer eye-catching varieties of purple potatoes. We know that certain recipes are best made with low-starch, waxy potatoes, while others require high-starch potatoes. We wondered where purple potatoes fell on the starch continuum.

We roasted Adirondack Blue, Purple Creamer, and Purple Majesty potatoes and found that all the samples tasted quite earthy and that they ranged in texture from fairly smooth to very grainy. Despite their differences, all three varieties seemed similar to Yukon Gold potatoes, a medium-moisture, medium-starch variety. To further explore how their starch levels would affect their use, we made home fries and gnocchi using russet, Yukon Gold, and the three types of purple potatoes. While all the purple potatoes made acceptable home fries, the purple gnocchi were dense and gummy across the board, due to their low starch levels. We recommend skipping purple potatoes in recipes where the starch content is critical to success, such as potato latkes or gnocchi. Instead, substitute them in recipes that call for Yukon Gold potatoes. –L.L.

PURPLE MAJESTY

PURPLE CREAMER

Shopping for Lo Mein

Our recipe for Beijing-Style Meat Sauce and Noodles (Zha Jiang Mian) (page 19) calls for lo mein noodles. These golden-colored strands are made from wheat and egg and contain a pair of salts (sodium carbonate and potassium carbonate) that raise the pH of the dough and strengthen its gluten network, giving the noodles their characteristic chewy texture and elastic spring. Fresh lo mein noodles are usually packaged as a loose, curly tangle and are found in the refrigerated section of Asian specialty markets and some high-end grocery chains.

If you can't find lo mein noodles, your best alternative actually comes from Italy: dried linguine. These noodles are close in size to lo mein and have a similar firm chewiness when cooked al dente, though they lack the elasticity of the alkaline noodles.

We also tested our recipe with various vacuum-packed "Chinese-style" fresh noodles from the refrigerated section of the grocery store, but we were disappointed in their gummy, pasty texture and do not recommend using them in this recipe. –K.S.

THE REAL DEAL
Fresh lo mein noodles

BEST ALTERNATIVE
Dried linguine

DON'T BUY IT
"Chinese-style" fresh noodles

DIY RECIPE Quick Candied Nuts

This sweet-salty treat is great for gifts; as a crunchy topping for our Chocolate Semifreddo (page 21), ice cream, yogurt, or salad; as a coating for truffles; as an accompaniment to a cheese plate; or even just eaten out of hand. We toast the nuts, which brings out their flavor and aroma, and then toss them in a mixture of sugar and salt that's been dissolved in hot water. Baking the nuts until they are crisp and dry to the touch (no longer tacky) ensures that they'll be crunchy once completely cooled. –A.P.

QUICK CANDIED NUTS
MAKES ½ CUP

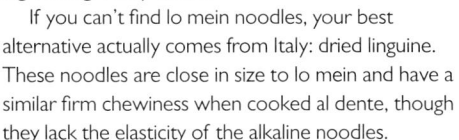

We like this recipe prepared with shelled pistachios, walnut or pecan halves, roasted cashews, salted or unsalted peanuts, and sliced almonds. If you want to make a mixed batch, cook the nuts individually and then toss to combine once you've chopped them.

- ½ cup nuts
- 1 tablespoon granulated sugar
- 1 tablespoon hot water
- ⅛ teaspoon salt

1. Adjust oven rack to middle position and heat oven to 350 degrees. Spread nuts in single layer on rimmed baking sheet and toast until fragrant and slightly darkened, 8 to 12 minutes, shaking sheet halfway through toasting. Transfer nuts to plate and let cool for 10 to 15 minutes. Do not wash sheet.

2. Line now-empty sheet with parchment paper. Whisk sugar, hot water, and salt in large bowl until sugar is mostly dissolved. Add nuts and stir to coat. Spread nuts on prepared sheet in single layer and bake until nuts are crisp and dry, 10 to 12 minutes.

3. Transfer sheet to wire rack and let nuts cool completely, about 20 minutes. Transfer nuts to cutting board and chop as desired. (Nuts can be stored at room temperature for up to 1 week.)

Add Just a Touch of Rose Water

Rose water, a widely used ingredient in Persian, Middle Eastern, and Indian cooking, is, as its name suggests, water infused with the flavor of roses. Traditionally enjoyed in sweets such as cakes, nougat, baklava, rice pudding, and the yogurt drink lassi, rose water is predominantly made with petals from the Damask rose (*Rosa* x *damascena*). Featuring an intensely floral aroma and flavor, it's typically used quite sparingly.

We substituted an equal amount of rose water for the vanilla in recipes for rice pudding and sugar cookies and found that an even swap delivered a rose flavor that was too intense for most tasters. Using 50 percent of the amount of vanilla called for in the recipe produced a more subtle, pleasant result. That said, if you really love the flavor of rose water, you may want to bump up the amount to 75 percent. –S.D.

Cooking with Carrot Tops

We like to buy carrots with their green tops still attached, as we've found they have deeper, more complex flavor than bagged carrots. We wondered whether we could put the tops to use, much like we do with the greens from beets, turnips, and radishes, which we sauté or braise. After sampling the feathery greens raw and sautéed, we found that they tasted grassy and slightly bitter in both applications. Ultimately, we liked carrot greens best when we treated them like we would an herb: finely chopped as a garnish or blended into pesto with an equal amount of basil. The fibrous stems can also be used to add a light vegetal flavor to stock. –A.P.

KITCHEN NOTES

BY STEVE DUNN, ANDREA GEARY, ANDREW JANJIGIAN, LAN LAM & ANNIE PETITO

WHAT IS IT?

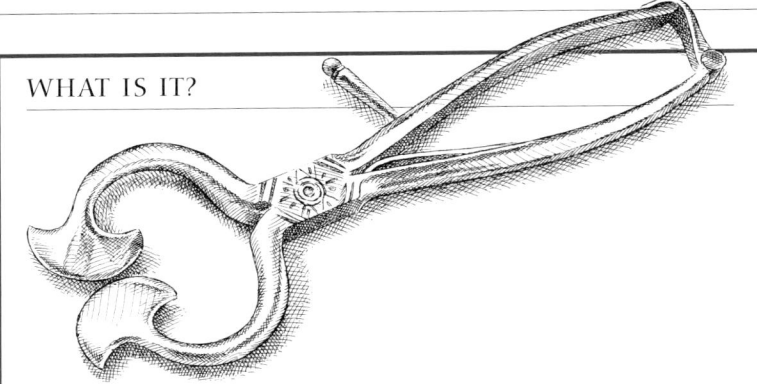

It may resemble an early 19th-century surgeon's tool, but this implement is actually a sugar nipper, a tool that was used to break down a sugarloaf for household use. Before sugar was sold as cubes (1843) or in granulated form (1853), it was sold in hard cones called sugarloaves that were developed by Venetians.

Sugarloaves were extremely hard and were difficult to break apart: Shopkeepers would likely have used a hammer and chisel to break off pieces from a larger loaf for customers to purchase. At home, a pair of nippers like these would be used to "nip" the sugarloaf into a more usable form. Small pieces could be dropped into a cup of tea or further broken down into granulated sugar using a mortar and pestle.

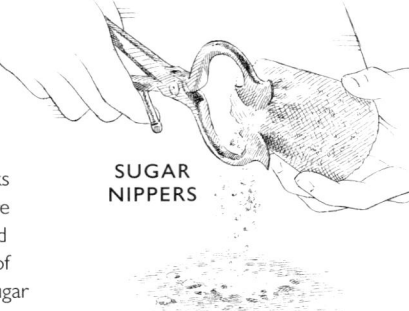

SUGAR NIPPERS

To test our nipper, we ordered a few sugarloaves from The Shop at Monticello, which stocks Jeffersonian-era replicas. While we're happy to live in the age of granulated sugar, the nipper made short work of breaking off some small pieces of sugar to sweeten our afternoon tea. –S.D.

How to Care for a Wooden Salad Bowl

Years of exposure to oily salad dressings can leave a wooden salad bowl with tacky, rancid residue. Here's how to make it new again—and keep it that way. –A.J.

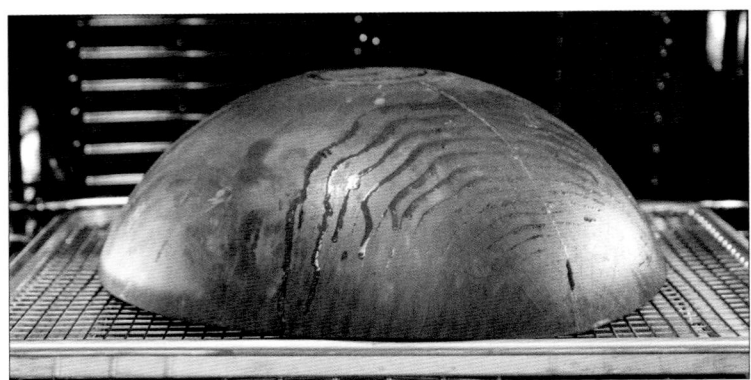

TO REMOVE STICKY BUILDUP: Adjust oven rack to middle position and heat oven to 275 degrees. Line rimmed baking sheet with aluminum foil or parchment paper and set wire rack in sheet. Place bowl upside down on rack. Turn off oven (don't forget this step or bowl might burn) and place sheet in oven. Within minutes, oils will start to bead on surface of bowl. After 1 to 2 hours, oils will run off bowl and onto sheet. Once bowl appears dry, remove sheet from oven and wipe down bowl with paper towels to remove any residue. (If bowl is still sticky, repeat baking process.)

TO RESEASON: Whenever bowl becomes dry or dull-looking, reseason it: Use paper towel to liberally apply mineral oil, which won't turn rancid like oils used in salad dressings, to all surfaces of bowl. Let stand for 15 minutes, then wipe away residue with clean paper towel.

TO CLEAN AND MAINTAIN: Use mild dish soap and warm water to clean well-seasoned wooden bowl. Always dry bowl thoroughly after cleaning. Never put bowl in dishwasher or let it soak in water, as it will warp and crack.

TECHNIQUE | THE BEST WAY TO FOLD

When folding an aerated ingredient, such as whipped cream, into a dense mixture as in our Chocolate Semifreddo recipe (page 21), we first whisk in part of the aerated component to lighten and loosen the dense ingredient before folding in the rest of the aerated ingredient. We found that this lightening technique gave our finished semifreddo a smooth texture and roughly halved the number of folds required to combine the whipped cream and custard (30 folds versus 57). Follow the steps below for efficient folding. –A.P.

1. In large, wide bowl, whisk approximately one-third of whipped component into denser base component until just combined.

2. Add remaining whipped component. Using flexible rubber spatula, start in center of bowl and cut through both components to bottom of bowl.

3. Pull spatula toward you, scraping along bottom and up side of bowl to edge.

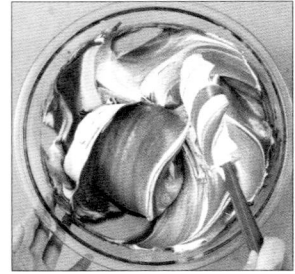

4. Once spatula has been lifted out of mixture, rotate it so any mixture clinging to blade falls back into center of bowl.

5. Rotate bowl quarter turn and repeat folding process until components are just combined, scraping down sides of bowl as needed.

How to Slice Tough, Thin Steaks

How you slice steak matters almost as much as how you cook it. Steak benefits from being sliced across the grain, which shortens its muscle fibers, making the meat more tender and easier to chew. Tough, thin cuts such as skirt, hanger, and flank steak should be sliced at an angle. This shows off a large cross section of the interior for more elegant presentation. –L.L

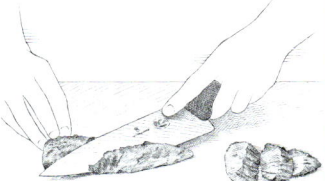

1. Hold knife perpendicular to grain of meat. Tilt spine of knife toward you.

2. Using sawing motion and applying slight downward pressure, slice meat thin.

Extend the Life of Leftover Pancakes

If you've got leftover pancakes, don't toss them. Use these simple tips to store and reheat them for another breakfast. –L.L.

How to Store: Place cooled pancakes in zipper-lock bag, separating them with pieces of waxed paper, parchment paper, or aluminum foil and pressing on bag to eliminate air pockets before sealing. Refrigerate for up to 3 days or freeze for up to 2 weeks.

How to Reheat: Place pancakes on rimmed baking sheet and heat in 325-degree oven (or toaster oven) until warmed through, 3 to 4 minutes if refrigerated and about 6 minutes if frozen.

SCIENCE Another Reason to Emulsify

An emulsion is a mixture of two liquids that ordinarily resist one another, such as the proverbial oil and water. (Vinaigrettes and mayonnaise are two classic examples.) Emulsions are creamier and thicker than nonemulsified sauces, which helps them coat and cling to food. We set up an experiment to demonstrate the mechanics at work in an emulsion.

EXPERIMENT

We made two batches of the butter sauce that accompanies our Buttery Spring Vegetables (page 22). For the first batch, we followed the recipe: We reduced the leftover cooking water with shallots, vinegar, salt, and sugar and then whisked in cold butter 1 tablespoon at a time to create an emulsified sauce. For the second batch, we simply combined the same ingredients in a saucepan over low heat until the butter was melted.

RESULTS

The first (emulsified) sauce had a thick, velvety consistency, while the second was thin and separated, with watery shallots below and liquid butter speckled with milk solids on top. When we dipped radishes into the two sauces, the emulsified sauce coated and clung nicely, but the second sauce slipped right off.

EXPLANATION

There are two types of emulsions: water-in-oil and oil-in-water. Solid butter is a water-in-oil emulsion—fat with tiny droplets of water suspended throughout. When butter simply melts, as in our non-emulsified sauce, the water and fat separate from each other so that the resulting sauce feels slippery and greasy and resists clinging to the surface of foods. But if you gradually whisk cold butter into hot liquid, as in our emulsified sauce, you can actually transform the sauce into an oil-in-water emulsion.

Here's how it works: The water droplets in butter contain remnants of the cream from which it was made—proteins. These proteins act as emulsifiers, coating and separating tiny fat droplets as they disperse into the liquid when the butter melts. Because these fat droplets are now separated by water, the resulting sauce is more viscous than either melted butter or water alone. It also clings to moist vegetables because the fat droplets are surrounded by water (remember, water is attracted to water but resists fat).

TAKEAWAY

Emulsifying might be a little extra work, but it comes with a big payoff. Emulsions are cohesive and creamy, which helps them to cling to food more effectively. –A.G.

THICK AND CLINGY
Emulsified sauce nicely coats.

THIN AND SLIPPERY
Nonemulsified sauce slides right off.

More Good Uses for Kitchen Shears

When sussing out the best pair of kitchen shears (page 32), we ran all the products through our standard kitchen shears tasks: butterflying a whole chicken, snipping herbs, and cutting sheets of parchment paper and lengths of kitchen twine. But using shears to perform tasks usually done with a knife can make these tasks faster, neater, and easier. Here are a few other good ways to put this essential tool to work. –A.P.

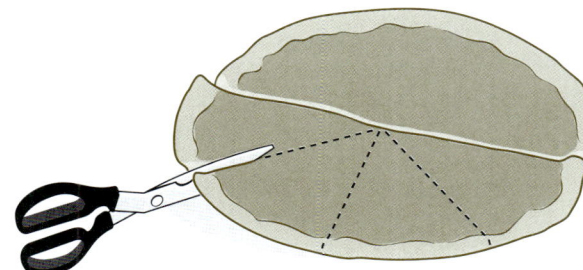
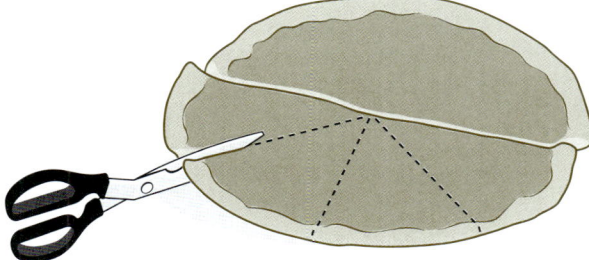

CHOP CANNED TOMATOES
Instead of chopping peeled whole tomatoes on a cutting board and creating a juicy mess, use shears to snip them into chunks right in the can.

CUT BREADS
Use shears to snip pizza, pita, or quesadillas into even wedges; cut focaccia into squares; or cut up stale bread for croutons.

PREP PRODUCE
Shears can cut cauliflower to size, trim artichoke leaves, section bunches of grapes, trim carrot and radish tops or fennel stalks, and snip stems from leafy greens.

SLICE MESSY STUFF
Shears make chopping sticky dried apricots and dates or slicing slippery raw bacon quicker, neater, and more pleasant.

EQUIPMENT CORNER

> BY MIYE BROMBERG, LISA McMANUS & LAUREN SAVOIE

RECOMMENDED

PHILIPS TurboStar Airfryer, Avance Digital
MODEL: HD9641/96
PRICE: $249.95

HIGHLY RECOMMENDED

OXO Good Grips Under Appliance Duster
MODEL: 1245400
PRICE: $15.51

HIGHLY RECOMMENDED

KERSHAW Taskmaster Shears
(Also sold as Shun Multi-Purpose Shears DM7300)
MODEL: 1120   PRICE: $26.30

RECOMMENDED

BEHMOR Connected 8-Cup Brew System
MODEL: GRT20C01CMC
PRICE: $167.00

RECOMMENDED

OXO Good Grips 8 Cup Smart Seal Rectangle Container
MODEL: 11174000
PRICE: $14.99

Air Fryers

Air fryers are large countertop appliances that offer a bold promise: perfectly fried food with very little oil (often less than a tablespoon). But these fryers don't actually fry; they bake food like a convection oven does, using a fan to circulate hot air. To see how they performed, we made oven-fried versions of French fries, chicken wings, and chicken Parmesan and compared them with the same recipes prepared in nine air fryers (priced from $60.20 to $249.95), making slight tweaks to cooking times and temperatures as needed. Impressively, every model we tried produced food that was just as good or better than oven-fried versions. Our favorite, the Philips TurboStar Airfryer, Avance Digital ($249.95), stood out thanks to its slimmer profile, automatic shutoff, easy cleaning, and intuitive digital controls. For a more affordable option, we recommend the GoWISE USA 3.7-Quart 7-in-1 Air Fryer ($75.15) as our Best Buy. Air fryers aren't for everyone, but if you frequently cook in small batches, prepare a lot of frozen foods, or have hungry teens who need an easy way to heat up after-school snacks, one of these products might deserve a place in your kitchen. –L.S.

Under-Appliance Dusters

Under-appliance dusters promise to remove dust bunnies and bits of food from tight spaces. We wanted to know if any of these products are worth owning, so we bought four, priced from $7.77 to $15.51, to clean under our test kitchen appliances as well as under a mock appliance built to mimic the space specifications beneath a home refrigerator. The heads and handles of most of the dusters were too bulky to fit into a 1-inch opening, the standard space under refrigerators and stoves. But the broad, relatively thin microfiber head of our winner, the OXO Good Grips Under Appliance Duster ($15.51), fit under our real and mock appliances and did a good job at collecting dust, flour, chickpeas, and rice. It was long enough to reach into far corners and even succeeded at sweeping up greasy flour. It's also machine washable. –M.B.

Kitchen Shears

Our longtime favorite shears, the Kershaw Taskmaster Shears ($26.30), which are also sold as Shun Multi-Purpose Shears, boast knife-like sharpness and a comfortable grip. They are also ambidextrous and can be taken apart for cleaning. To see how they compared with five other inexpensive models priced from $12.99 to $39.95, we snipped twine and herbs, cut parchment rounds, trimmed pie dough, cut heads of cauliflower into florets, and broke down whole chickens into parts. Some models had blades that were too short or too fat, lacked deep serrations, or were sharpened to wider angles, impairing cutting; others had uncomfortable handles. In the end, our previous favorite triumphed yet again. –M.B.

Behmor Connected 8-Cup Brew System

The Behmor Connected 8-Cup Brew System ($167.00) promises to be a "smart" coffee maker, with a mobile app that lets you turn it on remotely, conjuring up thoughts of brewing coffee before getting out of bed. It also encourages the coffee geek in you to customize how it operates by adjusting brew temperature and length of preinfusion. We put the machine through a number of tests and were impressed by the results. A big part of the Behmor's success is that it operates like an electric kettle, heating all the water to the selected temperature before brewing begins; if you set the temperature within the industry-standard range for good coffee (195 to 205 degrees), you're guaranteed a brew that isn't over- or underextracted, meaning it will be bold and flavorful but not harsh or too bitter. (Traditional automatic drip machines begin moving the water over the grounds before it hits that range, and by the end, it's boiling.) We also enjoyed tinkering with temperatures and found noticeable flavor differences when we brewed the same coffee at 190, 200, and 207 degrees. We appreciated the Behmor's intuitive design, which made it simple to fill and clean, and the ability to brew without the app simply by pressing a single button on the machine. A couple of downsides: The machine is slow, with all brewing cycles taking upwards of 13 minutes, about twice as long as our favorite automatic drip coffee maker, the Technivorm Moccamaster ($299.00). The app was also less intuitive than we'd have liked, and there was a small learning curve for testers. –L.M.

Glass Storage Containers

Plastic and glass food storage containers both have their advantages. While glass is heavier and more fragile than plastic, it also resists staining and warping, can go in the microwave without worry, and can be used in the oven. We tested five glass storage containers alongside six plastic containers (see related story on page 26). One product that was more like a covered dish—it lacked a silicone gasket or flaps to secure the lid—failed immediately, leaking water when we shook it. Two others leaked at different times during testing. Our winner, the OXO Good Grips 8 Cup Smart Seal Rectangle Container ($14.99), never dripped or let moisture in, even after we put it through 50 dishwasher cycles, froze water in it, and reheated food in it in both the microwave and the oven. The lid's large silicone gasket was easy to remove and replace for cleaning; faintly fishy odors and an orange tint on the lid from chili faded after a few dishwasher cycles. Also, with its 8-cup capacity, this loaf pan–like container held plenty of food; however, we'd have preferred a slightly wider, flatter shape to help foods heat and chill more uniformly. –L.M.

For complete testing results, go to CooksIllustrated.com/jun18.

INDEX
May & June 2018

RECIPES

MAIN DISHES
Beijing-Style Meat Sauce and Noodles (Zha Jiang Mian) 19
Chicken Caesar Salad 15
Deviled Pork Chops 11
Grilled Mojo-Marinated Skirt Steak 5
Perfect Poached Chicken for Salad 15
Roast Chicken with Warm Bread Salad 9
Roasted Whole Side of Salmon 7
Sichuan-Style Chicken Salad (Bang Bang Ji Si) 15
Thai-Style Chicken Salad with Mango 15

SIDE DISHES
Barley with Lemon and Herbs 18
    with Celery and Miso Dressing 18
    with Fennel, Dried Apricots, and Orange 18
Buttery Spring Vegetables 22

BREAKFAST
Easy Pancakes 13

DESSERT
Chocolate Semifreddo 21

ACCOMPANIMENTS
Arugula and Almond Pesto 7
Cherry Sauce 21
Cucumber-Ginger Relish 7
Ginger-Molasses Butter 13
Orange-Almond Butter 13
Quick Candied Nuts 29

BONUS ONLINE CONTENT
More recipes, reviews, and videos are available at CooksIllustrated.com/jun18

RECIPES
Beijing-Style Meat Sauce and Noodles (Zha Jiang Mian) for Two
Deviled Pork Chops for Two
Pumpkin Spice Butter

EXPANDED REVIEWS
Tasting Ground Turmeric
Testing Air Fryers
Testing Behmor Connected 8-Cup Brew System
Testing Glass Storage Containers
Testing Kitchen Shears
Testing Under-Appliance Dusters

▶ RECIPE VIDEOS
Want to see how to make any of the recipes in this issue? There's a free video for that.

FOLLOW US ON SOCIAL MEDIA
facebook.com/CooksIllustrated
twitter.com/TestKitchen
pinterest.com/TestKitchen
instagram.com/CooksIllustrated
youtube.com/AmericasTestKitchen

Roast Chicken with Warm Bread Salad, 9

Barley with Celery and Miso Dressing, 18

Roasted Whole Side of Salmon, 7

Deviled Pork Chops, 11

Buttery Spring Vegetables, 22

Easy Pancakes, 13

Grilled Mojo-Marinated Skirt Steak, 5

Thai-Style Chicken Salad with Mango, 15

Beijing-Style Meat Sauce and Noodles, 19

Chocolate Semifreddo, 21

America's Test Kitchen
COOKING SCHOOL

Visit our online cooking school today, where we offer 180+ online lessons covering a range of recipes and cooking methods. Whether you're a novice just starting out or are already an advanced cook looking for new techniques, our cooking school is designed to give you confidence in the kitchen and make you a better cook.

▸ **Start a 14-Day Free Trial at** OnlineCookingSchool.com

Cook's Illustrated on iPad
Enjoy *Cook's* wherever you are, whenever you want.

Did you know that *Cook's Illustrated* is available on iPad? Go to **CooksIllustrated.com/iPad** to download the app through iTunes. You'll be able to start a free trial of the digital edition, which includes bonus features including recipe videos, full-color photos, and step-by-step slide shows of each recipe.

Go to CooksIllustrated.com/iPad to download our app through iTunes.

PHOTOGRAPHY: CARL TREMBLAY AND DANIEL J. VAN ACKERE; STYLING: KENDRA McKNIGHT

NUMBER 153

JULY & AUGUST 2018

COOK'S
ILLUSTRATED

Grilled Chicken Thighs
Dead-Simple Method

Tacos Dorados
Ultimate Hard-Shell Tacos

Chewiest Granola Bars
Unlikely Secret Ingredient

How to Grill Tomatoes
Plus Three Bold Recipes

Mexican Corn Salad
Fast and Flavorful

Testing Instant-Read Thermometers
Finding the Fastest

Tasting Fresh Mozzarella
Top 12 Grilling Mistakes to Avoid
Peruvian Ceviche

CooksIllustrated.com
$6.95 U.S./$8.95 CANADA

Display until August 6, 2018

COOK'S ILLUSTRATED

JULY & AUGUST 2018

PAGE 14

2 Quick Tips
Quick and easy ways to perform everyday tasks, from pounding meat to storing dry goods.
COMPILED BY ANNIE PETITO

4 Grilled Chicken Thighs
Flavorful, meaty, inexpensive thighs should be the easiest part of the chicken to cook on the grill—not a direct path to an inferno. BY STEVE DUNN

6 Fresh Tomato Sauce
Tomato flavor is fleeting—which is why we examined every part of the fruit and our cooking method until we'd engineered a sauce that was bright, sweet, and aromatic. BY STEVE DUNN

8 Introducing Tacos Dorados
The hard-shell taco has been an American staple for more than half a century. When we traced its roots, we found a way to take it to a new, ultracrispy level. BY ANNIE PETITO

10 Vietnamese Pork with Rice Noodles
Bun cha—a one-dish meal featuring grilled pork patties, crisp vegetables, springy noodles, and a vibrant sauce—cooks as quickly as a burger but tastes much lighter. BY ANDREA GEARY

12 Better-Than-the-Box Granola Bars
We love the idea of chewy granola bars, but store-bought versions are overly sweet, contain mostly filler, and are soft, not chewy. We took matters into our own hands. BY ANDREA GEARY

14 How to Grill Tomatoes
Grilling enhances tomatoes with smoky char while preserving their summery taste. But don't simply throw them onto the fire or you'll end up with a mushy mess. BY ANNIE PETITO

16 Top 12 Grilling Mistakes to Avoid
Some of the most common practices are also the wrong ones. BY ELIZABETH BOMZE

18 Peruvian Ceviche
Bright citrus is great with fresh seafood—provided that the acid doesn't overwhelm its delicate flavor. We went fishing for more balance and found it in this regional version.
BY ANDREW JANJIGIAN

20 Mexican Corn Salad
Make this bright, creamy charred-corn salad without firing up the grill. BY LAN LAM

21 Dark Chocolate Fudge Sauce
We wanted a pourable, easily reheated sauce with a dark chocolate soul. BY STEVE DUNN

22 Peach Tarte Tatin
Yes, you can make a juicy, summery, peach-crowned version of the classic upside-down caramelized apple tart. No, you can't simply substitute peaches for apples. BY ANDREA GEARY

24 Tasting Fresh Mozzarella
What makes the best fresh mozzarella? It's all about balance. BY LAUREN SAVOIE

26 Testing Digital Thermometers
We've recommended a Thermapen for more than a decade, but there's new competition. Is it still the best option?
BY HANNAH CROWLEY

28 Ingredient Notes
BY ANDREA GEARY, ANDREW JANJIGIAN, LAN LAM & ANNIE PETITO

30 Kitchen Notes
BY STEVE DUNN, ANDREA GEARY & LAN LAM

32 Equipment Corner
BY MIYE BROMBERG, EMILY PHARES, LAUREN SAVOIE & KATE SHANNON

BACK COVER ILLUSTRATED BY JOHN BURGOYNE

Corn Products

CORN is one of the world's most essential food crops. While the corn silk is discarded from a cleaned ear, **CORN HUSKS** are harvested and dried. When reconstituted, they can be used to wrap tamales. Plump **HOMINY**, made by soaking dried yellow or white kernels in an alkaline solution to remove the hull and germ, can be added to dishes such as Mexican posole. It can also be ground and dried to make masa harina, which is mixed with water to make chewy, pliable yellow or **WHITE CORN TORTILLAS**. Cutting the tortillas into quarters and then crisping them in hot oil produces **TORTILLA CHIPS**. **CORN NUTS**, giant dried corn kernels that have been soaked, fried, and salted, are consumed both as a snack and as a garnish for ceviche. **CORNMEAL** is ground dried yellow or white corn kernels, from fine- and coarse-ground **POLENTA** to grits. The kernels of certain varieties of corn can be dried and used to make **POPCORN**. These **KERNELS** can be **YELLOW** or **CRIMSON** (the puffed corn does not retain the colors). Heat causes the moisture within them to build up steam pressure so that they explode into tender puffs.

America's Test Kitchen is a real test kitchen located in Boston. It is the home of more than 60 test cooks, editors, and cookware specialists. Our mission is to test recipes until we understand exactly how and why they work and eventually arrive at the very best version. We also test kitchen equipment and supermarket ingredients in search of products that offer the best value and performance. You can watch us work by tuning in to *America's Test Kitchen* (AmericasTestKitchen.com) and *Cook's Country from America's Test Kitchen* (CooksCountry.com) on public television and listen to our weekly segments on *The Splendid Table* on public radio. You can also follow us on Facebook, Twitter, Pinterest, and Instagram.

LETTER FROM THE EDITORS

ON COMMUNITY AND WOUND CARE

My mom's name is Martha, but she's always gone by Marty. Marty worked as a registered nurse on the cardiac-orthopedic floor of a local hospital for more than 40 years. When I was a kid, she'd come home from long shifts on her feet and cook dinner for my sister, my dad, and me. We'd sit down to eat her excellent from-scratch cooking—maybe cream of chicken and rice or her milky Maine-style fish chowder with crispy bacon. And she'd talk about what was on her mind: surgeries, needles, pandemics, bad falls, and the best practices for wound care.

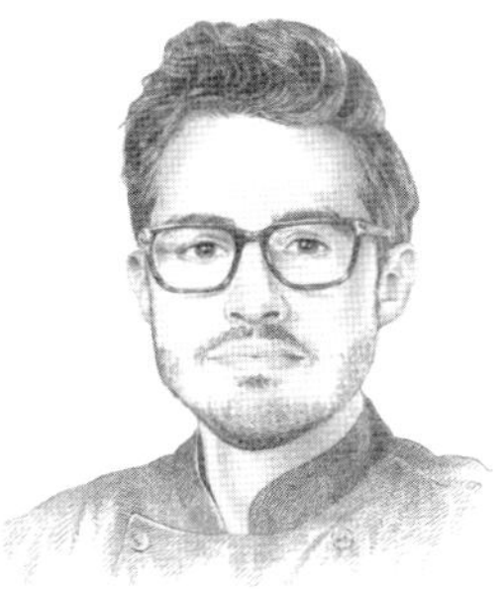

Within minutes the clatter of spoons on ceramic would cease. Marty, sensing the deep silence, would look up to see three faces, now as pale as her chowder, staring blankly back.

To this day my sister and I rag on my mom about her macabre dinner talk. But in truth, it wasn't her fault. We just weren't the right audience.

We weren't her community.

Before I started cooking professionally—wherein I was thrust, full bore, into an intense, passionate food community—I often felt like Marty at the dinner table. I wanted to debate the relative merits of a classic German-style chef's knife and a Chinese vegetable cleaver. I thought about the differences between yellow and white onions; I had an opinion about when to use each. Over Monday morning coffee I was eager to talk menu planning for Saturday's barbecue. My friends and loved ones would listen patiently and nod, but they never really got it.

Do you ever feel that way? Do you wish for a community of like-minded cooks where you can pose questions, ask advice, share photos, or argue about citrus juicers? Well, I have some good news for you. We've assembled one of the most vibrant online cooking communities in the United States. It's a private group hosted on Facebook that you can access only if you are a subscriber to *Cook's Illustrated* or *Cook's Country* or if you're a member of one of our websites.

Dan Souza

As of this writing, the group boasts a little more than 10,000 members. Among the ranks are various America's Test Kitchen staffers, including chief creative officer Jack Bishop, executive food editor Keith Dresser, and me. We often jump in to answer questions, add our opinions, or sometimes to just stir the pot. If that sounds appealing to you, I encourage you to visit CooksIllustrated.com/group to get your invitation. You might even see Marty in there from time to time. But don't worry—she's promised to keep it clean.

Dan Souza
Editor in Chief

QUICK TIPS

≥ COMPILED BY ANNIE PETITO ≤

Plunge Tomato Paste
Instead of spooning tomato paste from its small can, Gary Schwartz of Lake Elmo, Minn., "plunges" it out. He uses a can opener to cut the lids on both ends, removes the lid from only one side, and uses the freed-up lid on the opposite side to push the paste into a bowl.

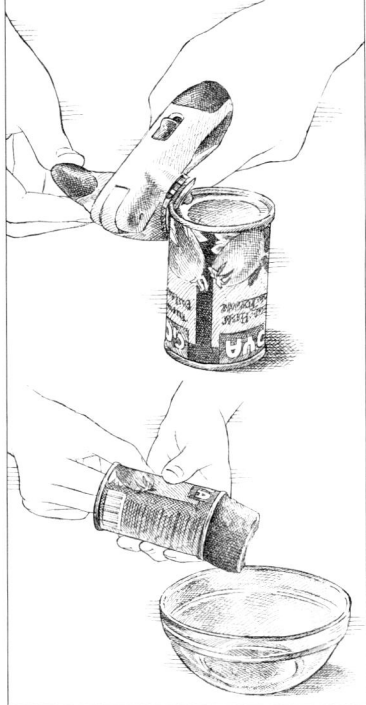

Crumple Parchment Paper for Blind Baking
Alice Hall of Chardon, Ohio, lines pastry shells with parchment paper when blind-baking but finds it difficult to position the stiff parchment snugly in the shell before adding pie weights. Crumpling the paper into a ball and then unfolding it helps it settle into the pastry.

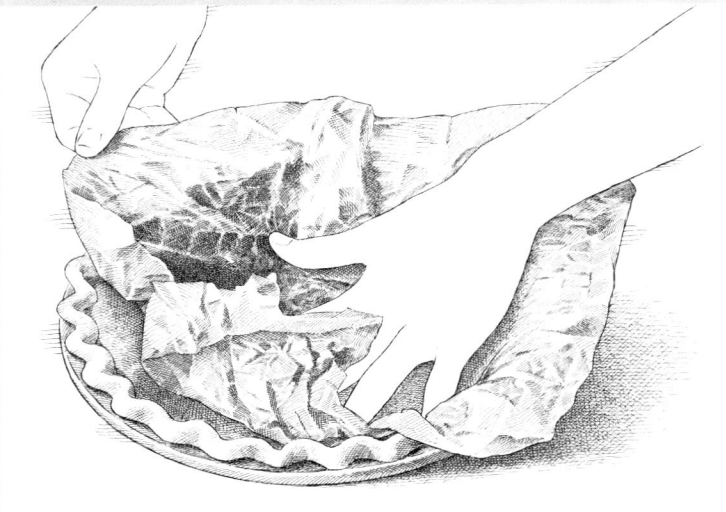

Pin Your Place in a Recipe
To avoid losing her place in a recipe when toggling between reading the text and cooking, Mary Gerber of Brunswick, Maine, clips a clothespin to the page. She moves it down the text as she cooks so she can quickly find her place.

Same Sheet for Raw and Cooked Meat
When transporting raw proteins to the grill on a rimmed baking sheet, Kristin Wianecki of Okemos, Mich., lines the sheet with aluminum foil or plastic wrap so that she can remove the liner and reuse the sheet to collect the cooked food.

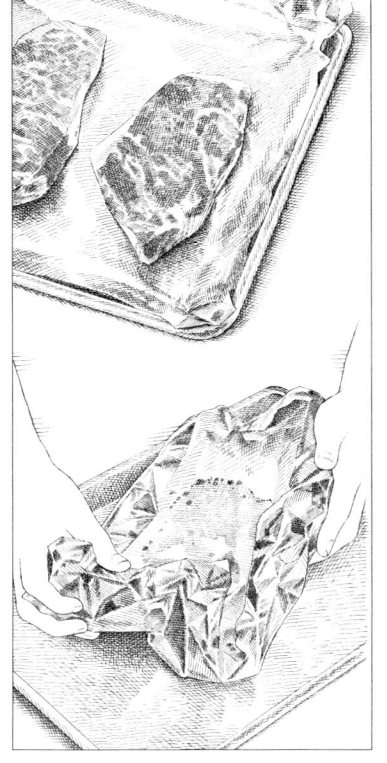

Watermelon "Sticks"
Eating watermelon wedges is messy, so Trisha Novy of Philadelphia, Pa., cuts the melon into sticks that are tidier to bite. First, she halves the melon crosswise. Then, working with one half at a time, she cuts 1- to 2-inch slices across the melon, rotates it, and cuts it again in a grid pattern.

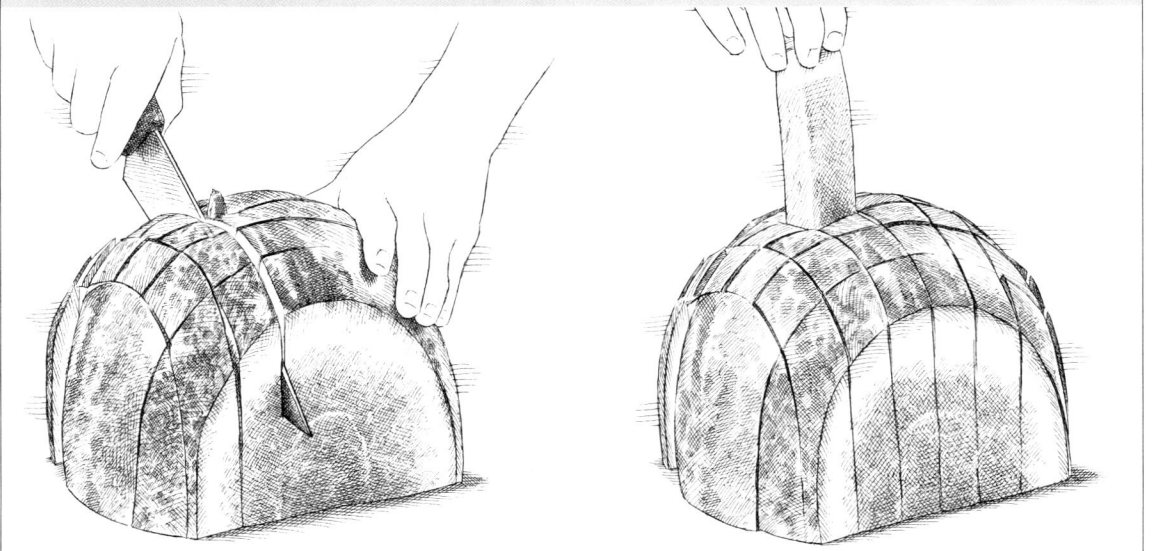

SEND US YOUR TIPS We will provide a complimentary one-year subscription for each tip we print. Send your tip, name, address, and telephone number to Quick Tips, *Cook's Illustrated*, 21 Drydock Avenue, Suite 210E, Boston, MA 02210, or to QuickTips@AmericasTestKitchen.com.

Save Time with Spice Kits
Nancy Immel of Bernalillo, N.M., saves herself prep time by putting together "spice kits" in advance for her favorite dishes and storing them in small zipper-lock bags to have at the ready when she cooks these recipes.

Makeshift Meat Pounder
Mandy Phillips of Omaha, Neb., doesn't own a meat pounder, so she uses the flat bottom of a small heavy skillet instead. After sandwiching the raw meat between sheets of plastic wrap, she pounds the meat to an even thickness.

An Easier Way to Clean Corn
When husking fresh corn, Carrol Bailey of Williamsburg, Va., dons clean rubber gloves to remove the clingy silk. The friction from the gloves helps her grab the fine threads, making them easier to pull away.

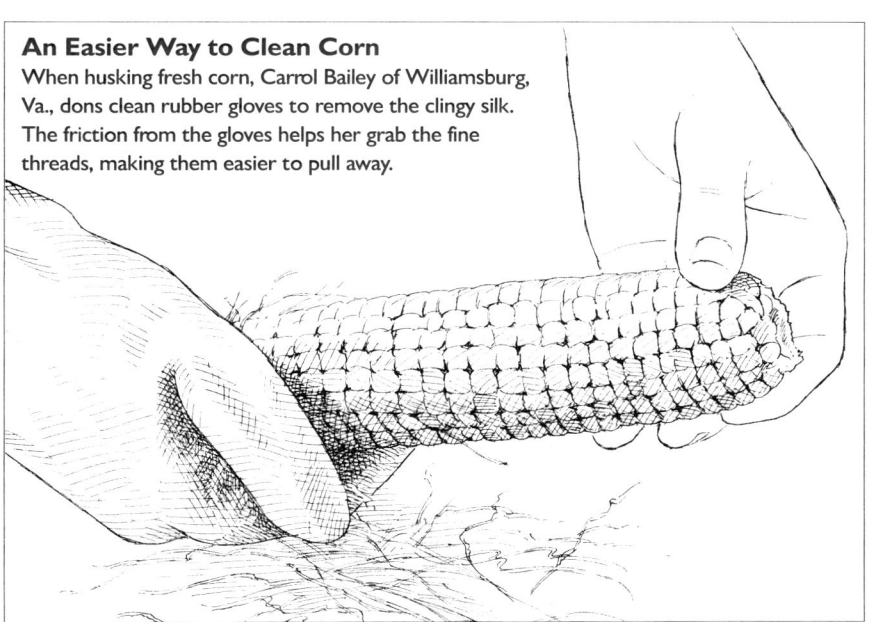

Salad Greens Boxes as Storage Bins
Sharon Morris of Austin, Texas, reuses large plastic salad greens containers as bins to consolidate dry goods such as pasta and rice in her pantry. The clear plastic means the contents are easily visible, and the flat containers can be stacked.

Mind the Gaps (in Your Bread)
When you use bread slices with large holes in the crumb to make grilled cheese sandwiches, melted cheese can drip through the holes and make a mess. Liz LeVan of San Antonio, Texas, plugs up the holes by tearing some of the soft crumb from the heel of the bread and stuffing the pieces into the gaps.

Grilled Chicken Thighs

Flavorful, meaty, inexpensive thighs should be the easiest part of the chicken to cook on the grill—not a direct path to an inferno.

≥ BY STEVE DUNN ≤

The flat layer of skin on thighs is ideal for crisping over the fire.

One of my earliest cooking memories is of my dad positioned at the grill, squirt bottle in one hand and grill tongs in the other, working furiously to rescue chicken thighs from a three-alarm blaze. In a rush to get dinner on the table, he would position the thighs directly over the fire to cook them quickly. Within minutes, their rendering fat dripped into the flames, ignited, and grew into a blaze that forced him to shuffle the chicken around the grate while he simultaneously tried to quell the fire with water from his squirt bottle. I can't lie: The pyrotechnics were pretty thrilling to watch as a kid. But eating the chicken was less thrilling—the chewy meat tasted of acrid smoke and was covered with rubbery, badly charred skin.

Chicken thighs have a lot going for them: They're more flavorful and less prone to overcooking than leaner breasts, boast a relatively high ratio of meat to bone, and have a flat layer of skin that is prime for browning and crisping. What makes them challenging to cook, especially over a live fire, is that they tend to have more subcutaneous fat than other parts of the chicken, which means the skin is at risk of not thoroughly rendering and remaining chewy and flabby, which will cause flare-ups.

My goal: a recipe that would produce juicy, flavorful meat and well-rendered, crispy skin—minus the inferno.

A Leg Up

My colleague Andrea Geary recently developed a recipe for Grilled Spice-Rubbed Chicken Drumsticks (May/June 2017) that I thought might be a good blueprint for thighs, too. The key is to cook the chicken over indirect heat for about an hour, during which time fat and collagen in the meat and skin render and break down, respectively, so that the meat is tender and the skin is primed for crisping. We also arrange the drumsticks in two rows alongside the fire and rearrange them halfway through cooking—those

▶ Mostly Hands-Off Chicken
A step-by-step video is available at CooksIllustrated.com/aug18

closer to the heat go to the outside, and those on the outside go closer to the heat—so that they all finish cooking at the same time. Then we move the drumsticks directly over the heat to briefly brown and crisp the skin.

I placed eight thighs skin side up over the cooler half of a grill, thinking that the fat in the skin would lubricate the meat as it rendered. After 20 minutes, I rearranged the pieces and then let them cook for another 15 to 20 minutes until they registered between 185 and 190 degrees. That's well past the point of doneness for white meat (160 degrees), but we've found that dark meat benefits from being cooked much more thoroughly, especially if it also cooks slowly. That's because the longer the meat spends cooking at temperatures above 140 degrees, the more of its abundant collagen breaks down and transforms into gelatin that lubricates the meat, making it seem juicy and tender.

The method was dead easy, and all seemed to be going well until I moved the thighs to the hotter side of the grill and flipped them onto their skin sides to crisp. Fat poured out from under the skin, dripped into the fire, and sent flames shooting up. I managed to salvage some of the thighs and was pleased that the meat was, indeed, quite tender and moist after the lengthy stint over indirect heat. But the skin wasn't nearly as nice to eat—not just because it was burnt in spots, but because it was still flabby and chewy beneath the surface.

Skin Treatment

Crispy, evenly bronzed chicken skin is a real treat, but it takes both ample time and heat to produce those results. That's partly because chicken skin—particularly the skin on thighs—is padded with fat that must render before the skin can crisp. But fat isn't the only factor that makes chicken skin flabby and chewy; skin, like meat, contains collagen that must break down in order for it to turn tender. Only once the skin is tender can it then crisp (see "What's Good for Tender Meat Is Good for the Crispiest Skin").

The thighs were already spending a long time on the grill, but maybe the skin wasn't getting hot enough to shed fat. So I spent the next several tests exposing the skin to more heat. Making a hotter fire helped but at the expense of the meat, which moved too quickly through the collagen

How to Portion the Paste

Our pastes add potent flavor, but it's important to apply them strategically. We found that too much paste on the skin prevented it from crisping, so we applied two-thirds of the paste to the flesh side and the remaining one-third to the skin side to ensure that the skin was seasoned but not wet.

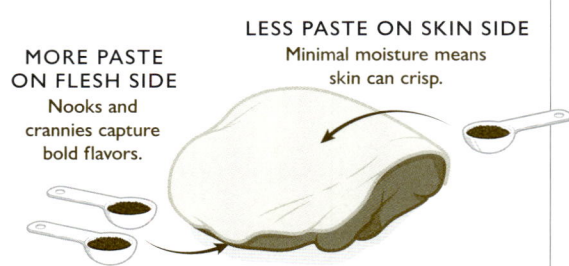

MORE PASTE ON FLESH SIDE
Nooks and crannies capture bold flavors.

LESS PASTE ON SKIN SIDE
Minimal moisture means skin can crisp.

SCIENCE: What's Good for Tender Meat Is Good for the Crispiest Skin

We know that cooking chicken thighs low and slow is a surefire way to produce tender meat. But it's also a great way to ensure crispy skin. Like thigh meat, chicken skin is loaded with collagen. During cooking—especially lengthy cooking at relatively moderate temperatures—collagen breaks down into a protein called gelatin. That gelatin forms a mesh that holds on to water and makes the skin soft and tender.

Then, when the tender skin is seared over high heat, the gelatin strands become rigid and the water evaporates out from among them so fast that it leaves behind tiny air spaces in the mesh—or, as we perceive it, crispiness.

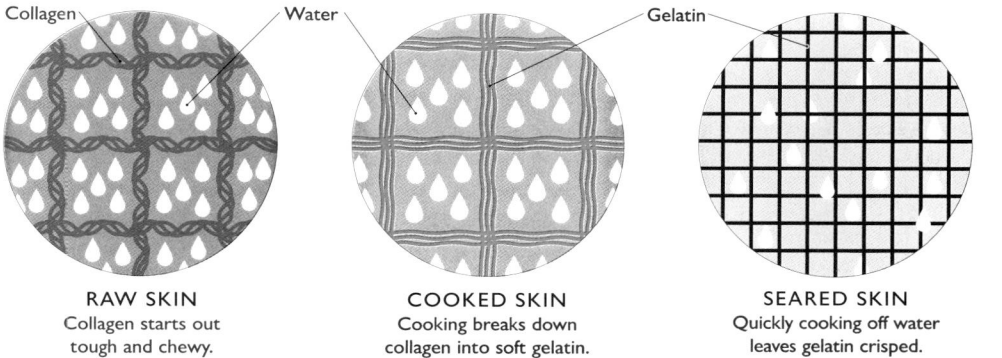

RAW SKIN Collagen starts out tough and chewy.

COOKED SKIN Cooking breaks down collagen into soft gelatin.

SEARED SKIN Quickly cooking off water leaves gelatin crisped.

---

breakdown zone and was thus not as tender. I had better luck turning the thighs skin side down midway through cooking instead of at the end; more direct (but still gentle) heat melted the fat, which now dripped out of each piece instead of puddling under the skin. But I got the best results yet when I cooked the chicken skin side down from start to finish. By the time the meat was tender, much of the skin's fat had rendered and the skin had become paper-thin and soft, so all I had to do to crisp it up was slide the thighs over to the hotter side for about 5 minutes. The method was so easy, and the results were perfect—if a bit plain.

Aced the Paste

I didn't want to thwart my skin-crisping efforts by dousing the thighs with a wet marinade, so I rubbed a few robustly seasoned pastes onto the chicken: a version that tapped into my love of Korean fried chicken with *gochujang* and soy sauce, a mustard and tarragon paste with loads of garlic, and an Indian version with garam masala and ginger.

The trick was applying it strategically, since even the moderate moisture in the paste could soften the skin. I found that spreading two-thirds of the paste on the flesh side of each thigh worked best; there were lots of nooks and crannies to capture the paste, and the remaining third that I rubbed over the skin seasoned and flavored it without adding so much moisture that crisping was inhibited. The only hitch: Since the chicken cooked skin side down the whole time, the paste on the flesh side looked and tasted a bit raw. So after the skin crisped over the hotter side of the grill, I flipped the pieces onto the flesh side for a minute or two to take the raw edge off the paste.

Perfectly tender, juicy meat; thin, crispy skin; bold flavor; and a method that requires practically zero work. Dinner's in the bag—not in the fire.

BEST GRILLED CHICKEN THIGHS
SERVES 4 TO 6

In step 1, the chicken can be refrigerated for up to 2 hours before grilling. Our recipes for Best Grilled Chicken Thighs for Two and Garam Masala Paste are available for free for four months at CooksIllustrated.com/aug18.

- 8 (5- to 7-ounce) bone-in chicken thighs, trimmed
- ½ teaspoon kosher salt
- 1 recipe paste (recipes follow)

1. Place chicken, skin side up, on large plate. Sprinkle skin side with salt and spread evenly with one-third of spice paste. Flip chicken and spread remaining two-thirds of paste evenly over flesh side. Refrigerate while preparing grill.

2A. FOR A CHARCOAL GRILL: Open bottom vent halfway. Light large chimney starter mounded with charcoal briquettes (7 quarts). When top coals are partially covered with ash, pour evenly over half of grill. Set cooking grate in place, cover, and open lid vent halfway. Heat grill until hot, about 5 minutes.

2B. FOR A GAS GRILL: Turn all burners to high, cover, and heat grill until hot, about 15 minutes. Leave primary burner on high and turn off other burner(s). (Adjust primary burner [or, if using 3-burner grill, primary burner and second burner] as needed to maintain grill temperature around 350 degrees.)

3. Clean and oil cooking grate. Place chicken, skin side down, on cooler side of grill. Cover and cook for 20 minutes. Rearrange chicken, keeping skin side down, so that pieces that were positioned closest to edge of grill are now closer to heat source and vice versa. Cover and continue to cook until chicken registers 185 to 190 degrees, 15 to 20 minutes longer.

4. Move all chicken, skin side down, to hotter side of grill and cook until skin is lightly charred, about 5 minutes. Flip chicken and cook until flesh side is lightly browned, 1 to 2 minutes. Transfer to platter, tent with aluminum foil, and let rest for 10 minutes. Serve.

GOCHUJANG PASTE
MAKES ABOUT ⅓ CUP

Gochujang, or Korean red chili paste, can be found in Asian markets or in the Asian section of large supermarkets.

- 3 tablespoons gochujang
- 1 tablespoon soy sauce
- 2 garlic cloves, minced
- 2 teaspoons sugar
- 1 teaspoon kosher salt

Combine all ingredients in bowl.

MUSTARD-TARRAGON PASTE
MAKES ABOUT ⅓ CUP

Rosemary or thyme can be substituted for the tarragon, if desired. When using this paste, we like to serve the chicken with lemon wedges.

- 3 tablespoons Dijon mustard
- 5 garlic cloves, minced
- 1 tablespoon finely grated lemon zest
- 2 teaspoons minced fresh tarragon
- 1½ teaspoons kosher salt
- 1 teaspoon water
- ½ teaspoon pepper

Combine all ingredients in bowl.

Perfect Results, Practically Zero Effort

We found that the best way to produce moist, tender meat and thin, crispy skin is also the easiest.

1. Cook, skin side down, over cooler side until last few minutes.

2. Transfer to hotter side and sear skin; flip and sear flesh side.

SET IT AND (ALMOST) FORGET IT

Fresh Tomato Sauce

Tomato flavor is fleeting—which is why we examined every part of the fruit and our cooking method until we'd engineered a sauce that was bright, sweet, and aromatic.

≥ BY STEVE DUNN ≤

High-end, tech-minded chefs and bartenders cheat the normal laws of cooking by using a contraption called a rotary evaporator (or "rotovap"). The device, which costs upwards of $8,000, works by gently heating a liquid, such as tomato juice, in a vacuum chamber. The vacuum lets the juice boil at near room temperature, which lets volatile flavors get extracted from the liquid and concentrated.

It's a tool that could revolutionize fresh tomato sauce, which has an inherent dilemma: Simmering cooks out the very thing that makes a ripe tomato so special—its bright, sweet, delicate flavor. On the other hand, if you don't cook juicy tomatoes long enough to evaporate a good bit of their liquid, the sauce won't have enough body to cling to pasta, and its flavor won't be intense enough.

Imagine: a fresh tomato sauce that actually tastes like a fresh tomato. I didn't have a rotovap. But I did have a garden chock-full of tomatoes, along with a test kitchen and a dream.

The Tomato Lab

I combed through a number of sauce recipes that called for fresh tomatoes (conventional round ones, not plum or cherry varieties), but I came away with more questions than I'd started with. Not only was there no consensus on which parts of the tomato should be included or eliminated (other than the core), but the cooking times ranged from just 20 minutes to as long as 2 hours. When I made some of the recipes, I wasn't surprised that the quick-cooked sauces retained much more fresh tomato flavor than those that simmered for longer. But there were also stark flavor differences among the lot—one-dimensional sweetness in some, balanced savoriness in others—that seemed to relate directly to which parts of the tomato I'd used.

That informed my next round of tests, in which I made batches of the same simple sauce (5 pounds of tomatoes, extra-virgin olive oil, and a little minced garlic) but varied which tomato components I used: For one batch I removed only the core, keeping the skin, the flesh, and the thick "jelly" and seeds; for another I cored the tomatoes and removed the skin; and for the third I cored the tomatoes and removed the skin, jelly, and seeds, using just the tomato flesh.

This vibrant-tasting sauce has a lighter consistency than most tomato sauces, so don't add any pasta cooking water or it will be too loose.

I roughly chopped the tomatoes and simmered each batch for about 40 minutes, by which point the sauces had enough body to coat pasta.

There was no question that using the whole tomato, sans the core, contributed to a more complex flavor in the sauce and that eliminating any single component could throw off the balance. Most notably, the batch that contained no skins or jelly was so sweet and one-dimensional that tasters likened it to tomato "candy." Leaving in the jelly and seeds yielded a sauce with better sweet-savory balance, and using the skins improved it even further. (For more information on what each part of the tomato contributes, see "Calibrating Balanced Tomato Flavor.")

A drawback to including the seeds and skins was that they marred the sauce's consistency. Also, many sources claim that tomato seeds impart bitterness, so I figured I'd make a seedless batch to find out. Seeding the tomatoes would be simple: After halving the tomatoes, I gently squeezed the jelly into a fine-mesh strainer that I'd set over a bowl, discarding the seeds and capturing the flavor-packed liquid to add to the sauce. Then I chopped the tomato flesh and, to break down the skins, pureed the pieces with their liquid in a blender until the mixture was smooth.

That yielded about 10 cups of tomato puree, which tasted sweet, savory, bright, and delicately aromatic. (Including the skins also made the recipe ultrasimple because there was no need to blanch,

▶ **Steve Keeps It Simple**
A step-by-step video is available at CooksIllustrated.com/aug18

Save Some Fresh Flavor for Later

Raw ripe tomatoes are loaded with flavor and aroma compounds that make them taste sweet, bright, and aromatic. But many of those compounds are volatile when heated, which is why cooking the fruit to a sauce-like consistency destroys its fresh flavor. To make a sauce that was thick enough to coat pasta but retained as much fresh tomato flavor as possible, we reserved some of the raw tomato jelly that we'd strained of its seeds and added it to the sauce at the end of cooking, along with fresh basil and some extra-virgin olive oil.

COOK'S ILLUSTRATED

RECIPE TESTING Calibrating Balanced Tomato Flavor

Did you know that the most concentrated source of fresh tomato flavor is in the fruit's skin? Neither did we, until we tasted batches of our Fresh Tomato Sauce made with varying parts of the fruit: skin, flesh, jelly, and seeds. (In each batch, we first discarded the core.) Our goal was to determine which elements of a tomato we should keep and which we should discard for a sauce that tasted sweet, bright, and aromatic.

➤ **The upshot:** The sauce that contained skin, flesh, and jelly delivered the most balanced flavor. (The seeds didn't contribute any noticeable flavor, but their texture was distracting, so we strained them out.) Here's a breakdown of the dominant flavor and aroma compounds in each component.

Skin: Aroma compounds (including terpenes, ketones, and aldehydes)

Flesh: Aroma compounds, sugars (glucose and fructose), and acids (citric and malic acids)

Jelly: Umami compounds (including amino acids), sugars, and acids

shock, and peel the tomatoes as many recipes require.) Notably, the seedless puree tasted no different from the previous batch, proving that the seeds hadn't contributed any significant flavor, bitter or otherwise. But achieving that flavor balance brought me only partway to my goal. I needed to reduce the puree by about half to achieve a sauce-like consistency, but many of the aromatic flavor compounds in the fruit that made the puree taste fresh and balanced are volatile, meaning they evaporate at a relatively low temperature. That's why simmering the sauce all but kills fresh tomato flavor.

Freshen Up

When making sauces or stews with ingredients that contain volatile flavors, such as wine, we often reserve a small portion to add at the end of cooking to reintroduce any flavors that were lost. So for my next test, I reserved 1 cup of the strained jelly to add back to the sauce. Happily, I found that it restored much of the tomatoes' bright sweetness. The only hitch was that the jelly thinned the sauce too much, so I made another batch in which I reduced the sauce to 4 cups instead of 5 cups to compensate for the liquid I'd be adding back. The result: a balanced sauce with just the right amount of body.

All I had left to do was polish the flavors, and I did so with a light touch to keep the tomato notes at the forefront. I sautéed dried oregano and red pepper flakes along with the garlic, and to reinforce the freshness, I added a couple of tablespoons of olive oil and a cup of shredded basil to the cooked sauce with the reserved tomato jelly.

The result boasted all the nuances of a ripe summer tomato—delicate sweetness, fragrant aroma, vibrant but balanced acidity—with just enough body to cling to pasta. (No rotovap necessary!) This is the sauce I'll be making every summer, and since the recipe makes a generous amount and can easily be doubled, I'll be stashing a supply in the freezer to enjoy in the dead of winter when I need to remind myself what a ripe tomato tastes like.

FRESH TOMATO SAUCE
YIELDS 5 CUPS; ENOUGH FOR 2 POUNDS PASTA

We developed this recipe using ripe in-season tomatoes. Supermarket vine-ripened tomatoes will work here, but the sauce won't be as flavorful. Don't use plum tomatoes; they are low in moisture and don't work well in this recipe. This is a light-bodied sauce, so don't adjust its consistency with reserved pasta cooking water as you would with most other pasta sauces or it will be too runny. This recipe can easily be doubled.

- 5 pounds ripe tomatoes, cored
- ¼ cup extra-virgin olive oil
- 2 garlic cloves, minced
- ¼ teaspoon red pepper flakes
- ¼ teaspoon dried oregano
-   Salt
- 1 cup fresh basil leaves, shredded

1. Cut tomatoes in half along equator. Set fine-mesh strainer over medium bowl. Gently squeeze tomato halves, cut sides down, over strainer to collect seeds and jelly, scraping any seeds that cling to tomatoes into strainer. Using rubber spatula, press on seeds to extract as much liquid as possible. Discard seeds. Set aside 1 cup liquid and transfer any remaining liquid to large bowl.

2. Cut tomatoes into rough 1½-inch pieces. Working in 2 or 3 batches, process tomatoes in blender until smooth, 30 to 45 seconds; transfer puree to large bowl with strained liquid (you should have about 10 cups puree).

3. Heat 2 tablespoons oil in Dutch oven over medium heat until shimmering. Add garlic, pepper flakes, and oregano and cook until fragrant, about 1 minute. Stir in tomato puree and 1 teaspoon salt. Increase heat to medium-high and bring to simmer. Reduce heat to medium-low and simmer, stirring occasionally, until reduced to 4 cups, 45 minutes to 1 hour.

4. Remove pot from heat and stir in basil, reserved tomato liquid, and remaining 2 tablespoons oil. Season with salt to taste. Use immediately or let cool completely before refrigerating or freezing. (Sauce can be refrigerated for up to 1 week or frozen for up to 3 months.)

You've Never Had Tomato Sauce Like This

If you've never tasted tomato sauce made from ripe summer fruit, prepare to be wowed. Unlike sauces made from canned tomatoes, which have a more concentrated, "cooked" flavor and heavier body, this version boasts a lighter consistency and vibrant, more aromatic flavor that actually tastes like a fresh tomato.

Don't Can It—Freeze It

If you have a bumper crop of tomatoes, the recipe for our Fresh Tomato Sauce can be easily doubled. But we don't recommend canning this sauce; doing so requires adding acid to make the sauce food-safe, which will distort its delicate, sweet flavor. Simply portion it into airtight containers or jars and freeze it for up to three months. Here are two tips that make the process easy.

1. To quickly cool the sauce, transfer it to a stainless-steel bowl, set the bowl over a larger bowl filled with ice, and stir the sauce until cool.
2. Be sure to leave at least ½ inch of headspace—that is, some space between the top of the food and the rim of the container—to account for the liquid's expansion as it freezes.

Introducing Tacos Dorados

The hard-shell taco has been an American staple for more than half a century. When we traced its roots, we found a way to take it to a new, ultracrispy level.

> BY ANNIE PETITO <

Maybe it's nostalgia—the first bite that cracks the shell, sending orange grease down your wrist. Or perhaps it's the satisfying combination of spiced meat, creamy cheese, and cool, crisp lettuce that makes hard-shell tacos so popular. Either way, Americans have an enduring love for this lunchroom and dinnertime staple.

Ease is a big part of the appeal: Relying on a packet of powdered taco seasoning and a sleeve of prefried taco shells means that dinner comes together in a flash. But when I recently prepared tacos using the contents of a supermarket kit, my middle school memories were obscured by a dust cloud of flat spices covering dry, nubbly meat.

Choose Your Shell Adventure

I'd followed the instructions for preparing the shells, baking them for a few minutes before serving, and they were fine, though not terribly flavorful. Frying your own shells into the proper U shape using corn tortillas produces better results—rich corn flavor and a light, crispy texture that's miles apart from the hard crunch of the prefab type—but the process is tedious and messy.

Not truly satisfied with either choice, I dug into the history of hard-shell tacos. It turns out that although commercially made hard-shell tacos are an American innovation, crispy-shell tacos have long existed in Mexico under the name *tacos dorados*, or "golden tacos." The way they're prepared is pure genius: Soft corn tortillas are filled, folded in half, and then deep-fried. At the table, the tacos are opened like a book and stuffed with garnishes.

After just one go-round with the filled-before-fried method, I was hooked. The fried shells were shatteringly crispy on their flat sides yet flexible at their spines, so they didn't break into a million pieces when I took a bite, and they boasted true corn flavor. This was what I had been craving; I just needed to come up with a low-fuss technique.

▶ **Watch: Crispiest Tacos Ever**
A step-by-step video is available at CooksIllustrated.com/aug18

Open the crispy fried shell like a book to load in shredded lettuce, cheddar cheese, sour cream, chopped tomatoes, pickled jalapeños, and hot sauce.

Beefing Up

Before I tackled frying the filled tortillas, I wanted to revamp the usual beef taco filling to work in my tacos dorados. I started with 90 percent lean ground beef, figuring that 85 percent would be on the greasy side. To ensure that the meat stayed tender and juicy, I used a test kitchen trick: raising its pH with baking soda to help the proteins attract and retain more water. I combined ¼ teaspoon of baking soda with 1 tablespoon of water so it would distribute evenly. I then stirred it into the raw beef and let the mixture sit.

Meanwhile, I sautéed finely chopped onion and added modest amounts of common taco seasonings—chili powder, paprika, ground cumin, and garlic powder—to bloom in the oil and release their flavors. Then I added the treated beef and cooked it until it lost its pink color.

It was a fine start, but I wanted a bolder spice flavor and more meaty depth. I increased all the spices to a total ¼ cup, and to boost the savoriness, I cooked a couple of tablespoons of umami-rich tomato paste in the skillet with the onion before adding the beef. My filling was now well spiced and rich-tasting. It was time to stuff the meat into tortillas and fry them up.

To ensure that the tortillas were pliable enough to be filled without cracking or falling apart, I borrowed a technique that we use for enchiladas: brushing each side with oil and then briefly baking the tortillas until they become flexible.

But even with tortillas that cooperated nicely, my filling was a little loose and tended to spill out. I tried binding it with flour and even with mashed canned beans, but ultimately it was easier to simply stir in some of the cheddar cheese I was already using as a garnish. I mixed ½ cup of the shredded cheddar into the beef while it was still hot. The cheese melted seamlessly, helping the beef stay put in the tortilla and enriching the mixture as well.

Finally, instead of deep-frying, which seemed fussy for these slender tacos, I simply shallow-fried them in the same skillet I'd used to cook the beef. I was able to fry 12 tacos in just ¼ cup of oil, and with some strategic arrangement in the skillet, I could complete the job in two batches of six.

As my colleagues eagerly pried open the tacos, added garnishes, and crunched away, I knew I had upped my taco game for good.

Shells That Don't Split

We've all eaten tacos that shatter at the first bite. That's why we were happy to find that stuffing tortillas with filling before frying them not only produces great-tasting tacos but also creates crispy yet flexible shells that stay intact when you dive in. To wit: We pried ours open to a 90-degree angle with no splitting or cracking, an impossible feat with store-bought shells.

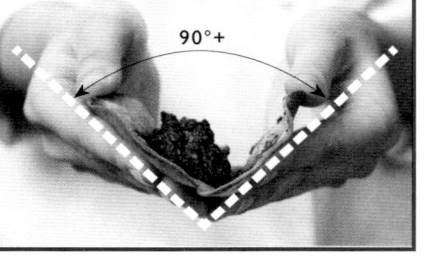

CRISPY TACOS (TACOS DORADOS)
SERVES 4

Arrange the tacos so they face the same direction in the skillet to make them easy to fit and flip. To ensure crispy tacos, cook the tortillas until they are deeply browned. To garnish, open each taco like a book and load it with your preferred toppings; close it to eat.

- 1 tablespoon water
- ¼ teaspoon baking soda
- 12 ounces 90 percent lean ground beef
- 7 tablespoons vegetable oil
- 1 onion, chopped fine
- 1½ tablespoons chili powder
- 1½ tablespoons paprika
- 1½ teaspoons ground cumin
- 1½ teaspoons garlic powder
  Salt
- 2 tablespoons tomato paste
- 2 ounces cheddar cheese, shredded (½ cup), plus extra for serving
- 12 (6-inch) corn tortillas

  Shredded iceberg lettuce
  Chopped tomato
  Sour cream
  Pickled jalapeño slices
  Hot sauce

1. Adjust oven rack to middle position and heat oven to 400 degrees. Combine water and baking soda in large bowl. Add beef and mix until thoroughly combined. Set aside.

2. Heat 1 tablespoon oil in 12-inch nonstick skillet over medium heat until shimmering. Add onion and cook, stirring occasionally, until softened, 4 to 6 minutes. Add chili powder, paprika, cumin, garlic powder, and 1 teaspoon salt and cook, stirring frequently, until fragrant, about 1 minute. Stir in tomato paste and cook until paste is rust-colored, 1 to 2 minutes. Add beef mixture and cook, using wooden spoon to break meat into pieces no larger than ¼ inch, until beef is no longer pink, 5 to 7 minutes. Transfer beef mixture to bowl; stir in cheddar until cheese has melted and mixture is homogeneous. Wipe skillet clean with paper towels.

3. Thoroughly brush both sides of tortillas with 2 tablespoons oil. Arrange tortillas, overlapping, on rimmed baking sheet in 2 rows (6 tortillas each). Bake until tortillas are warm and pliable, about 5 minutes. Remove tortillas from oven and reduce oven temperature to 200 degrees.

4. Place 2 tablespoons filling on 1 side of 1 tortilla. Fold and press to close tortilla (edges will be open, but tortilla will remain folded). Repeat with remaining tortillas and remaining filling. (At this point, filled tortillas can be covered and refrigerated for up to 12 hours.)

5. Set wire rack in second rimmed baking sheet and line rack with double layer of paper towels. Heat remaining ¼ cup oil in now-empty skillet over medium-high heat until shimmering. Arrange 6 tacos in skillet with open sides facing away from you. Cook, adjusting heat so oil actively sizzles and bubbles appear around edges of tacos, until tacos are crispy and deeply browned on 1 side, 2 to 3 minutes. Using tongs and thin spatula, carefully flip tacos. Cook until deeply browned on second side, 2 to 3 minutes, adjusting heat as necessary.

6. Remove skillet from heat and transfer tacos to prepared wire rack. Blot tops of tacos with double layer of paper towels. Place sheet with fried tacos in oven to keep warm. Return skillet to medium-high heat and cook remaining tacos. Serve tacos immediately, passing extra cheddar, lettuce, tomato, sour cream, jalapeños, and hot sauce separately.

A New Way to Make Tacos
A few changes to the usual routine result in the crispiest, tastiest tacos around.

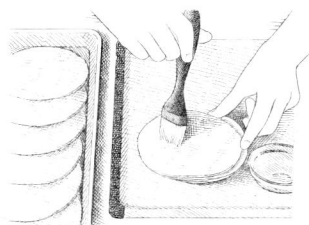
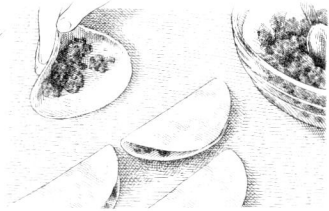

DUMP STORE-BOUGHT OR DEEP-FRIED SHELLS Brush the corn tortillas with oil; bake until pliable enough to stuff.

FILL 'EM FIRST Stuff the warmed tortillas with savory ground beef bound together with melted cheddar cheese.

SHALLOW-FRY IN MINIMAL OIL Fry the tacos in two batches until crispy. (Only ¼ cup of oil is needed for 12 tacos.)

Make It a Party with Micheladas

For this classic Mexican cocktail made with beer, lime, and savory seasonings, we found that a full ¼ cup of lime juice per drink was key. To balance the lime, we added doses of Worcestershire sauce and hot sauce, finding that a thicker hot sauce added a bit of body. To ensure that everything is blended, we combine the flavorful base ingredients before pouring in the beer.

MICHELADA (MEXICAN BEER AND LIME COCKTAIL)
MAKES 4 COCKTAILS

Use a well-chilled Mexican lager. Our favorite is Tecate, but Corona Extra or Modelo will also work. We recommend Cholula or Tapatío hot sauces for their flavor and thicker consistencies. If using a thinner, vinegary hot sauce such as Tabasco, which is spicier, start with half the amount called for and adjust to your taste after mixing. Do not use bottled lime juice here.

  Kosher salt
- ¼ teaspoon chili powder
- 1 cup lime juice (8 limes), plus lime wedges for serving
- 8 teaspoons hot sauce, plus extra for serving
- 2 tablespoons Worcestershire sauce
- 4 (12-ounce) Mexican beers, chilled

1. Combine 2 teaspoons salt and chili powder on small plate and spread into even layer. Rub rims of 4 pint glasses with 1 lime wedge to moisten, then dip rims into salt mixture to coat. Set aside glasses.

2. Combine lime juice, hot sauce, Worcestershire, and ¼ teaspoon salt in 2-cup liquid measuring cup, stirring to dissolve salt. Fill prepared glasses with ice cubes and divide lime juice mixture evenly among glasses. Fill glasses with beer. Serve with lime wedges, extra hot sauce, and remaining beer, topping off glasses as needed.

This tart, spicy cocktail is a refreshing accompaniment to our Crispy Tacos (Tacos Dorados).

Vietnamese Pork with Rice Noodles

Bun cha—a one-dish meal featuring grilled pork patties, crisp vegetables, springy noodles, and a vibrant sauce—cooks as quickly as a burger but tastes much lighter.

≥ BY ANDREA GEARY ≤

I usually start the summer months dreaming about ambitious grilling projects such as ribs and brisket, but when the evenings turn hot and humid, I find myself seeking out lighter, fresher options that I can make more quickly. That's how I learned about *bun cha*, a vibrant Vietnamese dish of rice noodles, grilled pork, and crisp vegetables, all pulled together with a light yet potent sauce.

In the street-food stalls of Hanoi, where the dish originated, cooks prepare fatty cuts such as pork shoulder or belly in two ways: They slice some into thin strips and marinate it in fish sauce, sugar, black pepper, and maybe some minced shallots or onions, and they finely chop the rest (*cha* refers to chopped meat), mix it with similar seasonings, and shape it into small patties. Then they grill all the pork over a box of hot coals and—here comes the genius bit—unload the sizzling meat into bowls of *nuoc cham*, an intensely flavored mixture of lime juice, fish sauce, sugar, water, and sometimes garlic and chiles. The nuoc cham picks up the meaty char flavor while every inch of the pork is bathed in zesty sauce. Then the pork is plucked from the bowl and served with a platter of cool, delicate rice noodles; tender greens; leafy herbs; and crisp cucumbers or bean sprouts. Diners assemble bowls of the components to their taste and drizzle more of the grilled meat–infused sauce over the top.

What makes bun cha so appealing to eat is that it's a one-dish meal with a brilliant contrast of flavors and textures. And as far as I could tell from the recipes I consulted, what makes this dish so appealing to cook is that it comes together relatively quickly and uses a small arsenal of mostly familiar ingredients.

Pat-a-Cake

Following the lead of one recipe I'd found, I sliced ½ pound of pork belly into strips and marinated them in a mixture of fish sauce, sugar, pepper, and minced shallots. I also finely chopped an equal amount of pork shoulder, folded in more of the seasonings, and shaped the mixture into small patties. To simulate the brazier over which the meat would traditionally be cooked, I piled a chimney's worth of hot coals on one side of my grill, dropped the cooking grate in place, and arranged the meat directly over the coals.

To serve, arrange the components on platters and allow diners to assemble individual bowls of meat, noodles, salad, and sauce.

▶ **Look: Bun Cha at Home**
A step-by-step video is available at CooksIllustrated.com/aug18

The pork belly released lots of fat, causing impressive flare-ups, so I had to move the strips around a lot and I lost about a quarter of them between the bars. Those that didn't fall through were nicely charred but very chewy. Ultimately, I decided to skip the strips altogether and stick with just the patties, which would make the recipe quicker to prepare. But the patties needed work, too. Though they were easier to maneuver on the grill and stayed more tender than the pork belly, they were dry inside by the time their exteriors had charred sufficiently—and a dunk in the sauce couldn't save them. Besides, finely chopping pork shoulder—a big, tough cut—had taken longer than it did to actually cook it.

I'd seen a few recipes that called for supermarket ground pork in place of the chopped meat. It wouldn't be as authentic, but taking the shortcut would make this dish a snap to prepare—something I could throw together any night of the week. Besides, my goal for the pork would remain the same: deeply savory, well-charred, rich meat that balanced the bright-tasting sauce, crisp vegetables, and noodles.

I mixed 1 pound of ground pork with the usual seasonings plus ½ teaspoon of baking soda—a favorite test kitchen trick. The baking soda boosts the meat's pH, which in turn enhances browning and inhibits the tendency of meat fibers to tighten up and squeeze out moisture as they cook. The result: patties that browned quickly and stayed juicy.

A World-Class Condiment

Nuoc cham—a salty-sour-sweet combination of fish sauce, lime juice, and sugar that is usually diluted with water and is often seasoned with garlic and/or chile—is as essential to Vietnamese cooking as salsa is to Mexican cuisine. It functions as a dipping sauce or dressing for countless dishes and is a snap to make. The key is flavor balance. We make sure to use hot water (which helps quickly dissolve the sugar) and to grind—not just mince—the garlic and chile so that their assertive flavors disperse evenly.

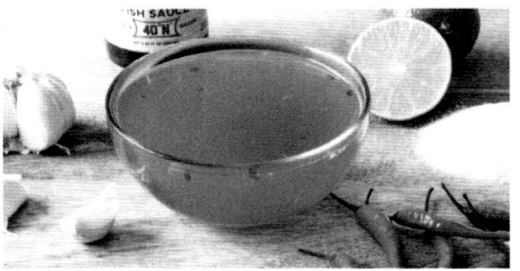

ESSENTIAL SAUCE
The salty-sour-sweet and spicy flavors of *nuoc cham* enhances countless Vietnamese dishes.

Sauce Does Double Duty

In bun cha, the assertively flavored sauce called nuoc cham is the element that brings together the various components of the dish. It functions as a postmarinade for the grilled pork, infusing the patties with salty, sour, sweet, and aromatic flavors. Then the meat-infused liquid is used as a sauce that dresses the rest of the components.

FLAVOR EXCHANGE
Dunking the grilled meat into the sauce enhances the flavors of both components.

Hot, Sour, Salty, Sweet

Nuoc cham, according to cookbook author Andrea Nguyen, is a dipping sauce that every good Vietnamese cook needs to master and is the element that brings together all the components in this dish and many others in Vietnamese cuisine. It's also a cinch to make. The tricks are to balance the saltiness of the fish sauce with the brightness of lime juice or vinegar and the sweetness of sugar and to add just enough water so that the sauce enlivens rather than overpowers whatever you're dressing. My placeholder version tasted balanced but spartan, so I tried incorporating the chile and garlic I had seen in some recipes.

However, I couldn't mince the chile and garlic finely enough to distribute their flavors evenly throughout the sauce, so some bites were fiery or pungent while others fell flat. But Nguyen makes a helpful suggestion in her version: Combine the aromatics with some of the sugar in a mortar and pestle. The granules act as an abrasive, helping speedily reduce everything to a paste that made every drop of the sauce taste more vibrant. (In lieu of a mortar and pestle, you can smear the sugar across the minced aromatics several times with the flat side of a chef's knife on a cutting board.)

Composing a Salad

When cooked, rice vermicelli, the bun in bun cha, should be fine and delicate yet resilient. My noodles softened after about 4 minutes in boiling water, at which point I drained them and rinsed them well with cold water to halt their cooking and wash away surface starch to minimize stickiness. Then I drained them again and spread them out on a platter to air-dry while I made the salad.

I tore a head of tender Boston lettuce into bite-size pieces and, per Vietnamese tradition, arranged the nuoc cham–moistened pork, remaining sauce, noodles, greens, herbs (mint leaves and delicate cilantro leaves and stems), and cucumber slices separately so that diners could compose their own salads.

Every bite was an extraordinary balance of smoky, juicy meat; tangy, salty-sweet sauce; cool, tender greens; and delicately springy noodles. And the kicker was that when I tallied up my over-the-heat cooking time—4 minutes to boil the noodles plus 8 minutes to grill the patties—it equaled just 12 minutes, making this an ideal dinner to cook on a sweltering summer night. Or on any night, for that matter.

VIETNAMESE GRILLED PORK PATTIES WITH RICE NOODLES AND SALAD (BUN CHA)
SERVES 4 TO 6

Look for dried rice vermicelli in the Asian section of your supermarket. We prefer the more delicate springiness of vermicelli made from 100 percent rice flour to those that include a secondary starch such as cornstarch. If you can find only the latter, just cook them longer—up to 12 minutes. For a less spicy sauce, use only half the Thai chile. For the cilantro, use the leaves and the thin, delicate stems, not the thicker ones close to the root. To serve, place platters of noodles, salad, sauce, and pork patties on the table and allow diners to combine components to their taste. The sauce is potent, so use it sparingly. Our recipe for Vietnamese Grilled Pork Patties with Rice Noodles and Salad (Bun Cha) for Two is available for free for four months at CooksIllustrated.com/aug18.

Noodles and Salad
- 8 ounces rice vermicelli
- 1 head Boston lettuce (8 ounces), torn into bite-size pieces
- 1 English cucumber, peeled, quartered lengthwise, seeded, and sliced thin on bias
- 1 cup fresh cilantro leaves and stems
- 1 cup fresh mint leaves, torn if large

Sauce
- 1 small Thai chile, stemmed and minced
- 3 tablespoons sugar
- 1 garlic clove, minced
- 2/3 cup hot water
- 5 tablespoons fish sauce
- 1/4 cup lime juice (2 limes)

Pork Patties
- 1 large shallot, minced
- 1 tablespoon fish sauce
- 1 1/2 teaspoons sugar
- 1/2 teaspoon baking soda
- 1/2 teaspoon pepper
- 1 pound ground pork

1. FOR THE NOODLES AND SALAD: Bring 4 quarts water to boil in large pot. Stir in noodles and cook until tender but not mushy, 4 to 12 minutes. Drain noodles and rinse under cold running water until cool. Drain noodles very well, spread on large plate, and let stand at room temperature to dry. Arrange lettuce, cucumber, cilantro, and mint separately on large platter and refrigerate until needed.

2. FOR THE SAUCE: Using mortar and pestle (or on cutting board using flat side of chef's knife), mash Thai chile, 1 tablespoon sugar, and garlic to fine paste. Transfer to medium bowl and add hot water and remaining 2 tablespoons sugar. Stir until sugar is dissolved. Stir in fish sauce and lime juice. Set aside.

3. FOR THE PORK PATTIES: Combine shallot, fish sauce, sugar, baking soda, and pepper in medium bowl. Add pork and mix until well combined. Shape pork mixture into 12 patties, each about 2 1/2 inches wide and 1/2 inch thick.

4A. FOR A CHARCOAL GRILL: Open bottom vent completely. Light large chimney starter filled with charcoal briquettes (6 quarts). When top coals are partially covered with ash, pour evenly over half of grill. Set cooking grate in place, cover, and open lid vent completely. Heat grill until hot, about 5 minutes.

4B. FOR A GAS GRILL: Turn all burners to high, cover, and heat grill until hot, about 15 minutes. Leave all burners on high.

5. Clean and oil cooking grate. Cook patties (directly over coals if using charcoal; covered if using gas) until well charred, 3 to 4 minutes per side. Transfer grilled patties to bowl with sauce and gently toss to coat. Let stand for 5 minutes.

6. Transfer patties to serving plate, reserving sauce. Serve noodles, salad, sauce, and pork patties separately.

SHOPPING Two Common Types of Rice Noodles

Dried rice noodles come in dozens of varieties, but there are two styles that you're likely to find at the supermarket.

Rice sticks are straight and flat and can be narrow like linguine or wide like pappardelle; they offer great chew and are typically used in noodle soups such as pho and stir-fries such as pad Thai.

Rice vermicelli are round strands that range in size from slightly wider than angel hair to about the thickness of spaghetti. They look wiry in the package but turn nicely springy when cooked; the noodles' diameter influences their cooking time, so check them for doneness early and often. They're the best choice for noodle bowls such as bun cha and for summer rolls. We prefer the more delicate springiness of vermicelli that are made from 100 percent rice flour to those that include a secondary starch such as cornstarch; however, if you can find only noodles that contain cornstarch, just cook them a bit longer.

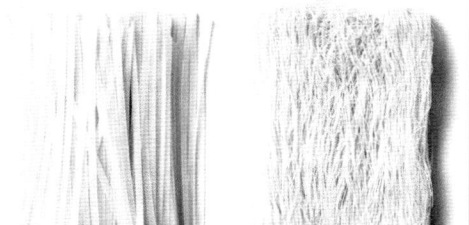

RICE STICKS RICE VERMICELLI

Better-Than-the-Box Granola Bars

We love the idea of chewy granola bars, but store-bought versions are overly sweet, contain mostly filler, and are soft, not chewy. We took matters into our own hands.

⇒ BY ANDREA GEARY ⇐

Every adult I know goes through the same mental checklist before leaving the house in the morning: Keys? Phone? Wallet? Granola bar? Okay, maybe that last one is just me.

But granola bars should be on your must-have list because they're tasty and easy to eat on the go. And because they contain fiber, protein, and healthy fats, they make great snacking alternatives to hastily grabbed cookies or chips. That said, buying granola bars can be disappointing. Many commercial bars are so sweet that they're really just undercover candy, and most are pretty light on hearty additions such as nuts, seeds, and dried fruit. Such stinginess is especially annoying because granola bars are pricey, even though most are largely composed of inexpensive oats.

I decided that the best way to be sure the granola bars in my bag were packed with satisfying nuts, seeds, and fruit; had just the right amount of sweetness; and kept costs in check was to make them myself. Mine would be of the chewy variety. Crunchy granola has its place (on top of Greek yogurt), but chewy bars are less likely to fall apart in my hand, and the physical act of chewing them reinforces the feeling that I've eaten something substantial. And I'm not alone: When I polled our readers on Facebook, 72 percent of them preferred chewy bars.

All Mixed Up

The first recipes I tried followed a similar procedure: I mixed oats, nuts, seeds, and, in some cases, chunks of dried fruit with a combination of sugar and a liquid sweetener—usually honey or maple syrup. Most recipes called for stirring in some oil or butter; many also called for peanut butter or almond butter. I spread the mixtures in pans and baked them. So far, so easy. It was only when I tried to cut the cooled slabs into individual bars that things literally fell apart.

▶ Watch: DIY Granola Bars
A step-by-step video is available at CooksIllustrated.com/aug18

Use a sharp chef's knife to cut the granola into neat, portable bars.

Most bars were unacceptably sticky to the touch yet, paradoxically, they refused to stick together. These bars were tender all the way through and were too yielding to be called "chewy." Other bars were drier and left my hands cleaner, but they were too hard and were prone to shattering into messy chunks. I wanted to make cohesive granola bars with varied textures, balanced sweetness, and plenty of chew, ideal for on-the-go snacking.

For the Birds

I started my own baseline recipe by toasting 2½ cups of oats, 1 cup of sunflower seeds, and 1½ cups of chopped walnuts in the oven to bring out their flavors. I transferred everything to a bowl and stirred in 1 cup of dried cranberries for pops of brightness. One cup of brown sugar and ½ cup each of peanut butter and honey made up my "glue." Because it's high in saturated fat, butter seemed antithetical to the granola bar concept, so I mixed in ½ cup of vegetable oil instead. (A bonus: Using oil instead of butter would allow the bars to keep longer at room temperature.) I pressed the mixture firmly into a foil-lined, greased baking pan and baked it for about 25 minutes. These bars tasted pretty good but, like many in my initial round of testing, were both tacky and crumbly.

Thinking that smaller particles might absorb some of the stickiness and hold together better, I coarsely ground the toasted oats and nuts in the food processor before mixing the next batch. This granola was more cohesive, which made it easier to cut into bars, but they felt grainy and pasty in my mouth and bore an unsettling resemblance to those blocks of compressed seeds you hang out for the birds when the weather turns cold. So the oats would have to stay whole. But having the food processor out reminded me of another technique I had seen: binding the bars with pureed dried fruit.

The Sticking Point

While my next batch of oats, nuts, and seeds toasted, I ground 1 cup of dried apricots with the brown sugar in the food processor. I added peanut butter, honey, and oil as the machine ran, and then I mixed the promisingly viscous mixture with the warm oat mixture and the cranberries. I also added some crisped rice cereal. I suspected that firm compression of the mixture before baking was going to be important for cohesion, so I hoped that the airy cereal would provide tiny pockets of lightness. After baking and cooling, these bars stood up to cutting better than any previous batches, but they were still rather tender and crumbly when I ate them. I was aiming for a bar so resilient that I could bend it into a shallow arc; this bar simply broke in two.

I knew that fat tenderizes baked goods. Was it possible that my formula was simply too high in fat? If so, I had two options: Nix the vegetable oil or nix the peanut butter. I decided to eliminate the latter so I could devise a nut-free variation later on.

Now I was getting somewhere: Without the peanut butter, the bars were distinctly chewy and definitely cohesive. They even passed the bend test.

Spend Less, Get More

Our granola bars cost about 50 percent less than commercial varieties. Plus, they contain more hearty nuts, seeds, and dried fruit.

How We Put the "Chew" in Our Chewy Granola Bars

"Too tender." "Too soft." "Too dense." We obsessed over getting the perfect chewy texture in our granola bars, meaning each bite should meet with repeated resistance as you chew. How did we achieve it? A mix of pureed dried apricots, brown sugar, oil, and water helped the bars' ingredients cohere. Using just the right amount of moisture was also key: We added enough to make the bars tender and to hold them together when they were bent or bitten—but not so much that they became soft and lost their chew.

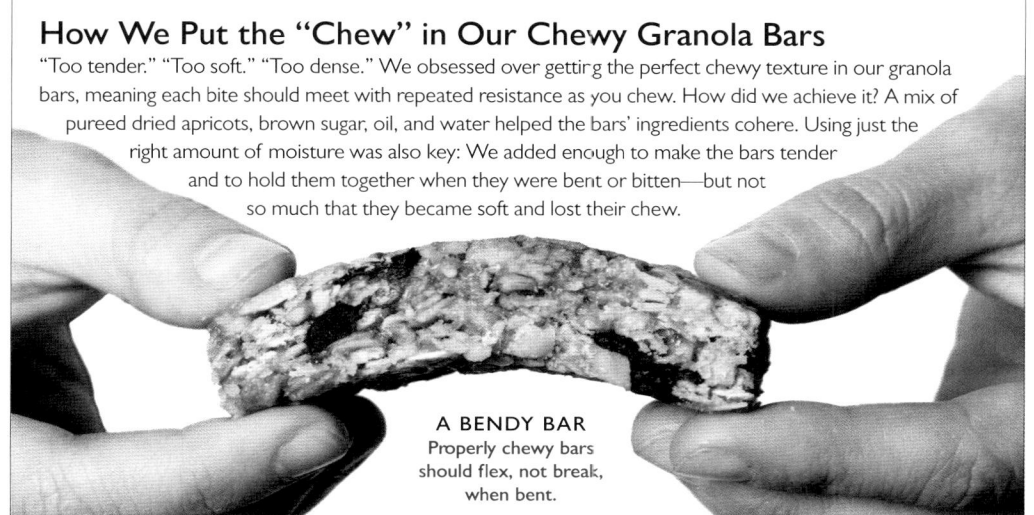

A BENDY BAR
Properly chewy bars should flex, not break, when bent.

Just Add Water

I knew I was getting close, but without peanut butter's salty richness, the bars were a bit too sweet and the honey flavor was especially obtrusive. Discouragingly, a batch made without honey was too dry and crumbly. I considered using corn syrup, which has very little flavor, in place of the honey because it seemed like some form of syrup was the key to a chewy, moist, cohesive texture. But was it?

Syrups are mostly sugar and water. In some cases, they're added to recipes, such as caramel, to inhibit crystallization, but that wasn't important in my granola bars. So maybe it wasn't a syrup that was the magic ingredient. Maybe it was something I had never seen in a granola bar recipe: water.

The ½ cup of honey had been contributing water, so I added a small amount to the next honey-free batch, streaming it into the food processor with the oil. Three tablespoons of water worked beautifully, producing bars that were chewy and cohesive without being sticky. The tart cranberries, nutty toasted oats, and crunchy walnuts were balanced by the sweetness of the apricots and brown sugar.

I was so happy with this recipe that I used it as a template for a hazelnut, cherry, and cacao nib bar so sophisticated that a box of them would make a luxurious gift, and a richly seeded, nut-free version.

Staying Power

Stored in an airtight container between sheets of parchment or waxed paper, our granola bars keep for three weeks. As your stock diminishes, transfer the bars to a smaller container to minimize their exposure to air, which can dry them out.

CHEWY GRANOLA BARS WITH WALNUTS AND CRANBERRIES
MAKES 24 BARS

We like the sweetness of Mediterranean or Turkish apricots in this recipe. Be sure to use apricots that are soft and moist, or the bars will not hold together well. Avoid using extra-thick rolled oats here. Light and dark brown sugar will work equally well in this recipe.

- 1½ cups walnuts
- 2½ cups (7½ ounces) old-fashioned rolled oats
- 1 cup raw sunflower seeds
- 1 cup dried apricots
- 1 cup packed (7 ounces) brown sugar
- ¾ teaspoon salt
- ½ cup vegetable oil
- 3 tablespoons water
- 1½ cups (1½ ounces) Rice Krispies cereal
- 1 cup dried cranberries

1. Adjust oven rack to middle position and heat oven to 350 degrees. Make foil sling for 13 by 9-inch baking pan by folding 2 long sheets of aluminum foil; first sheet should be 13 inches wide and second sheet should be 9 inches wide. Lay sheets of foil in pan perpendicular to each other, with extra foil hanging over edges of pan. Push foil into corners and up sides of pan, smoothing foil flush to pan. Lightly spray foil with vegetable oil spray.

2. Pulse walnuts in food processor until finely chopped, 8 to 10 pulses. Spread walnuts, oats, and sunflower seeds on rimmed baking sheet and toast until lightly browned and fragrant, 12 to 15 minutes, stirring halfway through toasting. Reduce oven temperature to 300 degrees.

3. While oat mixture is toasting, process apricots, sugar, and salt in food processor until apricots are very finely ground, about 15 seconds. With processor running, add oil and water. Continue to process until homogeneous paste forms, about 1 minute longer. Transfer paste to large, wide bowl.

4. Add warm oat mixture to bowl and stir with rubber spatula until well coated. Add cereal and cranberries and stir gently until ingredients are evenly mixed. Transfer mixture to prepared pan and spread into even layer. Place 14-inch sheet of parchment or waxed paper on top of granola and press and smooth very firmly with your hands, especially at edges and corners, until granola is level and compact. Remove parchment and bake granola until fragrant and just beginning to brown around edges, about 25 minutes. Transfer pan to wire rack and let cool for 1 hour. Using foil overhang, lift granola out of pan. Return to wire rack and let cool completely, about 1 hour.

5. Discard foil and transfer granola to cutting board. Using chef's knife, cut granola in half crosswise to create two 6½ by 9-inch rectangles. Cut each rectangle in half to make four 3¼ by 9-inch strips. Cut each strip crosswise into 6 equal pieces. (Granola bars can be stored at room temperature for up to 3 weeks.)

CHEWY GRANOLA BARS WITH HAZELNUTS, CHERRIES, AND CACAO NIBS

Substitute blanched hazelnuts for walnuts and pulse until finely chopped, 8 to 12 pulses. Substitute chopped dried cherries for cranberries. Stir in ½ cup cacao nibs with cereal in step 4.

NUT-FREE CHEWY GRANOLA BARS

Omit walnuts and cranberries. Toast 1 cup raw pepitas, ¼ cup sesame seeds, and ¼ cup chia seeds with oats in step 2. Increase cereal to 2 cups.

TECHNIQUE
PRESSING FOR SUCCESS

Using parchment or waxed paper to firmly press the raw granola mixture into the pan leads to a more cohesive mixture that is easier to slice into bars and, in turn, less messy to eat.

How to Grill Tomatoes

Grilling enhances tomatoes with smoky char while preserving their summery taste. But don't simply throw them onto the fire or you'll end up with a mushy mess.

⇒ BY ANNIE PETITO ⇐

Here's an idea for showcasing summer tomatoes that you may not have considered: Grill them. A stint over a hot fire softens the fruit's flesh and concentrates its sweetness. Meanwhile, the smoky char of the grill adds another dimension of flavor. If that's not enough to grab your attention, consider this: Tomatoes cook quickly, so you can grill them while your steak or other protein is resting and the coals are still hot.

For my first attempt, I used the easiest approach I could think of: simply placing 2 pounds of whole tomatoes on the grill. But by the time the fruit had sufficiently charred on the exterior, it was starting to turn mushy and disintegrate within. Plus, the interior didn't pick up any grill flavor to speak of.

It worked better to cut the tomatoes in half so that both the interiors and the exteriors could spend some time in contact with the grill grate. This way, there was lots of surface area available to quickly caramelize and char before the flesh started to break down too much. I also found that ripe but still firm tomatoes held their shape best during and after grilling—super-squishy ones fell apart. What's more, the way the tomatoes were cut had a huge impact on the results: It was essential to halve them along their equators, not pole to pole. Cut this way, the tomatoes stayed intact even as they began to soften (see "The Best Way to Halve Tomatoes for Grilling").

While the grill heated up—which took about 15 minutes—I sprinkled the raw tomato halves with salt and pepper and drizzled them with extra-virgin olive oil. Almost immediately, the salt began to draw liquid from the tomato flesh via osmosis, which is just what I wanted. The drier the tomatoes were, the more easily caramelization could occur.

Leaving the tomato liquid in the bowl, I placed the tomatoes skin sides down on the grill. After a few minutes, I flipped them—only to have warmed seeds and liquid flood the coals. The next time around, I grilled the halves cut sides down for about 5 minutes and then flipped them skin sides down and cooked them roughly 5 minutes longer. With this approach, the skins acted as cradles during the second half of cooking, helping contain the flesh as it continued to soften.

▶ **Annie Shares the Secrets**
A step-by-step video is available at CooksIllustrated.com/aug18

Clockwise from top left: Grill the tomatoes while your protein rests and serve them as a simple side. Or make Grilled Tomato Salsa, Grilled Tomato Gazpacho, or Marinated Grilled Tomatoes with Fresh Mozzarella.

When the skins were adequately charred and the juices were bubbling, I pulled the tomatoes off the grill. They tasted sweet and savory, with a light smokiness, but they lacked a bit of brightness. I realized that the liquid shed during the salting step was loaded with fresh, raw tomato flavor, so I drizzled it onto the grilled halves. The fresh tomato juice captured the true essence of summer and beautifully complemented the richer taste of the grilled flesh.

These tomatoes were great for just about anything, including pasta, sandwiches, salads, soup, and sauces. To show off their versatility even further, I developed a simple grilled tomato salsa with onion, jalapeño, cilantro, and lime juice, as well as a marinated mixture of fresh mozzarella cheese and the tomatoes. And for a deeply flavorful twist on gazpacho, I pureed the tomatoes with cucumber, aromatics, olive oil, vinegar, and a slice of bread for body.

GRILLED TOMATOES   MAKES ABOUT 2 CUPS

To serve the tomatoes as a simple side dish, top them with the reserved juice, 2 tablespoons of torn fresh basil leaves, 1 tablespoon of extra-virgin olive oil, and flake sea salt to taste. This recipe can easily be doubled.

1. Core 2 pounds ripe but firm tomatoes and halve along equator.

2. Toss tomatoes with 1 tablespoon extra-virgin olive oil, ½ teaspoon salt, and ¼ teaspoon pepper in large bowl. Let stand for at least 15 minutes or up to 1 hour. Reserve any juice left in bowl.

3. Place tomatoes, cut sides down, on clean, oiled grate of hot grill and cook (covered if using gas) until charred and beginning to soften, 4 to 6 minutes.

4. Using tongs or thin metal spatula, carefully flip tomatoes and continue to cook (covered if using gas) until skin sides are charred and juice bubbles, 4 to 6 minutes longer. Transfer tomatoes to large plate. (Tomatoes can be refrigerated for up to 2 days.)

For the best results, use in-season, round tomatoes that are ripe yet a bit firm so they will hold their shape on the grill. Plum tomatoes may be used, but they will be drier in texture. If using plum tomatoes, halve them lengthwise. Supermarket vine-ripened tomatoes will work but won't be as flavorful.

For the recipes in which the tomatoes were chopped, I initially slipped off the skins since their texture was distracting. But because some of the smokiness of the grill does transfer into the skins, discarding them meant discarding smoky flavor. It worked much better to chop the skins separately and include them. This way, their flavor could permeate the dish without their texture being bothersome.

These tomatoes are so full-flavored and versatile that I plan on making them all summer long.

GRILLED TOMATO GAZPACHO
SERVES 4

For the best flavor, refrigerate the gazpacho overnight before serving. Red wine vinegar can be substituted for the sherry vinegar, if desired.

- 1 recipe Grilled Tomatoes, room temperature, with juice reserved
- 1 small cucumber, peeled and cut into 1-inch pieces
- 1 slice hearty white sandwich bread, crust removed, torn into 1-inch pieces
- 1 small shallot, peeled and halved
- 1 small garlic clove, peeled and quartered
- 1 small serrano chile, stemmed and halved lengthwise
- Salt and pepper
- ½ cup extra-virgin olive oil
- 2 tablespoons finely minced fresh parsley
- 1 teaspoon sherry vinegar, plus extra for seasoning
- Water

Process tomatoes and reserved juice, cucumber, bread, shallot, garlic, serrano, and 1 teaspoon salt in blender for 30 seconds. With blender running, slowly drizzle in oil; continue to process until completely smooth, about 2 minutes longer. Strain soup through fine-mesh strainer into large measuring cup, using back of ladle or rubber spatula to press soup through strainer. Stir in parsley and vinegar. Add enough water to yield 4 cups soup. Cover and refrigerate for at least 2 hours to chill and develop flavors. Season with salt, pepper, and extra vinegar to taste. Serve.

GRILLED TOMATO SALSA
MAKES ABOUT 2 CUPS

For more heat, reserve and mince the jalapeño ribs and seeds and add them to the salsa.

- 1 recipe Grilled Tomatoes, room temperature, with juice reserved
- ¼ cup finely chopped onion
- 1 jalapeño chile, stemmed, seeded, and minced
- 2 tablespoons minced fresh cilantro
- 1–2 tablespoons lime juice
- Salt and pepper

Remove and reserve tomato skins; chop tomato flesh coarse and chop skins fine. Combine tomatoes, skins, reserved juice, onion, jalapeño, cilantro, and 1 tablespoon lime juice in medium bowl. Let stand at room temperature until flavors meld, about 30 minutes. Season with salt, pepper, and up to 1 tablespoon additional lime juice to taste. Serve. (Salsa can be refrigerated for up to 2 days; let come to room temperature before serving.)

MARINATED GRILLED TOMATOES WITH FRESH MOZZARELLA
MAKES ABOUT 3 CUPS

Serve this dish at room temperature by itself, alongside crusty bread, as a topping for bruschetta or grilled pizza, or as part of an antipasto platter.

- 1 recipe Grilled Tomatoes
- 8 ounces fresh mozzarella cheese, torn into bite-size pieces and patted dry
- ¼ cup extra-virgin olive oil
- ¼ cup chopped fresh basil
- 2 tablespoons red wine vinegar
- ¼ teaspoon salt
- ¼ teaspoon pepper
- Pinch red pepper flakes

Remove and reserve tomato skins; cut tomato flesh into ½-inch pieces and chop skins fine. Combine tomatoes, skins, mozzarella, oil, basil, vinegar, salt, pepper, and pepper flakes in bowl, ensuring that tomatoes and mozzarella are submerged in oil-vinegar mixture. Let stand at room temperature until flavors meld, up to 1 hour, stirring occasionally to ensure that tomatoes are evenly coated. Serve. (Mixture can be refrigerated for up to 2 days; let come to room temperature before serving.)

TECHNIQUE
THE BEST WAY TO HALVE TOMATOES FOR GRILLING

Moisture evaporates via open seed pockets.

How you halve a tomato affects how well it will hold its shape during grilling. Cutting it pole to pole leaves intact seed pockets that will burst when heated, causing the tomato to slump. However, cutting it along the equator slashes the seed pockets so that moisture can escape and the tomato stays intact.

Top 12 Grilling Mistakes to Avoid

Some of the most common practices are also the wrong ones.

BY ELIZABETH BOMZE

Ⓒ 1 Using lighter fluid
Lighter fluid can impart a chemical flavor to the food.
➤ **BEST PRACTICE** Light coals in a chimney starter.
Method: Place wadded-up newspaper in the bottom chamber and briquettes in the top. Light the newspaper. When the top coals are covered in ash, dump the coals into the grill.

Ⓒ 2 Packing too much paper into the chimney
Doing so blocks airflow, so the coals will take longer to ignite—or will not ignite at all.
➤ **BEST PRACTICE** Don't place more than two sheets of newspaper in the bottom chamber at one time.

Ⓒ 3 Pouring the coals before they are fully ignited
If the coals aren't hot enough, they won't cook food at the right rate. Or, worse, the fire can die out.
➤ **BEST PRACTICE** Don't pour the coals until the top layer is partially covered with ash—a sure sign that they're ready.

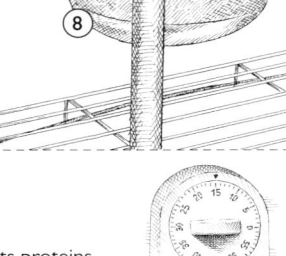

WINNING CHARCOAL MODEL:
WEBER PERFORMER DELUXE CHARCOAL GRILL ($399.00)
Maintains heat well; well-positioned vents; push-button gas ignition; roomy cart

Ⓒ Ⓖ 4 Skipping the preheat step
Meat placed on a cooking grate that's not sufficiently hot will stick aggressively because its proteins form a chemical bond with the metal.
➤ **BEST PRACTICE** Wait to add food until the metal is very hot. This will break the bonds (which are thermally unstable), preventing sticking. It will also produce much better color and char.

Charcoal Preheat Time: About 5 minutes
Gas Preheat Time: About 15 minutes

Ⓒ Ⓖ 5 Using one fire setup for all tasks
The fire setup—how much charcoal or how many burners you're using and where the heat is located in relation to the food—allows you to control the heat level and the rate of cooking. Using the wrong setup can cause food to burn before it's cooked through or cook through without developing any flavorful browning or char.
➤ **BEST PRACTICE** Use one of our three favorite fire setups.

SINGLE-LEVEL FIRE
Best for: Small, quick-cooking foods such as sausages, shrimp, fish fillets, and some vegetables.

Charcoal Setup: Distribute lit coals in even layer across bottom of grill.

Gas Setup: Turn all burners to high, cover, and heat grill until hot. Leave all burners on high.

HALF-GRILL FIRE
Best for: Foods that you want to cook gently but also sear, such as bone-in chicken parts and pork chops.

Charcoal Setup: Distribute lit coals in even layer over half of grill.

Gas Setup: Turn all burners to high, cover, and heat grill until hot. Leave primary burner on high and turn off other burner(s).

CONCENTRATED FIRE
Best for: Quick-cooking foods on which you want substantial char, such as burgers or thin steaks.

Charcoal Setup: Poke holes in bottom of large disposable aluminum pan, place pan in center of grill, and pour lit coals into pan.

Gas Setup: Concentrated fire setup is not possible on gas grill. To maximize heat, turn all burners to high.

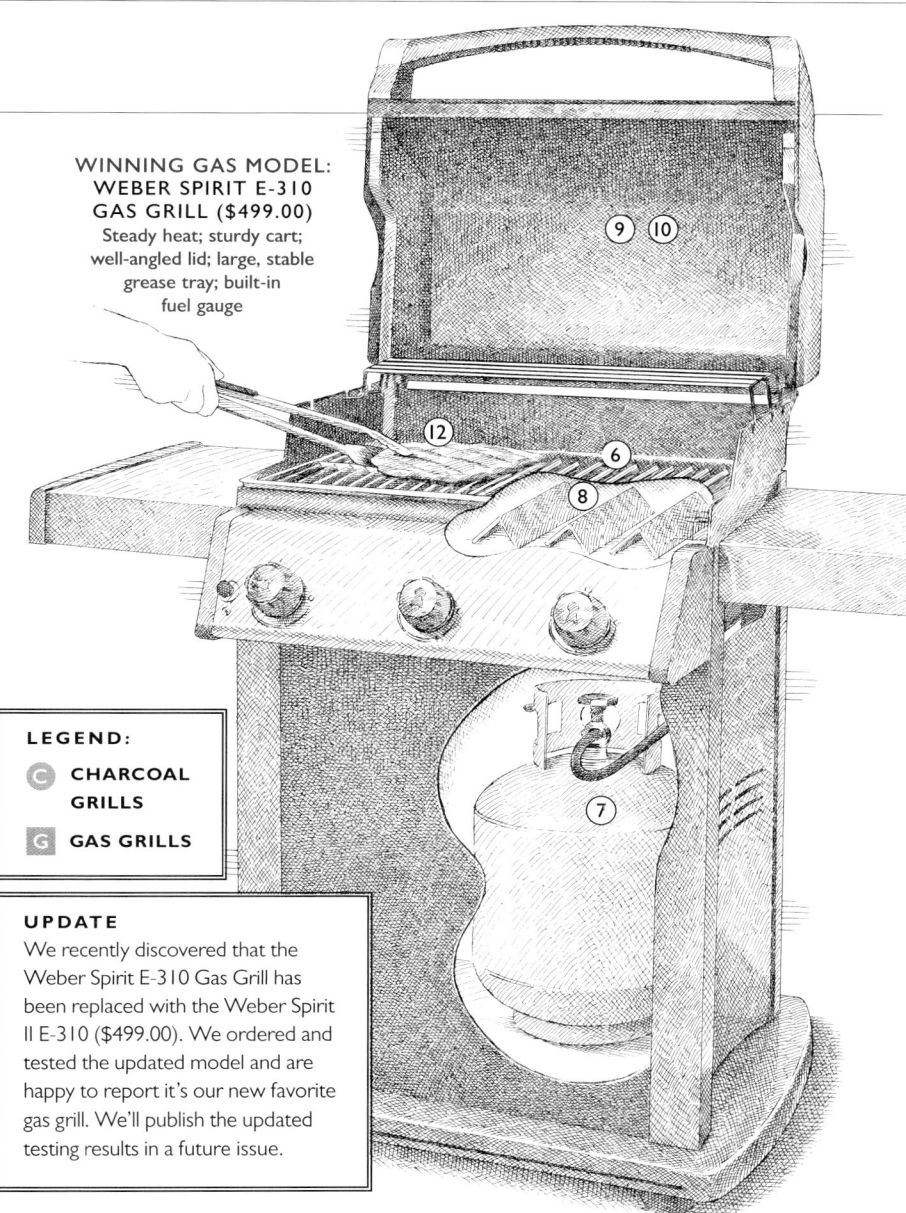

**WINNING GAS MODEL:
WEBER SPIRIT E-310
GAS GRILL ($499.00)**
Steady heat; sturdy cart; well-angled lid; large, stable grease tray; built-in fuel gauge

LEGEND:
C CHARCOAL GRILLS
G GAS GRILLS

UPDATE
We recently discovered that the Weber Spirit E-310 Gas Grill has been replaced with the Weber Spirit II E-310 ($499.00). We ordered and tested the updated model and are happy to report it's our new favorite gas grill. We'll publish the updated testing results in a future issue.

C G 8 Cooking on a gunked-up grill

Food debris, grease, and smoke that build up on various parts of the grill can cause sticking and impart off-flavors to food; full grease traps can ignite; and built-up grease on the interior basin and underside of the grill lid can carbonize and turn into a patchy layer that flakes off and lands on your food.

➤ **HOW TO CLEAN YOUR GRILL**
Grill grates: After preheating the grill, scrape the cooking grate clean with a grill brush.
Interior basin and lid: Lightly scrub the cool grill and lid with steel wool and water.
Ash catcher (charcoal only): Empty the cooled ash regularly.
Grease traps (gas only): Remove the cool shallow pan from under your grill and scrub it with hot soapy water. To make cleanup easier, line the pan with aluminum foil before use.

G 9 Leaving the lid open

Because gas grills deliver less heat output than charcoal models, grilling certain foods with the lid up allows too much heat to escape. **Note:** You should never light a gas grill with the lid down, which can trap gas and cause a dangerous explosion.
➤ **BEST PRACTICE** When directed in a recipe, keep the lid closed to trap as much heat as possible.

C G 10 Lifting the lid too often

This is equivalent to frequently opening the oven door. Heat will escape, which prolongs the grilling time.
➤ **BEST PRACTICE** Use a probe thermometer, which allows you to monitor food's doneness without opening the grill.

C 11 Ignoring the grill vents

If you're not using the vents, you're not controlling the heat output.
➤ **HOW GRILL VENTS WORK**
Grill vents are like the dials on your stovetop: They allow you to manipulate how hot the fire gets and how the food cooks. Charcoal grills have top vents on the lid and bottom vents on the underside of the basin. (Gas grills have vents, too, but they are not adjustable.) In general, opening the vents completely allows more oxygen to reach the fire so that it burns hotter and faster; partially closing the vents lowers the temperature and prolongs the fire's duration.

C G 6 Not oiling the cooking grate

Most cooking grates are made of steel or cast iron and must be oiled before grilling to keep food from sticking.
➤ **BEST PRACTICE** Using tongs, dip a wad of paper towels in vegetable oil and thoroughly wipe the preheated, scrubbed cooking grate before adding food.

G 7 Not checking the propane tank

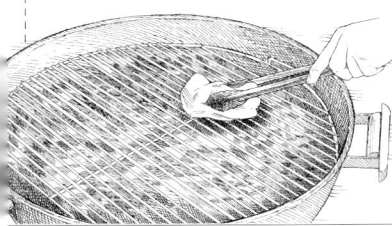

You don't want to end up with an empty propane tank in the middle of grilling—especially in the case of a lengthy project such as brisket or ribs.
➤ **HOW TO CHECK THE TANK**
If your grill does not have a built-in fuel gauge, you can buy an external one—for example, the intuitive Original Grill Gauge ($13.99). Or try this hot water trick: Boil 1 cup of water and pour it down the side of the tank. Feel the metal with your hand. Where the water has warmed the surface of the tank, it is empty; where the tank remains cool to the touch, there is still propane inside.

C G 12 Turning the meat too soon

Meat will stick to the cooking grate until the meat's surface is hot enough to release (see "Skipping the preheat step"). Lifting meat before it naturally releases will tear it.
➤ **BEST PRACTICE** Sear the meat without moving it until a substantial crust forms around the edges. If the meat doesn't lift easily, continue searing until it does.

Peruvian Ceviche

Bright citrus is great with fresh seafood—provided that the acid doesn't overwhelm its delicate flavor. We went fishing for more balance and found it in this regional version.

≥ BY ANDREW JANJIGIAN ≤

The bright, balanced dressing for our ceviche is packed with aromatics, herbs, and chiles. Its emulsified consistency coats every piece of fish.

In the summer, ceviche is one of my go-to dinners for three big reasons: It's easy and quick, it doesn't require turning on the stove or oven or even firing up the grill, and it's the only dish that truly allows the fresh, clean, delicate flavor of seafood to shine. Ceviche, of course, is the Latin American dish in which pieces of raw fish are "cooked" in an acidic marinade until the flesh firms and turns opaque.

Full disclosure: When I make ceviche at home, I don't normally use a recipe. I juice some limes, cut up the fish (usually a firm-fleshed white variety such as sea bass, snapper, or halibut—whatever is freshest at the market), and let the fish marinate in the lime juice until it just begins to turn opaque. Then I add minced garlic and chiles, chopped cilantro, some thinly sliced onion, creamy diced avocado, a glug of olive oil for some richness, and a generous pinch of salt. Some crunchy garnishes go in a bowl to be served alongside. When I started researching traditional recipes, I quickly realized how simplistic my understanding of ceviche was. Plenty of versions took an approach similar to mine, but the Peruvian recipes opened my eyes to a more sophisticated take.

A New Spin on Ceviche

Many Peruvian recipes call for blending the marinade ingredients—citrus juice, aromatics, and olive oil—before adding the seafood. But there's another component they often add to the marinade: fish. Some recipes call for a concentrated fish broth; others call for adding a small portion of fish before blending and straining. In both cases, the added seafood brings savory depth to the marinade, which is called *leche de tigre* ("tiger's milk"). This leche is sometimes poured over the the marinated fish before serving, like a sauce, or drunk as a beverage, either on its own or mixed into a cocktail (an alleged aphrodisiac).

With its creamy, rich consistency and balanced, nuanced flavor, the blended marinade is akin to an emulsified vinaigrette. Thanks to that emulsification, the silky marinade coats and clings to each piece of fish. (This was a sharp contrast to my usual unblended marinade, which always runs right off the fish, causing individual bites to feature too much sharp lime juice or an abundance of greasy oil.)

I began working on my version by slicing 1 pound of skinless red snapper into small pieces. To make the leche, I poured ½ cup of fresh lime juice into a blender along with two garlic cloves, ¼ cup of chopped cilantro, a couple of teaspoons of salt, and a tablespoon of olive oil. For a bit of heat, I added some *aji amarillo* paste, which is made from a fruity yellow pepper of the same name (see "Introducing Aji Amarillo Chile Paste" on page 28) and is traditional to many Peruvian ceviches (a seeded habanero chile can be substituted in a pinch). Finally, I added ⅓ cup of sliced snapper. After blending, I strained out any remaining solids.

The resulting leche had the creamy consistency I was aiming for, but the lime was so muted that I could barely taste it. Plus, blending the green cilantro with the yellow chile paste turned the leche an unappealing muddy brown. I made a new batch with ¾ cup of lime juice and no cilantro (I would add it as a garnish). This bright yellow leche had silky, rich body and bright, balanced flavor. It was time to figure out how long to "cook" my fish in this new marinade.

Firming Things Up

The acid in a ceviche marinade denatures (unravels) and coagulates (clumps together) proteins, giving the fish an opaque appearance and a slightly firm—yet still tender—texture (see "How Acid 'Cooks' Fish"). When fish is marinated in pure lime juice, it

▶ Andrew's Summertime Fave
A step-by-step video is available at CooksIllustrated.com/aug18

How Acid "Cooks" Fish

Acids denature and coagulate fish proteins, firming fish and turning it opaque just as hot cooking methods do. However, "cooking" with acid doesn't change the fish's taste—its clean, delicate flavor still shines. It also does not kill microbes, which underscores the importance of using the freshest seafood. Our *leche de tigre* is about three times less acidic than straight lime juice, so it affects the fish more slowly, giving us some breathing room in the marinating time. We marinated thin slices of fish in our leche to demonstrate how it affects the flesh over time.

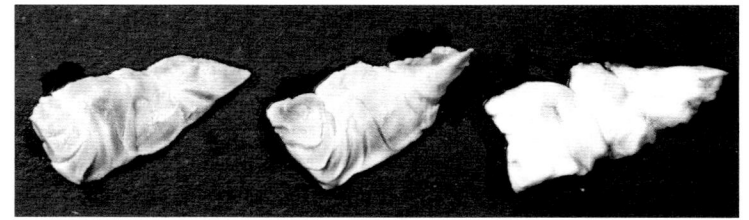

15 MINUTES Still too raw
30 MINUTES Just firm and opaque
90 MINUTES Dry and chalky

How to Buy the Freshest Fish

When making ceviche, using the freshest seafood possible is imperative for both flavor and food safety reasons. Here's what to look for:

➤ **CLEAN SMELL** The seafood (and the store or counter) should smell like the sea, not fishy or sour.

➤ **SHINY SURFACE** Fillets should look bright and shiny; whole fish should have bright, clear eyes.

➤ **FIRM TEXTURE** Fresh fish is firm. Ask your fishmonger to press the flesh with their finger; it should spring back.

➤ **ADVICE** Ask your fishmonger what's freshest that day, even if it's not what you originally had in mind. Ceviche works with many different varieties of fish.

Shrimp: The Starter Ceviche

Unlike with fish ceviches, many shrimp ceviches begin by lightly poaching the shellfish, making these versions a good entry point into the world of ceviche for the uninitiated. Shrimp proteins are slow to denature in acid as compared with fish (or scallops), so the quick poach firms the shrimp before they're marinated. We found that thawed frozen shrimp work just as well as fresh in this application, making it a great option when superfresh fish isn't available. Our version blends fresh tomato, jalapeño, and lime juice into the *leche de tigre*. After a 30-minute marinade, the poached shrimp are tossed with jícama, tomato, avocado, Vidalia onion, and cilantro. Our recipe for Peruvian Shrimp Ceviche with Tomato, Jícama, and Avocado is available for free for four months at CooksIllustrated.com/aug18.

turns opaque at the edges almost instantly and goes from tender to firm in minutes. In contrast, the leche's more tempered acidity affects the fish more slowly, providing a wider window for serving. For my snapper, I found 30 to 40 minutes to be the ideal marinating time. At around the 30-minute mark, it's just beginning to turn opaque and its texture is firm but easily yields as you bite into it. Those who prefer ceviche with a texture closer to that of fully cooked fish can marinate for 45 minutes to 1 hour, though beyond that I found the texture unpleasantly dry and chalky.

Salt First

Before cooking, we often season proteins, including fish, with salt and let them sit to season them throughout. Was this step necessary here, considering I had sliced the fish thin and exposed more surface area to the marinade? I tossed my next batch of sliced snapper with 1 teaspoon of kosher salt and refrigerated it while I made my leche. After a 30-minute soak, I tasted the presalted ceviche alongside an unsalted version (I still seasoned each batch before serving). The results were clear: Salting enhanced the flavor of the fish; it stood out against the other bold flavors in the ceviche. Further testing showed that a mere 10 minutes was all it took for the salt to have a noticeable effect on the small pieces of fish.

All that was left was sorting out the mix-ins: It's the layering of flavors and textures that makes a great ceviche. I liked the bright lime from the leche de tigre, but I thought it would be nice to bring in another citrus, so I added orange segments for sweet notes. Thinly sliced radishes added crisp texture and colorful contrast to the yellow leche and green cilantro. For salty, crunchy garnishes, I made a batch of popcorn (much to the delight of my colleagues) and set out a bowl of corn nuts. Both are traditional in Latin America.

Now that I've experienced this whole new world of elegant-yet-easy ceviches made with leche de tigre, I know what I'm making for dinner the next time it's too hot to cook.

PERUVIAN FISH CEVICHE WITH RADISHES AND ORANGE
SERVES 4 TO 6 AS A MAIN DISH OR 6 TO 8 AS AN APPETIZER

It is imperative that you use the freshest fish possible in this recipe. Do not use frozen fish. Sea bass, halibut, or grouper can be substituted for the snapper, if desired. For more information about cutting citrus segments, see page 29. *Aji amarillo* chile paste can be found in the Latin section of grocery stores (for more information, see page 28); if you can't find it, you can substitute 1 stemmed and seeded habanero chile. Serving the popcorn and corn nuts separately allows diners to customize their ceviche to suit their taste. Our recipes for Peruvian Scallop Ceviche with Cucumber and Grapefruit and Peruvian Shrimp Ceviche with Tomato, Jícama, and Avocado are available for free for four months at CooksIllustrated.com/aug18.

- 1 pound skinless red snapper fillets, ½ inch thick
- Kosher salt
- ¾ cup lime juice (6 limes)
- 3 tablespoons extra-virgin olive oil
- 1 tablespoon aji amarillo chile paste
- 2 garlic cloves, peeled
- 3 oranges
- 8 ounces radishes, trimmed, halved, and sliced thin
- ¼ cup coarsely chopped fresh cilantro
- 1 cup corn nuts
- 1 cup lightly salted popcorn

1. Using sharp knife, cut fish lengthwise into ½-inch-wide strips. Slice each strip crosswise ⅛ inch thick. Set aside ⅓ cup (2½ ounces) fish pieces. Toss remaining fish with 1 teaspoon salt and refrigerate for at least 10 minutes or up to 30 minutes.

2. Meanwhile, process reserved fish pieces, 2½ teaspoons salt, lime juice, 2 tablespoons oil, chile paste, and garlic in blender until smooth, 30 to 60 seconds. Strain mixture through fine-mesh strainer set over large bowl, pressing on solids to extract as much liquid as possible. Discard solids. (Sauce can be refrigerated for up to 24 hours. It will separate slightly; whisk to recombine before proceeding with recipe.)

3. Cut away peel and pith from oranges. Holding fruit over bowl, use paring knife to slice between membranes to release segments. Cut orange segments into ¼-inch pieces. Add oranges, salted fish, and radishes to bowl with sauce and toss to combine. Refrigerate for 30 to 40 minutes (for more-opaque fish, refrigerate for 45 minutes to 1 hour).

4. Add cilantro to ceviche and toss to combine. Portion ceviche into individual bowls and drizzle with remaining 1 tablespoon oil. Serve, passing corn nuts and popcorn separately.

Add Some Crunch (and Pop)

In Peru and Ecuador, where many different types of corn are grown, popcorn and corn nuts are often served alongside ceviche. Their salty crunch is the perfect complement to ceviche's bright, fresh flavors. Plantain chips (recipe on page 29) and tortilla chips are also popular accompaniments.

Mexican Corn Salad

Make this bright, creamy charred-corn salad without firing up the grill.

> BY LAN LAM <

If you're enjoying grilled corn only with butter and salt, you're missing out. Take just one bite of Mexican street corn, called *elote*, and you'll know why it has become wildly popular in the United States. A charred ear of corn is slathered with rich, tangy *crema*; coated with salty cotija cheese; sprinkled with chili powder; and finished with a squeeze of lime. This smoky, creamy, bright, salty ear has just one catch: It's messy to eat.

Some vendors offer elote in salad form (*esquites*), with charred kernels layered or tossed with the garnishes. You get the ideal ratio of flavors and textures in every bite but with the convenience of a fork. I wanted to find a way to make this flavor-packed side dish even when I'm not firing up the grill.

The broiler seemed a good place to start since its intense radiant heat is similar to that of a grill. I placed six ears of corn on a baking sheet and broiled them on the highest oven rack, rotating them every few minutes. Unfortunately, only the rows of kernels closest to the broiler browned; the rest turned dry and leathery. I thought that if I cut the kernels off the cob and spread them into an even layer, more of them might char, so I gave it a try. While more kernels browned, nearly all were overcooked. Because they

Handfuls of scallions and cilantro round out our salad.

were farther from the heating element, it had taken them much longer to develop any color.

It was time to try the stove. It seemed like cutting the kernels off the cob was still the way to go since it allows more kernels to come in contact with the heat. Plus, cut kernels release a starchy, sugary liquid that, in theory, would help with browning.

I grabbed a nonstick skillet and cooked the kernels in a little oil over high heat, without stirring them. The kernels touching the pan's surface charred beautifully and those in the middle were plump and perfectly cooked, but those on top remained raw and starchy. I was fine with some of the kernels not being charred so long as they were tender and plump, but what if I split the corn into two batches? This would put more kernels in contact with the hot skillet, and fewer kernels in the pan might lead to more even cooking.

I heated some oil in a fresh skillet, added half the kernels, and covered the skillet to trap steam. After 3 minutes, the corn on the bottom was perfectly charred and the rest was juicy and tender. After repeating the technique with the remaining kernels, I had plenty of charred corn to give my salad its signature flavor.

It was time to dress the dish. Mexican crema can be hard to find, but a combination of mayonnaise, sour cream, and lime juice produced a similar creamy tang and clung even better to the corn. To give my salad heat and bite, I stirred in some sliced serrano chile, chili powder, and garlic that I'd toasted in the empty skillet after cooking the corn. Finally, once the mixture had cooled, I tossed in cilantro, scallions, and some salty crumbled cotija cheese. The next time I'm craving my favorite way to eat corn, I can make a batch in less time than it takes to fire up the grill.

MEXICAN CORN SALAD (ESQUITES)
SERVES 6 TO 8

If desired, substitute plain Greek yogurt for the sour cream. We like serrano chiles here, but you can substitute a jalapeño chile that has been halved lengthwise and sliced into 1/8-inch-thick half-moons. Adjust the amount of chiles to suit your taste. If cotija cheese is unavailable, substitute feta cheese.

- 3 tablespoons lime juice, plus extra for seasoning (2 limes)
- 3 tablespoons sour cream
- 1 tablespoon mayonnaise
- 1–2 serrano chiles, stemmed and cut into 1/8-inch-thick rings
- Salt
- 2 tablespoons plus 1 teaspoon vegetable oil
- 6 ears corn, kernels cut from cobs (6 cups)
- 2 garlic cloves, minced
- 1/2 teaspoon chili powder
- 4 ounces cotija cheese, crumbled (1 cup)
- 3/4 cup coarsely chopped fresh cilantro
- 3 scallions, sliced thin

1. Combine lime juice, sour cream, mayonnaise, serrano(s), and 1/4 teaspoon salt in large bowl. Set aside.

2. Heat 1 tablespoon oil in 12-inch nonstick skillet over high heat until shimmering. Add half of corn and spread into even layer. Sprinkle with 1/4 teaspoon salt. Cover and cook, without stirring, until corn touching skillet is charred, about 3 minutes. Remove skillet from heat and let stand, covered, for 15 seconds, until any popping subsides. Transfer corn to bowl with sour cream mixture. Repeat with 1 tablespoon oil, 1/4 teaspoon salt, and remaining corn.

3. Return now-empty skillet to medium heat and add remaining 1 teaspoon oil, garlic, and chili powder. Cook, stirring constantly, until fragrant, about 30 seconds. Transfer garlic mixture to bowl with corn mixture and toss to combine. Let cool for at least 15 minutes.

4. Add cotija, cilantro, and scallions and toss to combine. Season salad with salt and up to 1 tablespoon extra lime juice to taste. Serve.

A Neat Way to Cut Corn

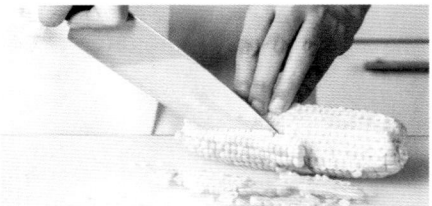

The most common method of cutting corn from the cob involves standing the corn up vertically, which causes the kernels to scatter. Here's an alternative that keeps the kernels more contained:
➤ Stand corn vertically and remove strip by slicing downward. Place corn horizontally on cut side.
➤ Use narrower front third of chef's knife to slice downward along cob and remove kernels. With less distance to fall, kernels don't scatter as far.

▶ Watch: Mexican Street Food
A step-by-step video is available at CooksIllustrated.com/aug18

Dark Chocolate Fudge Sauce

We wanted a pourable, easily reheated sauce with a dark chocolate soul.

≥ BY STEVE DUNN ≤

I recently questioned my colleagues about the hot fudge sauce they ate as kids, and their recollections were strikingly similar: It was more sweet than chocolaty and was so thick that it fell onto ice cream in globs. There are still plenty of sickly sweet, overly thick, barely chocolaty sauces out there, but our adult palates crave something less sugary, with darker chocolate and a luxurious, pourable consistency. Also, with the wisdom of age, we've learned that devouring an entire batch in one sitting isn't prudent, so an ideal sauce could be refrigerated and reheated multiple times.

Most fudge sauce recipes have a short ingredient list: bar chocolate and/or cocoa powder, sugar, and dairy. I planned on using a blend of cocoa powder and unsweetened chocolate so that I would have complete control over the amount of sugar. The former would add complexity, and the latter would contribute richness from its higher proportion of cocoa butter. I heated milk and sugar, whisked in the cocoa powder, poured this mixture over finely chopped chocolate, and then allowed the chocolate to melt so I could whisk the mixture to a saucy consistency.

It turned out that my starting ratio (½ cup cocoa powder to 2 ounces unsweetened chocolate) was too cocoa-heavy and produced a chalky texture. Dropping the cocoa to ⅓ cup and increasing the chocolate to 3 ounces provided enough additional cocoa butter to smooth the sauce. I evaluated sweeteners next, with confectioners' sugar, brown sugar, and corn syrup auditioning for the spot that granulated sugar currently held. Ultimately, I stuck with granulated sugar since we didn't notice a huge difference and it was the simplest choice.

I now had an easy-to-make sauce that delivered deep flavor with just enough sweetness, and it was nicely emulsified. But it wasn't thick enough. Swirling a few knobs of butter into a savory pan sauce thickens it. Would the same principle apply here? Indeed, incorporating 4 tablespoons of cold butter into the fudge sauce gave it body (and added a touch of richness). Here's how it works: Fudge sauce is an emulsion, a combination of two liquids—fat and water—that don't ordinarily mix. (In this instance, the liquids are cocoa butter and the water in milk.) Whisking transforms the melted cocoa butter into tiny droplets of fat, which are dispersed throughout the water to form an emulsion. Emulsifying proteins from the milk help keep it all stable. Butter made the sauce even thicker by dispersing even more fat droplets throughout the sauce. The fat in the butter also added shine: The more liquid fat there is in an emulsion, the glossier its surface will be.

After stirring in vanilla extract and a sprinkling of salt to help the chocolate flavor pop, I spooned the sauce over ice cream. It had just the right amount of flow, thickened slightly as it cooled but didn't seize or harden, and tasted like a molten dark chocolate bar.

Finally—and crucially—I found that the emulsion was sustained when I refrigerated and then gently reheated the sauce. It was important not to exceed 110 degrees, a little above body temperature, lest the sauce break and become greasy on top.

We celebrated the achievement late one afternoon in the test kitchen with a sundae bar to satisfy our adult tastes—and our inner children.

Our sauce can be refrigerated for up to one month and reheated whenever a craving strikes.

DARK CHOCOLATE FUDGE SAUCE
MAKES 2 CUPS

We like to serve this sauce over ice cream, but it can also be drizzled over fresh fruit. We prefer to use Dutch-processed cocoa powder here (our favorite is from Droste), but other cocoa powders will work. Our favorite unsweetened chocolate is Hershey's Unsweetened Chocolate Baking Bar. Our recipes for Dark Chocolate–Peanut Butter Fudge Sauce and Mexican Dark Chocolate Fudge Sauce are available for free for four months at CooksIllustrated.com/aug18.

- 1¼ cups (8¾ ounces) sugar
- ⅔ cup whole or 2 percent low-fat milk
- ¼ teaspoon salt
- ⅓ cup (1 ounce) unsweetened cocoa powder, sifted
- 3 ounces unsweetened chocolate, chopped fine
- 4 tablespoons unsalted butter, cut into 8 pieces and chilled
- 1 teaspoon vanilla extract

1. Heat sugar, milk, and salt in medium saucepan over medium-low heat, whisking gently, until sugar has dissolved and liquid starts to bubble around edges of saucepan, 5 to 6 minutes. Reduce heat to low, add cocoa, and whisk until smooth.

2. Remove saucepan from heat, stir in chocolate, and let stand for 3 minutes. Whisk sauce until smooth and chocolate is fully melted. Add butter and whisk until fully incorporated and sauce thickens slightly. Whisk in vanilla and serve. (Sauce can be refrigerated for up to 1 month. Gently reheat sauce in microwave [do not let it exceed 110 degrees], stirring every 10 seconds, until just warmed and pourable.)

DARK CHOCOLATE–ORANGE FUDGE SAUCE

Bring milk and 8 (3-inch) strips orange zest to simmer in medium saucepan over medium heat. Remove saucepan from heat, cover, and let stand for 15 minutes. Strain milk mixture through fine-mesh strainer into bowl, pressing on zest to extract liquid; discard zest. Return milk to saucepan and proceed with recipe, reducing cooking time to 3 to 4 minutes.

▶ **Look: Deep, Dark Chocolate**
A step-by-step video is available at CooksIllustrated.com/aug18

Butter Makes It Better
Butter plays three roles in our Dark Chocolate Fudge Sauce:
➤ Helps emulsify the ingredients
➤ Thickens the sauce by dispersing fat droplets throughout
➤ Adds attractive, glossy shine

Peach Tarte Tatin

Yes, you can make a juicy, summery, peach-crowned version of the classic upside-down caramelized apple tart. No, you can't simply substitute peaches for apples.

⋺ BY ANDREA GEARY ⋲

If you've got peaches, you should make a peach tarte Tatin. You say your peaches aren't quite ripe? You're allergic to long ingredient lists? You always fret that you've added the wrong amount of thickener to fruit pie filling, and fluting a fancy pie crust edge makes you feel graceless and inept? Excellent: This is the dessert for you.

But first a quick review of how the original apple version of tarte Tatin is made. You start on the stovetop, cooking a skillet full of apple chunks with butter and sugar. There's no thickener required because apples give off just a small amount of moisture when they're cooked, and it evaporates during this step. When the fruit is lacquered with a dark caramel, you place a disk of raw puff pastry or pie dough on top, transfer the skillet to a hot oven, and bake until the pastry is browned and crisp and gently molded around the fruit.

Here comes the plot twist: Rather than scoop the dessert straight from the skillet, you flip the whole thing onto a platter, revealing the apples in all their burnished, buttery splendor. The crust is now on the bottom, offering an intriguing dual personality: flaky and crisp on one side, soft and velveted with caramelized fruit juices on the other.

Despite its numerous charms, apple tarte Tatin isn't really a summer dessert, so I was eager to try a few of the many recipes I found in which peaches were substituted for the apples. They followed the same

For a glossy finish, brush some of the reduced peach juice (enhanced with a touch of bourbon) onto the tart before serving.

procedure: caramelize the peaches, cover with pastry (I opted for convenient store-bought puff), bake, and flip. But each one turned out too sweet, mushy, and/or flooded with watery juice. Simply swapping peaches for apples wasn't going to cut it.

Firm Peaches Are Preferable

This tart is the rare instance where perfectly ripe fruit isn't a must. In fact, we prefer firm, barely ripe peaches for the recipe because they don't require blanching to peel, and they taste just as good in the tart.

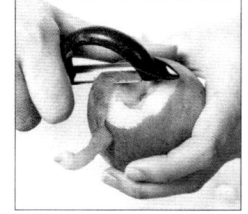

▶ **Andrea Shows You How**
A step-by-step video is available at CooksIllustrated.com/aug18

Juicy Fruit

I had an idea about how to deal with the excess juice, but first I got the caramelization process underway. Most recipes call for melting the butter and sugar in a skillet before arranging the peaches on top—a nasty burn waiting to happen. I kept things safe by smearing a cold skillet with 3 tablespoons of softened butter and then sprinkling it with ½ cup of sugar (and a pinch of salt). Next, hoping that a thickener might bind up the extra liquid, I tossed 2 pounds of peeled, pitted, and quartered peaches with cornstarch. I spiraled the chunks snugly on top of the sugar and placed the skillet over high heat. Ten minutes later, the butter, sugar, and peach juice had combined to make a rich caramel. I popped the puff pastry disk on top and placed the skillet in a 400-degree oven. Sadly, the cornstarch produced a gelled texture instead of the lightly sticky peaches I envisioned.

But without a thickener, the watery failures continued. Steam vents cut into the puff pastry proved ineffective. Withholding the pastry until later in the baking process allowed for some evaporation—but not enough. As each tart emerged from the oven, I quantified my failure by placing an inverted plate on top of the pastry and tilting the skillet over a liquid measuring cup. Each time almost a full cup of liquid poured out.

Instead of thickening the liquid, how about getting rid of it before the peaches went into the oven? I tossed the peaches with 1 cup of sugar and let them sit while the sugar pulled juice out via osmosis. It seemed promising: After 45 minutes, the peaches released ¾ cup of liquid, which I reserved. I proceeded with the caramelizing and baking, and while the tart was in the oven, I reduced the juice to a syrup, which I planned to brush onto the baked tart.

To my dismay, the postbake "tilt and drain" test still yielded almost ¾ cup of juice. Belatedly, I realized that much of what I had drained off before baking had been liquefied sugar, and indeed, after I brushed the syrupy reduction onto the tart, it was far too sweet. I considered halving the macerating sugar, but that would mean halving the osmotic force exerted on the peaches, so even less liquid would be released. It didn't seem worthwhile.

Full Tilt

It occurred to me that my tilting and draining move might be good for something beyond measuring my failures: I decided to skip macerating and simply bake the tart, drain off the accumulated juice, and then reduce the liquid and brush it onto the peaches.

Having taken no preemptive measures to decrease the excess liquid, I knew this tart would be a real slosh-fest when it came out of the oven. So, with safety in mind, I transferred it to a wire rack to cool for 20 minutes before draining the juice.

After I'd drained the juice, the tart, for once, was not drowning. And when brushed with the reduced juice, the peaches were pretty much perfect: soft but not too soft, with a lovely balance of sweetness and caramel-y bitterness.

SCIENCE Why Peaches Shed More Juice Than Apples

Peaches contain a bit more water than apples (88 percent and 84 percent, respectively), but that's not why peaches shed so much more juice during cooking. It's because peaches have very little pectin, while apples have it in abundance. When apples are cooked, they release water, but the pectin in their cell walls absorbs most of it instead of allowing it to leak out. Because peaches have far less pectin, they don't retain their juice nearly as well.

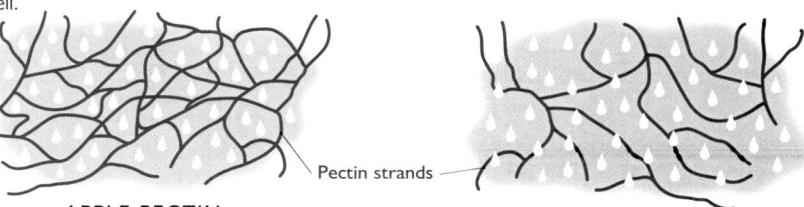

APPLE PECTIN
Abundant pectin traps juice to form a gel that makes it hard for juice to leak out.

PEACH PECTIN
Less pectin means that more juice can leak out.

Earning My Crust

Now that I had sorted out the juice problem, I could no longer ignore the fact that, except at the very edges, the underside of the puff pastry was kind of raw. So for my next test, I parbaked the pastry on a baking sheet while I caramelized the peaches and then married the two for a final bake.

But they remained very separate. The crust stayed awkwardly flat instead of molding itself around the peaches, and I never got that velvety interface where the fruit and crust met. And though the puff pastry expanded majestically in the oven, it collapsed under the fruit when I inverted the tart, so even though it was fully baked, it seemed dense and tough.

Given the special requirements of a peach Tatin, pie dough was a better option. I simply rolled out a disk of dough, folded the edge underneath itself to form a bit of a rim to contain the peaches, cut a few vents, and placed the pastry on top of the caramelized fruit. I brushed the dough with water and sprinkled it with sugar, so it would become extra crunchy when baked. As the tart baked, the pie crust absorbed more steam than the less-porous puff pastry had and did it without getting soggy, so there was a little less juice to drain.

Sensing that I was nearing the end of my quest, I celebrated by adding a bit of bourbon—for a little more complexity—to the reducing juice before brushing the mixture over the peaches. Finally, I whipped some lightly sweetened cream to serve alongside. Now that I have a summery peach version, I can make tarte Tatin all year round.

PEACH TARTE TATIN
SERVES 8

We recommend using our Foolproof All-Butter Dough for Single-Crust Pie for this recipe (available for free for four months at CooksIllustrated.com/aug18). Chill the dough for at least 1 hour before rolling it. We like using firm peaches in this recipe because they are easier to peel and retain their shape when cooked; yellow peaches are also preferable to white peaches. For instructions on peeling and pitting peaches, see page 31. When pouring off the liquid in step 4, the peaches may shift in the skillet; shaking the skillet will help redistribute them. Serve the tart with lightly sweetened whipped cream, if desired.

- 1 recipe single-crust pie dough, chilled
- 3 tablespoons unsalted butter, softened
- ½ cup (3½ ounces) plus 2 tablespoons sugar
- ¼ teaspoon salt
- 2 pounds ripe but firm peaches, peeled, pitted, and quartered
- 1 tablespoon bourbon (optional)

1. Invert rimmed baking sheet and place sheet of parchment paper or waxed paper on top. Roll dough into 10-inch circle on lightly floured counter. Loosely roll dough around rolling pin and gently unroll it onto prepared sheet. Working around circumference, fold ½ inch of dough under itself and pinch to create 9-inch round with raised rim. Cut three 2-inch slits in center of dough and refrigerate until needed.

2. Adjust oven rack to middle position and heat oven to 400 degrees. Smear butter over bottom of 10-inch ovensafe skillet. Sprinkle ½ cup sugar over butter and shake skillet to distribute sugar in even layer. Sprinkle salt over sugar. Arrange peaches in circular pattern around edge of skillet, nestling fruit snugly. Tuck remaining peaches into center, squeezing in as much fruit as possible (it is not necessary to maintain circular pattern in center).

3. Place skillet over high heat and cook, without stirring fruit, until juice is released and turns from pink to deep amber, 8 to 12 minutes. (If necessary, adjust skillet's placement on burner to even out hot spots and encourage even browning.) Remove skillet from heat. Carefully slide prepared dough over fruit, making sure dough is centered and does not touch edge of skillet. Brush dough lightly with water and sprinkle with remaining 2 tablespoons sugar. Bake until crust is very well browned, 30 to 35 minutes. Transfer skillet to wire rack set in rimmed baking sheet and let cool for 20 minutes.

4. Place inverted plate on top of crust. With 1 hand firmly securing plate, carefully tip skillet over bowl to drain juice (skillet handle may still be hot). When all juice has been transferred to bowl, return skillet to wire rack, remove plate, and shake skillet firmly to redistribute peaches. Carefully invert tart onto plate, then slide tart onto wire rack. (If peaches have shifted during unmolding, gently nudge them back into place with spoon.)

5. Pour juice into now-empty skillet (handle may be hot). Stir in bourbon, if using, and cook over high heat, stirring constantly, until mixture is dark and thick and starting to smoke, 2 to 3 minutes. Return mixture to bowl and let cool until mixture is consistency of honey, 2 to 3 minutes. Brush mixture over peaches. Let tart cool for at least 20 minutes. Cut into wedges and serve.

Put Your Peach Juice to Work

Because peaches throw off so much liquid during cooking, we had to find ways to make sure our tart didn't end up awash in it (as in the failed test above). At the same time, we put that excess juice to good use.

1. USE PIE DOUGH, NOT PUFF PASTRY Pie dough absorbs more steam than less-porous puff pastry, so the juice ends up a bit thicker.

2. DRAIN AND RESERVE JUICE Once the tart is baked, get rid of excess liquid by placing an inverted plate on the crust and draining off juice.

3. REDUCE JUICE INTO GLAZE Combine the peach juice with bourbon and reduce the mixture into a thick, flavorful glaze to brush onto the peaches.

Tasting Fresh Mozzarella

What makes the best fresh mozzarella? It's all about balance.

> BY LAUREN SAVOIE <

Mozzarella comes in many forms, including string cheese, dense blocks for shredding, and larger balls of "fresh" high-moisture mozzarella. You can also make it at home with a few specialty ingredients in less than an hour. According to the traditional method, milk, rennet, and an acid are heated until the curds separate from the whey. The curds are strained, salted, and plunged into hot water to make them flexible. Once removed from the water, they are stretched until they become smooth and elastic. Finally, the cheese is shaped into a block or a ball and cooled, and then it's ready to eat.

What Exactly Is "Fresh" Mozzarella?

For centuries, fresh mozzarella has been made in Italy using buffalo's milk. But since buffalo mozzarella is not aged and is usually produced with unpasteurized milk, its shelf life is only four to five days, making the cheese difficult to export to the United States.

While there are a few buffalo mozzarella producers in the United States, most domestic "fresh" mozzarella is made from pasteurized cow's milk. The term "fresh mozzarella" is not recognized by the U.S. Food and Drug Administration, but cheesemakers use it to denote a style of mozzarella that is higher in moisture and is eaten raw ("fresh") rather than cooked (with a few exceptions, such as pizza margherita).

We tasted the cheeses in three different applications, including our Cherry Tomato Caprese Salad.

With this in mind, we set out to find our favorite fresh mozzarella, focusing on cheeses labeled "fresh" and sold in shrink-wrapped balls or packed in brine. We rounded up eight nationally available products priced from $0.32 to $1.00 per ounce and tasted them plain, in our recipe for Cherry Tomato Caprese Salad, and melted onto miniature toasts. We didn't notice much difference in the cheeses when they were melted; however, flavor and texture differences were apparent in the plain and Caprese salad tastings.

Sodium played a big part in how we perceived flavor. The cheeses' sodium levels ranged from 50 to 110 milligrams per 1-ounce serving, and tasters found cheeses at the low end of the spectrum bland and boring. Mozzarellas at the higher end of the sodium spectrum fared a bit better, but a few tasters found them overly salty. We preferred products with a moderate amount of sodium (85 to 95 milligrams per serving); they were savory and flavorful without being overwhelmingly salty.

Zeroing in on differences in the tanginess of the cheeses took a bit more digging. During the mozzarella-making process, an acid is added to help the curds stretch. This acid can be vinegar, cheese culture (which causes natural bacteria to form and turn milk sugars into lactic acid), lactic acid, and/or citric acid. We looked at product labels and noticed a trend: Those with lactic or citric acid were at the bottom of our rankings, and those at the top used vinegar or cheese culture.

Mark Johnson, assistant director of the Wisconsin Center for Dairy Research at the University of Wisconsin–Madison, told us that citric acid is more effective at stretching the mozzarella, so less acid can be used. This means that the cheese ends up with a higher pH (it is less acidic) and tastes sweeter and not at all tangy. By contrast, more vinegar or cheese culture is needed to acidify mozzarella, so cheeses produced this way have a lower pH (they're more acidic) and a characteristic tang.

Lab tests confirmed this. The pH of the cheeses in our lineup ranged from 5.8 to 6.2, and we noticed that these slight variations in acidity can translate into big flavor differences. Tasters found the two highest-pH cheeses, which were acidified with lactic or citric acid, too bland and sweet; they found the two lowest-pH cheeses, which were acidified with vinegar or cheese culture, a bit too tart. Our favorite mozzarellas, which had a moderate pH (about 6.0) and were acidified with vinegar or cheese culture, were subtly tangy. These products may have been made using slightly less vinegar or cheese culture than the lower-pH cheeses, though other factors can influence pH, including naturally occurring bacteria, the cows' diet, and the original fat and moisture content of the milk.

Acid and Moisture Affect Texture

Variations in pH can also affect texture. Johnson explained that cheese is a tightly bound matrix of protein (called casein) and fat, and acid helps break down this tough protein. In general, this means that mozzarellas with a higher pH (less acidic) are relatively firm. Again, this tracked with our results; tasters found the higher-pH cheeses a bit dense and noted that one lower-pH cheese was too soft and slightly weepy. Our favorite products were soft, plush, and tender.

The two top-rated cheeses also had higher moisture content, more than 60 percent, that resulted in a melt-in-your-mouth creaminess when tasted uncooked. The driest product (with about 49 percent moisture) was dense and tough, similar to block cheese for grating. However, texture differences were less noticeable when we melted the cheeses; all were perfectly milky, stretchy, and chewy.

A Better Mozzarella

Our favorite cheese was BelGioioso Fresh Mozzarella ($7.99 for 8 ounces, in a vacuum-sealed ball), which had moderate tang, moderate sodium, and high moisture. These attributes combined to create a cheese with a savory, buttery richness; a tender curd; and clean, milky flavor.

Tracking pH and Sodium Levels

We found that cheeses with moderate amounts of sodium were full-flavored and savory. We also noticed a correlation between pH and flavor: Those cheeses that fell in the middle of our lineup's pH range were subtly tangy and slightly sweet. Tasters noted that our favorite cheese, with a pH of 6.0 and 85 milligrams of sodium per serving, had "balanced tang" and was "well seasoned."

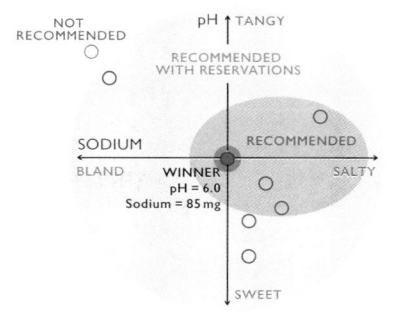

TASTING FRESH MOZZARELLA

Twenty-one America's Test Kitchen staffers sampled eight fresh mozzarellas plain (twice, to control for variability), in our recipe for Cherry Tomato Caprese Salad, and melted onto miniature toasts. We sent samples of each to an independent lab to have pH, moisture, fat, and protein levels calculated. Sodium level and type of acid were taken from ingredient labels. Sodium levels were standardized for comparison, using a serving size of 1 ounce. Products appear below in order of preference.

RECOMMENDED

BELGIOIOSO Fresh Mozzarella

PRICE: $7.99 for 8 oz ($1.00 per oz)
PACKAGE: Shrink-wrapped
INGREDIENTS: Pasteurized milk, vinegar, enzymes, salt
SODIUM: 85 mg
TYPE OF ACID: Vinegar
pH: 6.0
MOISTURE: 60.3%

COMMENTS: This "plush" mozzarella was "pillowy" and "tender," with a "melt-in-your-mouth" richness that tasters loved. It had a moderate amount of sodium and "balanced tang" as well as a flavor that was "buttery," "creamy," and "fresh." Overall, it's a "well-seasoned," "luscious" mozzarella.

LIONI Fresh Mozzarella

PRICE: $4.99 for 8 oz ($0.62 per oz)
PACKAGE: Shrink-wrapped
INGREDIENTS: Pasteurized whole milk, starter, cheese cultures, vegetable rennet, salt
SODIUM: 95 mg
TYPE OF ACID: Cheese culture
pH: 5.9
MOISTURE: 61.2%

COMMENTS: An all-around "balanced" cheese, this mozzarella was "tender but not too squishy" and "firm but not too dry." It had "the perfect amount of salt," and tasters also picked up on "grassy" notes of "cultured" milk (it uses cheese culture to acidify the curds). Its texture was "springy" and "soft," and we loved its "luxurious," "buttery" richness.

FRIGO Fresh Mozzarella Cheese

PRICE: $3.99 for 8 oz ($0.50 per oz)
PACKAGE: Shrink-wrapped
INGREDIENTS: Pasteurized milk, cheese cultures, salt, enzymes
SODIUM: 110 mg
TYPE OF ACID: Cheese culture
pH: 6.1
MOISTURE: 55.9%

COMMENTS: This "bold" mozzarella had plenty of sodium; most tasters found it "balanced," but a few thought it was "overseasoned." Its texture was "springy," "bouncy," and "smooth," and it had a "mild," "sweet" milkiness that contrasted with its more "savory" notes.

GALBANI Fresh Mozzarella

PRICE: $4.59 for 8 oz ($0.57 per oz)
PACKAGE: Shrink-wrapped
INGREDIENTS: Pasteurized milk, vinegar, salt, enzymes
SODIUM: 100 mg
TYPE OF ACID: Vinegar
pH: 5.9
MOISTURE: 57.9%

COMMENTS: This mozzarella was "soft," "moist," and "chewy," with "tangy vinegar notes" and a "buttery dairy flavor." Its "shaggy," almost "grainy" texture reminded a few tasters of "hand-pulled mozz." Though it was "a bit too salty and tangy" for some tasters, most liked this "fresh," "complex" cheese.

RECOMMENDED WITH RESERVATIONS

BOAR'S HEAD Fresh Mozzarella Cheese

PRICE: $4.99 for 8 oz ($0.62 per oz)
PACKAGE: Shrink-wrapped
INGREDIENTS: Pasteurized milk, vinegar, sea salt, rennet
SODIUM: 90 mg
TYPE OF ACID: Vinegar
pH: 5.8
MOISTURE: 58.3%

COMMENTS: This cheese, which was more "yellow" than the stark white we're used to with mozzarella, had a "buttery" and "fairly salty" flavor. Tasters were split on its texture, which was "soft" and "almost spreadable" when uncooked. While this cheese would be fine for a margherita pizza, it was a little atypical for a Caprese salad or for serving plain because of its softer texture.

CALABRO Fior Di Latte Ovolini

PRICE: $4.99 for 8 oz ($0.62 per oz)
PACKAGE: Brine
INGREDIENTS: Pasteurized milk, starter, rennet, salt
SODIUM: 90 mg
TYPE OF ACID: Cheese culture
pH: 5.8
MOISTURE: 59.5%

COMMENTS: One of two brine-packed cheeses in our lineup, this mozzarella was "moist" and "tender," with "vegetal," "fresh dairy" notes. Its interior was "soft" and "creamy" but a bit "loose," almost like "cottage cheese," likely because of its lower pH. This also meant that the cheese was more acidic, and many tasters noted "a hint of sourness," which they were divided on.

CRAVE BROTHERS Farmstead Classics Fresh Mozzarella Cheese

PRICE: $5.99 for 16 oz ($0.37 per oz)
PACKAGE: Shrink-wrapped
INGREDIENTS: Pasteurized milk, lactic/citric acid, salt, enzymes
SODIUM: 55 mg
TYPE OF ACID: Lactic and citric acids
pH: 6.2
MOISTURE: 48.8%

COMMENTS: With the lowest moisture content of any cheese in our lineup, this mozzarella was "firm" and "chewy"—more like low-moisture shredding mozzarella than fresh. Tasters also thought it was "a bit bland" and "slightly sweet" from its low levels of salt and acid. Still, many tasters applauded this cheese's subtle "fresh," "milky" flavors.

NOT RECOMMENDED

DI STEFANO Mozzarella Cheese

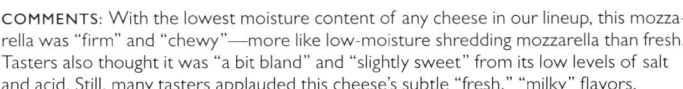

PRICE: $2.59 for 8 oz ($0.32 per oz)
PACKAGE: Brine
INGREDIENTS: Pasteurized milk, salt, lactic acid, culture rennet
SODIUM: 50 mg
TYPE OF ACID: Lactic acid and cheese culture
pH: 6.2
MOISTURE: 61.8%

COMMENTS: This mozzarella was "bland" and "rubbery," likely because of its low amount of sodium and high pH. Its "dense" yet "watery" and "gritty" texture confused tasters, with a few comparing it to a "wet sponge." In Caprese salad, it was "weepy" and "flavorless," disappearing among the stronger flavors of the tomatoes and basil.

Testing Digital Thermometers

We've recommended a Thermapen for more than a decade, but there's new competition. Is it still the best option?

≥ BY HANNAH CROWLEY ≤

If you cook or bake regularly, you should have a food thermometer. A good thermometer takes the guesswork out of cooking, telling you exactly what's going on inside your food. The old dial-faced ones are slow and imprecise: Digital is the only way to go.

We've highly recommended the ThermoWorks Thermapen Mk4 ($99.00) for years. But recently, competition has emerged, and many of the new models are less expensive. Could any top our old favorite? To find out, we gathered 11 digital thermometers priced from $11.95 to $99.95, including the Mk4 and the ThermoWorks ThermoPop ($29.00), our top-rated inexpensive model, and put them all through a series of tests to examine accuracy, speed, comfort, visibility, ease of use, and durability.

Accuracy and Speed Are Paramount

Our first tests were focused on accuracy: We used each thermometer to read the temperatures of a 32-degree ice bath, 212-degree boiling water, and a 125-degree *sous vide* water bath, repeating the first two tests three times and the third test 10 times. The least accurate models were off by about 2 degrees—not enough to ruin a dish but not exactly confidence-inspiring. Our top-rated thermometers were within 1 degree of accuracy every time. We also preferred those that gave us readings without decimal points, which we found distracting; it doesn't matter if your steak is cooked to 125 or 125.2 degrees.

Speed was crucial, too. The thermometers took, on average, from 2 seconds to just under 12 seconds to provide a reading. Twelve seconds may not seem long, but when our hands were hovering over a steaming pot of boiling water, it felt like an eternity. The best models read in just 2 to 3 seconds.

All the thermometers we tested have two basic parts: a metal probe that sticks into the food and a handle that houses the electronics and any controls. The size and design of both determined how comfortable and easy to use the thermometers were. Overall, we preferred models with big handles and long probes that opened like a switchblade (no separate covers to keep track of). A probe that measured at least 4 inches long was essential for reaching the center of a large roast or steak, and it kept our hands farther away from the heat.

As for the handles, the most comfortable ones were long and broad. This meant there was more room for us to grip the thermometer multiple ways with our full hand, like a handshake, which felt more secure than

The best thermometer gave us a reading in 2.2 seconds.

the pinch grip we had to use with smaller handles. We awarded more points to models with screens located near the probe. This meant there was more room on the back end of the handle to grip the thermometer without obscuring the display. We also liked models with minimal buttons.

Extra Features Made All the Difference

Most of the thermometers boasted extra features, but not all were created equal. For example, we found minimum and maximum buttons superfluous. (You don't need the thermometer to tell you the temperature range over the span of a few seconds if you're standing there looking at it.) However, we appreciated digital displays that rotate as you move the thermometer; this is great for lefties and anyone who needs to adjust their grip during use so that they don't have to read the temperature upside down. Some models rotated the digits two ways, flipping them 180 degrees; others rotated four ways so the digits could face all sides of the screen.

We also liked backlights, which were useful for grilling at night and reaching into dark ovens. Six models had them, but the Mk4 is the only one that turned on automatically in low light. (The OXO model has a black screen with white digits, making it easy to read even in the dark.) Another feature we valued was sleep mode, in which thermometers turn off when not in use. Even better was a sleep mode with an auto wake-up feature that turns the thermometer on when it's moved (if the probe is open).

After more than 50 hours of testing, we found a few decent models. But only one could hold a candle to the Mk4 and do so with a smaller price tag: The Lavatools Javelin Pro DUO ($49.99) is fast and accurate, with a big, clear display; a motion-activated backlight; a sleep mode with auto wake-up; and a 180-degree rotating display. It wasn't quite as comfortable as the Mk4, and its single button had three functions (hold, minimum, maximum), which testers found a bit confusing. Priced $50.00 less than the Mk4, it's a good deal; we're naming it our favorite midprice thermometer. The ThermoWorks Thermopop ($29.00), a very basic, fast, and accurate model, is again our winning inexpensive option. But in the end, the ThermoWorks Thermapen Mk4 ($99.00) is still the best. It's quick, precise, and intuitive as well as calibratable and waterproof, making it a worthwhile investment for any home cook.

TECHNIQUE | KEEPING YOUR THERMOMETER IN TIP-TOP SHAPE

The ThermoWorks Thermapen Mk4 ($99.00) is an expensive thermometer, so we like that it comes with a two-year warranty. You can protect your investment by cleaning it carefully and protecting it from prolonged exposure to heat.

Careful Cleaning: Spray an antibacterial cleaning solution onto a cloth or a paper towel and wipe the body and probe clean. Avoid cleaning wipes or solutions that contain isopropyl alcohol, which can damage the screen. Because the Mk4 is waterproof, you can also clean it under running water with soap, but avoid rotating the probe while doing so because it can damage the electronics.

YES, IT MELTS

Mind the Heat: Common resting places for kitchen thermometers, such as the space between the burners on a stove, can get hot enough to melt a thermometer; even prolonged periods of direct sunlight can cause damage. The manufacturer's rule of thumb is this: If it's too hot for your hands, it's too hot for your thermometer (and mind the sun).

TESTING DIGITAL THERMOMETERS

We tested 11 digital thermometers priced from $11.95 to $99.95. We ran a series of accuracy and speed tests and evaluated each model's comfort, ease of use, and durability while making caramel, roasted beef, seared steaks, and grilled chicken. We asked a series of testers to evaluate each thermometer's comfort and usability. Temperature ranges were reported by manufacturers; we calculated the average margin of error from all three accuracy tests. All thermometers were purchased online, and the top 10 appear below from left to right in order of preference.

 ThermoWorks Thermapen Mk4
 OXO Good Grips Thermocouple Thermometer
 Lavatools Javelin PRO Duo
 ThermoWorks ThermoPop
Lavatools Javelin
Polder Stable-Read Instant Read Digital Thermometer
 Maverick Rain Drop Waterproof Digital Thermometer
 Taylor Rotating Display Thermometer
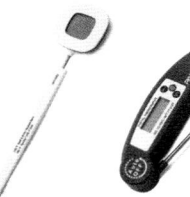 Palermo Instant Read Meat Thermometer
 EatSmart Precision Pro Digital Food Thermometer

ACCURACY:
We evaluated accuracy by taking the temperatures of a 32-degree ice bath, a 125-degree *sous vide* water bath, and 212-degree boiling water; models that were within 1 degree of accuracy at each temperature rated highest.

SPEED:
We timed how long it took for each thermometer to read temperature in the accuracy tests; those that read in 6 seconds or less rated highest.

EASE OF USE:
We rated how easy and comfortable each model was to use. We preferred those with spacious, grippy handles; long probes; and minimal buttons. Models with automatic wake-up, easy-to-read displays, and a single step for turning on and off also rated highest.

DURABILITY:
We monitored the thermometers throughout testing for both functional and cosmetic damage; those that emerged looking and operating like new rated highest.

▶ Hannah Tests the Thermometers
A free video is available at CooksIllustrated.com/aug18

HIGHLY RECOMMENDED

THERMOWORKS Thermapen Mk4
MODEL: THS-234-457 (blue) PRICE: $99.00
AVERAGE READ TIME: 2.2 sec
RANGE: -58°F to 572°F PROBE LENGTH: 4.3 in

ACCURACY: ★★★
SPEED: ★★★
EASE OF USE: ★★★
DURABILITY: ★★★

TESTERS' COMMENTS
Our old winner is still the best. It's dead accurate, fast, and comfortable, with a long handle that allows for multiple grips. The automatic backlight was useful for low light, and the rotating screen is handy for lefties and righties alike. It also comes with an auto wake-up function and is waterproof and calibratable.

RECOMMENDED

OXO Good Grips Thermocouple Thermometer
MODEL: 11204300 PRICE: $99.95
AVERAGE READ TIME: 3.85 sec
RANGE: -58°F to 572°F PROBE LENGTH: 4.25 in

ACCURACY: ★★★
SPEED: ★★★
EASE OF USE: ★★½
DURABILITY: ★★★

This newcomer had two unique features that we really liked: Its probe opened 225 degrees (instead of 180 degrees), enhancing viewability, and its display had white digits on a black screen, negating the need for a backlight. The downsides? There's no auto wake-up feature, the probe is a bit stiff, and the handle was too slick.

LAVATOOLS Javelin PRO Duo *BEST MIDPRICE OPTION*
MODEL: PX1D PRICE: $49.99
AVERAGE READ TIME: 3 sec
RANGE: -40°F to 482°F PROBE LENGTH: 4.35 in

ACCURACY: ★★★
SPEED: ★★★
EASE OF USE: ★★½
DURABILITY: ★★★

This fast, accurate thermometer had a large handle that kept us safely away from the heat, though it was slightly slick and a bit small. We appreciated its big, clear display; long probe; and easy operation. Its single button has three functions, which we sometimes found confusing, and it wasn't perfectly responsive.

THERMOWORKS ThermoPop *BEST LOW-PRICE OPTION*
MODEL: TX-3100-PK PRICE: $29.00
AVERAGE READ TIME: 3 sec
RANGE: -58°F to 572°F PROBE LENGTH: 4.5 in

ACCURACY: ★★★
SPEED: ★★★
EASE OF USE: ★★
DURABILITY: ★★★

Compared with fancier models, our former inexpensive winner felt like driving a standard car. The display rotates and has a backlight, but you have to press a button for both functions. It makes the best of its small lollipop-shaped head with a grippy, ergonomic design.

RECOMMENDED WITH RESERVATIONS

LAVATOOLS Javelin
MODEL: PT12 PRICE: $24.99
AVERAGE READ TIME: 3.9 sec
RANGE: -40°F to 482°F PROBE LENGTH: 2.8 in

ACCURACY: ★★★
SPEED: ★★★
EASE OF USE: ★½
DURABILITY: ★★★

This thermometer was intuitive, fast, and accurate, but its smaller size was a severe limitation. At 2.8 inches long, its probe couldn't reach the center of a large roast and, combined with its small handle, it sometimes put our hands dangerously close to the heat. It also lacked a backlight and a rotating screen.

NOT RECOMMENDED

POLDER Stable-Read Instant Read Digital Thermometer
MODEL: THM-389-90
PRICE: $15.99
AVERAGE READ TIME: 8.7 sec
RANGE: -49°F to 392°F
PROBE LENGTH: 4.2 in
ACCURACY: ★★½
SPEED: ★★
EASE OF USE: ★★
DURABILITY: ★★

MAVERICK Rain Drop Waterproof Digital Thermometer
MODEL: PT-55
PRICE: $39.99
AVERAGE READ TIME: 4.8 sec
RANGE: 4°F to 572°F
PROBE LENGTH: 3.9 in
ACCURACY: ★★½
SPEED: ★★★
EASE OF USE: ★
DURABILITY: ★★

TAYLOR Rotating Display Thermometer
MODEL: 9834
PRICE: $17.99
AVERAGE READ TIME: 7.2 sec
RANGE: -40°F to 482°F
PROBE LENGTH: 5.6 in
ACCURACY: ★★½
SPEED: ★★
EASE OF USE: ★
DURABILITY: ★★★

PALERMO Instant Read Meat Thermometer
MODEL: DTH-81
PRICE: $11.97
AVERAGE READ TIME: 9.7 sec
RANGE: -58°F to 572°F
PROBE LENGTH: 4.6 in
ACCURACY: ★★★
SPEED: ★½
EASE OF USE: ½
DURABILITY: ★★½

EATSMART Precision Pro Digital Food Thermometer
MODEL: ESFT-01
PRICE: $11.95
AVERAGE READ TIME: 7.9 sec
RANGE: -40°F to 450°F
PROBE LENGTH: 3 in
ACCURACY: ★★★
SPEED: ★★
EASE OF USE: ★
DURABILITY: ★½

INGREDIENT NOTES

≥ BY ANDREA GEARY, ANDREW JANJIGIAN, LAN LAM & ANNIE PETITO ≤

Tasting Burrata

Imagine slicing open a tender ball of fresh mozzarella to find a luscious, thick cream teeming with plush bits of curd. A mozzarella offshoot, burrata is made in much the same way, but before the ball is twisted and sealed, it's stuffed with a mixture of curd and cream. Cheesemakers in the Puglia region of Italy began making burrata in the early 20th century as a way to use up leftovers from the production of fresh mozzarella. Then, around the turn of the century, artisanal cheesemakers in the United States started crafting their own versions; large manufacturers eventually followed suit. We wondered if any domestic supermarket options could deliver the luxurious experience we associate with burrata, so we rounded up four nationally available products priced from $3.80 to $6.50 for 8 ounces. We sampled them plain and in our recipe for Heirloom Tomato and Burrata Salad with Pangrattato and Basil.

We immediately noticed the cheeses' varying ratios of shell to filling. Lower-ranking cheeses had thinner shells that disappeared into the filling (our least favorite was less than 20 percent shell). By comparison, our top two products had an equal amount of hefty shell and soft filling, which provided a nice textural contrast. Tasters also liked clean, milky, slightly salty flavor and favored products with at least 80 milligrams of sodium per serving. Our winner, Lioni Burrata con Panna, was bright-tasting and nicely salted, with a thick, luscious cream that tasters loved. It was lauded for its "luxurious," pillowy texture and fresh dairy flavor—proving that it is possible to get high-quality burrata from the supermarket. –Lauren Savoie

RECOMMENDED

LIONI Burrata con Panna
PRICE: $6.50 for 8 oz ($0.81 per oz)
INGREDIENTS: Pasteurized whole milk, cream, starter, cheese cultures, vegetable rennet, and salt
SODIUM: 80 mg   PERCENTAGE FILLING: 48%   PERCENTAGE SHELL: 52%
COMMENTS: "This is mozzarella from heaven," said one taster about this "buttery," "rich" product. Tasters singled it out as the "creamiest" and "saltiest" of the bunch. It also had a distinct shell, with a "balanced" amount of "thick" filling.

BELGIOIOSO Burrata
PRICE: $4.99 for 8 oz ($0.62 per oz)
INGREDIENTS: Pasteurized milk, cream, vinegar, enzymes, salt
SODIUM: 85 mg
PERCENTAGE FILLING: 44%   PERCENTAGE SHELL: 56%
COMMENTS: With our tasters' ideal shell-to-cream ratio, this "pillowy" burrata was "soft without being overly watery" and had "sweet dairy flavor." The inside was "tender" and "stringy," with "distinct" pieces that we liked in salad.

CALABRO Burrata
PRICE: $4.99 for 8 oz ($0.62 per oz)
INGREDIENTS: Pasteurized whole milk, pasteurized cultured cream, starter, vegetable rennet, packed in lightly salted water
SODIUM: 50 mg
PERCENTAGE FILLING: 73%   PERCENTAGE SHELL: 27%
COMMENTS: This burrata was "creamy" and "luscious," with a "mild" and "milky" flavor. The filling was on the thinner side, and while it produced a satisfying gush when we first sliced into the cheese, it was a little "watery" in salad. A few tasters also thought it was a bit "underseasoned" because of its lower sodium content.

*Sodium levels were standardized for comparison, using a serving size of 1 ounce.

Yellow versus White Peaches

Yellow peaches, with red-orange skin and golden flesh, and white peaches, with rosy-yellow skin and pale, butter-colored flesh, are the most common options in grocery stores and fruit markets. We wondered whether the two could be used interchangeably, so we sampled them plain; baked into a rustic, cobbler-like dessert called sonker; and in a fresh salsa. We found that their differences were more than skin-deep. Yellow peaches had a brighter, slightly more acidic taste that balanced the sweetness of the sonker, and their sturdier flesh held up better to baking than that of the white peaches. We also liked the brightness the yellow peaches brought to the salsa. The white peaches, meanwhile, had virtually no acidity, making the sonker taste overly sweet. Their softer flesh turned mushy in the oven, and their delicate floral taste was overwhelmed in salsa.

YELLOW PEACH
Great for baking

WHITE PEACH
Save for snacking

➤ **Bottom line:** We'll stick with yellow peaches for baking and cooking and enjoy the mild, floral flavor of white peaches for eating them out of hand. But if you do cook or bake with white peaches, know that their softer, smoother texture may affect the dish's consistency and you might need to add a bit of acid for balance. –A.P.

Don't Toss Expired Cocoa Powder

Some see a box of unsweetened cocoa powder six years past its expiration date and think "trash." In the test kitchen, we think "testing opportunity." Wondering if cocoa spoils or loses its flavor over time as spices do, we made hot cocoa and chocolate butter cookies with the six-year-old cocoa and a freshly opened box of the same product. When we tasted them side by side, only about half the tasters noted a difference, calling the samples made with the geriatric cocoa "duller," "weaker," and "more mellow." No one noted any off-flavors.

When we repeated the test using high- and low-fat cocoa powders one to two years past their expiration dates, again comparing them with samples made with fresh cocoa, tasters could not differentiate between the samples. The compounds that give cocoa powder its flavor are less volatile than those in ground spices, which lose much of their flavor and aroma after about a year. The more volatile the molecule, the more rapidly it evaporates and degrades.

➤ **The takeaway:** If you come across cocoa powder that's past its expiration date–even by a couple of years—it's fine to use. –A.G.

Introducing Aji Amarillo Chile Paste

Our Peruvian Fish Ceviche with Radishes and Orange (page 19) uses *aji amarillo* chile paste for heat and a hint of fruity flavor. Available in the Latin section of many grocery stores and popular in Peruvian and Bolivian cuisines, this paste is made from a vibrant yellow chile (*aji amarillo* translates as "yellow pepper") and typically salt and citric acid, the latter of which adds brightness and acts as a preservative. Tasters likened the chile paste's flavor to that of a habanero but with a moderate amount of heat. A few picked out a slightly sweet, vegetal finish reminiscent of red bell peppers.

UNMELLOW YELLOW
Medium heat, vibrant color

Use aji amarillo paste to punch up the flavor of marinades and dressings, stir it into mayonnaise to make a peppy spread for sandwiches, or fold a small amount into salsa or guacamole. –L.L.

Cucumber Primer

Gone are the days when supermarkets sold only one kind of cucumber. We tried four easy-to-find varieties plain and in bread-and-butter pickles. Below is a little background on each and what we learned. –A.G.

➤ **Pickling (Kirby):** Small and squat; dense, crunchy flesh; available late summer to late fall
Uses: Pickles, salads, crudités
Notes: This was the only variety we liked as pickles; its skin can be tough, so consider peeling it if eating it raw in salads.

➤ **Seedless (English/European/Hothouse):** Long and slim; sold shrink-wrapped; slightly sweet and melon-y; available year-round
Uses: Salads, crudités
Notes: The skins contain fewer bitter-tasting cucurbitacins than those of slicing cucumbers, and the seeds are tiny, so leave them in if you like.

➤ **Slicing (American):** Thick, with dark-green skin and plentiful seeds; crisp texture; mild flavor; available year-round
Uses: Salads, crudités
Notes: Remove the tough seeds, trim the ends, and remove the skin, which contains a relatively high concentration of cucurbitacins.

➤ **Mini (Persian):** Small and slim; similar to seedless cucumbers in flavor and texture; available year-round
Uses: Salads, crudités
Notes: There's no need to peel or seed mini cukes; they're typically more expensive than other varieties.

TEAM CUCUMBER
Clockwise from top left: pickling, seedless, slicing, mini

Technique: How to Segment Citrus

When slicing oranges, grapefruits, and other citrus fruits into segments, it's important to cut the sections free of the membranes and pith, which are fibrous and bitter. Here's how we do this in the test kitchen. –A.J.

1. TRIM Cut thin slice from top and bottom of fruit. Use paring knife to remove 1-inch-wide swaths of rind and white pith, cutting from top to bottom of fruit. (Working in small sections helps you follow contour of fruit, leaving more of flesh intact.)

2. SLICE Hold fruit over bowl to catch juice and segments. Insert blade of paring knife between membrane and side of segment. Carefully slice to center of fruit. One side of segment will be separated.

3. SEGMENT Insert blade between membrane and other side of segment. Again slice to center of fruit. Segment should release. If it does not, use knife to gently pry segment away from fruit. Repeat with remaining sections.

DIY RECIPE Plantain Chips

Plantain chips are expensive and are not always easy to find in stores, but they are a snap to make at home using our method. Slicing the plantains thinly and evenly ensures that they cook up crispy without burning, so we highly recommend using a mandoline for this recipe. Frying the plantains at a relatively gentle 325 degrees lets the interiors of the chips cook through before the exteriors begin to brown, so they are crispy inside and out. Enjoy plantain chips out of hand or serve them alongside salsas, guacamole, or our Peruvian Fish Ceviche with Radishes and Orange (page 19). –A.J.

PLANTAIN CHIPS
SERVES 4

Be sure to use plantains that are as unripe (dark green) as possible. To peel plantains, trim ½ inch from each end to expose the flesh and then use a paring knife to cut lengthwise through the skin. Use a spoon to peel back the skin along the cut and remove it. We prefer to slice the plantains using a mandoline, but they can be sliced using a sharp knife; just be sure to slice them precisely and evenly. Add the plantain slices to the oil a few at a time to prevent them from sticking together.

- 4 cups vegetable oil
- 3 unripe plantains, peeled and sliced on bias 1/16 inch thick
- Kosher salt

Line rimmed baking sheet with double layer of paper towels. Heat oil in large Dutch oven over medium-high heat to 325 degrees. Carefully add one-third of plantains and cook, stirring with slotted spoon or spider skimmer, until light golden brown, 5 to 7 minutes, adjusting burner, if necessary, to maintain oil temperature between 300 and 325 degrees. Using slotted spoon or spider skimmer, transfer chips to prepared sheet and season lightly with salt. Return oil to 325 degrees and repeat with remaining plantains in 2 batches. (Cooled chips can be stored at room temperature for up to 1 week.)

Mediterranean versus Mexican Oregano

Oregano is one of the few herbs that retains much of its flavor when dried, which is why we call for it in many recipes. Oregano's aroma compounds are less volatile than those of other herbs, meaning that more remain after the leaves are dried. There are two general categories of oregano: Mediterranean and Mexican, which come from different plants. Mediterranean oregano (*Origanum vulgare*) is a member of the mint family and a close relative of marjoram, while Mexican oregano (*Lippia graveolens*) is a member of the verbena family and a close relative of lemon verbena. Both plants contain a phenolic compound called carvacrol, which gives both herbs their distinctive, pungent flavor.

We tried both types in tomato sauce and *mojo*-marinated skirt steak and noticed minimal differences. The Mediterranean oregano was milder and faintly sweeter, while the Mexican type was stronger, with a hint of menthol.

As with other dried herbs, oregano's volatile compounds will eventually dissipate. Whichever kind you choose, be sure to store it in a cool, dry, dark place to preserve its flavor. Discard your oregano if it's faded in color or has lost its distinctive aroma. –L.L.

MEDITERRANEAN   **MEXICAN**

KITCHEN NOTES

BY STEVE DUNN, ANDREA GEARY & LAN LAM

WHAT IS IT?

Resembling the skeleton of an old umbrella, a *bois lélé* is the denuded twig from the so-called swizzlestick tree (*Quararibea turbinata*), which grows throughout the eastern Caribbean. Beginning in the late 19th century, British colonists in the Caribbean islands used the stick, which features short spikes radiating out from the end of a central pole, to mix a type of drink drink called a "swizzle."

We acquired a bois lélé from a local mixology shop and used it to mix a classic version of the cocktail. After filling a highball glass with crushed ice, orange and pineapple juices, dark rum, grenadine, and a dash of bitters, we inserted the bois lélé spiky side down and rapidly rubbed the upper portion between our palms to spin the stick (and spikes) and mix the drink. It worked beautifully. Of course, a long spoon or a modern swizzle stick will get the job done, too, but a bois lélé does it with more panache. –S.D.

BOIS LÉLÉ (SWIZZLE STICK)

Brush Up on Brushes

If you're equal parts cook and baker, consider keeping two brushes in your kitchen—a pastry brush with thin, natural-fiber bristles, and a sturdy silicone brush. –A.G.

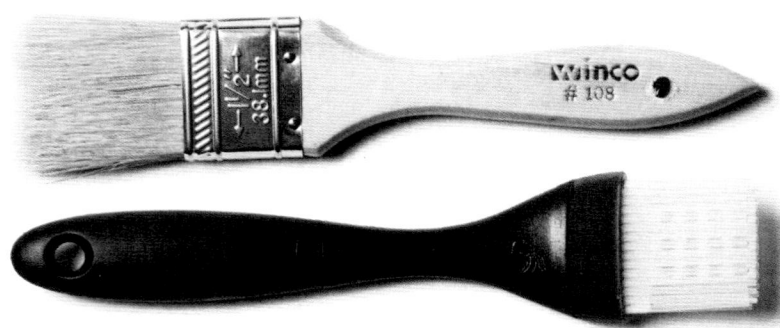

NATURAL-FIBER BRUSH	SILICONE BRUSH
Use for: Applying egg wash or glaze to delicate doughs and pastry or butter/oil to phyllo dough; brushing crumbs from cake layers	**Use for:** High-heat applications; basting meat or poultry; applying oil or melted butter to pans; applying anything with strong odor
Avoid: High heat, which can burn bristles and melt glue that secures them. Also avoid using with anything that has strong odor—smells cling to bristles, even after washing.	**Avoid:** Delicate items. Brush can damage fragile dough or fruit; its larger bristles can also leave visible lines on baked goods.
To clean: Rinse briefly to remove debris. Rub warm, soapy water into bristles and rinse thoroughly. Blot with towel and lay flat to dry. Replace brush if it begins to smell.	**To clean:** Place in top rack of dishwasher. Replace if silicone retains smells even after washing.

The Right Place for Leftover Pie

Where's the best place to store a pie? According to the U.S. Department of Agriculture (USDA), pies containing perishable ingredients such as eggs or dairy must be refrigerated once cool. But what about fruit pies? The USDA says they're food-safe at room temperature for up to two days because they contain plenty of sugar and acid, which retard bacteria growth. But does storage temperature affect the pies' texture or flavor?

To find out, we made two apple and two blueberry pies. We stored one of each in the refrigerator and the others on the counter overnight. The next day we tasted all four pies at room temperature. We expected the crusts on the refrigerated pies to be tough and chewy because cold typically hastens the staling of baked goods. But the pies were indistinguishable. The low moisture and high fat content of pie crust makes it resistant to staling in a way that leaner, moister items, such as breads, are not.

➤ **The takeaway:** Refrigerate leftover pie containing eggs or dairy right away. Fruit pies can be stored either at room temperature or in the refrigerator for up to two days (covering them with an overturned bowl is a handy way to keep them protected). –A.G.

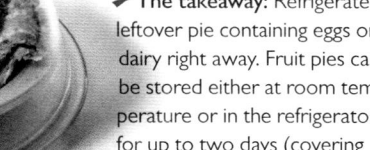

OVERTURNED BOWL = PIE PROTECTOR

Caring for Cast Iron, Inside and Out

We recommend oiling the interiors of cast-iron (and carbon-steel) pans after every use, but it's also important to maintain the exteriors of these pans, which are exposed to splatters, drips, and splashes during cooking. Without proper care, the exteriors can rust or develop tacky buildup.

To keep your pans looking spiffy inside and out, add this quick final step to your regular maintenance routine: After you've cleaned the whole pan and oiled and wiped out its interior, turn off the heat and flip the pan over. Wipe the bottom, outer edge, and handle with the trace oil remaining on the paper towels you used to oil the cooking surface. Do not add more oil to the paper towels, as excess oil on the pan bottom can leave a grease spot in your cabinet and cause excess smoking during the pan's next use. Let the pan cool completely before storing. –A.G.

NO ADDED OIL NEEDED

The Proper Way to Pour

Transferring liquid from one vessel to another can be tricky. Whether it's pouring a reduced sauce from a skillet into a measuring cup or stock from a saucepan into storage containers, most cooks' impulse is to bring the larger vessel as close as possible to the smaller one and pour slowly and carefully. But those tactics often lead to spills and splatters. We spent a few hours in the test kitchen honing our pouring skills. Here's what we learned. –L.L

➤ **Liquids pour from cookware in a wide stream that narrows as it falls:** Hold the pot or pan 3 to 4 inches from the top of the catch vessel. This is close enough to prevent splattering but far enough for the stream to narrow to a manageable width.

➤ **Cookware with a curved lip has the edge:** A curved lip helps prevent liquid from dribbling down the outside of the cookware by giving the stream a little arc as it leaves the pan.

➤ **For the liquid to pour in a neat stream, there should be some force behind it:** Commit to the pour instead of tilting the pot or pan slowly. This also prevents liquid from pouring down the outside of the cookware (and onto your counter).

➤ **The stiller the liquid, the easier the pour:** Sloshing liquid is far messier to pour than still liquid, so bring the catch vessel to your cookware rather than the other way around. Hold the cookware with your dominant hand (or both hands) and use the helper handle, if available, as you pour.

SCIENCE
Preventing Hot Milk from Sticking to Pans

When heating milk on the stovetop for custard, bread, homemade ricotta, or even hot chocolate, we're often left with a stubborn film of cooked—or scorched—milk on the bottom and sides of the pan. Constantly scraping the pan bottom as the milk heats to prevent the film from forming isn't practical, but we'd heard that wetting the pan with water before adding the milk would prevent the milk from sticking. We decided to put this bit of kitchen lore to the test.

EXPERIMENT
We pretreated three identical metal saucepans. In the first, we swirled 2 tablespoons of water around the saucepan's bottom and sides. We lightly sprayed the second saucepan's surface with vegetable oil spray. We rubbed the bottom and sides of a third saucepan with butter and left a fourth saucepan untreated. We added 2 cups of whole milk to each saucepan and then cooked each over medium-low heat for 10 minutes before pouring out the milk and examining them.

RESULTS
The saucepan misted with vegetable oil spray had just a tiny bit of milk residue (tasters did not notice any off-flavors from the oil), while the water-treated saucepan was almost as clean. The saucepan treated with butter was no cleaner than the untreated one, and stirring every 2 minutes produced a similar result.

EXPLANATION
When you add milk to a dry pan, it flows into microscopic imperfections in the pan bottom. As the milk heats, its proteins coagulate and stick to the pan and each other. Misting the pan with vegetable oil spray prior to adding the milk creates a thin film on the pan's surface, which acts as a barrier and makes milk proteins less likely to adhere.

TAKEAWAY
The next time we're heating milk, we'll save ourselves some cleanup and first mist the pan with vegetable oil spray (or swirl in some water if we don't want to add oil). –S.D.

TREATED

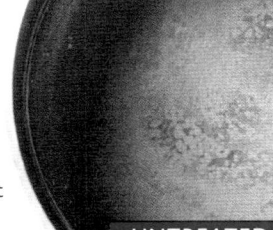

UNTREATED

Best Ways to Peel and Pit Peaches
What's the easiest, tidiest method for peeling a peach? It depends on the fruit's ripeness. –A.G.

For firm peaches: Use sharp vegetable peeler to remove circle of skin at top and bottom of peach, then remove remaining skin with top-to-bottom strokes of peeler.

For soft, ripe peaches: Cut shallow cross in skin at blossom end of each peach. Plunge peaches, few at a time, into large pot of boiling water for about 30 seconds. Transfer fruit to bowl of ice water until cool enough to handle, then strip away skins using your fingers (use paring knife for any stubborn bits).

To pit: Carefully cut peeled peach in half along equator, making sure to cut down to pit. Grasp both halves of peach and twist in opposite directions until 1 side pulls away from pit. Wiggle pit back and forth to loosen, then twist to remove. (For intractable pits, cut flesh from pit with vertical swipes of chef's knife, leaving pit encased in squared-off column of flesh.)

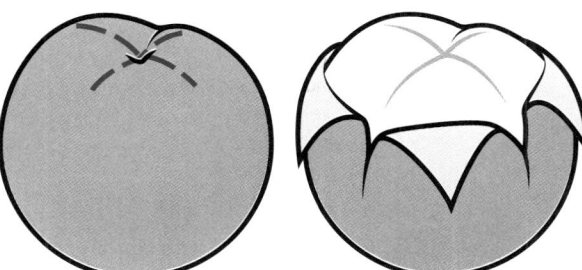

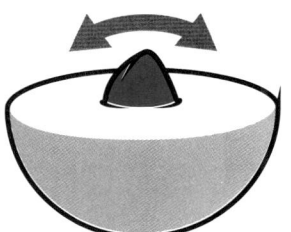

EQUIPMENT CORNER

≥ BY MIYE BROMBERG, EMILY PHARES, LAUREN SAVOIE & KATE SHANNON ≤

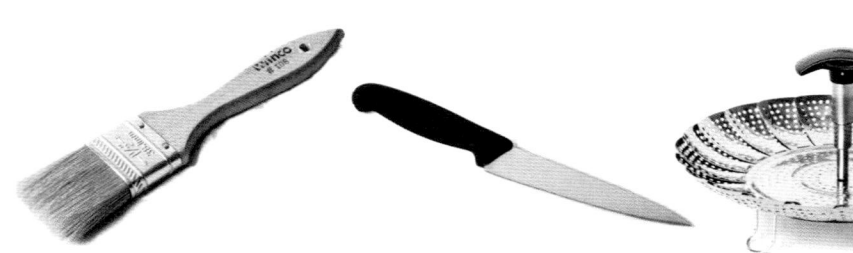

HIGHLY RECOMMENDED
OXO Good Grips 9" Tongs
MODEL: 28481
PRICE: $11.99

NOT RECOMMENDED
CUISINART Automatic Cold Brew Coffeemaker
MODEL: DCB-10
PRICE: $99.99

RECOMMENDED
WINCO Flat Pastry and Basting Brush, 1½ Inch
MODEL: WBR-15
PRICE: $6.93

HIGHLY RECOMMENDED
VICTORINOX Swiss Army Fibrox Pro 6" Chef's Knife
MODEL: 47570.US2
PRICE: $20.99

RECOMMENDED
OXO Good Grips Stainless Steel Steamer with Extendable Handle
MODEL: 1067247
PRICE: $17.95

9-Inch Tongs
We typically reach for 12-inch tongs to protect our hands from heat and messes in the kitchen. However, some cooks prefer the feel of a shorter pair, so we tested six pairs of tongs priced from $11.99 to $35.00, all 9 to 9.5 inches in length. We put each pair of tongs through a battery of kitchen tests—from portioning angel hair pasta to transferring a hot baked potato from baking sheet to cutting board—examining each pair's tension, precision, comfort, and locking mechanism. One pair, the OXO Good Grips 9" Tongs ($11.99), was comfortable to use, intuitive to lock, and could easily and securely pick up objects of all shapes and sizes. The uncoated, scalloped stainless-steel tips gave us a precise grip on everything we threw at them. –E.P.

Cuisinart Automatic Cold Brew Coffeemaker
Coffee aficionados swear by the cold-brew method for making smooth, nuanced iced coffee. But there's one drawback: The process takes 12 to 24 hours. The Cuisinart Automatic Cold Brew Coffeemaker ($99.99) promises to make ready-to-drink cold-brewed coffee in as little as 25 minutes. Designed like an automatic drip coffee maker, this machine has a water reservoir and reusable filter that sit atop a carafe. The filter spins on and off in 10-second intervals for 25, 35, or 45 minutes for "mild," "medium," or "bold" coffee, respectively. We compared coffee made with the bold setting with that made with concentrate from our favorite traditional cold-brew system, the Toddy Cold Brew System ($34.95). The Cuisinart's coffee was pale, thin, and weak-tasting and was also cloudy, with a film of bitter sediment. For now, it seems that quicker cold brew is too good to be true, so we'll stick with the Toddy. –L.S.

Pastry Brushes
Natural-fiber pastry brushes are useful for many delicate kitchen tasks, such as spreading egg wash, glaze, or melted butter on doughs or pastry. To find the best one, we bought six products priced from $5.32 to $15.95, all with 1½-inch-long brush heads, and evaluated them as we applied viscous egg wash to raw bread dough, slick olive oil to sheets of phyllo, and thick glazes to fruit tarts. And since these brushes are somewhat notorious for shedding bristles during use and washing, we kept track of the number of bristles lost during testing. All the brushes performed respectably, but minor differences in bristle length, uniformity, and density helped set some models apart. Our winning brush, the Winco Flat Pastry and Basting Brush, 1½ inch ($6.93), was agile and efficient. Its head had lots of bristles to wick up plenty of liquid but was not so dense that it bruised delicate berries or tore phyllo dough. Additionally, it had a varnished wooden handle that was comfortable to hold (though not as grippy as some) and it lost just two bristles during testing—the fewest of any of the models we tested. –M.B.

Chef's Knives For Kids
Standard chef's knives are too big for most kids, so we were pleased to discover kid-size versions a few years ago. These knives have smaller handles, shorter 2- to 4-inch metal or plastic blades, and built-in safety features such as blunt cutting edges or finger guards. With more kids' knives entering the market, we wondered if our old favorite from Opinel ($45.00) was still the best. We tested it alongside four other models priced from $7.36 to $58.50, as well as a 6-inch version of our winning 8-inch chef's knife from Victorinox ($20.99). We put the knives through some basic tests—dicing vegetables, mincing herbs, and slicing cheese—and eliminated two that seemed dangerous and ineffective. We then rounded up a group of children aged 8 to 13 with varying levels of cooking experience. We asked them to chop celery with the remaining knives and surveyed them on their favorite models. The 8- and 9-year-olds all liked our previous winner, the Opinel Le Petit Chef Cutlery Set ($45.00 for two-piece set), which features a wooden handle and a finger hole that encourages a safe grip. The 12- and 13-year-olds preferred the lightweight and nimble Victorinox Swiss Army Fibrox Pro 6" Chef's Knife ($20.99); its pointed tip required caution, but the children said they felt safe and adults reported feeling comfortable watching them use it. As for the 10- and 11-year-olds, their preference between the Opinel and Victorinox was influenced by their hand size and level of experience in the kitchen. We think either is an excellent addition to a young cook's toolkit. –K.S.

Steamer Baskets
Steamer baskets allow you to cook food quickly, consistently, and efficiently when set over as little as ½ inch of boiling water. They come in different styles, but we generally prefer collapsible versions, which are easier to clean and can be folded down after use for more compact storage. Since we last tested steamer baskets, our winner, the OXO Good Grips Stainless Steel Steamer with Extendable Handle ($17.95), was slightly redesigned. Curious to see if the new version held up to the competition, we pitted it against six other collapsible models (three metal, two silicone, and one plastic) priced from $8.41 to $28.52. We used each to steam broccoli and dumplings, hard-cook eggs, and poach chicken. All models cooked food evenly, but some—namely the silicone versions—were too small. The models also differed in the position and length of their handles; we preferred centered handles that were tall enough to grasp securely with tongs or an oven mitt but not so tall that they prevented us from securely placing the lid on the pot. Our winner solves this problem with a telescoping handle that extends from 2½ inches to 4 inches. The OXO Good Grips Stainless Steel Steamer with Extendable Handle ($17.95), the updated version of our old favorite, is a little finicky to clean (like other metal models), but its unique handle and large capacity allowed it to maintain its first-place ranking. –M.B.

INDEX
July & August 2018

MAIN DISHES
Best Grilled Chicken Thighs 5
Crispy Tacos (Tacos Dorados) 9
Peruvian Fish Ceviche with Radishes and Orange 19
Vietnamese Grilled Pork Patties with Rice Noodles and Salad (Bun Cha) 11

SIDE DISHES
Grilled Tomatoes 15
Marinated Grilled Tomatoes with Fresh Mozzarella 15
Mexican Corn Salad (Esquites) 20

SOUP
Grilled Tomato Gazpacho 15

SNACKS
Chewy Granola Bars with Walnuts and Cranberries 13
 Nut-Free 13
 with Hazelnuts, Cherries, and Cacao Nibs 13
Plantain Chips 29

DESSERT
Peach Tarte Tatin 23

DIP
Grilled Tomato Salsa 15

BEVERAGE
Michelada (Mexican Beer and Lime Cocktail) 9

SAUCES
Dark Chocolate Fudge Sauce 21
 Dark Chocolate–Orange 21
Fresh Tomato Sauce 7

SPICE PASTES
Gochujang Paste 5
Mustard-Tarragon Paste 5

BONUS ONLINE CONTENT
Go to CooksIllustrated.com/aug18 for more recipes.

Best Grilled Chicken Thighs for Two
Dark Chocolate–Peanut Butter Fudge Sauce
Garam Masala Paste
Mexican Dark Chocolate Fudge Sauce
Peruvian Scallop Ceviche with Cucumber and Grapefruit
Peruvian Shrimp Ceviche with Tomato, Jícama, and Avocado
Vietnamese Grilled Pork Patties with Rice Noodles and Salad (Bun Cha) for Two

▶ RECIPE VIDEOS
Want to see how to make any of the recipes in this issue? There's a free video for that. Go to CooksIllustrated.com/aug18 and click on videos.

FOLLOW US ON SOCIAL MEDIA
facebook.com/CooksIllustrated
twitter.com/TestKitchen
pinterest.com/TestKitchen
instagram.com/CooksIllustrated
youtube.com/AmericasTestKitchen

America's Test Kitchen COOKING SCHOOL
Visit our online cooking school today, where we offer 180+ online lessons covering a range of recipes and cooking methods. Whether you're a novice just starting out or are already an advanced cook looking for new techniques, our cooking school is designed to give you confidence in the kitchen and make you a better cook.

▸ Start a 14-Day Free Trial at OnlineCookingSchool.com

Cook's Illustrated on iPad
Enjoy Cook's wherever you are, whenever you want.

Did you know that Cook's Illustrated is available on iPad? Go to CooksIllustrated.com/iPad to download the app through iTunes. You'll be able to start a free trial of the digital edition, which includes bonus features such as recipe videos, full-color photos, and step-by-step slide shows of each recipe.

Go to CooksIllustrated.com/iPad to download our app through iTunes.

Chewy Granola Bars, 13

Fresh Tomato Sauce, 7

Mexican Corn Salad (Esquites), 20

Peach Tarte Tatin, 23

Vietnamese Grilled Pork with Rice Noodles, 11

Best Grilled Chicken Thighs, 5

Crispy Tacos (Tacos Dorados), 9

Peruvian Fish Ceviche, 19

Grilled Tomatoes, 15

Dark Chocolate Fudge Sauce, 21

PHOTOGRAPHY: CARL TREMBLAY; STYLING: KENDRA McKNIGHT

NUMBER 154 SEPTEMBER & OCTOBER 2018

COOK'S
ILLUSTRATED

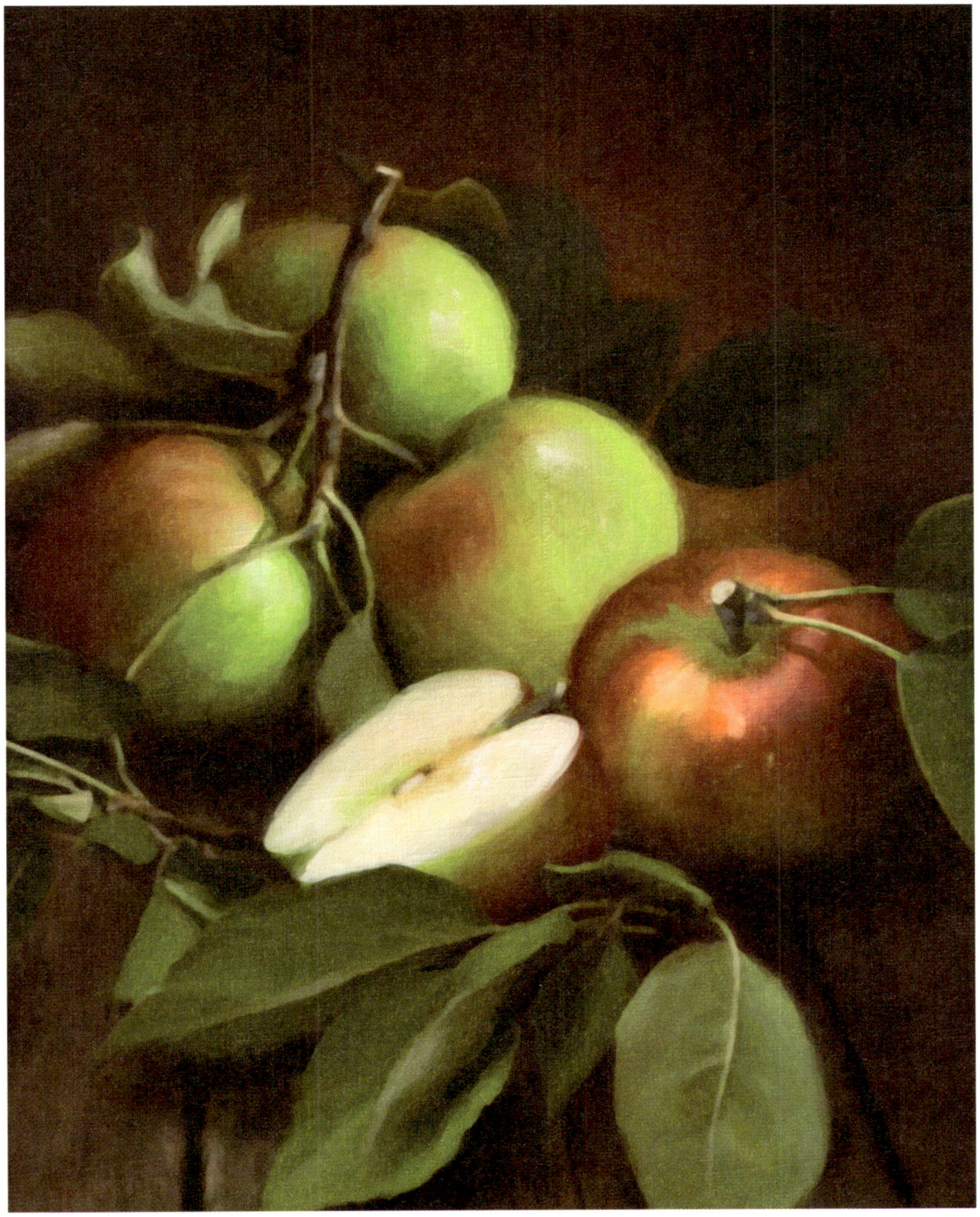

One-Pan Chicken
and Potatoes

Real Carne Adovada
Easiest-Ever Pork Braise

Ultimate Guide to
Roasted Vegetables

Skillet Green Beans
Embrace the Char

How to Cook
Swordfish
Treat It Like Meat

Falafel Done Right
Crispy, Tender, Flavorful

Why You Should
Make Pita Bread

Testing Dutch Ovens
How Much Do You
Have to Spend?

CooksIllustrated.com
$6.95 U.S./$8.95 CANADA

Display until October 8, 2018

COOK'S ILLUSTRATED

SEPTEMBER & OCTOBER 2018

2 Quick Tips
Quick and easy ways to perform everyday tasks, from neatly pouring oil to testing vegetables for doneness. COMPILED BY ANNIE PETITO

4 One-Pan Chicken and Potatoes
We produced a trio of heavy hitters—tender, crisp-skinned chicken; well-browned potatoes; and a garlicky white wine sauce—all in the same pan. BY ANDREA GEARY

6 Real Carne Adovada
Restraint is the key to the purest, most robust chile flavor in this classic New Mexican pork braise. It's also what makes it dead simple to prepare. BY ANNIE PETITO

8 Next-Level Grilled Steak
Anyone can throw a rib eye on the fire. But Japanese *negimaki* rolls the flavors of teriyaki and the stylish presentation of sushi into a make-ahead summer stunner. BY ANDREW JANJIGIAN

10 Fish for Meat Lovers
Most types of fish require a gentle temperature and a delicate touch. But for rich, meaty swordfish, it's best to crank up the heat. BY LAN LAM

12 Really Good Falafel
Loading up the chickpea batter with fresh herbs and aromatics is what makes falafel the world's greatest fritters. Too bad it also makes them a mess to handle and cook. BY STEVE DUNN

14 Why You Should Make Pita Bread
The tender chew and complex flavor of fresh-baked pitas are revelatory. Once you've experienced homemade, you'll swear off supermarket rounds for good. BY ANDREW JANJIGIAN

PAGE 6

16 Everyday Roasted Vegetables
Roasting is a great way to breathe life into whatever produce is in your crisper drawer. Plus, it's mostly hands-free. Here's a cheat sheet for doing it well.
BY ELIZABETH BOMZE AND KEITH DRESSER

18 Applesauce for Everyone
Transform just about any apple variety into flavorful, rosy applesauce in less than 30 minutes. Our secret weapon: the peels. BY ANDREA GEARY

20 Burn Your Beans
Skillet-charring produces deeply browned green beans with satisfying chew.
BY ANDREW JANJIGIAN

21 Pasta Salad Rehab
Our fixes: Overcook the noodles. Raid the pantry. Puree the dressing. BY ANNIE PETITO

22 Belgian Spice Cookies (Speculoos)
Passengers can't get enough of Delta Air Lines' in-flight snack of Biscoff, the commercial version of this Belgian confection. We took it to even greater heights. BY ANDREW JANJIGIAN

24 Tasting Basmati Rice
Its slender grains, nutty flavor, and popcorn-like fragrance are prized around the world. But when choices abound, how do you decide which basmati to buy? BY LISA McMANUS

26 Testing Dutch Ovens
Dutch ovens do it all. But which pot makes "it all" easiest? BY HANNAH CROWLEY

28 Ingredient Notes
BY STEVE DUNN, ANDREA GEARY, ANDREW JANJIGIAN, LAN LAM & ANNIE PETITO

30 Kitchen Notes
BY STEVE DUNN, ANDREA GEARY, ANDREW JANJIGIAN, LAN LAM & ANNIE PETITO

32 Equipment Corner
BY MIYE BROMBERG, LISA McMANUS, EMILY PHARES, LAUREN SAVOIE & KATE SHANNON

BACK COVER ILLUSTRATED BY JOHN BURGOYNE
French Breads
France lays claim to many of the world's great breads, most notably the lean, chewy, deeply browned **BAGUETTE**. Variations include **PAIN D'EPI**, in which the dough is cut into pointy lobes to resemble a wheat stalk. The name **BÂTARD** is often said to reference the loaf's torpedo-like shape—a "bastardization" of a slender baguette and a round *boule*. Cuts in **FOUGASSE** dough increase its crust-to-crumb ratio; many versions include olives, cheese, or seeds. The cuts in an **ÉCHELLE** loaf form a "ladder." A **COURONNE** is the French equivalent of pull-apart rolls. To make **CHAMPIGNON**, *boulangers* place a thin disk of dough on top of a roll to form the "cap." With its substantial crust and mellow tang, **PAIN AU LEVAIN** is a classic example of sourdough. **MICHE** rounds, which are sourdough-based, include whole-grain flours that lend them robust flavor. Buttery, eggy **BRIOCHE À TÊTE** is baked in a fluted tin and topped with a rounded "head" of dough. **PAIN DE MIE** is practically crustless and has a feathery crumb.

America's Test Kitchen is a real test kitchen located in Boston. It is the home of more than 60 test cooks, editors, and cookware specialists. Our mission is to test recipes until we understand exactly how and why they work and eventually arrive at the very best version. We also test kitchen equipment and supermarket ingredients in search of products that offer the best value and performance. You can watch us work by tuning in to *America's Test Kitchen* (AmericasTestKitchen.com) and *Cook's Country from America's Test Kitchen* (CooksCountry.com) on public television and listen to our weekly segments on *The Splendid Table* on public radio. You can also follow us on Facebook, Twitter, Pinterest, and Instagram.

EDITORIAL STAFF

Chief Executive Officer David Nussbaum
Chief Creative Officer Jack Bishop
Editor in Chief Dan Souza
Executive Editor Amanda Agee
Deputy Editor Rebecca Hays
Executive Managing Editor Todd Meier
Executive Food Editor Keith Dresser
Deputy Food Editor Andrea Geary
Senior Editors Andrew Janjigian, Lan Lam
Senior Editors, Features Elizabeth Bomze, Kristin Sargianis
Associate Editors Steve Dunn, Annie Petito
Photo Team & Special Events Manager Tim McQuinn
Lead Cook, Photo Team Dan Cellucci
Test Cook, Photo Team Jessica Rudolph
Assistant Test Cooks, Photo Team Sarah Ewald, Eric Haessler, Devon Shatkin
Senior Copy Editor Jill Campbell
Copy Editor Rachel Schowalter
Senior Science Research Editor Paul Adams

Executive Editor, Tastings & Testings Lisa McManus
Deputy Editor, Tastings & Testings Hannah Crowley
Managing Editor, Tastings & Testings Briana Palma
Senior Editors, Tastings & Testings Lauren Savoie, Kate Shannon
Associate Editor, Tastings & Testings Miye Bromberg
Assistant Editors, Tastings & Testings Carolyn Grillo, Emily Phares

Creative Director John Torres
Design Director Greg Galvan
Photography Director Julie Cote
Associate Art Director Maggie Edgar
Senior Staff Photographer Daniel J. van Ackere
Staff Photographers Steve Klise, Kevin White
Photography Producer Meredith Mulcahy

Executive Editor, Web Christine Liu
Managing Editor, Web Mari Levine
Associate Editor, Web Ashley Delma

Director, Creative Operations Alice Carpenter
Senior Editor, Special Projects Christie Morrison
Imaging Manager Lauren Robbins
Production & Imaging Specialists Heather Dube, Dennis Noble, Jessica Voas
Test Kitchen Director Erin McMurrer
Assistant Test Kitchen Director Alexxa Benson
Test Kitchen Manager Meridith Lippard
Test Kitchen Facilities Manager Kelly Ryan
Senior Kitchen Assistant Shopper Marissa Bunnewith
Senior Kitchen Assistant Receiver Heather Tolmie
Lead Kitchen Assistant Ena Gudiel
Kitchen Assistants Gladis Campos, Blanca Castanza, Amarilys Merced, Sujeila Trujillo

BUSINESS STAFF

Chief Financial Officer Jackie McCauley Ford
Senior Manager, Customer Support Tim Quinn
Senior Customer Loyalty & Support Specialist Rebecca Kowalski
Customer Loyalty & Support Specialist J.P. Dubuque

Chief Revenue Officer Sara Domville
Director, Sponsorship Marketing & Client Services Christine Anagnostis
Director, Integrated Partnerships & Business Development Eric Wynalek

Senior Director, Events & Special Projects Mehgan Conciatori
Partnership Marketing Manager Pamela Putprush
Event Coordinator Michaela Hughes

Chief Digital Officer Fran Middleton
Marketing Director, Social Media & Content Strategy Claire Oliverson
Social Media Manager Morgan Mannino

Director, Public Relations & Communications Brian Franklin

Senior VP, Human Resources & Organizational Development Colleen Zelina
Human Resources Manager Jason Lynott

Circulation Services ProCirc

Cover Art Robert Papp

PRINTED IN THE USA

LETTER FROM THE EDITOR

THE SUMMER OF JAWS

The summer after my sophomore year of college, I got braces—and my jaw broken. On purpose. My doctor called it preventive surgery, which made it sound prudent. My jaw had been growing out of alignment for years, and his description of a pain- and headache-free existence was enough to convince me to go for it. What he didn't dwell on was that my jaw would remain wired shut for seven weeks.

After surgery, it didn't take me long to put together a list of the things for which an open mouth is paramount. First, there's sneezing and coughing. With a closed mouth both feel like being slapped upside the head, but from the inside. And of course, there's yawning. No satisfaction or relief comes from a closed-mouth yawn. (Does it even count as a yawn?) Yet these physiological inconveniences paled in comparison to the real loss: solid food.

Forty-eight hours into my recovery, I'd already exhausted my tolerance for chocolate protein shakes. My anxiety level rose. My mom came to the rescue with her blender, delivering a burst of variety. Cream of chicken soup. Cream of mushroom soup. Cream of broccoli soup. Cream of asparagus soup. Cream of cauliflower soup. (You get the idea.) And it helped, for a short spell. When the monotony again set in, I got more creative.

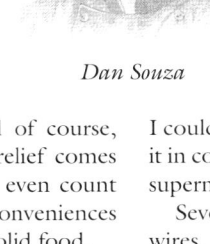

Dan Souza

I had a fantasy—a dream—of eating macaroni and cheese. So I cooked a batch from the box. I reveled in the smell of melted butter, the sound of noodles squishing past one another as I stirred the pot, and the sight of orange powder turning impossibly smooth.

Then I scooped it into the blender and added a glug of milk. After giving it a quick spin, I poured myself a thick cup and slipped a sip through my clenched front teeth. It was unspeakably awful. Having learned my lesson, I stuck to a near-monastic diet of soups and broths for the remainder of my recovery. And in that vacuum, my passion for anything related to food reached a fever pitch. I couldn't eat solid food, but I could watch it being prepared on TV, read about it in cookbooks, admire duotone images of it in the supermarket circular, and prepare it for my family.

Seven weeks after the surgery, my doctor cut the wires. Back home my dad asked me what I wanted to eat. It was rhetorical, as he'd already set the water to boil for the noodles. As I sat at the table waiting for my first bite all summer, I just smiled. I had a lot to be thankful for: a loving, supportive family; another school year just around the corner; a passion ignited. And solid food.

Dan Souza
Editor in Chief

FOR INQUIRIES, ORDERS, OR MORE INFORMATION

COOK'S ILLUSTRATED MAGAZINE
Cook's Illustrated magazine (ISSN 1068-2821), number 154, is published bimonthly by America's Test Kitchen Limited Partnership, 21 Drydock Avenue, Suite 210E, Boston, MA 02210. Copyright 2018 America's Test Kitchen Limited Partnership. Periodicals postage paid at Boston, MA, and additional mailing offices, USPS #012487. Publications Mail Agreement No. 40020778. Return undeliverable Canadian addresses to P.O. Box 875, Station A, Windsor, ON N9A 6P2. POSTMASTER: Send address changes to *Cook's Illustrated*, P.O. Box 6018, Harlan, IA 51593-1518. For subscription and gift subscription orders, subscription inquiries, or change of address notices, visit AmericasTestKitchen.com/support, call 800-526-8442 in the U.S. or 515-237-3663 from outside the U.S., or write to us at *Cook's Illustrated*, P.O. Box 6018, Harlan, IA 51593-1518.

CooksIllustrated.com
At the all new CooksIllustrated.com, you can order books and subscriptions, sign up for our free e-newsletter, or renew your magazine subscription. Join the website and gain access to 25 years of *Cook's Illustrated* recipes, equipment tests, and ingredient tastings, as well as companion videos for every recipe in this issue.

COOKBOOKS
We sell more than 50 cookbooks filled with recipes developed in our test kitchen, including *How to Roast Everything* and *Just Add Sauce*. To order, visit our bookstore at CooksIllustrated.com/bookstore.

EDITORIAL OFFICE 21 Drydock Avenue, Suite 210E, Boston, MA 02210; 617-232-1000; fax: 617-232-1572. For subscription inquiries, visit AmericasTestKitchen.com/support or call 800-526-8442.

QUICK TIPS

≥ COMPILED BY ANNIE PETITO ≤

Storing Butter "Orphans"
Whenever Elise Darrow of Denver, Colo., gets to the end of a stick of butter, she stores it in a clean, lidded plastic dairy container. (If the pieces are exact tablespoons, she leaves the measurement-marked wrapper on so that she can use them for cooking and baking.) This frees up her butter dish for a new stick, and the "orphans" don't absorb any unpleasant refrigerator odors.

Steady—Then Sanitize—Your Cutting Board
Mike D'Angelo of Rockville Centre, N.Y., has long used the trick of placing a dampened paper towel under his cutting board to stabilize it. Recently he improved upon the technique by spraying the paper towel with cleaner. When he's done cutting, he uses the sanitized towel to wipe the work surfaces clean.

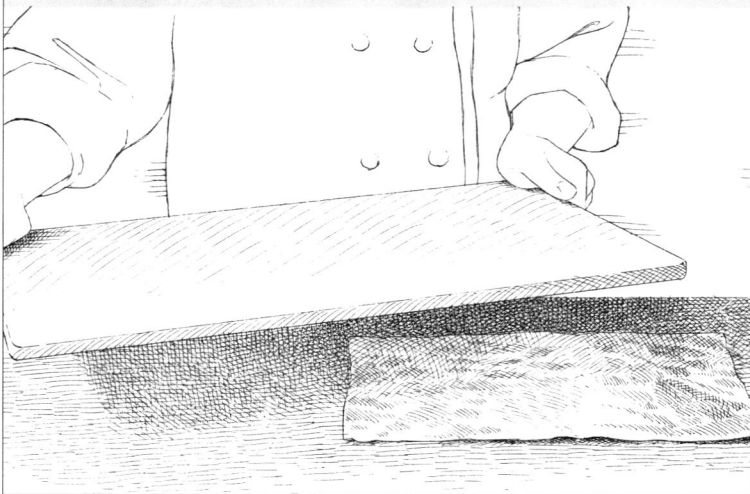

A Carrier for Hot Casseroles
When Troy Emerson of Somerville, Mass., brings a hot casserole to a friend's house, he makes it portable by lining a large, heavy-duty cardboard box with cutout handles in the sides (such as a box used for transporting liquor) with a towel and placing the hot dish inside. Besides acting as a trivet inside the box, the towel helps prevent the casserole from sliding around.

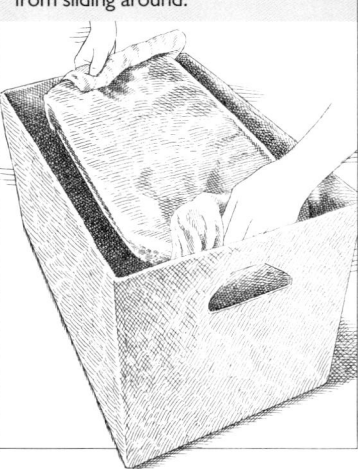

Mechanically Massaging Kale
Deborah Bernstein of Warwick, N.Y., uses her stand mixer to massage kale for salad. After adding the greens and the dressing to the bowl, she mixes them on low speed using the paddle attachment, which kneads the kale and breaks down its cell walls so that the pieces turn tender.

Save Space When Storing Pots in the Fridge
To fit her large covered Dutch oven in her refrigerator, Barbara Kram of Titusville, N.J., turns the lid upside down. That way, the vessel has more clearance on the shelf and she can even stack items on top of the lid for more storage.

Sock Up Bottle Drips
Judy Page of Centerville, Ohio, prevents wine or oil from dripping down the bottle by outfitting it with a clean long sock. She cuts a hole in the toe and pulls the narrow opening over the neck of the bottle to catch any spills.

SEND US YOUR TIPS We will provide a complimentary one-year subscription for each tip we print. Send your tip, name, address, and telephone number to Quick Tips, *Cook's Illustrated*, 21 Drydock Avenue, Suite 210E, Boston, MA 02210, or to QuickTips@AmericasTestKitchen.com.

"Rice" Water out of Thawed Spinach

Gerry McNamara of Concord, N.C., squeezes excess water from thawed chopped spinach with a potato ricer, which he finds less wasteful and more efficient than wringing it dry using paper towels or a clean dish towel.

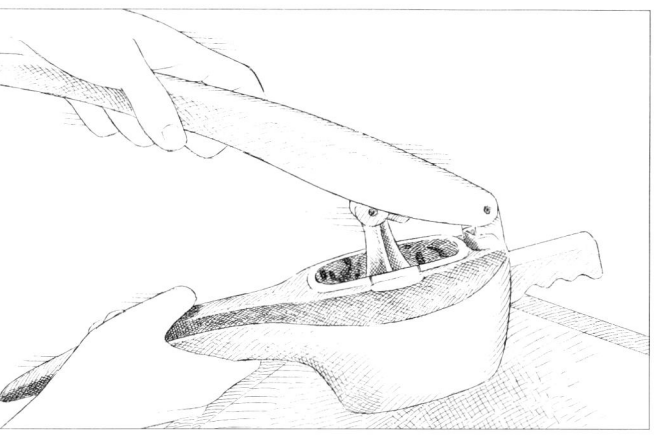

Oil Pour Control

Mary Jones of El Sobrante, Calif., doesn't tear away the foil seal on a bottle of oil. Instead, she uses a sharp paring knife to cut a V-shaped slit in it. When the narrow part of the V is facing downward, she can pour the oil slowly in a steady stream. When the wide end of the V is facing downward, she can pour the oil more quickly.

Devil Eggs in a Bag

To avoid messily transferring deviled egg filling from a mixing bowl to a pastry bag, Corinne Johnson of Wasilla, Alaska, mixes the hard-cooked yolks and seasonings directly in a zipper-lock bag.

1. After adding ingredients, seal bag and run rolling pin back and forth over bag to thoroughly combine ingredients.
2. Snip corner off bag and pipe filling into whites.

Piece-of-Cake Cutting

Alex Stefaniak of Somerset, N.J., slices ice cream cake with a bench scraper instead of a chef's knife. The tool's handle covers the metal blade completely, making it more comfortable to press down on the dessert, which can be dense and hard when cut straight from the freezer.

A Minimally Invasive Way to Test Doneness

Recipes often suggest testing the doneness of dense vegetables such as beets, squash, and potatoes by sliding the tip of a paring knife into the flesh to assess tenderness. Christina Boni of Somerville, Mass., prefers to use a metal cake tester, which is slimmer and barely disturbs the flesh.

One-Pan Chicken and Potatoes

We produced a trio of heavy hitters—tender, crisp-skinned chicken; well-browned potatoes; and a garlicky white wine sauce—all in the same pan.

≥ BY ANDREA GEARY ≤

Roast chicken and potatoes are near-universal favorites. Add a superflavorful pan sauce and you've got a slam dunk. A terrific example of this combination is chicken Vesuvio, a dish beloved in the Italian American restaurants of Chicago: Chicken and potatoes are cooked in a single skillet along with a garlicky white wine pan sauce that practically makes itself. So why aren't we all making chicken Vesuvio at home?

Before I answer, a look at how the dish comes together in a restaurant kitchen: A line cook makes each serving to order by searing a half chicken skin side down in an olive oil–slicked skillet and then adding potato wedges, which brown and crisp in the rendered fat. Everything is sprinkled generously with minced garlic and dried herbs, and then the chicken and potatoes are turned browned side up. Plenty of white wine goes into the pan, which is then transferred to a hot oven until everything cooks through.

With the cooked chicken and potatoes transferred to a warm plate, the sauce is briefly reduced in the skillet. A handful of peas or a sprinkling of parsley might be added before pouring the loose sauce around the chicken and potatoes. The whole process takes about 30 minutes.

Now, back to why Vesuvio isn't at the top of anyone's Tuesday night dinner list: None of the recipes I tried were particularly successful. They were all designed to serve at least four, which meant that the skillet was crowded. In cramped conditions, the chicken skin didn't render adequately, so it remained flabby, and the potatoes didn't brown well. Plus, the compact layer of chicken and potatoes acted like a lid, inhibiting evaporation of the sauce in the oven, which left it thin and sharp-tasting. Even after I reduced the sauce on the stovetop, it had a disappointingly watery consistency, with a layer of fat floating on top and all the garlic particles lurking at the bottom.

But the prospect of a chicken Vesuvio with enough crisp-skinned chicken, well-browned potatoes, and potent sauce to serve at least four was a powerful inducement. And if I could make the dish almost as quickly as a Chicago line cook? Even better. I pressed on.

The sauce ingredients—dry white wine, garlic cloves, oregano, and thyme—go into the pan once halved potatoes are browned in savory chicken fat.

▶ Look: Vesuvio at Home
A step-by-step video is available at CooksIllustrated.com/oct18

Sizing Up the Skillet

Most of the faults in my first round of testing could be attributed to a single factor: insufficient surface area. A restaurant cook makes each serving of chicken Vesuvio in its own skillet, so there is ample room for a half chicken and four or five wedges of potato to brown and for the sauce to cook down.

More servings required more surface area, but simultaneously wrangling two skillets seemed intimidating. Instead, I dug out my roasting pan, which was broad enough to accommodate all the ingredients, heavy enough to heat evenly, and tall enough to contain any sloshing of sauce.

Vesuvio Victories

Even with so much surface area at my disposal, a half chicken per person seemed excessive. Instead, I decided to go with just thighs. They cook up tender and juicy without salting or brining, they have plenty of skin for crisping, and they exude a good amount of fat, which would enrich the potatoes and sauce.

I placed the roasting pan over two burners set at medium-high heat. Instead of the traditional olive oil, which would lose its distinctive flavor over the heat, I added a tablespoon of vegetable oil and waited for it to shimmer. In went eight thighs, skin side down. After they'd released some fat, I added 1½ pounds of Yukon Gold potatoes (we liked this variety for its creamy texture) that I had halved crosswise, which made them sturdier than the wedges. What's more, they didn't occupy as much of the precious cooking

Are Some Dried Herbs as Good as Fresh?

We often prefer the flavor of fresh herbs in recipes, but dried oregano and thyme—the traditional choices in chicken Vesuvio—work fine here for two reasons. First, the ample amount of wine in the recipe provides moisture, which softens the herbs. The second reason has to do with the nature of the herbs themselves.

Delicate herbs such as basil and chives are native to wet, temperate regions. Their flavor compounds are more volatile than water, so they're gone before the leaves are fully dehydrated, leaving these herbs nearly flavorless in their dried form. But hardier oregano and thyme (as well as rosemary, bay, and sage) are native to hot, dry climates, so they've evolved to withstand warm, arid conditions. Their flavor compounds are less volatile, so they retain much of their flavor when dried.

HERBS THAT CAN TAKE THE HEAT
Herbs native to hot, dry climates—oregano, thyme, rosemary, bay, and sage—retain their flavor compounds when dried.

surface, and they required browning on only one side. I added a whopping 12 cloves of minced garlic, sprinkled dried oregano and thyme (see "Are Some Dried Herbs as Good as Fresh?") over the whole thing, and flipped the chicken. After turning all the potatoes browned side up, I poured in 1½ cups of dry white wine and moved the roasting pan to the oven. Twenty minutes later, I transferred the cooked chicken and potatoes to a platter, returned the roasting pan to the stovetop, and reduced the sauce, which took only about 4 minutes. I skipped the peas since they made the sauce sweet and vegetal, but I included a bit of parsley for color and freshness.

This was a huge improvement. The thighs were moist, tender, and crisp-skinned, and the potatoes were deeply browned. However, the sauce—although garlicky and bright—was still separated and thin, and the garlic detritus scattered throughout was irksome.

Garlic Gains

I considered skimming the fat from the sauce, but I didn't want to lose its rich flavor, which was a perfect foil for the wine's acidity. Stumped on that score, I turned my attention to those troublesome garlic bits.

For my next batch, I halved the garlic cloves instead of mincing them. My plan was to steep them in the sauce while it cooked and then fish them out before serving. But with their reduced surface area, they hadn't released much flavor. My sauce had gone from punchy to puny, and it was still greasy and thin.

Luckily, the softened garlic had made it only as far as my cutting board. I chopped it coarse, mashed it with the side of my knife, scooped it up, and whisked it back into the sauce. And then something unexpected happened: The fat that had been on the surface of the sauce was instantly incorporated, leaving nary a droplet behind. It turns out that garlic can be a powerful emulsifier (see "Bet You Didn't Know That Garlic Can . . ."). The garlic paste also added a bit of bulk, which gave the sauce even more body.

No Room for the Potatoes

In restaurants, one or two servings of chicken Vesuvio are prepared to order in a skillet. But when we made enough to serve four, the pan was so overcrowded that the chicken skin stayed flabby, the potatoes didn't brown, and the sauce failed to reduce. Our fix: a roasting pan. Its large surface provides ample room for eight chicken thighs and 1½ pounds of potatoes to brown and for the sauce to simmer.

FOUR SERVINGS JUST WON'T FIT

Bet You Didn't Know That Garlic Can . . .

. . . Be Tamed with Lemon Juice

Garlic cloves contain a compound called alliin, which has a mild flavor, and an enzyme known as alliinase. When the clove is whole, the two substances are kept in different parts of the plant's cells, but as soon as the garlic is cut and the cells are damaged, they mix. Within 30 seconds, the enzyme converts mild alliin into a third compound: pungent allicin, which gives raw garlic its bite. However, when an acidic ingredient such as lemon juice is quickly added to the cut garlic, the acid mostly prevents the enzyme from working, leaving the garlic with more of the mild—and less of the biting—compound.

Acid mellows the fiery taste of fresh garlic.

. . . Act as an Emulsifier

We've noticed that mashed garlic—whether raw or cooked—is an effective emulsifier, helping blend fat and water into a creamy sauce, possibly due to some of the sulfur compounds that are formed when its cells are ruptured (the 12 cloves of garlic also add bulk). Whisking mashed garlic into our sauce changes its texture from thin and separated to thick and uniform.

Our sauce boasts a thick, uniform texture thanks to mashed garlic.

The mashed garlic added a welcome note of nutty sweetness, but the sauce needed a little more zing. I minced two more cloves and mixed them with a bit of lemon juice. The acid limits the formation of the pungent compound allicin, the source of garlic's heat. Perfect: The sauce now had well-rounded, punchy garlic flavor, and whereas 12 minced garlic cloves had marred its texture, these final two cloves weren't noticeable. I poured the sauce around the chicken and potatoes so as not to obscure their beautiful brown hues.

Chicago has many attractions, but chicken Vesuvio is one that no longer requires a plane ticket.

CHICKEN VESUVIO
SERVES 4 TO 6

For this recipe you'll need a roasting pan that measures at least 16 by 12 inches. Trim all the skin from the underside of the chicken thighs, but leave the skin on top intact. To ensure that all the potatoes fit in the pan, halve them crosswise to minimize their surface area. For the most efficient browning, heat the roasting pan over two burners. Combining the garlic with lemon juice in step 1 makes the garlic taste less harsh, but only if the lemon juice is added immediately after the garlic is minced. Our recipe for Chicken Vesuvio for Two is available for free for four months at CooksIllustrated.com/oct18.

- 8 (5- to 7-ounce) bone-in chicken thighs, trimmed
- Kosher salt and pepper
- 1½ pounds Yukon Gold potatoes, 2 to 3 inches in diameter, halved crosswise
- 2 tablespoons vegetable oil
- 14 garlic cloves, peeled (2 whole, 12 halved lengthwise)
- 1 tablespoon lemon juice
- 1½ teaspoons dried oregano
- ½ teaspoon dried thyme
- 1½ cups dry white wine
- 2 tablespoons minced fresh parsley

1. Adjust oven rack to upper-middle position and heat oven to 450 degrees. Pat chicken dry with paper towels and sprinkle on both sides with 1½ teaspoons salt and ½ teaspoon pepper. Toss potatoes with 1 tablespoon oil and 1 teaspoon salt. Mince 2 whole garlic cloves and immediately combine with lemon juice in small bowl; set aside.

2. Heat remaining 1 tablespoon oil in large roasting pan over medium-high heat until shimmering. Place chicken, skin side down, in single layer in pan and cook, without moving it, until chicken has rendered about 2 tablespoons of fat, 2 to 3 minutes. Place potatoes cut side down in chicken fat, arranging so that cut sides are in complete contact with surface of pan. Sprinkle chicken and potatoes with oregano and thyme. Continue to cook until chicken and potatoes are deeply browned and crisp, 8 to 12 minutes longer, moving chicken and potatoes to ensure even browning and flipping pieces when fully browned. When all pieces have been flipped, tuck halved garlic cloves among chicken and potatoes. Remove pan from heat and pour wine into pan (do not pour over chicken or potatoes). Transfer pan to oven and roast until potatoes are tender when pierced with tip of paring knife and chicken registers 185 to 190 degrees, 15 to 20 minutes.

3. Transfer chicken and potatoes to deep platter, browned sides up. Place pan over medium heat (handles will be hot) and stir to incorporate any browned bits. Using slotted spoon, transfer garlic cloves to cutting board. Chop coarse, then mash to smooth paste with side of knife. Whisk garlic paste into sauce. Continue to cook until sauce coats back of spoon, 3 to 5 minutes longer. Remove from heat and whisk in reserved lemon juice mixture and 1 tablespoon parsley. Pour sauce around chicken and potatoes. Sprinkle with remaining 1 tablespoon parsley and serve.

Real Carne Adovada

Restraint is the key to the purest, most robust chile flavor in this classic New Mexican pork braise. It's also what makes it dead simple to prepare.

⇒ BY ANNIE PETITO ⇐

Before I take you on a deep dive into *carne adovada*, one of New Mexico's most celebrated dishes and quite possibly the easiest braise you will ever make, I need to back up and explain how hugely significant chiles are in New Mexican cuisine.

For one thing, the state claims its own unique chile cultivars. The relatively mild peppers, which are sold both fresh—either unripe and green or ripe and red—and dried were first released by New Mexico State University in 1913 and have since become one of the defining ingredients in the local cuisine—not to mention the state's most lucrative cash crop. New Mexico even passed a law declaring that only chiles grown in the state may be labeled as such. Dishes that feature the peppers typically contain few other seasonings so that the chile flavor can shine.

Carne adovada is a perfect example. To make it, cooks simmer chunks of pork in a thick sauce made from dried red New Mexican chiles; garlic; dried oregano; spices such as cumin, coriander, or cloves; vinegar; and a touch of sugar or honey. (*Adobada*, the Mexican preparation on which the dish is based, refers to meat cooked in an adobo sauce of chiles, aromatics, and vinegar.) When the meat is fall-apart tender, the rich, robust, brick-red braise is served with tortillas or rice and beans.

That's the purist's version, anyway. But there are also plenty of recipes for carne adovada that complicate the flavors by adding superfluous ingredients such as raisins, coffee, and/or a mix of other kinds of chiles so that the final result is reminiscent of a mole sauce. Many of these recipes, I found, are also plagued by typical braise problems, such as dry meat and over- or underseasoned sauce that is either too scant or too soupy.

I got to work on a minimalist braise—one that would feature moist, tender pork in a simple, potent sauce that tasted first and foremost of chiles.

What makes our *adovada* so simple? The chiles aren't toasted, the pork isn't seared, and the braising happens in the oven.

▶ See: It's All About the Chiles
A step-by-step video is available at CooksIllustrated.com/oct18

Seeing Red

Most of the recipes I found called for boneless butt roast, which is affordable, streaked with flavorful fat, and loaded with collagen that breaks down during cooking, rendering the meat tender. I cut the roast into 1½-inch chunks, which would be equally easy to eat wrapped in a tortilla or from a fork, and tossed the pieces with kosher salt so that the meat would be deeply seasoned. I didn't sear it since the meat above the surface of the liquid would brown in the oven.

Most of the simpler sauce formulas went something like this: Toast whole dried New Mexican chiles—as much as 8 ounces—and then steep them in boiling water until their stems soften, which takes about 30 minutes. Then, puree the chiles with enough water to form a thick paste and season it with garlic, spices, vinegar, and a sweetener.

Eight ounces of chiles was a massive pile that I wouldn't be able to toast or puree in a single batch, so I scaled down to a more manageable (but still generous) 4 ounces. After toasting and steeping them, I processed the chiles with 4 cups of the water they had soaked in, plus a couple of garlic cloves, Mexican oregano (less sweet than the Mediterranean kind), cumin, cloves, white vinegar, and sugar until it formed a loose puree. I poured the sauce over the meat in a Dutch oven, brought it to a boil on the stove, covered it, and (as we typically do with a braise) transferred it to the oven, where it would simmer gently and evenly with no stirring.

After about 2 hours of braising, the meat was fork-tender. But the sauce was way off—so loose and thin that it didn't cling to the meat. And despite the load of chiles it contained, the flavor was washed-out.

Reducing the water by half thickened the puree and made its flavor more concentrated, albeit one-dimensional. I'd have to think about tweaking the flavors. The bigger problem was that the chile seeds and skins hadn't broken down completely in

America's Oldest Cuisine

Often confused with Mexican and Tex-Mex cuisine, New Mexican cuisine is an amalgam of many influences that has evolved over hundreds of years and long predates the state's founding in 1912. Its earliest roots date back to Native American tribes (Pueblo, Apache, and Navajo), which settled in the area centuries before the pilgrims arrived at Plymouth Rock in 1620. The cuisine further evolved as new cooking traditions and ingredients were brought by Spanish settlers in the late 16th century, as well as by Anglo American and French newcomers who came to the area in the 1800s. As cattle ranching gained prominence in the 1800s, some cowboy got mixed in there, too.

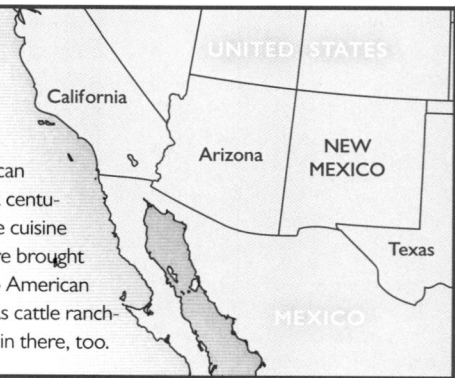

TECHNIQUE

BLENDING CHILES INTO A SMOOTH PUREE

To ensure that the tough skins on dried New Mexican chiles break down as thoroughly as possible in the blender, start by adding 1 cup of liquid—just enough to create a vortex while leaving enough friction to grind down the solids. Once the chiles are finely ground and the puree is smooth, blend in the remaining liquid.

the blender (New Mexican chile skins are particularly tough), and their texture was more noticeable now that there was less liquid.

Going forward, I made sure to seed the chiles before toasting them. As for the bits of skin, I tried straining them out to make the puree ultrasmooth, but it was a fussy step and the sauce suffered. Not only did it lack vibrancy in both color and flavor—chile skins contain high concentrations of flavor and aroma compounds that give them much of their astringent, floral, and fruity notes—but I found that the tiny insoluble particles of pureed skin and pulp were also responsible for making the sauce viscous enough to cling to the meat.

The trick to smoothing out the puree was refining my processing method. Instead of adding all of the water at the start, which left the skins swimming in liquid, I started with just enough liquid to keep the blender running before adding the rest. That way there was more friction to grind the solids.

The Toasting Is Toast

Back to refining the flavor of the sauce. Bumping up the amounts of garlic and vinegar, switching from sugar to the more nuanced sweetness of honey, and introducing a dash of cayenne pepper for subtle heat were all good moves. But the sauce still lacked the fruity brightness I was hoping for.

Toasting chiles is standard practice when you want to deepen their flavor; it can also add hints of char. But if I was after a sweeter, slightly acidic profile—which dried red New Mexican chiles naturally offer—maybe toasting them was the wrong move.

To find out, I held a side-by-side tasting of my adovada made with toasted and untoasted chiles. Sure enough, the untoasted batch boasted rounder flavor that was fruity, a touch sweet, and slightly astringent. Best of all, skipping the toasting step made the dish even easier to prepare.

The result was bright, rich, just a little spicy, and deeply satisfying—precisely the pure and simple adovada I'd had in mind. It's what I'll be making for dinner when I want a bold, hearty braise. And since those flavors also pair brilliantly with eggs and potatoes, I'll be sure to save the leftovers for breakfast.

BRAISED NEW MEXICO–STYLE PORK IN RED CHILE SAUCE (CARNE ADOVADA)
SERVES 6

Pork butt roast is often labeled Boston butt; to learn how to identify it, see page 28. For tips on trimming it, see page 30. For an accurate measurement of boiling water, bring a full kettle of water to a boil and then measure out the desired amount. If you can't find New Mexican chiles, substitute dried California chiles. Dried chiles should be pliable and smell slightly fruity. Kitchen shears can be used to cut them. If you can't find Mexican oregano, substitute Mediterranean oregano. Letting the stew rest for 10 minutes before serving allows the sauce to thicken and better coat the meat. Serve with rice and beans, crispy potatoes, or flour tortillas with shredded lettuce and chopped tomato, or shred the pork as a filling for tacos and burritos.

1	(3½- to 4-pound) boneless pork butt roast, trimmed and cut into 1½-inch pieces
	Kosher salt
4	ounces dried New Mexican chiles, wiped clean, stemmed, seeded, and torn into 1-inch pieces
4	cups boiling water
2	tablespoons honey
2	tablespoons distilled white vinegar
5	garlic cloves, peeled
2	teaspoons dried Mexican oregano
2	teaspoons ground cumin
½	teaspoon cayenne pepper
⅛	teaspoon ground cloves
	Lime wedges

1. Toss pork and 1 tablespoon salt together in bowl; refrigerate for 1 hour.

2. Place chiles in medium bowl. Pour boiling water over chiles, making sure they are completely submerged, and let stand until softened, 30 minutes. Adjust oven rack to lower-middle position and heat oven to 325 degrees.

3. Drain chiles and reserve 2 cups soaking liquid (discard remaining liquid). Process chiles, honey, vinegar, garlic, oregano, cumin, cayenne, cloves, and 1 teaspoon salt in blender until chiles are finely ground and thick paste forms, about 30 seconds. With blender running, add 1 cup reserved liquid and process until smooth, 1½ to 2 minutes, adding up to ¼ cup additional reserved liquid to maintain vortex. Add remaining reserved liquid and continue to blend sauce at high speed, 1 minute longer.

4. Combine pork and chile sauce in Dutch oven, stirring to make sure pork is evenly coated. Bring to boil over high heat. Cover pot, transfer to oven, and cook until pork is tender and fork inserted into pork meets little to no resistance, 2 to 2½ hours.

5. Using wooden spoon, scrape any browned bits from sides of pot and stir until pork and sauce are recombined and sauce is smooth and homogeneous. Let stand, uncovered, for 10 minutes. Season with salt to taste. Serve with lime wedges. (Leftover pork can be refrigerated for up to 3 days.)

Carne adovada for breakfast? You bet. The bright, robust chile sauce goes great with eggs, potatoes, and warmed tortillas.

INGREDIENT SPOTLIGHT
New Mexican Chiles

Chiles are as fundamental to New Mexican cuisine as soy is to Japanese cooking or potatoes are to Irish food. In fact, the state breeds and grows its own unique cultivars, which are sold both fresh and dried. Fresh chiles appear in everything from casseroles to burgers to rice; dried chiles appear in sauces for braised meats such as *carne adovada* or for enchiladas. Here's a rundown on the flavor and heat profile of the dried kind and how to substitute for them. (For information on shopping for, cleaning, and storing dried chiles, see page 29.)

Flavor: Fruity, sweet, slightly acidic
Heat: Relatively mild; Scoville rating: 0 to 7,000 (For reference: Bell peppers rate from 0 to 1,000; jalapeños rate from 1,000 to 50,000; and habaneros rate from 100,000 to 500,000.)
Appearance: Wrinkly; dark red; particularly shiny, tough skins
Substitute: Dried California chiles

Next-Level Grilled Steak

Anyone can throw a rib eye on the fire. But Japanese *negimaki* rolls the flavors of teriyaki and the stylish presentation of sushi into a make-ahead summer stunner.

≥ BY ANDREW JANJIGIAN ≤

These rolls, which can be assembled and refrigerated overnight before grilling, cook in about 30 minutes.

When was the last time you hosted a summer cookout and made a dish that your guests snapped up in minutes and raved about for the rest of the night? If you can't recall, consider this recipe—a popular Japanese preparation called *negimaki*—an opportunity to up your grill game.

The name may sound exotic, but its flavors and presentation are not. Negimaki is essentially a hybrid of beef teriyaki and rolled sushi, at least conceptually. To make it, cooks slice and pound a steak into thin strips, which they lay on a flat surface in an overlapping arrangement to form a rectangle. Then they roll the meat around a small bundle of scallions (*negi* means "scallion"; *maki*, "roll") to form a tight cylinder, fasten it with toothpicks, grill it over a hot fire, and brush it with a teriyaki-style glaze. Before serving, they slice the rolls crosswise into bite-size pieces and sprinkle them with toasted sesame seeds so that every beefy, grassy, salty-sweet bite pops with a nutty-rich, delicate crunch.

It's a dish you often see on Japanese restaurant menus alongside appetizers such as edamame and *gyoza*. But it's also great for home grilling: There are few ingredients; the rolls cook quickly—and, in the version I hoped to create, can be assembled ahead of time; and it functions equally well as an appetizer as it does alongside steamed rice and a vegetable as a complete meal.

High-Steaks Decision

Flavor and texture are two factors that I always consider when choosing a cut of beef. But here I also needed to consider the shape, size, and uniformity of the meat, since it needed to function as a "wrapper."

That's why I was surprised to find negimaki recipes that called for cuts such as tenderloin. For one thing, their leanness prevents them from charring quickly and makes them bland and prone to drying out. And when I tried slicing and pounding these cuts, I found that their exceptional tenderness made them too soft to roll into supportive wrappers. Plus, I wasn't about to splurge on a pricey tenderloin only to pound the daylights out of it. Same goes for other premium cuts such as strip steak and rib eye.

In the end, I chose flank steak. It's more affordable, flavorful, and mostly uniform. The drawbacks are that it tapers at one end and its edges are rounded; I'd have to devise a way to make an even wrapper out of the disparate pieces.

That's a Wrap

Producing a sturdy, tender wrapper is all about evenly slicing and pounding the steak and arranging the pieces in a rectangle with sides that are as straight as possible. I started by briefly freezing the steak to firm it up and make it easier to slice cleanly. Then I cut a few slices from the tapered end and pounded them about 3/16 inch thick. That left me with a roughly square piece of meat, which I halved along the grain to produce two slabs. I sliced the slabs crosswise and pounded those slices, too.

But pounding the slices exaggerated their rounded edges so that some pieces were irregularly shaped. I got around that by assembling the wrapper like a jigsaw puzzle, laying down one slice and then orienting two more around it to form straight edges on three sides. The rest of the assembly was a breeze: I laid a couple of whole raw scallions in each wrapper and rolled the package into a tight cylinder that I secured with toothpicks (see "Wrapping and Rolling Negimaki").

I grilled the rolls over a hot fire, turning them every 5 minutes so that they charred evenly. Partway through cooking, I brushed them with a glaze mixture of sake, mirin, soy sauce, and sugar.

Inside and Out

I couldn't track the meat's doneness by taking its temperature because the slices were too thin to probe with a thermometer, so I took a guess and pulled the rolls off the grill after about 20 minutes. At that point, the meat appeared to be cooked just beyond medium, which we've found is the ideal doneness for cuts with thick muscle fibers, such as flank steak.

But while the meat tasted good, most of the thin glaze had run off the meat as soon as I brushed it on. And the scallions, though pleasantly grassy and fresh against the beefy char, tasted sweeter or sharper depending on whether you ate a piece of negimaki that contained the whites or the greens.

▶ **Andrew Shows You How**
A step-by-step video is available at CooksIllustrated.com/oct18

TECHNIQUE

TEMP THE SCALLIONS
The meat is too thin to probe, so we take the temperature of the scallions instead.

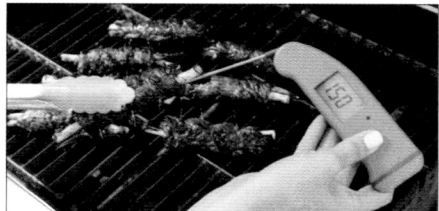

Insert the probe at the end of the roll into the scallion core. If the temperature registers between 150 and 155 degrees, the meat is done.

COOK'S ILLUSTRATED

To manage the scallion flavor, I halved each one crosswise and placed the halves inside each roll with the white parts at either end and the green parts down the center. I also let the whites hang over the roll ends. That way they could cook a little more to tame their sharpness and pick up some flavorful char over the fire.

But my most novel trick might have been this: monitoring the temperature of the middle of the rolls where the scallions were as a more reliable indication of the meat's doneness. Strange as that sounds, I discovered that when the scallions reached about 150 degrees, the steak was appropriately medium to medium-well.

As for the runny glaze, I reduced the mixture to a syrupy consistency before brushing it onto the rolls. The reduction clung nicely to the meat and boasted more concentrated flavor. I liked it so much that I made enough to drizzle over the finished rolls, too.

The result tasted great and looked even better. This is a dish I will pull out for company (samples in the test kitchen were gobbled up in seconds)—but it's also a dinner I'll throw on the grill any night, since the rolls can be assembled ahead of time.

Starter? Entrée? Your Choice

Negimaki is typically offered as appetizer fare in Japanese restaurants, but we found that it functions equally well as an entrée paired with simple sides. And since our version can be assembled and refrigerated for up to 24 hours before grilling, it can be a 30-minute dinner any night of the week. Below are some suggested accompaniments that Web subscribers can access at CooksIllustrated.com/oct18.

As part of an appetizer spread with: Shrimp Tempura, Chinese Pork Dumplings, Scallion Pancakes

As an entrée with: Sautéed Snow Peas with Ginger, Garlic, and Scallion; Chinese Restaurant–Style Rice

JAPANESE GRILLED STEAK AND SCALLION ROLLS (NEGIMAKI)
SERVES 8 TO 10 AS AN APPETIZER OR 4 TO 6 AS A MAIN DISH

Look for a flank steak that is as rectangular as possible, as this will yield the most uniform slices. Depending on how you slice the steak, you may end up with extra slices; you can grill these alongside the rolls or make several smaller rolls. Serve either as an appetizer or as a main dish with steamed white rice and a vegetable.

- 1 (2-pound) flank steak, trimmed
- ½ cup soy sauce
- ¼ cup sugar
- 3 tablespoons mirin
- 3 tablespoons sake
- 16 scallions, trimmed and halved crosswise
- 1 tablespoon sesame seeds, toasted

1. Place steak on large plate and freeze until firm, about 30 minutes.

2. Bring soy sauce, sugar, mirin, and sake to simmer in small saucepan over high heat, stirring to dissolve sugar. Reduce heat to medium and cook until slightly syrupy and reduced to ½ cup, 3 to 5 minutes. Divide evenly between 2 bowls and let cool. Cover 1 bowl with plastic wrap and set aside for serving.

3. Place steak on cutting board. Starting at narrow, tapered end, slice steak ⅜-inch thick on bias against grain until width of steak is 7 inches (depending on size of steak, you will need to remove 2 to 3 slices until steak measures 7 inches across). Cut steak in half lengthwise. Continue to slice each half on bias against grain. You should have at least 24 slices. Pound each slice to 3/16-inch thickness between 2 sheets of plastic.

4. Arrange 3 slices on cutting board with short side of slices facing you, overlapping slices by ¼ inch and alternating tapered ends as needed, to form rough rectangle that measures 4 to 6 inches wide and at least 4 inches long. Place 4 scallion halves along edge of rectangle nearest to edge of counter, with white tips slightly hanging over edges of steak on either side. Starting from bottom edge and rolling away from you, roll into tight cylinder. Insert 3 equally spaced toothpicks into end flaps and through center of roll. Transfer roll to platter and repeat with remaining steak and scallions. (Assembled rolls can be refrigerated for up to 24 hours.)

5A. FOR A CHARCOAL GRILL: Open bottom vent completely. Light large chimney starter three-quarters filled with charcoal briquettes (4½ quarts). When top coals are partially covered with ash, pour evenly over half of grill. Set cooking grate in place, cover, and open lid vent completely. Heat grill until hot, about 5 minutes.

5B. FOR A GAS GRILL: Turn all burners to high, cover, and heat grill until hot, about 15 minutes. Leave all burners on high.

6. Clean and oil cooking grate. Place rolls on grill (over coals if using charcoal) and cook until first side is beginning to char, 4 to 6 minutes. Flip rolls, brush cooked side with glaze, and cook until second side is beginning to char, 4 to 6 minutes. Cook remaining 2 sides, glazing after each turn, until all 4 sides of rolls are evenly charred and thermometer inserted from end of roll into scallions at core registers 150 to 155 degrees, 16 to 24 minutes total. Transfer rolls to cutting board, tent with aluminum foil, and let rest for 5 minutes. Discard remaining glaze.

7. Remove toothpicks from rolls and cut rolls crosswise into ¾-inch-long pieces. Arrange rolls cut side down on clean platter, drizzle with 2 tablespoons reserved glaze, sprinkle with sesame seeds, and serve, passing remaining reserved glaze separately.

STEP BY STEP | WRAPPING AND ROLLING NEGIMAKI

First we cut a few slices from the thin end and halve the chilled steak lengthwise. Then we slice, pound, and arrange the meat strategically to produce a sturdy, tight log.

1. SLICE chilled steak against grain on bias into 24 pieces.

2. POUND slices to 3/16-inch thickness.

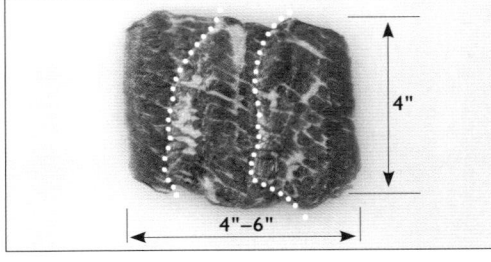

3. ARRANGE slices like jigsaw puzzle, overlapping them by ¼ inch to form rough 4- to 6-inch by 4-inch rectangle.

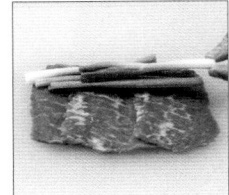

4. PLACE scallion halves head to toe on beef, letting white tips hang over edges.

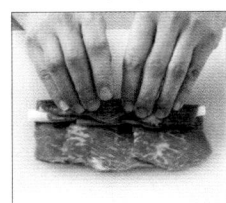

5. ROLL into tight cylinder and fasten with 3 toothpicks pushed through roll.

Fish for Meat Lovers

Most types of fish require a gentle temperature and a delicate touch.
But for rich, meaty swordfish, it's best to crank up the heat.

> BY LAN LAM <

It seems funny to admit that a fish was once my nemesis, but there was a spell back when I was a line cook when that was exactly the case. For five straight nights, I carefully prepared what appeared to be pristine swordfish steaks and began to plate them up, only to find that they were soft and mushy. The restaurant waitstaff then had to inform the diner that his or her entrée choice had been taken off the menu for the evening. Back then, I didn't know what to attribute the poor—not to mention wasteful—results to, and we ultimately stopped serving swordfish altogether. But I've long wondered why the texture of swordfish can sometimes be perfect—meaty, juicy, and tender—and other times so unpleasant. It was time to use a scientific approach to figure out why—and come up with a solution.

It would be a worthwhile effort: I knew that swordfish, unlike silky salmon or flaky halibut, at least had the potential to offer a unique dense meatiness. This distinctive texture, combined with a sweet, mild flavor, could excite even a staunch carnivore. In fact, swordfish steaks are similar enough to beef steaks that I decided to start my investigation by looking to one of the test kitchen's favorite methods for cooking steak.

We call it reverse searing: First, we gently cook the meat in the oven until it's perfectly juicy and tender, and then we transfer it to the stovetop to quickly brown the exterior. I seasoned four 8-ounce swordfish steaks with salt and cooked them gently in a 300-degree oven for about 45 minutes, until they were a few degrees shy of 140 degrees, a temperature

Go ahead and use tongs to flip the fish. Because of its firm, steak-like texture, swordfish is easy to maneuver and won't flake apart.

that the test kitchen likes for white fish. Next, I briefly seared the fish steaks in an oil-slicked nonstick skillet until they acquired a golden-brown crust and let them rest for a few minutes. They looked gorgeous, but I knew all too well that a good-looking swordfish exterior often hides a disappointing interior. Sure enough, although some tasters charitably described the fish as "too tender," most reported that it had the soft, tacky, almost mushy texture of canned tuna.

The Breakdown

After consulting with our science editor, I understood what was going on. Just like meats, fish contains enzymes called cathepsins. If the circumstances are right, the cathepsins will snip the proteins that give swordfish its sturdy texture, turning it soft. Although they're ultimately destroyed by heat, cathepsins are increasingly active at low cooking temperatures. By slowly bringing the swordfish steaks up to 140 degrees, I was giving the cathepsins plenty of time to take the flesh from meaty to mushy (see "Why Swordfish Can Turn Mushy").

Clearly, I needed to speed up the cooking. The fastest way to cook these (or any) steaks indoors would be to sear them in a skillet. The metal in the pan would conduct heat to the fish more rapidly than even the hottest oven or broiler. In a skillet, flipped once halfway through cooking, the steaks were done in just 16 to 18 minutes. Tasters agreed that this was a step in the right direction: Each bite was firmer since the enzymes hadn't been given much time to act. But I wasn't going to get off that easy. The swordfish was dry and tough just beneath the well-browned crust.

It made sense that the portions of the swordfish that had been nearest to the hot skillet were overcooked. The part of the fish that's in contact with the pan heats up very quickly because of the skillet's ability to transfer heat. That portion of the flesh must in turn transfer that heat to the layers adjacent to it. And most food, swordfish included, doesn't transfer heat quickly. The upshot is that as the interior slowly heats up, the exterior overcooks. But if gentle cooking turned these steaks to mush and a hard sear—necessary for preserving their texture—left them wrung out, where did that leave me?

Flipping Out

I had flipped the steaks only once during cooking. What if I flipped them more frequently? After the first flip, the steaks would cook from both sides. Simultaneously, the top side would get a reprieve from the hot pan, which could minimize overcooking (see "The Benefits of Frequent Flipping").

When my oiled skillet began to smoke, I added the swordfish steaks. I flipped them every 2 minutes, and after about 10 minutes, they hit 140 degrees.

SWORDFISH BASICS

SHOPPING: Swordfish steaks typically have a bloodline—a dark muscle rich in myoglobin—running through them. Since we found that the bloodline has an unpleasant mineral taste, we recommend looking for steaks with as minimal a bloodline as possible.

PREP: Thick, rubbery swordfish skin tightens up more than the flesh during cooking and can cause the steak to buckle. You can either ask your fishmonger to remove it for you or trim it off yourself using a thin, sharp knife.

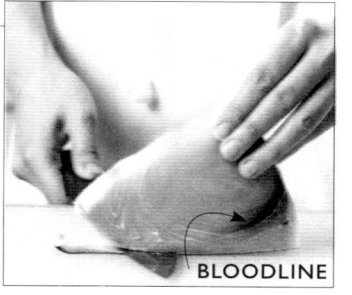

BLOODLINE

SCIENCE The Benefits of Frequent Flipping

We have noticed that frequently flipping swordfish (as well as beef steaks, pork chops, and tuna) during searing leads to faster, more evenly cooked results. To demonstrate this, we pan-seared nine swordfish steaks, nine strip steaks, and nine pork chops until they reached 130, 125, and 140 degrees, respectively. We flipped three of each protein every 30 seconds, three every 2 minutes, and three just once, recording how long it took each to reach the desired temperature.

The proteins flipped every 30 seconds cooked the fastest, while those flipped just once were the slowest. The 30-second and 2-minute samples were well browned and evenly cooked, whereas the once-flipped samples were also nicely browned but had a large band of overcooked flesh.

➤ **Here's why frequent flipping is efficient:** A hot skillet cooks food from the bottom up. When a protein is flipped, the seared side, which is then facing up, is also quite hot. Some of its heat dissipates into the air, and some of it cooks the protein from the top down. The more often a protein is flipped, the more it will cook from both the bottom up and the top down.

Though flipping pan-seared proteins every 30 seconds results in the speediest, most even cooking, it is impractical. However, flipping every 2 minutes cuts the cooking time by about 30 percent, which makes it well worth the effort.

This significantly cut the cooking time, and the steaks were much improved. They were cooked throughout and sported golden-brown crusts, and each bite was dense and meaty. There was just one problem: The fish oozed juices as it rested. A quick temperature check revealed the reason. The aggressive cooking had caused the fish to carry over to 150 degrees. And at such a high temperature, the proteins shrank and squeezed out juices. I seared another batch, this time pulling the steaks from the skillet when they registered just 130 degrees. That did the trick: During a 10-minute rest, they climbed to the target temperature of 140 degrees.

Though the rich, meaty, juicy steaks were great with just a squeeze of lemon, I wanted to celebrate the conquering of my nemesis (how I wish I knew then what I know now!) with a couple of sauces. One was a classic Italian swordfish accompaniment, an *agrodolce*-style relish based on piquant capers and sweet currants; the other was an ultragarlicky sauce with the unique addition of dried mint.

PAN-SEARED SWORDFISH STEAKS
SERVES 4

For the best results, purchase swordfish steaks that are ¾ to 1 inch thick. Look for four steaks that weigh 7 to 9 ounces each or two steaks that weigh about 1 pound each. If you purchase the latter, cut them in half to create four steaks. We've found that skin-on swordfish often buckles in the hot skillet. Ask your fishmonger to remove the skin or trim it yourself with a thin, sharp knife. Serve with Caper-Currant Relish or Spicy Dried Mint–Garlic Sauce (recipes follow), if desired. Our recipes for Pan-Seared Swordfish Steaks for Two and Harissa-Oregano Sauce are available for free for four months at CooksIllustrated.com/oct18.

- 2 teaspoons vegetable oil
- 2 pounds skinless swordfish steaks, ¾ to 1 inch thick
- 1½ teaspoons kosher salt
- Lemon wedges

1. Heat oil in 12-inch nonstick skillet over medium-high heat until shimmering. While oil heats, pat steaks dry with paper towels and sprinkle on both sides with salt.

2. Place steaks in skillet and cook, flipping every 2 minutes, until golden brown and centers register 130 degrees, 7 to 11 minutes. Transfer to serving platter or individual plates and let rest for 10 minutes. Serve with lemon wedges.

CAPER-CURRANT RELISH
MAKES ABOUT ½ CUP

Golden raisins can be substituted for the currants.

- 3 tablespoons minced fresh parsley
- 3 tablespoons extra-virgin olive oil
- 2 tablespoons capers, rinsed and chopped fine
- 2 tablespoons currants, chopped fine
- 1 garlic clove, minced
- 1 teaspoon grated lemon zest plus 2 tablespoons juice

Combine all ingredients in bowl. Let stand at room temperature for at least 20 minutes before serving.

SPICY DRIED MINT–GARLIC SAUCE
MAKES ABOUT ⅓ CUP

This sauce gets its spiciness from the raw garlic. If you are not using a garlic press, use a fork to bruise the minced garlic when stirring the sauce together.

- 4 teaspoons dried mint
- ¼ cup extra-virgin olive oil
- 2 tablespoons red wine vinegar
- 4 garlic cloves, minced
- ⅛ teaspoon salt

Place mint in fine-mesh strainer and use spoon to rub mint through strainer into bowl. Discard any solids left in strainer. (You should have about 1 tablespoon mint powder.) Add oil, vinegar, garlic, and salt to mint powder and stir to combine.

SCIENCE Why Swordfish Can Turn Mushy

Just as with land-bound critters, enzymes can have a profound impact on the texture of swordfish. To explore this, we cooked 12 swordfish steaks to 130 degrees—the temperature at which they need to be taken off the heat to carry over to a 140-degree serving temperature. We then held batches of four steaks at 130 degrees for 15 minutes, 45 minutes, and 1 hour and 45 minutes. Next, we measured the amount of force required to compress each sample ½ inch to quantify the experience of taking a bite. We found that the longer the fish stayed at 130 degrees, the softer it became. In fact, the force required to compress the fish at 15 minutes had decreased by about 15 percent after 45 minutes and 30 percent after 1 hour and 45 minutes.

➤ **Here's the explanation:** Enzymes in swordfish called cathepsins snip the proteins that hold the muscle fibers together. In fish, cathepsins are highly active at 130 degrees. When swordfish is cooked very slowly, its cathepsins have a long time to turn its flesh soft and mushy.

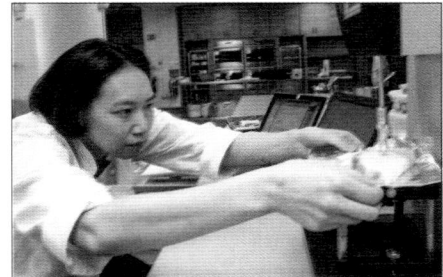

We used a highly sensitive machine called a CT3 texture analyzer to measure the amount of force required to compress each sample of fish.

Swordfish steaks, cooked for 15 minutes and held at 130 degrees for:	Force required to compress ½ inch
15 min	1,062 g
45 min	898 g
1 hr, 45 min	734 g

▶ Watch: Perfect Swordfish
A step-by-step video is available at CooksIllustrated.com/oct18

Really Good Falafel

Loading up the chickpea batter with fresh herbs and aromatics is what makes falafel the world's greatest fritters. Too bad it also makes them a mess to handle and cook.

≥ BY STEVE DUNN ≤

Rather than insert myself into the age-old debate over the origins of falafel—Egypt, Palestine, and Israel each claim it as a national dish—I prefer to think of it as a preparation with ancient roots and timeless universal appeal. But my recipe may prove to be divisive in another way: The key to its success comes from a technique associated with Asian bread baking. Before I explain how I landed there, however, it's important to understand why falafel is inherently tricky to make well.

Most falafel dough is nothing more than uncooked dried chickpeas or fava beans that have been soaked overnight so that they soften slightly before being coarsely ground in a food processor with onion, garlic, spices, and loads of fresh herbs (parsley and cilantro are typical). Grinding—not pureeing—the beans is what makes good falafel pleasantly nubbly and light, not pasty, and the abundant seasonings add freshness, warmth, and complexity to the otherwise starchy, neutral bean base. But both of those factors make forming and frying the fritters a real challenge. Binding up the coarse bean bits is like trying to make gravel stick together. The onion and herbs are full of water that helps make the falafel appealingly moist, but that moisture also makes the dough wet and often too fragile to pack into cohesive rounds or patties, never mind fry in a pot of vigorously bubbling oil.

That's why many recipes call for mixing starch into the dough—flour, cornstarch, and chickpea flour are all common additions. It's a surefire way to soak up that moisture and create a paste that helps bind the components so that the mixture is easy to handle and sturdy enough to withstand cooking. But the drawback, as I discovered when I made falafel with each of the three starches, is that when you use enough starch to act as a binder, it can render the falafel dense, dull-tasting, and overly dry.

No Can Do

Those competing goals are at the core of the problem and would be the focus of my testing. But before I jumped in, I wanted to give the admittedly rogue idea of using canned chickpeas a whirl to see if there was a way to eliminate the inconvenience of the overnight soak required by the dried kind. But these were a complete bust. Just a few spins in the food processor turned the drained canned beans into a sludgy puree that translated into falafel that were equally pasty and sludgy. I'd stick with the soaked dried chickpeas after all.

But how to make cohesive dough out of coarsely ground beans and loads of watery onion and herbs without drying out or otherwise ruining the falafel's texture? That was another matter—and where that Asian bread-baking technique came in handy.

Want the ultimate falafel? Make the pita (page 15), pickled vegetables (page 29), and tahini and tomato-chile sauces (page 13) yourself.

All About That Paste

It's called *tangzhong*. The gist is that you whisk together a little flour and water and briefly cook the mixture until it forms a smooth, pudding-like paste, which you then combine with the rest of the ingredients. In breads such as our Fluffy Dinner Rolls (January/February 2016), this cooked paste miraculously allows you to add extra water to the dough without making it too sticky or soupy to handle. Even more impressive is the exceptionally moist and tender final result.

A cohesive mixture that would cook up moist and tender was exactly what I needed for my falafel, so I experimented with the ratio of flour paste to chickpea base until the mixture was easy to form and stayed intact during frying. When I scooped a fritter from the hot oil and took a bite, I knew I was onto something: It was not only wonderfully moist and tender but also much lighter-textured than the batches I'd made with uncooked starches (for more information, see "How the Flour Paste Holds the Falafel Together").

The tangzhong method was a keeper, and I was able to lighten the texture of the fritters even more by adding a couple of spoonfuls of baking powder—an addition I saw in some modern falafel recipes—to the flour paste after microwaving. The only hitch was that by the time their exteriors were brown and crisp, these fritters, with their added moisture from the paste, were a tad raw at their cores. So I lowered the temperature of the oil from 350 to 325 degrees, which allowed them to fry longer without burning.

These falafel were killer: crisp and mahogany on the outside, with pleasantly nubbly, moist, and assertively seasoned centers. When I stuffed them into

COARSE GRIND

Keep It Coarse

To achieve falafel's desirably nubbly, open structure (right), it's crucial to grind the soaked dried chickpeas just until they're broken down into coarse bits (sesame seeds are a good visual reference). Processing them any further will result in a pasty dough and dense fritters.

COARSE INTERIOR

fresh Pita Bread (page 15) with traditional fixings such as Quick Pickled Turnips and Carrots with Lemon and Coriander (page 29), lemony tahini sauce, and a zingy tomato-chile puree, I felt convinced that nobody would fault me for introducing an Asian technique into a Middle Eastern classic. It may even go down in falafel history.

FALAFEL
MAKES 24 FALAFEL; SERVES 4 TO 6

This recipe requires that the chickpeas be soaked for at least 8 hours. Use a Dutch oven that holds 6 quarts or more. An equal amount of chickpea flour can be substituted for the all-purpose flour; if using, increase the water in step 4 to ½ cup. Do not substitute canned or quick-soaked chickpeas; they will make stodgy falafel. Serve the falafel with the tahini sauce as an appetizer or in Pita Bread (page 15) with lettuce, chopped tomatoes, chopped cucumbers, fresh cilantro, Quick Pickled Turnips and Carrots with Lemon and Coriander (page 29), and Tomato-Chile Sauce (recipe follows). Serve the first batch of falafel immediately or hold it in a 200-degree oven while the second batch cooks.

Falafel
- 8 ounces dried chickpeas, picked over and rinsed
- ¾ cup fresh cilantro leaves and stems
- ¾ cup fresh parsley leaves
- ½ onion, chopped fine
- 2 garlic cloves, minced
- 1½ teaspoons ground coriander
- 1 teaspoon ground cumin
- 1 teaspoon salt
- ¼ teaspoon cayenne pepper
- ¼ cup all-purpose flour
- 2 teaspoons baking powder
- 2 quarts vegetable oil

Tahini Sauce
- ⅓ cup tahini
- ⅓ cup plain Greek yogurt
- ¼ cup lemon juice (2 lemons)
- ¼ cup water
  Salt

1. FOR THE FALAFEL: Place chickpeas in large container and cover with water by 2 to 3 inches. Soak at room temperature for at least 8 hours or up to 24 hours. Drain well.

2. FOR THE TAHINI SAUCE: Whisk tahini, yogurt, and lemon juice in medium bowl until smooth. Whisk in water to thin sauce as desired. Season with salt to taste; set aside. (Sauce can be refrigerated for up to 4 days. Let come to room temperature and stir to combine before serving.)

3. Process cilantro, parsley, onion, garlic, coriander, cumin, salt, and cayenne in food processor for 5 seconds. Scrape down sides of bowl. Continue to process until mixture resembles pesto, about 5 seconds longer. Add chickpeas and pulse 6 times. Scrape down sides of bowl. Continue to pulse until chickpeas are coarsely chopped and resemble sesame seeds, about 6 more pulses. Transfer mixture to large bowl and set aside.

4. Whisk flour and ⅓ cup water in bowl until no lumps remain. Microwave, whisking every 10 seconds, until mixture thickens to stiff, smooth, pudding-like consistency that forms mound when dropped from end of whisk into bowl, 40 to 80 seconds. Stir baking powder into flour paste.

5. Add flour paste to chickpea mixture and, using rubber spatula, mix until fully incorporated. Divide mixture into 24 pieces and gently roll into golf ball–size spheres, transferring spheres to parchment paper–lined rimmed baking sheet once formed. (Formed falafel can be refrigerated for up to 2 hours.)

6. Heat oil in large Dutch oven over medium-high heat to 325 degrees. Add half of falafel and fry, stirring occasionally, until deep brown, about 5 minutes. Adjust burner, if necessary, to maintain oil temperature of 325 degrees. Using slotted spoon or wire skimmer, transfer falafel to paper towel–lined baking sheet. Return oil to 325 degrees and repeat with remaining falafel. Serve immediately with tahini sauce.

No More Fear of Frying
Using the right tools makes deep-frying a breeze: The WMF Profi Plus Spider Strainer 14" ($21) keeps your hands far from the hot oil and can scoop multiple pieces of food at a time. The ThermoWorks ChefAlarm ($59) clip-on probe thermometer monitors the oil temperature and transfers readings to a small countertop receiver.

THE FLY WAY TO FRY

TOMATO-CHILE SAUCE
MAKES ABOUT 1½ CUPS

Hunt's makes the test kitchen's favorite canned diced tomatoes.

- 1 (15-ounce) can diced tomatoes, drained
- ½ cup fresh cilantro leaves and stems
- 3 garlic cloves, minced
- 1 tablespoon red pepper flakes
- 1 tablespoon red wine vinegar, plus extra for seasoning
- 1 teaspoon ground cumin
- 1 teaspoon ground coriander
  Salt
- ½ teaspoon smoked paprika
- ⅛ teaspoon sugar
- 2 tablespoons extra-virgin olive oil

Process tomatoes, cilantro, garlic, pepper flakes, vinegar, cumin, coriander, ¾ teaspoon salt, paprika, and sugar in food processor until smooth paste forms, 20 to 30 seconds. With processor running, slowly add oil until fully incorporated, about 5 seconds. Transfer to bowl and season with salt and extra vinegar to taste.

SCIENCE How the Flour Paste Holds the Falafel Together

Adding lots of onion and fresh herbs to falafel makes them flavorful and moist—and usually so wet and fragile that they fall apart in your hands or during cooking. Adding flour holds the falafel together and soaks up the excess moisture but makes the fritters dull and dense. Instead, we add a paste of cooked flour and water that contributes moisture and binds the mixture without weighing it down.

➤ **Here's why it works:** When the paste is cooked, the flour's starch granules burst and form a gelatinous web that locks the water in the paste in place, preventing it from making the mixture even looser. Meanwhile, cooking the flour also greatly increases its ability to absorb water, so we can add less flour overall to act as a binder. The result: fritters that are well seasoned, moist, and easy to form.

▶ **Look: DIY Falafel**
A step-by-step video is available at CooksIllustrated.com/oct18

Why You Should Make Pita Bread

The tender chew and complex flavor of fresh-baked pitas are revelatory. Once you've experienced homemade, you'll swear off supermarket rounds for good.

⇉ BY ANDREW JANJIGIAN ⇇

If your only experiences of pita have been the dry, flavorless rounds from the supermarket, you might wonder how this ancient bread—which dates back thousands of years—has persisted. But I can think of several reasons. The first being that good, fresh pita is a revelation: soft, tender, and pleasantly elastic, with flavor that's both faintly sweet and reminiscent of the hearth on which it was baked. It's got broad functionality, too: Tear it apart and use it as a vehicle for swiping up dips; wrap it around sandwich fillings; or take advantage of its built-in pocket and stuff it with falafel (see our recipe on page 13). And compared to the precision and skill required for other breads, making pita is a low-tech, casual endeavor—basically, you flatten a swath of dough into a thin disk, toss it onto a ripping-hot stone, and watch it puff.

Despite these compelling reasons to make pita at home, the bread's one drawback is that its soft, tender chew is extremely ephemeral. Within hours of being baked, the rounds turn dull and dry—hence the lackluster options at most supermarkets. Maybe there was a way to prolong some of that fresh-baked tenderness and moisture. I also discovered when I tried out a few recipes that pita's inherent casualness leaves room for pitfalls such as breads that lack complexity and don't reliably puff. I would look for tricks for overcoming those issues, too.

From Pizza to Pita?

Since pita is a form of flatbread like pizza, I wondered if the dough for our Thin-Crust Pizza (January/February 2011) would also work here. Using roughly the same ratios with some tweaks to bump up the dough's flavor—after all, I wouldn't be topping every inch of it with sauce and cheese—I combined bread flour, yeast, and honey (more complex-tasting than sugar) in a food processor and then added olive oil and ice-cold water (see "Why Colder Water Makes Better Dough"

▶ **Andrew Perfects Pita**
A step-by-step video is available at CooksIllustrated.com/oct18

A strong yet pliable dough and a hot oven help our pita dough rounds inflate and form pockets.

on page 31), mixing briefly to form a dough. A 10-minute rest allowed the flour to hydrate and gluten formation to begin, at which point I added the salt (delaying this addition ensures good gluten development) and processed until a smooth dough formed, which took just minutes. I shaped the dough into eight balls, placed them on an oiled baking sheet, and let them proof overnight in the refrigerator. This long fermentation not only is convenient—you can make the dough one day and bake it the next—but also lets the yeast develop complex flavors without producing too much gas, which would result in an overly bubbly dough. It also makes for a less elastic dough that's easier to work with. Those bubbles lead to weak spots when the dough is rolled out—and, as I soon learned, weak spots are an enemy of properly pocketed pitas. The next day, I rolled out my pitas and baked them on a stone in a 425-degree oven for just a few minutes per side, until they had tanned and puffed.

Correction: until most of them had puffed, since several never did. Even those that did inflate were dry, so I took the surest route to increasing the perception of moisture: adding more fat. Starting cautiously, I doubled the 2 teaspoons I had been using and was rewarded with bread that stayed moist noticeably longer than my previous attempts. Encouraged, I kept going until I'd enriched the dough with ¼ cup of oil. Twenty-four hours later, the bread was still nicely moist and reheated impressively well, but its texture was not optimal in other ways. All that fat had compromised the dough's gluten development—that is, its ability to form a structural network—so much that the rounds lacked even a gentle chew, and my already-mediocre success rate with pitas that puffed dropped even lower.

Clearly, I'd overdone it. But backing down on the oil would mean losing the benefits of its rich flavor and moisture, so instead I balanced its tenderizing effect by adding more water. Doing so made the flour proteins more mobile and increased the gluten's ability to form a stronger network during mixing. More water also created more steam once the breads were in the oven, which helped them puff—though only somewhat more reliably than previous batches had.

SCIENCE How Pita Puffs

The way that pitas inflate in the oven looks like magic, but it's caused by some simple science. When a disk of pita dough hits the oven, the hot air quickly bakes the outermost layer, forming a thin "skin." Simultaneously, water in the dough turns to steam, pushing outward. The "skin" stretches and expands—small bubbles first form around the edge of the pita and eventually merge into a single large signature pocket.

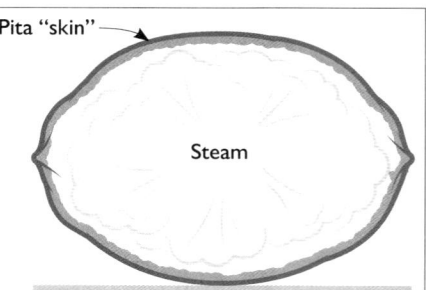

Puffed to Perfection

I couldn't solve the puffing problem until I figured out what causes the dough to inflate in the first place. The gist is that the oven's heat causes the dough's exterior to form a "skin" while steam from water in the dough causes the interior to expand. If the raw dough is perfectly smooth and taut, the skin that forms during baking is strong enough to withstand the steam pressure, and the dough expands impressively like a balloon. But if the dough has creases, thin patches, or other imperfections, as mine often did, they create weak spots where air can escape, preventing the signature puff.

Knowing that, I was careful to roll the proofed dough balls into flat, smooth, evenly thick disks. If the dough was insufficiently or unevenly coated with flour, it would stick to the counter or the rolling pin and could easily crease. I found a better way of thoroughly coating the dough with flour: Instead of dusting the counter with flour, I put the flour in a bowl and turned the dough in it (see "A New Way to Coat Your Dough"). That way, the dough was completely coated with flour even before it hit the counter. I still needed to use additional flour on the counter, too, since the dough becomes sticky again as it is rolled out.

But even my perfectly smooth dough rounds wouldn't always puff properly; some would inflate halfway and then frustratingly collapse, as if the top layer was too heavy for the steam to lift. When I examined the collapsed pitas, I saw that the top skins were quite thick—likely the result of baking too quickly. So I moved the baking stone from the middle rack to the lowest rack, which created more space between the pitas and the reflected heat at the top of the oven.

At last, every single round puffed beautifully—and all were gobbled up minutes after I pulled them from the oven. As a bonus, I tweaked the recipe to produce thick, plush Israeli-style rounds, and a nutty, more rustic version made with whole-wheat flour. That's a total of three compelling reasons why it's worth it to bake your own.

TAKE THE DOUGH FOR A DIP

A New Way to Coat Your Dough

To ensure that the dough is thoroughly coated in flour before it even hits the counter to be rolled out, we add flour to a bowl and turn each dough ball in it, brushing the excess right back into the bowl. Use this technique to coat other types of dough, such as pizza dough, before rolling out.

PITA BREAD
MAKES EIGHT 7-INCH PITA BREADS

We recommend weighing the flour and water. We prefer King Arthur bread flour for this recipe for its high protein content. If using another bread flour, reduce the amount of water in the dough by 2 tablespoons (1 ounce). If you don't have a baking stone, bake the pitas on an overturned and preheated rimmed baking sheet. The pitas are best eaten within 24 hours of baking. Reheat leftover pitas by wrapping them in aluminum foil, placing them in a cold oven, setting the temperature to 300 degrees, and baking for 15 to 20 minutes. Our recipes for double-thick Israeli-Style Pita Bread and Whole-Wheat Pita Bread are available for free for four months at CooksIllustrated.com/oct18.

- 2⅔ cups (14⅔ ounces) King Arthur bread flour
- 2¼ teaspoons instant or rapid-rise yeast
- 1⅓ cups (10½ ounces) ice water
- ¼ cup extra-virgin olive oil
- 4 teaspoons honey
- 1¼ teaspoons salt
- Vegetable oil spray

1. Whisk flour and yeast together in bowl of stand mixer. Add ice water, oil, and honey on top of flour mixture. Fit stand mixer with dough hook and mix on low speed until all flour is moistened, 1 to 2 minutes. Let dough stand for 10 minutes.

2. Add salt to dough and mix on medium speed until dough forms satiny, sticky ball that clears sides of bowl, 6 to 8 minutes. Transfer dough to lightly oiled counter and knead until smooth, about 1 minute. Divide dough into 8 equal pieces (about 3⅜ ounces each). Shape dough pieces into tight, smooth balls and transfer, seam side down, to rimmed baking sheet coated with oil spray. Spray tops of balls lightly with oil spray, then cover tightly with plastic wrap and refrigerate for at least 16 hours or up to 24 hours.

3. One hour before baking pitas, adjust oven rack to lowest position, set baking stone on rack, and heat oven to 425 degrees.

4. Remove dough from refrigerator. Coat 1 dough ball generously on both sides with flour and place on well-floured counter, seam side down. Use heel of your hand to press dough ball into 5-inch circle. Using rolling pin, gently roll into 7-inch circle, adding flour as necessary to prevent sticking. Roll slowly and gently to prevent any creasing. Repeat with second dough ball. Brush both sides of each dough round with pastry brush to remove any excess flour. Transfer dough rounds to unfloured peel, making sure side that was facing up when you began rolling is faceup again.

5. Slide both dough rounds carefully onto stone and bake until evenly inflated and lightly browned on undersides, 1 to 3 minutes. Using peel, slide pitas off stone and, using your hands or spatula, gently invert. (If pitas do not puff after 3 minutes, flip immediately to prevent overcooking.) Return pitas to stone and bake until lightly browned in center of second side, 1 minute. Transfer pitas to wire rack to cool, covering loosely with clean dish towel. Repeat shaping and baking with remaining 6 pitas in 3 batches. Let pitas cool for 10 minutes before serving.

STEP BY STEP | HOW TO SHAPE PITAS THAT RELIABLY FORM POCKETS

Shaping the dough into smooth, taut balls and rolling the proofed balls into even disks are the keys to pitas that reliably puff in the oven.

BEFORE PROOFING
1. Working in a circle, pull the edges of the dough into the center, forming a ball.

2. Holding the ball in your hand, pinch the seams together to seal, creating a taut surface.

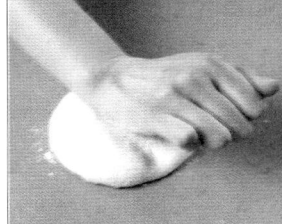

AFTER PROOFING
3. Use the heel of your hand to press the thoroughly floured dough ball into a 5-inch circle.

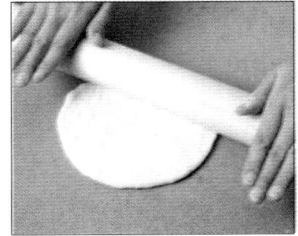

4. Roll the dough into a 7-inch disk. Roll slowly and gently to prevent any creasing.

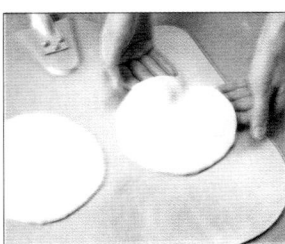

5. Before baking, make sure the side that was facing up when you began rolling is faceup again—this helps with puffing.

Everyday Roasted Vegetables

Roasting is a great way to breathe life into whatever produce is in your crisper drawer. Plus, it's mostly hands-free. Here's a cheat sheet for doing it well.

BY ELIZABETH BOMZE AND KEITH DRESSER

Something magical happens when you roast vegetables. The oven's dry heat drives off water to concentrate flavor while the fat encourages browning, transforming the raw vegetables into something entirely different. The trick is to use the right method for each vegetable and to keep a couple of simple garnishes in your back pocket so that you never get bored.

FIVE ROASTING RULES

These best practices apply to all vegetables and roasting methods.

1. **Use a sturdy rimmed baking sheet.**
   Flimsy sheets warp in a hot oven, causing oil to pool and food to brown unevenly.

2. **Evenly coat the vegetables with oil and seasonings.**
   Oil (use any neutral variety) encourages browning because it conducts heat efficiently from the metal of the sheet to the vegetable. Toss the pieces with oil and salt and pepper in a bowl to ensure they are evenly coated.

3. **Arrange the vegetables in a single layer.**
   Doing so ensures even cooking and deep browning on each piece.

4. **Don't crowd the sheet.**
   Leaving space between the pieces prevents a buildup of steam that thwarts browning.

5. **Don't flip too soon.**
   The side touching the sheet should be brown.

THREE EASY ROASTING METHODS

We use three basic methods for roasting most vegetables so that they emerge perfectly cooked on the inside with maximum surface browning.

METHOD 1
PREHEAT BAKING SHEET; ROAST UNCOVERED

Preheating the baking sheet ensures that relatively quick-cooking vegetables will develop flavorful browning by the time they are tender.

ASPARAGUS SERVES 4 TO 6
Amount and Prep: 2 pounds thick spears, bottom inch of each trimmed, bottom half peeled down to white flesh; 2 tablespoons oil
Oven Rack Position and Temp: Lowest; 500 degrees
Special Instruction: Don't move spears during roasting.
Cooking Time: 8 to 10 minutes
Keys to Success: Trimming and peeling the spears is less wasteful than snapping off the ends. Preheating the sheet on the lowest rack helps the spears sear upon contact; not moving them during roasting allows their undersides to brown deeply while the tops remain bright green.

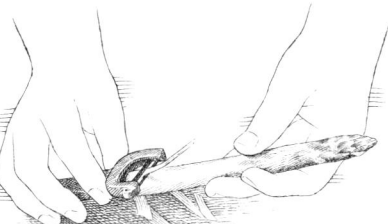

BROCCOLI SERVES 4
Amount and Prep: 1 large bunch (about 1¾ pounds), stalks peeled and cut into 2- to 3-inch lengths and each length into ½-inch-thick pieces, each crown cut into 4 to 6 evenly thick wedges; 3 tablespoons oil
Oven Rack Position and Temp: Lowest; 500 degrees
Special Instruction: Add ½ teaspoon sugar to oil.
Cooking Time: 9 to 11 minutes
Keys to Success: Cutting the crowns into wedges maximizes surface contact with the sheet to encourage browning. Adding sugar helps, too.

METHOD 2
ROAST UNCOVERED

The simplest roasting method works well for vegetables that will be sufficiently softened by the time their exteriors develop flavorful browning.

BUTTERNUT SQUASH SERVES 4 TO 6
Amount and Prep: 1 large (2½ to 3 pounds), peeled down to deep orange flesh, halved lengthwise, seeds removed, each half sliced crosswise ½ inch thick; 3 tablespoons oil (or substitute equal amount of melted unsalted butter for richer flavor)
Oven Rack Position and Temp: Lowest; 425 degrees
Cooking Time: 25 to 30 minutes, rotate sheet and roast 6 to 10 minutes longer, flip squash, roast 10 to 15 minutes longer
Key to Success: Peeling the squash thoroughly, to remove not only the tough outer skin but also the fibrous layer of white flesh just beneath, ensures supremely tender results.

CREMINI MUSHROOMS SERVES 4 TO 6
Amount and Prep: 1½ pounds, trimmed and left whole if small, halved if medium, or quartered if large; 2 tablespoons oil
Oven Rack Position and Temp: Lowest; 450 degrees
Special Instruction: Before roasting, brine mushrooms for 10 minutes in solution of 2 quarts water and 5 teaspoons salt. Dry well.
Cooking Time: 35 to 40 minutes, toss, 5 to 10 minutes longer
Key to Success: Brining the mushrooms seasons them evenly and helps them stay moist during cooking.

GREEN BEANS SERVES 4 TO 6
Amount and Prep: 1 pound, stem ends snapped off; 1 tablespoon oil
Oven Rack Position and Temp: Middle; 450 degrees
Special Instruction: Line baking sheet with aluminum foil or parchment paper, pressing liner into corners.
Cooking Time: 10 minutes, toss, 10 to 12 minutes longer
Key to Success: Lining the sheet prevents scorching and makes cleanup easy.

Dress Up Your Roasted Vegetables

A flavored salt or a compound butter is an easy way to add even more interest to roasted vegetables. Either pairs well with any vegetable and can be thrown together while the vegetables are cooking.

CHILI-LIME SALT
MAKES 3 TABLESPOONS

- 2 tablespoons kosher salt
- 4 teaspoons chili powder
- ¾ teaspoon grated lime zest

Combine all ingredients in small bowl.

BASIL AND LEMON BUTTER
MAKES ABOUT ½ CUP

- 6 tablespoons unsalted butter, softened
- 2 tablespoons minced fresh basil
- 1 tablespoon minced fresh parsley
- 1 teaspoon finely grated lemon zest
- ½ teaspoon salt
- ¼ teaspoon pepper

Combine all ingredients in small bowl.

METHOD 3
ROAST COVERED, THEN UNCOVERED

Initially covering the baking sheet with foil traps steam that helps dense vegetables soften and cook through. Uncovering the sheet allows moisture to evaporate so that the vegetables can brown.

BRUSSELS SPROUTS SERVES 4
Amount and Prep: 1¼ pounds, trimmed and halved; 2 tablespoons oil
Oven Rack Position and Temp: Middle; 500 degrees
Special Instruction: Add 1 tablespoon water when tossing sprouts with oil, salt, and pepper.
Covered Time: 10 minutes
Uncovered Time: 10 to 12 minutes
Keys to Success: Adding water to the oil helps the sprouts steam during the covered phase. Initially arranging the sprouts cut side down ensures that their flat surfaces brown deeply.

CARROTS SERVES 4 TO 6
Amount and Prep: 1½ pounds, peeled, halved crosswise, and cut lengthwise if necessary to create even pieces; 2 tablespoons oil (or substitute equal amount of melted unsalted butter for richer flavor)
Oven Rack Position and Temp: Middle; 425 degrees
Special Instructions: Line sheet with aluminum foil or parchment paper, pressing liner into corners.
Covered Time: 15 minutes
Uncovered Time: 30 to 35 minutes, stirring twice
Key to Success: Cutting the carrots into batons ensures that they cook evenly. Lining the sheet prevents scorching and makes cleanup easy.

CAULIFLOWER SERVES 4 TO 6
Amount and Prep: 1 medium head (about 2 pounds), outer leaves trimmed, stem cut flush with bottom, and head cut into 8 equal wedges so that core and florets remain intact; ¼ cup oil
Oven Rack Position and Temp: Lowest; 475 degrees
Special Instructions: Rub oil, salt, and pepper into each wedge. Line sheet with aluminum foil or parchment paper, pressing liner into corners.
Covered Time: 10 minutes
Uncovered Time: 8 to 12 minutes, flip, 8 to 12 minutes longer
Keys to Success: Leaving the core intact makes it easy to flip the pieces halfway through cooking. Rubbing the oil and seasonings into each piece ensures that the nooks and crannies are evenly coated.

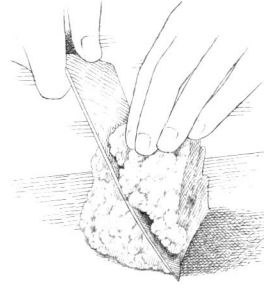

FENNEL SERVES 4 TO 6
Amount and Prep: 3 fennel bulbs, 3 to 3½ inches in diameter, stalks discarded, each bulb cut lengthwise through core (don't remove core) into 8 wedges; 2 tablespoons oil
Oven Rack Position and Temp: Lower-middle; 425 degrees
Covered Time: 15 minutes
Uncovered Time: 10 to 15 minutes, flip, continue to roast until core is tender and side touching sheet is browned, 5 to 10 minutes longer
Keys to Success: Cutting the bulbs lengthwise creates maximum surface area for browning. Leaving the core intact makes the halves easy to flip.

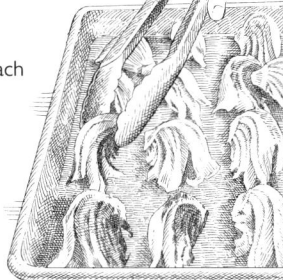

Applesauce for Everyone

Transform just about any apple variety into flavorful, rosy applesauce in less than 30 minutes. Our secret weapon: the peels.

≥ BY ANDREA GEARY ≤

As I began this project, I was often asked the question "Do adults actually eat applesauce?" My response: If they don't, they should, because applesauce is easy to make and it packs all the sweet-tart character of orchard-fresh apples into a deliciously concentrated format. Spooned warm and fragrant from a bowl, it's a cozy treat on its own, but it also makes a great accompaniment to roasted meat or potato pancakes. Don't let memories of that vaguely apple-flavored beige stuff from the supermarket turn you against applesauce. As a discerning adult, you deserve the real thing.

The traditional method for making applesauce is simple: Cut unpeeled apples into chunks; throw them into a saucepan with some water, a bit of sugar, and maybe a pinch of salt; and bring it all to a boil. Cover and simmer until the apples are soft, and then transfer everything to a food mill and crank away. As the blade smears the apples along the perforated floor of the mill, the flesh passes into the bowl below while the tough skins and seeds remain in the hopper. But I don't own a food mill, and a lot of other folks don't either, so I wanted to see if I could make equally flavorful applesauce without one.

I started with 3 pounds of McIntosh apples, which I chose for their balance of sweetness and acidity. It's a good middle-of-the-road variety, neither too tart nor too sweet, neither too firm nor too tender. Because I wouldn't have a food mill to filter out the undesirable bits, I first peeled and cored the apples before cutting them into big chunks. I cooked them in a saucepan with ¼ cup of sugar, a pinch of salt, and 1½ cups of water until they were soft, about 20 minutes. As I mashed them with a potato masher, I noticed an advantage to a food mill–free recipe: I could leave my sauce as chunky as I liked.

But irregular texture wasn't enough to redeem this sauce. Its pale appearance and bland, flat flavor made it nearly indistinguishable from the jarred stuff.

▶ Andrea Gets Saucy
A step-by-step video is available at CooksIllustrated.com/oct18

A potato masher makes applesauce as chunky—or smooth—as you like.

More Than a Peeling
The only difference between applesauce made with a food mill and my sad sauce was those discarded peels. Research revealed that the peels are the source of a lot of distinctive apple aromas (see "Apple A-peel"), so it made sense that the flavor of a sauce made without them was comparatively insipid. And there's another benefit to using the peels if they're red: The pigments transfer into the sauce during cooking, giving it a charming pink blush.

A Tedious Task
For my next batch, I cut the unpeeled apples in quarters and removed the cores from each wedge. I put them into a saucepan with sugar, water, and salt; and stirred occasionally over medium-high heat.

After painstakingly fishing out the skins and mashing the apples, I was disappointed to find that this sauce wasn't a huge improvement. The flavor was lackluster, and I could barely make out a hint of pink. Clearly I wasn't making the most of the peels. I started my next batch the same way, but instead of picking out the skins after cooking, I transferred everything to a blender and let it rip. When the peels were reduced to mere specks and the sauce had taken on a rosy hue, I took a taste. Those specks of skin, so tiny in the blender, felt huge on my tongue, and the rest of sauce was unnaturally smooth and uniform, with an odd stickiness.

Here's what went wrong: The cells of an apple are held together by pectin, a complex polysaccharide that acts as a sort of glue. When you mash cooked apples or pass them through a food mill, you break apart some of those clusters of cells, freeing the pectin that holds them together, but you leave a lot intact. That's why applesauce has a pleasantly nubbly texture. When I pureed the apples in a blender, I obliterated more of the cells, which released a lot more pectin into the mix. It gelled with the water in the sauce, giving it an unpleasantly sticky texture. But, texture aside, the flavor was fantastic: sweet and

Apple A-peel
Apple skin is chock-full of flavor and aroma compounds, which is why applesauce made with the peels tastes far more, well, appley. Cooking the peels in a small amount of water transfers flavor compounds and pigments to the liquid, which gets incorporated into our cooked applesauce.

ADD THE PEEL FOR MORE APPLE FLAVOR

Sweeter with Age
During storage, apples consume tart malic acid, meaning older apples are often perceived as sweeter than younger ones. Different apples require different amounts of added sugar to make a balanced applesauce, so we season ours to taste after cooking.

TECHNIQUE | HOW TO CORE AND PEEL APPLES

We use every bit of the apple by cooking the cores and peels separately from the flesh and then straining the mixture over the sauce.

WITH AN APPLE CORER
We prefer coring apples before peeling to ensure that no bits of skin remain on the apples' tops or bottoms.

1. Use corer to remove apple core. Reserve core.

2. Peel cored apple, working in wide strips. Reserve peel.

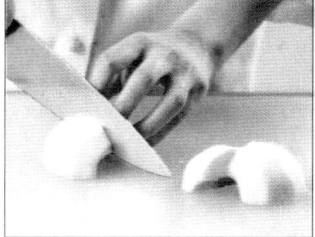

3. Cut apple into quarters.

WITHOUT AN APPLE CORER

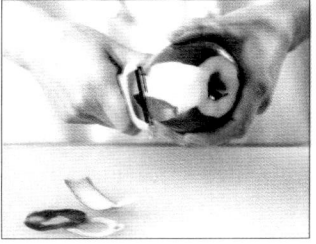

1. Peel apple top and bottom, then sides. Reserve peel.

2. Cut apple into quarters.

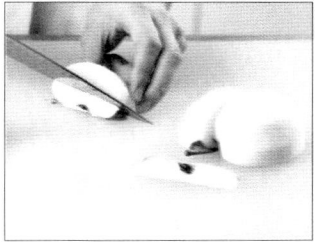

3. Cut away core from each wedge. Reserve core.

---

a bit tart, with just a touch of cleansing astringency. It must have come from the peels.

I was stuck. The gentle mashing approach yielded applesauce that was anemic in flavor and appearance, while the blender produced great flavor but the texture suffered. What about a hybrid approach?

I peeled and cored another batch of apples, but this time I put the skins in a separate saucepan with a cup of water. (I also added the cores to the pot along with the skins. After all, the cores have plenty of flesh on them to contribute flavor and pulp, so why throw them away? I then quartered the apples and put them in another saucepan with ½ cup of water and some sugar and salt. I brought both saucepans to a simmer and let them cook for about 15 minutes.

I periodically mashed the cores and peels and was gratified to see them turn pulpy and plum-colored. I mashed the softened apples and then placed a fine-mesh strainer over the saucepan. I poured the peel-and-core mush into the strainer and scraped it along the mesh with my spatula. Flesh from the cores and many of the flavor- and color-rich compounds from the peels passed through, and the tough stuff (including any seeds or seed pods) was left behind.

This batch had all the hallmarks of a great applesauce: rosy color, pleasantly chunky texture, and true, clear apple flavor. And it was just as good with a wide variety of apples (See "[Almost] No Bad Apples"). It's truly an applesauce anyone can make and everyone will love—adults included.

APPLESAUCE
MAKES 4 CUPS

We like the tart flavor of McIntosh apples in this recipe, but nearly any variety of apple can be substituted, except for Red or Golden Delicious. You may mash this applesauce until it's smooth or leave it chunky for a more rustic effect. If you have a food mill, we suggest preparing our Simple Applesauce; the recipe is available free for four months at CooksIllustrated.com/oct18. Our free recipe for Savory Applesauce with Parsnips and Mustard is also available.

- 3 pounds McIntosh apples, peeled and cored, peels and cores reserved
- 1½ cups water
- ¼ cup sugar, plus extra to taste
- Pinch salt
- Pinch ground cinnamon (optional)

1. Bring reserved peels and cores and 1 cup water to boil in small saucepan over medium-high heat. Reduce heat to medium, cover, and cook, mashing occasionally with potato masher, until mixture is deep pink and cores have broken down, about 15 minutes.

2. While peels and cores cook, cut apples into quarters and place in large saucepan. Add sugar; salt; cinnamon, if using; and remaining ½ cup water and bring to boil over medium-high heat. Reduce heat to medium, cover, and cook, stirring occasionally with rubber spatula, until all apples are soft and about half are completely broken down, about 15 minutes. Using potato masher, mash apples to desired consistency.

3. Transfer peel-and-core mixture to fine-mesh strainer set over saucepan of mashed apple mixture. Using rubber spatula, stir and press peel-and-core mixture to extract pulp; discard solids. Stir to combine. Sweeten with extra sugar to taste. Serve warm, at room temperature, or chilled. (Applesauce can be refrigerated for up to 1 week.)

DESSERT-WORTHY APPLESAUCE WITH BROWN SUGAR AND RUM

Substitute packed brown sugar for granulated sugar. Substitute ⅛ teaspoon ground nutmeg and pinch ground allspice for cinnamon. Stir 2 tablespoons gold rum into applesauce before serving. Serve warm with vanilla ice cream.

SAVORY APPLESAUCE WITH BEETS AND HORSERADISH
MAKES 2 CUPS

Decrease apples to 1¼ pounds and sugar to 2 tablespoons. Increase salt to ¼ teaspoon and omit cinnamon. Add 1 beet, peeled and grated (1 cup), to quartered apples with sugar and salt. (Beet will not completely soften.) Stir 2 teaspoons prepared horseradish into applesauce and season with salt to taste. Serve with roast beef or potato latkes.

(Almost) No Bad Apples

Our method works with just about any apple, even those that may have turned a little mushy. Keep in mind: Crisp, denser apples take longer to break down, and green or yellow apples make a beige sauce.

OUR FAVORITE
We love tart, sweet, colorful McIntosh.

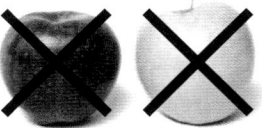

NOT SO DELICIOUS
Red Delicious were far too sweet, and Golden Delicious never fully broke down.

BARREL OF CHOICES
Experiment with different varieties to see which you like best.

Burn Your Beans

Skillet-charring produces deeply browned green beans with satisfying chew.

> BY ANDREW JANJIGIAN <

Sichuan cooks have a method for preparing green beans called "dry frying." It's a two-step approach in which the beans are deep-fried, and then stir-fried with aromatics and maybe a little ground pork. There's not much sauce because the beans are the real draw: blistered, with a soft chew and concentrated flavor. It's a technique I would use regularly if dry frying didn't require the hassle of, well, frying. Especially because the beans could pair well with so many flavors beyond the typical Sichuan profile.

Instead, I tried shallow-frying a pound of beans in a couple of tablespoons of oil. They were only spottily blistered after 10 minutes because the ends of the raw beans curled up and didn't make full contact with the oil. They were still firm inside, too, and showed no signs of softening even after 20 minutes.

It turns out that completely softening green beans is a lengthy process. That's because components in the beans' cell walls that give the raw vegetable its snap also take a while to soften during cooking (see "Green Beans Are Tougher Than You'd Think").

The advantage of deep frying, I realized, is that the beans are fully submerged in the hot oil, which softens them more quickly than shallow frying, where only part of the green is ever in contact with the oil. But what if I precooked the beans, which would wilt them enough so they'd at least make greater contact with what oil is in the pan?

Simmering the beans in water in a covered nonstick skillet was an obvious way to wilt them. Then I drained them, wiped the pan dry, got 2 tablespoons of oil smoking-hot, and added back the beans. This time, they blistered after 5 minutes. I shook the pan so that they would brown on the other sides, and after a few minutes they were downright charred. In fact, they boasted even richer flavor than typical dry-fried beans because the charring was deeper and because more of the beans' water had been driven off and their flavor concentrated.

But simmering the beans left a residue that stuck to the pan during the frying stage, which meant I had to stop and wash the pan. I found it easier to soften the beans in a covered bowl in the microwave (but we provide a method for doing it in a skillet as well). If I rinsed but didn't dry them, there was just enough water clinging to the beans to produce steam that softened them further.

Seasoning the beans with salt, pepper, and lemon was more than ample. But seasoned panko bread crumbs—finely crushed so that they clung to the beans—offered great contrast to their tender chew.

Dry-fried beans will still be my Sichuan restaurant order. But I dare say my charred beans might have them beat—especially since they're hassle-free.

▶ **Andrew Burns Beans**
A step-by-step video is available at CooksIllustrated.com/oct18

The secret to truly charred beans? Steam them first.

SKILLET-CHARRED GREEN BEANS
SERVES 4

Microwave thinner, more tender beans for 6 to 8 minutes and thicker, tougher beans for 10 to 12 minutes. To make the beans without a microwave, bring ¼ cup of water to a boil in a skillet over high heat. Add the beans, cover, and cook for 5 minutes. Transfer the beans to a paper towel–lined plate to drain and wash the skillet before proceeding with the recipe. Our Skillet-Charred Green Beans with Crispy Sesame Topping recipe is available for free for four months at CooksIllustrated.com/oct18.

- ½ teaspoon grated lemon zest plus 1 teaspoon juice
- ½ teaspoon kosher salt
- ¼ teaspoon pepper
- 1 pound green beans, trimmed
- 2 tablespoons vegetable oil

1. Combine lemon zest, salt, and pepper in small bowl. Set aside.

2. Rinse green beans but do not dry. Place in medium bowl, cover, and microwave until fully tender, 6 to 12 minutes, stirring every 3 minutes. Using tongs, transfer green beans to paper towel–lined plate and let drain.

3. Heat oil in 12-inch nonstick skillet over high heat until just smoking. Add green beans in single layer. Cook, without stirring, until green beans begin to blister and char, 4 to 5 minutes. Toss green beans and continue to cook, stirring occasionally, until green beans are softened and charred, 4 to 5 minutes longer. Using tongs, transfer green beans to serving bowl, leaving any excess oil in skillet. Sprinkle with lemon-salt mixture and lemon juice and toss to coat. Serve.

SKILLET-CHARRED GREEN BEANS WITH CRISPY BREAD-CRUMB TOPPING

Process 2 tablespoons panko bread crumbs in spice grinder or mortar and pestle until uniformly ground to medium-fine consistency that resembles couscous. Cook panko and 1 tablespoon vegetable oil in 12-inch nonstick skillet over medium-low heat, stirring frequently, until light golden brown, 5 to 7 minutes. Remove skillet from heat; add ¾ teaspoon kosher salt, ¼ teaspoon pepper, and ¼ teaspoon red pepper flakes; and stir to combine. Transfer panko mixture to bowl; set aside. Wash out skillet thoroughly and dry with paper towels. Proceed with recipe as directed, substituting panko mixture for lemon-salt mixture.

Green Beans Are Tougher Than You'd Think

Green beans are rugged. Their cell walls are rich in hemicellulose and pectin that make them firm enough to snap when fresh. Those components, plus a substance called lignin, also make them very resistant to heat, which explains why they can be cooked for a long time or over high heat, as we do for our Skillet-Charred Green Beans, without turning to mush. Instead, prolonged heat exposure gives them a silky yet stable quality.

FIT TO BE TIED

Pasta Salad Rehab

Our fixes: Overcook the noodles. Raid the pantry. Puree the dressing.

> BY ANNIE PETITO <

Mention pasta salad and most folks think of a hodgepodge of overly firm noodles, raw broccoli florets, and spongy canned black olives, all drenched in bottled Italian dressing. That's why my colleagues looked gleeful when I—not one of them—got the assignment of trying to rehab this sorry dish. But then I thought, I spend a lot of time perfecting hot pastas (often for this magazine), so why not give some attention to a cold one?

Before I started cooking, I settled on fusilli. Its corkscrew shape would trap dressing, and it's easy to spear with a fork. And right off the bat, I addressed the rubbery pasta problem. Instead of boiling the noodles until they were al dente, I cooked them longer until they were a little soft. Here's why: As pasta cools (whether in the refrigerator or under cold water), it goes through a process called retrogradation, in which the water in the pasta becomes bound up in starch crystals, making the pasta firm and dry. I made retrogradation work to my advantage by boiling the fusilli about 3 minutes past al dente and then running it under lots of cold water. As the pasta cooled, it went from almost mushy to just right.

Next up: mix-ins. Crunchy raw vegetables overshadow tender pasta and don't contribute much flavor. But I didn't want to take the time to grill or roast vegetables. Instead, I reached for pantry picks with less intrusive textures: chewy, sweet sun-dried tomatoes; briny kalamata olives and capers; and a whole jar of vinegary, spicy, slightly crunchy *pepperoncini*. For heartiness, I also included diced salami, and to balance its salty tang, bits of creamy fresh mozzarella. Finally, I mixed in arugula and basil for freshness and dressed everything with oil and vinegar.

The salad was punctuated with bold bites, but the pasta was bland since the oil and vinegar weren't clinging. I needed a potent mixture that was thick enough to coat the pasta, so I decided to puree some of the mix-ins into the dressing. I pulsed the capers and half the pepperoncini in a food processor. In place of vinegar, I drizzled in some of the piquant pepperoncini brine. Then, I gave the oil a flavor boost by microwaving it with garlic, anchovies, and red pepper flakes. As the oil bubbled, the garlic's raw edge disappeared and the oil took on the deep savoriness of the anchovies. I processed the infused oil into the other ingredients, creating a vibrant dressing with lots of body.

Giving pasta salad my full attention paid off: The thick, bold dressing settled into the grooves of the fusilli, and the mix-ins were ideal complements to the perfectly tender pasta. Now it was my turn to be gleeful.

Our hearty salad is chock-full of antipasto ingredients.

ITALIAN PASTA SALAD
SERVES 8 TO 10 AS A SIDE DISH

The pasta firms as it cools, so overcooking is key to ensuring the proper texture. We prefer a small, individually packaged, dry Italian-style salami such as Genoa or *soppressata*, but unsliced deli salami can be used. If the salad is not being eaten right away, don't add the arugula and basil until right before serving.

- 1 pound fusilli
- Salt and pepper
- ¼ cup extra-virgin olive oil
- 3 garlic cloves, minced
- 3 anchovy fillets, rinsed, patted dry, and minced
- ¼ teaspoon red pepper flakes
- 1 cup pepperoncini, stemmed, plus 2 tablespoons brine
- 2 tablespoons capers, rinsed
- 2 ounces (2 cups) baby arugula
- 1 cup chopped fresh basil
- ½ cup oil-packed sun-dried tomatoes, sliced thin
- ½ cup pitted kalamata olives, quartered
- 8 ounces salami, cut into ⅜-inch dice
- 8 ounces fresh mozzarella cheese, cut into ⅜-inch dice and patted dry

1. Bring 4 quarts water to boil in large pot. Add pasta and 1 tablespoon salt and cook, stirring often, until pasta is tender throughout, 2 to 3 minutes past al dente. Drain pasta and rinse under cold water until chilled. Drain well and transfer to large bowl.

2. Meanwhile, combine oil, garlic, anchovies, and pepper flakes in liquid measuring cup. Cover and microwave until bubbling and fragrant, 30 to 60 seconds. Set aside.

3. Slice half of pepperoncini into thin rings and set aside. Transfer remaining pepperoncini to food processor. Add capers and pulse until finely chopped, 8 to 10 pulses, scraping down sides of bowl as needed. Add pepperoncini brine and warm oil mixture and process until combined, about 20 seconds.

4. Add dressing to pasta and toss to combine. Add arugula, basil, tomatoes, olives, salami, mozzarella, and reserved pepperoncini and toss well. Season with salt and pepper to taste. Serve. (Salad can be refrigerated for up to 3 days. Let come to room temperature before serving.)

SCIENCE **Al Dente Pasta Is So Retro(grade)**

Just as leftover rice hardens when it is refrigerated, al dente pasta tastes overly firm once it cools. Retrogradation is to blame: As pasta cooks, its starch granules absorb water and swell. The chain-like starch molecules that formerly stuck together separate, allowing water to seep in among them. Then, as the pasta cools, the starch chains creep back together, forming tight microscopic crystals. The water that was keeping the molecules separate becomes bound up inside the crystals, and the pasta becomes overly firm because the starch is more rigidly compacted and the water is trapped.

➤ **Our solution:** When serving pasta cool, cook it until it is a little too soft. This way, when it retrogrades, it will firm up to just the right texture.

OVERCOOK IT
When chilled, the pasta will firm up to the perfect texture.

▶ **Annie Rewrites the Rules**
A step-by-step video is available at CooksIllustrated.com/oct18

Belgian Spice Cookies (Speculoos)

Passengers can't get enough of Delta Air Lines' in-flight snack of Biscoff, the commercial version of this Belgian confection. We took it to even greater heights.

≥ BY ANDREW JANJIGIAN ≤

There is a story floating around the internet about a grandmother who gobbled up her grandson's cookies as he slept beside her during a long flight. The motive for the 30,000-foot crime? Biscoff, the signature onboard snack of Delta Air Lines. The tempting cookie dates to 1932, when a Belgian bakery started selling *speculoos*. Fifty years later, the bakery began manufacturing speculoos for Americans under the name "Biscoff" and its popularity soared (see "How Biscoff Took Off").

The enthusiasm is understandable: Speculoos boast warm spice notes, nuanced caramel flavor, and a crisp, open texture that crumbles easily (the term of art here is "friable"). Imagine something between a delicate graham cracker and a hard gingersnap that nearly melts in your mouth.

I wanted to use the one-of-a-kind texture of Biscoff as a model for homemade speculoos. I also intended to mimic their caramel taste and improve the spice flavor—one place I found the packaged version lacking.

Speculoos Speculations

Speculoos recipes don't typically call for unusual ingredients or techniques: Simply cream sugar and softened butter in a stand mixer, add an egg (or not), and then mix in flour, spices, baking soda, and salt. Traditional recipes call for pressing the dough into shallow molds that serve the dual purpose of leaving a decorative imprint on the cookies and keeping them from spreading. I'd definitely be taking the more streamlined, modern route of simply rolling the dough thin so the cookies could bake up dry and crisp.

Small amounts of cardamom and cloves boost the sweet spiciness of the 5 teaspoons of cinnamon in our *speculoos*.

None of the recipes I tried produced the right texture, so I set out to establish my own. Since the dough would be rolled thin, I wouldn't need a lot of volume, so I started with just 1½ cups of flour. Most speculoos recipes call for roughly half as much butter as flour by weight, and sure enough, this made the cookies appropriately crumbly; any more butter made them too fragile. I kept the sugar in check so as to avoid the slight oversweetness of packaged Biscoff, and this also got me closer to a friable texture. That's because sugar is hygroscopic, meaning that it holds on to water, which creates chewiness in cookies. In the end, I landed on 1½ cups of flour, 8 tablespoons of butter, just ¾ cup of brown sugar, and 1 egg, which bound the dough without adding a lot of extra moisture.

As for the leavener, I started with ¼ teaspoon of baking soda, which didn't do much to enhance the crisp, open texture since it requires acid to react—and these cookies had only the slight acidity of brown sugar. Switching to baking powder successfully opened the internal structure (see "Producing the Distinctive Texture [and Taste] of Speculoos"). However, without the baking soda, the cookies lacked a certain savoriness, so I added it back in.

With the crumb of my speculoos just right, I investigated the sugar flavor. Most American speculoos recipes call for brown sugar, which is made by combining refined white sugar with molasses. But authentic speculoos are sweetened with Belgian brown sugar, which is made by adding caramelized sugar to refined white sugar, so it has a cleaner taste, with none of the bitterness of molasses. The one American speculoos recipe I found that acknowledged this difference was from Stella Parks, author of *BraveTart* (2017). She calls for toasting white sugar in the oven for 5 hours, which produced appealing, mild flavor but effort-wise was (quite literally) beyond the pale.

Turbinado sugar was a more efficient solution since it has the appropriate caramel-like notes (see "Sourcing Clean Caramel Flavor") straight from the bag. But turbinado crystals are larger than those of other sugars, so it gave the speculoos an underlying grittiness. My fix was to grind the turbinado in the food processor. With that, the cookies had the right honeycomb texture along with caramel undertones.

Now, how to nail the spice flavor? Speculoos recipes vary widely in their spice choices, but Biscoff contain only cinnamon. I followed that model, landing on a sizable 5 teaspoons. But something was missing. After some experimenting, I found that 1 teaspoon of cardamom and ¼ teaspoon of cloves made the cinnamon sing with warmth and sweetness without calling attention to themselves.

The Final Approach

To finish, I used a technique from our Easy Holiday Sugar Cookies recipe (November/December 2017): I rolled the just-mixed dough between sheets of parchment and then chilled it before cutting and baking. This was easier than having to either roll and cut a soft dough straightaway

> Try *speculoos* crumbled onto yogurt, ice cream, or pudding or ground to make a cookie-crumb pie crust.

Get a Decorative Edge

The fluted pastry wheel that we use to give our *speculoos* a scalloped edge can also be used to cut fresh pasta or ravioli dough, lattice strips for pie, cracker dough, or dough for turnovers, empanadas, or other filled pastries. **FLUTED PASTRY WHEEL**

Producing the Distinctive Texture (and Taste) of Speculoos

In baking, the term "crumb" is used to describe the internal structure of bread or cake. But cookies have a crumb, too. To achieve the proper friable (crisp, airy) crumb in our *speculoos*, we roll the dough thin so it can dry and crisp in the oven. And since sugar is hygroscopic (meaning that it holds on to water and makes cookies chewy), we use only enough to lightly sweeten the dough. Finally, we add both baking powder and baking soda. Baking powder reacts first when it gets wet and again when it is heated: Just ¼ teaspoon effectively puffed the dough, creating numerous big holes. Baking soda, on the other hand, provides lift when it reacts with acid. Our speculoos dough contains only a tiny bit of acid in the sugar, but it still made sense to include soda: It raised the dough's pH to promote browning reactions and gave the cookies a subtle toasty/savory quality that we missed when we left it out.

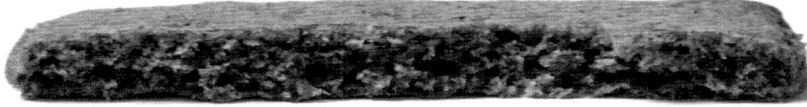

CRISP, AIRY, CRUMBLY

or wait for a disk of dough to chill to a workable consistency. After rolling the dough thin—⅜ inch was just right—I copied Biscoff's scalloped edges by using a fluted pastry wheel to cut it into rectangles. Finally, I gently baked the cookies in a 300-degree oven, which gave them ample time to thoroughly dry and crisp.

I had one more thought: Since I already had the food processor out to grind the turbinado, could I also use it to prepare the dough? Doing so would mean I wouldn't need to wait for the butter to soften since the processor's sharp blades can handle cold butter. To find out, I prepared the recipe in a stand mixer and in a food processor. Happily, the resulting cookies were identical; I would stick with the food processor.

With that, there was just one thing left to do: Step across the border to Holland, where speculoos are stamped with windmills and have almonds baked into the underside. I wasn't about to carve miniature windmills, but it was easy to roll sliced almonds into the bottom of my dough. With or without nuts, one thing was for certain: These speculoos were top-flight.

BELGIAN SPICE COOKIES (SPECULOOS)
MAKES 32 COOKIES

For the proper flavor, we strongly recommend using turbinado sugar (commonly sold as Sugar in the Raw). If you can't find it, use ¾ cup plus 2 tablespoons (6 ounces) of packed light brown sugar and skip the sugar grinding in step 2. In step 3, use a rolling pin and a combination of rolling and a smearing motion

How Biscoff Took Off

In 1986, Lotus, a Belgian bakery, began selling *speculoos* under the name Biscoff (so-called because the biscuits, or cookies, pair well with coffee) to Delta Air Lines to offer to their passengers on flights. Today, Delta serves roughly 80 million individual packages of the cookies annually on domestic routes.

to form the rectangle. If the dough spreads beyond the rectangle, trim it and use the scraps to fill in the corners; then, replace the parchment and continue to roll. Do not use cookie molds or an embossed rolling pin for the *speculoos*; they will not hold decorations.

- 1½ cups (7½ ounces) all-purpose flour
- 5 teaspoons ground cinnamon
- 1 teaspoon ground cardamom
- ¼ teaspoon ground cloves
- ¼ teaspoon baking soda
- ¼ teaspoon baking powder
- ¼ teaspoon salt
- ¾ cup (6 ounces) turbinado sugar
- 8 tablespoons unsalted butter, cut into ½-inch pieces and chilled
- 1 large egg

1. Whisk flour, cinnamon, cardamom, cloves, baking soda, baking powder, and salt together in bowl. Using pencil and ruler, draw 10 by 12-inch rectangle in center of each of 2 large sheets of parchment paper, crisscrossing lines at corners. (Use crisscrosses to help line up top and bottom sheets as dough is rolled.)

2. Process sugar in food processor for 30 seconds (some grains will be smaller than granulated sugar; others will be larger). Add butter and process until uniform mass forms and no large pieces of butter are visible, about 30 seconds, scraping down sides of bowl as needed. Add egg and process until smooth and paste-like, about 10 seconds, scraping down sides of bowl as needed. Add flour mixture and process until no dry flour remains but mixture remains crumbly, about 30 seconds, scraping down sides of bowl as needed.

3. Transfer dough to bowl and knead gently with spatula until uniform and smooth, about 10 seconds. Place 1 piece of parchment on counter with pencil side facing down (you should be able to see rectangle through paper). Place dough in center of marked rectangle and press into 6 by 9-inch rectangle. Place second sheet of parchment over dough, with pencil side facing up, so dough is in center of marked rectangle. Using pencil marks as guide, use rolling pin and bench scraper to shape dough into 10 by 12-inch rectangle of even ⅜-inch thickness. Transfer dough with parchment to rimmed baking sheet. Refrigerate until dough is firm, at least 1½ hours (or freeze for 30 minutes). (Rolled dough can be wrapped in plastic wrap and refrigerated for up to 5 days.)

4. Adjust oven racks to upper-middle and lower-middle positions and heat oven to 300 degrees. Line 2 rimless baking sheets with parchment. Transfer chilled dough to counter. Gently peel off top layer of parchment from dough. Using fluted pastry wheel (or sharp knife or pizza cutter) and ruler, trim off rounded edges of dough that extend over marked edges of 10 by 12-inch rectangle. Cut dough lengthwise into 8 equal strips about 1¼ inches wide. Cut each strip crosswise into 4 equal pieces about 3 inches long. Transfer cookies to prepared sheets, spacing them at least ½ inch apart. Bake until cookies are lightly and evenly browned, 30 to 32 minutes, switching and rotating sheets halfway through baking. Let cookies cool completely on sheets, about 20 minutes. (Cookies can be stored at room temperature for up to 3 weeks.)

BELGIAN SPICE COOKIES (SPECULOOS) WITH ALMONDS

Once dough has been rolled into rectangle in step 3, gently peel off top layer of parchment. Sprinkle ½ cup sliced almonds evenly over dough. Using rolling pin, gently press almonds into dough. Return parchment to dough, flip dough over, and transfer with parchment to sheet. Proceed with recipe as directed.

Sourcing Clean Caramel Flavor

Authentic *speculoos* are made from Belgian brown sugar, a blend of refined white sugar and caramelized sugar. American brown sugar, which is typically made by mixing refined white sugar with molasses (the syrup left over when cane juice is boiled down to make sugar), is the usual substitute. The amount of molasses in brown sugar isn't appropriate for speculoos. Instead, we call for turbinado sugar. It's produced by evaporating sugar cane juice to leave behind sugar crystals containing a very small amount of molasses residue, which results in a clean, light caramel flavor.

BELGIAN BROWN SUGAR    TURBINADO SUGAR

▶ Fill Your Cookie Jar
A step-by-step video is available at CooksIllustrated.com/oct18

Tasting Basmati Rice

Its slender grains, nutty flavor, and popcorn-like fragrance are prized around the world. But when choices abound, how do you decide which basmati to buy?

> BY LISA McMANUS <

Basmati rice is our go-to choice for pilaf, biryani, and the classic Persian dish called *chelow* and as a base for curry. In India, where basmati originated, it is considered part of the national heritage; in 2016 it was granted Geographical Indication (GI) status, similar to the European Union's protection for Champagne and Parmigiano-Reggiano. Indian cooks prize basmati for its fragrance as well as the extreme elongation and slenderness of the cooked grains. But in American supermarkets, it's one of several options for long-grain white rice, so it's easy to overlook.

To learn more, we bought eight nationally available white basmati rices, two grown in the United States and six from India and Pakistan. We sampled them plain, cooked according to package directions; in our recipe for Basic Rice Pilaf, where the grains are toasted in butter; and in our Chicken Biryani, which involves parcooking the rice in spice-infused water and then simmering it with layers of caramelized onions, chopped fresh herbs, and pan-seared chicken thighs. In each blind tasting, we rated the rice on flavor, aroma, texture, and overall appeal.

Growing Conditions Matter

Texture affected our preferences more than any other factor. Some products' grains were extremely long and slender, while others were thicker and shorter, or as one taster wrote, "more like regular long-grain generic stuff." Our tasters preferred grains that were smooth; some rices seemed "rough" and craggy. A few were quite soft, verging on "mushy," while our favorites retained some springiness and "al dente" firmness. Finally, our preferred rices were separate and fluffy, with very little of the stickiness we found in lower-ranked rices.

We used calipers to measure grains and found that our tasters preferred basmatis that were longer and thinner.

To understand these differences, we investigated factors that can determine a basmati's texture. Technically, only basmati from the traditional growing region of Northern India and Pakistan can be called basmati. And though the temperature and soil of the GI region may be ideal for producing quality rice, basmati is naturally delicate and low-yielding, which makes it labor-intensive and costly to produce. To bring down prices, many producers have attempted to breed higher-yield, hardier basmati, but with mixed results. We tasted two of these in our lineup; our panel noted that these basmati-like rices grown in Texas and California (labeled "Texmati" and "California basmati," respectively) were shorter, broader, and stickier than true basmati.

Aging Produces Quality Grains

Processing is another factor. After harvesting, basmati is cleaned, dried (mechanically or in the sun, to lower its moisture level), dehusked, and polished before being stored in varying conditions, from high-end temperature-controlled silos to simple covered boxes stacked on the ground for durations determined by manufacturers. This storage can be a form of deliberate aging to produce certain desirable qualities similar to aging fine wine or cheese; however, not all producers are willing to wait, since storing grain is expensive and increases the risk of loss to pests or spoilage. Finally, the rice is packed for sale.

> Only basmati from the traditional growing region of Northern India and Pakistan can be called basmati.

We asked manufacturers about aging and found that our top-ranked rices were aged, while the three lowest-ranked products (including the domestic, "basmati-like" rices) were not. Our favorite was aged for 12 to 18 months in temperature-controlled silos; cooler temperatures help prevent off-flavors and create the best conditions for flavor and texture development during aging.

Studies report that as all types of rice age, the grain undergoes structural changes and its cooked texture becomes less sticky, smoother, and firmer. Starch granules tighten while surface proteins on the rice grains oxidize, creating a shell-like exterior that is more resistant to absorption, helping prevent the grain from becoming mushy and controlling how much it can expand. While raw basmati is naturally long and slim, aging improves this trait so that as the rice cooks, it expands lengthwise and not widthwise. We measured the length and width of a small sample of each rice before and after cooking and found that the aged rices were longer and thinner and grew lengthwise by a higher percentage during cooking. Low-ranked rices, which were not aged, were shorter and fatter.

As for basmati's vaunted fragrance, some products

With Age Comes Length, Smoothness, and a Less-Sticky Texture

The aging process enhances the characteristics traditionally valued in basmati rice, including the long, slender shape of the grains and the smooth, firm, less-sticky texture when cooked. While preparing the rices for tastings, we noticed that all the aged rices had greater length-to-width ratios when cooked than did the nonaged products. As for the textures of the nonaged rices, the tasters found them sticky.

THE LONG AND SHORT OF IT
When cooked, aged basmati has a greater growth ratio than nonaged rice.

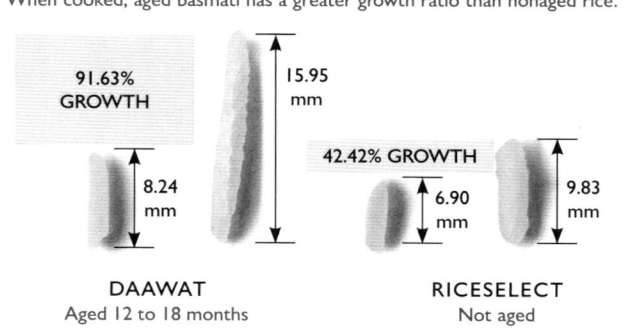

DAAWAT — Aged 12 to 18 months — 91.63% GROWTH — 8.24 mm → 15.95 mm

RICESELECT — Not aged — 42.42% GROWTH — 6.90 mm → 9.83 mm

TASTING BASMATI RICE

We bought eight basmati rices, six grown in India (one also sources from Pakistan) and two grown in the United States. We cooked them according to the stovetop directions provided on each package and tasted them plain; we also tasted them in our recipes for Basic Rice Pilaf and Chicken Biryani. Panels of 21 tasters sampled them blind, rating the flavor, aroma, texture, and overall appeal of each rice. The products were purchased in Boston-area supermarkets and online, and prices shown are what we paid. Information about origins and aging methods was obtained from manufacturers. We calculated the average length-to-width ratio (how much longer a grain is than it is wide) of cooked grains. Scores from the three tastings were averaged, and products appear below in order of preference.

RECOMMENDED

DAAWAT Basmati Rice
PRICE: $17.98 for 10 lb ($1.80 per lb)
AGED: 12 to 18 months   SOURCE: India
LENGTH-TO-WIDTH RATIO OF COOKED GRAIN: 8.04
AVERAGE GROWTH PERCENTAGE WHEN COOKED: 94%
COMMENTS: With "pleasantly chewy," "long, elegant, distinct, intact grains" with a "nice bite," this long-aged Indian-grown rice was "fragrant and tender, perfect" when eaten plain and in pilaf. When cooked in Chicken Biryani, "it contributes an earthy flavor," and the grains are very long, elegant, and toothsome." One taster simply wrote: "My favorite."

PRIDE OF INDIA Extra Long Indian White Basmati Rice
PRICE: $8.99 for 1.5 lb ($5.99 per lb)
AGED: 2 years   SOURCE: India
LENGTH-TO-WIDTH RATIO OF COOKED GRAIN: 8.80
AVERAGE GROWTH PERCENTAGE WHEN COOKED: 117%
COMMENTS: Despite tasters' praise for its "crazy-long grains!" and "floral" scent, this long-aged rice came in last in our plain tasting due to its "mushy" texture; we'd followed the package directions, which called for too much water. (We later tried tweaking the rice-to-water ratio, with minimal improvement.) But it was truly stellar in our Chicken Biryani, where tasters raved: "Delicious, slightly nutty flavor," and "Wow! I had no idea rice could be this flavorful." Our takeaway? We recommend it—but only if you ignore the package instructions.

GOYA Basmati Rice
PRICE: $19.99 for 11 lb ($1.82 per lb)
AGED: At least 1 year   SOURCE: India
LENGTH-TO-WIDTH RATIO OF COOKED GRAIN: 6.11
AVERAGE GROWTH PERCENTAGE WHEN COOKED: 81%
COMMENTS: "Fluffy, tender/firm, [and] aromatic," with "moderately" "long and slender," "very distinct" grains that tasted "nutty" and "toasty," this rice was "very fragrant," with a "buttery" aftertaste when eaten plain. In pilaf, tasters thought this rice was "beautifully tender" with "full flavor," but they noted that it seemed a little "mellow," even a bit "bland," in biryani.

RECOMMENDED WITH RESERVATIONS

RICESELECT Texmati White Premium Rice
PRICE: $5.99 for 2 lb ($3.00 per lb)
AGED: No   SOURCE: Texas
LENGTH-TO-WIDTH RATIO OF COOKED GRAIN: 3.71
AVERAGE GROWTH PERCENTAGE WHEN COOKED: 42%
COMMENTS: Tasters found this rice "chewy and slightly sticky. A little neutral in flavor, and texture is more like a short-grain rice." "Mildly fragrant, nutty, but also not remarkable." One wrote: "Are you sure this is basmati? The grains are short and fat. It looks like regular long-grain generic stuff." In pilaf and biryani, comments were similar, noting the "plumper, shorter, softer grains" that were "short and sticky for basmati," with a "mild, noncompeting flavor."

ROYAL Basmati Rice
PRICE: $23.16 for 10 lb ($2.32 per lb)
AGED: At least 1 year   SOURCE: India
LENGTH-TO-WIDTH RATIO OF COOKED GRAIN: 5.76
AVERAGE GROWTH PERCENTAGE WHEN COOKED: 58%
COMMENTS: "Gently fragrant," with "mild flavor" and "nice distinct grains," this rice was a bit "chewy" and "firm" when eaten plain. In pilaf, tasters enjoyed its "nice al dente texture" and "delicate" flavor with "grassy" notes, but some found that the "long, slim" grains had a "rough," "coral-like" surface. Cooked in biryani, it became a little too soft, and while some tasters enjoyed its "earthy" flavor, a few mentioned that it came across as a little "bland."

LUNDBERG FAMILY FARMS California White Basmati Rice
PRICE: $4.99 for 2 lb ($2.50 per lb)
AGED: No; stored for an average of 3 months   SOURCE: California
LENGTH-TO-WIDTH RATIO OF COOKED GRAIN: 4.16
AVERAGE GROWTH PERCENTAGE WHEN COOKED: 62%
COMMENTS: Tasters generally liked this American-grown rice, finding it "sweet," with "buttery flavor," but said "it looks much softer, clumpier, and fatter than I expected." It was "quite thick for basmati," with grains that were "short [and] sticky. This is not basmati." In pilaf, tasters found it "thicker, stickier, no fluff factor." "Not the profile I expect." One summed it up: "I can't really tell that this is basmati rice, specifically."

TILDA Basmati Rice
PRICE: $24.00 for 20 lb ($1.20 per lb)
AGED: A few months   SOURCE: India
LENGTH-TO-WIDTH RATIO OF COOKED GRAIN: 8.45
AVERAGE GROWTH PERCENTAGE WHEN COOKED: 108%
COMMENTS: With "long grains that are distinct without seeming dry," our previous winner didn't perform quite as well this time. Tasters praised its "clean flavor" but found it "a bit soft." In biryani, "it meshed nicely with the chicken" and had "a pleasant flavor on its own; it's not flavorless."

CAROLINA Basmati Rice
(also sold as Mahatma Basmati Rice)
PRICE: $3.99 for 2 lb ($2.00 per lb)
AGED: No   SOURCE: India and Pakistan
LENGTH-TO-WIDTH RATIO OF COOKED GRAIN: 5.40
AVERAGE GROWTH PERCENTAGE WHEN COOKED: 63%
COMMENTS: Tasters had several oft-repeated complaints about this rice, calling it "clumpy, sticky, mealy," with "superlight flavor." "Grains stick together. Seems shorter-grained than appropriate." In pilaf and biryani, it's "not very fragrant, not very flavorful, not much better than white rice." Perhaps most damning: "It's not terrible, but it does nothing truly well."

---

earned points for a pleasing aroma sometimes described as "buttery," "nutty," or popcorn-like. While this aroma has been traced to more than 100 volatile organic compounds, experts agree that the biggest source of the scent is a flavor molecule called 2-acetyl-1-pyrroline, or "2AP," which is enhanced by long-term storage under controlled conditions.

Our Favorite Basmati

When we compared scores across our three tastings, we had a winner that performed beautifully in all our tests. Imported from India, Daawat Basmati Rice is one of the longest-aged rices in our lineup. Its grains were among the longest after cooking, remaining slender and intact, rather than broken. Its texture was fluffy, smooth, and firm—not too soft, no matter how we prepared it. As one of the more aromatic rices in the lineup, Daawat Basmati contributed its own subtle flavor and fragrance to dishes, while other products were merely a blank slate. At about $1.80 per pound, it's also one of the most affordable.

Testing Dutch Ovens

Dutch ovens do it all. But which pot makes "it all" easiest?

⇒ BY HANNAH CROWLEY ⇐

Is there anything you can't do with a Dutch oven? We use these large, heavy-duty pots for boiling, searing, frying, braising, and baking food and for *sous vide* cooking. We turn them into smokers, steamers, coolers, and panini presses. They might just be the busiest pots in our kitchen.

Our longtime favorite from Le Creuset works perfectly, but at $367.99, it costs a pretty penny. At the other end of the spectrum is a classic cast-iron model that costs seven times less—and there's a pot in every price bracket in between. So how much do you need to spend to get a Dutch oven that will last for years, is capable of cooking everything you throw at it, and makes said cooking as easy as possible?

To find out, we chose 11 widely available models priced from $54.31 to $367.99, including the Le Creuset and our longtime favorite inexpensive option from Cuisinart ($83.70). Each held at least 6.5 quarts, a capacity that works well for all our recipes. We put them through a litany of tests, rating each pot on the quality of its food, how easy it was to use and clean, and how durable it was. At the end of testing, we concluded that all the pots are capable of making good food, but some were much easier to use. Here's what mattered.

Material Differences

Lighter, thinner Dutch ovens tend to scorch food because the heat zips right through them, so we focused on heavier ceramic and cast-iron models. The only ceramic model we tested weighed 9.75 pounds; the cast-iron pots ranged from 13.7 to 18.15 pounds. We had hoped that the ceramic might provide a lighter alternative to cast iron, but it proved too fragile for such a workhorse pot. We were nervous handling it, and the lid cracked when we firmly set it on the base from a mere 2 inches up. This left us with the cast-iron models and our next question: coated or uncoated?

All but one of the cast-iron pots were coated with enamel, a hard, smooth durable coating made by fusing powdered glass at a very high temperature to a metal surface; we tested one uncoated Dutch oven from Lodge, the maker of our winning traditional cast-iron skillet. It arrived fully seasoned, but it had to be dried and oiled immediately after washing.

In the past, when we tested the uncoated Lodge Dutch oven, we discovered that food cooked in it

▶ Watch Hannah in Action
See how the testing was done at
CooksIllustrated.com/oct18

It's much easier to monitor the browning of food in pots with light-colored interiors (left).

sometimes tasted metallic. This time around, though, tasters didn't notice any off-flavors, even after we simmered an acidic tomato sauce in it (acid can strip a pot's seasoning) and then cooked fairly neutral white rice and French fries. A Lodge representative said that the company is constantly working to improve its seasoning process.

Seeing the Light

Like the uncoated model, four of the enameled Dutch ovens had dark interiors. This made it difficult to monitor browning and to see how dark our fond got as we seared beef. It also made it more challenging to use our remote thermometer to track the temperature of oil during frying. That's because dark interiors prevented us from easily spotting the tip of the probe to ensure that it wasn't touching the pot, which can cause it to give a false reading. Overall, lighter interiors provided better visibility and were easier to cook in.

Some pots were tall and narrow; others were short and broad. We preferred those with generous cooking surfaces—at least 9 inches across. More usable surface area meant we could work faster, particularly when browning in batches. We also preferred low, straight sides, as tall or curved sides tended to partially block our view into the pot.

Handle style was another important factor, especially since we prefer heavier Dutch ovens. Our lineup included two styles: flat (like little tabs) and looped (semicircles). We much preferred the latter style because the loops allowed for a fuller, more secure grip; bigger loops were even better, especially when we were wearing oven mitts.

In the end, we're able to recommend all but two models; however, the Le Creuset ($367.99) is still the best. It is heavy enough to conduct heat well yet still the lightest of the cast-iron models. It has a broad, light-colored cooking surface; low, straight sides; and large looped handles.

We again recommend the Cuisinart Chef's Classic Enameled Cast Iron Covered Casserole ($83.70) as our Best Buy. It is shaped very similarly to the Le Creuset. It's 3 pounds heavier and has smaller handles but costs almost $300.00 less. Like most of the models in our lineup, both of these pots come with a limited lifetime warranty. But the Le Creuset held up better to the kind of everyday wear and tear not covered by the warranty; the Cuisinart pot chipped during our durability tests, while our winner emerged from testing looking as good as new.

What You Get for $368 versus What You Get for $84

We love our winning Dutch oven from Le Creuset, but it isn't cheap. Fortunately, we also love our more affordable runner-up from Cuisinart. It delivers many of the same features as the Le Creuset pot for a fraction of the cost.

LE CREUSET		CUISINART
$368	Price	$84
✓	Lower height	✓
✓	Light interior	✓
✓	Big surface area	✓
✓	Looped handles	✓
✓	Lighter weight	
✓	Durability	

TESTING DUTCH OVENS

We tested 11 widely available Dutch ovens, priced from $54.31 to $367.99. Nine were enamel-coated cast iron, one was uncoated cast iron, and one was ceramic. Prices shown are what we paid online. The 10 pots listed here appear in order of preference.

COOKING
We used each pot to boil water, cook rice, braise beef, make French fries, bake bread, and sear meatballs before simmering them in tomato sauce. All the pots we tested were able to make properly cooked food.

EASE OF USE
We evaluated how easy the pots were to cook in, to clean, and to move around. Medium-weight pots with large, comfortable looped handles; broad, light-colored cooking surfaces; smooth lids; and low, straight sides rated highest.

DURABILITY
To determine whether the pots could withstand years of heavy use, we put them through a series of abuse tests. We scrubbed each pot clean with an abrasive sponge 10 times, whacked each on the rim with a metal spoon 50 times, and firmly settled the lid onto the pot 25 times. Those models that didn't chip or crack rated highest.

KEY
GOOD ★★★
FAIR ★★
POOR ★

HIGHLY RECOMMENDED

LE CREUSET 7¼ Quart Round Dutch Oven
MODEL: LS2501-28   PRICE: $367.99
MATERIALS: Enameled cast iron, phenolic knob
WEIGHT: 13.7 lb   COOKING SURFACE DIAMETER: 9 in
INTERIOR COLOR: Light   INTERIOR HEIGHT: 4.5 in
COOKING: ★★★   EASE OF USE: ★★★   DURABILITY: ★★★

PROS: Ideal shape; medium weight; large, comfortable handles; light interior; superior durability
CONS: Price

RECOMMENDED

CUISINART Chef's Classic Enameled Cast Iron Covered Casserole
MODEL: CI670-30CR   PRICE: $83.70   **BEST BUY**
MATERIAL: Enameled cast iron
WEIGHT: 16.7 lb   COOKING SURFACE DIAMETER: 10.0 in
INTERIOR COLOR: Light   INTERIOR HEIGHT: 4.38 in
COOKING: ★★★   EASE OF USE: ★★½   DURABILITY: ★★½

PROS: Ideal shape, light interior, decently comfortable handles, price
CONS: Heavier and less durable than the Le Creuset model

RECOMMENDED

CROCK-POT 7 Quart Round Cast Iron Dutch Oven with Lid
MODEL: 69144.02   PRICE: $79.99
MATERIALS: Enameled cast iron, stainless-steel knob
WEIGHT: 14.35 lb   COOKING SURFACE DIAMETER: 8.88 in
INTERIOR COLOR: Light   INTERIOR HEIGHT: 5.19 in
COOKING: ★★★   EASE OF USE: ★★   DURABILITY: ★★★
PROS: Comfortable handles, durability, light interior
CONS: Tall and narrow shape

LAVA Signature 7 Qt. Enameled Cast Iron Round Dutch Oven
MODEL: LV Y TC 28 K2 BLU
PRICE: $134.95
MATERIALS: Enameled cast iron, stainless-steel knob
WEIGHT: 15.5 lb   COOKING SURFACE DIAMETER: 9.75 in
INTERIOR COLOR: Dark   INTERIOR HEIGHT: 4.31 in
COOKING: ★★★   EASE OF USE: ★½   DURABILITY: ★★★
PROS: Ideal shape; large, comfortable handles; durability
CONS: Dark interior, hard-to-clean lid

STAUB Cast Iron 7 Qt Round Cocotte
MODEL: 1102806   PRICE: $279.99
MATERIALS: Enameled cast iron, stainless-steel knob
WEIGHT: 14.95 lb
COOKING SURFACE DIAMETER: 9.38 in
INTERIOR COLOR: Dark   INTERIOR HEIGHT: 5.13 in
COOKING: ★★★   EASE OF USE: ★½   DURABILITY: ★★★
PROS: Ideal shape; large, comfortable handles; durability
CONS: Dark interior, hard-to-clean lid, price

LODGE Porcelain Enamel on Cast Iron Dutch Oven
MODEL: EC7D33   PRICE: $73.99
MATERIALS: Enameled cast iron, stainless-steel knob
WEIGHT: 18.15 lb   COOKING SURFACE DIAMETER: 8 in
INTERIOR COLOR: Light   INTERIOR HEIGHT: 4.38 in
COOKING: ★★★   EASE OF USE: ★½   DURABILITY: ★★★
PROS: Light interior; large, comfortable handles; durability
CONS: Heaviest in our lineup, smaller cooking surface

TRAMONTINA 6.5 Qt Enameled Cast-Iron Round Dutch Oven
MODEL: 80131/621DS   PRICE: $58.81
MATERIALS: Enameled cast iron, phenolic knob
WEIGHT: 15.10 lb   COOKING SURFACE DIAMETER: 8.5 in
INTERIOR COLOR: Light   INTERIOR HEIGHT: 4.75 in
COOKING: ★★★   EASE OF USE: ★½   DURABILITY: ★★★
PROS: Light interior, looped handles
CONS: Tall sides, handles slightly too fat for ideal grip, small cooking surface

LODGE 7-Quart Cast Iron Dutch Oven
MODEL: L10DOL3   PRICE: $54.31
MATERIAL: Cast iron   WEIGHT: 16.9 lb
COOKING SURFACE DIAMETER: 8.63 in
INTERIOR COLOR: Dark   INTERIOR HEIGHT: 4.38 in
COOKING: ★★★   EASE OF USE: ★½   DURABILITY: ★★★
PROS: Ideal shape; dark interior made exceptionally well-browned, crusty breads
CONS: Extra care required to maintain seasoning, small handles, dark interior made it hard to monitor browning

NOT RECOMMENDED

ANOLON VESTA Cast Iron 7 Qt. Covered Round Dutch Oven
MODEL: 51822   PRICE: $121.17
MATERIALS: Enameled cast iron, stainless-steel loop on lid
WEIGHT: 15.3 lb   COOKING SURFACE DIAMETER: 8.5 in
INTERIOR COLOR: Dark   INTERIOR HEIGHT: 4.63 in
COOKING: ★★★   EASE OF USE: ½   DURABILITY: ★★★
PROS: None
CONS: Small cooking surface, flat handles, dark interior, heavy lid

EMILE HENRY Flame Top Round Dutch Oven
MODEL: 794570   PRICE: $200.00
MATERIAL: Ceramic
WEIGHT: 9.75 lb   COOKING SURFACE DIAMETER: 8.5 in
INTERIOR COLOR: Dark   INTERIOR HEIGHT: 4.63 in
COOKING: ★★★   EASE OF USE: ½   DURABILITY: ★
PROS: Lightweight
CONS: Fragile, small cooking surface, dark interior, flat handles

INGREDIENT NOTES

> BY STEVE DUNN, ANDREA GEARY, ANDREW JANJIGIAN, LAN LAM & ANNIE PETITO

Tasting White Miso Paste

Miso paste is a powerhouse Japanese ingredient that adds complex, savory flavor to a variety of recipes, from soups and sauces to braised vegetables and grilled chicken. It starts with the cultivation of koji, a mold that is typically sprinkled over cooked rice and left to germinate for two to three days. The koji is then mixed with cooked soybeans, salt, and sometimes water and left to ferment, developing miso's trademark sweet and savory notes. Producers create different varieties of miso by altering the ratio of koji to soybeans as well as the length of fermentation. White miso paste, the kind we most frequently use in the test kitchen, is ready in just a few weeks or months and has a higher proportion of koji to soybeans for a milder, slightly sweeter flavor than other misos.

To find out which white miso paste delivers the best flavor, we purchased five widely available products priced from $4.80 to $7.49 per package ($0.34 to $0.92 per ounce). We sampled them in three blind tastings: plain, in miso soup, and in a marinade on broiled salmon.

Though darker-hued misos are generally more robust in flavor, color wasn't an accurate indicator of flavor. However, tasters did notice some subtle differences, especially in the plain tasting. Most products were "deeply savory" and "umami"-packed. Some tasted "funky" and "fermented," with distinctly "nutty" and sweet flavors of "browned butter" and "caramelized" sugar. One "fruit-forward" miso drew comparisons to "mango" and "banana." The best misos also had a moderate amount of sodium for balanced flavor that didn't overwhelm other ingredients in our recipes.

All five products earned our recommendation, producing good miso soup and salmon. Still, tasters did have a favorite: Hikari Organic White Miso ($0.43 per ounce) has a "caramelized sweetness" and plenty of "funky," "fermented" flavors to balance its moderate sodium level. Our top two products are shown below. –Kate Shannon

RECOMMENDED

HIKARI Organic White Miso
PRICE: $7.49 for 17.6-oz container ($0.43 per oz)
INGREDIENTS: Water, organic soybeans, organic rice, salt, yeast, koji culture
SODIUM: 675 mg   FERMENTATION TIME: About 6 months
SOURCE: Japan
COMMENTS: This toffee-colored miso combines intense "umami" with "tropical," "sweet," and "subtly tart" flavors. We especially liked it in glazed salmon; all the flavors were in "perfect balance." Its sodium level falls in the middle of our lineup, so tasters found it full-flavored but not overwhelmingly salty.

MISO MASTER Organic Mellow White Miso
PRICE: $6.99 for 8-oz container ($0.87 per oz)
INGREDIENTS: Organic whole soybeans, organic handmade rice koji, sun-dried sea salt, Blue Ridge Mountain well water, and koji spores
SODIUM: 540 mg   FERMENTATION TIME: 30 days
SOURCE: North Carolina, USA
COMMENTS: Our runner-up was very "nutty," with a "caramelized sweetness" that reminded us of "browned butter." We liked its distinctly "tangy," "tropical" fruitiness reminiscent of "banana" and "mango." With a moderate sodium content and a 30-day fermentation, it was "pleasantly" salty and fairly light in color.

Sodium levels are based on a 15-gram serving size.

Basmati versus Jasmine Rice

It's easy to confuse raw jasmine and basmati rices: They're both long-grain varieties, and both contain a compound that can give them a popcorn-like aroma. We prepared a batch of each and, once they were cooked, their differences became apparent. The basmati grains remained distinct and maintained their long, slim shape. The jasmine rice had a plush, moist texture; its grains collected in delicate clumps, perfect for eating with chopsticks.

BASMATI Best for pilaf

Why the difference? It's all about the two different molecules that make up starch. Basmati has a lot of amylose: a straight molecule that organizes into a tight formation, which helps each grain stay distinct when cooked, making basmati a great choice for pilaf. Jasmine rice's starch, by contrast, has less amylose and more of another molecule: amylopectin, which has bushy branches that prevent it from organizing itself tidily. That's what gives jasmine its clingy texture and makes it ideal for gently piling into a rice bowl and unmolding to make an impressive mound.

We love both of these fragrant rices, but they're a bit pricier than standard long-grain white rice. We'll save basmati for a refined pilaf and serve jasmine alongside our favorite Thai curries. –A.G.

JASMINE Clings to chopsticks

Pork Butt and Pork Shoulder: Deciphering the Difference

Pork butt and pork shoulder are frequently confused—and misleadingly named—cuts of meat. Both come from the shoulder of the pig, but pork butt is higher on the foreleg, while pork shoulder is farther down. As relatively tough and fatty cuts, both benefit from long, slow cooking methods such as roasting, stewing, and braising. But if we have a choice, we generally prefer the butt, which has better marbling and a more uniform shape. –A.P.

PORK BUTT   PORK SHOULDER

ALTERNATE NAMES	
• Boston butt	• Picnic shoulder; picnic roast

DISTINGUISHING FEATURES	
• Well-marbled with intramuscular fat • Often sold with fat cap intact • Rectangular, uniform shape • Typically sold without skin • Sold as bone-in and boneless	• Typically has less intramuscular fat and marbling • Tapered, triangular shape • Frequently sold with skin on • If boneless, typically sold in netting; when netting is removed, meat "unfolds" into uneven layer

Introducing Fresh Turmeric

Turmeric, the dried root (rhizome) of a plant in the ginger family, is most familiar as the spice that gives curry powder its yellow color; earthy, slightly bitter flavor; and touch of gingery heat. More supermarkets are stocking fresh turmeric, so we wondered how it compares to the more common dried ground version.

We compared rice pilaf, bread-and-butter pickles, and smoothies made with fresh and dried turmeric, substituting 3 parts fresh for 1 part dried. The fresh turmeric brought brightness and complexity to the smoothie, but it was difficult to differentiate from dried when heated for pilaf or pickles.

➤ **The takeaway:** We'll save the fresh stuff for raw applications and use dried when we're cooking. If you buy fresh turmeric, you can refrigerate it for three to four weeks in an airtight container or zipper-lock bag to keep it fresh.

➤ **Two tips for working with turmeric:** A spoon makes quick work of removing turmeric's thin skin, while a rasp-style grater breaks it down in a flash. –L.L.

Dried Chiles: Shopping, Cleaning, and Storing

We made our way through more than 250 dried chiles while developing our recipe for Braised New Mexico–Style Pork in Red Chile Sauce (Carne Adovada) (page 7) and learned a few tips along the way. –A.P.

➤ **Shopping:** Look for chiles that are pliable and smell slightly fruity. Avoid those that feel hard or crack when you try to bend them.

➤ **Cleaning:** Wipe chiles with a damp cloth or paper towel to remove dust or dirt.

➤ **Storing:** If not using straightaway, preserve the chiles' flavor and texture by sealing them in an airtight container or zipper-lock bag and storing them in a cool, dry place.

TAKE THESE HOME
Look for flexible dried chiles.

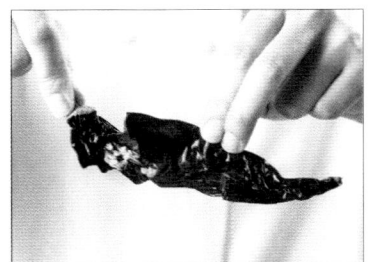

LEAVE THESE BEHIND
Avoid chiles that crack or tear when bent.

Does Iodized Salt Impact Flavor?

Iodized salt was created in the early 20th century to compensate for a lack of dietary iodine. Though an iodine deficiency is far less of an issue in the modern American diet, supermarkets still routinely carry iodized salt. We stock both iodized and noniodized salt in the test kitchen, and we've often wondered if there's a taste difference. To find out, we tasted a solution of 2 percent iodized salt in water (the maximum concentration in most foods) alongside an identical concentration of pure salt. The majority of tasters could not identify a difference. And when we made similar solutions using chicken stock in lieu of water, no one could tell them apart. Science supports this finding: One study reported that potassium iodide—the most common source of iodine in salt—is detectable only in concentrations thousands of times greater than the concentrations we would find in our food.

➤ **The takeaway:** Iodized salt is perfectly fine to stock in your kitchen; it won't affect the flavor of your food. –A.J.

DIY RECIPE Quick Pickled Turnips and Carrots with Lemon and Coriander

Crunchy, tangy pickled vegetables are a classic accompaniment to many Middle Eastern dishes, such as Falafel (page 13), hummus, and baba ghanoush, and make a great addition to a salad or cheese plate. Quickly toasting the spices to bring out their flavor and adding strips of lemon zest to the brine infuses these bright, crisp pickles with nuanced flavors. –S.D.

**QUICK PICKLED TURNIPS AND CARROTS
WITH LEMON AND CORIANDER**
MAKES ABOUT 4 CUPS

To ensure that the turnips are tender, peel them thoroughly to remove not only the tough outer skin but also the fibrous layer of flesh just beneath.

- 1 teaspoon coriander seeds
- 1 teaspoon mustard seeds
- 1½ cups cider vinegar
- ¾ cup water
- 1 tablespoon sugar
- ½ teaspoon red pepper flakes
- ½ teaspoon salt
- 1 pound turnips, peeled and cut into ½ by ½ by 2-inch batons
- 1 red onion, halved and sliced thin
- 2 carrots, peeled and sliced thin on bias
- 4 (3-inch) strips lemon zest

Toast coriander seeds and mustard seeds in medium saucepan over medium heat, stirring frequently, until fragrant, about 2 minutes. Add vinegar, water, sugar, pepper flakes, and salt and bring to boil, stirring to dissolve sugar and salt. Remove saucepan from heat and add turnips, onion, carrots, and lemon zest, pressing to submerge vegetables. Cover and let cool completely, 30 minutes. (Cooled vegetables can be refrigerated for up to 1 week.)

Convenience Garlic Products: Worth the Shortcut?

Supermarkets offer numerous options for garlic that's been prepped for cooking, including peeled cloves, jarred minced garlic, and even garlic paste in a tube. While such products are convenient, especially if you're making a recipe that calls for lots of garlic, we wondered how their flavor stacks up to that of fresh garlic that you peel and prep yourself. To find out, we used each raw in a gremolata with parsley and lemon zest and then in two cooked applications: garlic bread and spaghetti with garlic and oil. We compared each sample to a version made with garlic we'd peeled and prepped ourselves.

➤ **The upshot:** Garlic paste tasted weak, and the preminced kind had off-flavors. But peeled garlic cloves worked fine. One caveat: Make sure they're fresh. The cloves should be plump and creamy white in color and shouldn't smell like garlic. If they do, they've likely been damaged during transport or preparation and will rot quickly. –S.D.

PEELED
A fine option

MINCED
Too sharp and sour

PASTE
Weak flavor; too salty

KITCHEN NOTES

BY STEVE DUNN, ANDREA GEARY, ANDREW JANJIGIAN, LAN LAM & ANNIE PETITO

WHAT IS IT?

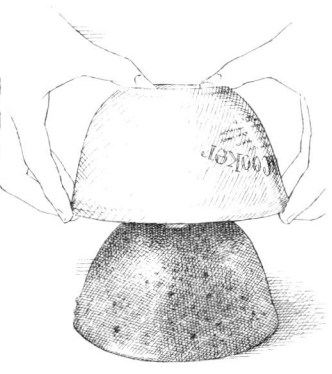

First introduced in Edwardian England around 1910, this lidded vessel was used to cook meat stews and steamed puddings. (Not to be confused with American custard-based puddings, British steamed puddings are most similar to cakes and can be sweet or savory.) Made of ironstone, a type of pottery similar to stoneware, the Grimwade's Quick-Cooker came in four sizes, with this 1-pint version being the smallest. Cooks would fill it with stew or pudding batter and then place a small piece of pastry dough over the center tube, creating a watertight seal once the lid went on. The sealed vessel cooked in a pot of simmering water; the device's central "chimney" promoted quick, even cooking by introducing heat to the center of the pudding or stew.

We tested this model, which we found at an antique sale, with a traditional British marmalade steamed pudding. How did it work? Bloody brilliantly! After a 2-hour bath in simmering water, the pudding emerged moist, tender, and evenly cooked. Served with a traditional custard sauce, the pudding was a hit. While 2 hours isn't exactly "quick," the Grimwade's Quick-Cooker certainly made easy work of this classic British dessert. –S.D.

GRIMWADE'S QUICK-COOKER

Three Other Grains to Cook in a Rice Cooker

Rice cookers produce perfectly cooked, fluffy rice because they're programmed to stop cooking once all the water has been absorbed by the rice. To see if other grains that we typically cook via the absorption method could work in this appliance, we cooked bulgur, millet, and quinoa in our winning rice cooker, the Aroma 8-Cup Digital Rice Cooker and Food Steamer. Once we established the appropriate amount of water to add, we found that all three did well in the rice cooker.

Next we tried three grains—pearled barley, farro, and wheat berries—that we normally cook via the pasta method (boiling in an abundance of water that we drain off). In the rice cooker, all three ended up requiring an hour-long presoak in boiling water to ensure that they were fully cooked by the time the water was absorbed—a big inconvenience that also meant the grains took a lot longer to prepare than on the stovetop.

Moving forward, we'll consider a rice cooker a viable option for quick-cooking grains such as bulgur, millet, and quinoa, but we'll stick with the pasta method on the stovetop for denser, heartier grains. (Note: If your rice cooker has multiple settings, choose the white rice option when cooking these other grains.) –L.L.

RICE COOKER–FRIENDLY
Bulgur, millet, and quinoa

RICE COOKER FAILS
Pearled barley, farro, and wheat berries

GRAIN (1 CUP)	WATER	SALT	APPROX. YIELD
Bulgur	1 cup	¼ teaspoon	3½ cups
Millet	1½ cups	¼ teaspoon	3½ cups
Quinoa	1 cup	¼ teaspoon	3 cups

Breaking Down Pork Butt

We often use pork butt (see page 28 for information on how this cut differs from pork shoulder) for stewing and braising because it's well marbled and contains lots of connective tissue, which breaks down during long, slow cooking, giving the meat a rich, moist texture. Efficiently trimming the fat from this large roast and cutting it evenly into smaller pieces, as we do in our recipe for Braised New Mexico–Style Pork in Red Chile Sauce (Carne Adovada) (page 7), can be a tricky endeavor. Here's an efficient way to tackle it. –A.P.

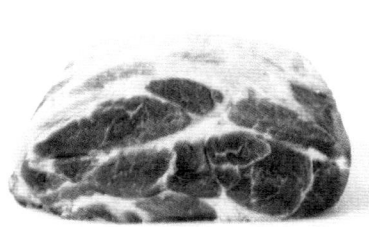

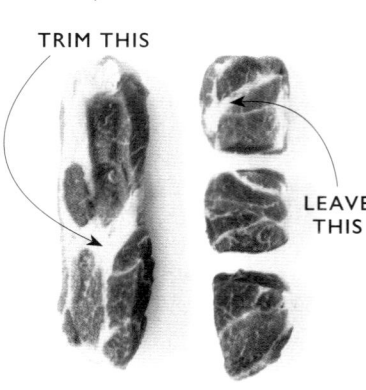

TRIM THIS / **LEAVE THIS**

Start by removing any hard, waxy fat from the surface of the meat, leaving just a thin layer. Don't worry about removing any interior fat at this point.

Slice the meat crosswise into slabs of the desired thickness. Then, cut the slabs lengthwise into strips of the desired thickness. Finally, cut each strip crosswise into cubes. As you work, remove any knobs of hard, waxy fat as they become accessible.

Don't worry about removing every last bit of fat: Focus on trimming the hard, waxy fat that becomes accessible as you break down the roast.

The Benefits of Being Dull

Is your baking sheet dull and matte from years of use and repeated scrubbing? Lucky you. We recently put a batch of pristine new sheets into rotation in the test kitchen and suddenly found that our recommended cooking times weren't getting the job done. Garlic bread was pallid and limp, and butternut squash emerged from the oven looking steamed instead of roasted. In the past, we've noted that dark-colored pans absorb and transfer heat more efficiently than lighter-colored pans. Could the same be true of dull pans, even if they were roughly the same color as the shiny new versions?

To find out, we placed gleaming new sheets and dull older ones in the oven with thermocouples attached to record the rates at which they heated. Sure enough, the older sheets heated rapidly, reaching just over 400 degrees in 15 minutes. The shiny new sheets were slower to heat, hitting only 350 degrees in the same amount of time. And they never got as hot as their duller counterparts, maxing out at 385 degrees after more than 30 minutes, which meant they would be far less effective for browning food.

So if your baking sheet has lost its luster, you should celebrate, not mourn. –A.G.

DULL PAN: NICELY BROWNED RESULTS

SHINY PAN: PALE BAKE

Why Colder Water Makes Better Dough

When making yeasted doughs that undergo a long, slow fermentation in the refrigerator, such as many of our pizza doughs and the dough for our Pita Bread (page 15), we use ice water. Keeping the dough cold during mixing—especially when friction from a food processor is involved—allows the yeast to ferment gradually when the dough is refrigerated. During this proofing period, the yeast develops complex flavors and creates just enough gas bubbles to make the dough pliable. If the dough becomes too warm during mixing, the yeast ferments too quickly and the dough will overproof, becoming sour-tasting and excessively bubbly. Those extra bubbles make the dough prone to tearing when stretched.

To prove what a difference a few degrees makes, we prepared two batches of pita dough: one using 35-degree ice water made by mixing equal volumes of ice and water and letting the mixture sit for 5 minutes before using and another with 55-degree water made by briefly stirring a handful of ice cubes into 2 cups of water.

After an overnight ferment in the refrigerator, the dough made with the 35-degree water had a smooth exterior, had expanded minimally, and stretched with ease once it came to room temperature. The dough made with 55-degree water had many large bubbles just beneath its surface and was about 25 percent larger. We found it difficult to shape and stretch evenly.

➤ **The takeaway:** For pizza, pita, and other doughs that ferment in the refrigerator, make sure your ice water is truly icy: Mix equal volumes of ice and water and let it sit for at least 5 minutes before using. –A.J.

ICY WATER = SMOOTH DOUGH   **COLD WATER = BUBBLY DOUGH**

SCIENCE Better Whole-Wheat Pie Dough

Adding whole-wheat flour to pie dough is a catch-22. It adds an appealing nutty flavor but can prevent the crust from developing shatteringly crisp, flaky layers. That's because whole-wheat flour doesn't form as much structure-building gluten as all-purpose flour does, so crusts containing too much whole wheat often bake up overly delicate and crumbly. The usual solution is to add only a small amount of whole wheat to the dough. But what if there were a recipe that needed less than half the flour to form gluten, while the remainder didn't need to contribute to structure at all? Our recipe for Foolproof All-Butter Pie Dough (January/February 2018) does just that: Only 40 percent of the flour forms gluten, and the crust bakes up beautifully flaky and crisp. We wondered if the technique we employ in that recipe would allow us to load up a pie dough with as much as 60 percent whole wheat without compromising its texture.

EXPERIMENT

We made three batches of Foolproof All-Butter Pie Dough, processing 60 percent of the flour with most of the butter to form a paste and breaking the paste into chunks before adding the rest of the flour and butter and finally the water. For the first batch we used all-purpose flour in the paste as a control. In the second batch, we used whole-wheat flour in the paste, and in the third batch—to really challenge our premise—we used gluten-free flour. We used all-purpose flour for the remaining 40 percent of the flour in all three doughs. We rolled, shaped, and blind-baked each crust before tasting.

RESULTS

All the crusts had plenty of shattery, crisp layers and were tender without being overly crumbly or fragile. These qualities were particularly remarkable in the 60 percent gluten-free crust, which had the potential to lack any structure at all.

EXPLANATION

The butter "waterproofs" the first portion of flour, meaning that it's unable to form a gluten network once water is added. Only the second portion of flour can do that. When baked, the glutinous portion forms a crisp, flaky framework for the non-gluten-forming portion, which contributes the richness and tenderness we expect of pie crust.

TAKEAWAY

Our novel method means you can create pie dough with 60 percent flavorful (but gluten-challenged) flour, such as whole-wheat, rye, or even buckwheat (which can't form gluten at all). The crusts will bake up with supercrisp, flaky layers, thanks to the gluten formed by the second portion of all-purpose flour. Our Foolproof Whole-Wheat Pie Dough and Foolproof Rye Pie Dough recipes are available for free for four months at CooksIllustrated.com/oct18. –A.G.

WHOLE-WHEAT CRUST

Don't Toss Fry Oil: Clean It with Cornstarch

A downside to deep frying is the large quantity of oil that's often required. But unless that oil smoked or you used it to fry fish, it's fine to reuse it once you strain it. Our usual method is to pour the oil through a fine-mesh strainer lined with a coffee filter, which can take hours. We found a speedier way: Add cornstarch to the oil, which attracts and traps solids for easy removal.

➤ **Here's how to do it:** For every cup of frying oil, whisk together ¼ cup water and 1 tablespoon cornstarch. Add mixture to warm or cooled oil. Heat oil gently over low heat (do not let it simmer), stirring constantly with heat-proof spatula, until starch mixture begins to solidify, 10 to 12 minutes. Remove oil from heat and strain through fine-mesh strainer (or use slotted spoon to fish out gelled mixture). Don't worry if oil appears cloudy; it will clear up once reheated. Refrigerate oil and reuse up to 3 times. –A.P.

EQUIPMENT CORNER

⇒ BY MIYE BROMBERG, LISA McMANUS, EMILY PHARES, LAUREN SAVOIE & KATE SHANNON ⇐

RECOMMENDED WITH RESERVATIONS

FORNO MAGNIFICO
Electric Pizza Oven
MODEL: FM-FB512
PRICE: $80.99

HIGHLY RECOMMENDED

WILLIAMS SONOMA
Junior Chef Oven Mitt
MODEL: 1701544
PRICE: $7.95 per mitt ($15.90 for 2)

RECOMMENDED

ZWILLING PRO 5.5"
Flexible Boning Knife
MODEL: 38404-143
PRICE: $99.95

RECOMMENDED WITH RESERVATIONS

HESTAN CUE Smart Cooking System
MODEL: 05404
PRICE: $499.95

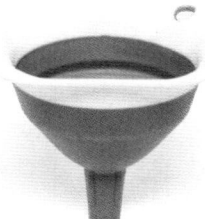

RECOMMENDED

PREPWORKS Thinstore Collapsible Funnel
MODEL: CF-15
PRICE: $9.11

Indoor Pizza Ovens

To make homemade pizza, we usually call for preheating a baking stone—the Old Stone Oven Pizza Baking Stone ($59.95) is our favorite—for 1 hour in a 500-degree oven. The baking stone transfers heat to the dough, resulting in crisp, golden-brown crusts and chewy interiors. Still, we were intrigued by indoor pizza ovens—midsize countertop appliances that minimize preheating time and can reach higher temperatures than conventional home ovens—so we purchased five models, priced from $34.52 to $169.99, including four electric ovens and one that works on a gas stovetop. We compared the pizzas (both homemade and store-bought frozen versions) made in each oven with the same pies baked in an oven on a stone. We also evaluated the machines on ease of use and maneuverability. Ultimately, they all fell short, and our winner, the Forno Magnifico Electric Pizza Oven ($80.99), is only recommended with reservations. Its high heat produced crisp crusts and evenly melted cheese, and it required just a 10-minute preheating period, but it wasn't significantly easier to use than a kitchen oven. Most damning: A majority of tasters preferred pizzas made in the oven to those made with this specialty appliance. –K.S.

Oven Mitts for Kids

Heat protection is one of the biggest safety considerations when kids are in the kitchen. And though we leave really hot jobs to the adults, little cooks still require protection for moderate-heat tasks such as removing a lid to stir food and putting baking sheets in the oven. With this in mind, we rounded up four oven mitts specifically designed for children, priced from $7.74 to $39.90 per pair (some sold individually). We adults did a preliminary safety check, monitoring how hot the mitts got and how quickly, as we gripped and carried hot pots and pans. We eliminated one product that failed to keep our hands cool for at least 30 seconds when we held a 350-degree baking sheet. Next, we brought in the kids and had them try the remaining models. Their favorite was the Williams Sonoma Junior Chef Oven Mitt, $15.90 for two (sold individually). These cotton mitts were snug but not too tight for providing good dexterity, and the kids found the fuzzy polyester lining to be comfortable. Most important, though, these mitts kept our hands cool for 35 seconds when we held hot pans, and at nearly 11 inches long, they protected kids' forearms, too. –L.S.

Flexible Boning Knives

With thin, narrow blades, boning knives are ideal for getting in between joints and for carving around larger bones. In the past, we've found that a 6-inch flexible boning knife is the most versatile option for home cooks. We resurveyed the options and selected six models, priced from $18.87 to $119.95, including our longtime favorite, the Victorinox Swiss Army Fibrox Pro 6" Flexible Boning Knife ($26.95). All did a serviceable job of boning chicken breasts, trimming tenderloins, and removing the bones from cooked pork shoulder roasts. Those that rose to the top of our rankings had blades that were very thin, narrow, and sharp and that maintained their sharpness throughout testing. We also preferred knives that were moderately flexible, affording us better control and precision. Our new winner, the Zwilling Pro 5.5" Flexible Boning Knife ($99.95), has a very sharp blade that is shorter than the others. That slightly shorter length ended up being a big asset, as it gave us even more control and precision. Our previous favorite is still an excellent entry-level choice for home cooks, and we've named it our Best Buy. –M.B.

The Hestan Cue Smart Cooking System

Imagine not having to worry about getting the temperature of your burner just right or forgetting to set a timer while you cook. This is the idea behind the Hestan Cue Smart Cooking System ($499.95), which includes two Bluetooth-enabled items: an induction burner and a skillet (a Chef's Pot saucier pan is sold separately for $299.95). All connect to a mobile app complete with step-by-step recipes. As you cook, the app automatically controls the burner's heat based on temperature sensors in the pans and burner. To see if the system worked, we tried a number of Hestan Cue recipes as well as manual cooking. We were pleased with the quality of the food and found the system mostly enjoyable to use, but it wasn't foolproof. For example, the app told us to measure only the thickest portion of a chicken breast and to input that number into the app. When we cooked it according to the instructions, the thinner parts of the breast were overdone. And while the pans are well constructed, they are small. The burner also proved to be fragile; during one test, water boiled over onto it and it shut down—permanently. As with any smart product, updates are planned for the Hestan Cue, but for now we can only recommend it with reservations. –L.M.

Funnels

A funnel can eliminate spills and minimize waste—if you have the right one. Since the winner of our last testing has been discontinued and there are new models on the market, we decided to retest. We selected seven funnels priced from $4.41 to $14.19, all with a capacity of at least 1 cup. We used each model to transfer foods and liquids with different textures into containers of varying sizes. The key to success was the spout. We preferred models with longer spouts, which anchored them inside the receptacle and allowed hands-free use. The size of the spout's opening was also important: Narrower spouts caused backups, but overly wide spouts didn't fit neatly inside a variety of containers. Our winner, the Prepworks Thinstore Collapsible Funnel ($9.11), had the ideal opening, just over ½ inch wide, and a long spout for good stability. As a plus, it's collapsible, so it can be easily stored in a kitchen drawer. –E.P.

INDEX
September & October 2018

RECIPES

MAIN DISHES
Braised New Mexico–Style Pork in Red Chile Sauce (Carne Adovada) 7
Chicken Vesuvio 5
Falafel 13
Japanese Grilled Steak and Scallion Rolls (Negimaki) 9
Pan-Seared Swordfish Steaks 11

SIDE DISHES
Italian Pasta Salad 21
Quick Pickled Turnips and Carrots with Lemon and Coriander 29
Roasted Asparagus 16
Roasted Broccoli 16
Roasted Brussels Sprouts 17
Roasted Butternut Squash 17
Roasted Carrots 17
Roasted Cauliflower 17
Roasted Cremini Mushrooms 17
Roasted Fennel 17
Roasted Green Beans 17
Skillet-Charred Green Beans 20
  with Crispy Bread-Crumb Topping 20

BREAD
Pita Bread 15

DESSERT
Belgian Spice Cookies (Speculoos) 23
  with Almonds 23

SAUCES AND CONDIMENTS
Applesauce 19
  Dessert-Worthy, with Brown Sugar and Rum 19
  Savory, with Beets and Horseradish 19
Basil and Lemon Butter 17
Caper-Currant Relish 11
Chili-Lime Salt 17
Spicy Dried Mint–Garlic Sauce 11
Tomato-Chile Sauce 13

BONUS ONLINE CONTENT at CooksIllustrated.com/oct18

RECIPES
Chicken Vesuvio for Two
Foolproof Rye Pie Dough for Double-Crust Pie
Foolproof Rye Pie Dough for Single-Crust Pie
Foolproof Whole-Wheat Pie Dough for Double-Crust Pie
Foolproof Whole-Wheat Pie Dough for Single-Crust Pie
Harissa-Oregano Sauce
Israeli-Style Pita Bread
Pan-Seared Swordfish Steaks for Two
Savory Applesauce with Parsnips and Mustard

Simple Applesauce
Skillet-Charred Green Beans with Crispy Sesame Topping
Whole-Wheat Pita Bread

▶ **RECIPE VIDEOS**
Want to see how to make any of the recipes in this issue? There's a free video for that.

▶ **BONUS VIDEO**
Testing Dutch Ovens

FOLLOW US ON SOCIAL MEDIA

facebook.com/CooksIllustrated
twitter.com/TestKitchen
pinterest.com/TestKitchen
instagram.com/CooksIllustrated
youtube.com/AmericasTestKitchen

America's Test Kitchen
COOKING SCHOOL
Visit our online cooking school today, where we offer 180+ online lessons covering a range of recipes and cooking methods. Whether you're a novice just starting out or are already an advanced cook looking for new techniques, our cooking school is designed to give you confidence in the kitchen and make you a better cook.

▸ Start a 14-Day free trial at OnlineCookingSchool.com

Do you have an iPad?
Download the CooksIllustrated.com/iPad app in iTunes.

Your free trial includes bonus features such as:
> Easy-to-follow videos for every recipe
> Step-by-step slide shows for every recipe
> Full-color photos

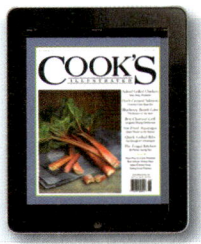

Chicken Vesuvio, 5

Skillet-Charred Green Beans, 20

Applesauce, 19

Braised New Mexico–Style Pork, 7

Falafel with Tahini and Tomato-Chile Sauces, 13, and Pita Bread, 15

Japanese Grilled Steak and Scallion Rolls, 9

Italian Pasta Salad, 21

Pan-Seared Swordfish Steaks, 11

Belgian Spice Cookies (Speculoos), 23

PHOTOGRAPHY: CARL TREMBLAY; STYLING: KENDRA McKNIGHT, ELLE SIMONE

NUMBER 155

NOVEMBER & DECEMBER 2018

25 YEARS
COOK'S
ILLUSTRATED

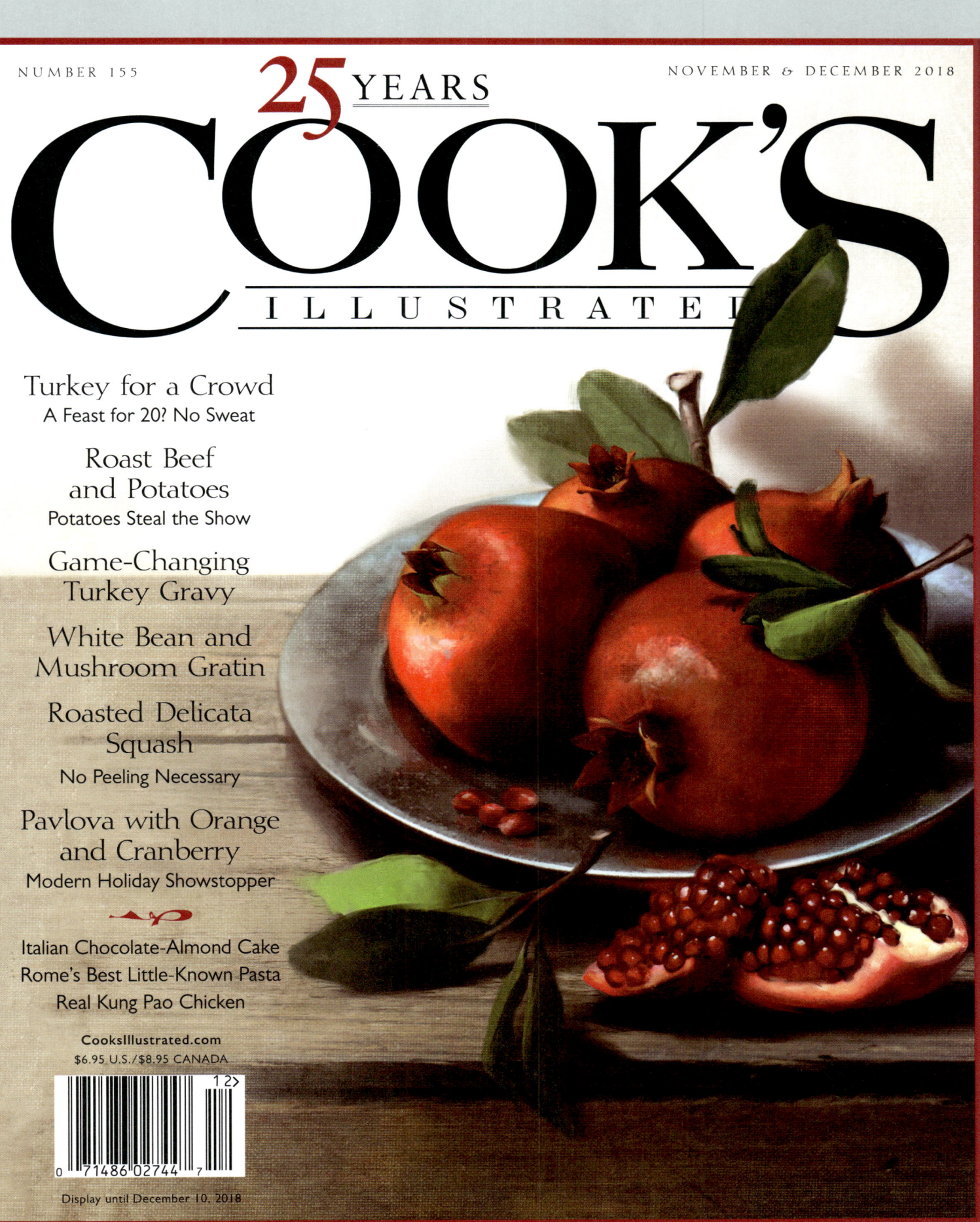

Turkey for a Crowd
A Feast for 20? No Sweat

Roast Beef
and Potatoes
Potatoes Steal the Show

Game-Changing
Turkey Gravy

White Bean and
Mushroom Gratin

Roasted Delicata
Squash
No Peeling Necessary

Pavlova with Orange
and Cranberry
Modern Holiday Showstopper

Italian Chocolate-Almond Cake
Rome's Best Little-Known Pasta
Real Kung Pao Chicken

CooksIllustrated.com
$6.95 U.S./$8.95 CANADA

Display until December 10, 2018

COOK'S ILLUSTRATED

NOVEMBER & DECEMBER 2018

PAGE 6

PAGE 19

PAGE 10

PAGE 14

PAGE 4

2 Your Quirkiest Quick Tips
Behold some of the most clever tips you've sent our way over the past 25 years. Keep them coming! COMPILED BY ANNIE PETITO

4 Low-Stress Turkey for a Crowd
Moist, tender meat; crisp, bronzed skin; and rich, full-flavored gravy for 20 people? No problem—if you think like a chef. BY STEVE DUNN

6 Roast Beef and Potatoes for Company
A tender, juicy roast isn't hard to pull off. Neither are creamy, golden-brown potatoes. But merging the two into a holiday centerpiece? That's where things get tricky. BY ANDREW JANJIGIAN

8 Game-Changing Turkey Gravy
Of course it had to taste great. But we also wanted a gravy that could be made in advance, didn't require drippings, and could accommodate dietary restrictions. BY LAN LAM

10 Rome's Greatest Little-Known Pasta
The porky-peppery flavors of *pasta alla gricia* deserve big recognition. BY ANNIE PETITO

11 The Easiest Winter Squash
Tired of struggling to peel and cut heavy-duty squash? Try something more delicate. BY LAN LAM

12 Real Kung Pao Chicken
Spicy chiles and tingly Sichuan peppercorns team up with lightly sauced chicken and peanuts in a stir-fry that's literally sensational. BY ANDREA GEARY

14 Creamy Dressings, Hold the Cream
A surprising ingredient quietly imparts the smooth richness of dairy or mayonnaise while letting the other ingredients shine. BY ANDREA GEARY

16 Ten Discoveries That Changed the Way We Cook
Over the past 25 years, we've performed countless tests in the pursuit of better, faster, easier, and more foolproof recipes. Here are a few of the game changers that transformed how we—and, dare we say, our readers—cook. BY ELIZABETH BOMZE

18 White Bean and Mushroom Gratin
Once you know the building blocks that create savory depth, you won't miss the meat. BY LAN LAM

19 Modern Holiday Showstopper
Pavlova is a drop-dead gorgeous dessert of marshmallowy, crisp-shelled meringue piled with lightly whipped cream and fresh fruit. Ours is as foolproof as it is beautiful. BY ANNIE PETITO

22 Italian Chocolate-Almond Cake
Flourless chocolate cake often trades on cloying fudge-like density and one-note chocolate flavor. Leave it to the Italians to whip up a version that's lighter and more nuanced. BY STEVE DUNN

24 The Best Unsalted Butter
Unsalted butter is one of the most basic ingredients for cooking and baking. What's the best one for everyday use? BY KATE SHANNON

26 Searching for a Superior Metal Spatula
This essential tool can be a cook's best friend—but only if you choose the right one. BY MIYE BROMBERG

28 Ingredient Notes
BY PAUL ADAMS, STEVE DUNN & LAN LAM

30 Kitchen Notes
BY STEVE DUNN, ANDREA GEARY, ANDREW JANJIGIAN & LAN LAM

32 Equipment Corner
BY MIYE BROMBERG, CAROLYN GRILLO, LISA McMANUS & EMILY PHARES

America's Test Kitchen, a real test kitchen located in Boston, is the home of more than 60 test cooks and editors. Our mission is to test recipes to learn exactly how and why they work and eventually arrive at the very best version. We also test kitchen equipment and taste supermarket ingredients in search of products that offer the best value and flavor. You can watch us work by tuning in to *America's Test Kitchen* (AmericasTestKitchen.com) and *Cook's Country from America's Test Kitchen* (CooksCountry.com) on public television and listen to our weekly segments on *The Splendid Table* on public radio. You can also follow us on Facebook, Twitter, Pinterest, and Instagram.

EDITORIAL STAFF

Chief Executive Officer David Nussbaum
Chief Creative Officer Jack Bishop
Editor in Chief Dan Souza
Executive Editor Amanda Agee
Deputy Editor Rebecca Hays
Executive Managing Editor Todd Meier
Executive Food Editor Keith Dresser
Deputy Food Editor Andrea Geary
Senior Editors Andrew Janjigian, Lan Lam
Senior Editors, Features Elizabeth Bomze, Kristina DeMichele
Associate Editors Steve Dunn, Annie Petito
Photo Team & Special Events Manager Tim McQuinn
Lead Cook, Photo Team Dan Cellucci
Test Cook, Photo Team Jessica Rudolph
Assistant Test Cooks, Photo Team Sarah Ewald, Eric Haessler, Devon Shatkin
Senior Copy Editor Jill Campbell
Copy Editor Rachel Schowalter
Senior Science Research Editor Paul Adams

Executive Editor, Tastings & Testings Lisa McManus
Deputy Editor, Tastings & Testings Hannah Crowley
Managing Editor, Tastings & Testings Briana Palma
Senior Editors, Tastings & Testings Lauren Savoie, Kate Shannon
Associate Editor, Tastings & Testings Miye Bromberg
Assistant Editors, Tastings & Testings Riddley Gemperlein-Schirm, Carolyn Grillo, Emily Phares

Creative Director John Torres
Design Director Greg Galvan
Photography Director Julie Cote
Associate Art Director Maggie Edgar
Senior Staff Photographer Daniel J. van Ackere
Staff Photographers Steve Klise, Kevin White
Photography Producer Meredith Mulcahy

Executive Editor, Web Christine Liu
Managing Editor, Web Mari Levine
Associate Editor, Web Ashley Delma

Director, Creative Operations Alice Carpenter
Senior Editor, Special Projects Christie Morrison
Imaging Manager Lauren Robbins
Production & Imaging Specialists Dennis Noble, Jessica Voas
Test Kitchen Director Erin McMurrer
Assistant Test Kitchen Director Alexxa Benson
Test Kitchen Manager Meridith Lippard
Test Kitchen Facilities Manager Kelly Ryan
Senior Kitchen Assistant Shopper Marissa Bunnewith
Senior Kitchen Assistant Receiver Heather Tolmie
Lead Kitchen Assistant Ena Gudiel
Kitchen Assistants Gladis Campos, Blanca Castanza, Amarilys Merced, Arlene Rosario

BUSINESS STAFF

Chief Financial Officer Jackie McCauley Ford
Senior Manager, Customer Support Tim Quinn
Customer Loyalty & Support Specialist J.P. Dubuque

Chief Revenue Officer Sara Domville
Director, Sponsorship Marketing & Client Services Christine Anagnostis
Director, Integrated Partnerships & Business Development Eric Wynalek

Senior Director, Events & Special Projects Mehgan Conciatori
Partnership Marketing Manager Pamela Putprush
Event Coordinator Michaela Hughes

Chief Digital Officer Fran Middleton
VP, Marketing Natalie Vinard
Senior Director, Social Media Marketing Claire Oliverson
Social Media Manager Morgan Mannino
Social Media Coordinators Charlotte Erritty, Sarah Sandler

Director, Public Relations & Communications Brian Franklin
Public Relations Coordinator Madeleine Cohen

Senior VP, Human Resources & Organizational Development Colleen Zelina
Human Resources Manager Jason Lynott

Circulation Services ProCirc

Cover Art Robert Papp

PRINTED IN THE USA

LETTER FROM THE EDITOR

COOKING FOR TWENTY-FIVE

Twenty-five years ago, the premier issue of this magazine hit newsstands and mailboxes. From day one, *Cook's Illustrated* stood out as a unique publication that, quite frankly, shouldn't have worked. Launched at a time when food magazines were glossy and laser-focused on the food of chefs and restaurants, *Cook's Illustrated* proclaimed—through hand-drawn illustrations, exhaustively tested recipes, and detailed explanations—that the home cook was king. The magazine's success and growth over the last quarter century is, to me, proof positive that Americans, now more than ever, care deeply about cooking, spending time in the kitchen, and feeding family and friends.

Our mission over the past 25 years hasn't been to make foolproof recipes; to perform rigorous, unbiased equipment reviews; or to explain the underlying science of everyday cooking. While these tenets form the backbone of our everyday work, our singular purpose has always been something a bit bigger. We strive to help home cooks be successful in the kitchen. Period. Over the past year we reached out to many of you and asked for your input on how we could make the magazine even more useful—how it could better support you in the kitchen. You had a lot to say. And we took your feedback to heart.

And so it is with great pride that I announce a number of exciting updates. Let's start on the cover. Our cover paintings are a signal of the changing seasons and an invitation to get into the kitchen and start cooking. With their canvas extended to the edges of the page, you get to see more detail and vibrant color. And that vibrancy continues inside, where all photography is now full color. Colorful food is obviously beautiful, but more important, a color photograph provides valuable detail about how a finished recipe should look. And speaking of recipes, you'll see a couple of important improvements in those as well. We've added total time to each so that you can see at a glance whether a recipe is an option for a busy weeknight or better suited to relaxed weekend cooking. We've also added nutritional information, which is available free for every recipe in this issue at CooksIllustrated.com/dec18/nutrition. You will even notice changes within the recipes themselves. When we use an ingredient more than once within the recipe, we'll note in the ingredient list that it is "divided" to help you with prep and organization. Finally, you'll see that we've included suggested recipe pairings from our archives for many of the main dishes.

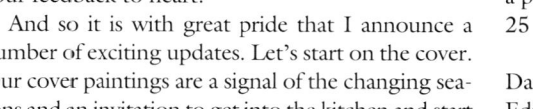
Dan Souza

Taken as a whole, these changes represent a significant step forward for the magazine. Not change for change's sake but improvements that I hope will make your time in the kitchen more productive and enjoyable. This issue is both a celebration of what we've accomplished over a quarter of a century and a promise of dedication and hard work for the next 25 years.

Dan Souza
Editor in Chief

FOR INQUIRIES, ORDERS, OR MORE INFORMATION

COOK'S ILLUSTRATED MAGAZINE
Cook's Illustrated magazine (ISSN 1068-2821), number 155, is published bimonthly by America's Test Kitchen Limited Partnership, 21 Drydock Avenue, Suite 210E, Boston, MA 02210. Copyright 2018 America's Test Kitchen Limited Partnership. Periodicals postage paid at Boston, MA, and additional mailing offices, USPS #012487. Publications Mail Agreement No. 40020778. Return undeliverable Canadian addresses to P.O. Box 875, Station A, Windsor, ON N9A 6P2. POSTMASTER: Send address changes to *Cook's Illustrated*, P.O. Box 6018, Harlan, IA 51593-1518. For subscription and gift subscription orders, subscription inquiries, or change of address notices, visit AmericasTestKitchen.com/support, call 800-526-8442 in the U.S. or 515-237-3663 from outside the U.S., or write to us at *Cook's Illustrated*, P.O. Box 6018, Harlan, IA 51593-1518.

CooksIllustrated.com
At the all new CooksIllustrated.com, you can order books and subscriptions, sign up for our free e-newsletter, or renew your magazine subscription. Join the website and gain access to 25 years of *Cook's Illustrated* recipes, equipment tests, and ingredient tastings, as well as companion videos for every recipe in this issue.

COOKBOOKS
We sell more than 50 cookbooks containing recipes all developed in our test kitchen, including *The Complete Mediterranean Cookbook* and *Vegan for Everybody*. To order, visit our bookstore at CooksIllustrated.com/bookstore.

EDITORIAL OFFICE 21 Drydock Avenue, Suite 210E, Boston, MA 02210; 617-232-1000; fax: 617-232-1572. For subscription inquiries, visit AmericasTestKitchen.com/support or call 800-526-8442.

YOUR QUIRKIEST QUICK TIPS

Behold some of the most clever tips you've sent our way over the past 25 years. Keep them coming!

≥ COMPILED BY ANNIE PETITO ≤

Pouring Boxed Broth
Boxed broth sometimes glugs and splashes out of the container, which can cause a bit of a mess. Dan Messier of Beacon, N.Y., found that by simply rotating the box so the spout is at the top of the container instead of the bottom, he can pour the broth without any splashing.

Thermometer Holder for the Grill
Avid griller Neil Macmillan of Nanaimo, British Columbia, came up with a convenient holder for the thermometer he sticks inside the grill vent to monitor the internal temperature—an ordinary wooden clothespin. It stays cool to the touch while also protecting the head of the thermometer from the hot metal surface of the grill.

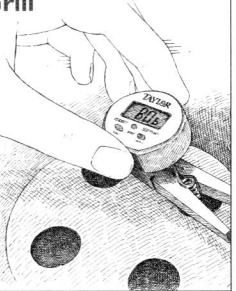

Impromptu Bowl Cover
Plastic wrap is the usual choice for covering leftovers for storage, but Kim Waters of Gainesville, Ga., discovered another option: a clean, unused shower cap (often found in complimentary toiletry packs in hotel rooms). It's big enough to fit most large mixing bowls, and it's reusable.

Cleaning Crevices
Cookware with tight crevices, such as panini presses and grill pans, can be hard to clean. Karen Pizzuto-Sharp of Seattle, Wash., found a solution in a compressed air duster. Designed to clean between the keys on a keyboard, the can's fine blast of air also lifts off crumbs in narrow cooking spaces.

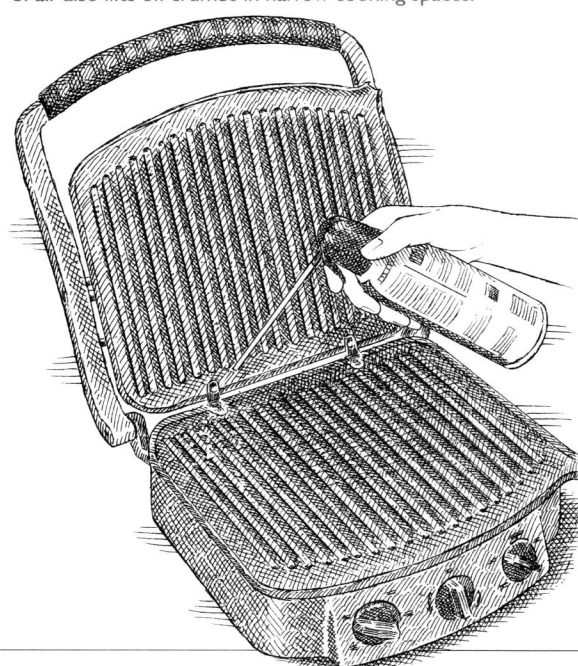

Chilling Beverages for a Party
When refrigerator space is at a premium, Melissa Lennon of Phoenixville, Pa., knows just what to do: She turns her washing machine into a makeshift icebox to chill drinks. She fills the washer's basket with ice cubes and nestles in the cans and bottles to have cold drinks at the ready. When the party's over and the ice is melted, she simply runs the washer's spin cycle to drain the water.

Aerating One Glass of Wine
Recalling that we had good results aerating a bottle of wine in a blender, Diane Kiino of Kalamazoo, Mich., turned to her electric milk frother when she needed to aerate just one glass. Buzzing the wine with the tiny whisk for just a few seconds improved its flavor.

SEND US YOUR TIPS We will provide a complimentary one-year subscription for each tip we print. Send your tip, name, address, and telephone number to Quick Tips, *Cook's Illustrated*, 21 Drydock Avenue, Suite 210E, Boston, MA 02210, or to QuickTips@AmericasTestKitchen.com.

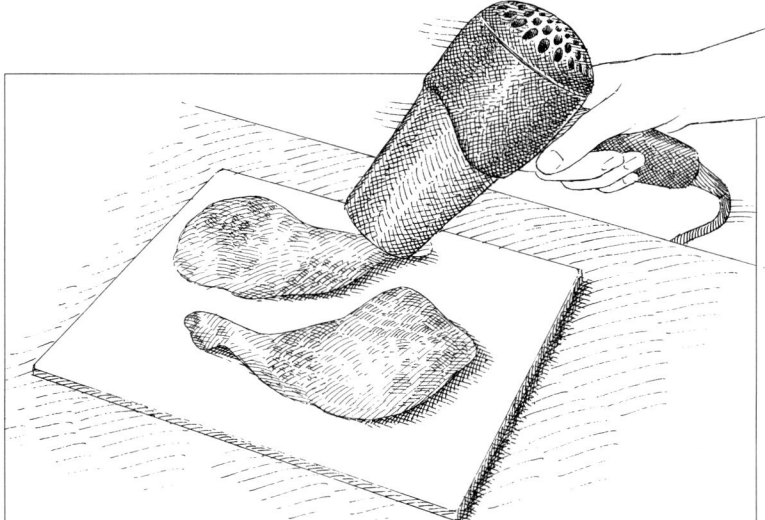

Dry Chicken Skin in a Flash
Salting skin-on chicken overnight helps dry the skin so it crisps up when cooked, but sometimes Ben Dahlberg of Houston, Texas, forgets to plan ahead, so he came up with a fast alternative: a hair dryer. He pats the chicken dry with paper towels and then waves a hair dryer set on high heat back and forth over the chicken pieces for about 2 minutes per piece, until the skin looks dry. It roasts beautifully, with very crispy skin.

Cut Slicing Time in Half
Individually halving cherry tomatoes, grapes, or pitted cherries is time-consuming. Marcia Lang of Two Harbors, Minn., found a way to speed things along.

1. Place a medium plastic lid, such as one from a cottage cheese container, on the counter with the lip side up. Place a single layer of the food to be sliced in the lid.
2. Place a second lid, lip side down, over the food. With one hand gently but firmly holding the top lid and your other hand holding a sharp chef's or serrated knife, slice horizontally between the lids, cutting the food in half.

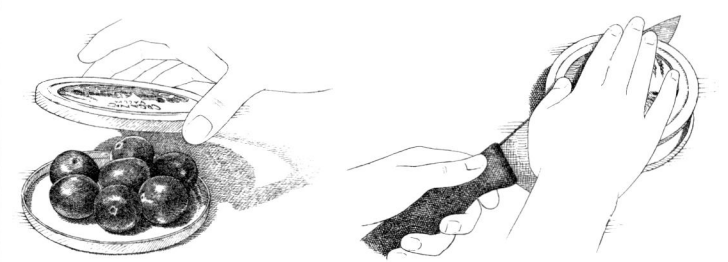

Rescuing Burnt Cookies
Even the best bakers sometimes produce cookies that are overbrowned or even burnt. This fate befell Lyn Babcock of New York, N.Y., but she managed to rescue the cookies that weren't too far gone by gently grating the burnt layer off the bottoms with a rasp-style grater.

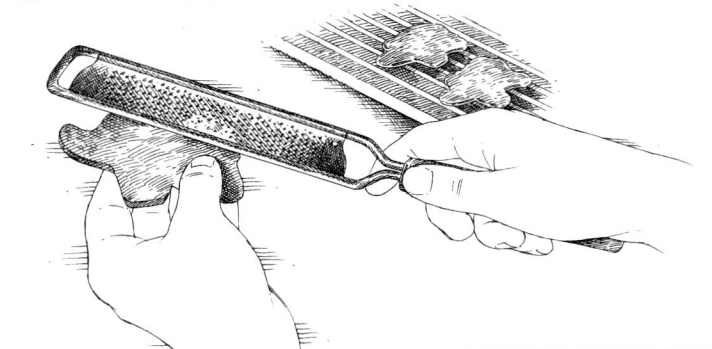

Halve or Halve Not
Andrew Pimlott of Seaside, Calif., discovered an ingenious way to accurately measure ½ cup of liquid with a 1-cup dry measuring cup.

1. Fill a straight-sided 1-cup measuring cup approximately halfway with liquid.
2. Tilt the cup diagonally. When the liquid touches the brim on one side of the cup and the edge of the flat bottom on the opposite side of the cup, you have measured exactly ½ cup. Use the same method to measure ¼ cup with a ½-cup measure, 2 tablespoons with a ¼-cup measure, and so on.

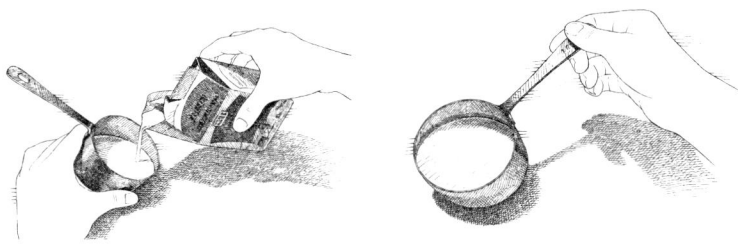

Handling Hot Pans
Pulling a hot baking sheet out of the oven while wearing oven mitts can be tricky, sometimes resulting in cookies with finger indents. Inspired by the cooks at his local pizzeria who use Channellock pliers to retrieve hot pizzas from the oven, John Watlington of Richmond, Va., put the tool to work in his own kitchen.

Spreading Cold Butter
Cecelia Rooney of Point Pleasant, N.J., often runs into this common problem: She wants butter for her toast but forgot to leave a stick out to soften. Crisis averted: She has discovered that a vegetable peeler will shave a thin ribbon that's easy to cut into smaller pieces before spreading.

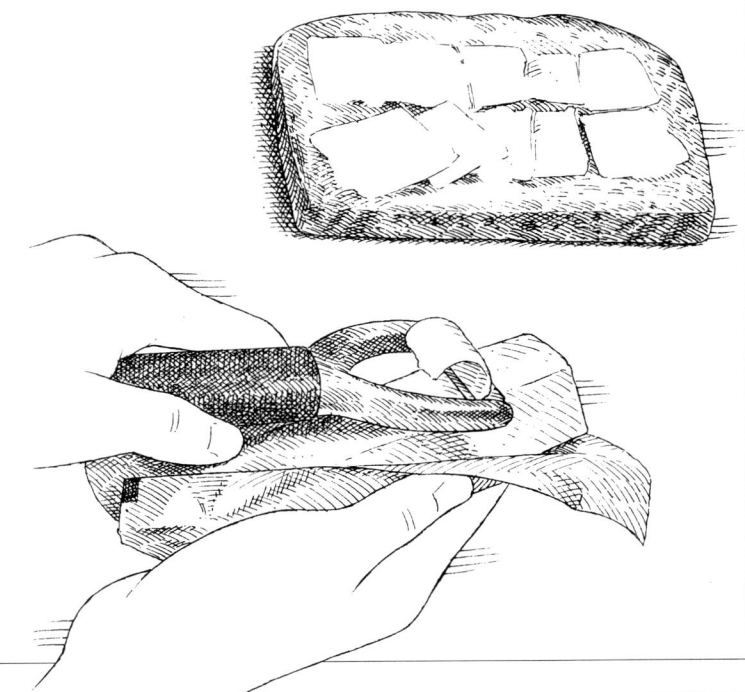

Low-Stress Turkey for a Crowd

Moist, tender meat; crisp, bronzed skin; and rich, full-flavored gravy for 20 people?
No problem—if you think like a chef.

⇒ BY STEVE DUNN ⇐

We ditch a whole turkey in favor of easier-to-manage parts. We braise the dark meat ahead of time, roast the breasts, and then reheat the dark meat and crisp its skin just before serving.

Hosting a big crowd on Thanksgiving has the potential to be disastrous. That's because the usual approaches—roasting two average-size birds or one enormous one—are fraught with issues. Two turkeys require dual ovens—a nonstarter for most. And a single large bird hogs the oven, making it off-limits for other dishes. A 20-pounder can also be a real challenge to maneuver in and out of the oven and nearly impossible to flip during roasting to promote evenly cooked white and dark meat. What's more, a large bird tends to overcook on the exterior while the interior comes up to temperature. And no matter how many birds you roast, there's still the last-minute scramble to make gravy from pan drippings. Finally, you must compose yourself for tableside carving.

But keep reading, because things are about to change. All the stress melts away if you think more like a professional chef. You see, a good chef is a master at breaking down complex dishes into simple components and then devising a timeline to prepare as much as possible in advance. Once I started thinking in those terms, all sorts of possibilities opened up.

My first move was the biggest game changer: Instead of roasting two whole turkeys, I separately cooked two bone-in breasts and four leg quarters. This meant that I could use different cooking techniques for each to guarantee juicy, tender results. Working with parts also presented some terrific make-ahead opportunities.

I sketched out a plan: I would start by braising the leg quarters up to a few days before the feast. Low, slow braising promises tender, moist dark meat since it gives the abundant collagen time to turn into supple gelatin—and the reheated dark meat would taste just as good as freshly made. What's more, a flavor-packed braising liquid (broth, white wine, fresh herbs, and aromatics) would be an ideal base for a big batch of gravy that I could also prepare in advance.

With the dark meat and gravy taken care of, I would salt the breasts the day before Thanksgiving to season the flesh and hold in moisture. Then, the only tasks left would be roasting the breasts (this takes 2 hours, freeing up precious oven space) and reheating the thighs, drumsticks, and gravy. Brushing the skin of the braised dark meat with melted butter and cranking the heat to 500 degrees would encourage browning and crisping so all the parts would arrive at the table looking as if they had come from two whole birds.

I executed my plan without a hitch. At serving time, the parts were a breeze to carve and made a gorgeous presentation on a platter. Moist, tender, well-seasoned white and dark meat? Check. Bronzed, crisp skin? Check. Sumptuous gravy? Check. Cool, calm, and collected host? Check, check, check.

▶ STEP-BY-STEP VIDEO AND NUTRITION INFORMATION
CooksIllustrated.com/DEC18

TURKEY AND GRAVY FOR A CROWD
SERVES 18 TO 20

This recipe requires refrigerating the salted turkey breasts for 24 hours. If using self-basting or kosher turkey breasts, do not salt in step 7, but season with salt in step 8. We used Diamond Crystal Kosher Salt; if you use Morton Kosher Salt, reduce the salt in step 7 to 2½ teaspoons per breast, rubbing 1 teaspoon onto each side and ½ teaspoon into the cavity. Covering the turkey with parchment and then foil will prevent the wine in the braising liquid from "pitting" the foil.

Turkey Legs and Gravy
- 3 onions, chopped
- 4 celery ribs, chopped
- 4 carrots, peeled and chopped
- 10 garlic cloves, crushed and peeled
- 3 tablespoons unsalted butter, melted, plus extra as needed
- 3 bay leaves
- 10 sprigs fresh thyme
- 10 sprigs fresh parsley
- 1 tablespoon black peppercorns
- 4 cups chicken broth
- 1 cup water
- 1 cup dry white wine
- 4 (1½- to 2-pound) turkey leg quarters, trimmed
- 3 tablespoons kosher salt
- ½ cup all-purpose flour

Turkey Breasts
- 2 (5- to 6-pound) bone-in turkey breasts, trimmed
- 2 tablespoons plus 2 teaspoons kosher salt, divided
- 7 tablespoons unsalted butter, melted, divided

UP TO 3 DAYS IN ADVANCE Braise Leg Quarters, Make Gravy TIME: 4 TO 4½ HOURS, PLUS 1 HOUR COOLING

DAY BEFORE Butcher and Salt Breasts TIME: 30 MINUTES, PLUS 24 HOURS SALTING

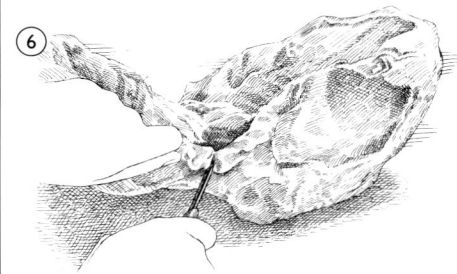

1. FOR THE TURKEY LEGS AND GRAVY: Adjust oven rack to lower-middle position and heat oven to 325 degrees. Toss onions, celery, carrots, garlic, melted butter, bay leaves, thyme sprigs, parsley sprigs, and peppercorns together in large roasting pan; spread into even layer. Place pan over medium heat and cook, stirring occasionally, until vegetables are softened and lightly browned and fond forms on bottom of pan, about 15 minutes. Add broth, water, and wine and bring to simmer, scraping up any browned bits. Remove pan from heat.

2. Cut leg quarters at joints into thighs and drumsticks, sprinkle with salt, and season with pepper to taste. Place pieces skin side up in pan (braising liquid should come about three-quarters of way up legs and thighs). Place 12 by 16-inch piece of parchment paper over turkey pieces. Cover pan tightly with aluminum foil. Place pan in oven and cook until thighs register 170 degrees, 2½ to 3 hours. Remove pan from oven. Transfer turkey pieces to large, shallow container and let cool completely, about 1 hour. Once cool, cover and refrigerate.

3. Using spatula, scrape up any browned bits from bottom and sides of pan. Strain contents of pan through fine-mesh strainer set over large bowl, pressing on solids with spatula to extract as much liquid as possible; discard solids.

4. Transfer liquid to fat separator and let settle for 5 minutes. Reserve ½ cup plus 1 tablespoon fat (if there is not enough fat, add extra melted butter to make up difference) and 8 cups liquid; discard remaining liquid.

5. Heat reserved fat in large saucepan over medium-high heat. Add flour and cook, stirring constantly, until flour is medium golden brown and fragrant, about 5 minutes. Slowly whisk in reserved liquid and bring to boil. Reduce heat to medium-low and simmer, stirring occasionally, until gravy is thickened and reduced to 6 cups, 15 to 20 minutes. Off heat, season gravy with salt and pepper to taste. Transfer to large container and let cool completely, about 1 hour. Once cool, cover and refrigerate.

6. FOR THE TURKEY BREASTS: Place breasts on cutting board skin side down. Using kitchen shears, cut through ribs, following vertical lines of fat where breasts meet backs, from tapered ends of breasts to wing joints. Using your hands, bend backs away from breasts to pop shoulder joints out of sockets. Using paring knife, cut through joints between bones to separate backs from breasts.

7. Flip breasts skin side up. Using your fingers, carefully loosen and separate skin from each side of 1 breast. Peel back skin, leaving it attached at top and center of each breast. Rub 1 teaspoon salt onto each side of breast, then place skin back over meat. Rub 1 teaspoon salt onto underside of breast cavity. Repeat with remaining breast. Place breasts on rimmed baking sheet and refrigerate, uncovered, for 24 hours.

SERVING DAY Roast Breasts, Reheat Dark Meat and Gravy, and Carve TIME: 2¾ HOURS

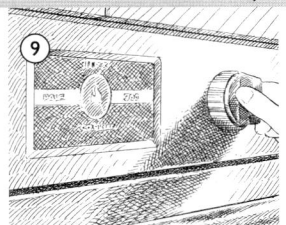
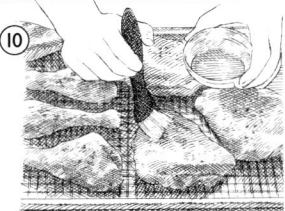

8. Adjust oven rack to middle position and heat oven to 325 degrees. Measure out 20-inch piece of foil and roll into loose ball. Unroll foil, place on second rimmed baking sheet, and top with wire rack (crinkled foil will insulate bottom of sheet to keep it from smoking during roasting). Place breasts, skin side up, on prepared wire rack; brush with 4 tablespoons melted butter and sprinkle each whole breast with 1 teaspoon remaining salt. Roast until thickest part of breast registers 130 degrees, about 1½ hours.

9. Remove breasts from oven and increase oven temperature to 500 degrees. When oven reaches temperature, return breasts to oven and roast until skin is deeply browned and thickest part of breast registers 160 degrees, 20 to 30 minutes. Transfer to carving board and let rest, uncovered, for 30 minutes. Pour any juices from sheet into bowl and set aside.

10. Adjust oven rack to upper-middle position. Place thighs and drumsticks skin side up on now-empty wire rack set in sheet and brush with remaining 3 tablespoons melted butter. Place in oven and reheat until skin is well browned and thighs register 110 degrees, 18 to 22 minutes. Transfer thighs and drumsticks to large platter.

11. While thighs reheat, bring gravy to simmer in large saucepan over medium-low heat, whisking occasionally. Add any reserved juices from breasts and season with salt and pepper to taste. Cover and keep warm.

12. Carve breasts and transfer to platter with thighs and drumsticks. Serve, passing gravy separately.

Roast Beef and Potatoes for Company

A tender, juicy roast isn't hard to pull off. Neither are creamy, golden-brown potatoes. But merging the two into a holiday centerpiece? That's where things get tricky.

⇒ BY ANDREW JANJIGIAN ⇐

Roasting beef with potatoes, a hallowed British tradition, sounds like it will produce the ideal holiday spread. While the meat cooks, the spuds sitting underneath or around it soak up the drippings and transform into a flavor-saturated side dish that impresses just as much as (if not more than) the roast itself. But as smart and serendipitous as that sounds, it's folklore. In my experience, cooking the meat and potatoes together rarely produces the best version of either one; in fact, it pits the two components against one another.

The problem is partly due to a lack of space. Most roasting pans can't accommodate a piece of meat large enough to feed a crowd plus enough potatoes to go alongside. So the options are to cram the potatoes into the pan, which causes them to steam, thwarting flavorful browning, or to include only enough to feed a few guests.

The more fundamental issue is that the two components require radically different cooking methods. Low-and-slow heat is the best way to ensure that a large roast cooks evenly and stays juicy, but it also makes for sparse drippings and, thus, bland potatoes. On the other hand, the only way to really brown and crisp potatoes in the oven is to crank the heat way up. But who's willing to risk overcooking a pricey roast for the sake of the spuds?

Finding a way to roast enough beef and potatoes for a crowd while allowing the roast to cook up juicy and tender (and release flavorful drippings to infuse and crisp the potatoes) would require real strategy.

Top Shop

I often default to prime rib for the holidays because of its well-marbled meat and fat cap, which crisps up into a thick crust, making it feel festive. But there are other good options, such as top loin roast. This is the cut that produces strip steaks (its alias is "strip roast"), so it, too, boasts well-marbled meat and a nice fat cap. Plus, it's boneless and uniform, which makes it easy to cook and slice (see "Strip Steak in Roast Form").

I crosshatched the fat cap to help it render and crisp and then salted the meat overnight to ensure that it would be well seasoned and juicy. And for the moment, I cooked the meat and potatoes separately

The roast cooks up nicely juicy and tender. But the beefy-tasting spuds—our take on French fondant potatoes—are the real stars of the dish.

(I'd tackle the merger later). I seared the roast, top and bottom, in a large roasting pan and then transferred it to a 300-degree oven, where it cooked gently until it reached 115 degrees. That's about 10 degrees shy of medium-rare, but the temperature of the meat would climb as it rested.

Potatoes won't crisp in a crowded pan even if the heat is blasting, so I scrapped that goal in favor of an old-school French preparation called fondant potatoes that creates marvelously flavorful results without crisping. To make them, you halve and brown the spuds on the cut sides and then braise them in fat and stock. The potatoes absorb the flavorful liquid, turning so velvety that they practically dissolve in your mouth (hence their nickname: "melting potatoes"). Not worrying about crisping also meant that I could pack plenty into the pan.

I browned 5 pounds of peeled, halved Yukon Gold potatoes (their starchy yet creamy consistency seemed ideal) in the rendered fat left in the pan, flipped them, poured beef broth around them, and returned them to a 500-degree oven. Thirty minutes later, they were plump and extremely tender. I transferred them to a platter and strained and defatted the remaining broth, which would make a nice jus for serving.

They tasted beefy on the outside but bland within—no surprise since commercial broth contains no fat and only moderate beef flavor. But the roast had those qualities in spades. Time for that merger.

Get Scrappy

One unique feature of top loin roast is the sinewy strips of meat and fat that run along either side of the roast. They're often left behind on the plate, but I decided to use them. I cut them off and sliced them into 1-inch pieces to brown alongside the roast.

The results were worth the minimal knife work: The trimmings gave up loads more fat and fond for the potatoes to soak up. (Starting the meat and trimmings in a cold pan maximized the amount of fat that was rendered, because the fat had time to melt thoroughly before the meat's exterior browned too much.) I even doubled their efficacy by simmering

---

SHOPPING
Strip Steak in Roast Form

Top loin roast, which comes from the short loin in the middle of the cow's back, is the roast that generates strip steaks (it's also called "strip roast"). The well-marbled, tender meat and ample fat cap make it a great alternative to other premium roasts, such as prime rib (it costs about $4 less per pound than prime rib, too). We trim off the strips of meat and fat that run along the sides of the roast and brown them with the roast to generate lots of flavorful juices for cooking the potatoes.

MEAT A DIFFERENT CUT
Top loin roast is a great alternative to prime rib.

the browned scraps with the broth before using it to braise the potatoes, which amped up its beefiness and the flavor of the spuds. Further doctoring the broth with garlic and herbs rounded it out; adding gelatin gave the reduced jus unctuous body.

Cooking the meat and potatoes together wasn't tricky once I had extracted all that flavor and fat from the trimmings. But it did require a strategic setup. After searing the meat and scraps, I laid the potatoes cut side down in the pan, keeping them in a single layer to ensure even cooking, and covered them with aluminum foil I poked holes in. That created a "rack" on which I placed the roast; it also allowed juices to drip through to the potatoes and trapped steam that helped the potatoes cook through. When the roast hit 115 degrees, I set it aside to rest; gingerly flipped the potatoes; added my beef-enhanced, strained broth (it simmered while the roast cooked); and finished the potatoes in a 500-degree oven.

It was a success: juicy, tender meat and creamy potatoes that tasted truly beefy.

BEEF TOP LOIN ROAST WITH POTATOES
SERVES 8 TO 10
TOTAL TIME: 2¾ HOURS, PLUS 6 TO 24 HOURS SALTING

Top loin roast is also known as strip roast. Use potatoes that are about 1½ inches in diameter and at least 4 inches long. The browned surfaces of the potatoes are very delicate; take care when flipping the potatoes in step 7. To make flipping easier, flip two potatoes and remove them from the pan to create space before flipping the rest.

- 1 (5- to 6-pound) boneless top loin roast
- 2 tablespoons plus 2 teaspoons kosher salt, divided
- 2 teaspoons pepper, divided
- 5 pounds Yukon Gold potatoes, peeled
- ¼ cup vegetable oil
- 5 cups beef broth
- 6 sprigs fresh thyme
- 2 small sprigs fresh rosemary
- 2 tablespoons unflavored gelatin
- 4 garlic cloves, lightly crushed and peeled

1. Pat roast dry with paper towels. Place roast fat cap side down and trim off strip of meat that is loosely attached to thicker side of roast. Rotate roast 180 degrees and trim off strip of meat and fat from narrow side of roast. (After trimming, roast should be rectangular with roughly even thickness.) Cut trimmings into 1-inch pieces. Transfer trimmings to small bowl, wrap tightly in plastic wrap, and refrigerate.

2. Using sharp knife, cut slits ½ inch apart and ¼ inch deep in crosshatch pattern in fat cap of roast. Sprinkle all sides of roast evenly with 2 tablespoons salt and 1 teaspoon pepper. Wrap in plastic and refrigerate for 6 to 24 hours.

3. Adjust oven rack to lowest position and heat oven to 300 degrees. Trim and discard ¼ inch from end of each potato. Cut each potato in half crosswise. Toss potatoes with remaining 2 teaspoons salt and remaining 1 teaspoon pepper and set aside.

4. Place oil in large roasting pan. Place roast, fat cap side down, in center of pan and scatter trimmings around roast. Cook over medium heat, stirring trimmings frequently but not moving roast, until fat cap is well browned, 8 to 12 minutes. Flip roast and continue to cook, stirring trimmings frequently, until bottom of roast is lightly browned and trimmings are rendered and crisp, 6 to 10 minutes longer. Remove pan from heat and transfer roast to plate. Using slotted spoon, transfer trimmings to medium saucepan, leaving fat in pan.

5. Arrange potatoes in single layer, broad side down, in pan. Return pan to medium heat and cook, without moving potatoes, until well browned around edges, 15 to 20 minutes. (Do not flip potatoes.) Off heat, lay 18 by 22-inch sheet of aluminum foil over potatoes. Using oven mitts, crimp edges of foil to rim of pan. With paring knife, poke 5 holes in center of foil. Lay roast, fat side up, in center of foil. Transfer pan to oven and cook until meat registers 115 degrees, 1 to 1¼ hours.

6. While roast cooks, add broth, thyme sprigs, rosemary sprigs, gelatin, and garlic to saucepan with trimmings. Bring to boil over medium-high heat. Reduce heat and simmer for 15 minutes. Strain mixture through fine-mesh strainer into 4-cup liquid measuring cup, pressing on solids to extract as much liquid as possible; discard solids. (You should have 4 cups liquid; if necessary, add water to equal 4 cups.)

7. When meat registers 115 degrees, remove pan from oven and increase oven temperature to 500 degrees. Transfer roast to carving board. Remove foil and use to tent roast. Using offset spatula, carefully flip potatoes. Pour strained liquid around potatoes and return pan (handles will be hot) to oven (it's OK if oven has not yet reached 500 degrees). Cook until liquid is reduced by half, 20 to 30 minutes.

8. Carefully transfer potatoes to serving platter. Pour liquid into fat separator and let settle for 5 minutes. Slice roast and transfer to platter with potatoes. Transfer defatted juices to small bowl. Serve, passing juices separately.

Make It a Mini Roast
No need to wait for a crowd to serve our Beef Top Loin Roast with Potatoes. With a smaller piece of meat and a 12-inch skillet, you can make one heck of a family dinner. Our recipe for Skillet Beef Top Loin Roast with Potatoes, which serves 4 to 6, is available for free for four months at CooksIllustrated.com/dec18.

KEY STEPS | BEEFING UP THE FLAVOR OF POTATOES

There are a few reasons the potatoes in this dish are so darn full of beefy flavor: We introduce beefy goodness to them three different times and in three different ways over the course of cooking.

BROWN IN RENDERED FAT After searing the roast and the trimmings, we sear the potatoes, broad side down, in the rendered fat to create deeply browned, beefy-tasting surfaces.

ROAST WITH BEEFY JUICES We cover the potatoes with a "rack" made from perforated foil and roast the beef on top so its juices drip down onto the potatoes.

BRAISE IN MEATY BROTH While the meat rests, we braise the potatoes, browned side up, in a quick enriched broth made from the trimmings, saturating them with more meaty flavor.

RECIPES TO MAKE IT A MEAL
Find these recipes in our archive: Citrus Salad with Watercress, Dried Cranberries, and Pecans (January/February 2013) and Chocolate Pots de Crème (November/December 2006).

STEP-BY-STEP VIDEO AND NUTRITION INFORMATION
CooksIllustrated.com/DEC18

Game-Changing Turkey Gravy

Of course it had to taste great. But we also wanted a gravy that could be made in advance, didn't require drippings, and could accommodate dietary restrictions.

⇒ BY LAN LAM ⇐

When there are pies to bake, potatoes to mash, and a turkey to carve, the gravy can become an afterthought, often thrown together at the last minute amid the chaos of getting all the food to the table. At that point, there's no time to eke out a flavorful stock for the base, and the roasted bird may or may not have generated the drippings you were counting on to infuse the gravy with rich turkey flavor. The result—whether gloppy, runny, greasy, or just plain dull—is a shame, since many of us drizzle gravy over the entire plate.

After spending weeks reimagining the gravy-making process from start to finish, I came away with an approach that produces a full-bodied gravy that truly tastes like turkey and can be almost entirely prepared days (or even weeks) ahead of time. Best of all, you don't need drippings to make it taste great (though you should certainly add them if you have them), and the recipe can be easily tweaked to accommodate guests with dietary restrictions. Read on and I'll review the important points.

Make a Seriously Flavorful Stock

Gravy is simply a sauce made by seasoning and thickening stock, so it's essential that the stock be full-flavored. Usually, that's accomplished by browning turkey parts (the neck and giblets—more about these later); adding chopped aromatics such as onions, carrots, and celery; deglazing the pot with wine; and adding several cups of liquid.

But I made our turkey stock even more flavorful by turning the process on its head: I skipped browning the turkey parts and instead simmered them straightaway in a couple of cups of chicken broth. The hot liquid surrounding the parts thoroughly extracted their flavorful fat and juices, which, when the liquid evaporated, created a more substantial layer of savory fond than I would have gotten by initially searing the turkey parts. (Fond is what's left in the pan when the proteins and sugars in the drippings undergo the Maillard reaction and brown, which creates hundreds of new flavor compounds. For more information, see "How We Built Gravy with Better Flavor.")

The stock can be made up to two days ahead, and the gravy can be made and refrigerated up to three days ahead or frozen for up to two weeks.

From there, I sautéed the aromatics, deglazed the pot with wine, added more broth, covered the pot to limit evaporation, simmered the stock for about 1 hour, and strained out the solids.

Use Broth, Not Water

Many gravy recipes call for a combination of chicken broth and water, but the latter dilutes flavor and requires reducing to concentrate savoriness. I used only broth.

Make Room for More Fond

More surface area in the pot allows a thin, even layer of the drippings to make contact with the hot pan and brown; this results in maximum fond development and a more flavorful stock. (In a narrower pan, a thicker layer of drippings forms and only those in contact with the pan bottom brown, so there's less fond development.) So instead of a large saucepan, which offers about 40 square inches of surface area, I opted for the 75 square inches of a large Dutch oven.

Use the Neck and Some Giblets

The neck, heart, and gizzard—parts usually found packaged in the bird's cavities—are flavor powerhouses that should be used to fortify the stock (see "Know Your Giblets" on page 28 for more information). Avoid the liver (it's large, shiny, and dark red); its strong mineral flavor ruins gravy.

Add Fat and Skin for Extra Flavor

In addition to adding the neck, heart, and gizzard, I enriched the stock's turkey flavor by trimming and adding excess skin from the top of the breast and excess fat from the bottom of the cavity. These bits and pieces should be trimmed away anyway for tidy presentation, and they contribute valuable turkey flavor to the stock. (For information on exactly where to trim, see "Trim Extra Bits for Extra Flavor.")

STEP-BY-STEP VIDEO AND NUTRITION INFORMATION
CooksIllustrated.com/DEC18

Trim Extra Bits for Extra Flavor

Like most gravies, ours relies on the neck, heart, and gizzard for building big turkey flavor. But we also trim excess skin and fat from the raw bird and add it to the stock to supplement those parts (it's easy to do with kitchen shears). The trimmings further enhance the stock's turkey flavor, and the roasted bird looks tidier.

See the illustration for exactly where to trim, and be sure to cut pieces of skin that are no larger than 1 inch (bigger pieces tend to curl up on themselves and stick out of the liquid). If your turkey does not have excess skin or fat, use kitchen shears to snip off the tail and cut it into three or four pieces.

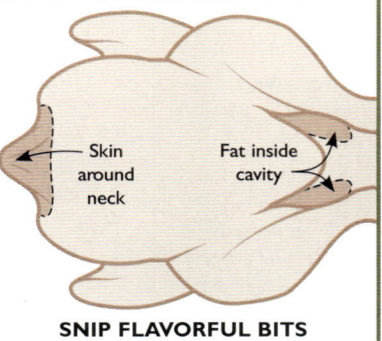

SNIP FLAVORFUL BITS

How We Built Gravy with Better Flavor

The rich turkey flavor in our gravy boils down to one critical component: fond, the flavor-packed browned bits and tacky layer of evaporated juices that form on the bottom of a pan when meat or vegetables are browned. The brown color is a sign that the proteins and sugars have undergone the Maillard reaction and transformed into hundreds of new flavor compounds that can add terrific savory depth when the fond is incorporated into a gravy or another sauce.

Most gravy recipes build fond by searing turkey parts such as the neck and giblets, but we came up with an approach that's more effective. Instead of initially searing the parts, we simmer them (plus turkey fat and skin for extra flavor) in chicken broth until the liquid evaporates. Simmering actually extracts the juices and fat much more thoroughly than searing does. The proof is visible on the bottom of the pot: Once the liquid evaporates, the entire bottom of the vessel (we use a Dutch oven for maximum surface area) is coated with a gorgeously browned layer of fond.

SIMMERED, THEN SEARED | **JUST SEARED**

Don't Defat the Stock

Gravy recipes often call for defatting the stock, but that's a mistake. In tests, I found that the bird's fat is integral to making gravy that tastes like turkey—not just generically like poultry—because an animal's fat is a repository for its unique aromatic compounds.

Be Sure to Brown the Roux

A roux, a cooked paste of roughly equal parts fat and flour, is what transforms the liquid stock into a full-bodied gravy. The key to making a good one is taking the time to cook the mixture until it's deep golden brown, since that color translates into a gravy with equally rich color and nutty depth. Browning the roux also yields a gravy that stays fluid longer (a boon to dinner guests who go back for second helpings) because the starches in the flour break down into smaller molecules that are slow to link up with one another as the gravy cools.

Add Drippings (If You've Got Them)

If you have them, drippings will make the gravy taste even better. Be sure to defat them first (the stock adds enough fat), and don't add more than ¼ cup or the gravy will be too thin.

Make It Ahead

To avoid as much last-minute work as possible, there are two make-ahead opportunities built into the recipe. The turkey stock can be prepared and refrigerated three days in advance or the gravy can be prepared and frozen up to two weeks ahead and gently reheated with the drippings (if using).

Make It Gluten- (or Alcohol-) Free

Flour and wine are traditional components in most turkey gravies, but my recipe works just fine with alternatives for both: a gluten-free flour blend and cider vinegar diluted with water, respectively. (Don't substitute cornstarch for the flour; because cornstarch contains less protein and a higher proportion of starch, it doesn't brown as well and yields gravy with a slippery consistency.)

OUR FAVORITE TURKEY GRAVY
SERVES 12 TO 16 (MAKES 4 CUPS)
TOTAL TIME: 2 HOURS 10 MINUTES

Much of this gravy's flavor is derived from the trimmed skin and fat plus the neck and giblets of a turkey. Use kitchen shears to cut away extra skin from the neck region (leaving enough to cover the opening) and any loose fat from the cavity. Cut large pieces of skin into 1-inch pieces. If your turkey does not have excess skin or fat, use kitchen shears to snip off the tail and cut it into three or four pieces to use as trimmings. Do not use the liver that is packaged with the giblets. The gravy's consistency can be adjusted to suit your taste: Simmer longer for a thicker gravy or thin with additional broth for a thinner gravy. This gravy is better with turkey drippings; you can add them either in step 4 or when reheating the gravy. To double the recipe, double all the ingredients including the trimmings and make the stock in two separate pots.

- 6 cups chicken broth, divided, plus extra as needed
- Reserved turkey neck and giblets
- Reserved turkey trimmings, cut into 1-inch pieces (⅓ cup)
- 1 onion, chopped
- 1 carrot, chopped
- 1 celery rib, chopped
- 8 sprigs fresh parsley
- 2 sprigs fresh thyme
- 2 garlic cloves, peeled
- ½ teaspoon pepper
- ¼ teaspoon salt
- ⅓ cup dry white wine
- 4 tablespoons unsalted butter
- 5 tablespoons all-purpose flour
- ¼ cup defatted turkey drippings (optional)

Listen for a Sizzle

There's no need to babysit the pot during the initial vigorous simmer; there's no chance of scorching since the liquid keeps the temperature well below the point where browning would occur. Only once you hear sizzling—an audible indication that only pockets of liquid remain and are turning to steam—has the temperature risen to the point where browning will occur and you need to start stirring.

1. Bring 2 cups broth, reserved neck and giblets, and reserved trimmings to simmer in Dutch oven over high heat. Cook, adjusting heat to maintain vigorous simmer and stirring occasionally, until all liquid evaporates and trimmings begin to sizzle, about 20 minutes. Continue to cook, stirring frequently, until dark fond forms on bottom of pot, 2 to 4 minutes longer.

2. Reduce heat to medium-high. Add onion, carrot, celery, parsley sprigs, thyme sprigs, garlic, pepper, and salt. Cook, stirring frequently, until onion is translucent, 8 to 10 minutes.

3. Stir in wine and bring to simmer, scraping up any browned bits. Add remaining 4 cups broth and bring to simmer over high heat. Reduce heat to medium-low, cover, and simmer for 1 hour. Strain stock through fine-mesh strainer set over bowl; discard solids. (You should have 3½ to 4 cups stock. Turkey stock can be refrigerated for up to 2 days.)

4. Melt butter in medium saucepan over medium heat. Add flour and increase heat to medium-high. Cook, stirring constantly, until mixture is deep golden brown, 5 to 8 minutes. Reduce heat to low and slowly whisk in strained stock. Increase heat to medium-high and bring to simmer. Simmer until thickened, about 5 minutes. Add drippings, if using, and thin gravy with extra broth, if desired. Season with salt and pepper to taste, and serve. (Gravy can be refrigerated for up to 3 days or frozen for up to 2 weeks; to reheat, bring to simmer over medium-low heat, stirring occasionally.)

OUR FAVORITE GLUTEN-FREE TURKEY GRAVY

The test kitchen's favorite gluten-free flour blends are King Arthur Gluten-Free All-Purpose Flour and Betty Crocker All-Purpose Gluten Free Rice Flour Blend. Do not use a gluten-free flour made with beans here.

Substitute gluten-free flour blend for all-purpose flour.

OUR FAVORITE ALCOHOL-FREE TURKEY GRAVY

Substitute ⅓ cup water and 2 teaspoons cider vinegar for wine.

Rome's Greatest Little-Known Pasta

The porky-peppery flavors of *pasta alla gricia* deserve big recognition.

≥ BY ANNIE PETITO ≤

Rome has four iconic—and outrageously good—pasta dishes: *cacio e pepe*, *amatriciana*, *carbonara*, and *gricia*. I've long been a huge fan of the more well-known first three but had never tried gricia, which features *guanciale* (cured hog jowls), ground black pepper, and tangy, salty Pecorino Romano. So when my colleague Sasha Marx, who grew up in Rome, offered to make it for lunch on a quiet day in the test kitchen, I couldn't refuse.

Sasha put a pot of rigatoni on to boil while he sautéed chopped guanciale in a skillet. When the pork was deeply browned but still retained a tender chew, he removed it, leaving behind its rendered fat. In went the drained rigatoni, which was only halfway cooked (also known as *al chiodo*, or "to the nail"), along with a lot of pasta water—roughly 2 cups. As he let the rigatoni simmer until it was al dente, he stirred it with the starchy water and pork fat to form a creamy sauce, a technique known as *mantecare*. Finally, he returned the browned guanciale to the mix, along with a few more splashes of pasta water, lots of pepper, and grated Pecorino.

It was a memorable lunch: The porky guanciale was at the forefront, followed by the heat of the pepper and the tang of the cheese; it all formed a rich yet delicately creamy sauce to coat the rigatoni.

But when I made the dish (using pancetta since guanciale can be hard to find), it became clear that the technique was more art than science: As the al chiodo pasta cooks through, it absorbs some of the pasta water and releases starch to help emulsify the water and fat into a creamy sauce. How much pasta water to add depends on knowing how much more cooking the pasta needs and how much water it will absorb. And if there isn't enough pasta water to maintain the emulsion, the sauce will be broken and greasy. I wanted to remove the guesswork for those times when I can't give dinner my undivided attention.

That would mean using the more straightforward approach of adding al dente pasta to a finished sauce. But rather than use the standard 4 quarts of water to boil the pasta, I scaled the water to 2 quarts (unsalted since the pancetta and Pecorino contributed plenty of salt). This way, the water would have double the starch, helping ensure emulsification.

I added 2 cups of the starchy pasta water to the rendered fat and boiled the mixture for a few minutes. This not only caused some evaporation to further concentrate the starch but also broke the fat into smaller, more numerous droplets. I stirred in the al dente pasta and the browned pancetta, followed by the Pecorino, transforming the liquid from thin and brothy to nicely emulsified.

This method was nearly foolproof, but I made a final tweak to guarantee consistent results. I boiled the fat-water mixture not for a specified time but to a specified volume: 1½ cups. This way, I'd always use the same amount of liquid to coat the pasta.

With this recipe for gricia at the ready, I couldn't wait until it was my turn to make lunch.

You're 30 minutes away from authentic Roman pasta.

PASTA ALLA GRICIA (RIGATONI WITH PANCETTA AND PECORINO ROMANO)
SERVES 6   TOTAL TIME: 30 MINUTES

Because this pasta is quite rich, serve it in slightly smaller portions with a green vegetable or salad. For the best results, use the highest-quality pancetta you can find. If you can find *guanciale*, we recommend using it and increasing the browning time in step 2 to 10 to 12 minutes. Because we call for cutting the pancetta to a specified thickness, we recommend having it cut to order at the deli counter; avoid presliced or prediced products. Our recipe for Pasta alla Gricia (Rigatoni with Pancetta and Pecorino Romano) for Two is available for free for four months at CooksIllustrated.com/dec18.

- 8   ounces pancetta, sliced ¼ inch thick
- 1   tablespoon extra-virgin olive oil
- 1   pound rigatoni
- 1   teaspoon coarsely ground pepper, plus extra for serving
- 2   ounces Pecorino Romano cheese, grated fine (1 cup), plus extra for serving

1. Slice each round of pancetta into rectangular pieces that measure about ½ inch by 1 inch.

2. Heat pancetta and oil in large Dutch oven over medium-low heat, stirring frequently, until fat is rendered and pancetta is deep golden brown but still has slight pinkish hue, 8 to 10 minutes, adjusting heat as necessary to keep pancetta from browning too quickly. Using slotted spoon, transfer pancetta to bowl; set aside. Pour fat from pot into liquid measuring cup (you should have ¼ to ⅓ cup fat; discard any extra). Return fat to Dutch oven.

3. While pancetta cooks, set colander in large bowl. Bring 2 quarts water to boil in large pot. Add pasta and cook, stirring often, until al dente. Drain pasta in prepared colander, reserving cooking water.

4. Add pepper and 2 cups reserved cooking water to Dutch oven with fat and bring to boil over high heat. Boil mixture rapidly, scraping up any browned bits, until emulsified and reduced to 1½ cups, about 5 minutes. (If you've reduced it too far, add more reserved cooking water to equal 1½ cups.)

5. Reduce heat to low, add pasta and pancetta, and stir to evenly coat. Add Pecorino and stir until cheese is melted and sauce is slightly thickened, about 1 minute. Off heat, adjust sauce consistency with remaining reserved cooking water as needed. Transfer pasta to platter and serve immediately, passing extra pepper and extra Pecorino separately.

The Roman Pasta Quartet

Four simple pasta dishes serve as pillars of Roman cuisine. Cooks debate the precise details, but the handful of ingredients that goes into each is well established.

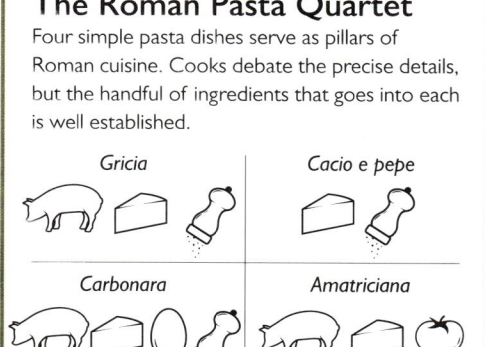

STEP-BY-STEP VIDEO AND NUTRITION INFORMATION
CooksIllustrated.com/DEC18

The Easiest Winter Squash

Tired of struggling to peel and cut heavy-duty squash? Try something more delicate.

≥ BY LAN LAM ≤

A few years ago, this magazine ran a tip on how to break down a large, dense winter squash such as Hubbard: Place it in a zipper-lock bag and drop it onto asphalt from chest height, smashing it to pieces. It sounds severe, but taking a knife to a giant rock-hard squash (even a modest-size butternut can be a struggle) isn't for the faint of heart, never mind that peeling its tough skin is a real chore.

Allow me to suggest an alternative: crenellated, creamy yellow delicata squash. These beauties, which are available from late summer through early winter, boast thin, edible striped skin that softens when cooked. Their small size means they are relatively easy to cut and seed, which makes preparation a snap. What's more, they offer a delicate, nutty taste that's entirely different from the pronounced sweetness of most winter squashes.

Mild delicata is complemented by flavorful browning. That can be achieved by sautéing slices, but doing so requires multiple batches since each flat side needs to be touching the pan to pick up color. Oven roasting is a better option since you can prepare enough squash to serve four on a single baking sheet. The squash can then be finished with fresh herbs or a simple sauce.

Most recipes call for simply arranging oiled squash slices on a baking sheet and roasting. But as the squash cooks, its water evaporates, leaving each piece with a leathery surface and a dry interior. I figured I'd have better luck with the technique that we use for other hard vegetables such as carrots: Oven-steam the squash until tender, and then brown the exterior.

I halved and seeded three squashes, sliced them ½ inch thick—skin and all—and tossed them with oil and salt. After spreading the slices into an even layer on a baking sheet, I covered the sheet with aluminum foil and placed it on the middle rack of a 425-degree oven. The foil trapped steam and helped the slices cook evenly without becoming desiccated. After half an hour, the slices were tender, so I removed the foil. Within minutes, any residual moisture evaporated and the starches and sugars on the surface of the squashes began to brown. After 15 minutes, I flipped the slices and then let the second side turn deep golden brown, which took about 15 minutes longer.

These squash slices were tender and moist, but I was sure I could speed up the cooking and coax an even fuller, richer flavor from the delicata. I moved the oven rack to the lowest position so that the baking sheet would be closer to the heat source. This shaved 15 minutes off the total time and deepened the browning.

Add butter near the end of cooking so it has time to develop nuttiness but not enough time to burn.

To reinforce the delicata's unique nuttiness, I dotted it with butter for the final 10 minutes—enough time for it to brown with no risk of burning. These tender, golden slices looked gorgeous, and each bite featured a slightly resilient strip of skin and toasty squash flavor—all without breaking a sweat.

ROASTED DELICATA SQUASH
SERVES 4 TO 6 TOTAL TIME: 50 MINUTES

To ensure that the flesh cooks evenly, choose squashes that are similar in size and shape. Delicata have thin, edible skin that needn't be removed; simply use a vegetable peeler to pare away any tough brown blemishes. For more preparation tips, see page 29. You can substitute chives for parsley, if desired. Serve the squash as is or drizzled with Basque-Style Herb Sauce (Tximitxurri) or Spicy Honey (recipes follow). Our recipe for Goat Cheese and Chive Sauce is available free for four months at CooksIllustrated.com/dec18.

- 3   delicata squashes (12 to 16 ounces each), ends trimmed, halved lengthwise, seeded, and sliced crosswise ½ inch thick
- 4   teaspoons vegetable oil
- ½   teaspoon salt
- 2   tablespoons unsalted butter, cut into 8 pieces
- 1   tablespoon minced fresh parsley

1. Adjust oven rack to lowest position and heat oven to 425 degrees. Toss squash with oil and salt until evenly coated. Arrange squash on rimmed baking sheet in single layer. Cover tightly with aluminum foil and bake until squash is tender when pierced with tip of paring knife, 18 to 20 minutes.

2. Remove foil and continue to bake until sides touching sheet are golden brown, 8 to 11 minutes longer. Remove sheet from oven and, using thin metal spatula, flip squash. Scatter butter over squash. Return to oven and continue to bake until side touching sheet is golden brown, 8 to 11 minutes longer. Transfer squash to serving platter, sprinkle with parsley, and serve.

BASQUE-STYLE HERB SAUCE (TXIMITXURRI)
SERVES 4 TO 6 (MAKES ½ CUP) TOTAL TIME: 20 MINUTES

For a sauce with some heat, substitute hot smoked paprika for the regular smoked paprika.

- ¼   cup minced fresh parsley
- ¼   cup extra-virgin olive oil
- 2   tablespoons sherry vinegar
- 2   garlic cloves, minced
- 1   teaspoon smoked paprika
- ¼   teaspoon salt

Stir all ingredients together in bowl and let stand for at least 15 minutes before serving.

SPICY HONEY
SERVES 4 TO 6 (MAKES ½ CUP) TOTAL TIME: 15 MINUTES

We prefer vinegary Frank's RedHot Original Cayenne Pepper Sauce here. Do not substitute a thick hot sauce, such as sriracha; it will make the honey too thick to drizzle. Microwaving in 20-second intervals will prevent the mixture from boiling over.

- ¼   cup honey
- 2   tablespoons hot sauce

Stir honey and hot sauce together in liquid measuring cup. Microwave until sauce comes to boil, about 1 minute. Continue to microwave in 20-second intervals until sauce is reduced to ¼ cup. Let cool for at least 10 minutes before serving.

▶ STEP-BY-STEP VIDEO AND NUTRITION INFORMATION
CooksIllustrated.com/DEC18

Real Kung Pao Chicken

Spicy chiles and tingly Sichuan peppercorns team up with lightly sauced chicken and peanuts in a stir-fry that's literally sensational.

≥ BY ANDREA GEARY ≤

Bite-size pieces allow kung pao chicken's hallmark sensations—spice, tingle, crunch, crispness, and juiciness—to be experienced all in one mouthful.

If you haven't eaten kung pao chicken in the past 10 years, there's a good chance you've never had the real thing. I hadn't, until recently.

In the '90s, the dish was my go-to Chinese restaurant order. The diced chicken and vegetables, peanuts, and vaguely sweet and sour sauce were cozily familiar, while the fiery dried chiles scattered throughout supplied an appealing undercurrent of danger. But eventually the novelty wore off, as did any urge to make it myself.

Then, a few months ago, I ordered kung pao in a restaurant and was delighted by the addition of Sichuan peppercorns, which imbued the dish with a woodsy fragrance and citrusy tang and created an intriguing tingling sensation on my lips and tongue, a perfect complement to the chiles' heat. In fact, the interplay of peppercorns and fiery chiles is so foundational to Sichuan cuisine that it has a name: *ma la*, which means "numbing heat." (See "Adding 'Pow' to Kung Pao.") Sichuan peppercorns were banned in the United States from 1968 to 2005 because they might carry a disease that could endanger the American citrus crop, so these tiny dried fruits of the prickly ash tree had been tragically absent from my '90s kung pao. But now, back where they belonged, they snapped the flavors of kung pao chicken into focus.

With my interest in the dish reawakened, I was eager to devise my own version of kung pao chicken. I knew that chiles and buzzy peppercorns weren't enough to ensure success, though. The chicken would have to be juicy and the peanuts crunchy, with a bit of crisp, cooling vegetable for contrast. And I wanted a potent glaze that lightly coated—not heavily sauced—each piece but still delivered flavor to every bite.

A Mild Start

Most recipes called for boneless, skinless chicken breasts or thighs. I went with thighs because they're not only more resistant to overcooking but also more flavorful, so they'd make a better match for the strong flavors of kung pao. I tossed the diced thighs in a marinade that, based on my research, appeared to be pretty universal: savory soy sauce; sweet rice wine; floral, earthy white pepper; and a bit of cornstarch that would help the marinade cling to the meat and lend some body to the glaze when cooked.

Vegetables aren't a major player in kung pao chicken, but a small amount adds welcome color and crunch. Celery and scallions are common, and I diced them to match the size of the smallest element of the dish: the peanuts. Cutting everything to the same size is a hallmark of kung pao chicken. It provides visual harmony and allows the diner to experience multiple flavors and textures in every bite. I also grated some ginger, minced some garlic, and whisked up a quick glaze composed of a bit more soy; complex, fruity black vinegar; dark brown sugar; and some toasted sesame oil to bolster the nutty flavor of the roasted peanuts. I kept the volume small so I'd end up with just enough glaze to coat all the components.

To start, I heated a tablespoon of vegetable oil in a nonstick skillet and added a generous handful of dried arbol chiles (a fine substitute for the traditional bright red *chao tian jiao*, or "facing heaven" chiles) and some ground Sichuan peppercorns. When they were fragrant and just starting to darken, I added the peanuts and then the garlic and ginger. The last two clumped up in the hot skillet, but I figured they'd disperse once I added the chicken.

Because the chicken pieces were a pain to turn constantly, I introduced an innovation: I covered the skillet. This way, the pieces cooked from the top as well as the bottom. When the chicken was mostly cooked, I added the celery. After pouring in the sauce and reducing it to a glaze consistency, I stirred in the scallions, killed the heat, and took a taste.

Let's start with the positives: The chicken thighs were tender and juicy throughout, the celery and scallions were crisp, and the dark glaze coated everything nicely. On the negative side, the peanuts were soggy and soft. And those sticky clumps of garlic and ginger hadn't spread out as I had hoped; they had instead collected all the Sichuan peppercorn dust, forming sneaky sensory bombs. As for the heat, despite my free hand with the chiles, it was almost nonexistent.

STEP-BY-STEP VIDEO AND NUTRITION INFORMATION
CooksIllustrated.com/DEC18

Hold the Sauce

Americans tend to like heavily sauced Chinese dishes to top their rice, but kung pao should not be swimming in liquid. The flavors of this dish are very potent, and a large volume of sauce would make it overwhelmingly spicy and salty. (Alternatively, reducing the potency of the sauce with ingredients such as broth and thickeners would dilute the overall flavor of the dish.) What's more, in China rice is typically eaten plain as a palate cleanser in between bites of assertively flavored food, not as a starchy base beneath a blanket of sauce.

Heating Things Up

I had a hunch about why my arbol chiles, which I knew to be impressively spicy, weren't imparting much "pow" to my kung pao. To test it, I touched an intact chile to my tongue. Nothing. Then I opened up a chile and tasted the interior. Ouch. There was plenty of heat on the inside since most capsaicin resides in the ribs and seeds of chiles, but there wasn't enough time or moisture in my recipe to coax that flavor through the tough skin.

So for my next batch, I halved the chiles lengthwise to expose as much of their spicy interiors as possible. (But to ensure that I didn't overwhelm my tasters with heat, I jostled the chiles until all the seeds fell out.) And to aid the distribution of the grated ginger and minced garlic, I put them in a small bowl and stirred in 1 tablespoon of oil.

I also tweaked the order of operations a bit. Because I wanted the peanuts to be as toasty and crunchy as possible, I first cooked them in a teaspoon of oil and then transferred them to a plate, where they would continue to crisp as they cooled. Then I stir-fried the halved chiles and the ground peppercorns and added the ginger and garlic, which dispersed with minimal persuasion thanks to their coating of oil. I added the chicken, covered the skillet, and, once the chicken was mostly cooked, tossed in the celery. I then stirred in the sauce, and only when it was fully reduced did I add the peanuts and scallions, so both would maintain their texture.

With its lightly glazed components and hallmark sensations of spice, tingle, crunch, crispness, and juiciness in every bite, this version of kung pao was as real as it gets.

KUNG PAO CHICKEN
SERVES 4 TO 6   TOTAL TIME: 40 MINUTES

Kung pao chicken should be quite spicy. To adjust the heat level, use more or fewer chiles, depending on the size (we used 2-inch-long chiles) and your taste. Have your ingredients prepared and your equipment in place before you begin to cook. Use a spice grinder or mortar and pestle to coarsely grind the Sichuan peppercorns. If Chinese black vinegar is unavailable, substitute sherry vinegar. Serve with white rice and a simple vegetable such as broccoli or bok choy. Do not eat the chiles. Our Kung Pao Chicken for Two recipe is available for free for four months at CooksIllustrated.com/dec18.

Chicken and Sauce
- 1½ pounds boneless, skinless chicken thighs, trimmed and cut into ½-inch cubes
- ¼ cup soy sauce, divided
- 1 tablespoon cornstarch
- 1 tablespoon Chinese rice wine or dry sherry
- ½ teaspoon white pepper
- 1 tablespoon Chinese black vinegar
- 1 tablespoon packed dark brown sugar
- 2 teaspoons toasted sesame oil

Stir-Fry
- 1 tablespoon minced garlic
- 2 teaspoons grated fresh ginger
- 2 tablespoons plus 1 teaspoon vegetable oil, divided
- ½ cup dry-roasted peanuts
- 10–15 dried arbol chiles, halved lengthwise and seeded
- 1 teaspoon Sichuan peppercorns, ground coarse
- 2 celery ribs, cut into ½-inch pieces
- 5 scallions, white and light green parts only, cut into ½-inch pieces

1. **FOR THE CHICKEN AND SAUCE:** Combine chicken, 2 tablespoons soy sauce, cornstarch, rice wine, and white pepper in medium bowl and set aside. Stir vinegar, sugar, oil, and remaining 2 tablespoons soy sauce together in small bowl and set aside.

2. **FOR THE STIR-FRY:** Stir garlic, ginger, and 1 tablespoon oil together in second small bowl. Combine peanuts and 1 teaspoon oil in 12-inch nonstick skillet over medium-low heat. Cook, stirring constantly, until peanuts just begin to darken, 3 to 5 minutes. Transfer peanuts to plate and spread into even layer to cool. Return now-empty skillet to medium-low heat. Add remaining 1 tablespoon oil, arbols, and peppercorns and cook, stirring constantly, until arbols begin to darken, 1 to 2 minutes. Add garlic mixture and cook, stirring constantly, until all clumps are broken up and mixture is fragrant, about 30 seconds.

3. Add chicken and spread into even layer. Cover skillet, increase heat to medium-high, and cook, without stirring, for 1 minute. Stir chicken and spread into even layer. Cover and cook, without stirring, for 1 minute. Add celery and cook uncovered, stirring frequently, until chicken is cooked through, 2 to 3 minutes. Add soy sauce mixture and cook, stirring constantly, until sauce is thickened and shiny and coats chicken, 3 to 5 minutes. Stir in scallions and peanuts. Transfer to platter and serve.

> **RECIPES TO MAKE IT A MEAL**
> Find these recipes in our archive:
> Chinese Restaurant-Style Rice (March/April 2018) and Sautéed Baby Bok Choy (March/April 2017).

Adding "Pow" to Kung Pao

The combination of numbing, tingly Sichuan peppercorns (*ma*) and fiery chiles (*la*)—or *ma la* ("numbing heat")—is a calling card of Sichuan cuisine. You'll find these trademark sensations in our Kung Pao Chicken as well as in our Sichuan Braised Tofu with Beef (Mapo Tofu) (September/October 2017) and Crispy Salt and Pepper Shrimp (November/December 2014).

TINGLY
Sichuan peppercorns contain the chemical hydroxy-alpha-sanshool, which stimulates receptors in our mouths, sending signals to our brains that we interpret as vibrations—even though the peppercorns don't actually vibrate our skin. They do, however, cause numbness and tingling.

FIERY
Arbol chiles are a good substitute for the traditional choice: *chao tian jiao*, or "facing heaven" chiles. Both varieties measure about 30,000 units on the Scoville heat scale.

GRIND AND SEED
Sichuan peppercorns need to be ground for even flavor distribution. After you slice the arbol chiles to expose their capsaicin-rich interior ribs, shake out their seeds for just the right amount of heat.

TECHNIQUE | LUBRICATE YOUR AROMATICS

The small bits of garlic and ginger in a typical stir-fry can clump up when you add them to the pan, preventing some bits from blooming in the oil and their flavors from distributing evenly throughout the dish. The easy work-around? Combine the aromatics with a tablespoon of oil and add this mixture to the pan.

OIL HELPS GARLIC AND GINGER DISTRIBUTE EVENLY

Creamy Dressings, Hold the Cream

A surprising ingredient quietly imparts the smooth richness of dairy or mayonnaise while letting the other ingredients shine.

≥ BY ANDREA GEARY ≤

Want to make a batch of dressing for the week? These thick, creamy concoctions keep well in the refrigerator for up to seven days.

Last year, the test kitchen published a vegan cookbook (*Vegan for Everybody*), so for a while there was a lot of dairy- and egg-free food around here. It's not a diet I've ever subscribed to, but watching (and tasting) the development process gave me a healthy respect for how flavorful and satisfying vegan cooking can be. In fact, it prompted me to retool a recipe category that typically relies heavily on dairy and eggs: creamy dressings and dips.

Vegan recipe authors tout all sorts of supposedly stealthy dairy alternatives, such as beans, tofu, avocado, and coconut milk. But if you ask me, most of them don't live up to their promise. I tried dressings with avocado, which was conveniently bland but visually obvious. Tofu and coconut milk worked aesthetically, but their flavors were too dominant. And beans tasted starchy.

But then I learned about nut cream, which is used as a starting point for vegan cheeses and creamy sauces. To make it, you simply soak raw nuts overnight to soften them and then drain them and process them in a blender until they form a puree that's creamy, smooth, and rich (nuts are a source of fat, after all). And here's a big perk: Unlike with tangy dairy products or mayonnaise, their neutral flavor lets seasonings come to the fore, producing results with potent flavor and creamy body all in one.

Soaked Through

Sources suggested a wide variety of nuts and seeds for the job, but I narrowed it down to cashews and blanched almonds because their pale color and subtle flavor (when raw) would make them easy to hide. I soaked the whole nuts overnight, drained them, and pureed each in a blender for 5 minutes, adding just enough water to keep things moving.

Both purees looked creamy, but the almond one tasted a bit grainy. I'd proceed with the smoother cashews (for more information, see "Cashews:

STEP-BY-STEP VIDEO AND NUTRITION INFORMATION
CooksIllustrated.com/DEC18

Cream of the (Nut) Crop"), but first I wanted to see if I could trim down that soaking time.

I wondered if creating more surface area on the cashews would help them absorb water more quickly, so I roughly chopped them and soaked them for only 3 hours. This yielded a smooth puree, so next I finely chopped them and soaked them for 1 hour. Success again, but could I skip the knife work altogether?

My next batch of cashews went straight into the blender, where I let the machine grind them until they looked like fine gravel mixed with sand. Then I transferred them to a bowl, covered them with water, and let them sit for just 15 minutes, after which I drained them in a fine-mesh strainer and returned them to the blender. One minute on low speed and 4 minutes on high turned them smooth and creamy. Time to make dressing.

I started out with a ranch-style herb dressing, the simplicity of which would test the cashews' anonymity. After grinding, soaking, and draining 1 cup of nuts, I returned them to the blender. I added just enough water to enable the mixture to form a vortex while blending, along with cider vinegar, shallot and garlic, salt and pepper, and a touch of sugar for balance.

After 4 minutes of churning, the mixture was silky and thick—the perfect consistency for dipping but too heavy for dressing greens, so I thinned it with water. It was also warm from the friction of blending, so I chilled it before stirring in minced chives and parsley to avoid wilting the delicate herbs.

This dressing was wonderfully creamy, and the neutral cashew base allowed the flavors of the herbs, alliums, and vinegar to emerge in a way that dairy hadn't. Delighted, I popped it into the refrigerator and, per test kitchen protocol, sent the recipe to volunteer testers (go to AmericasTestKitchen.com/recipe_testing for more information) while I dreamt up flavor variations. But my enthusiasm was premature. Some testers complained of harsh allium flavors; others reported that their dressing was watery and that it seemed wasteful to send so much of the ground nuts down the drain. The second comment confused me, since I'd only

---

The Power of Powdered Alliums

Seasoning our dressings with onion and garlic powders instead of fresh alliums might sound odd, but these pantry staples offer two perks that their fresh counterparts don't. First, measured amounts of these powders will yield more consistent flavor than garlic cloves and onions (or shallots), which can vary widely in size. Second, the flavors of these dehydrated products are more stable than those of fresh garlic and onions, since breaking the cells of the fresh vegetables causes them to develop sharp-tasting compounds that change in flavor over time. The upshot: Powdered alliums give our dressings more consistent flavor and a longer shelf life.

Cashews: Cream of the (Nut) Crop

Nut creams—purees of nuts that have been soaked and ground with water until smooth—are commonly used as a base for vegan cheeses and sauces. We made creams from nine different raw nuts—almonds, cashews, peanuts, pecans, walnuts, hazelnuts, pistachios, macadamia nuts, and Brazil nuts (all but the pecans and walnuts were blanched)—to see which puree had the best texture. All but one produced purees that were variously "gritty," "grainy," "foamy," and/or "chalky." Only the cashew cream stood out for a consistency so velvety that one taster called it "pure satin." Here's why: Cashews are uniquely low in fiber, which resists breaking down, and high in starch, the particles of which suspend nicely in liquid and provide body.

HAZELNUTS — Starches: 5 g; Fiber: 2.7 g; Grainy; weepy

BRAZIL NUTS — Starches: 7 g; Fiber: 2.1 g; Pulpy; chalky

MACADAMIA NUTS — Starches: 0.2 g; Fiber: 2.4 g; Foamy; finely gritty

WALNUTS — Starches: 1.3 g; Fiber: 1.9 g; Curdled; chalky

PISTACHIOS — Starches: 2.9 g; Fiber: 2.9 g; Loose; wet

ALMONDS — Starches: 0.9 g; Fiber: 3.3 g; Sawdusty

CASHEWS — Starches: 6 g; Fiber 0.9 g; Ultracreamy

---

ever drained away the soaking water. But then it hit me: Blenders and strainers vary, and a combination of a superfine grind and a coarse strainer would mean that fewer cashews were making it into the dressing, resulting in a thin consistency.

Fortunately, I saw a way to foolproof and streamline my method: "Soak" the cashews in the other dressing ingredients right in the blender jar so there was nothing to drain and no variation in consistency.

Fresh Isn't Always Best

Back to the complaints of overly potent allium flavor, which I initially attributed to personal taste and the use of larger-than-average shallots and garlic cloves. I opened the container of dressing I had made 48 hours earlier and was hit by a powerful waft of shallot and garlic. With all those allium cells broken during blending, their sharp flavors had continued to build during storage.

Our science research editor explained that the allicin that forms when garlic cells are ruptured breaks down over time, hydrolyzing into a variety of sulfide compounds with unpleasant flavors. The easy fix: substituting garlic and onion powders for fresh garlic and shallots, respectively. The flavors of these pantry alliums are standard and more stable over time, so the substitution increased the dressing's shelf life by several days (for more information, see "The Power of Powdered Alliums").

Finally, the variations. I started with classics such as ketchup-and-horseradish-based Russian dressing and herby, anchovy-rich Green Goddess, the latter of which was just as good on greens as it was on vegetables, grilled chicken, and fish. Then I went modern with roasted red peppers and tahini and ginger and miso, knowing that all these dressings were as creamy and rich as dairy- and egg-based ones but even more flavorful.

CREAMLESS CREAMY HERB DRESSING
SERVES 16 (MAKES 2 CUPS)
TOTAL TIME: 35 MINUTES, PLUS 45 MINUTES CHILLING

You'll need a conventional blender for this recipe; an immersion blender or food processor will produce dressing that is grainy and thin. If you use a high-powered blender such as a Vitamix or Blendtec, blending times may be shorter. Use raw unsalted cashews, not roasted, to ensure the proper flavor balance. This dressing works well drizzled over a hearty salad, but it can also be used as a dip for vegetables.

- 1 cup raw cashews
- ¾ cup water, plus extra as needed
- 3 tablespoons cider vinegar
- 1¼ teaspoons salt
- 1 teaspoon onion powder
- ½ teaspoon sugar
- ¼ teaspoon garlic powder
- 2 tablespoons minced fresh chives
- 1 tablespoon minced fresh parsley
- ½ teaspoon pepper

1. Process cashews in blender on low speed to consistency of fine gravel mixed with sand, 10 to 15 seconds. Add water, vinegar, salt, onion powder, sugar, and garlic powder and process on low speed until combined, about 5 seconds. Let mixture sit for 15 minutes.

2. Process on low speed until all ingredients are well blended, about 1 minute. Scrape down blender jar. Process on high speed until dressing is smooth and creamy, 3 to 4 minutes. Transfer dressing to bowl. Cover and refrigerate until cold, about 45 minutes. Stir in chives, parsley, and pepper. Thin with extra water, adding 1 tablespoon at a time, if desired. Dressing can be refrigerated for up to 1 week.

CREAMLESS CREAMY GINGER-MISO DRESSING

Decrease water to ⅔ cup. Substitute ¼ cup rice vinegar for cider vinegar, 2 tablespoons white miso for onion powder, 2 tablespoons grated fresh ginger for pepper, and 2 tablespoons soy sauce for sugar and add 1 teaspoon toasted sesame oil. Omit salt, garlic powder, chives, and parsley.

CREAMLESS CREAMY GREEN GODDESS DRESSING

Decrease cashews to ¾ cup. Substitute lemon juice for cider vinegar and ⅓ cup chopped fresh parsley, ⅓ cup chopped fresh chives, and 1 tablespoon chopped fresh tarragon for onion powder. Substitute 2 rinsed anchovy fillets for sugar. Decrease salt to ¾ teaspoon and pepper to ¼ teaspoon. Omit minced chives and parsley in step 2.

CREAMLESS CREAMY ROASTED RED PEPPER AND TAHINI DRESSING

Decrease cashews to ½ cup and increase garlic powder to ½ teaspoon. Substitute 1 (12-ounce) jar roasted red peppers, drained and chopped coarse, for water. Substitute sherry vinegar for cider vinegar and 3 tablespoons tahini for onion powder. Substitute 2 teaspoons toasted sesame oil for sugar and smoked paprika for pepper. Increase salt to 1½ teaspoons and garlic powder to ½ teaspoon and add pinch cayenne pepper. Omit chives and parsley.

CREAMLESS CREAMY RUSSIAN DRESSING

Substitute ¼ cup distilled white vinegar for cider vinegar and paprika for sugar. Substitute 2 teaspoons hot sauce; 2 teaspoons prepared horseradish, drained; and 1 teaspoon Worcestershire sauce for garlic powder. Decrease salt to ¾ teaspoon and onion powder to ½ teaspoon. Add ⅓ cup ketchup. Omit chives and parsley.

Dressing or Dip? You Choose

Right after blending, these dressings are thick and rich enough to use as dips, but they can also be thinned with water and drizzled over greens.

Ten Discoveries That Changed the Way We Cook

Over the past 25 years, we've performed countless tests in the pursuit of better, faster, easier, and more foolproof recipes. Here are a few of the game changers that transformed how we—and, dare we say, our readers—cook. BY ELIZABETH BOMZE

BEST PRETREATMENT FOR MEAT: SALT THERAPY — 1993

1 You may have missed our Roast Brined Turkey in 1993—the recipe that put brining on the map. But you can't have missed that brining and salting poultry and meat are two of our core techniques. Here's a refresher on why.

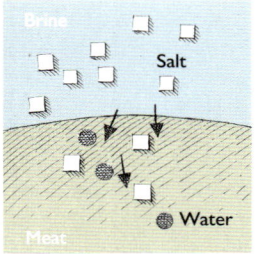

➤ **BRINING** adds moisture, which makes it a particularly good choice for lean proteins. The salt in the brine not only seasons the meat but also promotes a change in its protein structure, reducing its overall toughness and creating gaps that fill up with water and keep the meat juicy.

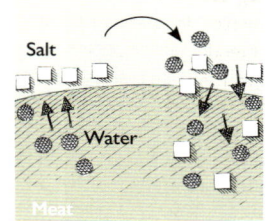

➤ **SALTING** helps proteins retain their natural juices and is the best choice for ensuring crisp skin or a crusty exterior. When salt is applied to raw meat, moisture inside the meat is drawn to the surface. The salt then dissolves in the exuded liquid, forming a brine that the meat eventually reabsorbs.

DON'T FEEL LIKE SEARING? YOU CAN SKIP IT

2 While making our Hungarian Beef Stew in 2008, we learned that there's no need to sear the meat if you're making a low-liquid braise that cooks in the oven. Over time, the dry surface of the meat that sits above the liquid will reach a high enough temperature for the meat to brown and form thousands of new flavor compounds.

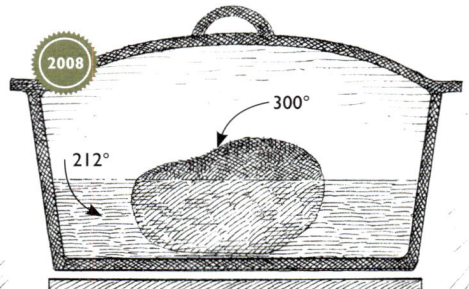

THIS GOOP MAKES BETTER BREAD — 2016

3 We didn't believe it either—until we applied the Asian bread-baking technique called *tangzhong* to our 2016 recipe for Fluffy Dinner Rolls and came away with an airy, feathery, ultramoist crumb that remained fresh and soft longer than any bread we'd made the conventional way. Incorporating this goop—a pudding-like paste made by cooking a portion of the recipe's flour with water—into the dough allows you to add more water to the dough than you could by simply combining the dry and wet ingredients. That's because flour can absorb twice as much hot water as cold water. The upshot: a superhydrated dough that bakes up incredibly moist and fluffy.

BROWNING MEAT BACKWARD KEEPS IT ROSY — 2007

4 The first step when cooking a steak or roast is to sear it, right? Wrong. When we dug deep into steak cookery in 2007, we realized that the best way to achieve a uniformly rosy interior and a deep crust is to "reverse-sear" the meat by first roasting it in a low oven until nearly done and then browning it in a hot skillet. The oven's gentle heat minimizes the temperature difference between the meat's center and edges, and the hot pan rapidly browns the warm, dry surface, so there's no time for the meat beneath it to overcook.

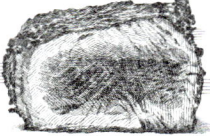

SEARED FIRST **SEARED LAST**

A "COLD" SKILLET LEADS TO MORE EVEN COOKING — 2004

5 Adding food to a ripping-hot skillet will quickly brown the exterior. But in 2004 we realized that if you want to brown a food that requires more than a flash of blazing heat to cook through or render fat—a pork chop, a skin-on chicken breast or salmon fillet, dense Brussels sprouts—it's best to place the food in a "cold" (not preheated) skillet and then turn on the heat. That way, the food's interior has more time to gently cook through (or render) before the exterior burns.

WE ACTUALLY TRIED THIS

Candling Eggs
While developing our recipe for Soft-Cooked Eggs (2013), we stood in a dark bathroom with a flashlight and an empty toilet paper roll, trying to locate the yolks within two dozen eggs. Then, if necessary, we shook the eggs to center the yolks, thinking that it might ensure even cooking. It didn't.

"Sedating" a Lobster
Nobody likes to watch a lobster thrash around after being eased into a pot of boiling water, so in 2013 we tried a few rumored methods to calm the lobster before cooking: rubbing its shell and standing it on its head, and soaking it in a cold saltwater bath scented with clove oil. Neither method helped.

AMP UP MEATINESS WITHOUT MEAT

6 When we added a few anchovies (per tradition) to our Daube Provençal in 2005, we didn't know exactly why it made the dish taste more complex. We later learned that anchovies are uniquely rich in compounds called glutamates and nucleotides, which individually enhance savory depth, or umami, in food but amp it up even more when present together. Nowadays we routinely slip anchovies into stews, soups, chilis, and even meatballs to boost meaty flavor. For vegetarian dishes, we might turn to tomato paste, soy sauce, or Parmigiano-Reggiano; to get that synergistic effect, we might also add dried mushrooms.

Glutamate-rich	Parmigiano-Reggiano
	Soy sauce
	Tomato paste
Nucleotide-rich	Dried porcini mushrooms
Glutamate- and	Anchovies
Nucleotide-rich	Dried shiitake mushrooms

OVERCOOKED DARK MEAT CHICKEN SEEMS JUICIER

7 Cardinal rule of preparing chicken: Don't overcook it, or the meat will be dry and stringy. But while developing a braised chicken thighs recipe in 2015, we realized that dark-meat poultry is the exception to the rule. While it is safe to eat at 160 degrees and moderately tender at 175, it tastes exceptionally juicy and tender when cooked to 195 degrees. That's because it's loaded with connective tissue, which dissolves into gelatin as the meat cooks, rendering it tender and especially juicy. Slowly cooking the meat to 195 degrees maximizes collagen breakdown so that it's not just tender but downright silky and succulent.

A MARINADE'S MOST IMPORTANT INGREDIENT IS SALT

9 Other recipes may call for soaking bland, chewy cuts in a marinade in the hope that it will tenderize or infuse flavor to the bone. Not ours. After dozens of in-house and independent lab tests, we declared in 2009 that marinades don't tenderize and most seasonings won't penetrate the meat, no matter how long it soaks.

The one ingredient that does make a big difference? Salt. As in a brine, salt in an overnight marinade is able to penetrate deep into the food to season the meat and enhance its juiciness. Other marinade must-haves include glutamate-rich soy sauce; water-soluble flavorings such as garlic and onion; and sweeteners, which add complexity and also encourage flavorful browning. While these ingredients won't penetrate as deep into meat as salt does, given enough time, they will move beyond its surface. Finally, oil dissolves the fat-soluble flavor compounds in most herbs and spices, allowing them to flavor the meat's exterior.

BAKING SODA ISN'T JUST FOR BAKING

8 Of course we use baking soda as a leavening agent. But page through the *Cook's Illustrated* archive and you'll see that it has a slew of other talents that can all be attributed to its alkaline properties.

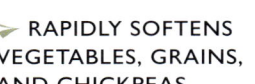

▶ **TENDERIZES MEAT** Briefly soaking ground beef or thin slices of meat destined for a stir-fry in a solution of baking soda and water raises the pH on the meat's surface, making it more difficult for the proteins to bond excessively, which keeps the meat tender and moist when it's cooked.

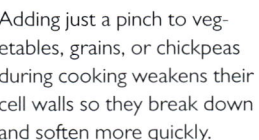

▶ **HASTENS BROWNING** Whether it's stirred into pancake batter or rubbed onto the surface of meat, baking soda creates a high-pH environment in which browning reactions occur more readily.

▶ **RAPIDLY SOFTENS VEGETABLES, GRAINS, AND CHICKPEAS** Adding just a pinch to vegetables, grains, or chickpeas during cooking weakens their cell walls so they break down and soften more quickly.

▶ **BOOSTS FLAVOR** Baking soda adds a salty, mineral flavor to baked goods and pancakes.

THE GENTLEST WAY TO COOK? NO HEAT

10 In 2008, we roasted an eye round for 24 hours at 130 degrees to see how tender this lean cut could be if cooked ultralow and slow. The results were exceptional, so we devised a faster, equally effective approach: cooking food partway at a moderate temperature and then shutting off the heat. As the heat of the cooking environment—an oven or a covered pot on the stovetop—declines, the temperature of the food gradually rises. In lean proteins, gentle heat prevents muscle fibers from getting too hot and squeezing out moisture and, in certain cases, can even increase enzymatic activity that helps tenderize the meat.

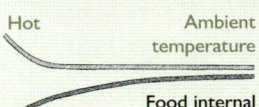

DWINDLING HEAT EQUALS TENDER MEAT

Pureeing Whole Pies

One of the saddest moments in the test kitchen was in 2013 when we baked three gorgeous pies just to buzz them to mush in a blender and send the samples to a lab. The objective of the test: to see how much alcohol remained in our Foolproof Pie Dough (which contains vodka) after baking. (Trace amounts remained.)

Smoking Nut Shells and Beans

Can anything rival the rich smoke flavor of smoldering wood chips? In 2014, we tried smoking a battery of pantry ingredients, including cinnamon sticks, dried garbanzo beans, and walnut shells, as well as smoker pucks and bricks, wood pellets, and sawdust. The answer was no.

White Bean and Mushroom Gratin

Once you know the building blocks that create savory depth, you won't miss the meat.

> BY LAN LAM <

Anyone who thinks that meatless bean dishes don't offer the heartiness of a meat-based meal should give the category another chance. As for those who think that meatless bean dishes tend to lack complexity and savory depth, I'm with you—and I have a recipe that will change your mind.

It's a bean-based gratin, and it's not loaded up with esoteric ingredients; in fact, you might have most of what you need on hand. Start to finish, you should be able to get this gratin on the table in just under 2 hours and have plenty of downtime to make a salad or green vegetable while it cooks.

I built the dish around creamy, nutty canned great Northern white beans. Canned beans are a real timesaver, and we've found that their quality can be more consistent than that of dried beans (see "Canned Beans: A Stellar Shortcut"). The other core elements are meaty cremini mushrooms, which I browned with salt in an olive oil–slicked skillet to help quickly extract their moisture, and chunks of carrots, which add earthy sweetness and an appealing pop of color.

Next, I gently sautéed some chopped onion. When it turned translucent, I stirred in minced fresh thyme and garlic along with tomato paste, a rich source of savory glutamates. As the aromatics browned, a sweet, savory, herbal fond developed. Since acid brings flavors into focus, I deglazed the skillet with dry sherry, a fortified wine that would boost complexity.

Finally, I stirred in the carrots; the beans and their well-seasoned, starchy liquid that would add body to the gravy; and some water and simmered the stew in a 300-degree oven until the carrots were tender, which took about 40 minutes. I wasn't surprised when the gravy tasted a bit lean and thin. In meat-based dishes, the meat is an important source of fat. To add richness, I upped the oil I was using to sauté the aromatics to a generous ¼ cup. I also thickened the gravy with a little flour.

For textural contrast, I took a cue from cassoulet, the French bean casserole crowned with a crisp layer of bread crumbs. I tossed cubes of a country-style loaf with ¼ cup of oil (I was generous here again) and some minced parsley and scattered them over the gratin's surface. I flipped on the broiler toward the end of cooking so the bread would toast evenly.

Crack through the crust and get a spoonful of

STEP-BY-STEP VIDEO AND NUTRITION INFORMATION
CooksIllustrated.com/DEC18

Creamy great Northern beans stay intact in the oven.

the rib-sticking, savory beans and vegetables that lie beneath. I promise you won't miss the meat.

WHITE BEAN AND MUSHROOM GRATIN
SERVES 4 TO 6 TOTAL TIME: 1¾ HOURS

We prefer a round rustic loaf (also known as a *boule*) with a chewy, open crumb and a sturdy crust for this recipe. Cannellini or navy beans can be used in place of great Northern beans, if desired.

- ½ cup extra-virgin olive oil, divided
- 10 ounces cremini mushrooms, trimmed and sliced ½ inch thick
- ¾ teaspoon salt
- ½ teaspoon pepper, divided
- 4–5 slices country-style bread, cut into ½-inch cubes (5 cups)
- ¼ cup minced fresh parsley, divided
- 1 cup water
- 1 tablespoon all-purpose flour
- 1 small onion, chopped fine
- 5 garlic cloves, minced
- 1 tablespoon tomato paste
- 1½ teaspoons minced fresh thyme
- ⅓ cup dry sherry
- 2 (15-ounce) cans great Northern beans
- 3 carrots, peeled, halved lengthwise, and cut into ¾-inch pieces

1. Adjust oven rack to middle position and heat oven to 300 degrees. Heat ¼ cup oil in 12-inch ovensafe skillet over medium-high heat until shimmering. Add mushrooms, salt, and ¼ teaspoon pepper and cook, stirring occasionally, until mushrooms are well browned, 8 to 12 minutes.

2. While mushrooms cook, toss bread, 3 tablespoons parsley, remaining ¼ cup oil, and remaining ¼ teaspoon pepper together in bowl. Set aside. Stir water and flour in second bowl until no lumps of flour remain. Set aside.

3. Reduce heat to medium, add onion to skillet, and continue to cook, stirring frequently, until onion is translucent, 4 to 6 minutes. Reduce heat to medium-low; add garlic, tomato paste, and thyme; and cook, stirring constantly, until bottom of skillet is dark brown, 2 to 3 minutes. Add sherry and cook, scraping up any browned bits.

4. Add beans and their liquid, carrots, and flour mixture. Bring to boil over high heat. Off heat, arrange bread mixture over surface in even layer. Transfer skillet to oven and bake for 40 minutes. (Liquid should have consistency of thin gravy.)

5. Leave skillet in oven and turn on broiler. Broil until crumbs are golden brown, 4 to 7 minutes. Remove gratin from oven and let stand for 20 minutes. Sprinkle with remaining 1 tablespoon parsley and serve.

> **RECIPES TO MAKE IT A MEAL**
> Find these recipes in our archive: Spinach Salad with Fennel and Apples (July/August 2010) and Best Butterscotch Pudding (January/February 2013).

Canned Beans: A Stellar Shortcut

Choosing canned beans over dried doesn't sacrifice quality. In fact, modern canning practices produce beans that are often more consistent than dried. Manufacturers clean, sort, and inspect dried beans before blanching them (similar in function to an overnight soak) and sealing them in cans with water and often salt, which seasons the flesh and tenderizes the skins. Most producers also add calcium chloride, which maintains firmness and prevents splitting. The final step is pressure-cooking the beans directly in their cans. The result is perfectly cooked, creamy, and intact beans. The "cooking liquid" in the can is great, too: We routinely use it to give body to bean dishes.

Modern Holiday Showstopper

Pavlova is a drop-dead gorgeous dessert of marshmallowy, crisp-shelled meringue piled with lightly whipped cream and fresh fruit. Ours is as foolproof as it is beautiful.

≥ BY ANNIE PETITO ≤

Anna Pavlova was known as the "incomparable" ballerina, captivating audiences not just in her homeland of Russia but across the entire world at the turn of the 20th century. It's no wonder, then, that chefs at the time immortalized her in recipes, including frogs' legs à la Pavlova in France, Pavlova ice cream in the United States, and most famously, the glamorous meringue, whipped cream, and fruit confection that's simply called pavlova.

Unlike meringue cookies, which are uniformly dry and crunchy throughout, the meringue for pavlova (which can be baked in a single large round or smaller individual disks) offers a range of textures: a crisp outer shell; a tender, marshmallowy interior; and a pleasant chew where the two textures meet. The meringue's sweetness is balanced by softly whipped cream and tart fresh fruit, which makes for a gorgeous jumble of flavors and textures—and a lightness that is ideal at the end of a rich meal.

Because of its dramatic appearance, you might think that pavlova is a real project. But you'd be wrong: It calls for only a handful of ingredients, and the meringue base can be baked in advance, leaving only cream to be whipped and fruit topping to be prepped before serving. Best of all, pavlova's unfussiness is part of its allure. More often than not, its shape is rustic and a few cracks are unavoidable, but there's beauty in these imperfections.

The meringue base is sure to crack as it bakes, but don't fret: Cracks are part of this dessert's rustic charm.

That said, there is one part of the process that can be intimidating: producing just the right texture for the meringue. So that's where I started my testing.

Whip It Good

Almost every pavlova recipe starts with a French meringue, which is made by whipping raw egg whites and sugar to stiff peaks and then folding in cornstarch and an acid, usually white vinegar (more on these ingredients later), along with a flavoring such as vanilla. The meringue is spread into a disk on a parchment-lined baking sheet and baked in a low oven until the outside is crisp. The oven is then turned off, and the meringue is left to continue drying out until the inside is no longer wet but still soft.

A French meringue is tricky because it requires adding the sugar to egg whites at just the right moment: too soon and the meringue won't inflate properly; too late and the meringue can be gritty.

To avoid that guesswork, I decided to switch to a style where the sugar is dissolved from the start. My two options were Italian and Swiss. The former requires the unnerving task of drizzling hot sugar syrup into the whites as they are whipped, so I opted for the latter: gently warming the whites and sugar in a bowl set over simmering water until the sugar is dissolved (many Swiss meringue recipes recommend heating to 140 degrees) and then whipping.

I heated six egg whites and 1 cup of sugar to 140 degrees; whipped the mixture to stiff peaks; added cornstarch, vinegar, and vanilla; and spread the meringue into a round. Unfortunately, it baked up with a pitted, coarse interior.

Our science research editor explained: Egg white proteins start out as separately wound little molecules, like balls of yarn. When heated and whipped, as in a Swiss meringue, the balls uncoil into linear strands (denature) and then slowly start to knit together (coagulate) at about 140 degrees. As the meringue bakes, the knitted proteins firm and contract, squeezing out water, which then evaporates. The more loosely knit the proteins are, the more they're pushed apart by the escaping steam, which can result in a coarse-textured dessert. Cooking the whites to a higher temperature—160 degrees—before baking would cause more coagulation. With the proteins knit into a finer, more cohesive mesh, the structure would not be as disrupted by escaping steam and the final product would be smoother.

When I thought about it, it made sense that I needed to alter the standard Swiss meringue. It's most often used as the base for buttercream frosting, not baked for pavlova. Sure enough, when I brought the whites and sugar to 160 degrees, I was rewarded with a smooth, fine texture. Its exterior was too soft, but I'd address that next.

STEP-BY-STEP VIDEO AND NUTRITION INFORMATION
CooksIllustrated.com/DEC18

RECIPE TESTING
Pavlovas on Parade

Our process for developing a recipe always starts with the same first step: choosing and preparing at least five published recipes, tasting each one, and noting our likes and dislikes.

NOVEMBER & DECEMBER 2018

Pavlova: A Trio of Fun-to-Eat Textures

Whereas a traditional meringue cookie is dry and crunchy throughout, the meringue for pavlova boasts three unique textures that keep things interesting as you eat.

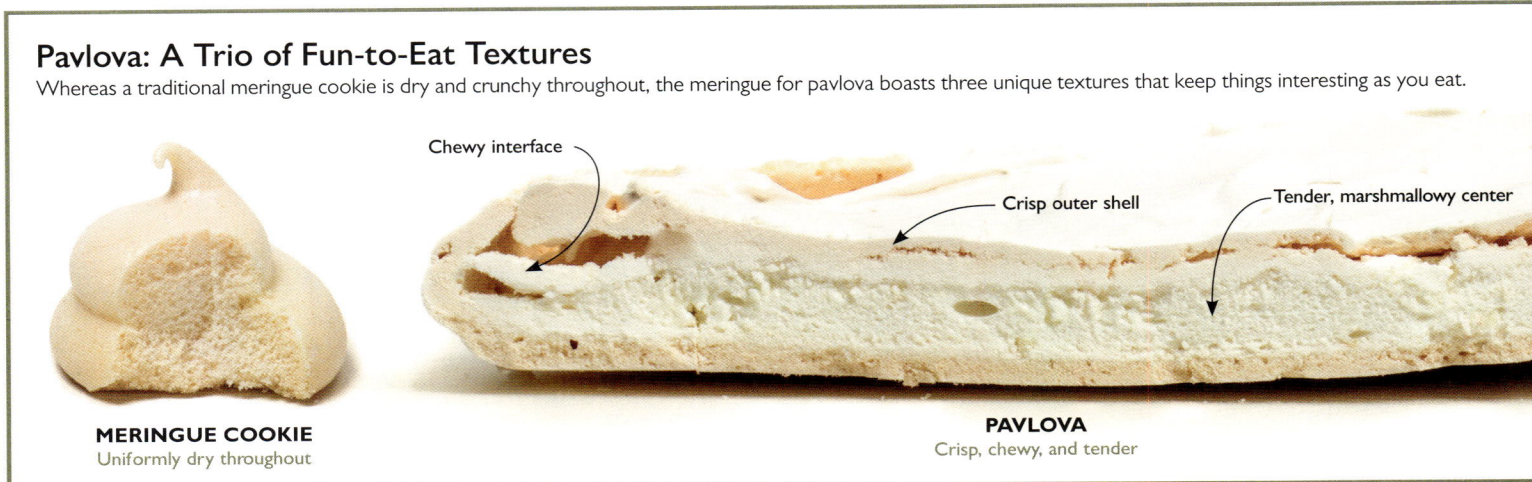

MERINGUE COOKIE
Uniformly dry throughout

PAVLOVA
Crisp, chewy, and tender

The Sweetest Thing

The exterior of the meringue was soft rather than crisp because it contained too much free water after baking. Adding sugar is the time-tested way to make sure a meringue crisps up: It draws water from the egg whites so they dry out during baking.

For my next set of tests, I made three batches of meringue with increasing amounts of sugar: 1 cup, 1¼ cups, and 1½ cups for six egg whites. The smaller amounts resulted in meringues with soft exteriors (they crisped after hours in the oven, but by then they were brown). I moved forward with 1½ cups of sugar, which resulted in a dry, crisp shell.

Pavlovian Response

Now, back to the vinegar and cornstarch. Many meringue recipes call for acid to be added to the egg whites. Pavlova meringue is unusual in that cornstarch is also typically mixed in and the vinegar is added after—not before—whipping. Recipes suggest that this combination is responsible for the meringue's tender/chewy texture.

To determine whether the presence of vinegar and cornstarch was dictated by tradition or function, I made five batches of meringue: one with just egg whites and sugar, one with cornstarch, one with vinegar, one with cream of tartar (a powder that's acidic like vinegar), and one with both vinegar and cornstarch. The plain sample seemed wet and slick on the inside. The starch-only interior was all chew, like a nougat, while the vinegar- and cream of tartar–based meringues were superdelicate and tender within. Only the batch made with acid and starch was just right: chewy at the edge and tender and marshmallowy inside. Since cream of tartar and vinegar performed identically, I chose to stick with tradition and call for vinegar since it's what most cooks keep on hand. I settled on 1½ teaspoons each of vinegar and cornstarch.

The Sum of Its Parts

I spread a thick layer of lightly sweetened whipped cream onto the cooled meringue disk. For a festive finish, I topped the whipped cream with sliced oranges, tart cranberries soaked in sugar syrup to cut their bitterness (for sparkle, I rolled some in sugar), and fresh mint. Slicing pavlova can be a slightly messy affair, which is part of the fun, but letting the dessert sit for just 5 minutes softened the meringue's crust just enough to make cutting easier.

Finally, to showcase the dessert's versatility, I developed a few topping options, including a mix of kiwi, blueberries, and mango as well as a strawberry version scented with basil.

Ladies and gentlemen, I present to you: the incomparable pavlova!

PAVLOVA WITH FRUIT AND WHIPPED CREAM
SERVES 10
TOTAL TIME: 1½ TO 2 HOURS, PLUS 1¾ HOURS COOLING

Because eggs can vary in size, measuring the egg whites by weight or volume is essential to ensure that you are working with the correct ratio of egg whites to sugar (see "Sizing Up Eggs"). Open the oven door as infrequently as possible while the meringue is inside. Don't worry when the meringue cracks; it is part of the dessert's charm. The inside of the meringue will remain soft. Our recipe for Strawberry, Lime, and Basil Topping is available for free for four months at CooksIllustrated.com/dec18.

Meringue
- 1½ cups (10½ ounces) sugar
- ¾ cup (6 ounces) egg whites (5 to 7 large eggs)
- 1½ teaspoons distilled white vinegar
- 1½ teaspoons cornstarch
- 1 teaspoon vanilla extract

Whipped Cream
- 2 cups heavy cream, chilled
- 2 tablespoons sugar

- 1 recipe fruit topping (recipes follow)

1. FOR THE MERINGUE: Adjust oven rack to middle position and heat oven to 250 degrees. Using pencil, draw 10-inch circle in center of 18 by 13-inch piece of parchment paper.

2. Combine sugar and egg whites in bowl of stand mixer and place bowl over saucepan filled with 1 inch simmering water, making sure that water does not touch bottom of bowl. Whisking gently but constantly, heat until sugar is dissolved and mixture registers 160 to 165 degrees, 5 to 8 minutes.

3. Fit stand mixer with whisk attachment and whip mixture on high speed until meringue forms stiff peaks, is smooth and creamy, and is bright white with sheen, about 4 minutes (bowl may still be slightly warm to touch). Stop mixer and scrape down bowl with spatula. Add vinegar, cornstarch, and vanilla and whip on high speed until combined, about 10 seconds.

4. Spoon about ¼ teaspoon meringue onto each corner of rimmed baking sheet. Press parchment, marked side down, onto sheet to secure. Pile meringue in center of circle on parchment. Using circle as guide, spread and smooth meringue with back of spoon or spatula from center outward, building 10-inch disk that is slightly higher around edges. Finished disk should measure about 1 inch high with ¼-inch depression in center.

A Sweet Rivalry

The history of pavlova is storied with an ongoing debate between New Zealand and neighboring Australia: Both countries lay claim to the dessert. As Kiwis have it, a Wellington chef created the dish in the prima ballerina Anna Pavlova's honor, citing her billlowy tutu as inspiration. But Australians insist that it was invented at a hotel in Perth and got its name when a diner declared it to be "light as Pavlova." More recently, it's been asserted that pavlova began life as a German torte and eventually traveled to the United States.

Sizing Up Eggs

We weighed 36 eggs from three separate cartons of eggs labeled "large." We weighed each egg whole and then separated each egg and weighed the white. The whole eggs ranged from 53 grams to 66 grams, while the whites ranged from 28 grams to 42 grams. For this reason, we recommend measuring the egg whites by weight or volume—not by egg count—to ensure just the right ratio of egg white to sugar in our meringue.

WHOLE EGGS Vary in weight by 22%

EGG WHITES Vary in weight by 40%

5. Bake meringue until exterior is dry and crisp and meringue releases cleanly from parchment when gently lifted at edge with thin metal spatula, 1 to 1½ hours. Meringue should be quite pale (a hint of creamy color is OK). Turn off oven, prop door open with wooden spoon, and let meringue cool in oven for 1½ hours. Remove from oven and let cool completely before topping, about 15 minutes. (Cooled meringue can be wrapped tightly in plastic wrap and stored at room temperature for up to 1 week.)

6. **FOR THE WHIPPED CREAM:** Before serving, whip cream and sugar in chilled bowl of stand mixer fitted with whisk attachment on low speed until small bubbles form, about 30 seconds. Increase speed to medium and whip until whisk leaves trail, about 30 seconds. Increase speed to high and continue to whip until cream is smooth, thick, and nearly doubled in volume, about 20 seconds longer for soft peaks. If necessary, finish whipping by hand to adjust consistency.

7. Carefully peel meringue away from parchment and place on large serving platter. Spoon whipped cream into center of meringue. Top whipped cream with fruit topping. Let stand for at least 5 minutes or up to 1 hour, then slice and serve.

ORANGE, CRANBERRY, AND MINT TOPPING
SERVES 10 (MAKES 4½ CUPS)
TOTAL TIME: 15 MINUTES, PLUS 1½ HOURS COOLING

You can substitute tangelos or Cara Cara oranges for the navel oranges, if desired. Valencia or blood oranges can also be used, but since they are smaller, increase the number of fruit to six.

- 1½ cups (10½ ounces) sugar, divided
- 6 ounces (1½ cups) frozen cranberries
- 5 navel oranges
- ⅓ cup chopped fresh mint, plus 10 small leaves, divided

1. Bring 1 cup sugar and 1 cup water to boil in medium saucepan over medium heat, stirring to dissolve sugar. Off heat, stir in cranberries. Let cranberries and syrup cool completely, about 30 minutes. (Cranberries in syrup can be refrigerated for up to 24 hours.)

2. Place remaining ½ cup sugar in shallow dish. Drain cranberries, discarding syrup. Working in 2 batches, roll ½ cup cranberries in sugar and transfer to large plate or tray. Let stand at room temperature to dry, about 1 hour.

3. Cut away peel and pith from oranges. Cut each orange into quarters from pole to pole, then cut crosswise into ¼-inch-thick pieces (you should have 3 cups). Just before serving, toss oranges with nonsugared cranberries and chopped mint in bowl until combined. Using slotted spoon, spoon fruit in even layer over pavlova. Garnish with sugared cranberries and mint leaves. Before serving, drizzle pavlova slices with any juice from bowl.

MANGO, KIWI, AND BLUEBERRY TOPPING
SERVES 10 (MAKES 5 CUPS)
TOTAL TIME: 10 MINUTES, PLUS 30 MINUTES RESTING

Do not use frozen blueberries in this recipe.

- 3 large mangos, peeled, pitted, and cut into ½-inch pieces (3 cups)
- 2 kiwis, peeled, quartered lengthwise, and sliced crosswise ¼ inch thick (about 1 cup)
- 5 ounces (1 cup) blueberries
- 1 tablespoon sugar

Toss all ingredients together in large bowl. Set aside for 30 minutes. Using slotted spoon, spoon fruit in even layer over pavlova. Before serving, drizzle pavlova slices with any juice from bowl.

INDIVIDUAL PAVLOVAS WITH FRUIT AND WHIPPED CREAM

Adjust oven racks to upper-middle and lower-middle positions and heat oven to 250 degrees. In step 4, spoon about ¼ teaspoon meringue onto each corner of 2 rimmed baking sheets. Line sheets with parchment paper. Spoon heaping ½ cup meringue into 5 evenly spaced piles on each sheet. Spread each meringue pile with back of spoon to form 3½-inch disk with slight depression in center. Decrease baking time in step 5 to 50 minutes. Top each meringue with ½ cup whipped cream, followed by ½ cup fruit topping.

KEY STEPS | MAKING A STUNNING DESSERT WITHOUT MUCH EFFORT

The baked, cooled meringue can be stored for up to a week, so all you need to do before serving is prepare the fruit topping and whip the cream.

WHIP 160-degree mixture of egg whites and sugar until stiff, glossy, and pure white, then add vinegar, cornstarch, and vanilla.

SCOOP meringue onto parchment and spread and smooth into 10-inch disk. Use back of spoon to create rim around edge.

BAKE for 1 hour, then turn off oven and prop door for 1½ hours, at which point meringue will be dry and crisp and lift cleanly from parchment.

TOP with lightly sweetened whipped cream and fresh fruit. Let pavlova sit for 5 minutes to 1 hour so that meringue softens slightly for neater slicing.

SLICE into wedges with serrated knife, using single decisive downward stroke. (Do not use sawing motion.)

Italian Chocolate-Almond Cake

Flourless chocolate cake often trades on cloying fudge-like density and one-note chocolate flavor. Leave it to the Italians to whip up a version that's lighter and more nuanced.

≥ BY STEVE DUNN ≤

Italian chocolate-almond cake (*torta caprese*) has a storied past—though it's not clear which (if any) story is true. One legend has it that the cake came to be when an Austrian princess visiting the island of Capri longed for the Sachertorte of her homeland. Not knowing how to make the dense Viennese chocolate layer cake, a local pastry chef added chocolate to his popular almond torte and hoped for the best. According to another tale, it was the accidental invention of an absent-minded baker who forgot to add flour to a chocolate-almond cake he made for a trio of Italian mobsters. And a third story tells of a sleep-deprived cook who confused cocoa powder for flour when he was mixing up almond cake batter.

What is certain: This torte, a classic dessert along the Amalfi Coast, can be a simple, elegant showstopper. When done well, it packs all the richness and depth of flourless chocolate cake, but it features finely ground almonds in the batter that subtly break up the fudgy crumb, making it lighter and less cloying to eat. It's also easy to make: Mix melted butter and chocolate with the ground almonds, lighten the batter with whipped eggs and sugar, pour it into a greased springform pan, and bake it for about an hour. There are no layers to assemble and no frosting to pipe and smooth. All it needs is a dusting of confectioners' sugar and maybe a dollop of whipped cream.

Simple ingredients, simple method. But making a great one takes a precise formula. The recipes I tried yielded a motley crew of cakes—some dry and dull like dilute cocoa, others as wet and dense as fudge—which made clear how important it would be to nail down just the right ingredient ratios and mixing method.

Batter Up

Butter and chocolate are typically the foundation of flourless chocolate cakes, and this one is no different. I melted 12 tablespoons of butter and 6 ounces of bittersweet chocolate in the microwave (easier and just as foolproof as melting chocolate over a traditional

STEP-BY-STEP VIDEO AND NUTRITION INFORMATION
CooksIllustrated.com/DEC18

The top of the cake forms a thin, dry shell during baking, so it's OK to dust the surface with confectioners' sugar several hours before serving.

water bath). Next came the eggs: Some recipes call for whipping just the whites with sugar, others for whipping the whites and yolks separately (both with sugar), and still others for whipping whole eggs with the sugar until the mixture is thick and pale. I tried the last, simplest route first. Finally, I blitzed sliced almonds to a fine meal in the food processor, blended them with the chocolate mixture, gently folded in the whipped eggs, poured the batter into the prepared pan, and baked it in a 325-degree oven.

The chocolate flavor was flat, but that was an easy fix with additions such as vanilla, salt, and cocoa powder to boost complexity. The bigger issue was the cake's consistency, which was downright dense.

Heavy Lifting

The tricky thing about flourless chocolate cakes is that they don't contain chemical leaveners. That's because the air created by a chemical leavener is useless unless it is trapped within the pastry's structure, typically by the flour. With no flour in the torta, the task of aerating my butter-, chocolate-, and nut-laden batter fell entirely to the eggs. The whipped whole eggs weren't providing enough lift or structure, so I made a couple more cakes in which I varied how I incorporated the eggs.

Whipping just the whites with sugar and folding them into the batter after I had whisked in the yolks didn't cut it either; the cake exited the oven proud and puffed but collapsed as it cooled. Only when I beat the whites and yolks separately in the stand mixer, each with half the sugar, were the two components able to aerate the heavy batter. Mixed this way, the center of the cake was moist, tender, and just a tad dense. And though the cake sank slightly as it cooled, it held its stature. (For more information, see "Whip the Entire Egg—in Two Parts.")

The other good news: The whipped yolks were so thick and stable that I discovered I could pour the chocolate-butter-almond mixture directly over them and mix everything in the stand mixer rather than by hand in a separate bowl as I had been doing. Even better, mixing the batter mechanically allowed me to incorporate a small portion of the whipped whites, which had been difficult to do with a spatula because of the batter's heft. But with the mixer's help, I was able to lighten the stiff batter just enough that I could then very gently fold in the rest of the whipped whites, preserving as much of their aerating effect as possible.

Make It a Meal

To make the cake's crumb just a tad tighter, I tried cutting back on the almond meal by 25 percent, which did the trick without noticeably affecting the flavor of the cake. While I was at it, I also discovered that commercial almond meal worked just as well as nuts I had ground myself—and it saved me the trouble of hauling out the food processor (see "Almond Flour versus Almond Meal").

Dusted with confectioners' sugar, the torta looked festive and elegant—a dessert fit for a princess, a mobster, or your favorite dinner guest. Serving it with infused whipped cream (I made one with Amaretto and another with orange liqueur and orange zest) brought it a step closer to its Italian roots and gave it further distinction from a typical flourless chocolate cake. And if you happen to have leftovers, you're in luck: It tastes great the next day.

TORTA CAPRESE

SERVES 12 TO 14
TOTAL TIME: 1¼ HOURS, PLUS 2½ HOURS COOLING

For the best results, use a good-quality bittersweet chocolate and Dutch-processed cocoa here. We developed this recipe using our favorite bittersweet chocolate, Ghirardelli 60% Cacao Bittersweet Chocolate Premium Baking Bar, and our favorite Dutch-processed cocoa, Droste Cacao. Either almond flour or almond meal will work in this recipe; we used Bob's Red Mill. Serve with lightly sweetened whipped cream or with Amaretto Whipped Cream or Orange Whipped Cream (recipes follow).

- 12 tablespoons unsalted butter, cut into 12 pieces
- 6 ounces bittersweet chocolate, chopped
- 1 teaspoon vanilla extract
- 4 large eggs, separated
- 1 cup (7 ounces) granulated sugar, divided
- 2 cups (7 ounces) almond flour
- 2 tablespoons Dutch-processed cocoa powder
- ½ teaspoon salt
- Confectioners' sugar (optional)

1. Adjust oven rack to middle position and heat oven to 325 degrees. Lightly spray 9-inch springform pan with vegetable oil spray.
2. Microwave butter and chocolate in medium bowl at 50 percent power, stirring often, until melted, 1½ to 2 minutes. Stir in vanilla and set aside.
3. Using stand mixer fitted with whisk attachment, whip egg whites on medium-low speed until foamy, about 1 minute. Increase speed to medium-high and continue to whip, slowly adding ½ cup granulated sugar, until whites are glossy and thick and hold stiff peaks, about 4 minutes longer. Transfer whites to large bowl.
4. Add egg yolks and remaining ½ cup granulated sugar to now-empty mixer bowl and whip on medium-high speed until thick and pale yellow, about 3 minutes, scraping down bowl as necessary. Add chocolate mixture and mix on medium speed until incorporated, about 15 seconds. Add almond flour, cocoa, and salt and mix until incorporated, about 30 seconds.
5. Remove bowl from mixer and stir few times with large rubber spatula, scraping bottom of bowl to ensure almond flour is fully incorporated. Add one-third of whipped whites to bowl, return bowl to mixer, and mix on medium speed until no streaks of white remain, about 30 seconds, scraping down bowl halfway through mixing. Transfer batter to bowl with remaining whites. Using large rubber spatula, gently fold whites into batter until no streaks of white remain. Pour batter into prepared pan, smooth top with spatula, and place pan on rimmed baking sheet.
6. Bake until toothpick inserted in center comes out with few moist crumbs attached, about 50 minutes, rotating pan halfway through baking. Let cake cool in pan on wire rack for 20 minutes. Remove side of pan and let cake cool completely, about 2 hours. (Cake can be wrapped in plastic wrap and stored at room temperature for up to 3 days.)
7. Dust top of cake with confectioners' sugar, if using. Using offset spatula, transfer cake to serving platter. Cut into wedges and serve.

Made to Be Made Ahead
This cake is so moist and tender that it still tastes great a few days after baking. Simply wrap it in plastic wrap and store it at room temperature.

SHOPPING Almond Flour versus Almond Meal
There are no official labeling standards for these products, but almond flour is typically made from skinless blanched nuts, while almond meal is most often ground from skin-on nuts. Luckily, both work equally well in our *torta*.

ALMOND FLOUR **ALMOND MEAL**

AMARETTO WHIPPED CREAM
SERVES 12 TO 14 (MAKES 2 CUPS)   TOTAL TIME: 5 MINUTES

For the best results, chill the bowl and the whisk attachment before whipping the cream.

- 1 cup heavy cream, chilled
- 2 tablespoons Amaretto
- 1 tablespoon confectioners' sugar

Using stand mixer fitted with whisk attachment, whip cream, Amaretto, and sugar on medium-low speed until foamy, about 1 minute. Increase speed to high and whip until soft peaks form, 1 to 3 minutes.

ORANGE WHIPPED CREAM
SERVES 12 TO 14 (MAKES 2 CUPS)   TOTAL TIME: 5 MINUTES

You can substitute Grand Marnier for the Cointreau, if desired.

- 1 cup heavy cream, chilled
- 2 tablespoons Cointreau
- 1 tablespoon confectioners' sugar
- ¼ teaspoon grated orange zest

Using stand mixer fitted with whisk attachment, whip all ingredients on medium-low speed until foamy, about 1 minute. Increase speed to high and whip until soft peaks form, 1 to 3 minutes.

RECIPE TESTING Whip the Entire Egg—in Two Parts

The eggs have a lot of heavy lifting to do in a flourless chocolate cake since they are the dessert's sole source of leavening and structure. Whipping them to incorporate air is thus essential. Whipping also causes the egg white proteins to unfurl and form a network that helps stabilize the air bubbles; the result is called an egg foam. But would we get the most leavening and structure by whipping whole eggs, just the whites, or the whites and yolks separately? Here's what we found:

Test: Whip whole eggs
Result: Dense, heavy cake
Explanation: The fat in the yolks inhibits the formation of the protein network in whites that traps air, so there's little foaming to help lighten the cake.

Test: Whip whites only
Result: Cake puffs, then collapses
Explanation: Even though the whites trap a lot of air to help the cake rise, they ultimately don't have enough structure to support the weight of the heavy batter.

Test: Whip whites; whip yolks
Result: Airy, sturdy cake
Explanation: Whipping the yolks with sugar traps more air and allows the sugar to draw in moisture, so the mixture becomes sturdier. The yolk mixture gets dispersed throughout the batter, giving the cake a more tender texture and strengthening the egg white foam.

The Best Unsalted Butter

Unsalted butter is one of the most basic ingredients for cooking and baking. What's the best one for everyday use?

≥ BY KATE SHANNON ≤

In the test kitchen, we go through 30 to 40 pounds of butter a week, relying almost exclusively on the unsalted type because we prefer to control the seasoning of our food. But which unsalted butter is best? A few years ago, we decided it was Plugrá, a high-fat product with a luscious texture. At almost $12 per pound, though, it's expensive. Although Plugrá is sometimes worth the splurge, we wanted a butter that was affordable and convenient for everyday use.

We assembled seven national top sellers, priced from $4.49 to $7.58 per pound. Two were cultured, which means that flavor-creating bacterial cultures had been added during production, and one of these butters was imported from Europe. The rest were domestic "sweet cream" butters, meaning no cultures are added. All were purchased in the user-friendly format familiar in America: individually wrapped ¼-pound sticks, sold in packs of two or four. All but one product had measurement markings on the sticks; the outlier had markings on the box. Tasters sampled the butters in three blind tastings: plain, in pound cake, and in sugar cookies.

A Complex Process

To better understand our lineup, we first looked at how butter is made commercially. According to *Better Butter* (2012), a technical manual by Robert Bradley of the University of Wisconsin's Center for Dairy Research, the process looks something like this: A tanker truck of cream arrives at the factory. The cream is pasteurized and then tempered, a complicated process of raising and lowering the temperature that alters the structure of the cream's fat globules so it can be churned more effectively. In the production of cultured butter, the bacterial cultures are added at this point.

Next, during churning, the cream crashes down on itself with enough force to burst the membranes that surround the fat globules and help keep them separate. The bits of fat begin to clump together, eventually forming a solid mass of butter. The liquid (now buttermilk) is drained, and then the butter is rinsed. At this point, additional ingredients may be added, including preservatives such as salt for salted butter and lactic acid for most unsalted butters. The butter is "worked," or kneaded, to incorporate the salt or lactic acid and to remove moisture. Once it's cohesive and has the prescribed moisture level, it is portioned and packaged.

We were pleased with the quality of the butters in our lineup; in fact, we recommend every product we tasted. Marianne Smukowski, an expert on food safety and quality at the University of Wisconsin's Center for Dairy Research, attributed the good scores across the board to two factors. First, today's butters are all made with good-quality cream. Second, modern churns work very well and produce very good, very consistent butters.

Battle of the Butters

There were some noticeable flavor differences among the products, especially with the two cultured butters, which were complex, with "grassy," "tangy," "floral," and even "cheesy" notes. We also noticed a "movie theater popcorn" flavor that may indicate the presence of diacetyl, an aroma compound with an intensely nutty, buttery flavor. It exists naturally in sweet cream butter and can occur in high levels when cream is cultured. It can also be included as an additive.

The two cultured butters also stood out for their markedly darker colors, a likely indicator that the milk came from cows that grazed on lots of grass. (Though the FDA does not require that butter labels state when food coloring has been added, both of these companies told us that their products do not contain coloring.) Grass contains the yellow pigment beta-carotene, and when cows eat enough grass, beta-carotene makes it into their milk (see "Many Shades of Yellow").

Packaging can also impact flavor, and all the experts we talked to agreed that the best way to prevent butter from picking up off-flavors is to wrap it in aluminum foil or special coated parchment paper—or a combination of both. Two of the top five products in our lineup had coated-parchment packaging. Manufacturers wouldn't offer specifics on these coatings, but (like aluminum foil) they really seemed to work. The butters wrapped in uncoated parchment, on the other hand, had a slightly "stale," "funky" flavor and hints of a "sour" aftertaste, indicating that their wrappers were more permeable.

Which Butter Should You Buy?

Although some of our tasters loved the complex, tangy flavors of cultured butters, most preferred the simple, straightforward taste of sweet cream butter, with Challenge Unsalted Butter ($4.49 per pound) leading the pack. It had a "milky sweetness" and clean dairy flavor. Its foil wrapper likely kept it tasting fresh. For everyday cooking and baking, this convenient, affordable butter is our new top choice.

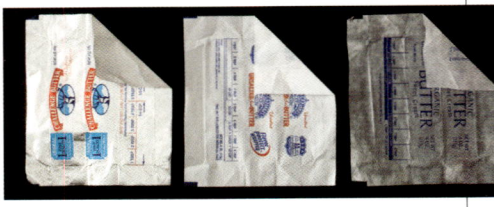

Packaging Matters

Two of the seven butters we tasted were wrapped in special coated parchment paper (middle), while our top two products were wrapped in aluminum foil (left). Tasters noted that some lower-ranked butters, which were wrapped in parchment (right), had a "stale" flavor and a "sour" aftertaste.

Many Shades of Yellow

As explained in *Butter: A Rich History* (2016) by Elaine Khosrova, grass contains yellow beta-carotene. When a cow eats grass, that beta-carotene is stored in her fat and ends up in the milk she produces. The membranes that surround particles of milk fat are white, so the milk is white. But when that milk is churned to make butter, the membranes surrounding the fat globules break and the pigment is released. That's why butter is yellow.

It's simple: Cows that eat more beta-carotene-rich plants produce milk that yields yellower butter. Other animals, such as goats and water buffalo, convert beta-carotene to vitamin A (which is colorless) instead of storing it in their fat, so butter made from their milk is naturally white—regardless of how much grass they eat.

A COW'S DIET IMPACTS A BUTTER'S APPEARANCE

TASTING UNSALTED BUTTER

We tasted seven top-selling unsalted butters, all sold in packages with individually wrapped ¼-pound sticks, priced from $4.49 to $7.58 per pound. Panels of 21 tasters sampled them in three blind tastings: plain, in pound cake, and in sugar cookies. Information on wrappers, ingredients, and the cows' diets was obtained from manufacturers and/or product packaging. Fat is reported per 1-tablespoon serving. Prices were paid in Boston-area supermarkets. Scores from the tastings were averaged, and products appear below in order of preference.

RECOMMENDED

CHALLENGE Unsalted Butter
PRICE: $4.49 per lb
INGREDIENTS: Pasteurized cream (milk), natural flavoring
FAT: 11 g
WRAPPER: Foil
STYLE: Sweet cream

TESTERS' COMMENTS

Made in California and well-known on the West Coast, this butter is now available in all 50 states. Its "clean," "strong dairy flavor" made it a crowd-pleaser when sampled plain. Describing pound cake made with this product, one taster said, "I can't imagine a better version." The sticks are wrapped in aluminum foil, which may protect them from picking up off-flavors during shipping and storage. The natural flavoring is lactic acid, which acts as a preservative.

KATE'S CREAMERY 100% Pure Butter, Unsalted
PRICE: $5.99 per lb
INGREDIENTS: Grade A cream, natural flavors developed by healthy dairy cultures
FAT: 11 g
WRAPPER: Foil
STYLE: Sweet cream

We loved the "good, fresh, slightly sweet flavor" of this butter, which is produced in Maine. Desserts made with it tasted "just about perfect." Lactic acid, which is used as a preservative, is derived from cultured milk and listed on the label as "natural flavors." However, no actual cultures are added to the butter; it's a sweet cream butter. It's wrapped in parchment-coated aluminum foil that may protect the butter's flavor, and though the foil doesn't have convenient measurement markings on it, the edge of the box does.

LAND O'LAKES Unsalted Butter
PRICE: $4.99 per lb
INGREDIENTS: Sweet cream, natural flavoring
FAT: 11 g
WRAPPER: FlavorProtect Wrapper (a proprietary coated parchment paper)
STYLE: Sweet cream

This well-known product wasn't boldly flavored, and that was fine with us. We enjoyed its "familiar," straightforward flavor in all three tastings. It produced "great, classic" pound cake and "rich, delicious" cookies. The manufacturer wouldn't disclose any details about its proprietary coated-parchment wrapper, but the butter had no off-flavors.

KERRYGOLD Unsalted Pure Irish Butter
PRICE: $7.58 per lb
INGREDIENTS: Cultured pasteurized cream
FAT: 12 g
WRAPPER: Parchment
STYLE: Cultured

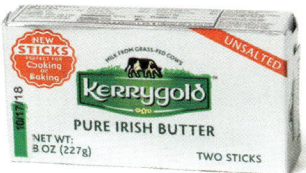

The sole European import we tasted, this Irish butter was a noticeably deeper yellow color than others in our lineup. It's likely that the cows ate a lot of fresh grass rich in the yellow pigment beta-carotene (a Kerrygold representative told us that the cows "graze outdoors for up to 300 days"). The combination of the cows' diet and the cultures resulted in an especially flavorful butter. Tasters called out "complex," "grassy" notes and a "tangy," "cheesy" quality.

ORGANIC VALLEY Cultured Unsalted Butter
PRICE: $6.99 per lb
INGREDIENTS: Pasteurized organic sweet cream (milk), microbial cultures
FAT: 11 g
WRAPPER: ButterLock (a proprietary coated parchment paper)
STYLE: Cultured

Like Kerrygold, this butter is both dark yellow (which indicates that the cows ate a lot of grass) and cultured. It was rich in "grassy," "vegetal," and "floral flavors" and tasted strongly of rich, tangy cream. The ButterLock coated-parchment wrapper, which is unique to Organic Valley, likely helped protect the butter's flavor.

CABOT CREAMERY Unsalted Butter
PRICE: $4.99 per lb
INGREDIENTS: Cream (milk), natural flavoring
FAT: 11 g
WRAPPER: Parchment
STYLE: Sweet cream

For the most part, this sweet cream butter was "unremarkable but acceptable." Desserts made with it struck the balance of butter flavor and vanilla-y sweetness that we wanted. But some tasters noticed funky off-flavors and a "plasticky" aftertaste, likely due to inferior parchment wrappers that let in odors. As one taster said, it "tastes like the box it was packaged in—or the fridge."

HORIZON Organic Unsalted Butter
PRICE: $5.99 per lb
INGREDIENTS: Organic grade A sweet cream (milk), lactic acid
FAT: 11 g
WRAPPER: Parchment
STYLE: Sweet cream

Although some tasters thought this butter was perfectly fine, it consistently scored at the bottom of the lineup. It's likely that the parchment wrapper, which let in odors, is to blame. When we tasted it plain, the butter had a mild but slightly "weird," "sour" flavor. That off-flavor was evident in baked goods, too. One taster summed up the cookies: "Tastes like butter that's soaked up fridge flavors."

Searching for a Superior Metal Spatula

This essential tool can be a cook's best friend—but only if you choose the right one.

⇒ BY MIYE BROMBERG ⇐

A good metal spatula is an essential part of any cook's toolkit. Often referred to as a turner or flipper, it's used to flip or transfer foods whenever we're working with metal cook- or bakeware. (When cooking in more delicate nonstick pans, we prefer plastic spatulas.)

It had been a while since we last reviewed metal spatulas and we wanted to know if our previous favorite, the Wüsthof Gourmet 12" Fish Spatula ($49.95), still held up to the competition. We bought 10 models priced from $4.53 to $49.95, including our old winner, and put them through their paces, using them to flip and transfer foods such as fried eggs, pancakes, burgers, fried fish, and home fries and to transfer sugar cookies from baking sheets to wire racks. We selected five conventional spatulas, featuring sturdy square or rectangular heads, some slotted and some solid. The other five models, including our previous winner, were fish spatulas. Often found in restaurant kitchens, fish spatulas feature long, tapered, slotted heads and, as their name implies, are intended to lift and support tender fish fillets, making an otherwise challenging task simple.

The good news? All the spatulas performed reasonably well and were able to get the food from point A to point B more or less intact. Still, a few factors made certain models easier, more comfortable, and generally more pleasant to use.

Fish Spatulas: They're Not Just for Fish

There's a reason that professional cooks swear by fish spatulas. The spatulas' head shape makes them versatile, allowing them to excel at flipping and moving not just delicate pieces of fish, but foods of a variety of shapes and sizes, including burgers, eggs, cookies, and everything else we tried. For one thing, the heads are roomy—on average, about 12 square inches compared to 11 for the conventional models. They are also long and slim, so they can nimbly navigate even the tightest spaces, such as the 8-inch cast-iron skillet we used to make over-easy eggs. The length of the fish spatulas' heads—5.5 inches on average for the models in our lineup—was particularly important. Longer heads act as more extensive landing strips for food to travel along.

By contrast, the heads of the five conventional metal spatulas in our lineup were squat and rectangular, making them a little awkward to maneuver in confined spaces. Because the heads are shorter than a fish spatula's (most were less than 4 inches long), fragile foods such as pancakes and soft cookies sometimes hit the back end and got dented if we slid the spatula

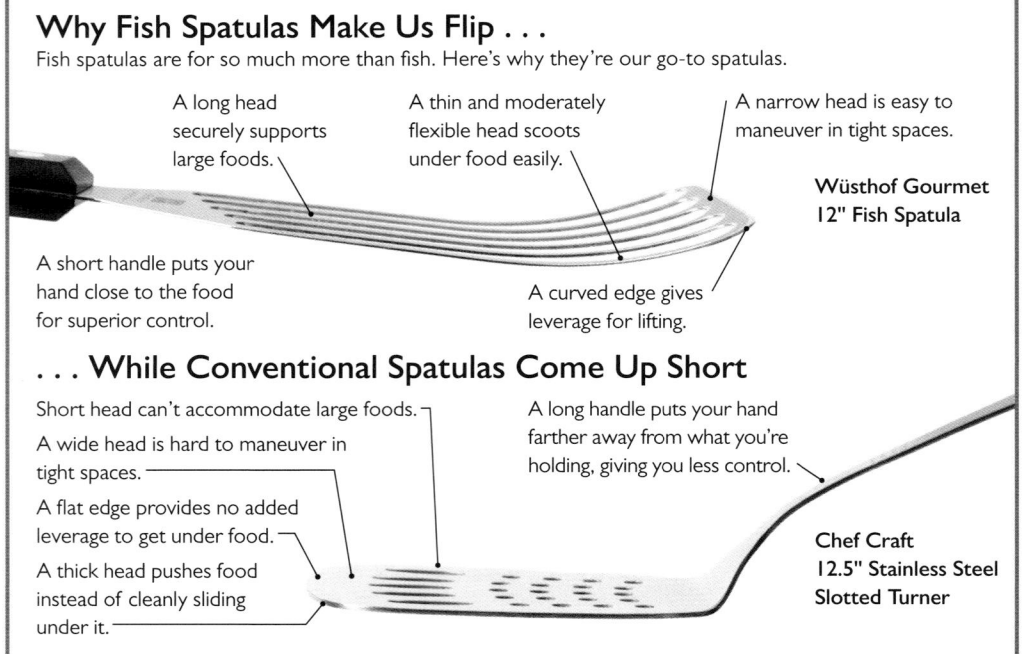

Why Fish Spatulas Make Us Flip . . .
Fish spatulas are for so much more than fish. Here's why they're our go-to spatulas.

- A long head securely supports large foods.
- A thin and moderately flexible head scoots under food easily.
- A narrow head is easy to maneuver in tight spaces.
- A short handle puts your hand close to the food for superior control.
- A curved edge gives leverage for lifting.

Wüsthof Gourmet 12" Fish Spatula

. . . While Conventional Spatulas Come Up Short

- Short head can't accommodate large foods.
- A wide head is hard to maneuver in tight spaces.
- A flat edge provides no added leverage to get under food.
- A thick head pushes food instead of cleanly sliding under it.
- A long handle puts your hand farther away from what you're holding, giving you less control.

Chef Craft 12.5" Stainless Steel Slotted Turner

under them too vigorously; heavier foods such as pub burgers simply fell backward onto the cooking surface. And these spatulas' smaller surface areas meant that long fish fillets and large pancakes sometimes draped over the sides a bit precariously.

In addition, most of the conventional spatulas' heads had one of two problems: they were either too rigid and thick (more than 1 millimeter), making it harder to get under food without damaging it, or they were too flexible and thin (0.2 millimeters), buckling slightly when we lifted the ½-pound pub burgers. Fish spatulas hit the sweet spot: At 0.8 to 0.9 millimeters thick, their moderately flexible heads hugged the cooking surface and slipped easily under all foods without tearing or bumping them, but they were still substantial enough to support heavier foods and do a little scraping.

Fish spatulas had advantages on the other end, as well. Their handles—all 4.5 to 5 inches long—moved our hands closer to the action and gave us more control for flipping and scooping. By contrast, the handles on conventional spatulas were simply too long (8 to 9 inches on the most unwieldy models), leaving us to poke clumsily at the food from afar.

More generally, we preferred handles of moderate thickness, about 2.5 to 3.25 inches around. Thinner, flatter handles cramped our hands after extended use, and thicker handles were hard for smaller-handed users to hold. We also liked handles made of textured wood or plastic, as these were easier to grasp than smooth metal, especially when wet or greasy.

Edging Out the Competition

By the conclusion of testing, one thing was clear: We significantly preferred fish spatulas to conventional models. Two products swam to the top of our rankings. They are nearly identical, with moderately long, comfortable handles made of easy-to-hold plastic. Both also have large, long heads that could lift any food without damaging it and had moderate flexibility for good control. Once again, our old favorite from Wüsthof had the edge—literally. The end of its head curves upward with a pronounced swoop, affording more leverage for prying up roasted potatoes or lifting the corner of a pancake to check its browning. The curved head also positions hands higher, keeping them at a safer distance over hot pans. At $49.95, it's not cheap, but we think it's a worthy investment, considering how frequently we use it. That said, our Best Buy, the MIU France Flexible Fish Turner—Slotted ($16.57), was a very close second. Its head is nearly flat, so it can't command quite the same amount of leverage as our winner and it brings your knuckles a little closer to the hot pan. But it performed almost as well—and at a third of the price.

TESTING METAL SPATULAS

KEY
GOOD ★★★
FAIR ★★
POOR ★

We tested 10 metal spatulas priced from $4.53 to $49.95, using them to flip and remove eggs, pancakes, burgers, fried fish, and home fries from a variety of cookware and to transfer sugar cookies from a baking sheet to a wire rack. We also asked users of different dominant hands and hand sizes to flip and transfer pancakes with each model. Models were evaluated on their overall performance, as well as head design and handle design. All models were purchased online and appear in order of preference.

PERFORMANCE:
We rated spatulas on how well they flipped and removed different types of food from a variety of cookware.

HEAD DESIGN:
We evaluated the design of the spatulas' heads, awarding points to those that maneuvered well in tight spaces, provided plenty of room to hold food securely, and were able to get underneath food easily without damaging it.

HANDLE DESIGN:
We evaluated the design of the spatulas' handles. Those that felt comfortable, grippy, and easy to control for testers of all hand sizes earned full marks.

SEE HOW THE TESTING WAS DONE
CooksIllustrated.com/DEC18

HIGHLY RECOMMENDED

WÜSTHOF GOURMET 12" Fish Spatula
MODEL: 4433 PRICE: $49.95
HEAD SURFACE AREA: 12.1 sq in
HEAD THICKNESS: 0.9 mm
PERFORMANCE: ★★★
HEAD DESIGN: ★★★ HANDLE DESIGN: ★★½

COMMENTS: Our favorite model's perfectly proportioned head supported foods of all shapes and sizes and maneuvered nimbly even in tight spaces. The head's pronounced curve provided extra leverage for prying up food and kept our hands higher above hot pans. Users found its handle easy to hold, but some wished it were grippier.

RECOMMENDED

MIU FRANCE Flexible Fish Turner–Slotted
MODEL: 90011 PRICE: $16.57
HEAD SURFACE AREA: 12.1 sq in
HEAD THICKNESS: 0.8 mm
PERFORMANCE: ★★★
HEAD DESIGN: ★★½ HANDLE DESIGN: ★★½

BEST BUY

COMMENTS: This spatula was nearly identical to our winner, but its head was almost flat, lacking the curvature that would allow users to summon that extra leverage and keep their hands higher above hot surfaces. It still excelled at every task we gave it and was comfortable to hold, although its handle was a bit too smooth.

VICTORINOX 3 x 6-Inch Chef's Slotted Fish Turner
MODEL: 40415 PRICE: $19.20
HEAD SURFACE AREA: 12.4 sq in
HEAD THICKNESS: 0.9 mm
PERFORMANCE: ★★★
HEAD DESIGN: ★★★ HANDLE DESIGN: ★★

COMMENTS: With a well-proportioned, nicely curved head of moderate thickness and flexibility, this model effortlessly flipped, transferred, and supported foods of all sizes. But testers were mixed on its handle: While the textured wood helped us keep our grip, a rough metal edge stuck out from that wood, digging into our hands and making the spatula unpleasant to hold for extended periods.

MERCER CULINARY Hell's Handle High Heat 6" x 3" Fish Spatula
MODEL: M33183 PRICE: $17.57
HEAD SURFACE AREA: 12.4 sq in
HEAD THICKNESS: 0.8 mm
PERFORMANCE: ★★★
HEAD DESIGN: ★★★ HANDLE DESIGN: ★★

COMMENTS: This fish spatula's head was moderately thin, flexible, and gently curved, allowing it to perform every task well. We liked the grippy plastic handle, which was easy to hold even when covered in grease. The only problem? The handle was quite thick, which made it slightly harder for even larger-handed testers to hold comfortably.

KUHN RIKON Flexi Spatula, 11"
MODEL: 2165 PRICE: $17.95
HEAD SURFACE AREA: 10.9 sq in
HEAD THICKNESS: 0.8 mm
PERFORMANCE: ★★½
HEAD DESIGN: ★★½ HANDLE DESIGN: ★★

COMMENTS: This turner performed ably, but its head and handle were a touch undersized next to the other fish spatulas in the lineup. Its smaller surface area made it feel less secure when flipping or transferring larger items such as pancakes. The metal handle was a bit short, narrow, and slick, which made it slightly harder to hold.

RECOMMENDED WITH RESERVATIONS

NORPRO Krona 12" Stainless Steel Solid Turner
MODEL: 1226 PRICE: $10.47
HEAD SURFACE AREA: 12.4 sq in
HEAD THICKNESS: 1 mm
PERFORMANCE: ★★½
HEAD DESIGN: ★★ HANDLE DESIGN: ★★

COMMENTS: This conventional spatula had plenty of surface area, so it did a fairly good job on most tasks, but its square head made it unwieldy to maneuver in tight spaces. Thick and rigid, it was tricky to slide under fragile foods such as pancakes and cookies. Finally, the metal handle was slicker and narrower than we preferred, which made it less comfortable to hold.

OXO Good Grips Flexible Turner-Stainless Steel
MODEL: 34491 PRICE: $7.99
HEAD SURFACE AREA: 10.8 sq in
HEAD THICKNESS: 0.2 mm
PERFORMANCE: ★★
HEAD DESIGN: ★½ HANDLE DESIGN: ★★½

COMMENTS: Faced with stiffer competition, our previous Best Buy fell in our rankings. Although it hugged the surfaces of pans closely and did a great job of sliding under food, its ultrathin head was too flimsy; holding a ½-pound burger felt like a risky proposition. It was also a bit small, so long fish fillets drooped over the edges and threatened to break.

FARBERWARE Professional Stainless Steel Slotted Turner
MODEL: 5084423 PRICE: $13.01
HEAD SURFACE AREA: 11.3 sq in
HEAD THICKNESS: 0.9 mm
PERFORMANCE: ★★
HEAD DESIGN: ★★ HANDLE DESIGN: ★½

COMMENTS: The head of this spatula was moderately thin, allowing it to slip under food fairly easily. But it was also on the smaller side, providing less surface area to support the food and allowing fish fillets and large pancakes to drape off the sides. Its squat profile made it feel clunky, and testers disliked its smooth metal handle.

CUISINART Steel Solid Turner
MODEL: CTG-08-SST PRICE: $9.63
HEAD SURFACE AREA: 8.6 sq in
HEAD THICKNESS: 1.1 mm
PERFORMANCE: ★★
HEAD DESIGN: ★½ HANDLE DESIGN: ★½

COMMENTS: The swoop of this spatula's ultralong handle was elegant but not very practical, encouraging users to hold the part closest to the head to summon more control when turning or moving food. Larger foods easily fell off the small head, which was thick and sometimes dented fragile pancakes and cookies.

CHEF CRAFT 12.5" Stainless Steel Slotted Turner
MODEL: 10211 PRICE: $4.53
HEAD SURFACE AREA: 11.3 sq in
HEAD THICKNESS: 1.3 mm
PERFORMANCE: ★★
HEAD DESIGN: ★½ HANDLE DESIGN: ★½

COMMENTS: This spatula's head was too small, thick, and rigid, so it was difficult to slip beneath large or fragile foods. Its handle was long, thin, and rough on the edges, which made it uncomfortable to hold for extended periods. Still, for the most part, it got the job done.

INGREDIENT NOTES

≽ BY PAUL ADAMS, STEVE DUNN & LAN LAM ≼

Tasting Crunchy Peanut Butter

Every major brand that makes a creamy peanut butter also manufactures a crunchy version. We wondered if the maker of our favorite creamy peanut butter would also produce our favorite crunchy one. To find out, we tasted nine crunchy peanut butters, priced from $2.69 to $6.91 per jar, plain, in peanut butter and jelly sandwiches, and in peanut butter cookies.

Crunchy peanut butters come in three styles: those made with hydrogenated vegetable oil and sugar, those that trade hydrogenated oil for palm oil (and are typically labeled "natural" since palm oil is naturally solid at room temperature), and those that are just peanuts and salt. Overall, tasters preferred peanut butters with added oil for their thick, uniform textures.

Tasters also liked extra crunch. When we separated the butter from the peanut chunks in each product, we learned that our favorites had about ¼ cup more peanut pieces per 16-ounce jar than lower-ranked products.

As for flavor, we liked a good balance of salt and sugar. The hydrogenated oil and palm oil peanut butters all had 3 grams of sugar per tablespoon of peanut butter, compared to just 1 to 2 grams in the simple peanuts-and-salt varieties, as well as a bit more salt to counter the sweetness.

Ultimately, the qualities that our tasters valued in creamy peanut butter held true for crunchy versions, too: hydrogenated oil for smooth, homogeneous texture; plenty of salt; and a generous helping of sugar. Made with a high percentage of peanut pieces for a hearty crunch, our favorite is Skippy Super Chunk Peanut Butter ($2.89 per 16.3-ounce jar), from the brand that also makes our winning creamy peanut butter. Our top two favorite products are shown below. –Lauren Savoie

RECOMMENDED

SKIPPY Super Chunk Peanut Butter
PRICE: $2.89 per 16.3-oz jar ($0.18 per oz)
INGREDIENTS: Roasted peanuts, sugar, hydrogenated vegetable oil (cottonseed, soybean, and rapeseed oil) to prevent separation, salt
STYLE: Hydrogenated oil
SUGAR: 3 g   SODIUM: 125 mg
PERCENTAGE OF PEANUT PIECES: 22%
COMMENTS: This product, from the same brand as our winning creamy peanut butter, was "very crunchy" and had a "salty/sweet balance" that tasters loved. Its texture was deemed the "perfect smooth and crunchy combo," a "light," "creamy" butter with "evenly dispersed" "good-size chunks." Tasters also liked its "toasty" flavor, which was punctuated by a "hint of sweetness."

JIF Extra Crunchy Peanut Butter
PRICE: $3.29 per 16-oz jar ($0.21 per oz)
INGREDIENTS: Roasted peanuts and sugar, contains 2% or less of: molasses, fully hydrogenated vegetable oils (rapeseed and soybean), mono and diglycerides, salt
STYLE: Hydrogenated oil
SUGAR: 3 g   SODIUM: 105 mg
PERCENTAGE OF PEANUT PIECES: 23%
COMMENTS: With a "light," almost "whipped" texture and a "balance of sweet and salty" flavors, this hydrogenated oil product had a "classic," "familiar" peanut butter profile. It had "lots of medium-size chunks" of peanut for a "very crunchy" texture that was still "balanced" and "spreadable."

Put Your Turkey Timing Worries to Rest

Every year we field the same question from readers: Won't my turkey get cold if I let it rest the standard 30 minutes before serving?

Letting turkey rest is essential to allow its juices to redistribute so that the meat is juicier when you carve it. But we decided to track how long it actually takes for the centers of the breast and thighs to cool to 130 degrees, the lowest temperature at which we consider meat optimally warm to carve and eat. We roasted two typical-size holiday birds: a 14-pounder and an 18-pounder, each cooked to about 160 degrees in the breast and about 175 degrees in the thighs. To avoid making the skin soggy, we did not tent the birds with aluminum foil while they rested.

After 30 minutes in our 78-degree test kitchen, the smaller bird's breast registered 158 degrees and the larger breast was 162; the thighs from each bird had cooled to just 167 and 169 degrees, respectively. After a full hour out of the oven, both birds were still plenty hot: The smaller turkey's breast was 142 degrees and its thighs were 150 degrees; meanwhile, the breast in the larger bird was 155 degrees and the thighs were 148. It took nearly 1½ hours for the smaller bird's temperature to drop below 130 and for the thighs in the bigger bird to do the same (its breast took close to 2 hours).

So if you're running behind schedule preparing the rest of your holiday meal, don't worry about the bird cooling down too fast. Its large size and rounded shape help it retain heat, and you can be confident that it will stay warm enough to eat well beyond the standard 30-minute rest –L.L.

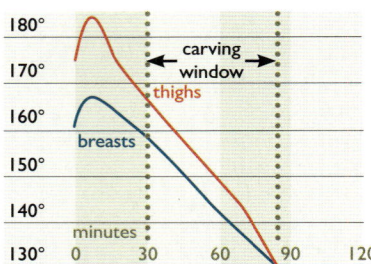

14-POUND TURKEY

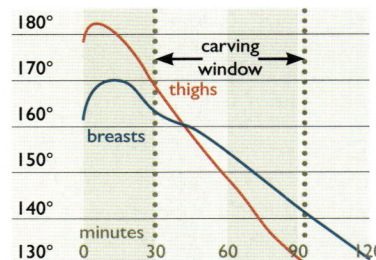

18-POUND TURKEY

Exact rates will vary, but as these graphs show, a turkey will stay in the ideal window for carving (above 130 degrees) for far longer than the standard 30-minute rest.

Know Your Giblets

One of the first tasks when roasting a turkey is to check the raw bird's cavities for the neck and giblets—the bundle of parts that often includes the heart, gizzard, and liver. You should remove these parts from the cavities and use all but the liver (which can impart a mineral, bitter taste to stock) for making gravy. –L.L.

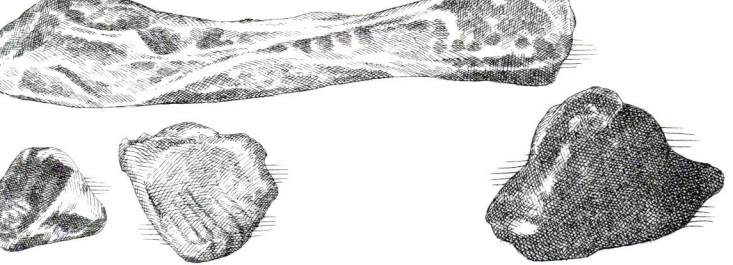

GREAT FOR STOCK
Clockwise from top: The neck, gizzard, and heart contribute meaty flavor to the stock we use to make gravy.

NOT FOR STOCK
The liver, identifiable by its amorphous shape and shiny, dark red exterior, can impart a mineral taste to stock and gravy.

Cooking with Wine? Pick Something Neutral

You've probably heard that you shouldn't cook with wine you wouldn't drink, but we wanted to test that advice for ourselves. So we made pan sauces and beef and chicken stews with red and white wines from a range of calibers and price points; some were lovely to drink, some were uninspiring, and some were downright terrible.

Our results turned the old adage on its head. Not only did some cheap bottles (a $4 Sauvignon Blanc and a $4 Cabernet Sauvignon) make perfectly good additions to our stews and sauces, but a few very fine drinking wines (a subtly sweet Riesling, an oaky California Chardonnay, a tannic Bordeaux, and a sweet Italian Lambrusco) actually imparted flavors to the food that we didn't like.

The important factor to consider isn't price or even how nice a wine is to drink but whether it features distinct characteristics that will become concentrated through cooking and distract from the flavor of the dish. In other words, the best wine for cooking is an unremarkable one. Bright, balanced flavors are good; distinctly tannic, sweet, or oaky flavors are not. For red wine, we recommend a blend such as Côtes du Rhône; a medium-bodied single varietal such as Pinot Noir, Merlot, or Grenache; or even a general table wine. For whites, Sauvignon Blanc, Chenin Blanc, Pinot Grigio, and Albariño are all good bets. And don't hesitate to reach for the cheap stuff! –S.D.

Digging Into Delicata Squash

If you're unfamiliar with this nutty-sweet vegetable with tender edible skin, here's what you need to know to make it as much of a go-to as butternut or acorn squash. And be sure to try our recipe on page 11. –L.L.

PREP:
➤ No need to peel the edible skin. Simply pare away any tough patches and trim off woody ends.
➤ To halve lengthwise, insert tip of chef's knife into center of squash, then cut down through flesh with blade. Rotate squash 180 degrees and repeat motion.

SHOPPING:
➤ Delicata is available from late summer through early winter.
➤ Choose squashes that are similar in size and shape to ensure even cooking.
➤ Small woody patches on the skin are okay, but avoid squashes with soft spots or bruises.

STORAGE:
Store as you would other winter squashes: at room temperature in a cool, dry spot. It will last at least 10 days.

DIY RECIPE Cultured Butter

With the help of friendly bacteria, you can make rich, tangy butter that's a lot more interesting than store-bought sticks. All it takes is cream, starter culture, and time. You'll also get buttermilk to add to your biscuits and pancakes. –P.A.

CULTURED BUTTER
MAKES ABOUT 2 CUPS BUTTER AND ABOUT 2 CUPS BUTTERMILK
TOTAL TIME: 45 MINUTES, PLUS 24 HOURS TO 1 WEEK RESTING

We prefer the flavor of butter made with pasteurized cream as opposed to ultrapasteurized cream. The ideal temperature range for churning butter is 55 to 60 degrees; colder and the fat is too firm and will stick to the sides of the food processor bowl; warmer and the fat is liquid instead of solid, leading to greasy butter. In step 2, chill the cream in the refrigerator or over an ice bath. For the most complex tangy flavor, we recommend aging the cream for a week. At that point the cream may smell quite pungent, but most of what you smell resides in the liquid that gets separated out, leaving the butter surprisingly mellow. This recipe requires cheesecloth.

- 4 cups heavy cream
- 2 tablespoons buttermilk
- ¼ teaspoon salt (optional)

1. Combine cream and buttermilk in clean lidded container. Cover container and let sit at room temperature until mixture smells tangy and buttery and thickens to sour cream–like consistency, at least 24 hours or up to 1 week.
2. Chill cream mixture to 55 to 60 degrees.
3. Process cream mixture in food processor until mixture turns from grainy whipped cream to lumps of butter splashing in liquid, 1 to 3 minutes. Stop processor immediately.
4. Fill medium bowl halfway with ice and water. Line fine-mesh strainer with triple layer of cheesecloth, leaving few inches of cloth hanging over sides of strainer, and set over a large bowl. Drain butter mixture in prepared strainer (buttermilk will collect in bowl). Lift cheesecloth by edges and twist and squeeze tightly over strainer to press out more buttermilk (stop when butter starts to squeeze through cheesecloth). Transfer cheesecloth-wrapped butter to ice bath until firm around exterior, about 2 minutes. Transfer buttermilk to airtight container.
5. Remove butter from cheesecloth and transfer to now-empty bowl. Stir and press with wooden spoon (metal utensil will conduct heat from your hands and make butter soft) to force out additional buttermilk from butter, 1 to 2 minutes. Drain buttermilk from bowl, add to buttermilk container, and refrigerate until ready to use. Knead salt, if using, into butter with wooden spoon. Transfer butter to second airtight container and refrigerate until ready to use. (Butter can be refrigerated for up to 2 months.)

Emergency Sub for Vanilla Extract

Have you ever started a dessert recipe only to find that you've run out of vanilla extract? We wondered if there was a solution that would let us avoid a trip to the supermarket. We traded liquor cabinet alternatives—straight bourbon and rum, both of which feature vanilla-like flavors—for the extract in pound cake, vanilla cookies, and vanilla pudding. Rum's flavor was too distinctive, but the bourbon was promising, though it was both too mild and too boozy.

The solution: We reduced ¼ cup of bourbon to 2 tablespoons in the microwave, which intensified its flavors and drove off some of its alcohol. While the concentrated bourbon didn't taste exactly like vanilla, it brought a pleasing complexity to all three recipes. (Note: We also found that for cake and cookies, simply omitting the vanilla led to acceptable results. But the additional flavor was essential to the pudding, which tasted too eggy without it.) –L.L.

KITCHEN NOTES

BY STEVE DUNN, ANDREA GEARY, ANDREW JANJIGIAN & LAN LAM

WHAT IS IT?

This tool is a vintage cookie press from Denmark, where pressed (and piped) butter cookies have long been a holiday tradition. Manufactured in the early 1900s from rolled steel and wood, this simple manual press calls for filling the hollow tube with cookie dough, screwing a shaping disk onto the end, and then pressing the wooden plunger through the tube to extrude dough onto a baking sheet. How well does it work? To be fair, perfectly pressed cookies can be tricky to make even with the latest gun-style presses. If the dough is too cold, it can jam up the press; too warm or loose and the dough won't hold its shape when extruded.

Nevertheless, using this manual-plunge press was especially challenging. Modern versions call for placing the press directly on the baking sheet for stability and then squeezing the handle to extrude a premeasured quantity of dough. This tool, however, requires you to "hover" the press above the sheet while pushing hard to extrude an adequate amount of dough. Even with practice, the antique press remained hard to use and my cookies were rarely perfectly formed. –S.D.

DANISH COOKIE PRESS

Faster, Easier White Rice

Want a fast way to make white rice that requires little attention and produces fluffy, separate grains every time? Use a pressure cooker. The interesting thing about cooking rice in a pressure cooker is that you need less water. In a traditional covered pot, water evaporates during the entire cooking time, so you need lots of water to compensate for that loss. In a pressure cooker, once the cooker has come up to pressure, it becomes a sealed environment that allows no further evaporation. So no matter how much rice you cook, you need to add only enough water to equal the volume of rice plus ¼ cup.

➤ **Here's how:** Place 1 cup long-grain white, jasmine, or basmati rice in fine-mesh strainer and rinse under cold running water until water runs clear, then transfer rice to stovetop or electric pressure cooker and add 1¼ cups water and ½ teaspoon salt, if desired. For each additional cup rice, add only 1 cup water (and additional ½ teaspoon salt). (Use 2¼ cups water for 2 cups rice, 3¼ cups water for 3 cups rice, and so on.) Cook rice at high pressure for 3 minutes, then remove pressure cooker from heat or turn it off and let pressure release naturally for 10 minutes. Open pressure cooker, fluff rice with fork, and serve. –A.G.

A Raisin to Revive Flat Champagne?

Rumor has it that dropping a raisin into an open bottle of flat champagne can bring back the bubbles; we ran a test to see if it was true. We dropped a raisin into a bottle that had been left open for four days and were hopeful when a stream of tiny bubbles appeared. We waited 2 minutes (the time recommended by most sources) and then tasted the "revived" sample alongside wine from another bottle that had also been open for four days; we also compared both to champagne from a freshly opened bottle.

➤ **The verdict:** Both four-day-old wines tasted less fizzy, less aromatic, and sweeter than the fresh champagne; furthermore, tasters couldn't tell which four-day-old wine had been "refreshed."

So why the appearance of bubbles? The raisin's wrinkly surface coaxed the carbon dioxide dissolved in the wine to form bubbles, which merely made the champagne look effervescent. But the raisin can't actually add carbon dioxide to the wine, which is necessary to restore fizz.

➤ **Bottom line:** A raisin won't restore the fizz. The best way to use up flat champagne? Cook with it. –L.L.

Trust Your Eyes When Judging Bread Doneness

Professional bread bakers judge the doneness of their loaves by looking for deep, even browning. They don't typically take the temperature of the crumb. That's because the internal temperature of bread doesn't tell the whole story.

To demonstrate how appearance is the critical factor when baking bread, we baked three loaves each of various styles, including enriched types containing fat and eggs and lean types containing just flour, water, and salt. We pulled one loaf of each type from the oven when it was 5 degrees shy of its recommended temperature (typically 190 degrees for enriched breads and 205 degrees for lean breads), one when it was 5 degrees past its recommended temperature, and one when it was right on the nose.

On the inside, all the loaves were just as they should be—neither too wet nor too dry and perfectly moist. But the exteriors were a different story: Many of the low-temperature loaves were soft-crusted and pale and lacked flavor, while some of the high-temperature ones were too hard and slightly burnt on the underside.

➤ **Bottom line:** There is a wider window for doneness on the inside of a loaf than on the crust, so when you're baking bread, trust your eyes first and foremost. Bake bread until it looks right. Feel free to use a thermometer for reassurance, but if the bread is still pale, keep baking it, even if it's at or above the recommended temperature. And if it looks good, don't keep baking it, even if it is 5 to 10 degrees below temperature on the inside. –A.J.

TOO LIGHT   **JUST RIGHT**   **TOO DARK**

SCIENCE: How Creaming Impacts Cake Texture

Ever wonder why different cake recipes call for different approaches to mixing the batter? Some layer cake recipes, for example, call for the creaming method (beating the butter and sugar together until light and fluffy before adding the remaining ingredients), while others call for the reverse creaming method (combining the butter with all the dry ingredients before mixing in the remaining ingredients). Since both approaches produce tender cake, does it really matter which method you use? —L.L.

EXPERIMENT

We made two layer cakes using the same ingredients (flour, sugar, salt, baking soda, baking powder, butter, milk, and egg whites) in the same proportions. We mixed one batter using the creaming method and the other via the reverse-creaming method. We then baked the cakes and asked tasters to compare the texture and appearance of each cake layer. Then, to get really geeky, we used a highly sensitive tool called the Brookfield Engineering CT3 Texture Analyzer to measure the firmness of each cake.

RESULTS

Tasters struggled to find any difference in tenderness between the two cakes. Even the texture analyzer measurements confirmed the firmness of the two cakes to be remarkably similar. That said, the cakes exhibited significant structural differences: The creamed version had a slightly domed top and a fluffy, more open crumb, while the top of the cake that we made using the reverse-creaming method was even and its crumb ultrafine and velvety.

EXPLANATION

When you cream butter and sugar, the sugar crystals help beat tiny pockets of air into the butter. The wet and dry ingredients are then gently added in alternating turns, limiting gluten development and ensuring tenderness. (The creaming itself has no impact on these.) Baking expands the air pockets created during creaming, giving the cake lift and an open structure.

When you reverse-cream, you're coating the flour with butter, which helps waterproof it. When the liquid ingredients are added, only some flour proteins can hydrate, limiting gluten development and ensuring tenderness. Little air gets incorporated during mixing, resulting in less rise and doming and a superfine, plush crumb.

TAKEAWAY

Both mixing methods produce equally tender results. Their differences boil down to the crumb's rise and structure. For everyday baking, fluffy, slightly domed creamed cakes are fine. For fancy cakes with multiple layers, the flat top and plush crumb of a reversed-creamed cake can be more desirable.

CREAMING
Fluffy, somewhat open crumb and domed top
WHEN WE USE IT: pound cake, cupcakes, everyday layer cakes

REVERSE CREAMING
Ultrafine crumb and flat top
WHEN WE USE IT: layer cakes (particularly those with more than two layers); coffee cakes with heavy toppings

---

Brine Turkey in a Cooler

Finding space in the refrigerator for a container large enough to hold a couple of gallons of brine and a turkey can be a tall order. One way to free up space is to place the turkey and brine in an oven bag and then stash the tightly sealed bag in a cooler or large Styrofoam box with ice. The key is to make sure the turkey and brine are well chilled (no warmer than 40 degrees) before placing them in the cooler. This allows all the ice's cooling power to go toward maintaining a food-safe temperature inside the cooler.

You'll need a turkey-size oven bag and 2 to 3 gallons of brine depending on the size of the turkey. The oven bag means you can use any size cooler that fits the bird; plus, you won't have to clean it. Combine the brine and turkey (thawed if frozen) in the bag and carefully remove as much air as possible before sealing the bag so that the bird is enveloped in brine. Place the bag and 15 pounds of ice in the cooler or Styrofoam box (any size large enough to hold the bag will do) and do not open it until you're ready to proceed with the recipe. We found that 15 pounds of ice was enough to keep a 20-pound turkey cool for more than 12 hours. —L.L.

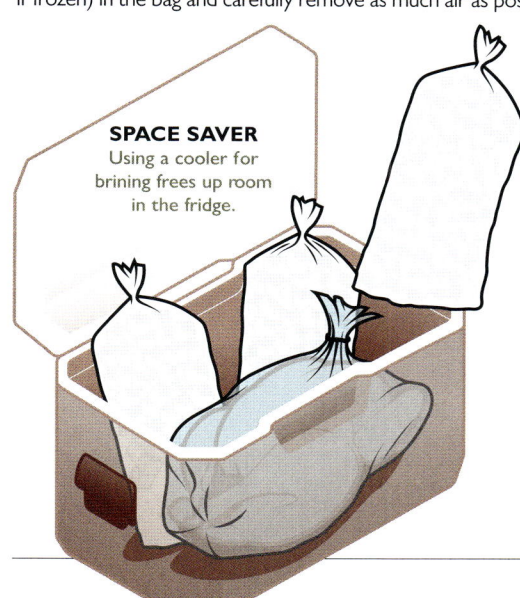

SPACE SAVER
Using a cooler for brining frees up room in the fridge.

Six More Reasons You Need a Bench Scraper

Any professional baker knows that the wide, flat blade of a bench scraper, with its heavy, easy-to-grip handle and deeply beveled edge, is indispensable for dividing dough or cleaning stuck-on flour from the "bench," or counter. But this inexpensive tool—our favorite is the Dexter-Russell 6" Dough Cutter/Scraper—Sani-Safe Series ($7.01)—has other handy uses that make it a must-have in any kitchen. —A.J.

SCOOP UP PILES
Push ingredients into piles and scoop from counter with blade.

CUBE BUTTER
Halve stick lengthwise, roll 1 turn, repeat. Then slice 4 cubes at a time.

MAKE DOUGH LOGS
Move scraper along length of dough to create smooth, even cylinders.

PORTION BAR COOKIES
Push down on blade to make series of straight cuts.

SMOOTH FROSTING
Hold scraper at 90-degree angle against frosting while slowly rotating turntable or plate.

MEASURE DRY INGREDIENTS
Dip measuring cup into container of flour, sugar, or other dry ingredient and level with scraper.

EQUIPMENT CORNER

≥ BY MIYE BROMBERG, CAROLYN GRILLO, LISA McMANUS & EMILY PHARES ≤

HIGHLY RECOMMENDED
JUNE Intelligent Oven
MODEL: 11-00001-00
PRICE: $1,495.00

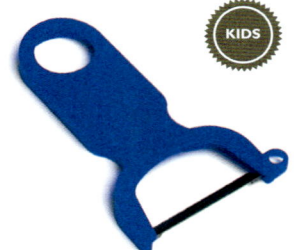

HIGHLY RECOMMENDED
KUHN RIKON
Original Swiss Peeler
MODEL: KHN 2771 (blue)
PRICE: $6.24

RECOMMENDED
OXO Good Grips
Salad Spinner
MODEL: 32480V4
PRICE: $29.99

RECOMMENDED
OXO Good Grips
Silicone Pastry Brush
MODEL: 1071062
PRICE: $7.99

RECOMMENDED
LIFEFACTORY
22 oz Glass Bottle with
Classic Cap-Orange
MODEL: LF230007C4
PRICE: $22.99

The June Intelligent Oven

The June Intelligent Oven ($1,495.00) bills itself as "the world's only intelligent convection oven" and offers technology to make cooking "faster, easier, and tastier." Its Food ID feature automatically recognizes many foods and carries out the appropriate cooking—all you have to do is press a button. It also comes with a built-in food scale and a food-temperature probe that plugs into the oven wall, plus a baking sheet and wire rack. We wondered if this oven was as smart as it claimed, so we brought it into the test kitchen. We tested Food ID and used the June with recipes from its app (the oven can be used with or without a subscription, which costs $4.99 per month or $49.00 per year) as well as our own recipe for cookies. Our verdict: We really like this little oven. Everything came out perfectly cooked, the oven and app are intuitive to operate, and cleanup was quick and simple. Yes, it is expensive, but the June Oven made preparing foods easier, and it was enjoyable to use, as it performed nearly flawlessly and operated seamlessly, with a clear, intuitive display and controls. For smaller households, we think it could easily take the place of a toaster oven and possibly even the full-size oven. –L.M.

Fruit/Vegetable Peelers for Kids

Kids can use a lot of standard kitchen equipment safely and comfortably, but sometimes they need their own tools. Recently, we noticed several peelers designed especially for children, with features such as rubber grips and plastic blades. Could we find one that was effective but also safe and easy for kids to use? We tested five models: three geared toward children, plus our favorite regular peeler from Kuhn Rikon and a "palm peeler" that slides onto the user's middle finger like a ring. After preliminary testing by adults in our test kitchen, we eliminated two models: a Y-shaped peeler with a plastic blade (it was ineffective and difficult to use) and the palm peeler, which we deemed unsafe for children. We brought in kids to test the remaining three models, and their preferences matched ours: They liked sharp peelers with comfortable handles. We recommend the Kuhn Rikon model ($6.24) for older children, but for younger kids or beginners in the kitchen, the Opinel Le Petit Chef Peeler ($17.00) is our pick; it includes a ring between the blade and handle where kids can rest their index fingers, giving them more control. –C.G.

Salad Spinners

There's no better tool than a salad spinner to make short work of cleaning and drying greens. To find the best one, we tested seven models, priced from $15.94 to $48.99, including the newest version of our former favorite, the OXO Good Grips Salad Spinner ($29.99), which was recently redesigned. All the models in our lineup operate similarly: A perforated plastic basket sits inside a larger, lidded bowl. You use a mechanism—a crank, plunger, lever, or pull cord—to spin the basket, creating centrifugal force to expel liquid, which collects in the outer bowl, leaving the basket contents dry. We tested each model with a variety of greens and found that overall capacity was important, as was the headway between the bottom of the spinner and the bottom of the basket (so plenty of water could collect without rewetting the greens). But easy spinning was the biggest factor: One model gave us more of an upper-body workout than we wanted, and two others had off-center cranks that made the machines wobble. However, the new version of our old favorite from OXO worked easily with just one hand. It was also the most efficient at removing water and was easy to clean. This model remains our winner. –L.M.

Silicone Brushes

We like to stock our kitchen with two kinds of brushes. Natural-fiber brushes are ideal for delicate applications such as glazing pastries and removing crumbs from layer cakes. But when it comes to higher-heat and more hygiene-sensitive tasks, we reach for a silicone brush. We wondered if our favorite silicone brush from OXO Good Grips was still the best, so we pitted it against six other models priced from $4.98 to $21.95. We used each brush to apply a thick glaze to meatloaf and melted butter to a hot skillet. We also tested them by applying egg wash to pie dough to see how they'd fare with a task where we'd typically use a natural-fiber brush. In the end, what mattered most was the flexibility of the bristles—we preferred those that were moderately flexible for good control and agility and overall comfort while in use; we liked models that were lightweight with grippy, moderately thick handles. Our previous favorite, the OXO Good Grips Silicone Pastry Brush ($7.99), ticked all the boxes and is once again our winner. –M.B.

Glass Water Bottles

When we previously tested water bottles, we excluded glass models because of weight and durability concerns. However, interest in alternatives to plastic is growing, and glass bottles have proliferated in the market. We decided it was time to examine them. We chose six popular models priced from $8.13 to $38.00, ranging in capacity from 16 to 22 ounces, and put them through a battery of tests. None of the bottles leaked, stained, or retained odors, so our preferences ultimately came down to how easy they were to use. The worst of the bunch included a model with seven separate pieces—which made it a pain to clean—and another with an uncomfortable metal strap and grating metal cap. Our favorite is the Lifefactory 22 oz Glass Bottle with Classic Cap ($22.99). This dishwasher-safe bottle had a wide mouth for easy filling and drinking and a comfortable handle; plus, it was durable, surviving three indoor drops. It's also available in a smaller 16-ounce size. –E.P.

INDEX
November & December 2018

PAGE 13

PAGE 11

SIDE DISH
Roasted Delicata Squash 11

DESSERTS
Pavlova with Fruit and Whipped Cream 20
　Individual Pavlovas with Fruit and Whipped Cream 21
　Mango, Kiwi, and Blueberry Topping 21
　Orange, Cranberry, and Mint Topping 21
Torta Caprese 23

DRESSINGS
Creamless Creamy Herb Dressing 15
　Ginger-Miso 15
　Green Goddess 15
　Roasted Red Pepper and Tahini 15
　Russian Dressing 15

SAUCES AND GRAVIES
Basque-Style Herb Sauce (Tximitxurri) 11
Our Favorite Turkey Gravy 9
　Alcohol-Free 9
　Gluten-Free 9
Spicy Honey 11

MAIN DISHES
Beef Top Loin Roast with Potatoes 7
Kung Pao Chicken 13
Pasta alla Gricia (Rigatoni with Pancetta and Pecorino Romano) 10
Turkey and Gravy for a Crowd 4
White Bean and Mushroom Gratin 18

ACCOMPANIMENTS
Amaretto Whipped Cream 23
Cultured Butter 29
Orange Whipped Cream 23

PAGE 23

PAGE 18

Find More Online
Our online extras include recipes, reviews, and a complete lineup of videos. Go to CooksIllustrated.com/DEC18

RECIPES
Goat Cheese and Chive Sauce
Kung Pao Chicken for Two
Pasta alla Gricia (Rigatoni with Pancetta and Pecorino Romano) for Two
Skillet Beef Top Loin Roast with Potatoes
Strawberry, Lime, and Basil Topping

VIDEO
Testing Metal Spatulas

NUTRITIONAL INFORMATION
CooksIllustrated.com/DEC18/nutrition

▶ RECIPE VIDEOS
Want to see how to make any of the recipes in this issue? There's a free video for that. Go to **CooksIllustrated.com/DEC18** and click on videos.

FOLLOW US ON SOCIAL MEDIA
facebook.com/CooksIllustrated
twitter.com/TestKitchen
pinterest.com/TestKitchen
instagram.com/CooksIllustrated
youtube.com/AmericasTestKitchen

AMERICA'S TEST KITCHEN COOKING SCHOOL

Visit our online cooking school today, where we offer 180+ lessons covering a range of recipes and cooking methods. Whether you're a novice just starting out or are already an advanced cook looking for new techniques, our cooking school is designed to give you confidence in the kitchen and make you a better cook.

▶ **Start a 14-Day Free Trial at OnlineCookingSchool.com**

Cook's Illustrated on iPad
Enjoy Cook's wherever you are, whenever you want.

For a digital version of Cook's Illustrated, go to **CooksIllustrated.com/iPad**. You'll be able to dowload the app through iTunes and start a free trial. Our digital edition includes bonus features such as recipe videos and step-by-step slide shows of each recipe.

▶ **Go to CooksIllustrated.com/iPad** to download our app through iTunes.

A Toast to 25 Years

A cocktail was once a mixture of spirits, bitters, water, and sugar that was consumed as a tonic, but modern-day mixed drinks signal celebration. The bitters-soaked sugar cube sunk into the flute of a **CHAMPAGNE COCKTAIL** sends sparkly bubbles to the surface. Salting the rim of a **MARGARITA** makes its citrus flavors pop. Name attributions behind the sharp, savory **BLOODY MARY** include a Palm Beach socialite and a scheming Scottish queen. The Great **TOM COLLINS** Hoax of 1874—a prank about a nonexistent trash-talking man by that name—likely inspired the name of the sparkling lemon cooler. Both a **MANHATTAN** and an **OLD-FASHIONED** are whiskey-based and often include a maraschino cherry; the former is sometimes finished with lemon, the latter with orange. Extract from the bitter *chinotto* orange flavors Campari, the red aperitif in a **NEGRONI**. A **MARTINI** can be "dry" (less vermouth), "dirty" (seasoned with olive brine), or garnished with a lemon twist. Egg white foam creates the frothy head on a **PISCO SOUR**. The official Kentucky Derby **MINT JULEP** contains 3 parts bourbon and 1 part mint simple syrup. A rum-based **MAI TAI** suggests a tropical escape.

BACK COVER ILLUSTRATED BY JOHN BURGOYNE　　　PHOTOGRAPHY: CARL TREMBLAY, STEVE KLISE; STYLING: KENDRA McKNIGHT, ELLE SIMONE, CHANTAL LAMBETH